Banking, Currency, and Finance in Europe
Between the Wars

This publication is the result of international research carried out between 1989 and 1993 within a scientific network on the *Economic History of Europe between the Wars*. The network was initiated and supported by the European Science Foundation.

Banking, Currency, and Finance in Europe Between the Wars

Edited by
CHARLES H. FEINSTEIN

CLARENDON PRESS · OXFORD
1995

Oxford University Press, Walton Street, Oxford OX2 6DP

Oxford New York
Athens Auckland Bangkok Bombay
Calcutta Cape Town Dar es Salaam Delhi
Florence Hong Kong Istanbul Karachi
Kuala Lumpur Madras Madrid Melbourne
Mexico City Nairobi Paris Singapore
Taipei Tokyo Toronto
and associated companies in
Berlin Ibadan

Oxford is a trade mark of Oxford University Press

Published in the United States
by Oxford University Press Inc., New York

British Library Cataloguing in Publication Data
Data available

Library of Congress Cataloging in Publication Data
Banking, currency, and finance in Europe between the Wars / edited
by Charles H. Feinstein
Includes bibliographical references
1. Finance—Europe—History—20th century.
2. Banks and banking—Europe—History—20th century.
3. Bank failures—Europe—History—20th century.
4. Europe—History—1918–1945.
I. Feinstein Charles, 1954–   .
HG186. A2B36 1995 95–5862
332'.094'09042—dc20
ISBN 0–19–828803–4

1 3 5 7 9 10 8 6 4 2

Typeset by Pure Tech India Ltd, Pondicherry, India
Printed in Great Britain
on acid free paper by
Bookcraft (Bath) Ltd, Midsomer Norton, Avon

Contents

List of Figures

List of Tables

List of Contributors

JEAN-CHARLES ASSELAIN, Professor of Economic History, Faculty of Economics and Management, University of Bordeaux 1, France.

THEO BALDERSTON, Lecturer in Economic History, Department of Economic History, University of Manchester, England.

LJUBEN BEROV, Professor of Economic History, Faculty of Economics, University of Sofia, Bulgaria.

FORREST CAPIE, Professor of Economic History, Department of Banking and Finance, City University Business School, London, England.

ISABELLE CASSIERS, Senior Research Fellow, Belgian National Foundation for Scientific Research, and Professor of Economics, Institute of Economic and Social Research, Catholic University of Louvain, Louvain-la Neuve, Belgium.

CONSTANTINE COSTIS, Assistant Professor of History, Faculty of Law, Economics, and Political Science, University of Athens, Greece.

GEORGE B. DERTILIS, Professor of History, Faculty of Law, Economics, and Political Science, University of Athens, Greece.

BARRY EICHENGREEN, JOHN L. SIMPSON Professor of Economics, Department of Economics, University of California at Berkeley, USA.

CHARLES H. FEINSTEIN, Chichele Professor of Economic History, University of Oxford, and Fellow of All Souls College, Oxford, England.

TARMO HAAVISTO, Lecturer in Economics, Department of Economics, Lund University, and Research Fellow, Nordic Economic Research Council, Uppsala, Sweden.

GERT HARDACH, Professor of Social and Economic History, Department of History, University of Marburg, Germany.

JOOST JONKER, Research Fellow, Institute for Netherlands History, The Hague, The Netherlands.

LARS JONUNG, Professor of Economics, Department of Economics, Stockholm School of Economics, Stockholm, Sweden.

ZBIGNIEW LANDAU, Professor of Economic History, Department of Economic History, Warsaw School of Economics, Warsaw, Poland.

MICHEL LESCURE, Professor of Economic History, Department of History, University François-Rabelais, Tours, France.

PABLO MARTÍN-ACEÑA, Professor of Economic History, University of Acalá and Fundación Empresa Pública, Madrid, Spain.

WOJCIECH MORAWSKI, Lecturer in Economic History, Department of Economic History, Warsaw School of Economics, Warsaw, Poland.

HELVIG NORDVIK, Professor of Economic History, Institute of Economic History, The Norwegian School of Economics and Business Administration, Bergen, Norway.

CORMAC Ó GRÁDA, Statutory Lecturer in Political Economy, Department of Political Economy, University College, Dublin, Ireland.

ALAIN PLESSIS, Professor of Economic History, Department of History, University of Paris X, Nanterre, France.

JAIME REIS, Senior Research Fellow, Institute of Social Sciences, University of Lisbon, Portugal.

BETH SIMMONS, Assistant Professor of Political Science, Department of Political Science, Duke University, North Carolina, USA.

PETER TEMIN, Elisha Gray II Professor of Economics, Massachusetts Institute of Technology, Cambridge, Mass, USA.

GIANNI TONIOLO, Professor of Economics, Department of Economics, University of Venice, Italy.

JAN LUITEN VAN ZANDEN, Professor of Economic History, Department of History, University of Utrecht, The Netherlands.

KATHERINE WATSON, Lecturer in Economic History, Department of Economics and Related Studies, University of York, England.

FRITZ WEBER, Lecturer in Economic History, Department of Economic History, Wirtschaftsuniversität, Vienna, Austria.

Introduction

In 1989 a meeting was convened under the auspices of the European Science Foundation to discuss the formation of a scientific network embracing economists and economic historians from a large number of European countries, and with some additional representation from the USA. The aim was to initiate a programme of research on the Economic History of Europe between the Wars.

The detailed planning of the network was taken forward a year later at a conference held at Var, in Provence, with the generous assistance of the Fondation des Treilles and the memorable hospitality of its President, Madame Anne Gruner Schlumberger. This in turn led to a series of conferences, one of which, held in Venice in January 1992 and supported by the Venice Committee for Economic Studies, was devoted to the theme Banking, Currency, and Finance in Europe between the Wars. Many of the papers included in this volume were initially presented at that meeting; others were specially commissioned for the volume or arose out of the comments of the rapporteurs and others at the discussions in Venice.

I should like to express my appreciation of the efficient assistance we received at every stage of our proceedings from the European Science Foundation, and in particular from Dr Gérard Darmon, the Scientific Secretary for the Humanities and Social Sciences. I also wish to acknowledge the valuable contribution made by members of the network's Co-ordinating Committee who participated actively in all our deliberations but are not represented in this study; in particular, Professor Françoise Caron, the President, and Professors Paul Bairoch, Wolfram Fischer, Rolf Ohlsson, and Herman Van der Wee.

The programme of research which has resulted in the present volume represents one outcome of the ESF network; the work of other groups will be published in F. Caron, P. Erker, and W. Fischer (eds.), *Innovations in the European Economy between the Wars* (De Gruyter and Co., 1995) and in a forthcoming special issue of the *Scandinavian Economic History Review*, edited by R. Ohlsson, on *The European Labour Market between the Wars*.

This collection of studies of banking, exchange rates, and domestic and international financial policy in Europe between the wars is arranged in three parts. In the first the major themes are set in a broad international context, and the experience of a large number of European countries and of the USA is brought to bear on the issues considered. Part II is devoted to comparative analyses of the specific exchange-rate policies of pairs of broadly comparable countries. In each of the chapters the experience of two such countries is examined to throw further light on the causes and consequences of their decisions to change or to defend the prevailing parities. Finally, in Part III the focus narrows again to examine the inter-war economic history of the banking system in a series of individual countries.

In the first of the overall studies Feinstein, Temin, and Toniolo provide a wide-ranging introduction to international economic relations in the inter-war period. They identify four key propositions which have been advanced by a number of scholars to account for the failure of policy and perform-ance in the inter-war years. These are: (i) the problems of structural imbalance arising from the disruptive effects of the First World War, and post-war changes in technology and in patterns of demand; (ii) the inabil-ity of the United Kingdom and the unwillingness of the USA to provide the central bank leadership necessary for the successful operation of the restored gold standard; (iii) the grip on policy-makers of out-moded political and financial ideologies, evident in the insistence on substantial payments of reparations and in the attachment to the gold standard; and (iv) the absence of international co-operation between the major powers and their reluctance to abide by the 'rules of the game' under the gold standard. The chapter examines the role played by these factors in the context of the successive financial and economic developments in inter-war Europe. It thus provides both a detailed survey of banking, finance, exchange rates, and international trade in the period, and an analysis of the causes of the problems encountered.

In Chapter 2, Jonker and van Zanden investigate the banking crises experienced in twelve European industrial countries and the USA. They attempt to establish a common pattern and to identify explanations for the timing and occurrence of the crises. They find that all crises occurred during years of deflation, but not every deflationary shock led to a run on the banks. In their view the reasons why banks in some countries were vulnerable to such shocks, and others were not, are closely related to the differing degrees of inflation experienced during and just after the First World War. There were two strategies which banks could adopt in response to the erosion of the real value of their assets by inflation. They could either convert nominal into real assets, thus accelerating the trend towards commitments to industry (investment banking) already present in many countries of continental Europe. Or they could increase the rate at which they expanded their acquisition of nominal assets, leading to increased competition with other banks and a greater danger of unsound loans.

The authors conclude from their study that the poor quality of the banks' assets and the reduction in their liquidity associated with the increased commitments to industry were a leading cause of banking crises, but that nevertheless this had been a rational policy for the banks in countries which had suffered rapid inflation during and after the war: there was method in their madness.

One of the principal features of the inter-war period was the massive movements of international capital to and from, and within, Europe. In Chapter 3, Feinstein and Watson explore the nature, scale, and direction of these flows. They present new data on international capital investment as measured by balance of payments statistics for each of the main lenders and borrowers in all parts of the world. These global estimates for all creditors and all debtors ought in principle to agree, but there is a substantial discrepancy between them, particularly in the 1930s. The authors suggest that one major explanation for this is the enormous flight of capital from Europe, seeking to evade exchange controls and other restrictions on the free movement of funds.

On the basis of these estimates they discuss the reasons for, and effects of the huge movements of capital. In the period 1924–30 at least $9 billion, and perhaps considerably more was invested abroad by the USA, Britain, France, and a number of smaller creditors. This international migration of capital reached a peak in 1928 and then diminished very rapidly; after 1930 there was no further net investment abroad by the major creditors as a whole, although the USA maintained a small net outflow for three further years. From 1931 the nature and direction of the movements in international capital changed dramatically. The overall dimensions of the process were roughly the same as in the previous phase, but the content and dynamics of the movement were completely different. The flood of long-term bonds and shares which had poured out of the capital markets in New York, London, and Paris dwindled to a thin and irregular trickle. In their place vast sums flowed from the less-developed nations to their former creditors, from countries with deficits on their balance of payments to countries in surplus, and from capital markets where interest rates were high to those where they were lower. The basis for these apparently perverse movements in short-term capital is shown to be the deterioration in economic conditions and the growing fears of war and political instability in Europe.

In the last of the international chapters Eichengreen and Simmons note the radical differences in the exchange-rate regimes, and associated monetary and fiscal policies, followed in Europe after the First World War. Some countries accommodated varying degrees of inflation by abandoning their pre-war gold parities; others subjected themselves to painful deflation in order to restore gold convertibility at the pre-war rates. Major policy differences were again evident in response to the Great Depression, with some eagerly abandoning the gold standard, others seeking at all costs to preserve it. Why did countries adopt such different policies?

In an innovative attempt to answer this question Eichengreen and Simmons investigate the relationship between economic policy and domestic political institutions. They study nineteen European countries and also the USA, Japan, and Canada, and find that countries with independent central banks, more stable governments, larger governing majorities, and—more surprisingly—left-wing parliamentary majorities were better able to resist currency depreciation in the 1920s. They then discuss some of the broader implications of these results, in particular the role of electoral systems based on proportional representation, and suggest further issues on which research is needed on the link between political institutions and economic policies.

The first of the four comparative studies of exchange-rate and monetary policies in Part II contrasts attitudes and policies in Germany with those in Britain. Balderston first examines the role and effectiveness of interest rates in the 1920s, and indicates the economic and political determinants of the monetary and fiscal policies adopted in the two countries. He then turns to the failure of the gold standard in 1931. In the case of Britain, he argues that public hostility to the adverse effects of high interest rates on credit conditions and employment made the authorities insufficiently resolute in their defence of sterling. The outcome may thus be seen as a deliberate choice of policy priorities. In Germany the discount rate was used more vigorously than in Britain to defend the currency, but the confidence this created was undermined by other aspects of the Reichsbank President's policy, notably his criticisms of government finance and his confrontational stance on reparations. There was thus an incoherence in the different aspects of policy which prevented a rational ordering of Germany's policy goals.

Balderston concludes from this study of the two countries that although the failure of central banks to co-operate hastened the collapse of the gold standard, it was in each case the uncertainty of market expectations with respect to the currencies which was of primary importance. Given this uncertainty, the level of support needed to maintain confidence in the two parities would have been much larger than in earlier gold standard crises (such as 1890 or 1907), and was probably not feasible.

The next two comparative studies deal with the experience of the three 'late stabilizers', France, Italy, and Belgium. Although the French and Belgian francs were initially undervalued and the lira overvalued, there were significant similarities in subsequent developments. All three countries remained on the gold standard after the departure of Britain and other countries in 1931, and all three were eventually forced to devalue after enduring a difficult period of deflation in the mid-1930s. In Chapter 6 Asselain and Plessis examine the effects of these decisions on trade and growth in France and Italy. In both the inter-war decades Italy appears to have been more successful than France in holding down the rate of inflation and preserving the value of the currency—the primary objective of monetary policy; and also in the attainment of a more rapid rate of economic growth. The authors attribute this primarily to the ability of the Fascist dictatorship to impose a consistent policy on the Bank of Italy and the commercial banks, to maintain effective exchange controls, and to enforce wage reductions on the workers. France was less successful in all these respects.

The central feature of the comparative analysis of the French and Belgian experience by Cassiers in Chapter 7 is the distinction between the international and domestic sectors of the two economies. She shows that in Belgium, as in France, the stabilization of the franc in 1926 brought a period of export-led growth to an end, so that further economic expansion rested on a boom in the domestic sector, with high profitability and a surge in private investment. The domestic sector remained relatively prosperous during the initial stages of the Great Depression, but the strict deflationary policies imposed in the attempt to sustain the gold standard eventually reduced domestic demand and the economy plunged into depression. Both countries were forced to devalue, but political and economic differences made the process more successful in Belgium than in France.

In the last of the comparisons, Haavisto and Jonung (Chapter 8) look at the contrasting experience of Sweden and Finland. The former went back to gold at the pre-war parity; the latter returned at the existing rate, accepting the depreciation of the markka which had occurred over the war and early post-war years. The authors use a quantity-theory framework to investigate the results of the divergent exchange-rate and monetary policies followed by the two countries. The Swedish economy was forced to undergo a severe contraction, with a sharp fall in industrial production and a rise in unemployment, while Finland escaped the need for such an adjustment at the cost of a higher rate of inflation, and enjoyed a post-war boom on the basis of its devalued currency. However, this was not the result of a deliberate choice on the part of the Finnish authorities: it was rather that the central bank lacked the resources needed to support the markka.

In Part III the focus narrows further, and the spotlight now falls on the banking systems in individual countries. There are twelve separate studies covering a range of countries at different stages of development, and with different economic and financial structures. The precise theme of each chapter naturally varies according to the specific circumstances and problems in the particular country, but common elements include the development of the commercial banks, the relationship between the financial and industrial sectors, control of the money supply, the role of the central bank as regulator and as lender-of-last-resort, the degree of intervention by the central government, and the extent to which the economy and the banks were affected by the Great Depression.

When the ESF network was established we specified four aspects which we thought deserved particular emphasis in our research: the importance of an international perspective; the enhanced insight to be gained from a comparative approach; the need to take full account of the experience of a wide range of countries, including the smaller ones and those not at the financial centre of events; and the role a study of the past can play in the illumination of key issues in contemporary policy concerns. In the course of our research and in our debates the significance of all of these aspects has emerged even more strongly, and we hope that this volume on the theme of banking, currency, and finance will make a distinctive contribution to wider knowledge and understanding of the economic history of inter-war Europe.

C. H. F.

PART I

The International Context

1

International Economic Organization: Banking, Finance, and Trade in Europe between the Wars

CHARLES H. FEINSTEIN, PETER TEMIN, and GIANNI TONIOLO

1. Introduction

Chaos, crisis, and catastrophe are terms which feature prominently in the economic history of inter-war Europe, applied to the functioning at various stages of prices and money supplies, foreign exchange rates, gold and capital movements, banking systems, and external trade. Early in the period there were several spectacular episodes of hyperinflation in central and eastern Europe, and many other countries suffered severe though less drastic inflation and corresponding depreciation of the external value of their currencies. There was a short-lived post-war boom followed by a slump, and a number of countries experienced serious banking crises in 1920–1. These inflationary and financial problems were a direct consequence of the First World War. So too was the colossal burden of inter-Allied debts, and the attempt of the Allies, particularly France, to extract huge sums in reparations from Germany. The struggle to cope with these enormous obligations was one of the critical factors in the financial instability of the 1920s. A further aspect of great significance was the widespread belief in financial and political circles that it was essential to return to the pre-war gold standard if the growth and prosperity of the pre-1914 era were to be re-established, whatever the sacrifices that would have to be made in order to force down wages and prices so that the pre-war value of the currency could be restored. The attempt to achieve this reconstruction of the gold standard dominated the financial policies of Britain, France, Germany, Italy, Belgium, the Scandinavian countries, Czechoslovakia, and many other Central and Eastern European nations.

An apparent measure of progress was achieved by the mid-1920s, and confidence and production revived. Improved economic understanding among the major powers was reflected in the acceptance in 1924 of the Dawes Plan for the future payment of reparations, and a new measure of political agreement was achieved with the ending of the French occupation of the Ruhr and the signing of the Locarno Pact. There was a brief interlude of relative stability and economic growth, but this could not be sustained.

In the mid-1920s agricultural producers were hit by falling prices, especially for wheat and sugar, and signs of impending recession were evident in Germany from 1928. The following year saw the beginning of a series of damaging banking panics and failures in Europe, culminating in 1931 in the collapse of the largest Austrian bank, and serious bank crises in Germany and the USA. This financial crisis merged with steeply falling commodity prices, and the collapse in output and employment in both industrial and primary producing countries to create the 'Great Depression', a world-wide cyclical decline of unprecedented intensity and duration. In September 1931 Britain was no longer able to meet her obligations to supply gold to her international creditors, and abandoned the gold standard. Numerous other countries followed her example and the international economic system established at such high cost in the 1920s was completely shattered at the beginning of the 1930s.

With the disintegration of the gold standard and the breakdown of international monetary co-operation, the world economy fragmented into hostile blocs, with mounting economic and political competition between the sterling area, the gold bloc, and the group of countries dominated by Nazi Germany. The period was marked by successive currency devaluations, the introduction of exchange controls, and the imposition of a wide variety of barriers to trade, all taking the major countries further away from the orthodox ideals of *laissez-faire*, free trade, and stable currencies. Britain and the Scandinavian countries, freed by devaluation from the need to protect their currencies, were able to initiate expansionary monetary policies and enjoyed five or six years of improving trade, rapid growth, and rising prosperity.

For other nations it was a time of considerable difficulty and slow recovery. This was true for the USA, even after the suspension of gold payments in 1933 and the devaluation of the dollar in early 1934. It applied, to an even greater extent, to those gold bloc countries who were determined to maintain their commitment to gold. As their competitive position deteriorated the attempt to cling to their pre-1931 gold parities became increasingly untenable, and they were finally compelled to devalue. Belgium capitulated to the speculative pressures in 1935, France late in 1936, swiftly followed by Switzerland and the Netherlands. The collapse of the French franc and a growing sense of the need for political solidarity on the part of the democracies, pushed a reluctant France, Britain, and the USA to take some limited and tentative steps back towards a more co-operative international framework. This was given formal expression in the Tripartite Agreement under which the three countries undertook to relax quotas and exchange controls and to avoid competitive devaluations. Germany and Italy stood outside this framework, with Hitler and Mussolini forcing their economies progressively further in the direction of state control, militarism, and autarky, dragging with them many of the countries of central and south-east Europe in a web of exchange controls, tariffs, and special bilateral trading arrangements.

The aim of this paper is to provide a brief description of these much-discussed events, and to analyse the primary causes of the successive financial and economic developments and of their interrelationship.[1] The Great Depression of 1929–33 and the financial crisis of 1931 are placed at the centre of the narrative, and are presented both as the culmination of the policies and practices of the 1920s, and as a powerful influence on the subsequent economic history of the 1930s. The unifying theme of the chapter is the impact of various forms and aspects of international economic organization on world economic stability. Four key propositions or hypotheses relating to the organization of international economic relations have been advanced by various writers to account for the failures of policy and performance in the years 1919–39. These recur throughout our account of this period, though with differing emphases in different phases, and we begin by briefly summarizing each of the propositions. We then revert to them and discuss their validity and applicability at appropriate points in the subsequent narrative.

Four propositions about international economic organization

For the early 1920s the traditional explanation for the depth and persistence of the widespread post-war difficulties is the problem of structural imbalance between countries. The origins of this dislocation are found in the changes in the composition of production and demand resulting from the wartime disruption of international trade, from the geopolitical effects of the Peace Treaty, and from post-war changes in technology and in patterns of demand. Although the effects of these changes are not always clearly spelled out, they may be taken to relate particularly to a misallocation of resources which was responsible for the high rate of unemployment in Europe in the 1920s, and which also made the adjustment process longer and more costly. The effects of these structural changes were felt in both labour and in product markets, in each of which, it is argued, there was appreciably less flexibility after 1918.

---

[1] There is a vast literature devoted to these topics and to the related political disputes. Recent general surveys of the economic issues in English include Moggridge (1989), Temin (1989), and Eichengreen (1992). The economic history of the 1920s has been covered by Aldcroft (1977) and the 1930s by Kindleberger (1973). There is also valuable material in earlier accounts such as those of Hodson (1938), Hawtrey (1939), Brown (1940) and the work done for the League of Nations, notably by Ohlin (1931) and Nurkse (1944). More specialized modern research is reported in Drummond (1981), Holtfrerich (1986), James (1986), McNeil (1986), Schuker (1988), Eichengreen (1990), James *et al.* (1991), Mouré (1991), and numerous other books and articles listed in the references at the end of this chapter.

The next explanation which has received prominence in relation to the late 1920s, notably in Brown (1940) and Kindleberger (1973), is the lack of central bank leadership in the operation of the restored gold standard: the proposition summed up in the phrase: 'no longer London, not yet Washington'. The diminished financial status of the United Kingdom meant that London was unable to act as sole conductor of the international orchestra; or—in more modern terminology—to operate as the hegemon, while the USA was not yet willing to take over this role despite the enormous improvement in its international economic standing. The ability of London to perform its traditional role as the dominant economic power was further undermined by the enhanced strength of France's relative financial position after the stabilization of the franc in 1926 and the large accumulation of gold by the Banque de France. The specific economic connotation of this lack of leadership was that there was no country able and willing to stabilize the global financial environment by acting as international lender-of-last-resort.

The third factor emphasized in the literature is the hold on policy-makers of old-fashioned political and financial ideologies. The former is seen as responsible for the insistence on substantial reparations. This produced a new pattern of international settlements that made the smooth functioning of international payments dependent upon the capability and willingness of the USA to continue lending indefinitely to Europe. The destabilizing potential of this 'arrangement' is self-evident. Even more important was the financial ideology reflected in the priority attached to the reintroduction of the gold standard, even where this could be achieved only by subjecting the economy to a severe programme of deflation and obstructing future trade by the imposition of an overvalued currency. Under the discipline which this doctrine enjoined—or the values it projected—country after country surrendered its 'monetary sovereignty' and restricted its ability to accommodate balance of payments disturbances by any means other than retrenchment.

Finally, the absence of international co-operation between the USA, Britain, France, and Germany, and the failure of the major nations to co-ordinate international economic policy, has been put forward as the primary explanation for the problems of the inter-war period. Clarke (1967) has argued this specifically in relation to the period from mid-1928 to the collapse of the gold standard in 1931, claiming that after the death of Benjamin Strong, governor of the Federal Reserve Bank of New York, the central bankers failed to achieve the necessary co-ordination of policy. More generally, Eichengreen (1985, 1992) has suggested this as a central feature of the entire period, manifest particularly in the attempt of each of the main powers to secure for itself a disproportionate share of the world's limited stocks of monetary gold. Prior to the collapse of the gold standard in 1931 their non-co-operative behaviour involved the imposition of tight monetary policies not only by countries in deficit, but also by those—notably the USA and France—which were in surplus. This added to the deflationary pressures on the world economy and also increased the vulnerability of the weak currencies, such as sterling and the mark, to speculative attack.

In other variants of this theme, the shortcomings of the inter-war adjustment mechanism are explained by the unwillingness of central banks to operate the gold standard according to the 'rules of the game', under which all movements in gold should have been fully reflected in compensating changes in domestic money supplies. The main reason for this tendency to neutralize changes in gold and foreign exchange reserves rather than allow them to influence internal monetary conditions, was that post-war governments were no longer willing to give unconditional support to external equilibrium and the defence of the reserves; democratic electorates increasingly required that they should attach greater weight to internal stability of prices and incomes. 'When the precepts of the gold standard ran counter to the requirements of domestic monetary stability, it was the latter that usually prevailed' (Nurkse, 1944: 105; see also Nevin, 1955). But the new position was not entirely symmetrical: there was always greater pressure to neutralize an outflow of gold than an inflow, and this imparted a deflationary bias to the whole system.

The inability of the powers to co-operate was dramatically symbolized at the World Monetary Conference in the summer of 1933, meeting in London shortly after the USA had abandoned the gold standard and allowed the dollar to depreciate. The gathering had been specifically convened to promote the co-ordinated stabilization of exchange rates, but in the middle of the proceedings Roosevelt announced that he was not willing to stabilize the dollar. He brusquely dismissed 'the specious fallacy of achieving a temporary and probably an artificial stability in foreign exchanges on the part of a few large countries only' (Hodson, 1938: 194). This disastrous meeting starkly exposed the total lack of any common ground between countries and hastened the further disintegration of the international monetary system. With global political relations also deteriorating rapidly the decade witnessed an epidemic of competitive currency depreciations, extended resort to exchange controls, the rise of protectionism, bilateralism, import quotas, and other barriers to trade, and the development of hostile, non-co-operating trade and currency blocs.

Elements of these four problems of international economic organization can be found throughout the inter-war period, but the first has dominated explanations of the early 1920s; the lack of central bank leadership has been particularly invoked to account for the developments of 1925–30; the role of financial ideology and the acceptance of the gold standard is seen as specially important in accounting for the Great Depression and the

propagation of the financial crises of 1930–5; and the inability of the major
nations to co-operate in the co-ordination of international economic policy
is given as a crucial factor, underlying both the disintegration of the attempt
to reconstruct the pre-1914 gold standard and the emergence of rival trade
and currency blocs.

The legacy of the First World War

It is impossible to understand the economic history of inter-war Europe and,
more specifically, that of its international economic organization, without
considering the long-lasting effects of a war which was first bitterly fought
on the battlefield and then continued, more subtly, in post-war political and
economic policies.

The First World War marked the true watershed between the nineteenth
and twentieth centuries. This is especially true when we consider our central
theme of international economic organization. In the nineteenth century this
was characterized by a relatively well-functioning international payment
system based on the gold standard, in which London played a pivotal and
stabilizing role, and the leading central banks co-operated as necessary
(Brown, 1940; Nevin, 1955; Bloomfield, 1959; Eichengreen, 1985). In addition, there was almost perfect mobility of factors of production reflected in
large-scale movements of labour and capital from Europe to the New
World, and relatively free movement of goods, due partly to free trade in
Britain and moderate tariff protection elsewhere, and partly to the existence
of large 'customs unions' such as the Habsburg and Tsarist empires within
which goods moved freely. The First World War brought down all three of
these pillars of the nineteenth-century international economic order.

The most enduring legacy of the war was instability. We have not the
space to concern ourselves here with social and political instability (seen in
its most extreme form in the forces which produced Mussolini in Italy,
Primo de Rivera and civil war in Spain, and Hitler in Germany) though this
played a major role in generating an unstable international economic
environment, but confine our attention to those consequences of the First
World War which adversely affected the post-war organization and activity
of the Continental economies, individually and collectively. Five such effects
deserve special mention.

1. The war caused a major disruption of the real economy, both on the
demand and on the supply sides. In every belligerent country there was a
swift change in production and consumption patterns under the pressure to
recruit men and women for the armed forces and provide military supplies
for the war economy. Heroic efforts were made to increase productive
capacity in war-related industries such as engineering, iron and steel, and
shipbuilding. Much of this became superfluous once the war was over, but

it proved exceptionally difficult to adjust to the required patterns of peacetime production. In part this was the consequence of the terrible devastation of transport networks and of fields, houses, factories, and mines during the fighting. The destruction was worst in France, Belgium, Italy, and Poland, but many other countries also endured considerable loss of fixed assets. In other cases the return to pre-war patterns was impossible because extra-European powers, notably the USA and Japan, had seized the opportunity created by the inability of British and other European manufacturers to maintain their normal trading activity, and had successfully invaded their markets. Japan, in particular, rapidly increased her sales to many Asian countries which had previously looked mainly to Britain for their imports. The war also stimulated domestic production, for example, of coal in Europe or of cotton textiles and other manufactures in India and Latin America, and so further reduced the markets on which the pre-war output of the exporting nations had depended.

2. Further disturbance to trade and production occurred as a result of the way in which the political map of Europe was redrawn by the post-war peace treaties. In many cases pre-1914 trading patterns, communications, and financial relations were disrupted, and the creation of smaller nation states in the territories of the former Russian and Austro-Hungarian Empires led to the creation of new currencies, additional trade barriers, and a less efficient allocation of resources. More generally, the imposition of tariffs (whether as a source of urgently needed revenue or as a means of protection), the loss of gold and exchange reserves, and the diminished possibilities for foreign borrowing by countries already overburdened by debts and/or claims for reparations, all helped further to restrict the scope for foreign trade.

3. Once the war was over, the greatest possible degree of flexibility in prices and practices was required in order to adjust to these devastating domestic and external shocks, but in fact the prevailing trend was towards greater rigidity. A long-run tendency for the flexibility of price and wage structures to decrease is likely to be a feature of all advanced democratic economies which give high priority to the stability of nominal incomes, prices, and employment, but the war considerably hastened the process. In the post-war labour market, wage flexibility was diminished as many more decisions were centrally negotiated in a greatly extended process of collective bargaining. Behind this change lay the growth of working-class militancy and the dramatic rise in the membership and strength of the trade union movement. In part this reflected the new mood of solidarity generated by the experience of the long and bloody battles fought side by side in the trenches. Other reasons, also related directly or indirectly to the war, were disappointment with the failure of the politicians to keep the promises which they had made when sacrifices were needed both from those who fought at

the front and those who worked at home to supply them with arms and equipment; the high levels to which unemployment soared abruptly from the middle of 1920; and the success of the Bolshevik Revolution.

In the goods market there was again a tendency to reduced flexibility of property incomes and of prices. The war contributed to this by an increase in government intervention in economic life, the formation or strengthening of trade associations, and the imposition of numerous controls; each of these features survived in varying degrees into the post-war period. More fundamentally, the war accelerated the trend towards larger business units, and in the extremely difficult circumstances of the 1920s many firms looked to collusion, to cartels, and to the exercise of monopoly powers to escape the consequences of increasing competition for shrinking markets. In Germany cartels and other forms of industrial combination were already well established before the war, and the increase in their scope and strength during the 1920s enabled them to resist falling prices by restricting production. In Britain a similar trend was strongly fostered by the government, which deliberately promoted legislation and other measures to reduce competition in industries such as cotton, shipbuilding, and coal-mining.

4. The financial sector was also greatly affected, with extensive interference in the peacetime patterns of both domestic and international markets. Most obviously, the war and its aftermath gave rise to unprecedented needs for revenue: it is estimated that the direct cost of the war in constant pre-war prices was the equivalent of five times the world-wide national debt in 1914 (Woytinski, 1955 quoted in Aldcroft, 1977: 30). In all countries note issues and bank credits were expanded by immense amounts, with little or no attempt either to raise taxes or to borrow from the public on the scale needed to offset the additional demand on resources generated by the enormous military expenditures. The United Kingdom did more than any other nation to impose additional taxes, but even this was sufficient to cover only one-third of its wartime expenditure; in France the proportion was about 15 per cent, in Germany at most 6 per cent (Morgan, 1952: 104; Patat and Lutfalla, 1986, English edn. 1990: 24; Holtfrerich, 1986: 105).

After the war further huge sums were required to service these swollen internal public debts, much of it short-term, and to meet the external demands for payment of war debts and reparations. Yet further large outlays were necessary in order to make good the terrible destruction which so many countries had suffered during the savage campaigns, especially in France and Belgium. A large body of literature exists on some aspects of this financial dislocation, especially on reparations, on inter-Allied debts (more generally on Europe becoming a net debtor) and on the new pattern of international lending—what Schuker (1988) calls American reparations to Germany. Less is known about changes in the web of international banking that provided the grass-roots connection for the international transfer of short- and long-term capital, as well as for the actual day-by-day functioning of an international payment system.

5. Finally, the classic gold standard was an early casualty of the conflict. Within a few months of the declaration of war almost all European central banks, including those in countries that were to remain neutral, had unilaterally suspended gold payments. During the war, the powers of the Entente developed their own payment system backed by the inter-Allied loans. This was designed to allow the belligerent countries to sustain the level of imports required to achieve the maximum military contribution to the common cause. However, once the war was over co-operation ceased almost overnight. Inter-Allied financial assistance was suspended, and creditor countries immediately made clear that they expected reimbursement of their war loans. At the same time, the victorious powers insisted on extracting an unrealistic amount of reparations from those they had defeated; with French retaliation for the terms which Germany had imposed on her after victory in 1870 as the dominant factor in preventing a more realistic settlement. A typical inter-war British view of the overall financial outcome is given in the following scathing comment by Lionel Robbins (1934: 6):

The inordinate claims of the victors, the crass financial incapacity of the vanquished, the utter budgetary disorder which everywhere in the belligerent countries was the legacy of the policies pursued during the war, led to a further period of monetary chaos.

We turn now to consider the way in which these and other consequences of the Great War took effect in the course of the financial and economic developments of the 1920s.

2. The Crises of the 1920s

Accelerating prices and hyperinflation

During the war years prices rose rapidly in all the belligerent countries as demands increased and supplies were disrupted, and the neutral countries could not remain immune from this process. The extent to which prices surged upwards between 1914 and 1918 is shown for a selection of countries in the first column of Table 1.1. There was a brief respite immediately after the armistice, when commodity prices fell, but from the spring of 1919 inflation resumed its course during a boom which lasted until the spring or summer of 1920, and was especially strong in the United Kingdom and some of the neutral countries, and in the USA. As can be seen from column

18   *C. H. Feinstein, P. Temin, and G. Toniolo*

(2) of Table 1.1 the extent of the inflation in 1920 varied widely, but the experience of rising prices was common to all countries.

TABLE 1.1.   *Consumer price indices, European countries, 1918–1926 (1914 = 100)*

	1918 (1)	1920 (2)	1922 (3)	1924 (4)	1926 (5)
Countries with hyperinflation until 1922 or 1923					
Austria	1,163	5,115	263,938	86[a]	103
Germany	304	990	14,602	128[a]	141
Countries in which inflation continued after 1920					
Belgium	1,434	—	340	469	604
Finland	633	889	1,033	1,055	1,078
Italy	289	467	467	481	618
France	213	371	315	395	560
Countries in which inflation was controlled after 1920					
Norway	253	300	231	239	206
Sweden	219	269	198	174	173
Switzerland	204	224	164	169	162
UK	200	248	181	176	171
Denmark	182	261	200	216	184
Netherlands	162	194	149	145	138

[a] Linked to base year via gold price. For Austria the index for 1923 on this basis was 76. For Germany the hyperinflation continued until late in 1923 and the price index for that year (1914 = 100) was 15,437,000,000,000.

Source: Maddison (1991: 300–3).

From the middle of 1920 the boom gave way to a world-wide slump and this continued until 1921 or, in some cases, a year later. The depression was particularly severe in the United Kingdom and the USA; Germany was one of the few countries which escaped. During this cycle and the subsequent years experience diverged sharply, and three distinct trends in the behaviour of prices can be identified. In one group of countries, represented in the upper panel of Table 1.1 by Germany and Austria, monetary stability was completely destroyed and inflation gave way to hyperinflation. In a second group, represented by Belgium, Finland, Italy, and France in the middle panel, inflation continued but was not allowed to get completely out of control. The third group, consisting of the Scandinavian countries, Switzerland, Britain, and the Netherlands, imposed strict deflationary policies of dear money and fiscal restraint, and by this means succeeded in actually reducing prices and wages until 1922 or 1923. Thereafter prices in this group of countries were broadly stable or falling.

Five countries proved totally unable to contain the war and post-war pressures and were ravaged by hyperinflation. These were Austria, Hungary,

Poland, Russia, and Germany. The latter was by far the most remarkable case, culminating in wholesale prices rising at the astronomical rate of 335 per cent per month from August 1922 to November 1923 (Holtfrerich, 1986: 17). Even as the inflationary spiral was gathering momentum there was heated controversy about its causes.[2] Within Germany almost all officials, bankers, industrialists, and a great many economists adopted the balance of payments theory, according to which the root cause of the inflation was to be found in the burden of reparations and occupation costs imposed on a defeated Germany. It was claimed that it was this which was primarily responsible for the magnitude of the deficit on the balance of payments, and that this deficit in turn caused the extraordinary depreciation in the external value of the mark and forced up import prices. As the accelerating costs and prices spread through the economy the authorities were compelled to expand the issues of paper money, thus fuelling the inflation. This analysis was supported by some foreign scholars, notably Williams (1922) and Graham (1930).

Opponents of this view reversed the causal chain and advocated a quantity theory explanation. They argued that it was the excessive issue of paper money which initiated the vicious circle, and traced this back to the size of the massive budget deficit. An authoritative inter-war exposition of the quantity theory explanation was given by Bresciani-Turroni (1937). He argued that the crux of the problem was to be found not in reparation payments but in the enormous increase in state spending. This sprang both from the heavy reliance on borrowing during the war, and from the huge outlays required by post-war economic and social programmes. The political parties were too weak to resist the pressure for this expenditure; the vested interests on either side were too bitterly divided to reach any agreement on how the necessary taxes should be allocated between labour and capital. The printing of paper money thus provided the only acceptable way out of the dilemma, and at least initially it could be argued by many of the contending social groups that the resulting inflation brought more benefits than costs.

The headlong expansion of the money supply in turn reduced the external value of the currency and so added further to the inflationary pressures. To make matters worse, the unexpectedly rapid pace of the inflation itself undermined attempts to balance the budget, since the real value of any revenue received was always less than had been anticipated when the taxes were imposed. Assessment of many taxes was also made more difficult in conditions of rapid inflation. The effect of the expanded note issue was then

---

[2] For a summary of the views of contemporary German participants in this debate, including the officials of the Reichsbank, see Bresciani-Turroni (1937: 42–7) and Holtfrerich (1986: 156–72). Other recent studies of the phenomenon include Laursen and Pedersen (1964), Feldman *et al.* (1982), and Webb (1989).

intensified by a steep rise in the velocity of circulation. From the outbreak of war until the summer of 1921 the currency in circulation and the internal price level had increased broadly in line (apart from a brief 'flight from the mark' in 1919) so that there was virtually no change in the real value of the paper money in circulation. But then the signing of the London Ultimatum and the imposition of what were seen to be excessive demands for reparations changed expectations. From the summer of 1921 the flight from the currency became continually quicker as first Germans and then foreigners lost confidence in the value of the mark. By the second half of 1922 the demand for real money balances was falling steeply (i.e. there was an abrupt rise in the velocity of circulation) and the acceleration in the rate of price increase outpaced even the exceptionally rapid growth of the money supply (Bresciani-Turroni, 1937: 162–75; Holtfrerich, 1986: 184–93).

This inability to cope with the abnormal fiscal problems created by the First World War and its aftermath was equally characteristic of post-war governments in the other hyperinflation countries. It also applied, though to a lesser extent, to many of the countries in the second and third groups mentioned above, and was largely responsible for the inflationary trends in those countries. Apart from the enormous costs of the war and the post-war restoration, the years of conflict had transformed social and political attitudes, weakening the old order and accelerating the rise of the working classes. In the tense and difficult situation created by defeat, devastation, and financial disorder the political parties in countries such as Austria, France, Belgium, and Italy could not agree on how the burden of taxation should be shared between the different social classes, and as in Germany distributional conflicts over taxes and incomes stand out as a principal source of financial instability in the post-war years.

Stability and crisis in the European banking systems

As noted above, the lively boom which followed the Armistice came to an end in the middle of 1920, and output, employment, and incomes began to fall in almost all countries; in a number of cases the recession proved to be fairly severe. Of the large countries of Europe, only Germany escaped a post-war slump due to the temporarily beneficial effects of hyperinflation: investment was encouraged by the fall in real interest rates and exports were stimulated as long as the depreciation of the mark outpaced the relative rise in German prices. A number of countries also experienced a banking crisis in this period. Whether or not such a crisis developed, and the extent of its severity, depended on three main factors: the organization of the banking system, the severity of the depression in the real economy, and the policy-stance of the central bank. Banks were more likely to fail in countries where they entertained close links with their industrial clients, on the German model of 'universal banking', where the real slump was more severe and accompanied by a price deflation, and where the central bank was unwilling or unable to act as a swift lender-of-last-resort. Where such crises occurred this, in turn, produced feedback effects on the real side of the economy.

Thus in Britain (see Chapter 15 by Capie) where there had been no panic or financial crisis since 1860, one would expect to find the highest degree of stability in the banking system, and 1920–1 was no exception. The separation between banks and industry was, by then, quite well established, so that banks did well in terms of profitability and currency/deposit ratios during the post-war depression; the depression itself was rather mild; and the Bank of England had developed such a reputation as lender-of-last-resort that it could defuse the possibility of banking panics by its very presence. The Irish system (described in Chapter 16 by Ó Gráda) also remained stable, both because of similar factors to those in Great Britain, and because of the close links between the two financial systems.

The French case, discussed in Chapter 11 by Lescure, is perhaps less clear-cut, but the reasons for the overall stability of its banking system may nevertheless be traced back to the three factors mentioned above. During and after the war, most French enterprises continued in their time-honoured tradition of self-financing from retained profits. Universal banking existed in France but was normally confined to small provincial banks. The crisis of 1921 made some enterprises less reluctant than before to resort to long-term bank credit but it was, on average, a rather limited phenomenon. Deposits fell in real terms during the first part of the 1920s as a response to inflation and to the high yields of state bonds, but the reaction of banks was prudent: they increased the liquidity of their portfolio. The Banque de France favoured this process by encouraging the placement of government securities with banks. The real recession was rather mild and—a very important point—was not coupled with price deflation.

The stability of the post-war German financial system, examined in Chapter 9 by Hardach, is particularly interesting, and contrasts sharply with the collapse of 1931. From this particular point of view, inflation was a 'blessing' since it resulted in growth rather than a slump in the real sector, and in the economy being oversupplied with liquidity. Given the fact that central bank credit financed most of the government's expenditure, there could be no question about lending-of-last-resort to financial institutions, which obviously proved to be unnecessary. Inflation also ensured the post-war stability of the Austrian and Polish banking systems (see Chapter 12 by Weber and Chapter 13 by Landau and Morawski). In Austria, however, the stabilization of the currency, with the necessary deflationary pressure, produced a stock exchange crash in 1924, and the resulting crisis in the real and financial sector of the economy caused widespread failures among small- and medium-sized universal banks.

Elsewhere bank failures were more common; they characterized the post-war economies of Italy, Spain, Portugal, and Norway (see the chapters in Part III by Toniolo, Martín-Aceña, Reis, and Nordvik). In Italy the third and fourth largest universal banks in the country became insolvent between 1921 and 1923, partly as a result of overtrading during and soon after the war, and the difficulties were exacerbated by the cyclical downturn of 1920–1. One of these banks was declared bankrupt at the end of 1921, but deposits were to a large extent guaranteed by the central bank, which also saved a metal-making and engineering concern—probably the most important in the country—owned by the bank. In the following year, fearing a run on deposits should another large bank go under, the central bank staged a large lending-of-last-resort operation in favour of the fourth largest bank in the country. Thus, a pseudo-financial crisis characterized post-war Italy, due to the active policy-stance of the central bank which gave priority to bank stability over other policy goals such as currency stabilization (Guarino and Toniolo 1993).

The Spanish central bank was not as ready as its Italian sister to accommodate the liquidity needs of credit institutions in serious difficulty. It, therefore, remained on the sidelines in 1920 when an early recession in manufacturing made a number of Catalan universal banks insolvent. The crisis hit the most developed region in the country, with the eventual failure of the oldest and most prominent Spanish credit institutions (see further Chapter 20 by Martín-Aceña). The crisis was very severe in Barcelona but its effect on Madrid and Bilbao, the two other financial centres in the country, was relatively mild. However, a new wave of runs on bank deposits unfolded in the second half of 1924; after years of persistently falling prices, both of goods and of financial assets (industrial shares), during which industrial companies required continuous assistance from credit institutions, a number of banks were dragged into insolvency. Again, the central bank remained passive, only in the case of the Banco Central, one of the largest in Spain, was it forced to yield to pressure from the Government of Primo de Rivera and provide enough assistance so that the Banco could actually overcome its problems.

In the Netherlands and in Scandinavia, bank failure followed the slump of 1920. In Denmark the central bank took a fairly active stance and was able to avoid a major confidence shock. The Bank of the Netherlands seems to have been less successful in this respect, and the failure of one of the largest commercial banks shook public confidence. As Nordvik shows in Chapter 17, the Norwegian case stands out for the length of its banking troubles, which lasted from 1923 to 1928. As the wartime boom in the real sector was particularly buoyant, the slump was relatively more serious than elsewhere, particularly given the strong deflationary policy imposed to stabilize the currency and return to gold. Given the links between manufacturing firms and banks, and the unwillingness of the central bank to let lending-of-last-resort jeopardize its monetary stance, it is not surprising that bank failures followed one after the other for a longer period than anywhere else. It is likely that institutional innovation embodied in the Bank Administration Act made things worse rather than better.

To sum up: the post-war slump in the real economy resulted in financial panics and runs on banks whenever (a) the latter had established close long-term relationships with their client firms of the kind that characterized the so-called universal banks, and (b) the central bank decided to refrain from providing the necessary liquidity either for policy reasons or for sheer prejudice. The story repeated itself on a larger scale ten years later, so that one may wonder why the lesson was not better learned.

Stabilization and the return to gold

As long as the post-war fiscal problems persisted, prices continued to increase and currencies to depreciate. Eventually, however, even those social groups who found some benefit in inflation began to fear its continuation, and the compromises necessary to reduce spending, raise taxes, and restrict the creation of credit were agreed. In many cases the process was assisted by foreign stabilization or reconstruction loans and by temporary credits, both mainly from London and New York, but in some cases arranged through the League of Nations. The issue of domestic loans to fund the excessive short-term debt was also important, notably in the French and Belgian stabilizations. At various dates between 1922 and 1927 the major countries in the first and second groups in Table 1.1 achieved the necessary degree of monetary and financial stabilization to restore the gold standard, with its commitment to sound money and fixed exchange rates. By the end of the decade only the Spanish peseta remained to be stabilized.

The dates at which this was achieved *de facto* (legal restoration was sometimes delayed for various reasons) are given in Table 1.2, together with a measure of the extent to which the foreign exchange value of each currency had depreciated as compared with its pre-war parity. The countries are again arranged in three groups which correspond to those in Table 1.1. The extreme cases of inflation and hyperinflation leading to stabilization of the currency at 10 per cent of the pre-war parity or less are in the upper group. At the other extreme, the six countries which imposed strict deflationary policies after 1920, and were able to return to gold at their pre-war parities, are covered in the lower group. In the middle group are examples of countries which allowed serious inflation to continue after 1920, but eventually stabilized their currencies at between 10 and 30 per cent of the pre-war rate.

The First World War had imposed heavy costs on Britain, but she had been less adversely affected than the Continental belligerents by physical destruction and financial disruption and, despite Keynes's forceful dissent, prevailing opinion strongly favoured a return to gold at the pre-war parity (Moggridge, 1972; Sayers, 1976). The objective, the method, and the price to be paid were clearly set out early in 1920 in a memorandum by the Bank of England to the Chancellor of the Exchequer (quoted in Howson, 1975: 18–19):

The first and most urgent task before the Country is to get back to the gold standard by getting rid of this specific depreciation of the currency. This end can only be achieved by a reversal of the process by which the specific depreciation was produced, the artificial creation of currency and credit, and for this the appropriate instrument is the rate of interest. The process of deflation of prices which may be expected to follow on the check to the expansion of credit must necessarily be a painful one to some classes of the community, but this is unavoidable.

TABLE 1.2.   *Post-war stabilization of European currencies, 1922–1929*

	Year of *de facto* restoration of gold standard (1)	New parity as percentage of pre-war (2)
Stabilization at less than 10% of pre-war parities		
Germany	1923	0.0000000001
Poland	1926	0.000026
Austria	1922	0.00007
Hungary	1924	0.0069
Romania	1927	3.1
Bulgaria	1924	3.8
Portugal	1929	4.1
Greece	1927	6.7
Yugoslavia	1925	8.9
Stabilization at between 10 and 30% of pre-war parities		
Finland	1924	13.0
Belgium	1926	14.5
Czechoslovakia	1923	14.6
France	1926	20.3
Italy	1926	27.3
Stabilization at pre-war parity		
Sweden	1922	100
Netherlands	1924	100
Switzerland	1924	100
United Kingdom	1925	100
Denmark	1926	100
Norway	1928	100

Sources: Brown (1940: 393–402; 919 and 1,028); League of Nations (1944: 116); Nötel (1986: 181–3).

None of the other belligerents shared this determination, but among the neutrals the Scandinavian countries, Switzerland, and the Netherlands were similarly committed to the restoration of the pre-war parity of their currencies. In Denmark voices were raised among politicians, businessmen, and economists recommending stabilization at about 75 per cent of the old parity, but they were unable to 'win the struggle for public opinion against the slogans of the deflationists who demanded return to "our old, honest krone" '; there was a parallel debate in Norway where an even greater appreciation of the currency was required (Lester, 1939).

In the event a very high price had to be paid for this belief in the virtues of the return to gold at the old parity. In Britain the collapse of the export industries, and the sustained downward pressure on wages, employment, and working-class living standards have frequently been seen as the sacrifice which the financial interests of the City imposed on industry in order to preserve the gold standard (Pollard, 1970; Ingham, 1984; Boyce, 1987). In Denmark and Norway it caused a depression lasting from 1925 to 1928 which was almost as severe as that in 1929–33, with sharply falling production and prices, an increased number of business failures, and very high unemployment (Lester, 1939). Sweden similarly experienced considerable difficulties at the beginning of the 1920s; the contrast with the developments in Finland which chose not to follow the deflationary path is brought out in Chapter 8 by Haavisto and Jonung. Italy, together with the two other 'late stabilizers', France and Belgium, initially enjoyed a brief period when their exports benefited from exchange rates more favourable than those of the countries which followed orthodox deflationary policies. However, once Mussolini had decided that the lira should be stabilized at the *quota novanta*, representing a substantial upward revaluation of the prevailing rate, it became necessary to impose painful deflationary measures, resulting in slower growth of output and investment, and higher unemployment (see Cohen, 1972 and Chapter 6 by Asselain and Plessis).

Once stabilization was achieved further problems were created by the extent of the relative over- and under-valuation of currencies resulting from the haphazard and uncoordinated process by which each country selected its parity. Some currencies, notably those of Britain, Italy, Denmark, and Norway were probably overvalued; in other cases, including France, Belgium, and Poland, the rate selected provided a degree of undervaluation. These disparities had important consequences for competitiveness in foreign trade. However, other powerful forces were also at work, and these too contributed to the very varied pattern of export performance in the 1920s. The data are given in Table 1.3, listed in the order indicated by the level achieved by 1929 relative to 1913.

In the case of Britain it has been generally accepted that the decision to return to gold at the pre-war parity of \$4.86 resulted in an overvaluation of the currency by about 10 per cent. It would, however, be wrong to see this as the primary reason for the decline of the export sector shown in Table

1.3. Coal, textiles, shipbuilding, and other major export industries were already confronted by an extremely difficult structural problem created by technological change, the growth of substitute products, and the opportunity which the war had provided for foreign competitors outside Europe, notably the USA and Japan, to capture a large share of Britain's traditional markets. Nevertheless, the overvaluation of sterling undoubtedly added significantly to the fundamental structural weakness, as did the high interest rates necessary to sustain the currency.

TABLE 1.3.   *Volume of merchandise exports, European countries, 1924–1929*
(1913 = 100)

	1924	1925	1926	1927	1928	1929
Denmark	142	138	147	170	179	181
Netherlands	125	135	140	161	166	171
Norway	111	122	130	141	143	167
Finland	125	139	142	160	156	161
Sweden	96	106	114	136	131	156
France	119	124	134	146	148	147
Italy	117	127	123	116	118	123
Belgium	—	73	76	96	108	107
Switzerland	87	90	87	98	101	101
Germany	51	65	72	73	82	92
Austria	76	82	77	87	92	86
United Kingdom	76	75	67	77	80	81

Source: Maddison (1991: 316–19).

As Table 1.3 indicates, the 1929 volume of British exports was still 19 per cent below its level in 1913. Of the other European countries which re-established their currencies at the pre-war parity against gold only Switzerland was unable to expand her exports above the pre-war level. Despite the probable overvaluation of their currencies, Norway increased the volume of her exports relative to 1913 by 67 per cent and Denmark by 81 per cent. Sweden and the Netherlands managed 56 per cent and 71 per cent respectively. For these countries, as for the less fortunate cases of Belgium, Germany, and Austria, other factors were clearly of more importance than the exchange rate.

The rules of the game

One consequence of the sequence of post-war financial developments and policies which was heavily emphasized in contemporary accounts of the period was the destabilizing effect of massive flows of capital, both short-term and long-term. The process gained its initial momentum early in the 1920s with the flight from currencies such as the German mark, the French franc, and the Italian lira, as those who could transferred their assets to what they perceived to be safer currencies. With the high interest rates necessary to defend the pound, London was a favoured haven. Once confidence in the stability of the French and other Continental currencies—and in their underlying public finances—was restored, the speculative funds flowed back again in eager anticipation of capital gains when the new parities were legally established. In 1925 and 1926 there was a large speculative movement which caused a sharp appreciation in the Danish and Norwegian krone in anticipation of their *de jure* restoration in January 1927 and May 1928 respectively (Lester, 1939: 197–8). Italy was similarly the recipient of a considerable capital inflow during the eighteen months preceding the *de jure* stabilization of the lira in December 1927.

From a British perspective the loss of gold as flight capital rushed back to France after the success of the Poincaré stabilization at the end of 1926 was always mentioned and often resented as a major cause of the weakening in Britain's external financial position. In the first place France had elected to stabilize the franc at one-fifth of its pre-war value, whereas Britain had accepted the discipline necessary to restore sterling at the pre-war parity, and this was seen as a major source of balance of payments disequilibrium. Secondly, there was a dramatic increase in French reserves, accumulated at first in foreign exchange and later in gold, but the authorities did not respond to this by inducing a corresponding increase in the money supply. If they had done so this should have stimulated the rise in prices which might have restored equilibrium. In June 1928 French gold reserves were only 29 billion francs; by the end of 1932 they had increased by 53 billion but the increase in the note circulation over the same period was only 26 billion francs (Mouré, 1991: 55–6). Instead, the returning French capital was mainly used for the purchase of government securities, either directly by the private sector or by the commercial banks as their deposits increased. The government in turn was able to repay a substantial part of its debts to the Banque de France. As a result, the large increase in the central bank's holdings of gold and foreign currency was to a considerable extent neutralized. As seen from London the gold standard was thus not operated according to the rules, and the necessary adjustment process was frustrated. The position was exacerbated by the very low level of foreign investment by France; with their pre-1913 assets largely wiped out by the war and the Russian Revolution, French *rentiers* had become extremely reluctant to trust any more of their savings to foreign governments and enterprises.

Treasury and central bank officials in Paris and London argued bitterly in public and private over the reasons for the movement of gold to France, over what action should or could be taken in order for the flow to be reversed, and over whose responsibility it was to take the corrective measures. Even when it was recognized that the final outcome was not the result of a French policy wilfully designed to sterilize the inflow of gold, it was still regarded as a failing in the system leading to a serious maldistribution in international holdings of gold (for a modern summary of the controversy see Mouré, 1991). Eichengreen (1986) emphasizes that the Banque de France could in theory have reduced their high reserve ratio by means of expansionary open-market operations, but were effectively precluded from doing so by statutory restrictions. These had been imposed by the 1928 stabilization law specifically to prevent a recurrence of the lax monetary policies which were held responsible for the searing inflation of 1922–6. The British thought these restrictions should be relaxed in the interests of international monetary co-operation; the French were determined to protect their currency from any possibility of renewed inflation.

Similar issues were debated with respect to the USA, the one other country to show a substantial increase in its gold holdings during the 1920s. In the early part of the decade the American banking authorities considered that since this inflow was the result of the abnormal post-war conditions in Europe most of the gold would in due course return to Europe and, therefore, should not be used as the basis for domestic credit creation in the USA. Neutralization was thus a deliberate policy, for which there were 'sound and compelling reasons' (Nurkse, 1944: 73–5). In the subsequent years the USA continued to neutralize any changes in the stock of gold, though on a less extensive scale, and in 1928 and 1929 the Federal Reserve Board actually initiated a progressive increase in interest rates in order to prevent what it saw as an alarming rise in speculation on the stock exchange. This action was taken regardless of its implications for the requirements of international stability. Countries such as Britain, which were running balance of payments deficits at this time, might well have asked, with the author of an official history of the *United States in the World Economy* (Lary, 1943: 166):

whether a more aggressive policy of credit expansion could have been safely followed with a view to supporting a higher level of prices and money incomes in the United States, thus helping to meet the foreign demand for dollars and relieving the strain on foreign exchanges and the general world deflationary pressure that developed in the latter part of the twenties.

Lary's answer was that, as was so often the case in the inter-war period, considerations of internal policy were given far higher priority, and 'the threat to international stability, although not overlooked, was regarded as a regrettable but necessary risk to be run in rectifying an unsound domestic situation'.

These controversies over the policies of the two surplus countries, France and the USA, are a special case of the more general debate about the degree to which the recurrent inter-war crises in the international monetary system could be attributed to the alleged failure of countries to operate the gold standard according to the rules followed in the pre-1914 era, thus depriving the system of its fundamental equilibrating mechanism. On a strict interpretation the traditional policy required not merely that changes in holdings of gold should be automatically reflected in corresponding changes in the domestic currency, but that further purchases or sales of domestic assets should be made by the monetary authority so that the impact of movements in gold was magnified in proportion to the central bank's reserve ratio.

In his League of Nations study of the behaviour of twenty-six countries during the years 1922–38, Nurkse (1944: 68) found that 'from year to year, central banks' international and domestic assets, during most of the period under review, moved far more often in the *opposite* than in the same direction'. The extent of the inverse correlation was even greater in the five-year period of fixed exchange rates when the restored gold standard was in operation: for 1927–31 international and domestic assets changed in the same direction in only 25 per cent of the possible cases, compared to 32 per cent for the inter-war period as a whole. Various qualifications need to be made to this finding, such as the possibility that the response to the flows of gold might have been delayed, or that movements of private short-term capital might have distorted the pattern, and it must also be recognized that even the classical gold standard was not quite as simple and automatic as the textbook models suggested (Bloomfield, 1959). Nevertheless, the broad conclusion was that there was an increasing tendency in the inter-war years to use gold reserves as a buffer to protect countries from the transmission of external shocks, rather than as the means by which fluctuations originating abroad were automatically transmitted to the domestic credit base.

Just as it would be wrong to attribute the apparently smooth and efficient operation of the classical gold standard to the virtues of theoretically built-in automatic adjustment mechanisms, so equally the collapse of the inter-war system should not be attributed to their absence. Eichengreen (1992) has stressed the dual importance of co-operation between central banks, and of the credibility of their commitment to gold, in explaining the good overall performance of the pre-war gold standard. Before 1914 each of the 'core' countries had an important stake in the stability of the entire system, so that while they would not necessarily co-operate routinely, they would certainly do so at times of major crises. Moreover, the role played by London as the *pivot* of the system was crucial in two respects: the dominant financial position of the City was enough to ensure the successful day-by-day operation of the classical gold standard, and, in an emergency, the existence of a *de facto* leader ensured stable results for the 'co-operative game'.

After 1919 none of the above conditions could be applied to the resurrected system. The Versailles Treaty created instability at the heart of international economic and political relations. Transaction costs in the movements of goods, capital, and labour were considerably increased; balance of payments adjustments became slower, thus requiring stronger rather than weaker co-operation if fixed exchange rates pegged to gold were to be maintained. The defeat of Germany, and in many respects of Europe as a whole, with the attendant provisions for reparations and debt payment, made the whole international monetary system entirely dependent on the ability or willingness of the USA to compensate for its trade surpluses by capital movements. These would inevitably be highly volatile. Neither governments nor public opinion understood the new situation well, much less did they know how to deal with it. Economists, with few exceptions, proved to be of little help; worse, they were often the slaves of dead teachers and their doctrines.

According to Kindleberger (1973) this situation required a higher degree of international leadership. Unfortunately, the international economic position of Great Britain had been gravely weakened by the war: it was no longer a net creditor for large amounts of capital; some countries—notably in Latin America—had left the economic orbit of the wider sterling area and joined that of the USA; Commonwealth countries had achieved a higher degree of economic independence. In these conditions Britain was no longer in a position to act as stabilizer of the international payment system. The USA, on the other hand, was not yet ready to assume this role. Isolationism was still a powerful factor in her foreign policy; the New York financial market did not possess London's experience or sophistication; the Fed, established only in 1913, was still feeling its way. In these conditions neither London nor Washington was able to exercise world leadership with the strength required by the unstable post-war situation.

Eichengreen (1992) carries this argument further. He agrees on the importance of leadership, as reflected in the success of both the pre-1914 gold standard and the post-1944 Bretton Woods system. If however, leadership implies that the leader is able to stabilize the world by its own action—such as world-wide last-resort lending—then no single country can possibly guarantee a stable international economic environment. As shown by international economic organization before the First World War leadership was indeed useful, perhaps necessary, in so far as it was a precondition for co-operation; but ultimately it was the co-operation which mattered. Moreover, the policy which the co-operation was designed to sustain had also to be credible. Before 1913 Britain, France, and other leading financial centres were willing to co-operate as necessary, and their commitment to the preservation of the gold standard was credible. After 1918 both these vital qualities were lacking.

The First World War produced conditions which both postulated and made impossible an even greater degree of co-operation than had been necessary in the late nineteenth century. Lack of leadership was of course a problem, but not the only one. The war itself had created the most uncooperative of all worlds. Behind the failure of the successive economic conferences, from Brussels in 1920 to London in 1933, lie rancour, vindictiveness, and all the problems created by the pursuit of misplaced patriotism and self-interest. The degree of international economic co-operation achieved in the second half of the 1920s by central bankers, led by Norman and Strong, was simply not enough. The war had also undermined the credibility of the commitment to gold. Domestic political pressures meant that governments could no longer permit their central bankers to give unquestioned priority to external stability, regardless of the consequences for the internal economy.

International capital movements

In addition to the speculative flows stimulated by current and anticipated exchange-rate fluctuations there were also enormous movements of international capital attracted by interest-rate differentials and the prospects of long-term gains. Interest rates in Europe were appreciably higher than in the USA, and those in Germany were among the highest in Europe. Capital flowed to selected European borrowers on a massive scale once stabilization had been achieved, and the adoption of the Dawes Plan provided—at least temporarily—a settlement of the dispute over reparations. In Europe, as elsewhere in the 1920s, it was the USA which was the dominant creditor, but the United Kingdom and France were also substantial net lenders. The gross inward flow (long- and short-term) to the seventeen principal European borrowing countries amounted to approximately $10,000 million in the seven years from 1924 to 1930, with almost $7,000 million going to Germany and the balance in much smaller sums to a number of other countries, notably Austria, Italy, Romania, Poland, Greece, and Hungary. At the same time some of these borrowers were themselves lending to others, and there was an outflow from Germany amounting to some $2,500 million (for further details see Chapter 3 by Feinstein and Watson).

This movement of American capital to Europe in the 1920s contributed to international monetary stability by recycling the funds which flowed out to pay for the Continent's current account deficits with the USA. In comparison with the pre-1913 period, Europe's trade balance had deteriorated because of the weakening in her relative industrial competitiveness. The net receipts on invisible account were also greatly reduced; in particular, because the loss of overseas assets as a result of the war and the Bolshevik Revolution eliminated a large part of the pre-war inflow of interest and dividends from abroad, while the inter-Allied debts increased the payments which had to be made to the USA. The import of foreign capital after stabilization thus helped to preserve the external value of the mark and and other currencies, and helped sustain Europe's commitment to the gold standard.

The huge sums which poured into Germany were frequently portrayed by German politicians and financiers as the inward transfer necessary to permit the payment of reparations, but in reality these payments accounted for at most one-third of the gross receipts from abroad. In the period 1924–30 the aggregate amount paid in reparations amounted to approximately $2,400 million (about 2.3 per cent of Germany's aggregate national income over these years), whereas the gross inflow of capital during the same period amounted to approximately $7,000 million, or 6.6 per cent of national income.[3] Thus as long as US bankers and investors remained eager to invest their capital in Germany the much-debated transfer problem created by the demand for payment of reparations to the Allies was effectively solved. There were, of course, expressions of concern both within Germany and outside that at a later date these loans would have to be repaid and Germany would then face an impossible double burden. But the hunger for external capital was too powerful to be stemmed by such remote considerations.

A number of recent American studies have developed the theme originally stated by Mantoux (1946) in opposition to the famous polemic by Keynes (1919). They argue that the domestic burden involved in raising the necessary sums through taxation was considerably exaggerated, and that after the downward adjustment made under the Dawes Plan—perhaps even before—the amounts were well within Germany's capacity to pay (see e.g. Marks, 1978; McNeil, 1986; Schuker, 1988). However, this analysis does not allow sufficiently for the prospect that payments could be progressively raised as the German economy expanded, or for the extreme reluctance of Germans to accept even a modest increase in taxation to meet what was universally regarded as an unjustified and oppressive imposition by hostile adversaries. Thus even if the economic aspects of the problem were not as crippling as had been assumed in the 1920s, the exaction of reparations was still of deep political and psychological significance for Germany. The payments were a paramount cause of instability and a barrier to international economic co-operation.

The figures quoted above show that the average annual capital flow to Germany net of reparations was equivalent to over 4 per cent of her

---

[3] The reparations payments and national income estimates are taken from Holtfrerich (1986: 152); the former are the series used in the official balance of payments statistics. The data on capital flows are taken from the tables in Ch 3. See also Schuker (1988: 106–15).

national income. Given the low level of domestic savings, the willingness of foreigners to fund German capital expenditure enabled the country to live markedly beyond its means. There were several reasons for the acute shortage of domestic capital. The years of war and hyperinflation had wiped out virtually all liquid capital, including most of the reserves of the banking system, and fear of inflation remained a deeply inhibiting factor even when stability was restored. There was also considerable misallocation of available funds to unprofitable industries, including agriculture, and to desirable but not revenue-yielding social amenities. Foreign capital thus permitted a higher level of investment and consumption than domestic resources would have supported; it enabled central and local government to spend more and tax less; the supply of imported goods was greater than it would otherwise have been; and the Reichsbank was able to add substantially to its reserves of gold and foreign exchange. The liquidity of the banking system was also greatly improved by the funds received from abroad, although the banks were following a risky strategy to the extent that they relied on short-term deposits to make long-term loans. The massive foreign borrowing contributed to Germany's industrial rationalization and revival, notably in the coal, iron and steel, electrical and chemical industries. However, only about 40 per cent of the long-term foreign capital issued in Germany in 1924–30 was taken by private enterprises, the remainder going to various public and semi-public bodies, such as the cities and municipalities. This enabled the local bodies to make substantial investments, partly in public utilities, urban transport, and housing, partly in social, cultural, and sporting facilities.

This position was stable only as long as the necessary imports of funds could be maintained, and the underlying problems and social conflicts meant that the economy was extremely vulnerable to any change in the preferences of American investors. The flow of long-term capital from abroad fell sharply in the first half of 1927, following a bitter attack on foreign borrowing by the Reichsbank president, Dr Schacht, and the withdrawal of the tax concessions previously enjoyed by foreign subscribers to German bonds. This subjected the economy to great pressures, and after a decline in gold reserves the tax exemption was reinstated and the bond flotations quickly revived. They reached a peak in the second quarter of 1928, then fell abruptly and had virtually ceased by the spring of 1929. The flow of capital from abroad recovered to a limited extent in 1930, but in 1931 the situation was transformed and there was actually a net outflow of over $600 million. Several factors contributed to America's unwillingness to continue sending capital to Europe on the scale of earlier years. Internally, the tightening of monetary policy by the Federal Reserve referred to above raised interest rates sharply, thus weakening the incentive to lend abroad; and with the stock exchange indices soaring upwards through 1927 and 1928 there was further strong encouragement to keep funds at home in the hope of more substantial gains from speculation on Wall Street. On the external side there was sharply growing alarm about the rising total of Germany's foreign liabilities, and her ability to continue to meet the obligations these imposed.

In the late 1920s Germany went into a slump of unparalleled severity. Real domestic product fell by 16 per cent between 1929 and 1932, industrial production by over 40 per cent, the value of exports by almost 60 per cent. Unemployment raced from 1.3 million in 1927 (less than 4 per cent of the labour force) to 5.6 million in 1932 (over 17 per cent).[4] The sudden contraction of capital imports from the USA is often cited as the critical factor which precipitated this catastrophe (Lewis, 1949; Falkus, 1975; Sommariva and Tullio, 1987). However, other scholars have argued strongly that the source of Germany's economic troubles was primarily domestic in origin (Temin, 1971; Balderston, 1983; McNeil, 1986). Their case is supported by the fact that nominal short-term interest rates were stable through the second half of 1928, and then fell in the first quarter of 1929, only moving up in the second quarter. If the exogenous view of the depression was correct it might have been expected that they would have risen sharply as soon as the foreign inflow was cut off, but the observed pattern is easily explained if the German economy was already moving into recession before the import of capital from the USA dried up.

Industrial production recovered strongly in 1927 after the depression of 1925–6, but then showed virtually no further growth in 1928 or 1929. Similarly unemployment dropped to 1,600,000 in the six winter months October 1927 to March 1928, and then increased sharply to 2,400,00 in the corresponding period of 1928–9. The same pattern is evident in the investment data. Gross fixed investment at current prices in the public sector (government and railways) expanded until 1927, and in other sectors the rise continued for a further year, though even at its peak in 1928 the investment ratio was low by comparison with the pre-war period. Moreover, information on investment intentions shows that series for both non-residential building permits and new domestic orders for machinery had already turned down in late 1927 or early 1928, well before the cessation of foreign lending. Balderston (1983) attributes the low level and early decline in investment primarily to an acute and persistent shortage of domestic capital, and claims that this provides a 'thoroughly endogenous explanation' for the decline in fixed investment. Borchardt (1979, English trans. 1991) also finds a domestic explanation for the Great Depression, but argues that the root of the trouble

---

[4] The sources for the data in this and the following paragraph are: GDP and unemployment, Maddison (1991: 212 and 1964: 220); industrial production and exports, Mitchell (1978: 180 and 304); interest rates, fixed investment, building permits, and new orders for machinery, Balderston (1983: 401–2 and 407).

was an excessive increase in wages relative to the growth of productivity, thus making the socio-political distributional conflicts which emerged in the aftermath of the Great War the focus of the analysis.

Although the virtual cessation of capital imports from the USA and the subsequent net outflow did not initiate the depression, it undoubtedly added greatly to the problems facing the German policy-makers and contributed to the adoption of measures which exacerbated the initial decline in activity. In principle their options were either to abandon the gold standard, boosting activity by allowing the mark to depreciate, or to follow orthodox policies of retrenchment, reducing imports and expanding exports by deflating the economy. In practice, the former was effectively ruled out, both by the powerful domestic fear of renewed inflation, and by international resistance to a reduction in the foreign currency value of reparations payments and of assets in Germany. The economy was thus gradually forced into a vicious spiral of restrictive financial policies and declining activity. Moreover, since the German 'mixed banks' had been borrowing short abroad and making long-term financial loans to domestic enterprises, the repatriation of foreign funds contributed to their liquidity problems which, in due course, fuelled the banking crisis of 1931.

From late 1929 long-term American capital was no longer available to sustain the budget deficits, but German investors—with the experience of 1922–3 still deeply etched in their memories—displayed great reluctance to purchase long-term government bonds (Balderston: 1982). The government and the Reichsbank were thus inexorably driven to resort to short-term borrowing; the more the short-term debt increased the greater the perceived threat to stability, and the more energetic the efforts of domestic and foreign asset-holders to withdraw their capital from Germany. The deterioration in the political situation provoked by the steadily deepening depression and the opposition to tax increases gave added grounds for distrust of the currency. The first of a succession of waves of capital flight occurred in the spring of 1929, and there were further massive losses of gold and foreign exchange in late 1930 and, on an even bigger scale, in 1931. The authorities were thus forced to adopt restrictive policies at precisely the point when the economy was in urgent need of counter-cyclical measures to stimulate revival. Short-term interest rates were raised in the second quarter of 1929, and the federal government, cities, and states initiated a succession of increasingly desperate efforts to raise revenues and restrict spending. From the end of 1930 and through 1931 Brüning introduced a succession of austerity decrees imposing progressively harsher increases in direct and indirect taxation. These were accompanied by reductions in civil service pay and in state welfare benefits. The descent into the Depression was cumulative and catastrophic.

Elsewhere in central and eastern Europe the end of the foreign lending boom was an even more significant factor helping to initiate the Depression and contributing to its severity. Unlike Germany, most of these countries (Czechoslovakia was the exception) relied primarily on exports of agricultural products for their foreign revenues, and were in trouble as soon as primary product export prices began to tumble. They had borrowed heavily during the 1920s, frequently in the form of loans at fixed interest, and even when the funds had been productively invested—by no means always the case—they found themselves unable to service their debts from the rapidly diminishing proceeds of their exports. Thereafter they could only meet their external obligations as long as they could continue to attract fresh capital. After 1929, when the inflow of foreign capital ceased, the position could no longer be sustained and painful adjustment was inescapable.

Hungary was one of the worst affected of the agrarian producers in this region and provides a good illustration of the difficulties they confronted. Together with Poland she had been the most active of the East European borrowers in the mid-1920s, and by the end of 1930 had an accumulated external debt of some $700 million, a large part of which had gone on unproductive expenditure (Berend and Ranki, 1974: 106–9). The export revenues on which she depended to service these debts came overwhelmingly from agricultural products, particularly wheat and maize. As their prices plunged the export proceeds went down with them; by 1931 their value was barely half the 1929 level and by 1932 less than a third (Nötel, 1986: 218). The resulting balance of payments problem was insuperable. In a period of some ten weeks from the beginning of May 1931 the central bank was compelled to pay out more in gold and foreign exchange than it had possessed in April: a drain only made possible because rescue credits of $50 million were obtained from abroad. With bankruptcy threatening urgent corrective measures were required.

By mid-1931 Poland, Romania, Yugoslavia, and Bulgaria were in a similarly untenable position. Yet all five countries were inhibited by fear of inflation from following the example of primary producers elsewhere, such as Australia and Argentina, and depreciating their currencies. The deep prevailing fear of inflation in the minds of both politicians and the public is well indicated in the following comment of a contemporary Polish economist, Edward Lipinski (quoted by Nötel, 1986: 228):

After this [repeated] collapse [of the Polish currency] its preservation became a sacrosanct principle of popular belief . . . It was duly realised that any devaluation could easily lead to panic, price manipulation, ruin of saving institutions, and a further sharpening of the crisis . . . Stability of the currency thus was turned into a popular myth.

Deprived of this solution they turned increasingly to moratoria, rigorous exchange controls, and commercial policy restrictions.

The problems which beset the agrarian producers emerged early in the cycle of events culminating in the Great Depression, and were particularly severe in the case of the two agricultural crops grown in this part of Europe, wheat and sugar. Australia, Canada, and the Argentine were also greatly affected. The underlying source of the trouble can again be traced back to the First World War, when European producers withdrew from the market and those elsewhere, particularly in North and South America, expanded their output in response to the rise in prices. After the war Europe attempted to restore the acreage previously under cultivation, and by 1925 it was impossible to find markets for the available supplies. The problem was made even more serious by various factors which tended to depress demand. It thus seems clear that in the case of agricultural foodstuffs a strong case can be made for the presence of overproduction, and for a downturn well before the break in activity in the industrial countries. The position was different for industrial raw materials, where it is more likely that the causal sequence ran from the decline in industrial activity to the fall in prices (Fleisig, 1972).

If all economic adjustments took place automatically and without friction this fall in agricultural prices would hardly matter from the standpoint of global economic stability. Any fall in the incomes of the producers of wheat would be offset by the rise in (real) incomes of the consumers of bread, and there would be no net effect on aggregate world demand. Unfortunately, this is not what happens in practice. The primary producing countries are forced to respond immediately to the deterioration in their international payments position, and do so by contracting activity and cutting their imports. By contrast, the consuming nations are slow to appreciate the improvement in their purchasing power and are under no urgent pressure to expand their activity.

The loss of income to the food-growing countries combined with the cessation of foreign lending thus had substantial adverse consequences for others as well as for themselves. In the sphere of trade the decline in their export revenues undermined their ability to purchase manufactured goods from abroad, significantly reducing the exports of their customary suppliers, especially Britain. In the financial sphere, many of them were forced to devalue their currencies in 1929 and 1930, thus precipitating the period of instability on the foreign exchanges. Others turned to tariffs, exchange controls, and bilateral trading agreements and contributed to the contraction in world trade. Countries with strong links to sterling, both those within the Empire, such as Australia and New Zealand, and those in Latin America such as Argentina and Brazil, had traditionally kept their surplus balances in London, but now that they were in difficulty they were forced to run down these balances, thus adding to the pressures on the UK reserves.

3. The 1931 Financial Crisis and the Great Depression

The crisis in Central Europe

After 1929 the downward slide in primary product prices continued relent-lessly, and in the industrial countries output and trade declined rapidly with unemployment rising to unprecedented heights. The USA ceased to supply capital on the previous lavish scale, and from 1931 was actually a net recipient of long-term capital fleeing from Europe in search of security. The only other country in a strong financial position was France, which attracted ever larger quantities of gold and foreign exchange. Both the American and the French authorities refused to take any steps to relieve the mounting crisis of confidence and liquidity in the rest of the world. The banking system was drawn inexorably into the gathering storm. As noted earlier, a succession of bank failures had occurred throughout the 1920s, and there were problems of varying magnitude in Spain in 1925, in Poland in 1926 and 1927, and in Norway in 1927 (see also Chapter 2 by Jonker and van Zanden). The problem then reached Germany in 1929, when the collapse of the Frankfurter Allgemeine Versicherungs was followed by the failure of smaller banks and withdrawals from savings banks in Frankfurt and Berlin.

However, the really serious troubles of the banking system emerged in Vienna in 1929 with the failure of the Bodencreditanstalt, the second largest Austrian bank. Under pressure from the government, the Rothschild's Creditanstalt agreed to a merger, but the rescuing bank was itself in a very weak position, and the enlarged institution could not provide a long-term solution. The Creditanstalt, Austria's largest bank, had unwisely operated during the 1920s as if the Habsburg Empire had not been broken up. In fact the Viennese banks had been cut off from their original industrial base, especially in Czechoslovakia. There was never a sound basis for their business in the 1920s, and their heavy commitment to unprofitable indus-tries meant that failures and losses were inevitable. In May 1931, after an auditor's report revealed the true position, the Creditanstalt went under and was forced to reorganize with the help of the Austrian government and of international credit and a partial standstill agreement with its foreign creditors. This collapse set off a run on the bank that spread to the Austrian schilling. The government quickly ran through its foreign-exchange reserves in a vain attempt to adhere to the gold standard and only belatedly imposed foreign-exchange controls (see Stiefel, 1989 and Chapter 12 by Weber).

The German banking system was heavily involved with Austria, and it went into crisis two months later when one of the major German banks, the

Darmstädter-und-Nationalbank (Danat) closed its doors. This threatened to precipitate the collapse of the entire German banking system, and a ruinous situation was only averted by government intervention and a banking moratorium. The German banking crisis of July 1931 is sometimes seen as the consequence of Austrian financial collapse in May. This presumption, however, has been hard to verify. The German crisis of July 1931 may well have been due to exclusively German causes, in which case the Austrian crisis foreshadowed—but did not cause—the more important German collapse.

German banks held the bulk of their reserves in cheques, bills of exchange, and Treasury bills that could be freely discounted at the Reichsbank. The bills earned more than deposits at the Reichsbank and were equally liquid as long as the Reichsbank stood ready to purchase them. The banks' reserve ratio fell sharply in June 1931, and again in July. Fully two-thirds of the fall in each month was accounted for by a reduction in the amount of bills held by banks. This reduction was concentrated almost entirely in the six great Berlin banks, and it was paralleled by a rise in the Reichsbank portfolio of virtually the same size. The large Berlin banks were selling their bills to the Reichsbank. They sold over half of their bill portfolio in those two months (Temin, 1989). The problem created by the withdrawals was not primarily that the banks were losing reserves, except for one bank heavily invested in a major failed firm. It was that the Reichsbank ran out of assets with which to monetize the banks' reserves as withdrawals continued (James, 1985). Despite some credits from other central banks, the Reichsbank had fallen below its statutory requirement of 40 per cent reserves by the beginning of July, and it was unable to borrow more. The Reichsbank could no longer purchase the Berlin banks' bills by mid-July.

The Reichsbank tried to replenish its reserves with an international loan, but tensions left over from the First World War disturbed the operation of the international credit market. The French, who had ample reserves to lend to the Reichsbank, were still fighting the First World War. They tied political strings around their offer of help that were unacceptable to the Germans. The Germans for their part tried to use the crisis to renegotiate the peace settlement and eliminate reparations, while the Americans pulled in the opposite direction to isolate the German banking crisis from any long-run considerations (Bennett, 1962). The absence of international co-operation was all too evident; no international loan was forthcoming.

Germany abandoned the gold standard in July and August 1931. A series of decrees and negotiations preserved the value of the mark, but eliminated the free flow of both gold and marks. In one of the great ironies of history, Chancellor Brüning did not take advantage of this independence of international constraints and expand. He continued to contract as if Germany was still on the gold standard. It is vivid testimony to the power of ideology that leaders like Brüning were induced to cling to orthodoxy even as the world economy collapsed, and continued to advocate gold standard policies after abandoning the gold standard itself.

As a consequence of the German moratorium the withdrawal of foreign deposits was prohibited, and huge sums in foreign short-term credits were frozen. As other countries saw that they would be unable to realize these assets they in turn were compelled to restrict withdrawals of their credits. Many other European countries suffered bank runs and failures in July, with especially severe crises in Hungary, where the banks were closely tied to those in Austria, and in Romania. As a result of the extensive foreign withdrawals from the Budapest banks it was again necessary to impose a partial moratorium on external obligations and to declare three days' 'bank holiday'. In the same month a leading Swiss bank had to be rescued by a take-over. In contrast, French banks were generally in a strong position by the end of the 1920s, and largely avoided the crisis of 1929–31, with only mild failures, largely confined to mixed banks, in 1930–1.

Disintegration of the gold standard

Almost immediately after Germany abandoned the gold standard the British pound was under pressure. The timing suggests that this was not the same process by which panic spread from Austria to Germany. German banks enjoyed a month of normal operation after the failure of the Creditanstalt. They felt pressure only after a delay and—we presume—from a new set of depositors. British banks had no such interlude. There was no internal drain. Pressure on the pound began as soon as the mark was restricted. Sales of sterling increased steadily after 14 July, and the Bank of England raised Bank rate on 22 July. The British troubles were accentuated when the standstill agreements froze some £70 million of British bankers' loans to Germany.

Although the banking crisis on the Continent had added to Britain's problems by simultaneously provoking a flight from sterling and freezing her foreign short-term assets, the extremely weak balance of payments position on both current and capital account was arguably a more fundamental cause of the inability to sustain the gold standard. Britain's external financial position in the 1920s was undermined by several factors. On the current account these included the abrupt transwar collapse of export markets for coal, cotton, and other staple products; the forced sale of a substantial fraction of her overseas investments to help meet the costs of the First World War; the overvaluation of sterling as a result of the decision to return to gold at the pre-war parity of $4.86; and the adverse impact on her traditional Empire and Latin American markets of the calamitous fall in primary product prices in the late 1920s.

The capital account was a further source of weakness because Britain had attempted to maintain her pre-1914 role as an exporter of long-term capital to the developing countries, but in the 1920s could no longer achieve this by means of a surplus on current account and was forced to offset the outflow by substantial borrowing from abroad. However, much of the capital attracted to London was short-term, leaving Britain very vulnerable to any loss of confidence in sterling. The increasing deficits on the current accounts of Australia and other primary producers who normally held a large part of their reserves in London compelled them to draw on these balances, thus further weakening Britain's position. By mid-1930 the United Kingdom held about £175 million in gold and foreign exchange reserves, and this could be supplemented by other liquid assets of approximately £150 million. Since the corresponding short-term liabilities amounted to roughly £750 million, Britain's defence against withdrawals was adequate only as long as confidence in the pound remained high.[5] When confidence drained away in the course of 1931 Britain could no longer cope with the pressure from foreign liquidation of sterling assets and, despite assistance from France and the USA in July and August, was forced to capitulate. On 20 September the Government announced that it had become necessary to suspend for the time being the operation of the clause in the Gold Standard Act of 1925 which required the Bank of England to sell gold at a fixed price.

As so often in the economic developments of the inter-war period, the history of the recent past played a critical role in shaping the attitudes which determined the course of events. Foreign concern about the scale of Britain's budget deficit had increased markedly with the publication of the Report of the May Committee in July 1931, and was the paramount reason for the final collapse in confidence in sterling. As Sayers (1976: 390–1) observed, it is difficult today to understand this obsession with the deficit given 'the relatively trifling sums under discussion':

The explanation lies . . . in memories of the currency disorders of the early twenties, which were, after all, less than ten years behind. In those troublesome times it had become accepted doctrine that an uncorrected budget deficit is the root of forced increase in the supply of money and depreciation of the currency, and that such depreciations become almost if not quite unmanageable. This view was not a mere academic fetish: it permeated the atmosphere in all financial markets . . . The Bank [of England] itself, in all the advice it tendered to the struggling central bankers of recovering Europe, year after year preached the gospel. It was not to be wondered

[5] Information about Britain's short-term liabilities to foreigners was first made public in the Macmillan Report in July 1931, but this covered only the sterling bills and deposits held by UK banks. A further sum of roughly £350m. was held by foreign banks and investors, so the true extent of Britain's position as a net short-term debtor was far worse than foreigners appreciated. See further Williams (1963) and Cairncross and Eichengreen (1983: 50–1).

at, that in 1931 the physician should be expected to heal himself—and that when he seemed unwilling to set about it, his life should be despaired of.

Even so, it has been argued (as Balderston does in Chapter 5) that the suspension of the gold standard was not inevitable and could have been averted if the authorities had been more resolute in their defence of the parity adopted in 1925. This would have required a much more aggressive policy to raise interest rates and reduce the level of domestic activity. Such a policy might have involved severe damage to employment and enterprise, and perhaps to political stability, but if firmly implemented would have shown speculators that the United Kingdom was determined to maintain the gold standard. However, international economic organization is intended to be a means to an end, not an end in itself, and it is not surprising that the British Government was ultimately unwilling to perist with its commitment to the gold standard regardless of the cost exacted in terms of lost output and increased unemployment.

In considering the factors underlying Britain's departure from gold much contemporary and subsequent British comment attributed considerable significance to the undervaluation of rival currencies, especially the French franc, but recent research has shown that the importance of this factor was considerably overstated. It was not the exchange-rate policy which was the basis for France's prosperity at the end of the 1920s, or for her successful resistance until 1931 to the slump from which almost all other countries suffered so grievously. Indeed the share of French exports in GDP was actually falling after 1927. Instead the strength of her economy should be attributed primarily to the 'crowding in' effect of Poincaré's fiscal policies, which induced an upsurge in domestic investment. Similarly in the case of Belgium, export growth on the back of a depreciated currency was not maintained after 1926, and the main sources of prosperity are to be found in the domestic economy associated with the expansion of the banking sector (Eichengreen and Wyplosz, 1990; and the analysis of the Belgian case in Chapter 7 by Cassiers).

The Bank of England, after an initial delay to rebuild its gold reserves, sharply reduced interest rates in 1932. As in Germany, British monetary authorities continued for a time to advocate gold-standard policies even after they had been driven off the gold standard. But while the grip of this ideology was strong in the immediate aftermath of devaluation, it wore off within six months. British economic policy was freed by devaluation, and monetary policy turned expansive early in 1932. But the British devaluation was hardly the basis for international co-operation. The British did not seek international leadership; instead they backed into devaluation, arguing they had no alternative. And while many smaller countries followed the British lead, the other major financial centres sought instead to protect themselves from British policy. The British devaluation was a good policy—it broke the suffocating grip of the gold standard on economic policy—but it did not point the way toward international co-operation.

By the time Britain was forced to abandon the gold standard seven other countries, including Australia, New Zealand, and Argentina had already done so. After her departure twenty-four other countries followed rapidly, including Sweden, Denmark, Norway, Finland, the Irish Free State, Greece, and Portugal. As a British writer noted mournfully (Waight, 1939: 1): 'If the foundations of the citadel of financial probity were unsound and the structure about to tumble, other centres could not remain for long un-affected.' In many other countries there was no formal suspension but the gold standard was made ineffective by the imposition of a range of exchange controls and restrictions. This applied ultimately to Germany, Austria, Hungary, Bulgaria, Czechoslovakia, Romania, Estonia, and Latvia (Brown, 1940: 1074). By the middle of 1932 the institution which had been generally accepted as the best guarantee of international stability, trade, growth, and prosperity had completely shattered. In Europe only France, Belgium, the Netherlands, Switzerland, Italy, Poland, and Lithuania remained on the gold standard, and only the first four of these were truly committed to its spirit, refraining from the imposition of exchange controls and allowing relatively free movement of gold. The inability to make the gold standard function successfully in the inter-war era was widely regarded as a symbol of failure even though the actual consequences for the real economy were largely highly favourable. Those countries which remained committed to gold did much less well subsequently than those which abandoned it (Eichengreen and Sachs, 1985).

At the same time as the gold standard was disintegrating there was also a renewed outbreak of tariff warfare provoked by the deterioration in eco-nomic conditions and by the introduction of the Smoot–Hawley tariff in the USA in 1930. Britain finally abandoned her long-standing commitment to free trade, and a temporary measure in late 1931 was followed a few months later by an Act imposing duties on almost all imports of manufacturers. Numerous countries—including France, Italy, the Netherlands, Norway, Spain, Portugal, and Greece, and many others outside Europe—increased their tariffs in a desperate attempt to protect themselves from the deepening depression and the collapse of any attempt at international co-operation. In the judgement of the League of Nations (*World Economic Survey, 1932/3:* 193–4):

There was probably never any period when trade was subject to such widespread and frequent alterations of tariff barriers. . . . Currency instability has led into a maze of new protectionist regulations and private trading initiative generally has given way to administrative controls.

The financial panic also spread from Britain to the USA, jumping instantaneously over the Atlantic Ocean in September 1931. Bank failures rose, and the Federal Reserve banks lost gold. There were both internal and external drains. In one of the most vivid acts of poor monetary policy in history, the Federal Reserve raised interest rates sharply in October to protect the dollar—in the midst of the greatest depression the world has ever known. This was not a technical mistake or simple stupidity; this was the standard response of central banks under the gold standard. It shows how the ideology of the gold standard transmitted and intensified the Great Depression. The pressure against the dollar eased, but the American economy accelerated its decline. The Federal Reserve Bank had chosen international stability over domestic prosperity. The result was intensified deflation and accelerated economic decline. Unlike Britain, which arrested the decline in 1932, the USA had to wait an additional painful year. This delay was not only costly for America; it added to the deflationary forces in Europe, delaying European recovery as well.

The banks in the Depression

Spain stands as the prime example of a country that avoided the worst excesses of the Great Depression by staying off the gold standard (Choudhri and Kochin, 1980). Spain tried to fix the peseta in the late 1920s as France and Italy stabilized their currencies, but the deflationists lacked the political muscle. The government continued to run deficits which were monetized by healthy banks. There was a run on Spanish banks contemporaneous with the failure of the Creditanstalt in Austria. Martín-Aceña (see Chapter 20) cites internal causes, but the peseta was under pressure as well. Very few banks failed, and the experience is not thought of as a panic. The Bank of Spain acted as a lender-of-last-resort, enabled to do so by two factors. The banks held large portfolios of government debt that could be sold for cash. And, unlike the Reichsbank, the Bank of Spain was not bound by the inflexible standards of the gold standard. It did have to raise Spanish interest rates to protect the value of the peseta, but it continued to lend freely—as Bagehot advised (Tortella and Palafox, 1984).

In Greece and Portugal the impact of the economic depression was relatively mild, and with minor exceptions the banks in each of these countries came through the period in reasonably good health (see further Chapter 18 by Dertilis and Costis and Chapter 19 by Reis). Where banking failures occurred in these and other countries it typically owed more to their involvement as universal banks with unsound or loss-making industries than to inherent financial difficulties. In Greece, as in Britain and other countries in which mixed banking was not the normal practice, the banks were much better able to sustain their liquidity and solvency, although problems were aggravated where the central bank was unable or unwilling to act as lender-of-last-resort (Mazower, 1991).

There were no general banking crises in Italy and Poland, even though they were on the gold standard. Differences in banking policy between them and others on the gold standard may well be the cause of the difference in financial outcomes between them and other, less fortunate countries. On the assumption that the direction of causality runs in this way, it is tempting to ask if Austria and Germany could have adopted the Italian and Polish policies. The Credito Italiano, one of two large German-style universal banks in Italy, found itself illiquid in 1930 as the economic downturn began. A holding company was formed to take the industrial assets of the bank, disguising its universal character without changing the fundamental financial status of the bank. This cosmetic change was not enough to deal with the problem. More action was needed at the start of 1931. The government reached an agreement with the Credito Italiano in February 1931, in which the bank gave up its holding company and its investment activities in return for a substantial grant of money from the government. The Credito Italiano was transformed from a universal bank to a commercial bank, but it was not allowed to fail.

The other 'German' bank needed help later in 1931. A similar agreement was reached with the Banca Commerciale in October. In return for an even larger infusion of cash, this bank too allowed itself to be restricted to short-term activities. The banks were transformed. The Government became actively involved in the finance of industry. But there was no banking crisis (Toniolo, 1980). Secrecy was absolutely critical to the success of this policy. Depositors did not panic or move into cash; they did not spread difficulties from bank to bank in a contagion of fear. The lira was not subjected to unusual pressure. The policy decisions had been undertaken by a small group of men, and word of them did not filter out to the financial community. This secrecy was possible in the Fascist Government that ruled Italy. We can all speculate on the reasons why the secrecy did not result in the kind of self-serving policies often associated with this kind of restricted decision-making (see Chapter 10 by Toniolo).

In Chapter 13 Landau and Morawski reveal a similar, although less spectacular, story in Poland. There was no secrecy, and there were no secret agreements in the face of collapse. Instead there was a gradual state take-over of troubled private banks. The first test of Polish banking policy came in 1925 as the result of an agricultural crisis. The State responded by taking over banks in difficulty. Another crisis came in 1929, at the start of the economic downturn. The world agricultural crisis caused prices to fall in Poland, threatening banks who had loaned on the security of crops. Again, the Government stepped in and took over troubled banks. A third crisis in 1931 followed the failure of the Austrian Creditanstalt, in which the pattern of government expansion continued. Private banks held 40 per cent of Polish deposits and investments in 1926, but only 20 per cent by 1934. The Polish policy was not undertaken by a small group of secret financiers; it was not composed of a few large grants to banks. It was instead a policy-stance extended to a large number of banks over a period of years. Its effectiveness came from the knowledge of its existence, that is, from the government's commitment to keeping credit markets stable.

Italy and Poland, therefore, were similar in the inter-war period in that their governments directly supported banks in trouble. The form in which this overall policy was implemented was vastly different—almost diametrically opposite—in the two countries. But government take-overs were common to both. Their common policies contrast sharply with those of Austria and Germany, in which failing banks were merged with other banks. This was a far less effective measure because the amalgamated banks then found themselves in trouble. It would be comforting to report that Italy and Poland were spared the worst excesses of the Depression as a result of their banking policies. But such was not the case. These countries were on the gold standard, and the gold standard was the primary transmission mechanism of the Great Depression. Unlike Spain, Italy and Poland experienced both deflation and falling production at about the rate of other gold-standard countries (Bernanke and James, 1991; and Chapter 2 by Jonker and van Zanden). Only by breaking the 'golden fetters' of the gold standard, to use Eichengreen's term, was it possible to break the deflationary spiral (Eichengreen, 1992).

The end of the contraction

Unhappily, it took a change of leadership to bring about a change in the policy regime. We can now see that restoration of the post-war gold standard was the problem not the solution in the 1920s, because it imposed monetary constraints which prevented the authorities from taking the action necessary to contain the banking panics and failures. These crises amplified relatively modest initial disturbances and undermined the financial stability of the leading centres. However, in the inter-war period the ideology of the gold standard was very strong, and it was extremely difficult for leaders to abandon it in this time of crisis. Not recognizing that this ideology was a large part of the problem, they instead held on to it as a drowning man holds on to a life raft. Alas, these 'golden fetters' only forced the European economy further under water. Only when national economies were freed of these constraints could the economic contraction be halted.

The change in policy regime can be seen most clearly in the USA. The Hoover administration followed a policy that became more orthodox over time. It was highly traditional in its support for the gold standard and its focus on efforts to bolster the credit markets rather than the economy directly. Although not initially deflationary, Hoover drew exactly the wrong lesson from the currency crisis of 1931 and became a strong deflationist. The Federal Reserve maintained a passive stance in the early stages of the Depression, replaced by active contraction in response to the run on the dollar in 1931. The Federal Reserve's steps toward expansion in March to July of 1932 were halted when the open-market purchases alarmed other central banks, and threatened the solvency of member banks by lowering the returns on bank portfolios (Epstein and Ferguson, 1984). The Glass–Steagall Act of 1932 reiterated support for the gold standard at the same time.

It was not clear during the presidential campaign of 1932 that Roosevelt would implement a change of policy regime. He had recently raised taxes in New York to balance the state budget, and he emphasized a balanced federal budget as well. He strongly criticized Wall Street, business, and utilities during the campaign and employed a generally anti-business rhetoric. These were not features of a candidate one would expect to help the business environment.

The first sign that a new policy regime was on the way came after the election, in December 1932, when Roosevelt torpedoed Hoover's efforts to settle war debts and reparations multilaterally, signifying his opposition to continuation of the existing meagre international financial co-operation. A change in regime became more tangible in February 1933, when the President-elect began a serious discussion of devaluation as part of an effort to raise commodity prices. This talk led to a run on the dollar and helped cause the bank holiday in March. The New York Federal Reserve Bank found its gold supplies running dangerously low at the start of March. It appealed to the Chicago Federal Reserve Bank for help. But the Midwestern bank refused to extend a loan to its New York cousin, its different view of the world echoing the contrast between the German and French attitudes when the Reichsbank appealed for a similar loan in July 1931. The New York Fed then appealed to Roosevelt to shut down the entire national banking system, a draconian way to force co-operation among the Federal Reserve banks (Wigmore, 1987).

Once inaugurated, Roosevelt responded by declaring the bank holiday. He also imposed controls over all foreign-exchange trading and gold exports. He ended private gold ownership and took control over the sale of all domestic gold production. These controls allowed Roosevelt to avoid speculative disequilibrium when he began to devalue the dollar. He did so in April when he announced that he would support the Thomas amendment to the Emergency Farm Mortgage Act of 1933; this allowed him to set the price of gold. At the same time he prohibited the private export of gold by executive order. The dollar, freed from its official value, began to fall. It dropped steadily until July, when it had declined between 30 and 45 per cent against the pound (Federal Reserve System 1943: 662–81).

The clarity of the change in policy was unmistakable. The USA was under no market pressure to devalue. Despite the momentary pressure on the New York Fed, the USA held one-third of the world's gold reserves, ran a chronic foreign trade surplus, and dominated world trade in modern manufactures like automobiles, refrigerators, sewing-machines, and other consumer durables. The devaluation was a purely strategic decision that appeared without precedent. Orthodox financial opinion recognized it as such and condemned it. Senator Carter Glass called it an act of 'national repudiation'. Winthrop Aldrich, the new chairman of the Chase National Bank, thought devaluation was 'an act of economic destruction of fearful magnitude' (Temin and Wigmore, 1990). This was a change of regime of the type described by Sargent in his account of the end of several hyperinflations (Sargent, 1983). It was a dramatic change, clearly articulated and understood. It was co-ordinated with fiscal and monetary policies. The new regime clearly was designed to increase both prices and economic activity. It was supported by a wide degree of consensus—professional, public, and congressional—despite the vocal opposition of some financial leaders. The remarks by Aldrich and Glass show that the shift in regime was clearly visible. They represent, however, only a minority opinion identified with the previous, failed regime. Aldrich himself quickly joined the bandwagon and became an enthusiastic proponent of the New Deal.

As with the British devaluation, the US action was the key to breaking free of the deflationary policies of the gold standard. It also was a national decision, taken without consultation or co-operation with other nations. Sequential devaluation was the best policy in the circumstances, but it was hardly a co-ordinated international response to the economic crisis. Devaluation was only one dimension of a multifaceted new policy regime. During Roosevelt's First Hundred Days, the passive, deflationary policy of Hoover was replaced by an aggressive, interventionist, expansionary approach. The New Deal has been widely criticized for internal inconsistency (Hawley, 1966; Lee, 1982). There was, however, a steadily expansionary bias in policy that added up to a marked change from the Hoover administration (Temin and Wigmore, 1990).

The story is similar, although not as clear-cut, in Germany. Chancellor Brüning was replaced by Papen in late May 1932. The Lausanne Conference effectively ended reparations and cleared the major political hurdle from Germany's path. Brüning's deflation was replaced by Papen's first steps toward economic expansion. Brüning had initiated a small employment programme that had little effect in the context of his deflationary policy regime. This programme was expanded by Papen and complemented by some off-budget government expenditures. In addition Papen introduced tax credits and subsidies for new employment (Hardach, 1980). These were steps in the right direction, but they did not alter the perception of the policy regime. They still appeared to be isolated actions, not regime shifts.

The new policy measures (like the Federal Reserve's open-market purchases earlier that year) nevertheless produced some effects. There was a short-lived rise in industrial production and shipments. The recovery was only partial, and the data are mixed, but there was a definite sign of improvement (Henning, 1973). These tentative results seem to have had an immediate political impact as well. The Nazis had leapt to prominence in the 1930 election and increased their seats in the Reichstag from 12 to 107. They then doubled their large representation in the Reichstag in the election of July 1932. But that was their high point in free elections. They lost ground in the second election of 1932, in November, garnering 33 per cent instead of 37 per cent of the vote and reducing their representation in the Reichstag from 230 to 196 seats (Hamilton, 1982; Childers, 1983).

Further economic improvement could well have reduced the Nazi vote even more. If so, we need to ask whether the recovery begun under Papen could have continued. For if it had, then the political courage to hold out a little longer with the Papen or Schleicher Governments might have spared Germany and the world the horrors of Nazism. The question then is not simply about the recovery. It is also whether Germany—and hence the world—was balanced on a knife-edge in 1933 between the continuation of normal life and the enormous costs of the Nazis.

There is, however, only a slim case for believing that the recovery could have been sustained. The instability of politics mirrored the instability of the economy. The policy regime was in the process of changing, but there was no clear signal of change like the American devaluation. There was no assurance that Papen's tentative expansionary steps would be followed by others. The recovery of 1932 consequently was neither sharp nor universal. Even though a trough can be seen in some data, other series show renewed decline into 1933. The economy fell back to its low point in the brief Schleicher administration, and it appeared that the Papen recovery was abortive.

For Nazism to have been a transitory aberration, the recovery would have had to resume in early 1933. It would have had to be strong enough to repair the damage to the political fabric caused by the social and political effects of extensive unemployment. The expansive policies already under-taken would have had to have further effects—which they probably did—and the American recovery would have had to spill over into Germany. Both factors are possible but neither was very strong, and the latter in addition could not have come for several months. One can argue that the future course of the German economy under elected governments would have limited the Nazis to continued minority status, but it is harder to argue that it would have led to a rapid decline in Nazi support.

Hitler was appointed chancellor at the end of January 1933, and sustained economic recovery began only thereafter. The advent of the Nazi Government heralded the presence—as in the USA—of a new policy regime. Instead of focusing on the clear political discontinuity in 1933, we need to expose the clear change in economic policy. The Nazi Government was truly a new (and horrible) regime, both politically and economically. The Nazis set out immediately to consolidate their power and destroy democracy. They obliterated democratic institutions. They turned away from international commitments to the restoration of domestic prosperity. And they gave their highest priority to the reduction of Germany's massive unemployment. Hitler conducted a successful balancing act. He reassured businessmen that he was not a free-spending radical at the same time as he expanded the job-creation programmes and tax breaks of his predecessors. The first Four-Year Plan embodied many of the new measures and gave them visibility as a new policy direction (Guillebaud, 1939).

Employment rose rapidly in 1933 as a result. The new expenditures must have taken time to have their full effects. The immediate recovery therefore was the result of changed expectations when the Nazis took power. It was the result of anticipated as well as actual government activities. Even though the specifics of the Nazi programme did not become clear—in fact were not formulated—until later, the direction of policy was clear. Hitler had been criticizing the deflationary policies of his predecessors for years, and the commitment of the Nazis to full employment was well known. As in the USA, a change in policy regime was sufficient to turn the corner, although not to promote full recovery.

4. A Divided World

The World Economic Conference

President Herbert Hoover of the USA had imposed a one-year moratorium on payments of reparations and war debts in an effort to avert the German crisis in July 1931. But the Hoover moratorium was not sufficient to end the German financial panic. A special advisory committee of the Bank for International Settlements reviewed economic conditions in Germany in late 1931 and found that the schedule for reparations payments established by the 1929 Young Plan was no longer feasible. The plan had expected trade expansion and recovery, not world-wide depression and the collapse of trade.

The British Government led an effort to convene a conference to discuss reparations. German Chancellor Brüning stated in January 1932 that Germany would seek complete cancellation of reparations at the upcoming conference. The French vehemently responded that they would not easily cede their right to reparations. The British and the Italians supported the Germans, leaving the French nearly isolated. The USA remained uninterested in reparations but adamantly opposed war-debt repudiation. Even in their last moments, reparations were a source of international discord. There was no international leadership and no co-operation.

Brüning's January statement and its repercussions in other capitals delayed the conference, as did impending elections in France and Germany, since neither Government would be in a position to make concessions prior to elections. The delay contributed to the collapse of Chancellor Brüning's Government. Brüning had launched Germany on a programme of deflation to end reparations by demonstrating to German creditors that the nation could not pay. He had succeeded in destroying the German economy along with reparations, a truly Pyrrhic victory.

The Lausanne Conference finally opened in June 1932 with statements of national views, with the French opposing substantial concessions, and the Italians, British, and Germans favouring a 'clean slate'. The proceedings at Lausanne were complicated by a disarmament conference concurrently meeting in Geneva, where the USA informed the United Kingdom and France that it would not allow European default on war debts while funds sufficient to cover the payments were being used for armament spending. The Germans expressed willingness to offer compensation, but they wished to avoid mention of the word 'reparations'. The British and the French favoured a clause linking reparations with an American war-debt settlement. Germany objected to the American argument that there was no link between the two obligations, and that an agreement had to be definite and independent of America (Wheeler-Bennett, 1933).

A breakthrough in negotiations led to the Lausanne Convention. An annexe to the agreement addressed the German reparations conflict, directing Germany to deposit bonds worth RM3 billion (£150 million) at the Bank for International Settlements. The bonds were to be issued by the BIS after a three-year moratorium if Germany was judged to be capable of paying. The allocation of the bonds was to be settled in a future meeting of the creditors. (The bonds, never issued, were burned in 1948.) Beyond the issue of these bonds, Germany was permanently relieved of reparations obligations.

Another annexe of the Convention called for a World Economic Conference to address the remaining major international economic issues. The British Treasury had favoured a world conference since late 1930. France had blocked Britain's attempts to co-ordinate an international economic conference in 1931, fearing both pressure to join in an artificial international redistribution of gold and German manipulation of the conference to obtain a reparations reprieve (Mouré, 1991). After the sterling devaluation of

September 1931 removed British pressure for gold redistribution, and the Lausanne Conference of June 1932 ended German reparations, these two obstacles to co-operation had been surmounted.

The French and British asked President Hoover to postpone the December 1932 war-debt payment, but Hoover refused. France and several other European nations defaulted on the instalment, and the English paid by earmarking gold in the Bank of England, angering American public opinion and increasing President-elect Roosevelt's determination to keep war debts off the agenda for the World Economic Conference. Despite agreement to end reparations with the face-saving bonds held by the BIS, war debts remained as an internationally divisive issue. Neither co-operation nor effective leadership was possible on the eve of the 1933 economic conference.

The Lausanne Convention had called for a committee of experts to meet in advance of the large conference to establish an agenda. The British staked out a position requiring higher prices and recovered trade as conditions for a stabilization agreement. The French cautiously guarded their continued adherence to the gold standard, which remained free of attack, and their trade barriers that provided protection from depreciated currencies. The Hoover Administration, represented at the meetings of the experts, sympathized with the French arguments, while Roosevelt, initially unsure, eventually drifted towards the English policies (Eichengreen, 1992).

Roosevelt was inaugurated as president at the beginning of March 1933. He invited representatives of fifty-three nations to the USA in April for preliminary discussions. But while the representatives of France and Britain were in transit to Washington, Roosevelt approved the Thomas amendment to the Agricultural Adjustment Act, allowing him to devalue the dollar. The US position had undergone a radical shift, making fruitful negotiations difficult if not impossible.

The Washington negotiations focused on war debts, a tariff truce, and monetary stability. The war-debt talks resolved nothing, and the tariff truce was blocked by stiff resistance from the French, who insisted on currency stabilization agreements, especially of the dollar. The Americans proposed a common fund to stabilize the major currencies, with the dollar devaluation limited to 15 per cent. The French delegation avoided a negative response to this proposal, but they also withheld approval because they feared that the British would object to a 15 per cent dollar devaluation and because they were unwilling to support the USA without knowing US economic policy. Feis recalled that while Roosevelt was sincere in the offer, he was actually relieved that his own proposal fell through (Feis, 1966: 146).

As the conference approached, prospects for success grew ever dimmer. As the value of the dollar fell during May, Roosevelt became less interested in stabilization, reversing the co-operative policies that he had advocated during the Washington discussions. Meanwhile, the French Government conveyed to the US and British Governments its belief that exchange stabilization was a prerequisite for success in London. 'The French sought not recovery, but security, in a world over which they exercised little control' (Mouré, 1991: 99).

Early in the course of the conference a conflict emerged regarding whether a representative of the USA or of France should head the financial committee. The French were opposed to a representative of a non gold-standard country presiding, and the Americans were opposed to a representative from a country that had defaulted on its war debts. The French completely defaulted on the 15 June war-debt instalment, drawing no immediate retribution from the Roosevelt administration, but lessening Roosevelt's sympathy for French appeals for stabilization. The major industrial countries were moving away from, not toward, agreement.

Central bank representatives from Britain, France, and the USA decided in June that exchange stabilization was possible. Each agreed to buy and sell gold to keep their currencies within prescribed limits of 3 per cent either way. The provisions of the stabilization were to be kept secret, and the agreement was null if the details were made public. Declarations were prepared stating that the three governments intended to limit fluctuations of the dollar and sterling for the length of the conference, that stabilization on gold was the ultimate objective, and that they would avoid measures that might interfere with monetary stability.

Unfortunately, the news of dollar stabilization leaked to the press, and American markets responded quickly. The dollar strengthened and commodity and stock prices fell as investors anticipated a return to deflation. Roosevelt telegraphed his negotiators in London to reject the agreement, claiming that he did not wish to restrict his domestic policy options and that he was not certain at what level the dollar belonged. Roosevelt then left Washington for a sailing vacation, hindering communications with both Washington and London. After attempts to sway the president failed, Roosevelt's rejection was announced at the World Economic Conference, causing turmoil and intensifying speculation against the Dutch florin and the Swiss franc, but restoring the recovery of American markets.

After the collapse of this agreement, the French concentrated pressure on the British to stabilize and join the gold countries, warning of impending monetary anarchy in Europe. In response, the British asked for a currency declaration, which was quickly drafted and approved by the gold countries. To the consternation of the French, however, the British invited American participation in the agreement. The US representative revised the document until the only remaining points were a call for monetary stability, recognition that an eventual return to the gold standard was desirable, and a statement that individual nations would take action to avoid speculation.

He advised Roosevelt to accept the document, fearing that the USA would be held responsible for the collapse of the conference. Roosevelt none the less sent a rejection to London on 1 July. His infamous 'bombshell' message was released to the conference and the public on 3 July. The message, loaded with inflammatory rhetoric, accused the stabilization discussion of interfering with the real issues that the conference should address. In Roosevelt's words: 'The world will not long be lulled by the specious fallacy of achieving a temporary and probably an artificial stability in foreign exchange on the part of a few large countries only. The sound internal economic situation of a nation is a greater factor in its well-being than the price of its currency' (Nixon, 1969: 269).

Roosevelt later admitted that the message was too heavy in rhetoric, but several economists agreed with his general argument; Keynes even said that Roosevelt was 'magnificently right' (Feis, 1966: 238). None the less, much of the logic of Roosevelt's message was contorted. His concerns about a US gold drain were offset by the American possession of one-third of the world's gold reserves. His qualms about only two or three nations stabilizing were contradicted by the fact that the rest of the world would stabilize in terms of the dollar, franc, and pound. And the distinction between governments and central banks he stressed was essentially irrelevant in considering a stabilization agreement. The central message that domestic conditions needed to be given priority was correct.

The failure and collapse of the World Economic Conference traditionally is attributed to Roosevelt's bombshell message. But the conditions for international economic co-operation were not present in mid-1933. Each of the major countries had its own view of the economic crisis and was trying to formulate its own remedies. Instead of initiating international co-operation or leadership, each of the major European industrial and financial powers would become the centre of a currency and trading block of its own.

The sterling area

Once Britain had devalued, the pressure to follow suit was especially great among countries with export-based economies for whom the United Kingdom was the primary market. Denmark, Sweden, Norway, and Finland followed Britain off gold, but did not immediately peg to sterling. By January 1932 Japan, Venezuela, and Bolivia were adopting policies that increasingly resembled basing on sterling. The countries that pegged to sterling between 1931 and 1933 formed the sterling area, composed of the colonial Empire and India, the Dominions excluding Canada, some semi-independent nations including Iraq and Egypt, and other foreign nations, particularly in Scandinavia (Drummond, 1981). The reasons for choosing to link with sterling varied among these groups. India and the colonial Empire were compelled to do so by Britain; this was not unusual, as a sterling peg had previously been used to stabilize these currencies. Australia and New Zealand had already suffered exchange depreciation, and needed to link to sterling to retain competitiveness in the British market. South Africa, after initially trying to maintain its gold parity, was forced to devalue and peg to sterling for similar reasons.

Many smaller European and Latin American countries chose to link to sterling both because Britain was a primary export market and because they held large reserves of sterling for exchange transactions. The Brussels Conference of 1920 and the Genoa Conference of 1922 had encouraged holding foreign currency instead of gold, and unless these countries devalued and repegged to gold, they would suffer large capital losses on their sterling reserves. Just as there were multiple reasons for pegging to sterling, there were multiple mechanisms for maintaining this new parity. The currency board system implemented for the colonial Empire, Egypt, and Iraq provided an automatic relationship with sterling. A system of semi-independence, in which the exchange rate was rigidly fixed and maintained through large sterling reserves, was maintained in India, Australia, New Zealand, South Africa, and Portugal. The third policy, an autonomous system of maintaining a target sterling parity without holding large sterling reserves, was attempted in Scandinavia (Drummond, 1981).

The British Government studiously avoided encouraging countries outside the colonial Empire and India to devalue or to peg to sterling because it wished to avoid responsibility for other nations' difficulties. Even though Britain avoided formal arrangements, it supported nations that voluntarily committed to the sterling area. In December 1931 the Bank of England provided a credit of £500,000 to the Bank of Finland, which was trying to maintain sterling parity through exchange controls. In the same month a credit of £250,000 was granted to Denmark. Throughout the 1930s Australia received sizeable credits which, while never used, demonstrated British willingness to stabilize exchange rates within the sterling area.

Soon after the devaluation of sterling in September 1931 British Treasury officials began to consider a monetary policy for the Empire. The British authorities shared the opinion of the leaders of the Empire that prices were too low, but they feared that the Empire countries might promote inflationary programmes of deficit monetization, public works, and deliberate credit expansion which could potentially destabilize sterling. In early 1932 the discussion of Empire monetary policy developed into preparations for the coming Ottawa Conference.

In the 1932 Ottawa meeting, the monetary policy issues of the conference were confined to a committee through which the British advanced their policies, reassuring the Dominions and India that monetary policy would be directed towards higher prices and recovery, but avoiding discussion of stabilization. The primary discussion at the Ottawa Conference considered trade agreements. In February 1932 the National Government of the United Kingdom had supported the Import Duties Act, a '10 per cent duty on all goods except basic foodstuffs, raw materials, and goods already subject to duty' (Howson and Winch, 1977: 98). The Ottawa Conference extended the British system of trade protection, granting preferential access to the British market to Commonwealth producers and giving preferential access to Commonwealth markets to British producers. The Commonwealth countries were unwilling to take any measures which would harm their emerging manufacturing industries, and despite her initial expectations the agreement did little to help increase Britain's sales of manufactured goods. It did, however, bring about a considerable shift in the direction of trade between Britain and the Commonwealth, at the expense of other countries. In 1929 Britain sold 51 per cent of its exports to the Commonwealth and the sterling area, and bought 42 per cent of its imports from these sources. By 1938, 62 per cent of her exports and 55 per cent of imports involved these countries.

When the World Economic Conference ground to a halt following Roosevelt's attack on attempts to stabilize currencies, the formation of the gold bloc led by France, with its intention of deflating world prices, caused alarm among the primary producing nations of the sterling area; they feared that the British might join the gold bloc. The Chancellor of the Exchequer's response was to reaffirm his commitment to cheap money and higher prices, but also to express concern that Europe, which eventually must abandon gold, should not fall apart in chaos during the conference (Drummond, 1981: 176–7). The British Commonwealth Declaration was signed on 27 July 1933 resolving to raise prices, to ease credit and money except for monetizing government deficits, to eventually restore the gold standard, and to keep exchange rates stable within the sterling area. The declaration succeeded in quieting talk of public works and further depreciation in the Empire, in distracting attention from the general failure of the World Economic Conference, and in reaffirming the Ottawa agreements.

As the dollar became more unstable and the USA did little to encourage pegging to the dollar, this declaration formalizing the sterling area made it a more attractive option for countries seeking to stabilize their exchange rates. Denmark, Sweden, and Argentina formalized their sterling pegs soon after the British Commonwealth Declaration. Norway had officially pegged to sterling in May 1933, having devalued 9.5 per cent from the sterling gold parity rate (see further Chapter 17 by Nordvik). From late in 1933 to 1938, the sterling to dollar exchange rate was reasonably stable, meaning that a large part of the world enjoyed five years of exchange stability. Following devaluation of the franc in September 1936, France associated with the sterling area by trying to maintain a fixed sterling rate, much as the Scandinavian countries had from 1931 through 1933. In late September both Greece and Turkey devalued slightly and pegged to sterling, and Latvia moved from a franc peg to a sterling peg with a substantial devaluation.

The cheap credit policies of Britain allowed the sterling system to accommodate the cheap money policies of Scandinavia, Australia, South Africa, and other devaluing nations. London facilitated the operation of the system by supplying sterling-area nations with the sterling reserves they needed. The stability of the pound throughout the decade encouraged a willingness to hold sterling balances, and the combination of increased production from South African mines and dishoarding in India supplied gold to the sterling area, ensuring convertibility. While British policy could not create the international co-operation necessary to initiate world-wide recovery, recovery was possible for any nations that wished to join the sterling area.

The Nazi trading area

After the banking and currency crises of July 1931, the German Government allowed banks to reopen only after freezing foreign deposits and limiting foreign-exchange transactions to the Reichsbank. These initial exchange controls were ineffective, and were replaced in September, after the sterling devaluation, with more stringent controls. These required owners of gold and foreign assets to sell them to the Reichsbank, restricted the amount of foreign exchange available to importers, and required exporters to surrender their foreign exchange proceeds to the Reichsbank (Ellis, 1941).

Following the devaluation of sterling, foreign advisers advocated a German devaluation to restore equity in international markets, possibly in conjunction with joining the sterling area. The maintenance of the gold-standard parity hurt exporters, especially as other nations devalued and protectionism increased, but depreciation of the mark was avoided. Historians differ on the question of whether another choice was possible. Those who say no point to the association of depreciation with the hyperinflation of the 1920s (Borchardt, 1984, 1990). Others point to the British example of successful devaluation (Temin, 1989). By contrast, the bilateral trading agreements that the Germans pursued offered the trade balance advantages of devaluation while giving the government control over the composition of imports and providing an instrument for international diplomacy (James, 1986).

In January 1933 Adolph Hitler and the Nazi Party came to power in Germany. Many of the Nazis' policies, including exchange control, work-creation projects, government intervention in banking, and agriculture intervention were inherited from the Weimar Republic. Germany had always had a high degree of government involvement in the economy and in foreign trade policy. But the Nazis used terror, the threat of concentration camps and possible death, to enforce compliance with economic controls, including exchange and trade controls (Temin, 1991).

The deterioration of world trade in the 1930s was magnified in Germany by the devaluations of sterling and the dollar, by the rise of protectionism, and by capital flight resulting from Jews fleeing persecution and from domestic and foreign response to Nazi policies (see further Chapter 3 below by Feinstein and Watson). For the short term, the response in 1934 was increased foreign-exchange restrictions and a moratorium on interest payments on debt to foreigners. A long-term strategy was devised with the New Plan of Hjalmar Schacht, the president of the Reichsbank and the minister of finance, which encouraged autarky by restricting imports and provided commodity boards to create greater administrative control of trade. In 1935 a scheme was initiated to extend subsidies to German exports that were not competitive on world markets because of the overvalued mark.

The trade policies of the Nazis, moving towards autarky, were unique among the Western economies because they were directed towards preparing for a war economy. German goals included military preparedness and administrative control over the domestic population, with politics taking precedence over economics. The price paid for this was fewer available import goods and increased labour intensiveness.

The Nazis initiated bilateral trade agreements that were to take several forms during the decade. One of the first systems was the private compensation procedure which created agencies that attempted to balance imports and exports by matching private exporters and importers to ensure offsetting trade. One characteristic of this system was the use of blocked marks, frozen funds held by foreigners and used at a discount to buy German exports. Through the use of blocked marks, German exporters could obtain higher prices in terms of marks for their products, and foreign importers purchasing these marks at a discount could purchase German exports at a lower price in terms of the foreign currency. Because this system was highly profitable for German exporters, its use was limited to 'additional exports', those goods that were not competitive in foreign markets due to the overvalued mark (Kitson, 1992).

A second, more flexible method was the bilateral exchange clearing system which attempted to balance credits and debits on a national level. The mechanism of this system was conducted through clearing accounts in the Reichsbank. German importers paid marks to the Reichsbank account of the trading partner, where the funds were held until they could be used to pay German exporters for goods sold to the other country. If the accounts held insufficient funds, the exporters had to wait for imports to increase, and if there were excess funds, importers had to wait for increased exports. The central bank of the trading partner held similar clearing accounts for its exporters and importers. After the initial agreement with Hungary, arrangements of this type were made between Germany and Estonia, Latvia, Bulgaria, Greece, Yugoslavia, Romania, Czechoslovakia, and Turkey. While the details of each arrangement were different, all of these clearing agreements shared the common goal of opening trade controls to help export industries (Kitson, 1992).

The central banks of Germany's trading partners with clearing balances were forced to intervene to prevent the blocked marks from depreciating, which would decrease the competitiveness of the trading partner's exports in the German market. One alternative, pursued by Hungary and Bulgaria, two nations politically favourable to Germany, was to pay exporters in domestic currency for their holdings of blocked marks. A second alternative, pursued by Romania and Yugoslavia, two nations wary of German influence, was to allow the blocked marks to depreciate slightly until domestic importers purchased German goods and depleted the balance of blocked marks. Hungary, following the financing principle, experienced consistent trade surpluses with Germany, while Romania, following the waiting principle, experienced alternating surpluses and deficits. Germany's trading partners 'found political opposition to Germany economically costly and acquiescence rewarding' (Neal, 1979: 392).

Germany's trade with Western Europe, traditionally an area of export surpluses, was limited by the decline in international trade and the rise of exchange controls. Germany negotiated Sondermark agreements with Denmark, Switzerland, Sweden, Italy, France, Belgium-Luxembourg, the Netherlands, Norway, Finland, Spain, and Portugal to preserve these valuable export markets. The Sondermark agreements involved partial rather than full clearing systems, with the establishment of clearing accounts for 'additional trade'. Normal levels of trade were conducted according to foreign-exchange quotas, and the special accounts for additional trade, the trade that developed beyond normal levels, operated in the same manner as the bilateral exchange clearing agreements between Germany and south-east Europe.

In 1934 the ASKI (Ausländer Sonderkonten für Inlandszahlung) procedure was introduced, replacing the private compensation procedure which had been less restrictive and had been used to avoid strict exchange controls. The ASKI procedure established accounts at German banks where foreign exporters' proceeds were held. Foreign exporters needed to secure permission from German exchange control authorities to trade with Germany, with German imports limited to only those deemed necessary by the commodity control boards. ASKI balances could be used to purchase certain non-essential German goods, but the goods had to be shipped to the country of the account-holder. Two types of ASKI accounts developed: accounts for individual foreign exporters, and accounts for foreign commercial banks which represented a group of foreign traders.

The New Plan also created a system of payment agreements with Great Britain, Belgium-Luxembourg, Canada, France, and New Zealand. These agreements provided for the release of free foreign exchange to pay for imports and to transfer payment on old German debts. In addition, Germany agreed to import goods equal to a specified fraction of its exports to each country. The effect of the New Plan was to extend and develop the exchange controls of the early 1930s, replacing the ineffective ones with more stringent controls.

The exchange control system in place after the New Plan consisted of three different arrangements: the stringent ASKI agreements, the more moderate clearing agreements, and the more lax payments agreements. Germany's free trade was limited to only a small group of countries, including the USA, because the overvalued mark doomed Germany to a trade deficit where trading agreements were not in effect (Neal, 1979; Kitson, 1992).

Germany's bilateral trading agreements accounted for 50 per cent of Germany's trade by 1938. German trade with south-east Europe is often overemphasized, as the Balkans bought only 7 per cent of Germany's exports in 1935 and 11 per cent by 1938. While these parts of Europe were regarded as prime areas for German economic and trade expansion, there was significant resistance to any kind of limiting relationships with Germany. Germany incurred trade deficits with most of her Balkan neighbours during the 1930s, and the largest German trade was conducted with Western Europe, Latin America, and the Middle East (Overy, 1982).

Kitson (1992) concludes that Germany sacrificed terms-of-trade advantages that could have been won from its position as monopolist in export markets and monopsonist in import markets. Other objectives replaced terms-of-trade gains, as isolation from the world market, reduced dependence on imports, and the reorientation of trade to safe, adjacent countries took precedence. According to Neal (1979: 392) 'it was relatively costless, and often politically rewarding, for Germany to forgo the advantages of monopoly exploitation'.

While the United Kingdom, France, the Netherlands, and other economic powers increased trade within their empires, Germany, which had no empire, was forced to develop a currency bloc, altering its pattern of trade. German trade was reoriented in favour of southern and eastern Europe, the countries with which it conducted the stricter policies of ASKI and clearing agreements. As trade between Germany and south-east Europe increased, these nations became more dependent on Germany for their markets for basic foodstuffs and raw materials. These countries were isolated in the post-Depression trade world, and Germany, paying prices 20–40 per cent above world prices for agricultural commodities, was the most attractive market. A trading bloc was effectively established, providing Germany with a dependable source of necessary commodities. Between 1929 and 1938 German exports to south-east Europe rose from 5 to 13 per cent of total German exports, and her imports from this region rose from 5 to 12 per cent of the total (Kindleberger, 1973: 282). Although successful in reorienting German trade, the Nazi policies never made south-eastern Europe one of Germany's major trading partners, and some of the increase which did occur was simply the re-establishment of older trading patterns broken by the inflations of the 1920s and the Depression of the 1930s. Comparably, over the same period the share of German trade with the United Kingdom, France, the Netherlands, Belgium, and Scandinavia fell as these countries turned to the sterling area.

The gold bloc

The gold bloc of the 1930s had its origins in the Latin Monetary Union of 1865, in which the French, Belgian, and Swiss francs were established at equal parities (Kindleberger, 1973). In response to Roosevelt's message to the World Economic Conference and the turmoil that emerged in its aftermath, the representatives of France, Belgium, Holland, Switzerland, Italy, and Poland released a joint declaration that their governments would strive to maintain the gold standard and the stability of their currencies at their current parities, both to create a stable gold platform for the recovery of international exchange-market stability and to promote social progress at home. Representatives of their central banks met in Paris, and on 8 July they pledged to support each other's currencies, reimbursing each other in currency or gold.

While the gold bloc was to develop a reputation for possessing 'little cohesion and no organization' (Mouré, 1991: 110), its initial declaration successfully ended the speculation against the Dutch florin and the Swiss franc that had persisted during the proceedings of the World Economic Conference. Despite this strong beginning, however, the gold bloc remained a symbolic organization. No progress was made in developing the connections between the central banks or the government policies of the member nations after the 8 July meeting.

Of all the trading blocs that emerged in the aftermath of the London Economic Conference, the gold bloc was the only one still constrained to follow the stringent deflationary policies demanded by the gold standard. The continuing efforts in these countries to hold their economies to this harsh course produced ever more economic declines. The commitment to the gold standard revealed by these actions in the presence of the beginning of recovery in other countries was deep indeed. It is no wonder that this misguided ideological purity prevented international co-operation and inhibited the emergence of leadership.

Within the constraints of the existing gold parities, countries had only two options to protect their trade balances: exchange controls and deflation. Among the central European nations, including the emerging Axis trading bloc, tariffs were supplemented by exchange controls, nominally leaving the countries on the gold standard but effectively rendering the system meaningless. The gold bloc regarded exchange controls as incompatible with the workings of the gold standard and completely against the spirit of the system. Continued deflation was its policy.

Czechoslovakia, a minor member of the gold bloc, devalued its currency in February 1934. Unemployment in Italy had risen to levels at which deflationary measures were no longer feasible. Mussolini placed pride in the stability and strength of the lira and was unwilling to devalue. Italy therefore gradually imposed exchange controls, maintaining only the illusion of retaining gold-standard parity. In July 1935 the Italian Government prohibited gold exports. Not all the original members of the gold bloc could stand the strain of deflation for very long, as discussed in Chapter 6 by Asselain and Plessis.

The other gold bloc nations pursued policies of stringent deflation. The French had been successful in the early years of the decade in keeping their current account deficit small through trade barriers, but by 1933 the situation was steadily growing worse. The decline in economic activity was accompanied by lower government revenues, resulting in budgetary deficits that caused great alarm among the French populace who still bore the memory of the inflationary cycles of the mid-1920s. The political effects of expenditure cuts and new taxes created a situation of turmoil in which there were four governments in 1932, three in 1933, and four in 1934. Even though the decline in prices left the real wages of pensioners, veterans, and government employees higher than their original levels, attempts to reduce fiscal expenditures by cutting payments to these groups were highly unpopular.

Within the gold bloc, the high prices resulting from the overvalued gold-standard parities of the currencies discouraged trading among the bloc's members. French trade with Belgium decreased 13 per cent between 1933 and 1934, and French trade with Switzerland decreased by 40 per cent. To encourage trade among themselves, the gold bloc nations met in Geneva in September 1934 and signified their agreement to increase trade and tourism within the bloc and arrange another conference to meet in Brussels in October to discuss trade policy. Poland was not allowed to participate in either the Geneva or the Brussels conferences, ostensibly because its economy was structured differently from those of the other members of the gold bloc, but more likely because the other members were reluctant to include a nation whose economy was in as desperate need of assistance as Poland's in 1934.

The Brussels conference convened in an atmosphere of pessimism and reluctance. The Italians were not interested in the conference and tried to use the absence of Poland as a pretext for postponing or cancelling the conference. Eventually Italy sent only one delegate to Belgium. The Dutch were reluctant to limit their preferential trade agreements to the members of the gold bloc. They favoured extending any trade barrier reductions to Germany and Britain, especially as they were concerned about German retaliation which might cost them the German steel market, one of their most important export markets. The Belgians, hosting the conference, were openly discussing devaluation, and there was speculation in the French Government that the Belgian Government wanted the conference to fail to provide justification for devaluation. France was constrained by limitations similar to those placed on the Dutch. While the French were interested in promoting the gold bloc, their most important export markets were in countries in other exchange blocs. The French were limited by most-favoured-nation trade agreements in the concessions that they could offer to their gold bloc trading partners.

The conference opened with the Italian and Dutch delegations expressing reluctance to reaffirm their countries' commitment to maintain the gold standard and their currency parities. Under French guidance the conference was brought to a close with an agreement for gold bloc countries to continue bilateral negotiations to allow for a 10 per cent increase in gold bloc trade by 30 June 1935. The conference therefore was successful to the extent that the gold bloc survived intact. But the results of the proposed negotiations were not the least bit encouraging for gold bloc unity. The French agreed in principle to increase Belgian trade, but the proposed 10 per cent rise was unattainable.

Belgium had been severely hurt by its loss of competitiveness in British markets with the sterling devaluation in 1931. In September 1934 the Belgian Government asked for French assistance, but neither loan arrangements nor proposals to lower French quotas on Belgian goods were enacted. In March 1935 the British Government limited steel imports, worsening Belgium's plight. In desperation, the Belgian Government reopened talks with France to seek economic assistance. Again, the French could not offer more than token relief. Returning from Paris essentially empty-handed, the Belgian Government was forced to impose exchange controls. A new government devalued the Belgian franc on 30 March, repegging it 28 per cent lower at a level calculated to restore the prices of Belgian goods to the level of Britain and the USA (see further Chapter 7 by Cassiers).

When the gold bloc was officially declared in the aftermath of the World Economic Conference, French opinion was firmly opposed to devaluation of the franc as an alternative to deflation. As the disparity between the recovery of countries with depreciated currencies and the stagnation of gold bloc countries became apparent, individuals within French political and journalism circles began to support devaluation, although public opinion remained strongly opposed. The primary danger to the franc was perceived to be the budget deficits that threatened to resurrect the debt monetization and the resulting inflationary cycles that had caused the economic chaos of the 1920s. Fearing these consequences, successive French governments struggled with programmes to reduce expenditure and augment decreasing revenues, but economic contraction and budget deficits persisted.

The Popular Front, a coalition of the Radical, Communist, and Socialist Parties led by Léon Blum, took office in June 1936 with a plan to restore economic growth with a French 'New Deal'. Blum renounced deflationary policies, but did not devalue. France consequently suffered serious depletion of its gold reserves. The Popular Front introduced a shortened work-week of forty hours without a reduction in wages, and it raised wages to stimulate consumption and ignite the economy. The Matignon Accords, which forced employers to sign a package of wage increases, were the Popular Front's solution to widespread labour unrest.

By mid-1936, there was widespread support for devaluation among politicians, publicists, and banking and financial experts, but still not among the general populace. The opposition to devaluation during 1934 and 1935 had so effectively convinced the French public that devaluation would cause a return of inflation that this opinion persisted through 1936.

The Tripartite Agreement

As French gold losses mounted in the spring of 1936, Blum's Popular Front Government, whose appeal was largely based on its repudiation of deflation, was forced to make emphatic declarations that it opposed any change in the value of the franc. Even while Blum was defending the franc by publicly announcing that he would not devalue, his opinions were drifting in that direction and he privately began to explore the possibilities of an international accord to prevent competitive devaluation of the dollar or the pound in the event of a French devaluation. To defend the French gold reserves, the government was faced with a choice between deflation, devaluation, and exchange control. Deflation was eliminated as an option by its failure to achieve recovery, or even stability, during its many reincarnations in the first half of the decade. Faced with the choice between exchange control and devaluation, the financial and banking communities favoured devaluation as the lesser of two evils. Imposition of exchange controls would lead to French autarky, isolating France from its allies, the Western democracies. Exchange control was regarded as a fascist option, requiring extensive controls and administration, and severe penalties to be effective.

While many members of the right-wing press and of financial circles favoured devaluation, the French public remained resolutely opposed, as were the Communist Party and many Radicals and Socialists.

The French Government's problem was unprecedented in the need to negotiate internationally *before* devaluing. Unlike the devaluations of the dollar and sterling, which were relatively simple, largely domestic decisions, the franc devaluation was jeopardized by the prospect of competitive devaluations or increased trade barriers in the devalued nations. The floating pound and the dollar were likely to respond to a change in the value of the franc.

The USA asked France in the summer of 1936 whether a joint American and British statement that the dollar and the pound would not depreciate in the event of a reasonable france devaluation would ease the process of lowering the value of the franc. The French opposed such a tripartite declaration as merely amounting to a unilateral devaluation, which the Blum Government could not readily accept after campaigning on the promise not to devalue. The British also did not want any commitment that would force them to support the franc and would link the pound to gold. They did not want France pegging to sterling; they wanted France to peg the franc on gold to allow continued British operations in francs. The British did express their willingness unofficially to keep the pound as stable as possible, while retaining control of the sterling rate, and in the spirit of co-operation they agreed to devise some formula for the rates, preferably a meaningless one (Clarke, 1977).

France did not pursue negotiations immediately, expecting an improvement in the domestic situation, but the anticipated calm never developed. The government announced a 21 billion franc rearmament programme in September 1936 and proceeded to experience a massive gold outflow. France then responded by presenting a draft pre-stabilization agreement to Britain and the USA. This called for nations to direct monetary policies toward maintenance of stability and consideration of the international effects of domestic policies. Washington and London objected to the excessive references to co-operation and stability; they also disliked any reference to the gold standard. In addition, the USA objected to a reference to social classes, which would not be palatable to the American public, and to a formula for the French devaluation that would adjust the franc to world prices. The British were uneasy that the new French proposal did not clearly define the extent of the franc devaluation, which the Treasury feared might exceed 100 francs to the pound.

A revised French draft offered a compromise suggesting that the French and British co-operate daily, allowing them to convert holdings of the other's currency into gold. This compromise was the basis of what became known as the 24-hour gold standard. The two exchange authorities subsequently agreed that each morning they would inform each other if they intended to engage in currency operations during the day. If they agreed on the operation and the rates that would be used, a gold price would be established at which currency could be redeemed for gold at the end of the day (Clarke, 1977).

The USA rewrote the second French proposal and submitted it to Britain and France on 19 September. The American version, which was to form the basis of the final agreement, retained flowery French allusions to peace and liberty, while offering reasonable dollar stability, accepting the French devaluation, and promising co-operation with the French and British Governments. But with an agreement appearing imminent, an American confusion emerged to jeopardize the negotiations. The American officials had misinterpreted the British position on stabilization of currencies.

Washington informed London that the USA was interested in a $5 pound, plus or minus ten cents. US officials assumed that the British would consider it a reasonable level, as $5 had been the average rate for the past year while the British Exchange Equalization Account managed the exchanges. In fact, the British disliked the $5 parity, but had maintained that rate to avoid forcing devaluation of the franc and other gold bloc currencies. They immediately protested against the American message, claiming that no such agreement had ever been implied or arranged, and that there would be no stabilization of the dollar–pound exchange. To salvage the Tripartite Agreement, the Americans responded by agreeing to disagree: they retained the view that a $5 pound was appropriate, but were willing to concede the point to allow the announcement of the three declarations (Drummond, 1981).

The British, French, and American Governments released their Tripartite Declarations on 26 September 1936. A large fraction of the declarations was devoted to avowals of belief in peace, prosperity, increased living standards, and truth, beauty, and goodness that the French favoured. While the British were sceptical of this phraseology, the Americans took it seriously. Secretary of the Treasury Morgenthau believed that the declaration would be of value in restoring peaceful conditions to the world. More significantly, the declaration included the references to relaxing quotas and exchange controls that the British wanted, although France was not specifically mentioned, and the French did very little to lower trade barriers after the release of the agreement. The British agreed not to retaliate against the French devaluation, but there were no promises about rates because the British refused to constrain their domestic policy. The agreement also included announcements calling for increased co-operation among the central banks and the equalization funds of the Tripartite Powers.

The tangled negotiations needed to produce even this minimal agreement showed the tattered condition in which international organization existed at the end of the 1930s. Limited and partial co-operation was possible among the three principal democratic powers with great strain, but more was unattainable. There was 'little tripartite consultation and less co-operation' in the management of the franc after September 1936: 'As far as France was concerned the tripartite understanding remained in existence only because Britain and the United States were prepared to ignore the way in which France ignored it.' Much the same was true for sterling (Drummond, 1979, 1981). The French and British were too weak to provide effective leadership; the USA had turned inward, providing more of an obstacle than a stimulus to co-operation. The prevailing spirit is vividly illustrated by the note in which the deputy governor of the Banque de France recorded the basis of the understanding reached in discussions with Britain leading to the Tripartite Agreement: 'ni accord, ni entente, uniquement co-opération journaliere' (quoted in Sayers, 1976: 480). Germany and Italy remained outside even this limited agreement: they were not interested in co-operation, nor welcome in international forums. A few of the smaller countries sought to respond to the invitation to co-operate made in the British declaration; but nothing of any consequence followed from this.

The Tripartite Agreement did avoid a round of competitive devaluation at the end of the decade, though it would have been far better for all of Europe if an agreement for a co-ordinated devaluation could have been concluded five years earlier. Currency movements were generally mild in the few remaining years of peace. The Agreement might perhaps be seen as some advance in international understanding as compared with the early 1930s, and it had significant political implications as the Nazi threat became more alarming. But, contrary to some assessments, it was neither a serious step towards genuine international co-operation nor the precursor of Bretton Woods. It 'brought a shadow of international co-operation, but not its substance' (Drummond, 1981: 223).[6]

The Netherlands and Switzerland followed France off the gold standard, officially ending the gold bloc, three years after its inception. Recovery was quick in these two nations, as it had been in Belgium. Export markets recovered and expansionary policies were implemented. The Italian Government used the occasion of the French devaluation as an excuse to devalue the lira and reduce exchange controls, and Czechoslovakia devalued the crown a second time. The Tripartite Agreement was received negatively in France, where it was commonly believed that the Blum Government had reneged on its promises not to devalue, and where the international accord was seen as a sham hiding the French devaluation.

[6] For a somewhat more favourable view of the Tripartite Agreement see Kindleberger (1973: 257–61) and Rowland (1976: 51–6 and 250–1).

The benefits of devaluation were largely offset in France by the increase in French prices. In June 1937, under the pressure of gold losses and budget deficits, the Blum Government resigned and was replaced by a government that allowed the franc to float. The economy remained stagnant from 1936 to 1938 until a new government ended the forty-hour working week, imposed new taxes and budgetary economies, and attacked fiscal fraud. The French economy rebounded rapidly, but it was too late. The Nazi menace was about to put an end to the period between the wars.

5. Concluding Remarks: The Past and the Present

As the Second World War was slowly drawing to a close, policy-makers began to concern themselves with peacetime economic issues. The shade of depression and unemployment loomed large; in spite of wartime full employment the future of the economy looked uncertain. It was not clear whether democratic capitalism would be able to compete with central planning and dictatorship, right- or left-wing, in generating sustained growth and full employment once the war economy had been dismantled. In this intellectual climate, it was natural to turn to recent history in the hope that a better understanding of the past would show what mistakes should be avoided in the future. In such a vein the Royal Institute of International Affairs invited H. W. Arndt to analyse the previous decade's economic policies; his deservedly famous study was published in 1944 under the significant title *The Economic Lessons of the Nineteen-Thirties*. His contention was rigorously Keynesian: the Great Depression originated in a lack of aggregate demand and was made so exceptionally long and severe by misguided 'orthodox' policies. The better-than-average performance of Sweden, Britain, and Germany in the 1930s could be explained precisely by their decision to break away from such policies. Emphasis on Germany may seem peculiar. Arndt, nevertheless, was in good company: at the time, Balogh, Kaldor, and others were deeply impressed by the apparent success of German economic policies in fighting unemployment, and discussed how similar policies could be implemented in the context of the democratic political environment.

The concern for renewed depression and unemployment after the war proved to be misplaced, thanks partly to the understanding of history shown by the Allied Powers in avoiding some of the worse mistakes which had been made at the Versailles Conference of 1919. As a result, when another authoritative Keynesian-flavoured interpretation of the Great Depression appeared in 1954 (Svennilson's *Growth and Stagnation in the European Economy*), it was already much less in touch with the current interest of policy-makers and public opinion than its predecessor.

For the following twenty-odd years, the study of the inter-war decades lost most of its appeal to economists and politicians alike: unprecedented growth led to full employment in a context of stability never seen before or since. It became the common belief that an adequate mix of monetary and fiscal policies could free mankind from future depressions; some economists went so far as to speak of the 'conquest of the business cycle'.

The fortune of such visions was short-lived: the so-called 'first oil shock' showed conclusively that cycles had not been eliminated. By the mid-1970s, the intellectual climate had almost taken a U-turn: a question about the 1930s, unthinkable ten years earlier, had resurfaced: 'can it happen again?' Economists and historians turned enthusiastically to a search for lessons to be drawn from the inter-war years. The resulting intellectual effort generated a quantum leap forward in the understanding of the period: the findings of the resulting work constitute the basis for many of the points made in the previous pages of this survey chapter.

There was a brief spell of optimism in the 1980s, lasting only the *éspace d'un matin;* but now, at the moment of writing these lines, the European economy is burdened with the highest level of unemployment since the 1930s. Is it time again to turn to Clio's lessons? As economists we are inclined to think so. As historians we are aware that the dictum *historia magistra vitae* has been too often abused in mechanical transpositions of the past into the present. History seldom imparts simple lessons, but it can provide a useful framework in which pertinent questions about the present can be posed, and its value is enhanced when it is matched with relevant economic theory.

The most striking similarity between the present state of distress in the international economic setting and that of the 1920s, is that in both cases the end of a long-established 'international order' produced destabilizing effects. In section 1 of this chapter we discussed five consequences of the First World War which resulted in a major upset to the preceding *status quo*. Is the end of the cold war and the collapse of the Soviet empire likely to have equally far-reaching effects?

All five of the deleterious effects of the First World War noticed above are to some extent present again after the cold war. In particular, the real economy of Europe and the world has been distorted by the huge arms build-up of the past half-century. Massive shifts of resources need to be made. Political boundaries have been redrawn in Eastern Europe, and indeed are still unsettled; trade flows have been upset by the collapse of Comecon; migration waves pose a major challenge to social stability at the very heart of Western Europe. The banking systems of Europe appear to be more fragile than they were in the past. And like the gold standard after the First World War, the European Monetary System has not withstood the strain of developments since the end of the cold war, in particular of German unification.

Adjustments are needed in the 1990s as they were in the 1920s. But the need for economic change can create new demands which provide an opportunity for continued prosperity or, as in the inter-war years, it can be the source of disaster. In the introduction to this chapter we set out four propositions which have been suggested as explanations for the failures of policy and performance in the inter-war period. To what extent do similar factors inhibit creative economic policy today?

The first factor relates to the magnitude of the post-war imbalance in the real economy and to the disruption in commodity and factor flows noted above. Western Europe and the USA need to shift resources from weapons production to the manufacture of civilian goods. Eastern Europe has the much larger task of establishing an effective market economy. The victors in the cold war need to show a breadth of vision similar to that which enlightened policy-making after the Second World War. Resources hitherto allocated to armaments and the prosecution of the cold war should be used for the development of the 'defeated' Eastern European economies. Certainly, conditions there are very different from those of Western Europe in 1945. Nevertheless, the contrast between the attitude of the winning powers in 1919 and in 1945 is so striking, and the consequences for the policy outcomes so evident, that it should stimulate both generosity and intelligence in creating viable ways to provide the support necessary for the reconstruction of democracy and market economies.

The second complicating factor in the inter-war period was the decline of Britain as an economic hegemonic power, and the inability or unwillingness of the USA to assume leadership in world economic affairs. Here again we find analogies with the situation today. While the American economy is still large and vigorous, economic policies are constrained by the large debt accumulated to fight the cold war during the 1980s, as British flexibility was hampered in the 1920s by the weakness of its post-war economic position. The objectives of American foreign economic policy—and of its foreign policy *tout court*—seem at times to be uncertain and blurred, while new isolationist tendencies are apparent at the grass roots of American society. Germany and Japan are occupied with their internal problems and do not possess the economic strength and the international political status to take on the hegemonic mantle. If the world economy needs a single strong leader, then there are danger signs here.

Are we too prisoners of outdated economic ideologies, the third inhibiting factor of the inter-war period? This is obviously an issue that only prophetic minds and future generations will be able to clearly decide. Some suspicions, however, cannot be avoided. There are more than a few similarities between

September 1992 and September 1931. The tie to the gold standard during the Great Depression seems to have been echoed by ties to the European Monetary System (EMS) in our day. Does the obsessive defence of the exchange rate of the DM resemble in any way the poor monetary policy pursued by the Federal Reserve Bank in October 1931? Is the current obsession with inflation, deriving from the two-digit figures of the 1970s, in any way constraining policy, as the similar obsession with recent experience did in the early 1930s? We hope that the answers to these questions will turn out to be negative, given the implicit potential consequences if they are not. But these and similar issues surely need continuous monitoring and discussion in the light of the inter-war history.

The last of our four factors, international co-operation, is still a vital issue today. In the post-cold-war environment, co-operation may turn out to be more difficult (or, at least, to appear less crucial) for European countries than it was when the continent was divided into two conflicting camps. Moreover, depressed activity levels and high unemployment make the temptation to resort to protectionism and competitive devaluations more difficult to resist. This is especially a problem for individual governments which come under pressure from their electorates to produce short-term stimuli to the economy. However, if there is one clear 'lesson' from the 1930s, it is precisely that such temptations should be resisted at any cost, and that governments should help each other in avoiding such myopic policies that in the medium term are sure to result in a negative-sum game. This is, in our opinion, a broad but safe conclusion.

For the rest, the scope for central bank co-operation remains large, despite the *de facto* collapse of the EMS. The European Monetary Institute which started operating on 1 January 1994 is explicitly designed to foster cooperation: it is a novel institution with no precedents in the economic history of Europe. Its success, however, rests on the political willingness of individual governments to accept the consequences of co-operation in monetary matters. As we have seen, the history of the 1920s and 1930s is full of conferences ending with well-worded communiqués praising and promising co-operation, soon followed by non-co-operative moves. While responsibility for co-operative behaviour rests on the shoulders of all the participants in the game, the history of the inter-war years indicates that some form of leadership should be exercised by the largest and most powerful player.

History does not repeat itself, and the present situation, for all its analogies with the 1920s, is in many ways distinct from that of the inter-war period. Nevertheless, the presence of a substantial amount of dislocation now as then gives us pause. Will we be more successful in dealing with our problems than the inter-war generation were with theirs? We hope so and are cheered by one great difference. We, after all, have experienced the world-wide collapse known as the Great Depression. Policy-makers of the inter-war period did not know such a thing was possible. We hope that this added historical experience—described in detail in this volume—will impart wisdom to our leaders. We take comfort in the successful navigation of the economic shoals after the Second World War.

REFERENCES

Aldcroft, Derek H. (1977), *From Versailles to Wall Street* (London: Allen Lane).

Arndt, H. W. (1944), *The Economic Lessons of the Nineteen-Thirties* (London: Oxford University Press).

Balderston, T. (1982), 'The Origins of Economic Instability in Germany, 1924–1930: Market Forces versus Economic Policy', *Vierteljahrschrift für Sozial und Wirtschaftsgeschichte*, 69: 488–514.

—— (1983), 'The Beginning of the Depression in Germany, 1927–30: Investment and the Capital Market', *Economic History Review*, 36: 395–415.

Bennett, Edward W. (1962), *Germany and the Diplomacy of the Financial Crisis* (Cambridge, Mass.: Harvard University Press).

Berend, Ivan T., and Ranki, Gyorgy (1974), *Hungary, A Century of Economic Development* (Newton Abbot: David & Charles).

Bernanke, Ben, and James, Harold (1991), 'The Gold Standard, Deflation and Financial Crisis in the Great Depression: An International Comparison', in R. Glen Hubbard, (ed.), *Financial Markets and Financial Crises* (Chicago: NBER).

Bloomfield, Arthur I. (1959), *Monetary Policy under the International Gold Standard, 1880–1914* (New York: Federal Reserve Bank of New York).

Borchardt, Knut (1979, Engl. trans. 1991), 'Constraints and Room for Manœuvre in the Great Depression of the Early Thirties: Towards a Revision of the Received Historical Picture', in Knut Borchardt, *Perspectives on Modern German Economic History and Policy* (Cambridge: Cambridge University Press).

—— (1984), 'Could and Should Germany have Followed Great Britain in Leaving the Gold Standard?', *Journal of European Economic History*, 13: 471–98.

—— (1990), 'A Decade of Debate about Brüning's Economic Policy', in J. Baron von Kruedener (ed.), *Economic Crisis and Political Collapse: The Weimar Republic 1924–1933* (New York: Berg).

Boyce, Robert W. D. (1987), *British Capitalism at the Crossroads, 1919–1932* (Cambridge: Cambridge University Press).

Bresciani-Turroni, C. (1937), *The Economics of Inflation* (London: Allen & Unwin).

Brown, William Adams (1940), *The International Gold Standard Reinterpreted, 1914–1934* (New York: NBER).

Cairncross, Alec, and Eichengreen, Barry (1983), *Sterling in Decline: The Devaluations of 1931, 1949 and 1967* (Oxford: Blackwell).

Childers, Thomas (1983), *The Nazi Voter: The Social Foundations of Fascism in Germany, 1919–1933* (Chapel Hill, NC: University of North Carolina Press).

Choudhri, Ehsan U., and Kochin, Levis A. (1980), 'The Exchange Rate and the International Transmission of Business Cycle Disturbances', *Journal of Money, Credit and Banking*, 12: 565–74.

Clarke, Stephen V. O. (1967), *Central Bank Cooperation, 1924–31* (New York: Federal Reserve Bank of New York).

—— (1977), *Exchange-Rate Stabilization in the Mid-1930s: Negotiating the Tripartite Agreement*. Princeton Studies in International Finance, No. 41 (Princeton: Int. Fin. Section, Princeton University).

Cohen, Jon S. (1972), 'The 1927 Revaluation of the Lira: A Study in Political Economy', *Economic History Review*, 25: 642–54.

Drummond, Ian M. (1979), *London, Washington, and the Management of the Franc, 1936–39*, Princeton Studies in International Finance, No. 45 (Princeton: Int. Fin. Section, Princeton University).

—— (1981), *The Floating Pound and the Sterling Area, 1931–1939* (Cambridge: Cambridge University Press).

Eichengreen, Barry (1985), 'International Policy Coordination in Historical Perspective: A View from the Interwar years', in Willem Buiter and Richard Marston (eds.), *International Economic Policy Coordination* (Cambridge: Cambridge University Press): 139–78.

—— (1986) 'The Bank of France and the Sterilization of Gold, 1926–32', *Explorations in Economic History*, 23: 56–84.

—— (1990), *Elusive Stability, Essays in the History of International Finance, 1919–1939* (Cambridge: Cambridge University Press).

—— (1992), *Golden Fetters: The Gold Standard and the Great Depression, 1919–1939* (Oxford: Oxford University Press).

—— and Sachs, Jeffrey (1985), 'Exchange Rates and Economic Recovery in the 1930s', *Journal of Economic History*, 45: 925–46.

—— and Wyplosz, Charles (1990), 'The Economic Consequences of the Franc Poincaré', in Barry Eichengreen, *Elusive Stability* (Cambridge: Cambridge University Press), 153–79.

Ellis, H. S. (1941), *Exchange Control in Central Europe* (Cambridge, Mass.: Harvard University Press).

Epstein, Gerald, and Ferguson, Thomas (1984), 'Monetary Policy, Loan Liquidation and Industrial Conflict: The Federal Reserve Open Market Operation of 1932', *Journal of Economic History*, 44: 957–84.

Falkus, M. E. (1975), 'The German Business Cycle in the 1920s', *Economic History Review*, 28: 451–65.

Federal Reserve System (1943), *Banking and Monetary Statistics* (Washington, DC: Government Printing Office).

Feis, Herbert (1966), *1933: Characters in Crisis* (Boston: Little, Brown & Co.).

Feldman, Gerald D. *et al.* (1982), *The German Inflation Reconsidered: A Preliminary Balance* (Berlin: de Gruyter).

Fleisig, Heywood (1972), 'The United States and the Non-European Periphery during the Early Years of the Great Depression', in Herman Van der Wee (ed.), *The Great Depression Revisited* (The Hague: Nijhoff), 145–81.

Graham, Frank D. (1930), *Exchange, Prices and Production in Hyperinflation in Germany, 1920–1923* (Princeton, NJ: Princeton University Press).

Guarino, G., and Toniolo, Gianni (1993), *La Banca D'italia e il sistema bancario, 1919–36* (Rome: Bari).

Guillebaud, Claude W. (1939), *The Economic Recovery of Germany* (Cambridge: Cambridge University Press).

Hamilton, Richard (1982), *Who Voted for Hitler?* (Princeton, NJ: Princeton University Press).

Hardach, Karl (1980), *The Political Economy of Germany in the Twentieth Century* (Berkeley, Calif.: University of California Press).

Hawley, Ellis (1966), *The New Deal and the Problem of Monopolies: A Study in Economic Ambivalence* (Princeton, NJ: Princeton University Press).

Hawtrey, Ralph G. (1939), *The Gold Standard in Theory and Practice*, 4th edn. (London: Longmans).

Henning, Friedrich-Wilhelm (1973), 'Die zeitliche Einordnung der Überwindung der Weltwirtschaftskrise in Deutschland', *Schriften des Vereins für Sozialpolitik*, NS 73: 135–73.

Hodson, H. V. (1938), *Slump and Recovery, 1929–1937* (Oxford: Oxford University Press).

Holtfrerich, Carl-Ludwig (1986), *The German Inflation, 1914–1923: Causes and Effects in International Perspective* (Berlin: de Gruyter).

Howson, Susan (1975), *Domestic Monetary Management in Britain, 1919–1938* (Cambridge: Cambridge University Press).

—— and Winch, Donald (1977), *The Economic Advisory Council, 1930–1939* (Cambridge: Cambridge University Press).

Ingham, Geoffrey (1984), *Capitalism Divided? The City and Industry in British Social Development* (London: Macmillan).

James, Harold (1985), *The Reichsbank and Public Finance in Germany, 1924–1933* (Frankfurt am Main: Knapp Verlag).

—— (1986), *The German Slump: Politics and Economics, 1924–1933* (Oxford: Clarendon Press).

—— Lindgren, Hakan, and Teichova, Alice (eds.) (1991), *The Role of Banks in the Interwar Economy* (Cambridge: Cambridge University Press).

Kindleberger, Charles P. (1973, 2nd edn. 1986), *The World in Depression, 1919–1939* (London: Allen Lane).

Kitson, Michael (1992), 'The Move to Autarky: the Political Economy of Nazi Trade Policy', Working Paper No. 9201 (DAE, University of Cambridge).

Lary, Hal B. (1943), *The United States in the World Economy* (Washington, DC: US Dept. of Commerce).

Laursen, Karsten, and Pedersen, Jorgen (1964), *The German Inflation, 1918–1923* (Amsterdam: North-Holland).

League of Nations (1933), *World Economic Survey 1932/33* (Geneva: League of Nations).

Lee, Bradford A. (1982), 'The New Deal Reconsidered', *Wilson Quarterly*, 6: 62–76.

Lester, Richard A. (1939), *Monetary Experiments, Early American and Recent Scandinavian Experience* (Princeton: Princeton University Press).

Lewis, W. Arthur (1949), *Economic Survey, 1919–1939* (London: Allen & Unwin).

Maddison, Angus (1964), *Phases of Capitalist Development* (Oxford: Oxford University Press).

—— (1991), *Dynamic Forces in Capitalist Development, a Long-Run Comparative View* (Oxford: Oxford University Press).

Mantoux, Étienne (1946), *The Carthaginian Peace—or the Economic Consequences of Mr Keynes* (Oxford: Oxford University Press).

Marks, Sally (1978), 'The Myths of Reparations', *Central European History*, 3: 231–55.

Mazower, Mark (1991), 'Banking and Economic Development in Interwar Greece', in Harold James, Hakan Lindgren, and Alice Teichova (eds.), *The Role of Banks in the Interwar Economy* (Cambridge: Cambridge University Press), 206–31.

McNeil, William C. (1986), *American Money and the Weimar Republic* (New York: Columbia University Press).

Mitchell, Brian R. (1975, abridged edn.), *European Historical Statistics* (London: Macmillan).

Moggridge, Donald (1972), *British Monetary Policy, 1924–1931* (Cambridge: Cambridge University Press).

—— (1989), 'The Gold Standard and National Financial Policies, 1913–1939', in Peter Mathias and Sidney Pollard (eds.), *The Cambridge Economic History of Europe*, viii. *The Industrial Economies: The Development of Economic and Social Policies*, (Cambridge: Cambridge University Press), 250–314.

Morgan, E. Victor (1952), *Studies in British Financial Policy, 1914–1925* (London: Macmillan).

Mouré, K. (1991), *Managing the Franc Poincaré: Economic Understanding and Political Constraint in French Monetary Policy, 1928–1936*, (Cambridge: Cambridge University Press).

Neal, Larry (1979) 'The Economics and Finance of Bilateral Clearing Agreements in Germany, 1934–8', *Economic History Review*, 32: 391–404.

Nevin, Edward (1955), *The Mechanism of Cheap Money* (Cardiff: University of Wales Press).

Nixon, Edgar B. (ed.) (1969), *Franklin D. Roosevelt and Foreign Affairs, January 1933–February 1934*, (Cambridge, Mass.: Harvard University Press).

Nötel, R. (1986), 'International Credit and Finance', in Michael C. Kaser and E. A. Radice (eds.), *The Economic History of Eastern Europe, 1919–1975*, ii (Oxford: Oxford University Press): 170–295.

Nurkse, Ragnar (1944), *International Currency Experience: Lessons of the Interwar Period* (Geneva: League of Nations).

Ohlin, Bertil (1931), *The Course and Phases of the World Economic Depression* (Geneva: League of Nations).

Overy, R. J. (1982), *The Nazi Economic Recovery 1932–1938* (London: Macmillan).

Patat, Jean-Pierre, and Lutfalla, Michel (1990, Eng. trans.), *A Monetary History of France in the Twentieth Century* (London: Macmillan).

Pollard, Sidney (ed.) (1970), *The Gold Standard and Employment Policy between the Wars* (London: Methuen).

Robbins, Lionel (1934), *The Great Depression* (London: Macmillan).

Rowland, Benjamin M. (1976), *Balance of Power or Hegemony: The Interwar Monetary System* (New York: New York University Press).

Sargent, Thomas J. (1983), 'The Ends of Four Big Inflations', in Thomas Sargent (ed.), *Rational Expectations and Inflation* (New York: Harper & Row), 40–109.

Sayers, Richard S. (1976), *The Bank of England, 1891–1944* (Cambridge: Cambridge University Press).

Schuker, Stephen A. (1988), *American 'Reparations' to Germany, 1919–33: Implications for the Third World Debt Crisis*, Princeton Studies in International Finance, No. 61 (Princeton: Int. Fin. Section, Princeton University).

Sommariva, Andrea, and Tullio, Giuseppe (1986), *German Macroeconomic History, 1880–1979* (London: Macmillan).

Stiefel, Dieter (1989), *Finanzdiplomatie und Weltwirtschaftskrise: Die Krise der Credit-Anstalt 1931 und ihre wirtschaftlich-politische Bewaltigung* (Frankfurt am Main: Knapp Verlag).

Svennilson I. (1954), *Growth and Stagnation in the European Economy* (Geneva: UN Economic Commission for Europe).

Temin, Peter (1971), 'The Beginning of the Depression in Germany', *Economic History Review*, 24: 240–8.

—— (1989), *Lessons from the Great Depression* (Cambridge, Mass.: MIT Press).

—— (1991), 'Soviet and Nazi Economic Planning in the 1930s', *Economic History Review*, 44: 573–93.

—— and Wigmore, Barrie A. (1990), 'The End of One Big Deflation', *Explorations in Economic History*, 27: 483–502.

Toniolo, Gianni (1980), *L'economia dell'Italia Fascista* (Rome: Bari Laterza).

Tortella, Gabriel, and Palafox, Jordi (1984), 'Banking and Industry in Spain, 1918–1936', *Journal of European Economic History*, 13: 81–111.

Waight, L. (1939), *The History and Mechanism of the Exchange Equalisation Account* (Cambridge: Cambridge University Press).

Webb, Steven B. (1989), *Hyperinflation and Stabilization in Weimar Germany: Policies, Politics and Market Reactions* (Oxford: Oxford University Press).

Wheeler-Bennett, John W. (1933), *The Wreck of Reparations* (London: Allen & Unwin).

Wigmore, Barry (1987), 'Was the Bank Holiday of 1933 Caused by a Run on the Dollar?', *Journal of Economic History*, 47: 739–55.

Williams, David (1963), 'The 1931 Financial Crisis', *Yorkshire Bulletin of Economic and Social Research*, 15: 92–110.

Williams, John H. (1922), 'German Foreign Trade and Reparations Payments', *Quarterly Journal of Economics*, 36: 482–503.

Woytinsky, W. S., and Woytinsky, E. S. (1955), *World Commerce and Government* (New York: Twentieth Century Fund).

2

Method in the Madness? Banking Crises between the Wars, an International Comparison

JOOST JONKER AND JAN LUITEN VAN ZANDEN

Financial crises are often described as if propelled by the erratic side of the human mind, from mania via boom to panic and finally crash, to summarize Kindleberger (1984: 270–6). Seen exclusively in this light the European banking stage of the inter-war years appears to be crammed with crazy creditors putting their money into foolhardy ventures and toppling one country after another into financial crisis, culminating first in a wave of banking crises, then in the profound aberrations of hyperinflation, and finally in the resounding crashes of the complete banking system in Germany and Austria in 1931.

Of course there is a deeply fascinating irrational side to financial crises and crashes. But the recurrence of certain themes and particular problems in various countries suggests a common pattern. In this chapter we want to compare banking crises in thirteen industrial countries—twelve European countries[1] and the USA—to establish that common pattern and explain the curious fragility of the financial system during the inter-war years. After having defined (various types of) banking crises, we give an inventory of banking crises in the inter-war period (sections 2–3).[2] Next an attempt is made to explain the resulting pattern: why did some countries have 'their' crisis in the 1920s, others in the 1930s, and why did no banking crisis occur in UK and Finland? This results in a number of hypotheses about the connection between inflation and changes in the banking system (section 4). Section 5 contains a first test of these hypotheses.

1. What is a Banking Crisis?

To start with, the concept of a banking crisis has to be defined. Banking crises are a subspecies of 'financial crises', shocks threatening the stability of the (inter)national financial system. This includes a (stock-market)

---

[1] Denmark, Norway, Sweden, Finland, Great Britain, the Netherlands, Germany, Belgium, France, Switzerland, Austria, and Italy.

[2] Many of the points summarized here are elaborated more fully in the individual country studies in Part III of this volume.

crash—a sudden fall in the price of certain commodities or shares—and a
foreign exchange crisis—a shock which threatens the stability of the exchange rate, especially under the gold standard. A banking crisis may be
defined as a run on banks, a 'scramble for high-powered money ...
precipitated by actions of the public that suddenly squeeze the reserves of
the banking system' (Schwartz, 1986: 11; Kindleberger, 1982: 2).

A banking crisis is the outcome of the interaction between (*a*) a decline in
public confidence resulting in an increase in the public's currency : deposit
ratio, and (*b*) financial distress of banks, which is aggravated by the panic.
The interaction of these two developments may result in a massive run on
the banks; this process can be stopped by actions of a lender-of-last-resort
guaranteeing the liquidity and solvency of the banks. On this basis three
kinds of banking crisis may be distinguished:

1. A 'hidden' crisis, in which the real financial problems of the banks
remain secret and are solved by covert actions of the central bank and/or
the government; Italy in 1931 is the perfect example of a 'hidden' banking
crisis.

2. A 'panic', a run on the banks, which is not the result of real financial
problems of the banks but of a sudden decline in public confidence, caused
for instance by the outbreak of war (1914), rumours about the financial
difficulties of banks, etc.

3. A real banking crisis, the result of the interaction of changes in public
confidence and real financial problems of the banks.

Cagan (1965) has shown that, at least in the USA, banking crises do not
precipitate a downturn in the economy, but occur after the downturn. Through
their effects on the money supply and the general confidence of the public,
banking crises tend to accelerate the downturn and aggravate the depression, a
point which is clearly demonstrated by Bernanke and James (1992).

To establish whether a banking crisis has occurred, we have relied on one
hand on (descriptive) accounts of the financial and monetary history of the
thirteen countries, on the other on data on the composition of the money
supply, especially the development of the currency : deposits ratio. The
quantitative criterion used was that a banking crisis was characterized by a
sudden jump in this ratio as a result of the run on banks or, as seems to
have occurred in a number of countries in the 1930s, a more gradual and
less chaotic process of converting deposits into cash (see section 3). Only
year-to-year figures were used, which of course seriously restricts the scope
of the analysis.

The close connection between deflation and banking crises throughout the
inter-war period can be followed with the help of these data. They make it
quite clear that no banking crisis occurred in the UK, and that the USA,
Germany, and Austria went through a very severe one after 1929–30. But

many cases are in between these extremes and are more difficult to classify. As a rule it would seem as if crises occurred in countries which, following the collapse of the post-war boom, implemented deflationary policies in the run-up towards restoration of the gold standard. Countries postponing currency stabilization also avoided its dangerous consequence, only to experience a worse crisis in the 1930s, as the Depression hit a banking system weakened by the prolonged inflation. This general division would seem to run along the line between belligerents and neutrals in the First World War, and further subdivisions can be made following reaction patterns to the threats of inflation, deflation, and banking crises.

2. Banking Crises in the 1920s: The Former Neutrals

During the First World War all neutrals experienced rapid economic growth, fostered by the increased demand for goods and services from the belligerent countries. As transport difficulties curtailed imports, the balance of payments surplus swelled, creating large gold reserves and extreme liquidity in banking, trade, and industry alike. Any investment seemed to promise good returns; the stock exchanges boomed, fuelled by banks keenly competing to promote expansion and investors falling over themselves to secure the richest pickings. The liberation of transport after the Armistice speeded up the whole carousel by releasing pent-up demand, until a downturn set in during the autumn of 1920.

From this point the path of the former neutrals starts to diverge somewhat. In Denmark, Sweden, and the Netherlands deflationary policies were introduced which combined with the depression to produce banking crises. Between 1920 and 1923 the price level in these countries fell by 21 per cent, 23 per cent, and 27 per cent respectively (Maddison, 1991: app. E). The banking systems immediately came under pressure; the cash : deposits ratios in the Netherlands and in Denmark rose sharply.[3] On the surface Sweden forms the exception, since the cash : deposits ratio did not rise, but it did follow the rest of the pattern. Two bank failures there in 1919–20 heralded the storm, though apparently unconnected with it. At about the same time rumours started to circulate about the Rotterdamsche Bank, the biggest in the Netherlands, being overstretched (Larsson, 1991: 86; Larsson and Lindgren, 1992: 348–51). In 1921 four Swedish banks failed and rumours caused an unsuccessful run on an Amsterdam savings bank (Larsson, 1991: 87; De Vries, 1991: 233–5). The worst of the weather came the following year. Two Dutch and five Swedish banks, plus the biggest

---

[3] Calculated from data from League of Nations, *Money and Banking, Commercial Banks* (various issues), and CBS, *Vijfenzeventig jaren statistiek in tijdreeksen*, 1974.

bank in Scandinavia, the Danish Landmandsbanken, all suspended payments. After one year of relative calm another trough occurred with the
Rotterdamsche Bank, several Dutch credit co-operatives, and two large
Danish banks running aground in 1924–5 (Hansen, 1991: 37–9; De Vries,
1991: 233–5).

Unfortunately the present figures do not allow a direct comparison
between the countries on the impact of the crisis, and we can only present
diverse national data. From 1920 to 1932 thirty-five Danish banks liquidated with losses of about 887.9 million kroner (Hansen, 1991: 37). Fourteen
banks failed in Sweden in the period 1921–5 (Larsson, 1991: 88). No less
than fifty-nine banks were hit by the crisis in the Netherlands, though some
of them survived; one conservative estimate puts the losses at 200 million
florins in 1920–2 alone (De Vries, 1991: 230–64).

For all its violence, this short, sharp shock would seem to have cured the
banking systems in these countries. They experienced no real difficulties
during the deflation of the 1930s, Denmark and Sweden by devaluing early,
the Netherlands by acting as a refuge for capital from abroad. Banks did of
course get into difficulties: the Danish Handelsbanken faced a run in 1931;
several banks in Sweden suffered under the Kreuger crash of 1932; the
Netherlands witnessed the very heavy losses and reorganization of the
Nederlandsche Handel-Maatschappij (1934) and the collapse of Mendels-
sohn & Co. (1939). But the systems themselves never came under threat after
1925. This separates these three countries from Norway, where extreme and
protracted deflationary policies led to a prolonged economic and banking
crisis. No fewer than 129 banks collapsed from 1922 to 1928, with
commercial bank losses running to 1,500 million kroner, or 37 per cent of
the loans outstanding in 1920 (Knutsen, 1991: 55–6). Despite early devaluation another round of failures hit the system in the 1930s, and the
continuing decline in the cash : deposits ratio shows that public confidence
did not recover until about 1933.

There are three exceptions to this general pattern among the former
neutrals, all of them explained by particular circumstances. Finland did not
attempt to return its currency to pre-war parity and thus escaped the
deflationary shock (Lester, 1939: 221–2). Spain headed towards the familiar
crisis, but returned from the brink when Primo de Rivera seized power in
1923 and introduced strongly interventionist and protectionist policies.
These created a boom until Primo de Rivera's fall in 1930. The turn of the
political and economic tide then produced a depression which forced one
major bank to close its doors, but the economic isolation protected Spain
from the cold wind of deflation and banking crises blowing elsewhere
(Tortella and Palafox, 1984: 89–91, 94–5, 103–6).

Switzerland followed an altogether different path, explained by the
banking system's particular course of development. After the war the

rigorous policies of the Nationalbank pushed prices down by 25–30 per cent until the return to parity in 1924. No banking crisis occurred however, since the wheat had already been separated from the chaff just before the war during seven years of profound restructuring. In keeping with this difference in phase, depression and deflation in the 1930s did lead to a crisis. The balance total of the big banks more than halved from 1930 to 1935; one major bank failed, and the collapse of public confidence forced the government to introduce regulatory legislation (Cassis and Tanner, 1992: 296, 304–12; Ritzmann, 1964: 256–61).

In short, the former neutrals followed a familiar pattern of debt deflation after the war. As prices fell, the banks became squeezed between clients unable to pay their debts and falling asset prices coupled with erosion of their own capital value. The reasons for these countries avoiding a banking crisis in the 1930s are less clear. In some countries, as for instance the Netherlands, banks translated the experience of deflation into an excessive concern for liquidity and a refusal to return to the mixed banking embraced just before and during the war (Jonker, 1991). The return to a normal, even, economic development and the absence of inflation during the remainder of the inter-war years probably explains the rest.

3.   Banking Crisis in the 1930s: The Former Belligerents

With the major exception of Britain all members of this group postponed deflation and currency stabilization to the second half of the 1920s, thus avoiding the first wave of banking crises, only to be hit by a worse one in the 1930s. Of course in grouping these countries together a distinction must be made between France and Belgium on one hand with moderate inflation, Germany and Austria on the other experiencing hyperinflation, and Italy conveniently sitting somewhere in between. But the importance of that difference would seem to disappear before the similarity of their vicissitudes in the 1930s.

The first post-war governments in Belgium confidently expected the franc to return automatically to its pre-war parity, and borrowed a way out in the meantime. Taken as a whole the economy prospered under this misguided optimism. Rising inflation and crumbling international confidence sent the exchange rate ever more quickly downwards, however, until in 1926 a wide-ranging programme of financial reconstruction stabilized the franc at about 14 per cent of its pre-war value against the pound. An economic boom followed, but it was too short to repair the erosion from years of inflation. Sensing the danger inherent in their traditionally deep commitment to industry, the banks reacted to the Depression in 1929 by frantically trying to raise their liquidity. The Belgian Government's determination to defend the franc by deflation undermined these efforts, however. Several banks had to be supported by the National Bank in 1932 and 1933; the full scale of the problems surfaced a year later when two medium-sized banks failed, forcing the Government to step in, provide safeguards for depositors to restore confidence, set up a company to mobilize the banks' frozen loans, and prohibit mixed banking in Belgium (Vanthemsche, 1991: 110–11; Kurgan-Van Hentenryk, 1992: 326–8).

France followed a similar course of optimistic reconstruction based on borrowing, continuing inflation, and currency depreciation, followed by stabilization in 1926–8 at 20 per cent of the pre-war parity. And again the government's commitment to keeping the franc at par by deflation squeezed a banking system weakened by the preceding inflation, leading to two waves of bank failures in 1930–2 (Bouvier, 1984: 34–41, 51–5).

Italy fits in the middle between France and Belgium on one side and Germany and Austria on the other. But, perhaps befitting a late entrant to the war, its development resembles the neutrals' pattern as well, with mild deflation squeezing the banking system in 1920–1. The country then turned around to experience a remarkable spate of growth, fuelled by unprecedented banking and stock-exchange activities, until the overheated economy started to falter in 1926, and deflation set in under Mussolini's efforts to boost the lira. A banking crisis was forestalled, however. The influx of foreign loans after stabilization propped up the banks' liquidity, and a consortium to support share prices eased the heavy burden of industrial securities by shifting it to the Bank of Italy. Pressure increased with the withdrawal of foreign capital from 1930. Again the Bank of Italy stepped in, providing loans to the equivalent of 57 per cent of currency in circulation by 1932. In the meantime the government set up a secret scheme to defuse the looming crisis by a large-scale transfer of frozen bank assets to two public holding companies, a solution very similar to the one chosen in Belgium (Ciocca and Toniolo, 1984).

The dramatic hyperinflation in Germany and Austria will be too familiar to need extensive treatment here. The particular effects of inflation on the banking system as experienced by all former belligerents stand out as if under a magnifying glass: spiralling costs and sharp competition, continuing concentration accompanied by diminishing administrative control, and more importantly a gradual erosion of the banks' operating base by inflation outstripping the growth of balance-sheet figures. After stabilization these underlying weaknesses were camouflaged in both countries by the influx of foreign capital, and in Austria in particular by merging the problems into ever bigger proportions, to wreak havoc when the withdrawals started in 1929–30 (Feldman, 1991: 49–50; James, 1992: 267–8; Hardach, 1984: 206–13).

The major exception in this group is of course the United Kingdom. Alone amongst the former belligerents it took the neutrals' route of deflation and currency stabilization, and still managed to avoid a crisis during the inter-war period though the tests facing the banking system were real enough. The post-war boom tempted the banks to increase their advances to industry in Britain as well, and the chill of the early 1920s equally froze these into unwanted assets. But it looks as if the problems were small and localized, connected to the staple industries of cotton, steel, and shipbuilding in the north, compared to the commitments across the country and the economy bogging down some Continental banking systems. Several regional banks and one clearer got into difficulties; advances to staple industries took up 10–20 per cent of the advances of three of the Big Five in 1928. But the reserves were big enough or the problems small enough for the problems to surface only towards 1925, when the worst had already passed for the Continental countries going through deflation and crisis (Cottrell, 1992: 55–7). Early devaluation eased the pressure of the 1930s, though after the standstill agreements of 1931 the London bill market only kept going by the sanctioned fiction of German acceptances being sound rather than frozen credits (Sayers, 1976: 504–10).

A tentative explanation for the absence of a banking crisis would therefore rest on Britain's lucky course between the threats of inflation and deflation. The banks probably steered clear of crisis during the 1920s because they had avoided running up the all-embracing commitments before, during, and after the war which confronted the neutrals with the damage from debt deflation; in the 1930s because they did not suffer the prolonged erosion which undermined the other belligerents' banking systems, and benefited from the early devaluation of sterling. If it is tempting to see this crisis avoidance as the benefit of the British banks' traditional concern with liquidity and financial stability on one hand, and British industry's preference for self-finance on the other, it would have to be balanced by considering the cost of those attitudes. After all there can be little doubt that the banking policies on the Continent in times of inflation, misguided though they may have been from a purely financial viewpoint, did stimulate industrial regeneration on a large scale, an advantage not lost when deflation caught up with the banks, and this was reflected in the vociferous complaints of businessmen once the tide turned again. But that issue would lead us too far away from the subject at hand.

4. Hypotheses about the Increased Fragility of the Banking System

In the preceding sections we stressed the connection between deflation and banking crises: all crises occurred during years of deflation, but not every deflationary shock led to a run on the banks. Such a shock seems to have been a necessary precondition for a crisis, but not a sufficient one.

The literature mentions several other specific factors contributing to the vulnerability of banks in particular countries, and most of them recur across Europe: the decentralized nature of the banking system in Norway and in the USA (Knutsen, 1991: 32; Bordo, 1986: 230–8); reckless overlending to one client or to industries trading on wartime conditions in the Netherlands (De Vries, 1991: 242–7); failure of administrative control compounded by mergers, as in Austria; lack of experience and fraud in several countries; and competition and increased lending to industry in all. This suggests that the problems sown in the period of inflation during and just after the war, and uncovered by deflation, were equally rooted in common experiences.

The common element is of course the inflation in the years after 1913 which undermined the solidity of the banking system. In this section we analyse the connection between inflation and the ability of banks to absorb deflationary shocks in more detail. In all countries the price level increased rapidly after 1913, but the rate and extent of the inflation varied enormously, with the hyperinflation of Austria and Germany as the most extreme cases.

This inflationary wave had a number of consequences for the banks. Unlike most other industries, which see the value of their assets, capital, and products rise almost automatically in periods of inflation, banks have to increase their real activities rapidly in order to keep up with the rising price level. This is, we think, of fundamental importance: because the banks' own resources are invested in assets—loans to industry and trade in particular—with a nominal value, a rise in the price level will automatically mean a decline in the real value of the banks' resources. Inflation almost automatically means that the solvency of the banks decreases and that the relative economic strength in relation to industry and trade tends to decrease, because the latter are not confronted with an automatic decline of their own resources.

The inflation of the years after 1913 had another, perhaps even more important effect on the banks. The creation of excess liquidity by governments and central banks was probably the main driving force behind the inflation. This meant that the cash reserves of the banks increased rapidly, and banks were almost forced to expand lending at the same pace.

To meet these pressures, banks could opt for two strategies, or a mix of both: (*a*) to convert nominal assets into real ones, i.e. loans into shares, as a protective measure against inflation; (*b*) to expand lending rapidly, much more rapidly than before the onset of the inflation. The first strategy, which to a certain degree was chosen in almost all countries—the UK is the most obvious exception—meant the acceleration of a trend which already existed in most countries of continental Europe, the rise of investment banking. Especially in the countries that remained neutral, bank advances to industry increased very rapidly during and after the war. The conversion of these loans into shares protected the banks against the rise of the price level, but made them very vulnerable to the deflation that occurred after 1920 (and again after 1929).

The second strategy resulted in increasing competition between banks—all banks faced the same problem: to invest profitably the excess liquidity—which weakened the bargaining position of the banks towards industry and trade. Because of the strong pressure to expand rapidly, banks found it increasingly difficult to apply prudent, orthodox lending policies. As inflation progressed and large changes in relative prices, real wages, and exchange rates occurred, it became almost impossible to distinguish between firms that were profitable in the long run and firms that were dependent on inflation-induced windfall profits. The combination of these developments probably led to a decline in the quality of the assets of the banks.

In short, during an inflationary boom banks had to choose between sticking to financial orthodoxy—and dwindling in relative size—or expanding lending aggressively, and sailing ever closer to the wind of bankruptcy. When the boom ended and the price level started to decrease, the windfall profits disappeared and the quality of the assets was put to the test. Moreover, deflation pushed down share prices and the value of collateral on loans, and forced the bankruptcy of clients dependent on speculative profits. This in turn undermined confidence in the banks, and set into motion the banking crisis.

We think this picture is quite accurate for describing developments in the group of countries that went through a banking crisis after 1920 (the Netherlands, Denmark, Sweden, Norway). In Austria and Germany the time-lag between the end of hyperinflation in 1923 and the breakdown of the banking system in 1931 may partially be explained by the access to foreign (American) credit during these years (which also played a part in forestalling the post-1926 crisis in Italy). Austrian banking between 1924 and 1931 offers a special explanation for the time-lag: one bank after another got into difficulties, but was taken over by or merged with another bank, until in 1930 one very big bank, the Creditanstalt, was formed, which collapsed in 1931. In France, Belgium, and the USA the inflationary boom lasted until 1929. There are indications that the quality of the assets of American banks deteriorated seriously in the second half of the 1920s, although this has been contested in part by Friedman and Schwartz (1963: 246–7, 354).

Two countries did not experience a banking crisis. Finnish banking was never confronted with a deflationary shock; even between 1929 and 1931 the price level decreased only modestly. Britain is the most interesting exception. The large London banks maintained orthodox lending policies after 1913 and did not join the European-wide movement towards lending to industry. The gap between industry and the City remained and perhaps became even wider, which may explain why British banking was hardly affected by the deflationary shocks of 1920 and 1929. In the Netherlands the same occurred after the reorganization of the banking system in 1921–4. The Dutch banks returned to the financial orthodoxy of the pre-war period—which they had left between 1913 and 1920—and stopped lending to industry (Jonker, 1991: 124–6). Because the dubious assets were liquidated and the banks re-organized in the 1920s, the banks could face the deflation of 1929–35 almost without difficulty.

5. Testing the Hypothesis

In this section we try to test the hypothesis that the increased fragility of the banking system was caused by changes in the banking system during the inflation in the post-1913 years. The first step is to measure the instability and fragility of the banks in the inter-war period. The League of Nations has published figures of the 'net profit or loss as a percentage of capital' of the commercial banks in twelve of the countries of our sample—only data for Belgium are missing. These and other data collected and published by the League (and used below) are of course not completely reliable. In some cases, they probably give a better picture of international differences in accounting practices and the problems of properly defining the various categories of assets and liabilities than of existing international differences in the structure of banking systems. Yet they do give a rough idea of the general evolution of the profitability of the banks in the period 1920–37. To illustrate this, in Figure 2.1 these data are presented for three countries, England and Wales, the USA, and the Netherlands. The amazing stability of British banking is clear from these statistics, as are the banking crises in the Netherlands in 1921–4 and in the USA in 1931–4. Table 2.1 draws on these figures to show the average profitability and the standard deviation for 1920–37. These figures clearly show the very large international difference in the degree of instability of the banks, with, on the one hand, England and Wales with an extremely stable system and, on the other hand, Austria, Italy, Germany, and Norway as examples of very unstable systems.

The next step was to explain this pattern. In order not to mix up cause and effect—Bernanke and James (1992) for instance demonstrated clearly that banking crisis affected the development of prices and production—we decided to concentrate on the changes in the banking system in the period 1913–20, that is before the first deflationary shock. We tried to predict the international differences in the instability of the banks on the basis of data on the changes in the general price level and on the solvency and liquidity of the banks between 1913 and 1920. The hypotheses we tested are that:

TABLE 2.1. *Average and standard deviation of the yield on bank capital, twelve European countries and the USA, 1920–1937 (%)*

	mean yield	s.d. yield	missing years
England and Wales	7.78	0.7	
Finland	7.83	4.8	
Norway	− 15.83	27.7	
Denmark	0.72	14.4	
Sweden	3.60	7.5	
Netherlands	4.17	4.1	
Austria	− 25.60	112.0	1924, 1937
Germany	7.45	46.0	1923
Italy	− 2.17	27.1	1922, 1935–7
Switzerland	4.68	2.3	
France	7.24	4.2	
USA	5.69	6.0	

Source: League of Nations (see Appendix).

(*a*) a (more than average) *decrease* in solvency between 1913 and 1920 will result in (more than average) instability after 1920;

(*b*) a (more than average) *increase* in liquidity between 1913 and 1920 will result in (more than average) instability after 1920; and

(*c*) a (more than average) *increase* in the price level between 1913 and 1920 will also result in (more than average) instability.

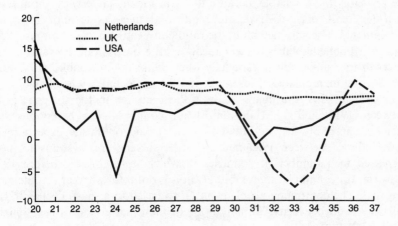

FIG. 2.1 Yield on banking capital in the Netherlands, England and Wales, and the USA, 1920–1937(%)

TABLE 2.2.   Development of the solvency ratio and the cash ratio of the (big) commercial banks in twelve European countries and the USA, 1913–1929.

	Solvency ratio (%)[a]			Cash ratio[b]		
	1913	1920	1929	1913	1920	1929
England and Wales	10.1	6.5	7.4	29.1	22.9	24.8
Finland	22.0	24.9	19.4	3.2	4.7	4.1
Norway[c]	18.3	24.2	12.2	3.0	5.3	5.3
Denmark	30.8	14.7	17.5	4.1	4.3	5.1
Sweden	32.0	18.7	18.6	4.3	4.1	3.6
Netherlands	52.8	29.4	28.0	7.3	6.7	6.7
Austria	33.3	7.5	15.1	3.5	10.6	3.6
Germany	30.3	4.0	7.5	8.2	7.3	4.1
Italy	31.1	7.8	14.5	7.3	7.3	10.1
Switzerland	21.7	16.7	15.2	2.6	3.6	3.0
Belgium	24.3	15.1	25.6	5.7	13.4	12.5
France	19.8	8.9	8.3	10.1	13.7	15.1
USA	19.8	12.0	15.4	19.9	11.5	12.6
unweighted average	26.6	14.6	15.7	8.3	8.9	8.5

[a] Banks' own resources/public liabilities (%).
[b] Cash + items of a cash nature/total deposits (%).
[c] After 1925: excluding banks under public administration or liquidation.

Source: League of Nations, Commercial Banks, 1913–1929.

On the basis of data collected by the League of Nations it is possible to get a rough idea about the development of the liquidity and the solvency of the (large) banks in the period 1913–29 (Table 2.2). The figures of the cash ratio are probably fairly reliable, because the data for the underlying variables—cash (+ items of a cash nature) and total deposits—cannot be easily manipulated. The solvency ratio, the ratio between the banks' own resources and their public liabilities, is dependent on an estimation of the value of the assets of the banks, which, especially when banks are in trouble, will almost certainly be manipulated. These data are, therefore, much less reliable.

In spite of this, the figures show a clear decline in the solvency ratio between 1913 and 1920 in almost all countries—the exceptions are Norway (probably heavily inflated by much too optimistic expectations) and Finland. Between 1920 and 1929 the solvency ratio seems to have increased in a number of countries in which it fell heavily before 1920 (Austria, Italy, and Germany), but again it is doubtful whether this increase was real. The continuing problems in Norway led to a sharp decline in the solvency ratio between 1920 and 1929; in the other countries it stabilized (Table 2.2).

Developments in the cash ratio do not show a clear pattern; there is no general worsening of the liquidity of the banking system. The decline of the cash ratio in Sweden and the USA, for instance, is part of a long-term decline in this ratio, which had already started after 1870 (Bordo, 1986: 224, 228) and does not seem to be connected with the problems of the inter-war years. Nor did other indicators of the degree of vulnerability of the banking system—the share of sight deposits in total deposits and the share of long-term investments in total assets—show a clear trend.

Summing up, the variables used in the regressions are:

Dependent variables
(1) *myield*, the average profitability in 1920–37 (column 2 in Table 2.1); (2) *sdyield*, the standard deviation of profitability in 1920–37 (column 3 in Table 2.1).

Independent variables
(1) *solv13/20*, the solvency ratio of 1920 as a percentage of the 'normal' solvency ratio of 1913 (Table 2.2);[4] (2) *cash13/20*, the cash ratio of 1920 as a percentage of the 'normal' cash ratio of 1913 (Table 2.2); and (3) *infl13/20*, the price level of 1920 as a percentage of the price level of 1913 (from Maddison, 1991: app. E).

The results are presented in Table 2.3; because of a high degree of multicollinearity between *cash13/20* and *infl13/20* no regressions containing both variables are presented. All the variables have the expected signs, with the exception of *solv13/20* in (2). To find out whether this was caused by the inflated value of the solvency ratio of Norway in 1920, a dummy for Norway (*dummo*) was entered into the equation. This changed the sign of *solv13/20* in the explanation of *myield* (regression (3)), and gave, in combination with *cash13/20*, a satisfactory explanation of myield (regression (4)). Regression (4) can be interpreted to state that an increase in the cash ratio of 1 per cent between 1913 and 1920 probably had the effect of lowering average profitability in 1920–37 by 0.114 per cent; the increase in the price level between the same years by 1 per cent may have led to a decrease in profits of about 0.006 per cent (regression (2)).

The explanation of *sdyield*—probably the best indicator of instability— was also satisfactory: the independent variables had the expected signs and the inclusion of the dummy for Norway gave very neat results (regressions (8) and (9)). It may be concluded that the instability of the banking system was clearly connected with the increase in the price level and/or the cash ratio between 1913 and 1920 and with the decrease in the solvency ratio.

Summarizing the results, the regressions presented in Table 2.3 support the view that developments in the banking system between 1913 and 1920

---

[4] Experiments with the absolute level of the solvency ratio and the cash ratio in 1920 did not produce results, Bernanke and James (1992).

are able to explain the instability after 1920. Because in a large number of countries inflation went on after 1920, and hyperinflation did not start in Germany and Austria until 1922–3, this may be considered a very restrictive test of the hypothesis about the relations between inflation and changes in the banking system. Of course, it should be stressed that because of the small number of 'cases'—twelve countries—and the limited reliability of the data used, the regressions do not offer more than a first test of the hypothesis.

TABLE 2.3. *Explanation of the instability of the banks in the period* 1920–1937 (as measured by myield and sdyield)

Dependent variables		Independent variables				R^2 (corrected)
		solv13/20	*cash13/20*	*infl13/20*	*dumno*	
myield	(1)	.005 (.09)	− .133 (4.60)			.64
	(2)	− .092 (1.39)		− .0064 (3.82)		.53
	(3)	.157 (1.53)			− 30.21 (2.42)	.25
	(4)	.111 (2.10)	− .114 (5.19)		− 20.09 (3.03)	.81
sdyield	(5)	− .408 (3.21)	.384 (5.71)			.78
	(6)	− .101 (.91)		.020 (7.23)		.85
	(7)	− .725 (2.31)			64.31 (1.69)	.24
	(8)	− .365 (5.47)		.019 (14.86)	46.10 (6.02)	.97
	(9)	− .582 (3.79)	.352 (5.52)		33.06 (1.71)	.82

Sources: Tables 2.1 and 2.2; Maddison (1991, app. E).

6. Conclusion

A central feature in the literature on European banking during the inter-war period is the discussion on the merits and dangers of mixed banking, or more precisely the close involvement of banks with industry. These ties are identified as contributing to industrial strength, but blamed at the same time for the wave of crashes which characterized inter-war banking development. Some contemporaries took the breakdown of the German and Belgian systems, the archetypes of mixed banking, as conclusive proof of the basic unsoundness of this concept, smugly praising their own healthy concern with liquidity and holding industry at arm's length as the recipe for avoiding disaster (Jonker, 1991: 128).

Our findings suggest there may be a wider canvas for this discussion. There need be no doubt that the banking crises across Europe were rooted in heavy commitments to industry. But that happened to be the form which the common experience of prolonged and severe- to hyper-inflation assumed, the common experience of banks fighting the erosion of their business by lending for anything which promised a return. As a result the quality of assets and liquidity fell, to be exposed by the abrupt deflationary shocks after 1920 and 1929, with these two waves explained by the different timing of currency stabilization. Though going against common opinions on sound banking policy, the banks' behaviour was perfectly rational in the circumstances, and one would expect to see it returning elsewhere in times of inflation, suggesting that when banking crises coincide with the onset of deflation, there's method in the madness.

References

Bernanke, B., and James, H. (1992), 'The Gold Standard, Deflation and Financial Crises in the Great Depression: An International Comparison', in R. G. Hubbard (ed.), *Financial Markets and Financial Crises* (Chicago: NBER, Chicago University Press).

Bordo, M. D. (1986), 'Financial Crises, Banking Crises, Stock Market Crashes and the Money Supply: Some International Evidence, 1870–1933', in Capie and Wood (1986).

Bouvier, J. (1984), 'The French Banks, Inflation and the Economic Crisis, 1919–1939', *Journal of European Economic History*, 13.

Cagan, P. (1965), *Determinants and Effects of Changes in the Stock of Money, 1875–1960* (New York: Columbia University Press).

Capie, F., and Wood, G. E. (eds.) (1986), *Financial Crises and the World Banking System* (London: St Martin's Press).

Cassis, Y. (ed.) (1992), *Finance and Financiers in European History, 1880–1960* (Cambridge: Cambridge University Press).

—— and Tanner, J. (1992), 'Finance and Financiers in Switzerland, 1880–1960', in Cassis (1992).

Central Bureau of Statistics (1974), *Vijfenzeveventig jaren statistiek in tijdreeksen* (The Hague: CBS).

Ciocca, P., and Toniolo, G. (1984), 'Industry and Finance in Italy, 1918–1940', in *Journal of European Economic History*, 13.

Cottrell, P. L. (1992), 'The Domestic Commercial Banks and the City of London, 1870–1939', in Cassis (1992).

Feldman, G. D. (1992), 'Banks and the Problem of Capital Shortage in Germany, 1918–1923', in James *et al.* (1992).

Friedman, M., and Schwartz, A. J. (1963), *A Monetary History of the United States, 1867–1960* (Princeton: Princeton University Press).

Hansen, P. H. (1991), 'From Growth to Crisis, the Danish Banking System from 1850 to the Interwar Years', *Scandinavian Economic History Review*, 39.

Hardach, G. (1984), 'Banking and Industry in Germany in the Interwar Period', *Journal of European Economic History*, 13.

James, H. (1992). 'Banks and Bankers in the German Interwar Depression', in Cassis (1992).

——, Lindgren, H., and Teichova, A. (eds.) (1991). *The Role of Banks in the Interwar Economy* (Cambridge: Cambridge University Press).

Jonker, J. P. B. (1991), 'Sinecures or Sinews of Power? Interlocking Directorships and Bank–Industry Relations in the Netherlands, 1910–1940', *Economic and Social History in the Netherlands*, 3.

Kindleberger, C. P. (1982), Introduction in C. P. Kindleberger and J. P. Laffargue (eds.), *Financial Crises* (Cambridge: Cambridge University Press).

—— (1984), *A Financial History of Western Europe* (London: Allen & Unwin).

Knutsen, S. (1991), 'From Expansion to Panic and Crash, the Norwegian Banking System and Its Customers 1913–1924', *Scandinavian Economic History Review*, 39.

Kurgan-Van Hentenryk, G. (1992), 'Finance and Financiers in Belgium, 1880–1940', in Cassis (1992).

Larsson, M. (1991), 'State, Banks and Industry in Sweden, with Some Reference to the Scandinavian Countries', in James *et al.* (1991).

—— and Lindgren, H. (1992), 'The Political Economy of Banking: Retail Banking and Corporate Finance in Sweden, 1850–1939', in Cassis (1992).

League of Nations, *Commercial Banks* (various issues).

—— *Money and Banking* (various issues).

—— *Monetary Review* (various issues).

Lester, R. A. (1939), 'The Gold Parity Depression in Norway and Denmark 1925–1928 and the Devaluation in Finland, 1925', in R. A. Lester (ed.), *Monetary Experiments.* (Princeton: Princeton University Press).

Maddison, A. (1991), *Dynamic Forces in Capitalist Development* (Oxford: Oxford University Press).

Ritzmann, F. (1964), 'Die Entwicklung des schweizerischen Geld- und Kredit-systems', *Schweizerische Zeitschrift für Volkswirtschaft und Statistik*, 100.

Sayers, R. S. (1976), *The Bank of England 1891–1944* (Cambridge: Cambridge University Press).

Schwartz, A. J. (1986), 'Real and Pseudo-Financial Crisis', in Capie and Wood (1986).

Tortella, J., and Palafox, J. (1984), 'Banking and Industry in Spain, 1918–1936', *Journal of European Economic History*, 13.

Vanthemsche, G. (1991), 'State, Banks and Industry in Belgium and the Netherlands, 1919–1939', in James *et al.* (1991).

Vries, J. de (1991), *Geschiedenis van de Nederlandsche Bank*, i, *Visserings tijdvak 1914–1931* (Amsterdam: De Nederlandsche Bank).

Appendix

TABLE 2.A1. *Yield on banking capital, twelve European countries and the USA, 1913–1937 (Net profit or loss as percentage of capital and reserves)*

	1913	1920	1921	1922	1923	1924	1925	1926	1927	1928	1929	1930	1931	1932	1933	1934	1935	1936	1937
England and Wales	9.3	8.6	9.3	8.2	8.0	8.1	8.5	8.2	8.1	8.0	8.2	7.3	7.9	6.9	7.0	6.9	6.7	7.0	7.1
Finland	8.1	9.7	-1.2	9.6	10.7	11.0	12.2	13.6	11.8	12.1	10.8	8.6	-2.6	4.8	-0.3	7.2	7.5	7.6	6.9
Norway[a]	7.7	7.7	-5.0	-13.9	-70.6	-22.8	-68.1	-50.5	-60.7	-14.8	4.8	5.0	-19.3	3.4	2.6	3.9	3.4	4.7	6.4
Denmark	7.3	14.4	3.9	-35.9	-0.2	5.5	-36.4	5.7	4.7	-8.0	6.4	6.0	-1.9	7.7	9.9	9.8	4.9	7.9	8.5
Sweden	7.8	8.8	0.9	-14.8	6.3	5.6	5.1	5.6	6.3	6.8	7.5	4.5	3.6	-17.1	2.4	1.5	5.2	9.4	13.0
Netherlands	8.5	15.7	4.4	1.9	4.6	-5.8	4.9	5.1	4.5	6.1	6.1	4.8	-0.5	2.1	1.6	2.5	4.4	6.2	6.5
Austria	8.2	13.3	27.6	33.9	21.2	—	8.2	7.3	9.0	8.6	5.6	-33.8	-34.4	-438.7	-17.7	-23.4	0.9	3.1	—
Germany	9.1	23.3	19.7	145.6	—	8.4	7.5	10.2	9.0	9.9	7.0	4.5	-118.3	-15.0	-2.9	3.6	3.8	4.6	4.9
Italy	6.6	11.4	-86.4	—	8.5	11.0	9.5	9.3	9.0	8.8	8.7	6.3	4.6	3.4	-36.7	2.2	—	—	—
Switzerland	6.1	4.0	5.5	4.8	5.7	6.4	6.6	6.7	7.1	7.3	6.8	6.5	3.6	1.6	-1.4	2.7	2.1	3.5	4.7
Belgium[b]																			
France	7.5	8.7	7.0	8.4	9.0	9.5	9.6	12.6	11.9	12.4	9.3	8.8	-5.3	5.5	2.4	5.0	5.3	4.6	5.6
USA	8.4	12.8	9.4	7.8	8.5	8.1	9.0	9.5	9.2	9.0	9.4	5.3	0.2	-5.1	-7.7	-4.8	4.5	9.9	7.1

[a] after 1928: excluding banks under public administration or liquidation.

[b] no data are available for Belgium.

Source: League of Nations, *Commercial Banks, 1913–1925, 1925–33; Monetary Review, 1936/37–1941/42.*

3

Private International Capital Flows in Europe in the Inter-War Period

CHARLES H. FEINSTEIN AND KATHERINE WATSON

1. Introduction

Both the magnitude and the character of the movements of international capital in the 1920s and 1930s make the changes in foreign investments and debts an essential element in any study of the banking and financial history of inter-war Europe. The sums which came flooding into the Continent in the 1920s, and went racing away in the next decade, were enormous by any historical standard, and their potential impact on both lenders and borrowers was correspondingly great. As the First World War ended the controversies began, with intense conflicts over the payment of war debts by the allies and of reparations by the defeated enemies. When attention shifted to commercial loans and private capital flows, the bitter disputes and polemics continued between economists, politicians, financiers, and industrialists.

At the very beginning of the period Keynes expressed his prophetic doubts about whether the prospective American investment in Europe could indeed be considered comparable with the pre-1914 investments abroad by Britain and other creditors (Keynes, 1922: 162):

If European bonds are issued in America on the analogy of the American bonds issued in Europe during the nineteenth century, the analogy will be a false one; because, taken in aggregate, there is no natural increase, no *real* sinking fund out of which they can be repaid. The interest will be furnished out of new loans, so long as these are obtainable, and the financial structure will mount always higher, until it is not worthwhile to maintain any longer the illusion that it has foundations.

The tone of most subsequent studies of capital movements in the 1920s has been similarly critical, even in the case of long-term investment, blaming

We have received a great deal of help from friends and colleagues in the preparation of this chapter. Patrick Nefors, Gert den Bakker, and Pierre Sicsic generously allowed us to make use of their unpublished estimates. We are also indebted to Theo Balderston, Forrest Capie, Anne Digby, James Foreman-Peck, Angus Maddison, Avner Offer, Peter Solar, Peter Temin, Gianni Toniolo, Herman van der Wee, and Gerardo della Paolera for providing references and for their extremely useful comments and suggestions. None of them has any responsibility for deficiencies in the present results and the way in which they are presented.

the USA for ill-judged and excessive lending, and the borrowers, especially Germany, for squandering much of the capital on unproductive and extravagant public amenities (Harris, 1935: 4–5; RI IA, 1937: 10–14). Many other features of inter-war foreign investment have been the subject of equally adverse comment. They include the British practice of 'lending long and borrowing short' in the late 1920s; the abrupt withdrawal of funds from Germany when US investors switched from foreign to domestic securities in 1928–9; the huge movements of French capital out of the franc in the mid-1920s and back again, with ultimately devastating consequences for sterling, in 1928–31; the destabilizing nature of the large-scale movements of short-term funds in 1930–3; and the mass flight of capital from continental Europe to the USA and the UK in the later 1930s. Looking back on the period when it had ended, Bloomfield (1950: viii) roundly condemned the 'erratic and perverse behavior of capital movements in the inter-war period' as:

Massive, sweeping, and highly capricious transfers of short-term funds, blessing neither the countries that gave nor the countries that received . . . Far from serving a useful function, they left nothing but disturbance and damage in their wake, and appear in retrospect to have been a luxury which few countries can afford in the future.

The principal objective of the present chapter is not to re-examine these contentious issues (many of which are discussed in the chapter above by Feinstein, Temin, and Toniolo, and in the individual country studies in Part III of this volume), but to make a fresh survey of, and new estimates from, the available data. Our basic aim is to provide as accurate an estimate as the sources permit of the nature, scale, and direction of the inter-war flows of capital, both within Europe, and between Europe and the USA. On the basis of this information we attempt to summarize the developments in each of the main phases of foreign investment, and to indicate the major characteristics of the movements in each phase.

The focus of our attention is on the years from 1924 to 1937. The early post-war years are excluded because of the highly abnormal conditions which many European countries suffered after the war. Export markets collapsed, with steeply declining output and employment, and there was severe disruption of economic activity, acute problems of inflation, and widespread financial and political instability. In these circumstances, private capital flows were relatively modest,[1] and capital movements were dominated by a series of large intergovernmental loans which lie outside the scope of this chapter. A second and more pragmatic reason for commencing in

---

[1] Bond issues for Europe by the six leading creditors amounted in total to some $800m. in 1919–23, including $120m. for the 1923 government-guaranteed Austrian loan under the auspices of the League of Nations. As an annual average this was less than one-third of the level in the remainder of the decade.

1924 is that the restoration of stability which most countries achieved at about this stage was also associated with an improvement in the supply of the essential statistical series on which our study is based.

In the following section we introduce the topic with a broad survey of the pattern of foreign investment. We look first at the position prior to 1919 and then, in a little more detail, at the inter-war period, and give a preview of our main findings on the nature and scale of the international flow of private capital. This is followed by a review of the different types of international capital movements and of the data available for their measurement. In the core of the chapter we assemble and comment on the available information on the flows of international investment as measured by balance of payments statistics for each of the principal creditors and debtors. This both serves as a basis for an appraisal of the reliability of the estimates derived from these data, and also provides a detailed picture of the sources and destinations of the global flows of capital in each year. In the final section the focus of attention narrows to the European scene which is our principal interest. We look first at the details of the balance of payments estimates of the flows to and from the Continent, and then consider an alternative and more elaborate set of estimates based directly on evidence of various categories of long- and short-term capital transactions. This provides a further check on the balance of payments data, and also extends our understanding of the pattern of investment. However, it can only be done for the 1920s because so much of the international movement in the following decade consisted of fugitive capital which was deliberately concealed from the authorities and thus left only blurred traces in the records.

2. An Overview of Foreign Investment

On the eve of the First World War long-term foreign investment in Europe amounted to about $12 billion, a little over a quarter of the total foreign assets accumulated by the world's creditor nations.[2] The basic estimates for 1914 are summarized in columns (1) and (2) of Table 3.1.[3] Britain's interest in the Continent had declined in the late nineteenth century, as her investors

---

[2] All estimates in this chapter are given in US dollars; for years from 1934 onwards these are at the new parity of $35 per fine ounce of gold and not—as in the pre-war League of Nations tables—the old parity of $20.67 per fine ounce. All estimates can be converted to a very approximate equivalent in present-day prices by multiplying by twelve; this very crude measure is based on the rise from 1924–37 to 1990 in weighted consumer price indices (Maddison, 1991: 300–7) for the USA (weight 2), Germany (1), and the UK (1).

[3] Estimates in this and other tables are rounded (in this case to the nearest $50m.), but this does not imply that they are regarded as accurate to that degree.

TABLE 3.1. *Long-term foreign investment, 1914 and 1938 ($m. to nearest $50m.)*

	1914		1938	
	Total investment (1)	*of which* in Europe (2)	Total investment (3)	*of which* in Europe (4)
Creditors				
UK	20,000	1,050	22,900	1,750
France	9,700	5,400	3,850	1,050
Germany	5,800	2,550	700	250
Netherlands	1,200		4,800	1,650
Belgium			1,250	300
Switzerland	4,300		1,600	800
		3,000		
Sweden			400	350
Italy	1,400		400	100
Other Europe[a]			650	150
Total Europe	42,400	11,300	36,550	6,400
USA	3,500	700	11,500	2,350
Other countries	200	—	4,750	600
TOTAL	46,100	12,000	52,800	9,350

[a] 1938 includes $400m. for Portugal, $100m. for Spain, and $150m. for Czechoslovakia (all of it in Europe).

Sources: For 1914, Woodruff (1966: 150–5) except for France, for which Cameron (1961: 486). For 1938 Lewis (1945) as quoted in Woytinski and Woytinski (1955: 213).

switched their attention to the Empire and the developing regions of North and South America. By 1914 her holdings of European securities in 1914 were little more than $1 billion, only 5 per cent of the UK total, and half what it had been forty years earlier.

In sharp contrast to this, the other European creditors had allocated some 40–50 per cent of their much smaller total foreign investment to Europe. France was by far the largest source of foreign capital on the Continent, with European holdings amounting by 1914 to some $5.4 billion. Almost $2.5 billion of this was invested in Russia, with loans both to the Tsarist government and to joint-stock banks and industrial companies. The total German investment outstanding on the Continent in 1914 was about $2.5 billion, with the largest share allocated to Austria-Hungary, and less than $500 million in Russia. The remaining countries, including Belgium, the Netherlands, Switzerland, and Sweden, had total holdings in Europe of some $3 billion, but there is no information about the countries in which it was invested. The USA had as yet ventured into Europe on only a modest scale, with assets of some $700 million, almost all in the form of direct investment in manufacturing, oil distribution, and other commercial activities (Lewis, 1938: 605–6).

The First World War and its immediate consequences played havoc with these investments. France and other holders of Russian securities lost their entire capital when the Tsarist regime was overthrown by the Bolsheviks. Investments in enemy countries either became worthless or were very severely depreciated. According to one estimate, only a quarter of the nominal value of France's pre-1914 foreign securities in Europe surived in 1919 (Meynial, quoted in RI IA, 1937: 131). German losses were even more striking, and by the end of the war almost nothing remained of her previous holdings of foreign securities. Britain was left with little more than a third of its investments in Europe; and was also compelled to sell over $3 billion of her pre-war dollar securities in order to meet wartime obligations for equipment purchased in the USA. In total the foreign assets lost by the three main European creditors may have exceeded $12 billion, over a third of the investments they had accumulated abroad over the preceding century (RI IA, 1937: 131; UN, 1949: 4–5; Woytinski and Woytinski, 1955: 199–200). While European assets were thus being sharply diminished by these wartime losses and sales, the USA greatly strengthened its economic position. In 1914, long-term private foreign borrowing by the USA exceeded her investments abroad by over $3 billion. By 1919 the USA emerged from the war with foreign long-term assets of $6.5 billion, and liabilities of only $2 billion, and was from then on a substantial net creditor in respect of private long-term capital (US Department of Commerce, 1975: 869).

The inter-war period

A preliminary and partial indication of the subsequent investment experience of the main creditors can be gained from a comparison with the long-term private investment outstanding at the end of the inter-war period, shown in columns (3) and (4) of Table 3.1.[4] By 1938 the estimated total was approximately $53 billion, only about 15 per cent higher in nominal terms than it had been in 1914, and perhaps 50 or 60 per cent above the 1919 level.[5] However, as a result of inflation during and after the First World War

---

[4] The comparison between the two estimates of the outstanding stock is not a reliable indication of the net flows of capital in the intervening period. The difference also reflects changes between the two dates in the market value of company securities and in the book value of direct investments; exchange-rate revaluations, and the loss of government securities through defaults or wartime disposals.

[5] The estimates for 1938 in Table 3.1 are based on the aggregation of foreign loan and credits as shown by the creditors; an alternative compilation of foreign obligations as shown by the debtors (also by Lewis, 1945) is some $2 bn. higher. This is the estimate used by Woodruff (1966: 156–7). However, even the lower estimate may be too high. According to Woytinski and Woytinski (1955: 211) the estimates—particularly those for the UK—include considerable

the general level of prices was significantly higher in 1938 than in 1914 (for the UK the rise was 60 per cent, for the USA about 40 per cent), so the real value of the accumulated foreign assets was well below its pre-war level, though higher than in 1919. Neither France nor Germany rebuilt their pre-1914 portfolios of foreign long-term assets, and even in nominal terms their 1938 holdings were well below the previous level. The UK and the Netherlands do show a small nominal increase, but the most striking change is the threefold rise in the long-term external assets of the USA. Despite this the UK remained the largest overall creditor, with long-term foreign assets double those of the USA.

The amount invested in Europe on the eve of the Second World War is estimated at a little over $9 billion, less than a fifth of the overall total. Of the pre-First World War European creditors, only the UK shows any advance, even in nominal terms, on the 1914 level. However, Europe remained of limited interest to British investors and, as in the pre-1914 period, the greater part of the long-term capital outflow from the UK was directed to the Dominions and India. US capital in Europe had increased to over $2.5 billion by 1938, outstripping investments of about $1.7 billion each for the UK and the Netherlands. The principal European borrowers from the USA were Germany, the UK, Poland, and Italy.

The 1938 figures in Table 3.1 provide a useful record of the level of foreign investment as it stood at the end of the period, and the comparison with 1914 is also revealing in certain respects. However, the net change between the two bench-marks actually conceals some of the most crucial features of the capital flows in the inter-war period. First, it relates only to long-term investment. In 1914 short-term liabilities (and corresponding assets) were small even for the UK, and were closely related to the financing of trading activities and to London's central position as banker for much of the world.[6] During the inter-war period the extent and character of these short-term investments changed enormously: they grew very much larger and became far more volatile. The changes indicated by Table 3.1 omit all record of these developments, and thus give no indication of the violent fluctuations in short-term capital which occurred during the inter-war years. Secondly, the character of the capital flows, both short-term and long-term, differed very markedly in the successive decades of the 1920s and the 1930s, with radical changes in their origin, direction, motivation, and effect. Estimates of the stock of capital at the beginning and end of the period are thus a very

amounts of debt which were in default though not officially repudiated, and show some depreciated stocks and bonds at parity rather than market price. In their view 'a more realistic estimate of total international loans and investments in 1938 is likely to lie not far from $50 bn.'.

[6] For a broad indication of the position of the UK as a short-term creditor in 1914 and the changes over the First World War see Morgan (1952: 331–4, 342–3). See also Conolly (1936: 353–4).

inadequate basis for a full appreciation of the nature and causes of international capital movements in the intervening years.

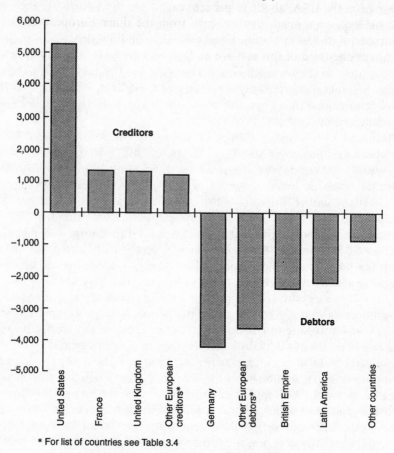

* For list of countries see Table 3.4

FIG. 3.1   Composition of the global capital flows, 1924–1930 ($m.)

For a more complete picture we must resort to other information, covering the actual movements of capital within the period. We shall discuss below the details of the various estimates and the large problems raised by the deficiencies in the available data, but for the moment we present a broad overall view.[7] The major sources of international finance and the destinations to which it went are shown in Figure 3.1 for the period 1924–30. In these seven years the flow of capital from the creditor nations, as measured by their records, amounted to at least $9 billion (equivalent in present-day

[7] The following summary is based on Tables 3.2–3.5, and Figure 3.2, with the qualifications noted in the discussion of these results later in the chapter.

prices to around $100 billion), and may have been appreciably more than that, perhaps between $10 and $11 billion. Almost 60 per cent of this sum came from the USA, about 15 per cent each from the UK and France, and the balance, on a much smaller scale, from the other European creditors: Switzerland, the Netherlands, Czechoslovakia, and Sweden.

About one-third of this massive outflow was invested in Germany, and a further quarter in the other European countries. The four British Dominions and India together received a little under one-fifth, as did the countries of Central and South America. Much of this was intended as long-term investment, but changes in bank deposits and other forms of short-term investment also made a very significant contribution to the increased indebtedness of the borrowing countries. Indeed, within Europe, the net addition to the two types of capital were of approximately equal magnitude over the period 1924–30.

The high point of this international migration of capital occurred in 1928; it then fell away very rapidly and, after 1930, there was no further net investment abroad by the major creditors as a whole. This aggregate movement conceals an apparent difference between the USA, which maintained a small net outflow for three further years, and the major European creditors, all of whom became net importers of capital from 1931. However, the outflow from the USA consisted predominantly of the withdrawal of foreign short-term assets in response to fears that the dollar would depreciate (as it did from April 1933 until the formal devaluation announced by Roosevelt at the end of January 1934); on long-term capital the USA was also a net recipient.

From 1931 the nature and direction of the movements in international capital changed dramatically. The overall dimensions of the process were about the same as they had been in the previous phase, but the content and dynamics of the flows were completely different. In the 1920s the net movement of capital was predominantly from the rich creditor countries to the less-developed debtors in Europe and elsewhere. Borrowing countries wished to exploit the greater wealth and balance of payments surpluses of the creditors to enhance their domestic savings and develop their economies; while private investors in the USA, Britain, France, and the other creditor nations chose foreign bonds and shares in preference to comparable domestic securities with the expectation that these would yield higher returns. This pattern of international capital movement thus conformed very broadly to that of pre-1914 foreign lending, even though it was supplemented to an unprecedented degree by short-term investments. In the 1930s, however, this traditional pattern was sharply reversed. Vast sums now flowed from the less-developed nations to their former creditors, from countries with deficits on their balance of payments to countries in surplus, from capital markets where interest rates were high to those where they were lower.

The flood of bonds and shares which had poured out of the capital markets in New York, London, Paris, and other financial centres now dwindled to a thin and irregular trickle. Potential lenders retreated in the face of the rapid deterioration in economic conditions and prospects, damaging financial crises, and numerous defaults by debtors unable to cope with the collapse of primary product prices and of their foreign earnings. The occasional new issues of long-term capital which were made in the 1930s were outweighed by the amortization of former loans by those debtors who maintained their repayments. The migration of capital characteristic of the new phase consisted predominantly of short-term funds, moving swiftly and on a vast scale, and determined almost entirely by speculative forces and the threat of war.

At the beginning of the decade the banking crises of 1930 and 1931, and the loss of confidence in the stability of various economies and the value of their currencies, played the major role in stimulating the seemingly perverse flows of 'hot money' from the debtors to the creditor countries. Enormous sums were withdrawn by asset-holders, who simply wished to preserve their investments in the face of currency depreciation and the domestic inflation associated with it. These movements were swelled by a very high level of activity by speculators: some trying to avoid losses when they anticipated depreciation of their own currencies, others looking for capital gains from the short-term purchase of a foreign currency which was expected to appreciate. To protect their limited reserves of gold and foreign exchange against these mounting pressures more and more countries were compelled to impose exchange controls, and this in itself provoked further withdrawals before the available loopholes were closed. Repatriation of German and other securities was made increasingly profitable by the widening disparity between the prices quoted for these securities on domestic exchanges, and the lower levels at which they were valued abroad. The strong recovery of security prices on Wall Street from the spring of 1935 provided a further inducement to move capital to the USA.

From the middle of the decade these economic factors were powerfully supplemented by political concerns. A succession of developments, including the Italian invasion of Ethiopia, the German reoccupation of the Rhineland, and the Spanish Civil War, raised the alarming prospect of world war, with its attendant dangers to wealth from seizure or destruction by the enemy, and from the imposition of increased taxes, capital levies, and exchange restrictions. As the panic spread, Great Britain and the USA came to be seen increasingly as the only safe and reliable havens for capital.

The result of these tendencies was a transfer of capital to the USA of almost $5.5 billion from 1934 to 1937, and further large movements across the Atlantic in 1938 and 1939. The flow towards the UK began a little earlier, and over the seven years 1931–7 the net import of funds amounted to roughly $4 billion. In the same period there was also a small net movement of about $600 million to Switzerland, Sweden, and the Netherlands. The countries responsible for sending these vast sums cannot be identified reliably from the available data, but it seems likely that the great bulk of this capital, perhaps $6–7 billion, was an outflow from continental Europe, with France, Germany, and Belgium leading the exodus. Switzerland and the Netherlands also remitted large sums to the USA though much of this may have come initially from other sources (Bloomfield, 1950: 7–10, 16).

3. Measurement of Inter-War Capital Movements: Definitions and Sources

The available data on inter-war capital movements are incomplete and of limited reliability. No one set of records provides all the information we require, and it is necessary to use a variety of different sources and types of information. However, by comparing and reconciling these independent datasets we can attempt both to get an indication of the reliability of the different sources, and to build up a more comprehensive picture.

There are two major types of information to be considered. First, there are estimates for all the principal countries of the balance of payments on current account (covering merchandise trade; services, remittances and other transfers; and interest and dividends) and movements in official reserves of gold and foreign exchange. These estimates are available in official or private studies for individual countries, and in the statistics compiled by the League of Nations (detailed sources are given in Appendix 1). Under this definition gold is included both as an ordinary export of the producing countries (or as merchandise for use by industry and the arts by importing countries), and as a movement in international currency reserves. The treatment of foreign currency reserves is discussed more fully below. The combined series for the current account, gold, and foreign exchange yields annual estimates of the net movement—inflow or outflow—of capital. For example, the overall international payments of a country with a balance of payments surplus partly offset by an increase in official reserves will be balanced by an export of capital; a country with a deficit as well as an increase in reserves will have a corresponding import of capital equal to the total outflow of currency. The balance of payments data are probably the most reliable of the existing sources on net international capital movements, but offer no further evidence of the gross flows in each direction, or of the source or destination of the flows, and no means of distinguishing between long-term and short-term investments.

For this more detailed information we rely on the other major dataset: direct evidence on transactions in international debts and claims. Under this heading we have three categories of foreign investment, for each of which there may be information on annual flows and/or on the stock of outstanding assets and liabilities at selected dates. Seen from the side of the creditors, the first category covers long-term portfolio investment, the second relates to long-term direct investment by companies in their foreign subsidiaries or associates, and the third takes the form of short-term holdings of foreign assets.

In relation to the first category the starting-point is estimates of varying degrees of reliability of the amount of long-term capital subscribed each year to new issues of bonds and shares. These securities may have been issued either by central and local governments and municipalities, or by public utilities, industrial companies, and other private corporations. Information on such issues is available for the six major lending countries: the USA, the UK, France, the Netherlands, Switzerland, and Sweden. These series can provide very detailed and valuable information about the borrower responsible for floating the issue, and about the purpose for which the capital was raised. However, the issues are normally reported individually in the financial press, and have to be aggregated and classified. There are invariably inconsistencies in the way this is done by the different authorities who have compiled such series, even within the same country; the problem is particularly acute in the case of France (cf. RIIA, 1937: 210–15).

Given these series, allowance must then be made for the fact that the securities are typically issued for less than their par value. Ideally, some estimate should also be made to cover the extent to which a loan floated in, say, the USA for Germany, is subscribed for by German nationals and/or by other foreigners. Conversion and refunding issues which create no net addition to the flow of capital should also be excluded. A deduction must then be made from this outward flow of new issues from the creditors to allow for repayment of outstanding debts, either under formal amortization arrangements or because economic circumstances make it profitable for nationals to repurchase their foreign bonds. Finally, outward (inward) long-term portfolio investment may also take the form of purchases (sales) of existing foreign securities, but information on such transactions is poor for all countries except the USA.

The second category of long-term capital movements covers direct investment. This refers essentially to investments made not by individuals or collective bodies such as insurance companies and investment trusts, but by business firms with an interest either in a supply of raw materials or in increasing sales by production abroad or through selling organizations. The definition normally assumes that the firm has a substantial interest in the foreign subsidiary or associate and is able to exercise a significant degree of managerial control. By its nature such investment is not normally reported publicly, and information is usually available only where specific enquiries have been undertaken. The USA has compiled good estimates of outward direct investment by American firms in the inter-war period, and there is some information on inward investment in certain countries derived from balance sheets of foreign companies. The UK data do not include any measure of direct investment inwards or outwards, and statistical coverage of this category is generally very poor.

For both portfolio and direct investment information on the annual flows can be supplemented by estimates of the accumulated stock of overseas capital, compiled by enquiries in either the lending or the borrowing countries. These estimates vary a great deal in their frequency, definitions, and completeness, but can be a valuable indication of the total amount lent or borrowed at a particular date. However, even when compiled on a consistent basis by the same authority over a period of time, they cannot be used without considerable qualification as an indication of the changes between the survey dates (see n. 4 above).

The third category of overseas investment relates to changes in short-term assets (or the corresponding liabilities) held by (owed to) banks, trading concerns, and private individuals. These are normally defined as claims due for repayment within less than one year, though they may be renewed and thus approximate more to long-term investments. They include holdings of government floating debt, commercial bills of exchange, deposits with commercial banks and other institutions, acceptance credits, and other forms of short-term trade credit. By far the largest component of this short-term indebtedness arises from the need to employ funds in the financing of foreign trade. In addition, there are balances held abroad for a variety of other financial motives: by debtors to meet interest, dividend, and amortization payments; as balances arising from security dealings; and as speculative capital hoping to avoid exchange-rate depreciation or economic disaster, or to profit from an expected appreciation of currencies.[8]

This latter category is naturally subject to violent fluctuations and was of particular importance in the inter-war period. The available information on both stocks and flows of short-term capital is extremely limited for the 1920s but, as the importance of this type of investment increased, more data were collected, notably by the Bank for International Settlements (e.g. 4th *Annual Report*, 1934: 27–9; 5th, 1935: 31–5; 6th, 1936: 35–44; see also Conolly,

---

[8] For some purposes short-term investments would also cover the movements in foreign currency reserves of central banks and other monetary authorities but, as explained at the end of this section, changes in these items are not treated as part of the flow of capital on the definition used in the present chapter.

1936), and there are good estimates for the USA and Britain for the 1930s, and for Germany and a number of other countries for particular dates.

In making our estimates we have drawn heavily on the inter-war work of the Economic Intelligence Service of the League of Nations, as recorded in their annual publication *Balances of Payments*, and on the revision and updating of these statistics published by the United Nations (1949). We should also like to acknowledge our debt to the unknown authors of an unpublished League of Nations paper, *Europe's Capital Movements, 1919–1932: A Statistical Note.* (The typed copy in the library of Nuffield College is dated June 1943 and has a note that it was received from the Princeton Institute of Advanced Studies.) We found this extremely useful both as a guide to some of the main statistics for the inter-war period, and as a source of estimates and information.

Our estimates include, in principle, all forms of long- and short-term portfolio investment by the private sector, and all private direct investment. They exclude all transactions relating to inter-Allied war debts and reparations (including the Dawes and Young Loans to Germany), official short-term credits such as those granted to Britain by the USA and France in the summer of 1931, and certain small loans made by the UK and US Governments. Movements of capital arising from loans issued by governments but subscribed for by private investors are included as private flows. Our main concern is with the experience of Europe, and its relationship with the USA, but in order to evaluate the balance of payments data for these countries we need to place them in a global context, and for this purpose we have also to consider estimates for other parts of the world.

In our presentation of the results the European countries are divided into two groups. The first group comprises the UK, France, the Netherlands, Switzerland, Sweden, and Czechoslovakia. Five of these countries were already significant creditor nations in 1914 and continued to add to their holdings of overseas investment in the 1920s; Czechoslovakia was a net exporter of capital in the 1920s although still on balance a debtor country. For brevity we generally refer to this group as 'the creditors', ignoring the qualification regarding Czechoslovakia. The second group contains seventeen countries which are classified as 'the debtors' on the basis of their net borrowing in the 1920s, although some, notably Germany and Belgium, had been substantial lenders before 1914, and Belgium remained an overall creditor. The major omissions are Spain and Portugal, for which no balance of payments estimates are available.

There are two main reasons for the differences between the present balance of payments estimates and those published by the United Nations (1949) as the culmination of the inter-war studies by the League of Nations. First, it is now possible to make or use revised estimates for a number of major countries, including Austria, Belgium, France, Italy, the Netherlands, and the UK, as well as for India, China, Australia, Japan, and other countries outside Europe. These revisions cover the current account, and also movements in gold and foreign currency reserves, for which some previously confidential information is now available. A full account of the sources used is given in the detailed notes in Appendix 1.

Secondly, in the present study changes in foreign exchange reserves are treated in the same way as those in gold, not as part of the movement of capital. Our justification for adopting this approach, rather than that of the League and the United Nations, is that under the gold exchange standard it is misleading to have regard to only one of the two types of reserve asset. This applies both when countries operated in the spirit of the gold exchange standard, allowing deficits (surpluses) on current and capital account to be offset by reductions (increases) in foreign currency rather than gold; and again at the point when they abandoned it and converted their holdings of foreign currency to gold, as France and Belgium did after the devaluation of sterling. It is thus normally changes in gold and currency reserves *taken together* which can be regarded as induced movements, and the combination of this total with the balance on current account which gives the appropriate measure of the flow of capital.[9]

The difference in treatment can lead to quite substantial differences in the estimates. For example, in 1927 French holdings of foreign exchange increased by some $700 million, and this was financed by roughly $350 million from the current account surplus and export of gold, and by a similar amount from the net *import* of capital. However, if the movement in currency is omitted, as in the League of Nations presentation, the result appears as a net *export* of capital of $350 million. Conversely, in 1932 when there was a current account deficit of almost $200 million, French holdings of gold soared by more than $650 million, so the League definition shows a net import of capital of over $850 million. However, the acquisition of gold was offset by a corresponding reduction in French foreign exchange reserves; when this is taken into account the import of capital is reduced to less than $200 million.

4. Global Balance of Payments Statistics, 1924–37

The balance of payments statistics are the primary source of information for an overview of the inter-war capital flows. Our purpose in studying them is partly to get an overall picture of the movements in international capital, and partly to check the reliability of these series. If the data were both

---

[9] In certain circumstances autonomous movements of gold would occur as part of arbitrage operations; see e.g., Bloomfield (1950: 133–42).

accurate and complete the net outward movement from all capital-exporting countries would exactly balance the net inward movement to all capital importers. In practice, of course, the series satisfies neither requirement, but it is instructive to consider the size and sign of the discrepancies which emerge when all the data available for a global survey are assembled.[10]

TABLE 3.2. *Balances on current account, gold and foreign currency: comparison of global estimates for creditors and debtors, 1924–1937ᵃ ($m. to nearest $10m.)*

	Creditors (1)	Debtors (2)	Errors and omissions (3)
1924	1,630	−1,810	180
1925	1,460	−1,370	− 90
1926	810	−1,480	670
1927	1,250	−2,560	1,310
1928	1,980	−2,620	640
1929	1,420	−1,890	470
1930	510	−1,510	1,000
1931	−870	790	80
1932	−590	190	400
1933	−340	90	250
1934	−820	−180	1,000
1935	−1,760	860	900
1936	−2,870	1,850	1,020
1937	−2,610	760	1,850

(+) = Net capital export, (−) = Net capital import

ᵃ For the composition of the two series see Tables 3.3 and 3.4; France is included with the creditors in 1924–32 and with the debtors in 1933–7.

Source: See App. 1.

The main results of an investigation on this basis are given in Tables 3.2 and 3.3 and are presented visually in Figure 3.2. Column (1) in Table 3.2, drawn as the solid line in the chart, shows the movement of capital each year as recorded by the creditors. The positive values reflect their export of capital from 1924 to 1930, and the negative values indicate the transfer of capital to these countries in the 1930s. The countries covered by this series are the USA, the UK, Switzerland, the Netherlands, Sweden, and Czechoslovakia; and France is also included until 1932. After that French investors parted company from their fellow creditors, and joined Germany and other major debtors in transferring substantial sums abroad, first to the UK and then to the USA. We have therefore included France with the debtors from 1933 onwards in order to get a better indication of the scale of the transfer to the other creditors.

[10] For an earlier but more limited exercise on these lines, using the series for current account balances and gold assembled by the United Nations, see North (1962).

Column (2) of Table 3.2, and the dotted line in the chart, show the corresponding movements as recorded by the debtors: Germany and the other European countries (plus France for 1933–7), together with those in the British Empire, South America, and the major Asian countries. For this debtors' series the conventional signs adopted elsewhere in this chapter are reversed in Figure 3.2, so that the positive values indicate an *inflow* of capital, and negative values an *outflow* from the debtors. The composition of these aggregate series for the flows to and from the creditors and debtors is shown for the major countries or regions in Table 3.3.

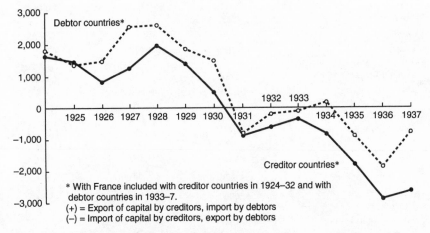

FIG. 3.2   Global capital flows, 1924–1937 ($m.)

Two major conclusions may be drawn from this presentation. The first finding—which is very reassuring—is that these two series, derived from completely independent data, agree remarkably well with respect to the general pattern of international investment in the inter-war years. They indicate the same broad movement, with capital first flowing from the creditors to the debtors and then from debtors to creditors; and also agree on the timing of the changes within these successive phases. Both series show that the outflow from the creditors reached a peak in 1928, then declined abruptly, with 1930 as the last year in which the group as a whole made a net transfer to the debtors. The reverse flow from debtors to creditors started in 1931, diminished in the next two years, increased strongly in 1934–6, and then declined slightly in 1937 though it remained at a very high level.[11]

---

[11] Apart from France, there were a few countries among the debtors (e.g. Austria, Greece, Australia, and China) which also deviated from this general pattern, and continued as net importers of capital in the 1930s. However, the sums involved were quite small, and it seemed unnecessary to complicate the story even more by further changes in the composition of the two groups.

TABLE 3.3. *Balances on current account, gold and foreign currency: composition of the global estimates, 1924–1930 and 1931–1937 ($m. to nearest 10m.)*

	1924–30	1931–7	1924–37
	(1)	(2)	(3)
Creditors			
United States	5,250	– 4,620	630
United Kingdom	1,300	– 4,000	– 2,700
France[a]	1,340	– 690	650
Other[b]	1,180	– 560	620
TOTAL	9,060	– 9,860	– 800
Debtors			
Germany	– 4,190	1,010	– 3,180
France[a]	—	2,190	2,190
Other Europe[c]	– 3,600	– 20	– 3,620
Australia	– 1,310	– 200	– 1,510
Other British Empire[d]	– 1,060	580	– 480
Argentine	– 770	180	– 590
Other Latin America[e]	– 1,430	180	– 1,250
Other countries[f]	– 880	440	– 440
TOTAL	– 13,240	4,360	– 8,880
Errors and omissions	4,180	5,500	9,680
TOTAL	– 9,060	9,860	– 800

(+) = Net capital export, (–) = Net capital import

[a] France is included with the creditors for 1924–32 and with the debtors for 1933–7; the estimates cover the French overseas territories, except Indo-China for 1924–30.

[b] Netherlands, Switzerland, Sweden, and Czechoslovakia.

[c] See Table 3.4.

[d] Canada, India, New Zealand, and South Africa.

[e] Includes Bolivia, Brazil, Chile, Colombia, Cuba, Mexico, Peru, Uruguay, Venezuela, and other countries in Central and South America; as explained in Appendix 1 these estimates are not based on balance of payments data.

[f] China, Japan, Netherlands Indies, and Turkey (for 1924–33).

Source: See App. 1.

The other feature of these results is equally striking but more disturbing. It is immediately evident from the chart that except for 1925 the estimates based on the statistics of the creditors are always below those for the debtors. Because the series switch from positive to negative this means that the estimates of capital received by the countries importing capital persistently exceeded those derived from the countries exporting capital. This holds both in the 1920s, when it was the debtors who were the importers, and again in the 1930s when the creditors became the importers.

From 1924 to 1930 the estimates for the creditors show an average inflow of $1,300 million per annum, but the balance of payments estimates for the debtors put the amount received $600 million above that. Then in the 1930s, when the USA, Britain, and other former creditors (excluding France) become the recipients of a massive capital inflow, estimated from their data to average $1,400 million per annum, the annual average outflow of capital recorded in the accounts of the former debtors was almost $800 million less than that. Over the inter-war period as a whole the apparent errors and omissions in the estimates (see column (3) of Table 3.2) thus averaged approximately $700 million, with discrepancies significantly below average in 1924–5 and 1931 and above average in 1927, 1930, and 1934–7.

Explanations for the discrepancies

It seems unlikely that any substantial part of this large and persistent difference is attributable to an export of capital from the countries which have been omitted from Table 3.2.[12] Two other factors are more likely to provide the principal explanation. First, it is inevitable that there will be appreciable margins of error in balance of payments data: this must always be the case with a series derived as the difference between two very much larger items. For example, on merchandise trade alone, an error of only 5 per cent in the data for world exports would make a difference of over 50 per cent to the aggregate global flow of capital estimated in this way. There are also likely to be errors in our interpretation and presentation of the primary data, in particular, the complex adjustment of the numerous separate currencies, with their changing parities, to a common dollar denomination.

In addition to these unintended errors, there may also have been a more systematic form of bias. The League of Nations statisticians (1937: 20) thought that the current account estimates for the major creditors tended to overstate their deficits and understate surpluses: 'Where the information on account of foreign transactions is incomplete, there is frequently a tendency to estimate receipts on the low, and payments on the high, side.' If, as is possible, this applies equally to the estimates for the debtors, the true figure for the 1920s would lie somewhere between the understated surplus of the creditor nations and the overstated deficit of the debtors. (In the 1930s, it would fall between the overstated deficit of the creditors and the understated

---

[12] The main omissions are Spain, the USSR, Portugal and her African colonies, all of Britain's African colonies, the Belgian Congo, Egypt and other countries of the Middle East, Malaya, the Philippines, and (for 1924–30) French Indo-China. With the exception of Portugal, these countries were all net debtors, and the addition of estimates for them would thus raise the global import of capital in the 1920s and increase the discrepancy. The position in the 1930s is less clear-cut. Several of these countries conformed to the typical debtors' pattern and were, on balance, repaying earlier loans, but others, for example Iraq and Iran, were importing capital from abroad. The net effect on the global estimates is uncertain but would be small. (These comments are based on the stock of foreign investments at the end of 1930 and 1938: RI IA, 1937: 142 and 186; Woytinski and Woytinski, 1955: 213–14; and on very incomplete estimates in the annual League of Nations, *Balances of Payments*).

surplus of the debtors.) There are also likely to be erratic errors of estimation in particular years.

We believe that the second major explanation for the discrepancy is the flight of private capital evading exchange controls and other restrictions on the free movement of funds. In the 1920s this occurred on a substantial scale before the stabilization of the French, Belgian, Italian, and other currencies (see further the chapter by Feinstein, Temin, and Toniolo). In the case of the large-scale escape from the French franc which occurred in 1924 and 1925 it was observed that there were laws in force forbidding all forms of capital export, but 'it did not prove very difficult to evade them. The easiest way to increase balances abroad was to reinvest in other countries the proceeds from exported merchandise' (RIIA, 1937: 204).

In the 1930s, when the average discrepancy was appreciably larger, the pressure to export capital in contravention of exchange controls was even greater. First sterling, after Britain's departure from the gold standard in 1931, and then the dollar, as it depreciated in 1933, became progressively more attractive compared to the overvalued currencies of the gold bloc countries. Economic motives for moving funds out of currencies threatened by devaluation and inflation were progressively reinforced by the deteriorating political conditions in Europe and the looming menace of war. The Nazi campaign against the Jews created a further powerful inducement, and tax avoidance was also a motive for some illicit movements of capital.

One indication of the extent of this unreported movement of funds is the exceptionally large size and positive sign of the entry for errors and omissions in the balance of payments estimates for the USA and the UK (Sayers, 1976: iii. 312–13; US Department of Commerce, 1975. 867; Bloomfield, 1950: 3 and 25). The authorities in these countries had accurate information about the gold they received in the 1930s, but much of the capital which gave rise to this accumulation was evading exchange controls in the countries from which it came, and was either held privately as gold or converted into assets which were not disclosed to the American and British authorities. As the League of Nations observed (1937: 24):

There can be no doubt that there has existed a considerable clandestine capital export from countries applying exchange control, and that large quantities of gold and currency are held by inhabitants of these countries in the European creditor countries and the United States. The nature of these holdings is such that they are likely to escape record to a considerable extent.

A variety of ingenious methods were adopted to achieve this illicit transfer of funds, and large-scale evasion typically involved falsification of invoices to create either overvaluation of imports or undervaluation of exports. For example, exports would be invoiced at less than their true cost, and an obliging trading partner (sometimes a subsidiary company) in the importing country would then pay the difference into a foreign currency account which would be held for the subsequent use of the exporter.[13] Other forms of evasion included smuggling of banknotes, gold, precious stones, securities, and other assets which could be sold abroad; juggling of blocked accounts and mutually compensating transfers between bank accounts of foreigners and nationals so that funds could be applied for prohibited purposes; and repatriation of domestic securities purchased abroad with foreign currency acquired illegally.[14]

It is relevant in this connection to note also that there appears to have been very substantial hoarding and dishoarding of gold in the 1930s. According to estimates by the Bank for International Settlements (8th *Annual Report*, 1938: 37–45), over the period from January 1931 to September 1936 the amount of newly mined gold, plus the dishoarding by India and China, exceeded the reported increase in official gold reserves by the considerable sum of $3.5 billion (measured at $35 per fine ounce). The bank estimated that about $1.7 billion of this was incorporated into the undeclared holdings of official exchange funds, but that the remainder represented private hoards in Europe, with about two-thirds held in the London market. In the following nine months (October 1936 to June 1937) it was estimated on the same basis that more than $1 billion was taken out of private hoards. These holdings, together with any private European hoarding prior to 1931, thus provided a very large reservoir from which unreported capital could flow when alternative locations seemed more attractive to the owners.

In the light of these considerations and of the observed pattern of the year-to-year discrepancies, one plausible—but necessarily highly speculative—interpretation of the data would run as follows. A significant component of both the unintended errors, and the bias towards caution in estimation noted above, is likely to be broadly constant from year to year. This is because of the widespread practice of relying on an initial estimate made for a particular date (e.g. for the adjustment to merchandise imports required for smuggling and other unrecorded trade, or for the receipts from services such as tourism or shipping for which no regular statistics were

---

[13] For a very thorough discussion of the operation and evasion of exchange controls in Germany, Austria, and Hungary in the 1930s see Ellis (1941: esp. 40–4, 142–8, 166–8, 305–9). James (1986: 131–2, 298–301) discusses some of the techniques adopted for the evasion of the controls imposed by Germany. Guarneri (1953), the inter-war head of the Italian Ministry for Foreign Exchange, recalls in his memoirs a variety of methods adopted to circumvent the state monopoly of all foreign exchange imposed by Italy at the end of 1934; we are indebted to Gianni Toniolo for this reference.

[14] Evasion through repatriation of securities was a serious weakness in the Hungarian system of exchange controls. Germany also bought back securities on a large scale, but this was done with the approval of the authorities and did not represent illegal capital flight (Klug, 1993).

collected), and then either extrapolating the bench-mark by a rough indicator or simply repeating the initial ratios or values.

What might be an appropriate magnitude for such persistent errors of estimation? If we set the correction at 20 per cent for the years 1924–30, reducing the surpluses of the creditors and raising the deficits of the debtors by this proportion each year, this would be more than enough to account for the average annual discrepancy of approximately $600 million in this period. This would imply that the effects of all other sources of error and of unreported capital flight happened to be mutually compensating; this seems intrinsically unlikely. Moving to a lower level, a margin of error of only 10 per cent seems implausibly low for a residual item such as the current account balance. We are thus led to the conclusion that the adjustment should probably be more than 10 per cent but less than 20 per cent; and we shall use a compromise 15 per cent as the likely order of magnitude. For 1924–30 a correction to both series of this proportion would eliminate four-fifths of the overall discrepancy, and the two estimates would converge on a global flow of capital from creditors to debtors averaging between $1,400 and $1,600 million per year in this phase, or between $10 and $11 billion in aggregate. This still leaves significant discrepancies in individual years within this period; and explanations for these would have to be found in random errors, unrecorded flights of capital, and other special factors. In 1927, for example, the estimated export from the UK, Switzerland, and the Netherlands may not allow fully for the massive repatriation of funds to France after the Poincaré stabilization.

There is, of course, no necessary reason to make the same proportionate adjustment to both series. It is possible that the estimates provided by the creditors were more reliable than those for the debtors—statistical services were presumably more advanced in countries like Britain, Sweden, and the USA than in many of the less-developed borrowing countries. However, the comparison in the following section with direct information on capital transactions broadly supports the balance of payments estimates for 1924–30 for Germany and the other European debtors (see Table 3.5 below). Furthermore, the data for the UK (though not for the other major creditors) show a large positive residual: this may be a rough measure of unidentified short-term imports and of repurchases by foreigners of existing securities, but it could also point to an understatement of the surplus on current account.[15]

---

[15] The positive sign of the balancing item for the UK could of course be the result of an even larger unidentified import of capital offset by an *overestimate* of the surplus on current account. In the same way, the negative sign of the balancing item for the USA, France, and other creditors in 1924–30 does not preclude the possibility that their current account balances were understated, if unidentified capital exports were even greater than the residual.

For the 1930s, a continuing correction of 15 per cent for persistent error would account for a much smaller proportion of the average annual discrepancy in these years ($800 million). It would raise the estimated flow from the debtors to just over $700 million per annum, but that would still be a very long way below the adjusted inflow to the creditors of $1,200 million. However, given the extent of unrecorded capital flight in this decade, this corrected estimate from the side of the creditors is likely to provide a better indication of the international migration of capital. Over the seven years the overall discrepancy remaining after the adjustment would aggregate to almost $3.5 billion, and this may be a rough measure of the scale of the unreported flight to the USA and the UK in these years.

5. European Lending and Borrowing

Our aim in this section is to provide a slightly more detailed picture of the flows of capital to and from Europe. We approach this in two stages. In the first, we continue with the previous dataset and show the extent of the net inflows and outflows for each country as indicated by their balance of payments data for the contrasting phases 1924–30 and 1931–7. In the second we relate the balance of payments estimates for the debtors to alternative estimates of the international movement of capital derived directly from data on new issues and other specific categories of long- and short-term capital. This is done for 1924–30, the years of heavy borrowing by these countries, and the alternative data serve as a check on the balance of payments estimates, and also help to fill out the picture of the nature and scale of the capital movements in this period.

The relevant balance of payments statistics for the individual European borrowers and lenders for the two periods 1924–30 and 1931–7 are summarized in columns (1) and (2) of Table 3.4.

In the first period the records of the debtors show an immense net inflow of some $7.8 billion, an average rate of over $1.0 billion per annum, though, as noted in our earlier discussion of the global statistics, the true figures might be roughly 15 per cent lower than this. The movement of capital was dominated by foreign lending to Germany, which received more than $4 billion, over 50 per cent of the gross flow to Europe. Most of this capital came from the USA, and for a while it seemed that there was no limit to the appetite of American issuing houses and their investors for German bonds, regardless of the purposes for which the loans were raised, or for the interest to be earned from placing money on short-term deposit with German banks. The next largest destinations, a long way behind, were Austria and Italy, which together obtained about $1.5 billion. Roughly $1.3 billion was invested in Eastern Europe, especially Romania, Poland, and

TABLE 3.4. *Balances on current account, gold and foreign currency: European creditors and debtors, 1924–1930 and 1931–1937 ($m. to nearest $10m.)*

	1924–30 (1)	1931–7 (2)	1924–37 (3)
Europe: creditors			
UK	1,300	− 4,000	− 2,700
France[a]	1,340	− 690	650
Netherlands	380	− 290	90
Switzerland	370	− 340	30
Czechoslovakia	250	90	340
Sweden	180	− 20	160
TOTAL	3,820	− 5,250	− 1,430
Europe: debtors			
Germany	− 4,190	1,010	− 3,180
France[a]	—	2,190	2,190
Austria	− 860	− 150	− 1,010
Italy	− 710	− 50	− 760
Romania	− 440	− 110	− 550
Poland	− 400	70	− 330
Hungary	− 320	20	− 300
Greece	− 310	− 120	− 430
Belgium	− 240	230	− 10
Norway	− 140	0	− 140
Yugoslavia	− 80	− 50	− 130
Bulgaria	− 50	20	− 30
Finland	− 40	150	110
Denmark	− 40	60	20
Estonia, Latvia, and Lithuania	0	40	40
Ireland	30	− 130	− 100
TOTAL	− 7,790	3,180	− 4,610
TOTAL EUROPE	− 3,970	− 2,070	− 6,040

(+) = net capital export, (−) = net capital import

[a] France is included with the creditors for 1924–32 and with the debtors for 1933–7; the estimates cover the French overseas territories, except Indo-China for 1924–30.

Source: See App. 1.

Hungary, and these were quite large sums relative to their national economies, giving foreign capital a significant role in their inter-war economic and political history.

On the other side, the payments accounts of the principal European creditors show a capital export of $3.8 billion, with France and the UK each contributing approximately $1.3 billion and the Netherlands and Switzerland each a little under $400 million. As in the nineteenth century Europe was a relatively unimportant outlet for British investors, most of whose funds were still directed to the Empire and South America, but their own continent accounted for a larger share of the foreign lending by France and the other European creditors. Taking the figures as they stand, there appears to have been a net inward flow for Europe as a whole during these seven years of about $4 billion but, as suggested earlier, it is likely that the estimates are subject to a bias tending to understate the outflow from the creditors and overstate the inflow to the debtors, so the actual net import of capital by Europe from the USA was probably considerably lower than this.

For Germany the peak year for the inflow of capital was 1928, when it reached $1 billion. It then dropped very sharply. Wall Street stock prices, which had started to climb in 1927, were surging upwards in 1928, luring more American investors away from foreign lending in the hope of a quick fortune at home. More seriously, there were growing doubts in the USA about the rapid expansion of Germany's external obligations and the unproductive purposes for which some of the foreign capital had been raised; doubts partly stimulated from within Germany by those concerned about the increase in the country's indebtedness. From 1930, with the accession of Brüning, the adoption of deflationary policies intensified the economic depression, and after the success of the National Socialists in the general elections in September of that year the sense of impending political crisis was a major deterrent to further foreign investment.

For the other European debtors the peak came a year earlier, when Austria, Italy, Poland, and Yugoslavia all raised large sums in the USA. Sizeable new bond issues were still possible for a few countries in 1928, including Denmark, Norway, and Italy in New York, and Greece and Hungary in London, but the boom was over and during the following years new lending fell away very rapidly. Economic conditions in many areas were already deteriorating, particularly in the agricultural regions of central and eastern Europe. A sharp decline in prices for their wheat, sugar, and other farm products drove down export revenues and drastically weakened the ability of these countries to service their foreign debts. For the European debtors as a whole the capital inflow dropped from about $1.7 billion in 1927 and 1928, to $1 billion in 1929, and less than half that a year later.

The flow of finance then turned completely around, and from 1931 to 1937 there was a reverse movement from the debtors to the creditors. As emphasized earlier, the scale of this movement was very much larger than is indicated by the estimates for the debtors in Table 3.4. As the economic climate darkened both foreigners and nationals became increasingly anxious to transfer their funds to stronger and safer currencies, and the resulting withdrawal of short-term capital put the central monetary authorities under enormous pressure. In Germany, Austria, Hungary, Poland, Italy, and many other countries the inevitable step was the imposition of progressively more stringent and comprehensive exchange controls. In itself this further intensified the eagerness of asset-holders to escape from such currencies, and the extent to which they succeeded in doing this will not be reflected in the records of the debtor nations, but can be seen in the massive accumulation of gold by the recipients, notably the UK and, after the stabilization of the dollar, the USA.

Two powerful forces explain most of this enormous outflow from continental Europe. Initially, speculative activity played the main role in stimulating the flight from Europe; for example, the movement of funds away from the gold bloc as the likelihood increased that these currencies would be devalued. Then, in the closing years of the decade, political dangers and the menace of war became the dominant factor. The change in France's international financial position was particularly striking. In the late 1920s, the undervaluation of the franc and the weakness of sterling enabled France to make massive additions to its reserves of gold and foreign exchange, and also to lend abroad, albeit on a modest scale—French investors having lost much of their enthusiasm for foreign investment after their experiences in 1917. From 1931, when Britain left the gold standard and devalued the pound, the franc lost its strength, and capital ebbed away as investors became progressively more pessimistic about future economic and political conditions in France. Table 3.4 shows an outflow in 1931–7 of over $2 billion, and the true figure may have been considerably larger.

The German accounts show a net outward movement in this period of over $1 billion. For the most part this was not the result of speculative flows, but a deliberate programme for the reduction of foreign indebtedness. The transformation of exchange controls from 'an emergency measure to a totalitarian institution' (Ellis, 1941: 158) gave the regime tight control over all current and capital account payments, and provided the context in which securities could be repurchased and debts repaid.

Financial conditions were also problematic and painful for many of the other European debtors even though the net capital movements were relatively small. Belgium experienced similar problems to France and was forced to devalue in 1935; and there were net outflows from Finland, Poland, and a number of other countries. However a few of the debtors continued to receive a net import of capital against the general trend. In the case of Austria this reflected the success of her economic policies, the reduction in external debt, and the abolition of exchange controls from 1935. In the following two years 'Austria was unique in being able to secure again short-term credits on the London market' (Ellis, 1941: 55). Romania continued to attract direct investment for the expansion of oil production, and Greece was also a net importer of capital, reflecting the more favourable economic circumstances she enjoyed during and after the Great Depression.

The nature of the capital flows to the European debtors, 1924–30

The estimates in Table 3.4 provide a broad overall indication of the net flows of capital which occurred in the years 1924–37. But they offer no further clue to the nature of the factors underlying these movements, or to the scale of possible offsetting inward and outward movements of different categories of long-and short-term capital. In order to make a more detailed analysis of the capital movements we need to go behind these net flows, and attempt to build up a more elaborate balance of movements in different types of capital. This can be done by examination of the alternative data sources, covering separate categories of foreign investment in either direction: new issues of long-term shares and bonds for foreign borrowers, purchases and sales of existing securities and of real property, amortization and repayment of debts, direct investment, and changes in short-term international indebtedness. There are serious gaps in the data which make it impossible to cover all items as fully or as accurately as would be desirable, but sufficient information exists to provide a useful supplement to the story told by the balance of payments data.

Estimates on this alternative basis were compiled for each of the seventeen European debtors for the period of massive inward capital flow from 1924 to 1930. The results are given in column (1) of Table 3.5 for Germany and in column (2) for the other European debtors as a group. Before turning to the details of the table we can consider the outcome of the comparison between the two sets of data. Total capital movement as measured by the balance of payments data is given in row 3, and as measured by the capital transactions in row 12. The difference is shown in the final row as errors and omissions. The remarkably small size of this residual must be partly the fortuitous outcome of compensating errors in various components of the two estimates and, in column (2), in the estimates for the different countries. It is, nevertheless, an encouraging result, and suggests that the overall results are broadly reliable despite all the numerous uncertainties in the two sets of figures.

Much the largest individual discrepancy occurs in the figures for Austria, where the $500 million of identified capital transactions is some $320 million below the net import derived from the balance of payments records. However, we have only a very rough indication of the extent of the net short-term borrowing prior to 1930, and we have not found any direct evidence on the value of Germany's direct and portfolio investment in Austria in the 1920s; it is thus possible that our rather arbitrary allowance for both these items may be too low. The two other cases where there is a significant shortfall in the identified capital imports are Italy and Greece (the gaps are $140 million and $100 million respectively), but for both countries the data on the increase in short-term liabilities are again too frail to sustain any implication that it is the balance of payments estimates which should be discarded.

We turn finally to the content of the additional information in Table 3.5. Row 4a of the lower panel shows that almost $3.5 billion of new long-term finance was obtained by the European debtors from external bond issues in

TABLE 3.5. *Comparison of the balance on current account, gold and foreign currency with direct estimates of capital transactions, European debtors, 1924–1930 ($m. to nearest $10m.)*

	Germany (1)	Other European debtors[a] (2)	Total (3)
Balance of payments			
1. Current account balance	− 3,620	− 2,810	− 6,430
2. Gold and foreign currency	− 570	− 790	− 1,360
3. TOTAL CAPITAL MOVEMENT	− 4,190	− 3,600	− 7,790
Capital transactions			
Long-term capital			
4(a). New bond issues abroad			
Central and provincial governments	470	1,030	1,500
Municipalities	160	210	370
Corporations	980	550	1,530
Total	1,610	1,790	3,400
4(b). New share issues abroad	90	240	330
5. *Less*: Repayments of debt	− 260	− 530	− 790
6. Direct inward investment	120	200	320
7. Foreign purchases of domestic securities and real property	1,350	0	1,350
8. Other capital inflows	30	420	450
9. *Less*: Investment abroad by debtors	− 1,050	− 150	− 1,200
Net long-term capital movement	1,890	1,970	3,860
Short-term capital			
10. Increase in assets	− 1,050	n/a	n/a
11. Increase in liabilities	3,450	n/a	n/a
Net short-term capital movement	2,400	1,150	3,550
12. TOTAL CAPITAL MOVEMENT	4,290	3,120	7,410
Errors and omissions	− 100	480	380

[a] See Table 3.4 for list of countries.

Notes: balance of payments: (−) = deficit or increase in assets = net capital import; capital transactions: (+) = decrease in assets/increase in liabilities; (−) = increase in assets/decrease in liabilities. Rows 4–6 cover the import of capital from the six main creditors; row 8 covers all forms of capital import from other countries, e.g. by Austria from Germany (offset by the increase in Germany's assets in row 9) or by Romania from Czechoslovakia.

Source: See App. 2.

the capital markets of the major creditors. The lion's share of this, 58 per cent, came from the USA; the UK provided 18 per cent, the Netherlands 9 per cent, Sweden 7 per cent, and Switzerland and Sweden each 4 per cent. This classification of the origins of the long-term bond finance must, however, be qualified by the observation that it is possible to identify only the immediate, not the ultimate source of the funds. Thus, if a loan was issued in Switzerland, but the shares were mainly purchased by French or German investors, our statistics would still show this as capital from Switzerland. For Germany, about 40 per cent of these loans were floated for governments and municipalities, and 60 per cent for private corporations; in the other countries corporate borrowing was responsible for only 30 per cent, and the bulk of the new issues was made by central and local government.

These bond issues were supplemented by small sums raised by issues of shares in companies not under the control of the creditors (row 4*b*), and by inward direct investment (row 6); and partially offset by some $800 million required for amortization and repayment of outstanding debts (row 5). Row 7 covers a further significant source of capital, an inflow of almost $1.4 billion, in the form of purchases by foreigners of German stock-exchange securities, real property, and mortgages. An estimate for this item is available only for Germany, but it is not likely that investments of this type in the other countries were significant. Investment in Germany from countries other than the six major creditors (for example loans from Belgium or Italy), and in other European countries from Germany and Czechoslovakia, are shown in row 8. The $450 million which we have allowed for the estimated inflow under this heading is very uncertain.

The last entry relating to long-term capital is in row 9. This covers the estimated outward movement of capital from these debtors, for example investment elsewhere in Europe by Germany, and by Belgium or Italy in Africa. (The foreign lending by Germany is offset by row 8 to the extent that it was a movement of capital to the other European debtors.) The aggregate of these six categories of long-term capital shows an estimated net movement of just under $4 billion, divided about equally between Germany and the other debtors. Within the latter group Italy imported about $400 million, Austria, $300 million, and Belgium, Hungary, and Poland each about $200 million.

The enormous sums involved in short-term capital movements over this period are indicated in rows 10 and 11. On the one hand there was a substantial outflow as banks and other concerns built up their private external holdings of floating assets. In the case of Germany this amounted to over $1 billion. It is not possible, unfortunately, to give a comprehensive figure for the other countries, but there is some evidence of appreciable outflows under this heading for a number of countries including Austria,

Poland, Italy, and Belgium. However, this movement was swamped by the increase in short-term indebtedness, with an increase of foreign liabilities of $3.5 billion for Germany, and perhaps something approaching $1.5–2 billion for the other countries. As a result there was a net inflow of $2.4 billion for Germany and over $1 billion for the other countries. For Germany, this increase in net short-term finance was significantly more important than the supply of long-term capital, and accounted for about 55 per cent of the total inflow in 1924–30. For the other countries the proportion was rather smaller, but short-term capital still made up about 37 per cent of the total inflow.

Thus, even in the 1920s, when the behaviour of international capital movements was relatively 'normal', flows of short-term finance occupied a far more prominent position than they had done before 1914. They were not yet rushing between currencies with the destructive and destabilizing effects which were to develop in the following decade, but the potential for this had been created.

Appendix 1. Notes and Sources for Balance of Payments on Current Account, and Changes in Gold and Foreign Currency

Unless otherwise stated: (*a*) the current account balance is taken from United Nations (1949: 10–12, 18–21, and 41–4), with a few missing figures (e.g. for Yugoslavia and Turkey in 1924 and 1925) interpolated on the basis of trade statistics; (*b*) movements in gold were based on the estimates given by the United Nations (1949: 10–12) and the League of Nations, *Balances of Payments* (*BP*), or on the net trade in gold as given by the League of Nations, *International Trade Statistics* (*ITS*); and (*c*) changes in holdings of foreign currency were based on League of Nations, *Statistical Yearbook* (*Stat. YB*) or Nurkse (1944: 234).

All estimates in national currencies were converted to dollars using the exchange rates given in Federal Reserve System (1943: 660–82).

Australia: Current account, gold and foreign currency: *Australian Historical Statistics* (1987: 191–2).

Austria: Current account: Monatsberichte des Österreichischen Institutes für Wirtschaftsforschung (1965: 41).

Belgium: Current account: provisional unpublished estimates kindly made available by Patrick Nefors, adjusted to include reparations payments received from Germany (*The Economist*, 1932).

Gold and foreign currency: calculated from the change in the total holdings of the Banque Nationale de Belgique and the Belgian government (Dupriez, 1939: 292–4; see also van der Wee and Tavernier, 1975: 424–31); with adjustments to exclude effects of devaluations in 1934 and 1936, and of acquisition of gold from domestic hoards in 1935 (League of Nations, *BP*, 1936: 69).

Canada: Current account, gold and foreign currency: *Historical Statistics of Canada* (1965: 159–64) and, for 1924–5, Sinclair (1993: 23).

China: Current account: for 1924–32 based on trade balance (League of Nations, *ITS*) and estimates for services and payments of interest and dividends made on the basis of data for 1928–30 in Remer (1932) and League of Nations (*BP*, 1931–2). For 1933–7 based on League of Nations (*BP*, 1936) adjusted to include Manchuria.

Gold and foreign currency: net trade in gold adjusted to cover unrecorded exports and exports from Hong Kong (Bank for International Settlements, *8th Annual Report*, 1938: 42).

France: Gold and foreign currency: for 1926–35 based on Rist and Schwob (1939: 548–9) and Sicsic (1993: 18) with certain corrections and additions kindly communicated in correspondence by Pierre Sicsic (letter of 18 January 1994). The Sicsic figures are derived from material in the archives of the Banque de France, and adjust the published series for transactions with members of the public and for certain concealed transactions by the Bank.

Germany: Gold and foreign currency: This estimate covers changes in Reichsbank holdings of gold in Germany plus the private trade in gold (League of Nations, *ITS*), plus movements of Reichsbank gold held abroad and changes in Reichsbank holdings of foreign currency (League of Nations, *BP*, and *Stat. YB*).

Greece: Current account: 1924–8 from the League of Nations (1943).

Ireland: Current account: for 1924–32 each of the main components of the initial estimates published by the League of Nations (*BP*) were adjusted in the light of revised estimates subsequently published for 1931.

India: Current account and gold: Bannerji (1963: 147).

Italy: Current account: Istituto Centrale di Statistica (1957: 254).

Gold and foreign currency: net trade in gold (League of Nations, *ITS*) and change in holdings of foreign exchange (League of Nations, *Stat. YB*).

Japan: Current account, gold and foreign currency: Ohkawa and Shinohara (1979: 335).

Latin America (other than Argentina): There are no balance of payments estimates for this large group of countries, but because of their importance as international debtors in the inter-war period it was essential to include their contribution to the global flows. The principal source of capital for this region was the USA, and a series for the annual new dollar loans (net of repayments), both short- and long-term, was taken from Lewis (1938: 619–29). This was raised by 80 per cent to cover (*a*) direct investment by the USA (estimated to be 62 per cent of US portfolio investment in 1924–30); and (*b*) all forms of investment by the UK and other creditors; see UN (1955: 7–10 and 154–7) and RIIA (1937, 146).

The Netherlands: Current account: these estimates were kindly made available by G. P. den Bakker of the National Accounts Research Division of the Netherlands Central Bureau of Statistics. They are taken taken from work done for his Ph.D. thesis, 'The Dutch Interwar Economy Revisited'.

Romania: Current account: very approximate estimates based on various sources quoted in Lampe and Jackson (1982: 514–16) and Notel (1986: 184–8, 220–2, 242).

South Africa: Gold and foreign currency: United Nations (1949) adjusted for gold held abroad and foreign currency (League of Nations, *BP* and *Stat. YB*).

UK: Current account, gold and foreign currency: Sayers (1976: 312–13). Movements in government long-term capital, and the official short-term credits received from the USA and France in 1931 and repaid in 1932, are excluded from the estimated capital flow.

USA: Current account, gold and foreign currency: US Department of Commerce (1975: 867; see also Lary, 1943). Movements in government long- and short-term capital are excluded from the estimated capital flow.

Appendix 2. Notes and Sources for Estimates of Capital Transactions

Long-Term Capital

4a. New bond issues abroad. Aggregate estimates of new bond issues are given in a number of sources, but these seldom provide more than a very broad classification by area. For the six main creditors there is an invaluable compilation in the unpublished League of Nations study (1943: app. Tables 3C–3I). This gives annual figures for each of the six major creditors classified both by borrowing country and by government, municipal, or corporate borrower. The main underlying sources from which this was derived were Lewis (1938: 632–9) for the USA; the *Statist* for the UK; a yearly article 'Balance des payments' by Meynial in *Revue d'economie politique* for France; an annual article on capital issues in the *Monthly Review* of the Rotterdamsche Bankvereeniging for the Netherlands; the *Schweizerisches Finanzjahrbuch* for Switzerland; and *The Economist* (29 March 1932) and Kommerskollegium, *Kommersiell a Meddelanden* (15 December 1934 and 15 January 1935) for Sweden.

For the UK and the Netherlands the new issues are recorded in these statistics at the price of issue; for the remaining countries the statistics are for nominal values and we have reduced the figures by 10 per cent to get a better estimate of the actual sums raised by the borrowers. This is the proportion shown for all long-term bond issues for Europe in the USA (Lewis, 1938: 645).

4b. New share issues abroad. The League of Nations study (1943: app. Table 3B) gives figures from the same sources for share issues with a classification by borrowing country, but only for the period 1919–31 as a whole. We used information in Lewis (1938: 654) and League of Nations (1943: notes to Tables 3A–3I: 2) to obtain an estimate for the years 1924–30 only.

5. Repayment of debts. For the USA detailed information is given in Lewis (1938: 619–29); for the other creditors we assumed that repayments by each borrower were the same ratio to total new issues 1919–31 as for the USA.

6. Direct inward investment. For the USA official estimates are available for the total annual outward movement, and for the aggregate stock of direct investment in each country at end-1924 and end-1929. The proportion invested in the European debtors at the latter date was applied to the annual flow series. For the UK direct investment is partly covered by the new issue statistics (which include domestic concerns operating abroad), and a small notional allowance was made for any additional UK capital and for the remaining creditors.

7. *Foreign purchases of domestic securities and real property.* The figure for Germany is based on the estimate given in the Wiggin Report (*The Economist*, 22 Aug. 1931: 6; see also Harris, 1935: 8–9 and 94 and the RIIA 1937: 236). No estimate has been found for the other debtors.

8. *Investment by other creditors.* For Germany this is a small allowance to cover loans by countries other than the six main creditors; see e.g. the figures in Harris (1935: 95). For the other debtors this covers the import of long-term capital in all forms from Germany and Czechoslovakia. The total foreign investment by Germany in this period is known (see row 9) but the only information we have found on its allocation by country relates to all of Europe at the end of 1938 (Woytinski and Woytinski, 1955: 213), and we have no proper basis for the total allowed for under this heading, still less for the allocation among individual countries. For foreign investment in Europe by Czechoslovakia we were guided by the comments in Teichova (1974: 25).

9. *Investment abroad.* The estimate for Germany is taken from the Wiggin Report (*The Economist*, 22 Aug. 1931: 6). We have added a rough allowance for foreign investment by Belgium, Italy, and others.

Short-Term Capital

10 and 11. Increase in short-term assets and liabilities. The estimates for these items are very uncertain.

The estimate for Germany's end-1930 short-term assets was taken from the Wiggin Report (*The Economist*, 22 Aug. 1931: 6) excluding the Reichsbank foreign exchange reserves. The corresponding liabilities were about RM 14.5 billion (Conolly, 1936: 356; Kindleberger, 1973: 138). The end-1930 level of net liabilities was then taken as equivalent to the increase since 1924 on the assumption that net liabilities at the end of 1923 had been effectively wiped out by the hyperinflation and economic disruption of the preceding years.

For Bulgaria, Denmark, Hungary, Norway, Poland, and the three Baltic States our estimates are based on the series for net short-term capital movements in the League of Nations, *Balances of Payments*.

For Austria, Finland, Greece, Italy, Romania, we used estimates of assets and liabilities at the end of 1931 compiled by the League of Nations (1943: 22–4, 29–30 and App. Table 5); for Italy and Romania the liabilities were said to be 'very incomplete', and an arbitrary allowance was made for this. These figures were corrected to exclude official reserves and adjusted, very roughly, for the change in 1931 in the light of the global estimates for end-1930 and end-1931 and the related discussion in Conolly (1936: 362–4; see also League of Nations, 1943: 36–7). As in the case of Germany the end-1930 levels of net liabilities were taken as equivalent to the increase since 1923 except for Finland.

For the three remaining countries (Belgium, Ireland, Yugoslavia) we have been unable to find a satisfactory basis for an estimate.

References

Official publications and international organizations

Banque Nationale de Belgique (1946), *Statistiques Économique Belge, 1929–1940* (Brussels).
Bank for International Settlements (1931–38), *Annual Reports* (Basle: Bank for International Settlements).
Federal Reserve System (1943), *Banking and Monetary Statistics* (Washington, DC: Government Printing Office).
Istituto Centrale di Statistica (1957), *Annali di Statistica, Indagine Statistica sullo Svilluppo del Reddito Nazionale dal 1861 al 1956*, 86 (8th series), vol. 9 (Rome: Istituto Centrale di Statistica).
League of Nations (1927–1938), *Balances of Payments* (Geneva: League of Nations).
—— (1943), 'Europe's Capital Movements, 1919–1932: A Statistical Note' (Princeton: unpublished typescript).
—— (annual), *International Trade Statistics* (Geneva: League of Nations).
—— (annual), *Statistical Yearbook* (Geneva: League of Nations).
Monatsberichte des Österreichischen Institutes für Wirtschaftsforschung (1965), *Österreichs Volkseinkommen, 1913 bis 1963* (Vienna).
United Nations (1949), *International Capital Movements during the Interwar Period* (Lake Success, NY: United Nations).
—— (1955), *Foreign Capital in Latin America* (New York: United Nations).
US Department of Commerce (1975), *Historical Statistics, Colonial Times to 1970* (Washington, DC: Government Printing Office).

Books and Articles

Banerji, A. K. (1963), *India's Balance of Payments* (London: Asia Publishing House).
Bloomfield, A. I. (1950), *Capital Imports and the American Balance of Payments* (Chicago: University of Chicago Press).
Cameron R. E. (1961), *France and the Economic Development of Europe, 1800–1914* (Princeton, NJ: Princeton University Press).
Conolly, F. G. (1936), 'Memorandum on the International Short-Term Indebtedness', in Carnegie Endowment-International Chamber of Commerce, *The Improvement of Commercial Relations between Nations* and *The Problems of Monetary Stabilization*, (Paris: International Chamber of Commerce).

Dupriez, L. H. (1939), 'L'Évolution Monétaire de la Belgique de 1925 a 1938', *Bulletin d'information et de documentation*, 14 (Brussels: Banque Nationale de Belgique)

Economist (1931), Wiggin–Layton Report, Special Supplement, 22 Aug.

—— (1932), Reparations and War Debts, Special Supplement, 23 Jan.

Ellis, H. S. (1941), *Exchange Control in Central Europe* (Cambridge, Mass.: Harvard University Press).

Guarneri, F. (1953), *Battaglie economiche tra le due guerre* (Milan: Garzanti; new edn. Bologna: Il Mulion, 1988).

Harris, C. R. S. (1935), *Germany's Foreign Indebtedness* (Oxford: Oxford University Press).

James, H. (1986), *The German Slump: Politics and Economics, 1924–1933* (Oxford: Clarendon Press).

Keynes, J. M. (1922), *A Revision of the Treaty* (London: Macmillan).

Klug, A. (1993), *The German Buybacks, 1932–1939: A Cure for Overhang?* Princeton Studies in International Finance, No 75 (Princeton: Int. Fin. Section, Princeton University).

Lampe, J., and Jackson, M. (1982), *Balkan Economic History, 1550–1950* (Bloomington, Ind.: Indiana University Press).

Lary, H. B. (1943), *The United States in the World Economy* (Washington, DC: Government Printing Office).

Lewis, C. (1938), *America's Stake in International Indebtedness* (Washington, DC: Brookings Institution).

—— (1945), *Debtor and Creditor Countries: 1938, 1944* (Washington, DC: Brookings Institution).

Maddison, A. (1991), *Dynamic Forces in Capitalist Development, a Long-Run Comparative View* (Oxford: Oxford University Press).

Morgan, E. V. (1952), *Studies in British Financial Policy, 1914–1925* (London: Macmillan).

North, D. C. (1962), 'International Capital Movements', in R. F. Mikesell (ed.), *U.S. Private and Government Investment Abroad* (Eugene, Oreg.: University of Oregon Books).

Nötel, R. (1986), 'International Credit and Finance', in M. C. Kaser and E. A. Radice (eds.), *The Economic History of Eastern Europe, 1919–1975*, ii (Oxford: Oxford University Press), 170–295.

Nurkse, R. (1944), *International Currency Experience: Lessons of the Interwar Period* (Geneva: League of Nations).

Ohkawa, K., and Shinohara, M. (eds.) (1979), *Patterns of Japanese Economic Development: A Quantitative Appraisal* (New Haven: Yale University Press).

Remer, C. F. (1932), *Foreign Investments in China* (New York: Macmillan).

Rist, L., and Schwob, P. (1939), 'Balance des paiements', *Revue d'économie politique*, 53: 528–50.

Royal Institute of International Affairs (RIIA) (1937), *The Problem of International Investment* (London: Oxford University Press).

Sayers, R. S. (1976), *The Bank of England, 1891–1944* (Cambridge: Cambridge University Press).

Sicsic, P. (1993), 'The Inflow of Gold to France from 1924 to 1934', Banque de France, *Notes d'études et de recherche*, 22.

Sinclair, A. M. (1993), 'Balance of International Payments, 1870–1925', in M. C. Urquhart (ed.), *GNP, Canada, 1870–1926* (Kingston: McGill-Queen's University Press).

Teichova, A. (1974), *An Economic Background to Munich* (Cambridge: Cambridge University Press).

Urquhart, M. C. (ed.) (1965), *Historical Statistics of Canada* (Toronto: Macmillan).

Vamplew, W. (ed.) (1987), *Australian Historical Statistics* (New South Wales: Fairfax, Syme & Welden.

Van der Wee, H., and Tavernier, K. (1975), *La Banque Nationale de Belgique et L'histoire monétaire entres les deux guerres mondiales* (Brussels: Banque Nationale de Belgique).

Woodruff, W. (1966), *Impact of Western Man, A Study of Europe's Role in the World Economy* (London: Macmillan).

Woytinsky, W. S., and Woytinsky, E. S. (1955), *World Commerce and Governments: Trends and Outlook* (New York: Twentieth Century Fund).

4

International Economics and Domestic Politics: Notes on the 1920s

BARRY EICHENGREEN AND BETH SIMMONS

1. International Economics

Recent research on the inter-war years points to the importance of international economic policies for the macroeconomics of the 1920s and 1930s. The chapters, in the second section of this volume are no exception. Tarmo Haavisto and Lars Jonung show how the deflation associated with Sweden's return to its pre-war gold parity in 1922 was associated with a severe contraction of output, but how Finland escaped those costs by accepting as permanent the depreciation of its currency. Isabelle Cassiers shows for Belgium and France how the decision to remain on the gold standard explains the depth and duration of the Great Depression in both countries, and how Belgium's abandonment of convertibility in March 1935, a year and a half in advance of France, accounts for the precocious recovery (by French standards) of its exports and production. Jean-Charles Asselain and Alain Plessis compare France not with its northern European neighbour, Belgium, but with its hot-blooded Mediterranean rival, Italy. While the very different structures of the French and Italian economies render the comparison problematic, once again international monetary policies emerge as key for understanding the course of the Depression. Both France and Italy suffered initially due to their allegiance to gold and their defence of increasingly overvalued exchange rates. Recovery commenced earlier in Italy than in France due to Mussolini's initiation of expansionary monetary policies under the cover of exchange controls. Perhaps the better comparison for Italy is Germany, as the chapter by Theo Balderston shows: in Germany, as in Italy, the inception of recovery coincided with the inauguration of expansionary policies (or at least the termination of contractionary ones), again under the protection afforded by exchange controls, although

This chapter began as a comment on the chapters in this volume by Asselain and Plessis, Balderston, Cassiers and Haavisto and Jonung. We thank Charles Feinstein for encouraging us to expand it into the present chapter. The work described here reports early findings from an ongoing project, the full results of which will be presented elsewhere.

more radical reflationary stimulus was ruled out by fears of inflation rooted in the experience of the 1920s.[1]

These and the other European experiences considered in this volume can be seen as special cases of a general pattern linking domestic economic performance to international economic policies. These links have been emphasized by, among others, Choudri and Kochin (1981), Temin (1989), Eichengreen (1992), and Bernanke and James (1992).[2] In the 1920s, these authors argue, the course and contours of recovery and readjustment were conditioned by the decision of whether or not to return to gold at the pre-war parity.[3] Countries like Britain and Sweden returning to gold at pre-war rates of exchange had to engineer a reduction of wages and prices sufficient to reverse the wartime inflation, or at least to reduce prices to the levels that US prices had scaled. Other countries, like France, Belgium, and Italy, which ultimately returned to gold at parities below those prevailing before the war, were unable to prevent inflation from persisting into the mid-1920s.

The inflationary and deflationary consequences of these international economic policies exercised a powerful influence over economic recovery in the 1920s. Countries that accommodated moderate inflation by abandoning their pre-war gold parities surmounted the disruptive after-effects of the First World War more quickly than did countries which subjected themselves to radical deflation in order to restore gold convertibility at pre-war rates.[4]

The mechanisms linking inflation and economic activity were the ones emphasized by Keynes in his *Tract on Monetary Reform* (1923). Inflation stimulated output and employment by reducing real wages and real interest rates. Keynes's assertion that it is a 'commonplace' of economics textbooks that wages tend to lag behind prices in periods of inflation and deflation has been a subject of debate among economists ever since. Whatever the validity of the generalization, the fact is that wages did exhibit such a tendency in the special circumstances of the 1920s, except where explosive hyperinflation led workers and employers to jettison existing wage contracts and conventions. The reason was obvious enough: it was costly to throw out contracts before they expired and to supersede prevailing labour-market conventions.

---

[1] Eichengreen (1991) emphasized the tendency for countries imposing exchange controls, which were often the same ones that had experienced high inflation a decade before, to fail to capitalize on their newfound freedom by dramatically expanding their money supplies.

[2] Two surveys of the relevant literature are Eichengreen (1992b) and Temin (1993).

[3] This paragraph draws on and summarizes the argument of Eichengreen (1986).

[4] This leaves aside countries where price-level increases degenerated into hyperinflation, with pronounced negative consequences. This stratification raises the question, of course, of how long moderate inflation can remain moderate without degenerating into an explosive inflationary spiral.

So long as it was still possible that price increases might be reversed and the pre-war parity restored after all, inflation and real wage reductions might prove temporary; this in turn minimized the incentive to recontract. It followed that output recovered more quickly in countries like France and Belgium where employers enjoyed an inflation-induced reduction in labour costs during the critical phases of post-war reconstruction, and that in countries like Britain and Sweden the deflation associated with restoring the pre-war parity heightened labour cost disadvantages.

Besides raising real labour costs, deflation increased the burden of business debts. Keynes emphasized the capital gains and losses accruing to business as a result of changes in the price level. Inflation not reflected in a commensurate increase in interest rates reduced the value of corporate liabilities by inflating away a portion of outstanding debts. The entrepreneur, his burden lightened, was willing to borrow more in order to expand the volume of production. Deflation that failed to lower interest rates similarly increased the weight of debt burdens, discouraging new borrowing to finance investment and production.

Critical to the operation of this mechanism was that inflationary trends were unanticipated, for otherwise they would have been incorporated into interest rates. That the permanence of inflationary trends was imperfectly anticipated was surely the case in the early 1920s, when there remained widespread confidence in governments' commitment to restoring pre-war parities and in their ability ultimately to do so. This was the dominant evaluation even of German prospects as late as 1920–1.[5]

Once inflation and deflation slowed and currencies were stabilized, either at their pre-war parities or at depreciated levels, the real wage and output trends of the preceding period were reversed. If wages had lagged behind rising prices during the inflation, trade unions used the lull following stabilization to make up lost ground. If real wages had risen as a result of the tendency for money wages to lag behind falling prices, employers now insisted that wages rise less quickly than productivity. In the immediate post-stabilization period, as a consequence, the cost of production generally fell in countries that had succeeded in restoring pre-war parities and rose in countries that had failed—the opposite of the pattern that had prevailed prior to stabilization.

To document these regularities, we reproduce a pair of tables from Eichengreen (1986), estimated on data for a cross-section of countries. These regress first real wages and then output on current and lagged inflation.[6] The

---

[5] This point is documented by Holtfrerich (1986), among many others. For an analysis of the political conditions that undermined this confidence, see Simmons (1994).

[6] Table 4.1 utilizes data for the UK, France, Norway, Sweden, Belgium, Italy, Denmark, Holland, Finland, Switzerland, Canada, USA, Australia, and Japan. Table 4.2 drops Finland and Switzerland for lack of data.

results show the tendency for current inflation to erode real wages and stimulate output, and for lagged inflation to induce an offsetting catch-up effect.

TABLE 4.1. *Cycles of inflation and real-wage growth, 1921–1927*

Equation	Sample period		Constant	π	π_{-1}	R^2	n
1.	Dependent variable	1921–7	1.35 (12.06)	−0.24 (2.28)	0.001 (0.58)	.33	14
	π:	1921–7					
	π_{-1}:	1920–1					
2.	Dependent variable	1922–7	0.93 (3.33)	−0.28 (3.58)	0.54 (1.60)	.54	14
	π:	1922–7					
	π_{-1}:	1921–2					
3.	Dependent variable	1923–7	1.33 (0.57)	−0.46 (2.56)	0.28 (1.03)	.48	14
	π:	1923–7					
	π_{-1}:	1921–3					
4.	Dependent variable	1924–7	1.55 (15.66)	−0.86 (5.32)	0.42 (2.67)	.76	14
	π:	1924–7					
	π_{-1}:	1921–4					
5.	Dependent variable	1925–7	1.42 (16.89)	−0.51 (3.84)	0.19 (1.85)	.74	14
	π:	1925–7					
	π_{-1}:	1921–5					

Note: t-statistics in parentheses. Dependent variable is the ratio of real wages at the end and the start of the period. π is the change in wholesale prices.

Source: Eichengreen (1986).

The offset is only partial, however. The coefficient on lagged inflation, in other words, is consistently (and significantly) smaller than that on current inflation. This may reflect the need for more time than that encompassed by these regressions for catch-up to be completed, that is, for the downward-sloping short-run Phillips curve to rotate to its vertical long-run position. Alternatively, it may indicate that the long-run Phillips curve was not vertical in this period. The latter is not a view to which most economists would subscribe, although it is necessarily one that must be adopted by those who would insist that national decisions to go back to the gold standard at 'wrong' exchange rates caused persistent economic problems throughout the post-stabilization period.

Once the Great Depression struck, these same mechanisms again came into play.[7] All countries suffered a deflationary shock to the price level,

[7] Here we draw on and summarize the analysis of Eichengreen and Sachs (1985).

which raised real wages and increased the weight of debt burdens, through both channels placing downward pressure on production. In 1931, however, the industrial world bifurcated into two monetary blocs that subsequently followed very different macroeconomic paths. One set of countries, led by France and including Belgium, Switzerland, the Netherlands, Czechoslovakia, and initially the USA, clung to their gold-standard parities, deflating as necessary for their currencies' defence. Others, led by Britain and including Scandinavia and the members of the British Commonwealth and Empire other than South Africa, abandoned the gold standard, either voluntarily or under duress. This removed the imperative of pursuing deflationary policies, allowing monetary and fiscal stringency to be relaxed. These policy shifts ameliorated the severity of the slump in countries with

TABLE 4.2. *Cycles of inflation and economic growth, 1921–1927*

Equation	Sample period		Constant	π	π_{-1}:	Start/ 1913	R^2	n
1.	Dependent variable	1921–5	0.24 (0.64)	1.52 (4.92)	−0.003 (1.76)	−0.44 (4.46)	.91	12
	π:	1923–5						
	π_{-1}:	1920–3						
2.	Dependent variable	1921–5	−0.83 (1.62)	2.15 (4.14)	−0.002 (0.58)		.69	12
	π:	1923–5						
	π_{-1}:	1920–3						
3.	Dependent variable	1921–6	0.88 (3.27)	0.99 (5.30)	−0.006 (1.98)	−0.42 (2.92)	.88	12
	π:	1923–6						
	π_{-1}:	1920–3						
4.	Dependent variable	1921–6	0.29 (1.20)	1.19 (5.00)	−0.005 (1.36)		.75	12
	π:	1923–6						
	π_{-1}:	1920–3						
5.	Dependent variable	1921–7	1.37 (4.68)	0.81 (2.48)	−0.18 (0.52)	−0.52 (3.29)	.72	12
	π:	1924–7						
	π_{-1}:	1920–4						
6.	Dependent variable	1921–7	0.93 (2.50)	1.00 (2.17)	−0.50 (1.04)		.34	12
	π:	1924–7						
	π_{-1}:	1920–4						

Note: t-statistics in parentheses. Dependent variable is the ratio of industrial production at the end and the start of the period. π: is the change in wholesale prices.

Source: Eichengreen (1986).

newly depreciated currencies relative to its continued intensity in the
countries of the gold bloc.

The mechanisms through which these different exchange-rate regimes and
the associated monetary and fiscal policies transmitted their effects were the
same as in the 1920s. On the supply side, countries which abandoned the
gold standard, for whatever reason, and allowed their currencies to depreciate, reduced real wages and enhanced the profitability of manufacturing
production. Regression analysis based on data for a cross-section of
countries suggests that the depreciation of sterling (which reduced the gold
content of the pound by about 40 per cent) lowered real wages in Britain by
about 10 per cent relative to the level which would have prevailed in 1935
had the country clung to the gold standard with the tenacity of Holland and
France. If wages had been 10 per cent higher, industrial production would
have been 5 per cent lower, *ceteris paribus*.[8] On the demand side, countries
that depreciated their currencies succeeded in improving the competitiveness
of their exports and enhancing the incentive to invest.

The question raised by these observations is why countries pursued such
very different policies. If the benefits of currency depreciation and inflation
were clear to see, then why were some countries so inclined to close their
eyes to their advantages? Why were others more willing to meet the
recessionary shock with depreciation and reflation?

Countries' historical experiences with inflation and deflation in the 1920s
may have been the single most important proximate determinant of the
policies pursued in the 1930s.[9] Those nations which had succeeded in
restoring their pre-war parities in the 1920s were least hesitant to devalue in
the 1930s. Conversely, those which had suffered persistent, socially divisive
inflations less than a decade before were least inclined to risk a repetition.
Ultimately, then, as with many questions in inter-war economic history, one
is drawn back to the immediate post-First World War years.

2. Domestic Politics

The international economic policy choices of the early 1920s—choices that,
according to the preceding argument, had such powerful and enduring
effects—were political choices. It was a political decision to pursue the
policies needed to deflate and restore the pre-war gold-standard parity, or
to refuse to implement the needed policies and to allow inflationary
tendencies to persist. International economic policy choices in the first half

[8] These elasticities can be read off figures 2 and 3 of Eichengreen and Sachs (1985).
[9] See Eichengreen (1992*a*), esp. ch. 1.

of the 1920s were thus profoundly shaped by partisan struggles, political instabilities, and governmental institutions.[10]

An immense literature describes the politics of the 1920s and their implications for policy.[11] Yet economic historians have made little progress—indeed, they have invested surprisingly little effort—in systematically incorporating political factors into the analysis of post-First World War economic policies. The reason for this reticence is not hard to find. The literature on post-First World War politics is a literature dominated by powerful individuals, national idiosyncrasies, and chance events. It is written in terms of the personalities of Winston Churchill and Raymond Poincaré and the attitudes of Montagu Norman and Benjamin Strong. This material resists efforts to identify systematic determinants of economic policy outcomes. Social scientists seek regularities driven by stable structural determinants. These, to put the point mildly, are not clearly visible in the literature on post-First World War politics.

One place to start in attempting to systematize these connections is the new political economy. Work flying under this banner (surveyed and extended by Grilli *et al.*, 1991) shows how cross-country patterns in inflation rates, budget deficits, and public-debt levels bear a seemingly stable and predictable relationship to a small number of political variables such as the political orientation of the government and its longevity. This, at least, is the conclusion that seems to emerge from the analysis of data for recent decades. Contributors to this literature suggest further that the ability of governments to translate their preferences into policy have depended on a small number of well-defined factors such as the size of the government's majority and the statutory independence enjoyed by policy-making institutions such as the central bank.

It is possible to pursue a parallel analysis for the 1920s. We focus here on the political determinants of the rate of currency depreciation in the first half of the decade. In Table 4.3 we report regressions of the percentage rate of currency depreciation in a given country in a given year on various proxies for political conditions.[12] The exchange rate is defined as US dollars per unit of domestic currency. Four political variables are considered. One is a measure of government instability: the number of times each year in which there was 50 per cent turnover of cabinet members or a significant change in prime minister.[13] The sign of this variable should be negative if government instability is conducive to depreciation. (Recall that the

---

[10] See Simmons (1994) for a detailed discussion.
[11] The single richest introduction to this literature is Maier (1975).
[12] Data on exchange rates are taken from Federal Reserve Board (1944).
[13] Our data on cabinet turnover are constructed from Banks (1971). There exist previous studies of patterns of governmental instability in inter-war Europe. See Zimmermann (1988).

exchange rate is defined as dollars per domestic currency unit, so a change in the negative direction indicates a depreciation.) The logic is that ephemeral governments should be less willing to pursue policies of short-term sacrifice in order to reap the long-term gains associated with stabilization.

The second variable is an index of central bank independence.[14] This is constructed as the average of four sub-indices: one which measures the government's capacity to appoint or otherwise influence the choice of the central bank head and governing board; one which indicates the severity of any prohibitions on central bank advances to the government; one which measures whether the executive or parliament may participate or otherwise intervene in the central bank's decision-making process; and one which indicates the extent to which the central bank is publicly or privately owned. The sign on this index should be positive if central bank independence enhances the ability of the monetary authorities to resist financing government budget deficits and otherwise bowing to inflationary pressures.

The third political variable is the size of the governing majority, proxied for by the percentage of seats in parliament held by parties included in the governing coalition.[15] Its sign should be positive if larger majorities are better able to implement the painful policies required for stabilization, while smaller ones are susceptible to political fragmentation and deadlock.

The final political variable is the percentage of seats in Parliament or Congress held by left-wing parties, defined as Social Democrats, Socialists, Communists, and other working-class parties.[16] US Democrats and Canadian Liberals are debatably included in this category. The sign of this variable is ambiguous *a priori*. Where labour contracts were structured such that wages were able to keep pace with inflation, workers should have been insulated from many of its costs, producing a positive association between left-wing representation and inflation. Conversely, where wages lagged behind price increases but renters were able to insulate themselves from their effects by altering the term structure of their assets toward Treasury bills and other financial instruments with short terms to maturity, the association is likely to be negative. In so far as the results of the previous section suggest the existence of considerable nominal inertia in labour markets, we are inclined to anticipate a negative sign on this variable.[17]

---

[14] This variable is constructed on the basis of data in Kirsch and Elkin (1928).

[15] Our measures are constructed from Flora (1983) and McHale (1983).

[16] This variable was constructed from the same sources as the size of the governing majority.

[17] A more sophisticated treatment would allow the preferences of left- and right-wing parties to vary over the business cycle, as in Simmons (1994); e.g. parties of the left might be less concerned about inflation-associated reductions in real wages during periods of high unemployment, on the grounds that policies of demand stimulus that produced inflation also reduced unemployment.

Information on these variables was assembled for nineteen European countries, the USA, Canada, and Japan. Regressions were run on pooled data for 1921–6. Given the nature of the argument, we excluded observations for countries with non-democratic governments in particular years. The number of observations differs across regressions because of missing data. Fixed effects for countries and years were included but not reported. Along with the four political variables we consider one measure of economic performance: the lagged rate of economic growth. Our prior is that governments in rapidly growing economies where the size of the distributional pie was expanding should have found it easier to push through the painful compromises required for stabilization.[18]

TABLE 4.3. *Political determinants of rate of exchange-rate depreciation, 1921–26* (Dependent variable is % change in domestic currency units per dollar)

Explanatory variable	(1)	(2)	(3)
Constant	− 0.97	− 1.11	2.04
	(4.36)	(4.59)	(5.00)
Government instability	− 0.07	− 0.07	− 0.10
	(2.12)	(1.85)	(2.58)
Central bank independence	0.12	0.12	0.15
	(5.22)	(5.31)	(5.94)
Governing majority		0.01	0.01
		(1.13)	(0.67)
Per cent left-wing			0.02
			(2.52)
Lagged output growth			0.30
			(1.90)
n	103	93	76
Standard error	0.199	0.196	0.184

Note: *t*-statistics in parentheses. All equations include country and year dummy variables.

With one exception, the political variables enter with their expected signs. Countries with independent central banks, more stable governments, and larger governing majorities appear to have been better able to resist exchange-rate depreciation in the 1920s. The first two of these variables are statistically significant at standard confidence levels.[19] As expected, countries

[18] Eichengreen and Casella (1993) have analysed a war-of-attrition model to identify the precise conditions under which an increase in national income will in fact accelerate the termination of a distributional conflict.

[19] That not all three variables are significant follows from the degree of multicolinearity between governmental instability and the size of the majority, a pattern emphasized previously by Zimmermann (1988).

in which recovery had been proceeding rapidly (as proxied by lagged output growth) were better able to resist exchange-rate depreciation.[20]

The coefficient on the percentage of representatives with a left-wing affiliation also enters significantly, though not with the predicted sign. According to these regressions, left-wing governments were more rather than less likely to resist exchange-rate depreciation in the 1920s. This is not due to the coding of American and Canadian parties, for the result is the same when the observations for these countries are dropped.

This finding is surprising given the historical association of left-wing governments with inflation.[21] The Belgian and French inflations were both presided over by left-wing governments, and stabilization in both countries coincided with a political consolidation that brought centrist prime ministers to power. (In Belgium, the Government of National Union was a three-party coalition with a significantly more centrist cast than its predecessor. It was led by Henri Jaspar, a member of the Catholic Party, and dominated by the financially conservative Emile Francqui as minister without portfolio. In France, depreciation was halted and stabilization took hold only when the conservative Raymond Poincaré replaced the left-leaning Edouard Herriot as head of government.) It could be that membership in social democratic, socialist, communist, and other working-class parties is not a sufficiently precise measure of distributional preferences for the 1920s. Alternatively, it may be that this association between left-wing governments and currency depreciation in post-First World War Europe was less general than previously thought.

These results clearly point to an agenda for research. In addition to the left-wing paradox, the sources of governmental instability and majority–minority status remain to be explained. While it is clear that both of these variables had a causal association with exchange-rate policy outcomes, we still need to know what was responsible for governmental instability and minority status themselves, a task which would involve exploring the possibility of reverse causation running back from exchange-rate instability to political outcomes.

Much of the literature on post-First World War politics appeals to the turbulence of the political environment—to the entry into the political arena of new political parties and, in defeated countries, to the discrediting of long-standing ones. In many countries the war had led to a broadening of the franchise; it was no longer possible to send workers off to war and yet to deny them the vote. These factors predictably strengthened the position

---

[20] This variable is lagged to minimize simultaneity bias. Readers still concerned about simultaneity bias should note that the argument of the preceding section, that depreciation should stimulate output growth, predicts a negative correlation between the two variables rather than the positive one reported in the Table.

[21] See once again Maier (1975).

of labour, socialist, and communist parties and weakened those of parties that had traditionally been dominated by landowners and industrialists. A larger electorate and a more powerful popular media promoted the growth of splinter parties representing narrow special-interest groups.

All this was a recipe for political instability. The proliferation of parties led to parliamentary fragmentation, unstable coalitions, minority governments, and inexperienced leadership. The exchange-rate instability of the 1920s was the predictable consequence.

There is a sense, however, in which such generalizations fail to get us very far. Some countries were clearly more susceptible than others to potential sources of political disarray. Despite functioning in the same turbulent international environment, the USA and the UK had relatively few significant changes in government between 1920 and 1926 (two and five, respectively, by the measure utilized in this chapter), whereas France and Germany were much more prone to governmental instability (the comparable statistic for both was eight). The USA and UK tended to have majority governments (1924 in the UK was an exception, but the share of seats commanded by the governing party averaged 63 per cent in the UK and 58 per cent in the USA), but not so France (where the Government commanded just 47 per cent of seats on average) or Germany (where the comparable figure was only 38 per cent).

Why this difference? One potential explanation is cross-country differences in electoral institutions. Historians are sympathetic by inclination to the notion that institutions play a role in shaping historical outcomes. Why should political institutions and political outcomes be an exception?

Electoral systems differ along many dimensions; the one we highlight here is the distinction between majority and proportional representation. In a pure proportional system, each party's representation in parliament is proportional to its share of the vote.[22] If a party receives 2 per cent of votes nation-wide, it receives 2 per cent of parliamentary seats. Such outcomes are most likely in systems with large electoral districts, party lists, and two ballots, although they also tend to obtain in a variety of similar institutional settings.

In a majoritarian system, in contrast, the individual candidate receiving the largest number of votes in a given district (a plurality or, if a majority is required, as a result of a second run-off ballot) gains the seat, and parties receiving smaller shares of the vote remain unrepresented. Electors are discouraged from casting their ballots for minority parties, since such votes are unlikely to affect the outcome of the election. Hence, majority representation systems are likely to result in the electoral and parliamentary dominance of a few (often two) large parties. This result is most likely in

---

[22] A good introduction to the various electoral systems is Lipjhart (1977). The definitive recent analysis from a political science vantage-point is Taagepera and Shugart (1989).

single-member district-plurality systems, although it can also obtain in a variety of similar settings.

The notion that majority representation favours two-party systems while proportional representation encourages multipartism is a stylized fact of political science known as 'Duverger's Law'.[23] The inter-war period provides clear illustrations of its operation. In Britain, a country with a majoritarian system, the 1920s saw the rise of the Labour Party and the decline of the Liberals. While the Liberals continued to garner a substantial fraction of the popular vote, they (and their potential supporters among the electorate) quickly found themselves severely underrepresented in Parliament. Although various governments, notably those of Labour, required Liberal support, Britain's traditional two-party system of Liberals and Conservatives was able to transform itself with a minimum of fragmentation and political deadlock into what was essentially a new two-party configuration of Labourites and Conservatives.

Germany is the obvious contrast. There a system of exceptionally pure proportionality encouraged the entry of small parties, rewarding them for generating a small share of the vote with a commensurate share of parliamentary seats. Given the proliferation of political parties, Weimar governments were necessarily coalition governments, coalitions which often succeeded in commanding only minority support. This political weakness was a recipe for governmental instability, which in turn encouraged governments to adopt short horizons when formulating economic policy. The incoherence of the resulting policies then fed back negatively on the political environment, inducing further fragmentation and chaos. F. A. Hermens, a leading critic of Weimar's electoral system, concluded that proportional representation 'was an essential factor in the breakdown of German democracy'.[24]

Whatever the ultimate political consequences of proportional representation in Germany, there is a striking correlation across European countries between its presence and short-run economic policy outcomes. Austria, Belgium, France, Italy, and Poland, as well as Germany, all employed forms of proportional representation in the 1920s and suffered inflation and currency depreciation. In contrast, countries like the UK and the USA, whose electoral systems were based on majority representation, were able to take the hard policy decisions needed to effect the restoration of their pre-war parities.

The spread of proportional representation was yet another change wrought by the First World War. When fighting erupted, there were doubts about whether the working classes would enlist in a conflict pitting rival

[23] See Duverger (1954: 217, 226 and *passim*).
[24] Hermens (1941: 293). Subsequent authors have been critical of his conclusion; see e.g. Lipjhart (1977).

capitalist economies against one another. Workers could hardly be expected to rush to the defence of institutions in which they had little voice. Hence the franchise was extended and wealth and property tests were relaxed or eliminated in virtually all the belligerent countries. Proportional representation became the risk-averse strategy for the old governing élites, who feared that the rise of labour and socialist parties might otherwise result in their complete loss of power. A further implication drawn from a war that first flared up at the fringes of the Austro-Hungarian Empire was the importance of giving voice to ethnic, religious, and national minorities. Proportional representation was a means to this end.

In a situation like that of the 1920s, when stabilization required painful distributional sacrifices, proportional representation could be a significant obstacle to the formulation and implementation of coherent policies. Inflation and depreciation in the first half of the 1920s were symptomatic of the failure of countries and their elected representatives to achieve a consensus on how to balance government budgets and to remove the need for central bank monetization of deficits. The war had transformed the distribution of incomes and tax obligations and challenged long-standing conventions underlying public discussion of these matters. The question of whose taxes to raise and whose favoured public programmes to cut was consequently up for grabs.

Proportional representation could make it that much more difficult to achieve a consensus on such matters. Governments were often minority governments and almost always multi-party coalitions. Coalition partners were willing to bring down the government, repeatedly if necessary, to prevent the adoption of policies with undesirable distributional consequences. This was a recipe for deadlock. And deadlock over the budget guaranteed inflation and exchange-rate depreciation.

The political consequences could be devastating, and not only in Germany. Austria suffered through no fewer than twenty governments under ten different chancellors in the fifteen years of proportional representation brought to a close in 1934 by the abolition of parliamentary government. In Poland, an extended political deadlock was broken only by General Pilsudski's seizure of extra-parliamentary powers in 1926. In Italy, four years of proportional representation saw the formation of no fewer than eight cabinets under five prime ministers. Between 1897 and 1919, Italian parliaments, elected under a majoritarian system, had an average duration of more than four years; the first post-war parliaments, elected by proportional representation, had an average life-span barely 25 per cent as long. Given the deadlocked parliament's inability to reach decisions, laws in many cases had to be enacted by royal decree, a practice which had been exceedingly unusual in earlier years. Economic stabilization was completed only after Mussolini seized dictatorial powers. Even in France there were calls, with the deterioration of the economic and political climate in 1925–6, to suspend Parliament's powers and install an autocratic leader to impose unilaterally the policy changes necessary for stabilization.

The plausibility of this argument is buttressed by the subsequent decisions in many countries to reform the political system so as to reduce the degree of proportionality. In the Netherlands, where unfettered proportionality led to a proliferation of political parties, the electoral system was already modified in the early 1920s to raise the threshold share of the national vote which parties had to garner before receiving parliamentary representation. France's system of proportional representation was abandoned once it became clear how much power it vested in fringe parties, particularly on the left; thus, the elections of 1928, 1932, and 1936 were held under the old system of single-member constituencies with two ballots.[25]

This hypothesis of an association between proportional representation and the incoherence of policy is not universally accepted. Lipjhart (1977) argues that the implications for policy of alternative electoral systems depend on the social, political, and economic context in which they are embedded. Katzenstein (1985) suggests that a number of small European countries succeeded in using proportional representation as an effective strategy of power-sharing and political compromise after the Second World War. Rogowski (1987) lauds proportional representation for being conducive to political stability and coherent policy in recent decades.

While it is hard to dispute the conclusions of any of these authors, neither are their views necessarily incompatible with the preceding characterization of the effects of proportional representation in the 1920s. No one has disputed that the low entry barriers facing small political parties in proportional representation systems are conducive to coalition government. Any one of a number of small parties can in principle defect from the coalition and topple the government. But the parties involved presumably weigh the benefits of defecting against the costs of shattering the coalition, aggravating the climate of political instability, and acquiring a reputation as an unreliable coalition partner. When the distributional stakes are high, in the sense that different policies have very different implications for income distribution, the benefits of blocking the adoption of an undesirable policy are likely to dominate the costs associated with bringing down the government. When the distributional stakes are low, on the other hand, the costs attached to bringing down the government provide an incentive for compromise conducive to stability. Thus, the effects of an electoral system should depend on

---

[25] The French system had always been particularly complicated. Under the law governing the 1919 and 1924 elections, if a party or group of parties obtained a majority in a particular district, it received all the seats; otherwise, seats were distributed according to proportional representation. Thus, the French system was at most a diluted form of proportional representation.

the policy environment—or to put it another way, on the political, social, and economic context within which that system operates.

In many European countries, the 1920s was a period of unparalleled political polarization, when distributional conflict was intense and the distributional consequences of policy choices were profound. In such circumstances, coalition partners were willing to bring down governments, repeatedly if necessary, to prevent the adoption of policies with undesirable distributional implications. Proportional representation was therefore a recipe for political deadlock, which meant the perpetuation of budget deficits and the persistence of inflation and currency depreciation.

The Netherlands and the Scandinavian countries can be invoked as exceptions that prove the rule. While these countries were among those adopting systems of proportional representation, they did not experience persistent inflation and currency depreciation. But as wartime neutrals they had not experienced the same degree of fiscal turbulence. Existing fiscal conventions had not been overturned as a result of hostilities. They did not emerge from the second decade of the century with large public debts and deficits in desperate need of finance. Since the distributional stakes were lower, the costs of acquiring a reputation as an unreliable coalition partner were an effective deterrent preventing fringe parties from repeatedly bringing down the government. Proportional representation may still have created a bias in favour of maintaining the fiscal and distributional *status quo*, but in the Netherlands and Scandinavia, unlike France, Belgium, Italy, and Poland, that did not necessarily imply inflation and exchange-rate depreciation.

3. Implications for Research

Much of economic history, like economics, is a search for plausible identifying restrictions. But in the richness of history, many of the standard identifying assumptions of economics lose their appeal. Economists frequently attempt to identify the effects of economic policies by assuming that policy initiatives can be taken as exogenous with respect to their consequences.[26] But in the underlying general equilibrium model historians have in mind, not just the effects of policy initiatives but the decision to take them must be treated as being determined within the model.

From this fact emanates the search for deeper historical structures with the capacity to influence both the policy decisions and their outcomes. In this note we have suggested that political institutions comprise one such set

[26] A particularly sensitive attempt to implement this approach is Romer and Romer (1989).

of structures. In truth, all we have done is to provide this suggestion. Much research remains to be done to establish the nature and robustness of the link running from electoral institutions in particular, and political institutions in general, to economic policy decisions and outcomes.

References

Banks, Arthur S. (1971), *Cross-Polity Time-Series Data* (Cambridge, Mass.: MIT Press).

Bernanke, Ben, and James, Harold (1991), 'The Gold Standard, Deflation and Financial Crisis in the Great Depression: An International Comparison', in R. Glenn Hubbard (ed.), *Financial Markets and Financial Crises* (Chicago: University of Chicago Press): 33–68.

Casella, Alessandra, and Eichengreen, Barry (1993), 'Can Foreign Aid Accelerate Stabilization?' unpublished manuscript, University of California at Berkeley.

Choudri, E., and Kochin, Levis (1981), 'The Exchange Rate and the International Transmission of Business Cycle Disturbances', *Journal of Money, Credit and Banking*, 12: 565–74.

Duverger, Maurice (1954), *Political Parties*, 2nd edn. (New York: John Wiley).

Eichengreen, Barry (1986), 'Understanding 1921–1927: Inflation and Economic Recovery in the 1920s', *Rivista di Storia Economia*, NS 5: 34–66.

—— (1991), 'Relaxing the External Constraint: Europe in the 1930s', in George Alogoskoufis, Lucas Papademos, and Richard Portes (eds.), *External Constraints on Macroeconomic Policy: The European Experience* (Cambridge: Cambridge University Press), 75–117.

—— (1992a), *Golden Fetters: The Gold Standard and the Great Depression, 1919–1939* (New York: Oxford University Press).

—— (1992b), 'The Origins and Nature of the Great Slump Revisited', *Economic History Review*, 45: 213–39.

—— (1993), 'The Endogeneity of Exchange Rate Regimes', in Peter Kenen (ed.), *Understanding Interdependence* (Princeton: Princeton University Press (forthcoming).

—— and Jeffrey Sachs (1985), 'Exchange Rates and Economic Recovery in the 1930s', *Journal of Economic History*, 45: 925–45.

Federal Reserve Board (1944), *Banking and Monetary Statistics* (Washington, DC.: Federal Reserve Board).

Flora, Peter (1983), *State and Society in Western Europe 1815–1975* (London: Macmillan).

Grilli, Vittorio, Masciandaro, D., and Tabellini, Guido (1991), 'Political and Monetary Institutions and Public Financial Policies in the Industrial Countries', *Economic Policy*, 13: 342–92.

Hermens, Ferdinand A. (1941), *Democracy or Anarchy? A Study of Proportional Representation* (Notre Dame, Ind.: University of Notre Dame Press).

Holtfrerich, Carl-Ludwig (1986), 'U.S. Capital Exports to Germany, 1919–1923 compared to 1924–1929', *Explorations in Economic History*, 23: 1–32.

Katzenstein, Peter (1985), *Small States in World Markets* (Ithaca, NY: Cornell University Press).

Keynes, John Maynard (1923), *Tract on Monetary Reform* (London: Macmillan).

Kirsch, H., and Elkin, W. A. (1928), *Central Banks: A Study of the Constitutions of Banks of Issue* (London: Macmillan).

Lijphart, Arend (1977), *Democracy in Plural Society* (New Haven: Yale University Press).

Maier, Charles S. (1975), *Recasting Bourgeois Europe: Stabilization in France, Germany and Italy in the Decade after World War I* (Princeton: Princeton University Press).

McHale, Vincent E., and Skowronski, Sharon (eds.) (1983), *Political Parties of Europe: Greenwood Historical Encyclopedia of the World's Political Parties* (Westport, Conn.: Greenwood Press).

Rae, Douglas W. (1967), *The Political Consequences of Electoral Laws* (New Haven: Yale University Press).

Rogowski, Ronald (1987), 'Trade and the Variety of Democratic Institutions', *International Organization*, 41: 203–24.

Romer, Christina, and Romer, David (1989), 'Does Monetary Policy Matter? A New Test in the Spirit of Friedman and Schwartz', *NBER Macroeconomics Annual*, 4: 121–70.

Simmons, Beth (1994), *Who Adjusts? Domestic Sources of Foreign Economic Policy During the Interwar Years* (Princeton, NJ: Princeton University Press).

Taagepera, Rein, and Shugart, Matthew Soberg (1989), *Seats and Votes: The Effects and Determinants of Electoral Systems* (New Haven: Yale University Press).

Temin, Peter (1989), *Lessons from the Great Depression* (Cambridge, Mass.: MIT Press).

—— (1993), 'Transmission of the Great Depression', *Journal of Economic Perspectives*, 7: 87–102.

Zimmermann, Ekkart (1988), 'The Puzzle of Government Duration: Evidence from Six European Countries during the Interwar Period', *Comparative Politics*, 20: 341–57.

PART II

Comparative Studies of Exchange
Rates and Monetary Policy

5

German and British Monetary Policy, 1919–1932

THEO BALDERSTON

1. Summary of the Argument

The argument of this chapter may be summarized as follows:

1. For some time after the war (much shorter in Britain than in Germany) monetary policy in both countries was ancillary to an inflationary fiscal policy, and its main task was to minimize the cost to the State of the national debt.

2. In Britain the way in which the decisions for restoring the gold standard were taken suggests that policy-makers were aware of the potential divisiveness of their action. In Germany, stabilization was postponed as long as it was largely an economic question and pursued only when the self-destruction of the German currency seemed to threaten the survival and integrity of the German State.

3. In both countries the main policy tool between 1924 or 1925 and 1931 remained discount-rate manipulation. In both active capital-market policies were employed to influence the capital balance with abroad, and thus modify (if in different ways) the action of discount-rate policy. In both, though only slightly in Germany, open-market operations were attempted. In both there was sporadic intervention on the foreign-exchange market; in both 'gold devices' were occasionally employed.

4. In both countries the gold standard failed in 1931. Why?

(i) In neither is it proven that the policy tools were inherently unequal to the task of maintaining convertibility.

(ii) In Britain the tools were used too irresolutely for too long, because of powerful domestic hostility to the effects of higher discount rates on credit conditions and employment. Thus the markets had good reason by 1931 to doubt whether the Bank would use all means to defend the exchange rate in a crisis.

I am indebted to Professor R. Millward and participants in the ESF Workshop on Money and Banking between the Wars for comments on earlier drafts; they are not responsible for remaining defects. The Bank of England and the Institut für Zeitgeschichte, Munich, gave permission to use their archives. Research for the paper was supported by the University of Manchester and the Nuffield Foundation.

(iii) In Germany the discount rate was used vigorously to defend the exchange rate, thus tending to build confidence in the currency. Other parts of Reichsbank President Schacht's policy, however, tended to weaken this confidence, especially his criticisms of government finance and his confrontational reparations stance. The intrinsic contradiction between monetary policy on the one hand, and reparations policy and the fiscal process on the other, intensified after Schacht resigned in March 1930. See 5 below.

(iv) Thus in both countries, if in different ways, the trumpet of monetary policy gave an uncertain sound, and the market uncertainty this generated may be held chiefly responsible for the destabilizing flows afflicting the German exchanges after 1927 and sterling from the last months of 1930.

5. In Britain it is possible to discern a rational *ex post* relation of employment and debt policy to exchange-rate policy, which prevented too single-minded a pursuit of the last goal at the expense of the first two. Thus the abandonment of the gold standard, disorderly as it was, may be seen as the outcome of a *choice* not to prioritize exchange-rate policy over credit and employment policy.

In Germany, especially after 1929, the problem was rather the incoherence of the different policy areas which prevented a rational ordering of policy goals. In particular, this was prevented by the intrinsic irrationality of fiscal and reparations policy. Recurrent fiscal and reparations crises generated uncertainty in the currency markets and provoked periodic flights from the mark, despite the firmness of monetary policy *per se*. These eventually undermined confidence in the solvency of the banks, precipitating the 1931 crisis and, ultimately, exchange controls.

6. A more credible monetary regime in Germany would have prevented the banking crisis of 1931 and lessened the unemployment of 1932. It is not clear, however, that a more credible defence of $4.86 would have eased Britain's problems.

7. In Germany after 1931 devaluation could not have made exchange controls redundant or permitted an easier monetary policy than that followed.

8. Whilst recognizing that in 1931 the failure of co-operation among central banks hastened the collapse of the gold standard, the emphasis placed here on the uncertainty of market expectations implies that the level of support needed to rekindle confidence in parities would have been much larger than in 1890 or 1907, and was probably not feasible.

2. Definition of Comparable Periods

British monetary history from 1920 to 1931, can be regarded as a unified whole dominated by the gold standard: until April 1925 by the aim of restoring it, and thereafter by the aim of defending it (Sayers, 1976: i. 110). Prior to this, a short initial period can be separated out, running from the end of the war until December 1919, during which, though all concerned paid lip-service to the objective of return to gold, in actuality this policy took a back seat, since the Treasury refused to permit interest-rate increases. The result of this was to torpedo the Bank of England's hopes of an early resumption of fixed-parity gold payments.

These two periods—of (i) 1919, (ii) 1920 to 20 September 1931—are of obviously unequal length, but they can be used to structure the comparison with German monetary history. The first corresponds to the period of the German inflation, from the end of the war until, perhaps, the formation of the great coalition in August 1923. The second corresponds to the period of stabilization and of the convertible gold standard: August 1923 to July 1931.

We can now proceed to a period-by-period comparison of monetary policy, its environment, and its outcomes, in the two countries.

3. The Gold Standard in the Back Seat: Britain 1919, Germany 1919–1923

Howson and Sayers agree that when the Treasury refused to countenance the wishes of the 'dear money party' in March 1919 and overruled the Bank of England (Howson, 1975: 11–16; Sayers, 1976: i. 110–15) it was out of fear of the repercussions of higher interest rates on the market for government debt and on the state of trade and employment. Behind the last two concerns lurked the deeper fears of the political radicalization of the working classes (Wrigley, 1990: 80–173).

In such circumstances, monetary policy was briefly an annexe of fiscal policy, and the preoccupations of the Bank of England resolved themselves into two: (i) matters of day-to-day management—of the reserves, of the sale of Treasury bills, and of the market for the national debt; (ii) longer-term attempts to influence the government in the direction of 'sounder money' (Howson, 1975: 14–23). Manipulation of the exchange rate was not, it seems, a major policy preoccupation.

The dilemma of German monetary policy after the war differed in degree rather than in kind from the British. The Reichsbank, publicly subservient to the Reich, privately recommended monetary restriction from the end of the war (Holtfrerich, 1986: 162–3). But prior to the Erzberger fiscal reforms of 1920 the Reich lacked an adequate revenue base to sustain the burden of war-debt servicing, of war pensions, and of the swelling social outlays of the 'social' republic. And on top of these burdens loomed the liability whose determination lay outside German control: reparations. Contrary to common opinion, the real value of the German national debt at the end of hostilities stood little higher in relation to real 1913 national income than the corresponding ratio in Britain (though real national income probably fell further in Germany between 1913 and 1918). (Inferred from Balderston, 1989: 226; Hoffmann *et al.*, 1965: 826; and Feinstein, 1972, T12, col. (5).) However the many threats in 1919 to the survival of the new republic, and its obvious incapacity to balance its budget, provoked a collapse in the demand for marks. The funded debt of the Reich proved unsaleable, and a vast expansion of the floating debt, much of it directly monetized at the Reichsbank, joined with the collapsing demand for money to produce the rapid inflation of that year (Holtfrerich, 1986: 192–3).

The Erzberger fiscal reforms in 1920 changed the Reich's revenue resources less than is sometimes supposed; for while they gave the Reich power to set the *rates* of direct taxation, the *revenues* raised thereby were still largely transferred to states and local authorities under the provisional Apportionment of Revenues (*Der Finanzausgleich*, 1931). Nevertheless the real reason for the unsteady, but ultimately explosive course of inflation lay not in the inherent inadequacy of the tax system to function under *stable* prices, nor in an impossible debt burden, but in the market's assessments, based on current political news, of the government's capacity to deliver future budget surpluses. Pessimism regarding this caused asset-holders to change debt into money and money into real goods, reducing the real burden of public debt, but also reducing real government revenue relative to expenditure, creating further deficits and fresh issues of Treasury bills (Webb, 1989: 37–44).

In Germany, as in Britain in 1919, monetary policy during the inflation was an annexe of budgetary policy. It had three main aspects:

1. Matters of day-to-day management. Of these the Reichsbank's role as residual purchaser of the part of the Treasury bill stock which the market did not wish to hold at the current, pegged, discount rate (Holtfrerich, 1986: 67–8, 73) was maybe its principal function. This proportion remained less than one-half until the end of 1921, after which it rose rapidly. Scarcely less important in the Reichsbank's eyes was the duty of supplying the private sector with credit, particularly in 1922, as the accelerating inflation caused shrinkage of firms' real balances, hence shortages of working capital—and as rising inflationary expectations caused rising demand for credit. In meeting these demands by readier direct rediscounting of bills drawn on larger firms, the Reichsbank was acting upon the 'real bills' doctrine which had guided its practice from its foundation (Holtfrerich, 1986: 64–71; Webb, 1989: 27–9).

2. The Reichsbank also intermittently sought to pursue an exchange-rate policy in disregard of budgetary policy. Most notably, in spring 1923 it pegged the exchange rate successfully for several weeks, hoping thereby to

thwart bear speculation and deter it in the future. Eventually, however, the worsening diplomatic and political crisis, and the unchecked budget deficits defeated its efforts (Holtfrerich, 1986: 68, 311).

3. Lastly, the Reichsbank sought to persuade the government to reform the budget, as the foundation for monetary stabilization. Whilst publicly mouthing the 'balance of payments' explanation of the inflation, its private advice to the government stressed the 'quantity theory' with its budgetary implications (Holtfrerich, 1986: 163–72). These attempts to persuade were fairly constant immediately after the war, but as the diplomatic crisis worsened, they ceased, even although new legislation in 1922 made the Bank constitutionally autonomous from the Reich.

4. The Restoration of Monetary Control

In Great Britain there were two decisive moments in the restoration of monetary control: the imposition of the 7 per cent bank rate in April 1920, and the 'resumption of gold payments' in April 1925. Both decisions really represented recognition of the logic of policy lines laid down previously, and were not in themselves decisive policy switches. Howson showed that the 7 per cent bank rate represented the outworking of what she called the 'Bradbury trick' of December 1919 (Howson, 1975: 13–14, 17). And it would have been more radical for Churchill in 1925 to have proposed the renewal of the Gold Embargo Act of 1920 (Brown, 1940: i. 185) which was due to expire at the end of the year, than to advance by nine months or so the return to gold, which the Act's expiry in any case entailed (cf. Moggridge, 1972: 39–41). Putting a term on the gold embargo in 1920 had both eased acceptance of the measure at the time, and facilitated the subsequent return. As 1925 approached, the Act having created market expectations of return, those who now opposed it were put in the position of advocating costs (possibility of abrupt loss of confidence in the exchanges) which their alternative would not otherwise have implied (Moggridge, 1969: 41, 50). In some respects, too, the decision to return at $4.86 can be construed as a line of least resistance. There were those who agitated for a lower parity (Boyce, 1987: 41, 45–6, 73–5; *Macmillan*, 1931b: i. 190–1) and the controversy persisted after 1925 (cf. the echoes in Gregory, 1926). But in the crucial deliberations between the Bank, the 'experts' and the chancellor, the matter was not squarely addressed (Moggridge, 1969: 25–54). *As a matter of decision-taking* it was easier to duck the parity question than to open Pandora's box by discussing the matter.

In Britain the return to gold was a freely chosen policy. In Germany stabilization may be regarded as mere recognition of the inevitable. The decision to stabilize was effectively taken by the great coalition which briefly held office between August and November 1923. But it was taken because the inflation was in any case burning itself out. In the autumn of 1923 the real value of the mountainous papermark circulation may be calculated at between 80 and 800 million gold marks, whereas the circulation of notes and coin in 1914 had been about 6 milliard marks (Holtfrerich, 1986: 313). The shrinkage of the 'gold' value of papermark deposits was even more dramatic (Balderston, 1991: table 2). The papermark, having shed its function as a store of value some time since, was rapidly losing its role as a unit of account now that most wages and retail prices were fully index-linked via the dollar exchange-rate. Only its function as a means of payment survived, and this, too, was being eroded, as firms, to a perhaps disputable extent, were going over to hard-currency invoicing (Webb, 1989: 15–16 *contra* Holtfrerich, 1986: 75, 304), and as a variety of emergency moneys, some denominated in commodities, were appearing. The quantitative extent of these substitute moneys is not as important as the trend they revealed. The transactions costs incurred in using the paper mark were becoming so great as virtually to entail that Germany would shortly repudiate it, perhaps for foreign currency substitutes, which would eliminate the possibility of an autonomous German monetary and state-debt policy, forfeit the potential of seigniorage, and deliver Germany up to the monetary policies and possible tricks of countries still perceived as hostile. In monetary terms, what the stabilization of the mark achieved was not so much stable prices in themselves, as a currency which reserved to Germany much (though not all, given foreign controls under the Dawes Plan) of the limited sovereignty over economic policy that countries on the gold standard can enjoy. Perhaps more importantly, in political terms, with the Ruhr still under occupation, with signs of separatism in the Rhineland and Bavaria, and with communist participation in the governments of Saxony and Thuringia, the surrender of a German currency seemed likely to hasten the end of the German State (Holtfrerich, 1986: 334).

Not even the choice of parity was at the discretion of the German policy-makers. True they chose, in an imaginative step, to stabilize the papermark at 4.2 trillion to the dollar, thus permitting, once the zeros were cancelled, the apparent restoration of the pre-war dollar exchange-rate. But if they had instead stabilized at, say, 12 trillion to the dollar, a rate briefly touched on uncontrolled exchanges in the second week of November 1923 (*Die Reichsbank*, 1929: 160), prices and wages would simply have stabilized at higher papermark rates, since they were fully index-linked to the dollar. The *real* mark–dollar exchange-rate was determined by the markets, and was not at the policy-makers' discretion. To argue whether the mark was over- or under-valued at stabilization is therefore unreal.

Whereas sterling's 'return to gold' could be effected by decisions in the monetary sphere in practical autonomy from other spheres of State decision-making, the stabilization of a *German* currency required not merely resolute monetary action but also contemporaneous and co-ordinate decisions in the fiscal and diplomatic spheres (Webb, 1989: 65–74; cf. Garber, 1982). The first essential corollary was fiscal stabilization, which a series of emergency decrees passed between October 1923 and February 1924 were designed to bring about (Netzband and Widmaier, 1964: 118 ff.). So vigorous were these measures that a running budget surplus was already displayed by the Reich's accounts for December 1923. This surplus was only provisional, however; it depended on a temporary non-payment of reparations and could be made permanent only if a definite and tolerable schedule of future reparations payments could be agreed with the Allies. Thus the second essential corollary of stabilization was the evident change of heart on both sides at the end of 1923 which made it possible to set up the 'Experts' Committees' to renegotiate reparations. Renewed American interest in the matter probably assured the markets of an amicable outcome (Eichengreen, 1992: 142–52).

One further action was needed to make mark stabilization 'stick'. This was the Reichsbank's so-called *Kreditstopp* of 7 April 1924. From February 1924 paper mark quotations against the dollar had been slipping on uncontrolled foreign exchanges. This was not caused by a simple excess supply of marks, for ever since November 1923 the Reichsbank had been severely rationing foreign exchange against paper marks (Müller, 1934: 199). Rather the slippage seems (judging by the remedial action thought appropriate by the Reichsbank) to have been precipitated by the rapid increase of the Reichsbank's portfolio of domestic bills. This increase was produced by the rapidly recovering demand for cash balances following currency stabilization, but it gave rise to fears that, following the 'real bills' doctrine which had traditionally guided its actions, the bank would regulate the expansion of the currency with more regard for 'the legitimate needs of trade' than for the state of the exchanges. The Reichsbank's reaction was to announce, on 7 April, a 'stop' to the discounting of bills (Hardach, 1976: 33–40, 51–3; Northrop, 1938: 332–60). The value of its bill portfolio was to be stabilized at the current level and fresh bills would be discounted only as existing bills ran off. There was some force in the Bank's argument that in the current circumstances the demand for discounts was inelastic with respect to discount-rate increases, so that the rawer method of credit restriction could not be avoided. The *Kreditstopp* also had the virtue of the clarity of its announcement effect. By signifying a clean break with the 'real bills' doctrine, it unmistakably announced the priority which the Reichsbank

TABLE 5.1. *Reichsbank bill holdings*[a] 1924–1930 (deseasonalized) (RM. million)

Bimonthly average	1924	1925	1926	1927	1928	1929	1930
Jan.–Feb.	1,264	1,694	1,113	1,315	2,285	1,946	2,189
Feb.–Mar.	1,713	1,629	1,019	1,481	2,238	2,049	2,107
Mar.–Apr.	1,927	1,433	832	1,648	2,205	2,323	1,970
Apr.–May	2,105	1,443	856	1,937	2,191	2,838	1,944
May–June	2,067	1,433	870	2,165	2,032	2,955	1,790
June–July	1,898	1,434	818	2,262	1,944	2,679	1,625
July–Aug.	1,840	1,580	841	2,308	1,972	2,478	1,607
Aug.–Sep.	1,842	1,560	798	2,266	1,885	2,344	1,569
Sep.–Oct.	2,001	1,435	782	2,334	1,820	2,298	1,840
Oct.–Nov.	2,052	1,311	830	2,260	1,723	2,240	2,027
Nov.–Dec.	1,995	1,164	946	2,255	1,739	2,313	2,056
Dec.–Jan.	1,825	1,128	1,121	2,338	1,848	2,285	2,091

[a] *Wechsel-und Lombardanlage.*

Source: Calculated from G. Hardach (n.d.: 249). I am grateful to the author for the loan of his copy.

henceforth accorded to the strength of the exchange rate (cf. *Die Reichsbank*, 1929: 137–43). The restriction remained in force till the end of 1925, by which time the alternative of cheaper foreign refinancing had made it redundant.

In this account of German stabilization, as in most others, the actual introduction of a new 'gold' currency—the reichsmark—in autumn 1924 appears only as a kind of appendix (Hardach, 1976: 51). What is central to the British story—the restoration of gold convertibility—is only an epilogue in the German.

5. The Goal of Monetary Policy 1924/1925–1931

(Question 3) . . . The principal duty of the Central Bank is to maintain in the general interest of the community the stability of the national monetary unit . . . Now in a gold standard world, [this] means, I take it, the maintenance of its stability in relation to gold as the common international denominator.

(Question 7512) . . . I should say at this stage that we regard the Bank Rate as our principal weapon for carrying that policy into effect . . . Now, what are the guides which prompt the Bank to make use of the weapon of Bank Rate? I should say they were the state of the Bank's reserves, the condition of the money market . . . and, thirdly, the position and trend of the foreign exchanges. (*Macmillan*, 1931*b*).

I should now state the criteria for fixing the level of the discount rate, i.e. the rate of interest at which the Reichsbank supplies money . . . The first criterion is of course the relation of the reserves to the note issue, that is, the legal requirement laid on the

TABLE 5.2. Reichsbank holdings of gold and foreign exchange, 1924–1931 (deseasonalized) (RM. million)

Bimonthly average	1924	1925	1926	1927	1928	1929	1930	1931
Jan.–Feb.	590	2,025	2,160	2,446	2,221	2,727	2,599	2,336
Feb.–Mar.	611	2,047	2,337	2,254	2,260	2,680	2,727	2,361
Mar.–Apr.	663	1,973	2,441	2,229	2,361	2,496	2,865	2,462
Apr.–May	767	1,912	2,384	2,128	2,489	2,131	2,927	2,546
May–June	1,063	1,878	2,376	2,091	2,705	2,149	3,060	2,348
June–July	1,338	1,773	2,378	2,071	2,818	2,409	3,101	1,875
July–Aug.	1,497	1,658	2,426	2,027	2,865	2,548	3,040	
Aug.–Sep.	1,526	1,613	2,504	2,192	2,916	2,584	3,010	
Sep.–Oct.	1,408	1,628	2,627	2,224	3,018	2,619	2,706	
Oct.–Nov.	1,487	1,713	2,640	2,327	3,053	2,583	2,503	
Nov.–Dec.	1,785	1,844	2,517	2,165	3,017	2,496	2,532	
Dec.–Jan.	1,943	1,994	2,579	2,148	2,880	2,501	2,452	

Source: Calculated from G. Hardach (n.d., 248).

Reichsbank to hold a stated proportion of gold and foreign-exchange cover. A further, important criterion is the state of the exchange rates, which measure the value of the German currency against other currencies. (*Die Reichsbank*, 1929: 145)

The first two paragraphs above are replies given in later 1929 and 1930 by Sir Ernest Harvey, deputy governor of the Bank of England; the third was a reply given in 1926 by Hjalmar Schacht, president of the Reichsbank, to the Money and Credit Committee of the Commission of Investigation of the German Economy. Moggridge's gloss on Harvey applies equally to Schacht: 'Throughout the period after 1925 the Bank [of England] recognized its primary duty as being the maintenance of the international exchange value of the pound' (Moggridge, 1972: 145; cf. Sayers, 1976: i. 71; and Abramowski, 1988: 594).

If this was so for both central banks, then it follows that both had to abandon their objective in 1931, when Britain suspended gold payments and Germany instituted exchange controls. The main purpose of the following sections is to ascertain why they failed. Three possible reasons may be distinguished:

1. The policy tools at the central banks' command may have been inherently ineffectual in this period.
2. The policy-makers' use of the tools at their command may have been defective.
3. The policy goals of the monetary authorities may have been unclear, because the above apparently clear statements of these were obscured by other actions.

Any or all of these may have contributed to the policy failures of 1931. I shall now consider each in turn.

5. Effectiveness of Policy Tools, 1924/5–1931

In both countries discount rate was the principal policy tool of the central bank. In investigating the power of this tool to maintain the exchange rate, one must not get confused by the parallel question of its power over domestic credit conditions. In particular, if a single 'world interest rate' (equal to the New York market rate in this period perhaps) dominates a country's (e.g. Germany's) domestic money market, then the central bank will have asymmetric powers over domestic credit conditions: by underbidding the world rate it will be able (though only temporarily) to ease them, but it will not be able to make credit dearer than the world-market rate. The condition for this state of affairs is that money balances are perfectly elastic across the exchanges with respect to the interest-rate differential between the home-market rate and world-market rate. However this condition *implies* perfect confidence in exchange-rate stability, certainly for the period of the loan transaction; and this confidence would rest, *inter alia*, on confidence in the intention and power of the central bank to maintain the exchange rate. Thus the impotence of the discount rate to tighten domestic credit may be testimony to its perceived power over the exchanges.

Under less extreme assumptions, the imperfect elasticity of money balances across the exchanges will, given supply and demand for them, create an equilibrium interest-rate differential at which there is no net flow of such balances.

The application of this theory also depends on the relative sizes of the two money markets, under all conditions of less-than-perfect elasticity of money balances with respect to interest-rate differentials. In the British case we might *a priori* expect bank rate to have greater power over the domestic credit conditions than Reichsbank discount rate had over German, because the volume of funds employed on the London money market was so much larger, relative to that employed on the American, than in the German case (Hawtrey, 1932: 250). Thus, granted less than perfect elasticity of money balances, the attraction of US funds to London in sufficient quantity to reduce London rates would tighten New York rates, and the process of mutual accommodation would give the Bank of England its power to tighten domestic credit.

On the basis of this theory, we can conclude in respect of Germany that, from early 1925 at the latest until March 1929, Reichsbank discount-rate policy could control the exchange rate and the flow of balances across the exchanges. But thereafter it lost control on three occasions: April–May

1929, September–October 1930, and finally after May 1931, with fatal consequences for convertibility.

The first period (early 1925–March 1929) can itself be divided into two. Up to January 1927 the effect of a high Reichsbank discount rate was that money balances flooded into the country, powerfully reinforced by large-scale bond flotation in the USA. This, together with the effect of the 1925–6 slump in reducing the demand for transactions balances, progressively eroded the short interest differential between the two countries to a minimum of less than 1 per cent in autumn 1926, at which level the Reichsbank's deseasonalized foreign reserves were approximately constant. See Tables 5.2, 5.3, and 5.4.

In such circumstances, the Reichsbank could not conduct an independent monetary policy (Hardach, 1974; cf. *Die Reichsbank*, 1929: 203; Lansburgh, 1928: 205). The Reichsbank had scant alternative means of enforcing its discount rate. Its own stock of securities was small, particularly on account of the severe restrictions on its holdings of government paper; but its subsidiary, the Golddiskontbank, did issue promissory notes to RM100m. as a form of open market sales (Abramowski, 1988: 595). The Reichsbank believed that its loss of market control was largely caused by the independent short-term deployment of public-sector surpluses (generated variously by the budgetary reforms of 1924, by foreign flotation of public bonds, and by the fragmented cash-management by public bodies). The Bank campaigned (with some success) to gain control of the deposit of these public balances (Abramowski, 1988: 1243–4). However, seeing that the loss of control was as much caused by large foreign deposits with German banks

TABLE 5.3. *Reichsbank international reserves as a proportion of the note issue, 1924–1931 (%)*

	1924	1925	1926	1927	1928	1929	1930	1931
Jan.		123.9	86.5	85.2	58.4	68.6	61.8	60.8
Feb.		118.0	93.8	75.9	60.5	67.7	64.3	60.6
Mar.		104.5	91.5	71.0	58.5	63.1	65.6	61.2
Apr.		89.0	84.0	64.7	58.7	54.1	65.8	61.3
May		75.6	81.4	58.3	60.9	44.2	66.7	63.8
June		71.3	80.8	54.6	62.8	48.8	69.4	47.0
July		66.3	80.4	54.1	63.5	54.4	66.7	57.9
Aug.		63.5	79.9	56.8	65.5	55.6	68.1	39.6
Sept.		60.9	82.2	56.4	65.0	55.6	65.2	38.2
Oct.	82.2	62.1	85.8	55.6	58.6	57.2	55.7	28.7
Nov.	104.1	70.9	85.9	59.2	60.4	58.2	61.3	26.8
Dec.	115.9	77.6	81.7	55.6	71.5	56.3	61.6	25.2
Annual ave	100.7	82.0	84.5	62.3	62.0	57.0	64.4	47.6

[a] Gold and eligible foreign-exchange balances.

Source: G. Hardach (n.d.: 250).

TABLE 5.4. *The differential between the market discount rate on prime bills in Berlin and New York, 1925–1932 (%)*

	1925	1926	1927	1928	1929	1930	1931	1932
Jan.	5.31	2.64	0.51	2.89	1.05	2.39	3.19	4.06
Feb.	4.95	1.83	0.54	2.70	0.68	1.73	3.44	3.86
Mar.	4.75	1.37	0.96	3.22	0.93	1.99	3.26	3.59
Apr.	4.81	1.48	0.99	2.95	1.13	1.52	3.15	3.63
May	4.78	1.50	1.27	2.66	1.99	1.39	3.65	3.87
June	4.50	1.27	1.76	2.56	2.00	1.45	5.21	3.87
July	4.63	1.16	2.34	2.49	2.27	1.52	(7.72)	3.83
Aug.	4.43	1.05	2.70	2.06	2.05	1.36	(10.82)	3.75
Sept.	3.68	1.00	2.77	2.15	2.05	1.42	7.06	3.50
Oct.	3.59	0.96	3.50	2.08	2.15	3.08	5.75	3.21
Nov.	3.28	0.82	3.51	1.78	2.70	2.91	4.94	3.38
Dec.	3.25	0.92	3.68	1.85	3.10	2.95	4.32	3.50

Sources: Balderston (1993: 147).

TABLE 5.5. *The reichsmark–dollar exchange rate (New York quotations), 1924–1932 (cents per mark/reichsmark)*

	1924	1925	1926	1927	1928	1929	1930	1931	1932
Jan.	22.6[a]	23.80	23.80	23.72	23.83	23.77	23.88	23.77	23.65
Feb.	21.8[a]	23.80	23.81	23.70	23.86	23.73	23.87	23.77	23.74
Mar.	22.0[a]	23.80	23.80	23.71	23.90	23.72	23.86	23.81	23.78
Apr.	22.0[a]	23.80	23.80	23.70	23.91	23.70	23.87	23.81	23.74
May	22.8[a]	23.80	23.80	23.69	23.93	23.76	23.86	23.80	23.79
June	23.4[a]	23.80	23.81	23.69	23.90	23.84	23.85	23.73	23.69
July	23.9[a]	23.80	23.80	23.74	23.86	23.83	23.87	23.28	23.92
Aug.	23.8[a]	23.80	23.81	23.79	23.83	23.81	23.89	23.66	23.78
Sept.	23.8[a]	23.80	23.81	23.80	23.83	23.81	23.82	23.42	23.78
Oct.	23.8[a]	23.80	23.80	23.86	23.81	23.87	23.81	23.24	23.77
Nov.	23.80	23.81	23.75	23.86	23.82	23.92	23.83	23.68	23.75
Dec.	23.80	23.81	23.80	23.89	23.83	23.94	23.84	23.79	23.79

[a] Paper 'billmarks'

Source: *Banking and Monetary Statistics* (1943: 671).

(Balderston, 1991: 568–70), even had Schacht's campaign succeeded (or had he been able to conduct effective open-market policy) he could not have prevented the dominant influence of the US rate of interest on the German money market in this period. In this period the conditions more or less conformed to the 'perfect elasticity' model outlined above.

On 11 January 1927 the Reichsbank reduced its discount rate to 5 per cent—its minimum for the 1924–32 period—thereby reducing the market differential against New York to 0.5 per cent. This was evidently less than the equilibrium differential (as Schacht himself stated, Abramowski, 1988:

TABLE 5.6.   Changes in Reichsbank discount rate, 1924–1932

Date		New rate (%)	Date		New rate (%)	Date		New rate (%)
(1924)[a]		(10)	(1928)[a]		(7)	1931	13.5	7
							16.7	10
1925	26.2	9	1929	12.1	6.5		1.8	15
				25.4	7.5		12.8	10
1926	12.1	8		2.11	7		2.9	8
	27.3	7					10.12	7
	7.5	6.5	1930	14.1	6.5			
	6.6	6		5.2	6	1932	9.3	6
				8.3	5.5		9.4	5.5
1927	11.1	5		25.3	5		28.4	5
	10.6	6		20.4	4.5		22.9	4
	4.10	7		21.5	4			
				9.10	5			

[a] The rate shown obtained throughout the year.

Source: Konjunktur–Statistisches Handbuch (1936: 109).

595), for the exchange rate dropped below parity and the Reichsbank's reserves ebbed rapidly (see Tables 5.2–5.5). However, by the time the Reichsbank raised its rate again to 6 per cent on 10 June, the equilibrium differential had evidently risen too, for the reserve position scarcely improved and the exchange rate not at all (Abramowski, 1988: 1238). Nevertheless, money balances were still responsive to changes in the interest differential: a further hike of the official discount rate to 7 per cent on 4 October (assisted by the famous FRBNY cut of August 1927) seemed to do the trick; and at the expense of a 3.5 per cent market differential (not paralleled again until 1931) the exchange rate strengthened rapidly, and the reserves slowly. Two per cent seems to have been an equilibrium differential in later 1928, to judge by reserves and exchange rate; and when the Reichsbank shaded its rate by 0.5 per cent on 12 January 1929, the resultant reduction of the market differential caused the exchanges to weaken and reserves to fall (Vogt, 1970: 418–19).

This analysis seems to confirm that in this period German discount policy could 'turn the exchanges'. But such discount-rate policy had different implications for domestic credit in the two halves of the period. Between early 1925 and January 1927 it had next to no effect. Out of this the Money and Credit Committee of the Commission of Investigation inferred the powerlessness of discount-rate policy to influence domestic credit conditions, and saw verified the dominant pre-war theory, that the official discount could do no more than 'confirm' (konstatieren) the market rate (Die Reichsbank, 1929: 63–7). However after the middle of 1927 the postulate of perfect elasticity of response to market interest-rate differentials was no longer satisfied, and the protection of the exchange rate entailed dearer domestic credit (see Table 5.4).

Beginning in April 1929, three episodes of panic flight from the mark revealed that the discount-rate policy could no longer be counted on to 'turn the exchanges' (see Table 5.2). The first began because of the near-breakdown of the Reparations Conference in Paris (James, 1986: 77–9), and was ended, not by the discount-rate rise to 7.5 per cent on 25 April, nor by the credit restriction imposed about the same time (*Der Bankkredit*, 1930: 145–6), but because Schacht compromised on the reparations schedule, thus saving the reparations consensus. The second period of flight started in August 1930, seemingly as reaction to the July fiscal crisis, but greatly accelerated when the implications of the Reichstag elections of 14 September 1930 sank in, and ended not when the discount rate was raised on 9 October, but (I suppose) once it became clear that the Brüning government and its policies had survived. The third episode was the banking crisis: and it could be mended neither by discount policy nor credit restriction; instead, disequilibrium across the exchanges was institutionalized by exchange controls and standstill agreements.

Discount-rate policy in Germany was supplemented by use of a variety of other forms of intervention in the foreign exchange and capital markets. These were mainly used to modify the undesired tendency of a high discount-rate policy to stimulate the influx of capital. Thus, as we shall see, the Reichsbank used these supplementary tools partly to offset the international repercussions of a vigorous discount-rate policy, but not to spare the domestic economy; whereas the Bank of England used them to strengthen the international effects of a timorous bank rate policy and to soften its domestic impact.

First, intervention in the foreign exchange and gold markets. Until August 1926 the Reichsbank had intervened continuously to maintain a steady rate of 4.20. But in August 1926 the Bank suspended its intervention, permitting the risk of exchange-rate movements between the gold points, and thus reducing the attractiveness of the German money market without cutting the discount rate (a fixed dollar exchange-rate had made it too cheap for German banks to finance their end-of-month cash requirements abroad) (*Die Reichsbank*, 1929: 76; Abramowski, 1988: 579). However the effect on the inflow of short capital was imperceptible. In October 1927, simultaneously with raising its discount rate to 7 per cent, the Reichsbank reduced its buying price of gold from RM 2,790 to RM 2,784 per kilogram, thus effectively raising the gold import point (*Die Reichsbank*, 1929: 77–8; cf. Abramowski, 1988: 1245). The Bank steadfastly refused to intervene on the forward market, on the argument that by reducing its variability it would encourage speculation (*Der Bankkredit*, 1930: 87–8; cf. Bank of England Archive, OV34/81, Documents 99C, 100, 101C).

More importantly and notoriously the Bank, and particularly its President, consistently aimed to control the influx of long-term capital (McNeil, 1986). It was a prominent advocate of the establishment in December 1924 of the Advisory Board for Foreign Credits (*Beratungsstelle für Auslandskredite*), a committee of the Reich, states, and the Reichsbank designed to vet local authorities' plans for foreign-bond flotation, to which the states also voluntarily submitted their foreign loan plans. (Private foreign issuing was uncontrolled on the argument that the discipline of profit-seeking automatically ensured its justifiability.) Initially Schacht was in favour of foreign borrowing thus controlled. But by 1926 he had come to want more general restriction. He was therefore instrumental in persuading the government to suspend, in December 1926, the exemption from German capital yield tax, which had normally been accorded to foreign loans up to that date (Abramowski, 1988: 594). This action seems to have been responsible for a virtual cessation of German flotations in New York in the first half of 1927—a period of unusual strength in the New York bond market (see Table 5.10). But later in 1926 Schacht also thought that foreign investment in German equities (common stocks) was excessive, both from the standpoint of exchange-rate stability and of the health of the equities market. He also blamed the equity speculation partly on excessive lending by the commercial banks. Having tried for some months by simple 'moral suasion' to persuade the banks to cut stockmarket lending, (Abramowski, 1988: 588–90) on 11 May 1927 Schacht at length added the threat of credit restriction (of which, more below). The result was 'black Friday' on the Berlin stock exchange on 13 May when, following a banks' communiqué announcing cuts in their stock-market lending, share prices and turnover collapsed. (Abramowski, 1988: i. 893; ii. 1237–8; Benning, 1929; *Die Reichsbank*, 1929: 190–209).

The weakness of the mark following the stock-market collapse, (Table 5.5), which persisted despite the increase of Reichsbank discount rate to 6 per cent on 6 June, prompted a partial reintroduction of tax exemptions on foreign loans. Schacht now turned to two other means of controlling foreign-bond issuing. He sought to strengthen the Reichsbank's control over the Advisory Board's decisions (Abramowski (1988); i. documents 260, 286, 301, 310, 312, and esp. 313). And he launched into a noisy public criticism of 'profligate' local-authority spending. In this he found himself in paradoxical alliance with the Agent-General for Reparations (McNeil, 1986: 165–91; cf. Weber, 1927). In 1928, however, Schacht's campaign ran up against the dictates of electioneering: with Reichstag elections looming, the government, which had hitherto sat on the sidelines of the battle between Schacht and the local authorities, sanctioned the foreign issuing of part of the backlog of municipal bonds.

In 1929, when the Wall Street boom had brought German foreign-bond flotation to a halt, he turned his attention to the Reich's efforts to ease its acute cash problems by borrowing from a US–German bank consortium. His opposition to this, unsuccessful in May, managed to prevent a second foreign credit in December, and to force on the government a fiscal reform which torpedoed the programme of tax cuts devised as recently as September to meet the bitter and rising attacks on income and property taxes by business and the wealthy (Balderston, 1993: 275–85; Maurer, 1973: 80–107).

It is debatable whether the actions of the Advisory Board for Foreign Credits reduced the aggregate supply of German foreign debt by very much; and they may have even enhanced the demand for the loans it sanctioned. But the Schacht–Gilbert propaganda campaign against municipal debt probably weakened the foreign demand for it, to judge by the fact that from autumn 1927 German bond prices on New York fell relative to US bond prices, revealing that the decline of German issuing there cannot be wholly blamed on the 'Wall Street boom' (see Table 5.10; cf. McNeil, 1986: 176 ff).

I have left till last the most important of Schacht's policy innovations—credit restriction, which was resorted to on three occasions—April 1924, May 1929, and June–July 1931—and threatened on one other, May 1927 (cf. James, 1985b). On the three occasions when it was actually used, this was because of doubts regarding the efficacy of discount policy. A further object was to force commercial banks and others to sell their own stocks of foreign exchange (believed to be plentiful) thus reducing the pressure on the Reichsbank's. It was a rough measure which did not spare the discounters whose bills were now refused, and in all cases of actual use it may also have been designed to increase the clarity with which the Reichsbank's 'monetary regime' was signalled to the markets. But it presupposed a strong financial system, otherwise the very attempt to strengthen the reichsmark by signalling the Reichsbank's commitment to the parity could weaken it by aggravating doubts about the solvency of German financial institutions. This makes the more puzzling its use on 22 June and 10 July 1931. In fact this measure was forced on the Reichsbank by foreign central banks as a condition for a central bank credit (James, 1986: 304–7): foreign central bankers were seemingly unaware of the weakness of German commercial banks, believed they and other Germans still had plentiful foreign reserves of their own, and thought that at all costs the Reichsbank must seek to maintain its reserve ratio (see Balderston 1994).

On the occasion when it was threatened but not used (May 1927) its object, as already stated, was rather different: to force the banks to act to break a stock-market boom and thus to deter the influx of speculative balances from abroad.

This section has argued that Reichsbank was capable of defending the parity between late 1924 and the spring of 1929. This argument is at odds with the prevalent view which would regard the apparent efficacy of

Reichsbank discount policy as illusory, or at most an epiphenomenon, riding upon the forces beyond German control which were propelling foreign capital into Germany up to 1927, and sucking it out thereafter.

This flow and ebb of foreign balances could be explained by a simple theory of portfolio adjustment. The argument would be, that US portfolios, empty of German debt in 1924, were beginning to reach equilibrium holdings of it by early 1927, and could be persuaded to take more only if offered differentially more attractive returns. And still later, knowledge of Germany's large overhang of foreign short debt necessarily created fears of exchange-rate risk which inevitably rendered discount-rate policy ineffectual. A major difficulty with this theory is that the German balance of payments was adjusting rapidly and strongly in a stabilizing direction after 1928: the current account balance was becoming highly active, and German exports continued to perform more strongly than American and British exports (Hoffmann, 1965: 818–19; Balderston, 1993: 99–128): it is therefore not clear what simple balance of payments considerations could have caused money-balance holders to fear increasingly for the stability of the exchange rate. It is more common to argue, of course, that in the later 1920s the portfolio preferences of American investors changed. Their brief flirtation with cosmopolitanism in the middle of the decade turned into introversionist speculation in US equities towards its end (Kindleberger, 1974: 72–6).

The main immediate reason why the Wall Street boom affected the rest of the world so badly was that the rest of the world mainly sold fixed-interest securities on Wall Street and these including US bonds, did badly during the equity speculation. What is puzzling, however, is why the US equity speculation did not spill over into demand for German equity. This was not just some 'structural feature' of US investment preferences. For as stated above, between mid-1926 and mid-1927 US interest in German equities had reportedly been strong. If this interest had revived in 1929, the history of the inter-war world economy might have been very different. Seeing that in Germany the 'new industries', whose stocks were the focus of the Wall Street speculation, were also performing strongly, and that German markets were largely the still-prosperous lands of Europe, it is all the more puzzling that the German equity index was actually falling in 1929, whereas in Britain it was at least rising weakly (*Konjunktur-Statistisches Handbuch*, 1936: 115; Capie and Collins, 1983: 113–15). The provisional conclusion must be that American investors' aversion from Germany at the end of the 1920s was at least in part caused by events in Germany.

One reason for US failure to buy German equities may have been infection with the deep if scarcely explicable mood of pessimism which began to sweep across German enterprise in 1929 (Balderston, 1993: 382–3); and German central banking policy could do little about this. However, it is also very likely that the Reichsbank intervention of May 1927 to break the stock-market boom had long-term consequences: neither foreign nor domestic interest in German equities was likely to revive as long as Schacht was thought likely to repeat his actions against 'speculation'.

The argument, then, that the Reichsbank was not able to control the parity depends on the belief that the outflow of foreign capital from 1927–8 was determined by events outside German policy control. But I have shown the grounds for believing that German policy did have quite a part in repelling it.

So much for the changing efficacy of monetary policy in regard to the German exchange rate. As regards Britain, William Adams Brown began his account of the defence of sterling between 1925 and 1931 with a section on 'the weakening of Great Britain's basic pull over the exchanges' (Brown, 1940: i. 603–15)—a theme in fact also dominating subsequent sections of his long analysis. The argument has much *a priori* plausibility. Precisely sterling's 'key currency' status exposed it to the effects of changing portfolio choice, as between gold and foreign reserves, of other central banks, such as the French and, he alleges, the German. The structure of Britain's external balance, too, had changed, as 'lending long' had to be balanced, to a greater extent than pre-war, by 'borrowing short'. Narrower, technical changes in the discount market may also have worked to reduce the power of discount rate to 'turn the exchanges'. In this connection Brown emphasizes the decline in the supply of good trade bills, the substitution of the forward exchange market for the finance bill as the means of controlling exchange risk, and the rise of the Treasury bill, whose supply is insensitive to market discount-rate. The deteriorating balances of payments of the 'outer sterling area' countries are often also cited as having weakened the stability of sterling (Cairncross and Eichengreen, 1983: 47 ff., 50).

In this period the Bank of England supplemented discount-rate policy by a variety of other operations designed to strengthen the exchanges (Moggridge, 1972: 159–227; Sayers, 1976: i. 297–313). Norman sought to ease pressure on sterling by appealing to Moreau, Schacht, and Strong when their markets were drawing gold from London; and his more general attempts to persuade foreign central bankers to substitute reserve currencies for gold may *inter alia* have served the same object. The Bank intervened on the spot and forward foreign exchange markets in support of sterling. In summer 1929, it raised its gold-buying price in order to attract gold without raising bank rate, and in 1930 delivered gold bars of reduced fineness thus lowering the gold export point (Sayers, 1957: 74; Cairncross and Eichengreen, 1983: 58). (In both cases the object was the opposite of the Reichsbank's use of 'gold devices' in October 1927.) More significant than these palliatives were attempts to control the capital balance with abroad by informal pressure on the issue of new foreign long-term stocks. This policy was applied only sporadically. If pursued systematically it would have

antagonized the issuing houses and conflicted with the imperial and diplomatic interests of the government; and the Bank lacked the means, in the
long-term capital market, to give 'bite' to its 'suasion'. The bank also used
open-market operations to make its discount rate effective, especially after
the fusion of the 'currency' and 'bank' note issues in 1928 enlarged its stock
of Treasury bills.

It has been commonplace, too, to argue that monetary policy exercised
not only a weaker 'power over the exchanges', but also over domestic prices
and costs; and thus weakened the exchange rate in the long run. The poor
performance of British exports, and weakening of her external current
account—both in marked contrast to contemporaneous German developments—may be advanced in support of this argument. To the extent that
the long-term interest-rate governed domestic investment and stood in no
simple relation to the short (Howson, 1975: 47–51, 167–72), bank-rate policy
may have been powerless to deflate costs.

TABLE 5.7. *Gold and foreign-exchange reserves of the Bank of England,* 1925–1931
(end of first week of each month) (£ million).

	1925	1926	1927	1928	1929	1930	1931
Jan.		148	171	195	171	166	171
Feb.		150	172	198	168	168	166
Mar.		154	174	202	169	168	172
Apr.		155	178	201	172	170	173
May		156	180	204	177	178	179
June		158	181	207	185	172	183
July		161	183	216	178	178	193
Aug.		166	181	212	165	178	146
Sept.		171	181	212	163	178	148
Oct.	161	170	188	202	153	181	147
Nov.	153	170	190	193	154	185	135
Dec.	149	171	192	181	154	180	

Source: R. S. Sayers (1976: iii. 349 ff).

In particular, it has been argued that the weakening British balance of
payments in 1930–1 made the parity unsustainable (Moggridge, 1972:
110–16, 127–9). Markets will, however, not refuse to finance temporarily a
deficit which they perceive as cyclical, so this argument must further specify
why some bank rate would not have attracted such financing. One reason
could be that the markets attributed the widening trade deficit to a
permanent deterioration of British competitiveness. Another could be that
they attributed it to failure of the multilateral payments system on which
the British balance of payments depended: the diminishing surpluses of
Britain's export markets with Europe and the USA. In any case,

Eichengreen showed the limits of this line of explanation (Cairncross and Eichengreen, 1983: 72–83).

TABLE 5.8.   *Bank of England bank-rate changes* 1919–1932 (%)

1919			1924			1930		
before	6 Nov.	5	All Year	4		6 Feb.	4.5	
	6 Nov.	6				6 Mar.	4	
1920			1925			20 Mar.	3.5	
	15 Apr.	7	5 Mar.	5		1 May	3	
			6 Aug.	4.5				
			1 Oct.	4		1931		
1921			3 Dec.	5		14 May	2.5	
	29 Apr.	6.5	1926			23 July	3.5	
	23 June	6	All Year	5		30 July	4.5	
	21 July	5.5				21 Sept.	6	
	3 Nov.	5	1927					
			21 Apr.	4.5		1932		
1922						18 Feb.	5	
	17 Feb.	4.5	1928			10 Mar.	4	
	21 Apr.	4	All Year	4.5		17 Mar.	3.5	
	15 June	3.5				21 Apr.	3	
	13 July	3	1929			12 May	2.5	
			7 Feb.	5.5		30 June	2	
1923			26 Sept.	6.5				
	5 July	4	31 Oct.	6				
			21 Nov.	5.5				
			12 Dec.	5				

Source: W. Adams Brown (1940: i. 713).

It will be argued in this chapter that these familiar theses about the declining efficacy of bank rate may have much truth, but that they are not proven, because in fact bank-rate policy was not pursued with the resoluteness needed to test its inherent efficacy. Certainly the thesis of 'weakening pull over the exchanges' cannot tell the whole story. A cursory glance at movements of bank rate, the market discount differential against New York, the dollar exchange-rate, and the Bank of England's reserves (see Tables 5.7–5.9) seems clearly to reveal that when bank rate was reduced to 4 per cent on 1 October 1925, thus reducing the market differential against New York to less than 0.25 per cent, reserves were rapidly lost, compelling the raising again of bank rate on 3 December 1925, which rapidly reversed the exchange losses. The widening of the differential created by the FRBNY discount-rate cut of August 1927 was followed by a substantial strengthening of the dollar rate of sterling and of the bank's foreign currency reserves. The substantial drop in bank reserves from the middle of 1928, and simultaneous weakening of the dollar exchange-rate seem to show a clear connection with the reversal of the market differential against New York during those months, and also with the large negative differential against Germany, the reduction of which, through the German discount-rate cut of 12 January 1929 may explain the stabilization of Bank of England reserves in that month, despite a continued reverse differential against New York.

TABLE 5.9. *The differential between market rates of discount in London and New York, 1925–1932 (monthly average; + = London > New York)*

	1925	1926	1927	1928	1929	1930	1931	1932
Jan.	0.86	1.18	0.51	0.83	− 0.41	0.17	0.72	2.60
Feb.	0.83	0.72	0.55	0.72	− 0.04	0.04	1.16	1.87
Mar.	1.27	0.79	0.75	0.64	− 0.04	− 0.34	1.13	0.19
Apr.	1.15	0.98	0.46	0.31	− 0.23	− 0.46	1.09	0.70
May	1.43	1.25	0.32	0.01	− 0.27	− 0.31	1.26	0.50
June	1.23	1.03	0.75	− 0.23	− 0.16	0.20	1.22	0.17
July	1.15	0.92	0.82	− 0.24	0.26	0.50	1.72	0.18
Aug.	0.74	0.93	1.24	− 0.32	0.44	0.34	3.44	0.03
Sept.	0.23	0.70	1.24	− 0.25	0.48	0.21	3.94	− 0.16
Oct.	0.13	0.83	1.17	− 0.16	1.01	0.22	3.53	0.25
Nov.	0.46	0.95	1.13	− 0.12	1.10	0.31	2.85	0.43
Dec.	1.23	0.77	1.11	− 0.14	0.90	0.45	2.96	0.71

Note: UK: three-month bankers' bills; US: prime bankers' acceptances, 90 days.

Sources: Brown (1943: i. 713); *Banking and Monetary Statistics* (1943: 450–1).

Yet even in this period, when bank rate had an obvious 'pull over the exchanges', it was not used to signal clearly to the markets that defence of the parity was the overriding objective. In 109 of the 197 weeks between 1 June 1925 and 31 March 1929, that is, the period when the discount rate did demonstrate 'pull over the exchanges', the pound rate was below $4.86 (Brown, 1940: 719; cf. Cairncross and Eichengreen, 1983: 37).

From 1929 the simple relations traced out in earlier years were not so evident. The strengthening of the reserves in April and May, despite the rise of US market rates in relation to London, may merely reflect seasonal factors, or it may represent the backwash of the contemporaneous reparations crisis. The weakening of reserves between June and October 1929 and their recovery thereafter, which stand in no clear relation to the market differential against New York, presumably reflect the Wall Street boom and crash. And the weakening tendency of bank reserves from about November 1930, despite a rising differential against New York, seems further to point to a 'weakening pull of discount policy over the exchanges'—which could variously be connected with gold policy abroad (France, USA) or with reactions to the weakening of the British balance of payments on current account. But if judged by the strength of the parity, the Bank was scarcely less successful than in the 1925–9 period: sterling was below $4.86 in 65 of the 128 weeks between 1 April 1929 and 20 September 1931 (Brown, 1940: i 719).

These arguments brings us to the next class of possible causes of failure of exchange-rate policy in 1931—the defective use of policy instruments which, rightly used, would have been perfectly capable of defending the exchange rate.

7. Defective Use of Policy Tools 1924/5–1931

It is commonly said that, after the return to gold, Bank of England discount-rate policy was hobbled by sensitivity to its reaction on the burden of government debt service, and hence taxation policy; and on the state of trade. '[A]t a very early stage political considerations moved [Norman] towards ease in 1925' (Moggridge, 1972: 174–5; Sayers, 1957: 76–8). In 1927 Norman told Moreau that he could not raise bank rate for fear of the effects on industry (Clay, 1957: 230; cf. 293). Because of the political backlash, Norman usually waited for some event which could serve as public justi-fication for raising bank rate, rather than responding simply to evidence of sterling weakness (Moggridge, 1969: 36; Boyce, 1987: 135; Clay, 1957: 241); for example, in the summer of 1929, despite the haemorrhaging of reserves, he did not raise bank rate until the Hatry scandal provided 'cover' (Cairncross and Eichengreen, 1983: 39, 46, 49, 63). As a result bank rate changed far less frequently than pre-war, because the Bank feared to reduce rates lest political considerations obstruct a subsequently needed rise. It is questionable however whether the result of this immobilization was a bank rate which was on average excessively high from an exchange-rate point of view, given the evidence, cited above, that in more than half the weeks of the period the pound was below $4.86. 'The resulting rates were never high enough to effect adjustment or low enough to avoid criticism and the Bank ended up, in a sense, falling between two stools' (Moggridge, 1972: 165). The deference of bank rate to the state of trade was obvious to foreigners (Abramowski, 1988: 204). The argument that Norman sought to shield the home economy from over-high bank rates because he thought that the problem lay abroad rather than at home (Williamson, 1984: 112) will not explain the immobility of bank rate.

Thus in Britain the supplementary means of influencing the exchange rate were employed as substitutes for the partially immobilized discount rate, but they were not employed vigorously enough to make up for its inactivity. Given the *a priori* argument at the beginning of the section 'Effectiveness of policy tools', that the relative sizes of the British and American money markets gave the Bank of England power over domestic credit even when elasticity was quite high, I conclude that the authorities were unwilling, rather than unable, to tighten credit to the extent needed to bring the real economy into line with the gold-standard parity. In fact the bank counteracted the intrinsic effects of exchange-rate support on the monetary base by its policy of 'offsetting'. This was the policy of replacing foreign reserves sold in support of the exchanges by an equivalent purchase of sterling securities (*Macmillan*, 1931*b*: Q. 7596). This served to conceal the support action (both foreign reserves and sterling securities appeared in the bank's balance sheet under 'Other securities'), but it prevented the contraction of the monetary base which the sale of foreign exchange to sterling-balance holders would otherwise have caused. And to the extent that 'moral suasion' in the markets for both long- and short-term capital was also designed to ease the pressure on the real economy which would have effected the necessary adjustment of the current account to the exchange rate, or was seen as having this intention, it could only weaken confidence in the parity in the long run. In so far as the deterioration of the trade balance during the slump was attributed to domestic costs, then bank policy was partly responsible.

The Reichsbank's employment of its policy instruments was in striking contrast to the Bank of England's. This is true first of discount rate. Whereas the legal minimum proportionate cover of the note issue by gold and foreign reserves was 40 per cent (and had generally been 50 per cent pre-war (*Die Reichsbank*, 1929: 146), the annual average of this proportion slipped below 60 per cent in only one year between 1924 and 1930: 1929 (Table 5.3). It appears that a drop of the published ratio to 55 per cent was the signal for a prompt increase of Reichsbank discount rate in June and October 1927, April 1929, and October 1930. And on the other hand discount rate was not eased following the Wall Street crash until 2 November, until, that is, the ratio was well clear of the 55 per cent 'working minimum'. The long stability of the Bank's discount rate at 7 per cent between 4 October 1927 and 12 January 1929 does not betray special tenderness towards the home economy, but, if anything, the reverse.

In consequence of this energetic use of discount policy, the Reichsmark stood above its dollar parity, on average, during fifty-seven of the seventy-three months between May 1924 and May 1931 (Table 5.5). By this prompt reaction to reserve and exchange-rate change, the Reichsbank clearly signalled that the 'monetary regime' which it desired to pursue, was one which gave overriding priority to maintenance of the mark's value in a free foreign-exchange market.

It has been also sufficiently shown above, I think, that Schacht's capital-market policy was pursued with far greater resolution and energy than Norman's. Its principal limitation lay in the principles of the gold standard itself: more effective intervention would have entailed controls on the short-term borrowing which the impediments to long-term borrowing tended to increase. But to be effective, this would have entailed exchange controls (*Die Reichsbank*, 1929: 113).

8. Obscurity of 'Policy Regime'

It follows from the argument advanced in the last section that the Bank of England's actions were at some variance with its policy pronouncements, and this contradiction may well have caused the markets to doubt whether the bank really would defend the parity in a crisis. Underlying this irresolution was the relentless public criticism of the return to gold, of its effects on domestic credit conditions, and of the wage adjustments which it seemed to demand (cf. *Macmillan*, 1931*a*: 6–9). From later 1928 such criticism apparently intensified, and whereas the Labour Government taking office in May 1929 placed the conduct of economic policy in the unpliable, orthodox hands of Philip Snowden, sections of the Party and of the trade-union movement expressed vehement criticism of the gold standard and the commercial banks. To placate these Snowden established the Macmillan Committee on Finance and Industry, and his announcement of it at the party conference in October 1929 was at least partly designed to meet the outcry against the rise in bank rate at the end of September (Williamson, 1984: 114–15; Boyce, 1987: 280 ff.). Statements of intent in periods of calm may be quite orthodox; but no rational and informed sterling-balance holders had grounds for certainty, long before August 1931, that in a crisis, when hard choices must be made, a Labour Government would prioritize defence of the parity.

Criticism of credit policy was equally trenchant from the industrialists' side, as represented by the Federation of British Industries. Before return in 1925 they had sent the government a clear plea not to hasten the resumption of gold payments at the expense of burdening industry with adjustments; and in its later representations to the Macmillan Committee the FBI advocated a conjunction of the gold standard with price-level stability, through the medium of an international conference to organize world reflation. This being Utopian, it was clear that the FBI preferred price stability to the gold convertibility (*Macmillan* 1931*b*: Q. 3078 ff. and preceding statement). Thus there were divisions in the Conservative Party too.

Indeed, long before its Report was published with its revelation of the extent of British short indebtedness, the fact of the Macmillan Committee was a symbol of doubt about commitment to the parity in so far as it prioritized the better provision of domestic credit facilities. The tardy increase of bank rate in July (Cairncross and Eichengreen, 1983), was presumably interpreted in the light of six years' history of bank rate pusillanimity. Doubtless the budgetary prognoses of the May Report also weakened confidence in the pound. In Britain, as in Germany, the lack of a strict fiscal policy ever since 1925 may have unsettled the markets, and certainly aggravated the task of bank rate. But since not even the formation of a National Government and announcement of its economy programme saved the pound, and the landslide re-election of the National Government on 28 October 1931 merely ushered in a renewed sharp slide in sterling, it seems unlikely that the budget was the root cause of the failure of the gold standard in Britain; but rather, the bank's irresolution. Kunz believed it possible to infer that the bank was not 'forced' off the gold standard, but chose to sacrifice it rather than to eat into her gold stock or take further central bank credits (Kunz, 1987: 133–9).

In the German case, the goals of monetary policy were apparently stated and pursued with all clarity and determination. But this apparent clarity begins to cloud over when one considers Schacht's capital-market policies.

Had Schacht's sole concern been the (very reasonable) fear that excessive foreign borrowing endangers the long-run exchange stability of the borrowing country, it would have been rational to try to reduce only the supply of debt by German borrowers. To weaken the demand for it would merely advance the very exchange instability which it was hoped to avert. But his campaign also had a reparations angle. Whilst as a central banker Schacht doubted that the transfer of the 'Dawes' schedule of reparations annuities was consistent with long-run monetary stability, he also had nationalist policy goals regarding their abrogation. In his campaign against reparations, he was not merely indifferent to the means whereby foreign borrowing was reduced; he had an actual interest in alarming the lenders about the safety of their loans, because, if he could do this, he could perhaps mobilize them against reparations, whose transfer jeopardized the transferability of their debt charges. The hope that he could turn Germany's financial liabilities into her diplomatic assets was one reason behind his agreement to the 'Young' round of renewed reparations negotiations in Paris in the spring of 1929. And here his reparations objectives most starkly clashed with the objective of short-run exchange stability, when his brinksmanship as leader of the German delegation to the talks nearly broke up the conference and thus caused panic flights from the mark. In the end, the desire to maintain convertibility triumphed over the demand for reparations reductions: the flight from the mark, and the need not to lose the chance of foreign support for the currency, forced Schacht to compromise. None the less, the incident showed that Schacht had rising political goals which he was willing to pursue at some cost to the currency (ten Cate, 1988; Müller, 1972).

Schacht's campaign against municipal foreign borrowing was also partly actuated by his objections to the conduct of the public finances. The fiscal situation had clear parallels to the reparations issue: it also had an innate tendency to jeopardize monetary stability. The strong surplus with which the Reich appeared to emerge from fiscal year 1924–5 was actually something of a sham. It rested on the fact that the year's reparations annuity was entirely paid for out of the Dawes Loan. In future years larger annuities were scheduled, but no repetition of the loan. As a result the Reich never again had a true budget surplus, though for some years it could maintain the fiction of budgetary balance through progressive application to current deficits of the residue of the 1924–5 surplus. The Agent-General for Reparations exposed this sham in his Reports (Balderston, 1993: 231–50).

TABLE 5.10. *German foreign and US domestic bond prices* 1927–1929 (indexes of bond prices: Jan.–July 1927[a])

	German foreign			US municipal			US corporate[b]		
	1927	1928	1929	1927	1928	1929	1927	1928	1929
Jan.	99	98	97	99	103	96	100	103	100
Feb.	101	99	98	99	103	94	99	103	100
Mar.	100	99	97	100	103	92	100	103	99
Apr.	100	99	96	101	102	93	100	103	99
May	100	99	96	101	99	94	101	102	99
June	100	99	95	100	98	94	100	101	97
July	99	99	97	99	97	93	100	100	97
Aug.	99	98	96	100	96	93	101	100	97
Sept.	100	98	96	101	96	92	101	100	97
Oct.	100	98	95	102	96	93	102	100	97
Nov.	98	97	93	102	96	94	102	100	97
Dec.	98	98	95	102	96	95	103	100	99

[a] 1926 annual averages: German foreign: 95; US municipal: 98; US corporate: 98.
[b] i.e. Moody's 'Aaa'.

Sources: *Die Wirtschaftskurve*, 1927–1930; *Banking and Monetary Statistics* (1943: 469–70).

Given the history of the inflation, it would not have been surprising for Schacht to fear the effects of the fiscal tendencies on monetary stability. If the Bank's only objective had been monetary stability, then its best strategy would have been quiet attempts to persuade the authorities, without alarming the markets. Schacht *did* try private persuasion (e.g. Abramowski, 1988: 811) as had the pre-1922 Reichsbank and as Luther, too, would try. But Schacht supplemented it by a noisy public campaign which, as in the case of his reparations policy, aggravated the very consequences, as president of a central bank, he might have been thought most desirous of preventing. The fact that he acted thus, seems to indicate that he wanted to use money-market instability to force the Reich to retrench. (There are parallels with the Bank of England's policy towards the government in August 1931 (Kunz, 1987. 133–9).) It may be that in his eyes he was sacrificing short-term monetary peace for the longer-term security which budgetary control would promise. But most historians suspect that a deeper, more political opposition to parliamentary government already underlay his actions.

And thus we may conclude, as regards Reichsbank policy under Schacht, that whilst its two main branches—money-market policy and capital-market policy—were severally pursued with clarity and determination, the latter tended to call in question the stability of the 'policy regime' which the former sought to establish (see Lansburgh's view of Schacht: *Die Bank*, 1930: 401 ff., 426).

I have traced this contradictoriness of policy to the diversity of Schacht's monetary and political goals. But, at a deeper level, it was inherent in the dynamics of German political and diplomatic relations. For the contradictions grew worse, rather than better, once Schacht abruptly resigned in March 1930 and was replaced by Hans Luther. Luther collaborated closely with the incoming Brüning government, did not criticize fiscal policy publicly (and little in private either); nor did he conduct a reparations policy. But already by 1929 it no longer took an irascible Reichsbank president or officious Agent-General to point out the problems of public finance, for there was now an open fiscal crisis. This crisis was not caused (as in Britain in 1931) by publication of fiscal statistics, but by the painful problems of trying to finance the—fairly modest—deficits (cf. Vogt, 1970: ii. 1211).

In explaining the repercussions of the fiscal crisis on monetary stability, the size of the deficit matters less than its causes. The Reichstag had a long tradition of failure to assemble taxing coalitions before 1914, which neither the institution of parliamentary responsibility for the budget in the republic, nor the Erzberger fiscal reforms could eliminate: even the coalition parties often showed scant loyalty to their governments. And to these long-standing obstacles to budgetary control was now added the disruptive influence of reparations: an *ex post* analysis suggests that the revenues of the Reich in fact rose more or less to match rising home expenditures between 1924–5 and 1928–9, but not to match rising reparations liabilities. Moreover, revenues rose in this period largely because tax yields rose with economic recovery, not because tax rates rose: as the decade progressed the opposition of the business and propertied classes to the current rates of taxation reached near-hysterical proportions.

Markets will presumably tolerate deficits better if they believe that the government has the power to throw the levers of fiscal policy into reverse when need be. German fiscal history between 1924 and 1929 suggested that the government lacked this power. Historical fiscal and monetary analysis too often neglects the crucial distinction between a controlled budget deficit, and failure of fiscal control: Germany exemplified the second case. The exceptions proved the rule. The only two periods of fiscal deflation in Germany between *c.* 1905 and 1945 were the brief period of the turn of

1923–4 and the period from December 1929 to January 1933. In the first, and in most of the second, fiscal control was ensured by bypassing the Reichstag under emergency legislative procedures. And in both periods the parties consented—barely and uncertainly—to their own emasculation chiefly out of fear that the alternative was literal state bankruptcy.

A connection can perhaps be traced between the sharp but temporary widening of interest differentials against those abroad from summer 1927 and the Schacht–Gilbert criticisms of the Reich's finances from summer 1927 (though the cut in the Reichsbank's gold-buying price also played a part); and also between the renewed widening of interest differentials later in 1929 and the fiscal crisis (communes and Reich) of that period. Likewise a connection may be seen between the abrupt falls in bank deposits in August 1930 and the second rejection of Brüning's first emergency fiscal decree in July 1930, and also between the fall in bank deposits in June 1931, and the attempts in that month to frustrate the so-called Second Emergency Fiscal and Economic Decree. The failure of fiscal control threatened a double bind: if Reichsbank monetary policy remained resolute, it threatened public bankruptcy, with catastrophic consequences for the banking system; and if it relaxed, it indicated abandonment of the monetary regime on which mark stability had been founded. In atomized markets balance-holders have to guess the reactions of others to such a prospect, and take prudent precautions: and this can easily lead to an avalanche of destabilizing withdrawals, as happened in 1931.

Likewise with reparations. It is easy with hindsight to calculate the smallness—or even the absence (Schuker, 1988) of the true reparations burden; but taxation rests on a moral consensus between taxer and taxed, and when this is absent, small burdens have large fiscal and political consequences. The persistently high interest-rate differential of 1928 may reflect apprehension about the forthcoming 'Young' round of reparations negotiations. The panic withdrawals of September and October 1930 were not unconnected with the fears for German governability and hence fiscal control. But they were also precipitated by fears of a confrontational foreign and reparations policy. And one of the aggravations of the 1931 panic was Brüning's 'reparations' declaration' of 6 June.

Throughout the period 1924–31 mark stability was maintainable only within a triangle bounded on its three sides by (i) resolute monetary policy, (ii) fiscal discipline, and (iii) consensus with the Allies over reparations. If any one of these 'sides' was breached, mark stability was endangered. The establishment of these three sides had been essential to stabilization in 1923–4, as we have seen. The appearance of fiscal strength, and the 'spirit of Locarno' had conjoined with firmness of monetary policy in producing a strong mark in the mid-1920s. But the progressive breaching of (ii) and (iii), with the cumulative repercussions of this on the perceived solvency of the German commercial banks, was the reason for the failure of convertibility in 1931. In Britain departure from gold in 1931 represents the rational outworking in the long term of choices made by the authorities long before. In Germany the element of policy choice was very much more restricted: the irrationality of fiscal and reparations policy inherently contradicted the 'monetary regime'.

9. Some 'Might-have-beens'

Because the execution of policy did not clearly signal the monetary regime being followed, it cannot be proved that a gold-standard regime, clearly pursued, would have ended in the 1931 crisis, or even have caused the Great Depression. Though these may seem probable conclusions (Temin, 1989; Eichengreen, 1990*b*) they are not immediately relevant to the actual history. This section does not enter upon these global questions, but considers some limited counterfactuals.

1. Supposing that the markets had believed that the German government could exercise reliable fiscal control, and that reparations questions would be resolved amicably, Germany would not have had a financial crisis, or nearly such high interest rates between August 1931 and the end of 1932. This judgement is founded on the belief that the banking crisis was caused more by deposit instability than by the illiquidity or deterioration of bank assets (Balderston, 1994). The flaw in the 'counterfactual' is, however, that it must presuppose a wholly different political constellation, which would imply a different Germany; it is impossible to isolate 'pure' economic-policy aspects.

2. It is harder to judge the effects of a credible British monetary policy. These would depend on the elasticity of foreign short balances with respect to higher bank rate; and on the longer-term implications of a larger British short indebtedness to other countries; on the malleability of wages in both 'sheltered' and 'unsheltered' industries, given tighter credit conditions; and on the effect of a higher British bank rate and weaker British import demand on world commodity prices. It is not possible, therefore, to assert that more credible defence of the parity would have been better for Britain. However, a lower parity in 1925, resolutely defended, would doubtless have been a better option.

3. Should the Reichsmark have been devalued in 1931? (cf. Borchardt, 1991). Following the devaluation of sterling, the hitherto enormous German trading surplus with other countries shrank rapidly; and it may well be that doubts about the mark, despite exchange controls, played their part in the large and persistent market-interest differential against New York, whilst the London differential narrowed rapidly from January 1932. Thus, it may be argued that the decision to force through domestic price and cost deflation (in Brüning's notorious Fourth Emergency Fiscal Decree of

8 December 1931) as a conscious alternative to devaluation, was the main cause of the catastrophic unemployment in Germany in 1932, with serious economic repercussions throughout central Europe.

However, it is unlikely that even with devaluation Germany could have done without exchange controls. This is because whilst the banks' liquidity crisis had been resolved by the measures of summer 1931, their deeper solvency crisis was resolved only by reconstructions which were not completed until early 1932. Even with controls bank and savings-bank deposits continued to haemorrhage away for years after July 1931, and it is highly probable that without controls deposit-holders would have transferred their balances to safer banks abroad. (Devaluation would in any case have weakened the banks' assets relative to liabilities.) Not one of the 'respectable' proposals for credit expansion, which proliferated after the imposition of exchange controls, advocated devaluation (cf. Bombach 1976–81: vol. ii) Lastly, the apparent ease of sterling's abandonment of the gold standard probably owed a good deal to inelastic market expectations: in Germany, at any rate until about early November, the sterling suspension was thought likely to be temporary (cf. *Die Bank*, 1931: 1358, 1394, 1525, and especially 1539 ff.) and it seems plausible to connect the sharp fall of sterling in November and December 1931 with the extinction of that hope. Meanwhile, the initial inelasticity of hopes served to cushion sterling's landing: by the time they were extinguished, the market had some weeks of evidence that the floating pound could be controlled. This story should further caution us against too readily accepting the argument that had the mark been devalued and made freely convertible, its passage to a floating state would have been trouble-free.

Nor should we easily suppose that devaluation would have removed the impediments to internal credit and fiscal expansion. The reason why the government could impose its stern fiscal discipline on the Reichstag was the power of the threat that the alternative was State bankruptcy. This threat was never more powerful than in the winter of 1931–2 (Schäffer Diary: entries for 6, 9, 10, and 11 November 1931), and it rested, not least, on the fear, grounded in actual exchange-rate tendencies, of a severely adverse reaction of the foreign-exchange markets, even despite controls, to the appearance of fiscal indiscipline. Had the threat of this reaction been removed, rationally controlled reflation would not have been the outcome, but rather a budget out of cabinet control. In the circumstances, renewed panic flights from the mark would have been expected.

4. Were gold reserves an irrational 'fetish', so that gold shortage and maldistribution unnecessarily caused the world slump? The tendency of my argument is that what money-balance holders really looked for was evidence of the policy-makers' commitment to the parity, which adequate exchange reserves would have as well served to display as large gold stocks.

As far as holders of Reichsmarks were concerned, this certainly seems to have been what the policy-makers thought the market believed. They seem to have acted on this principle when they re-established the pre-war dollar parity as the central act of mark stabilization, and also in their continuous intervention in the foreign-exchange markets up to August 1926, to maintain the strict 4.20 relationship. And, as already stated, it is not without significance that most accounts treat the actual reintroduction of a 'gold' currency in early autumn 1924 as merely a kind of appendix to the tale of stabilization. The legal obligation upon the Reichsbank to pay gold for Reichsmarks remained in suspension until April 1930 (Northrop, 1938: 32): the bank merely acted upon a *de facto* commitment; and this, too, suggests that the relationship to gold was not viewed by the authorities as essential to a stable demand for marks. Thus, the Reichsbank Law's stipulations regarding gold cover were probably too restrictive from the point of view of the demand for Reichsmarks, which in itself might have been as content with a large dollar reserve as with a large gold reserve.

However there was another rationale to the demand for gold—that of the German authorities themselves. In the years 1924–31 Germany subscribed verbally to the idea of the 'gold-exchange standard'. However the *Realpolitik* of money limited their implementation of it. Whereas the Reichsbank Law permitted up to 25 per cent of the gold- and foreign-exchange cover of the note issue to be in foreign exchange, in fact gold never fell below 85 per cent of the reserves shown even in its internal tabulations (James, 1985a: 337 ff.; cf. Northrop, 1938: 32). W. A. Brown discerned two phases in the Reichsbank's reserves policy: a first co-operative phase, in which the Bank was more willing to accumulate foreign exchange, and a second, when it more actively bought gold (Brown, 1940: i. 486–9). These phases are hard to see in the reserve statistics (to which he did not have access). None the less it seems probable that once a renewed round of reparations negotiations seemed likely, the Reichsbank did start to accumulate reserves as a precaution, and by late 1928 was drawing gold from England (Bank of England Archives, G1/414; Schacht–Norman correspondence of 11 and 15 December 1928; cf. Vogt, 1970: 204–5).

This case indicates why the Reichsbank could hardly have done other than hold its reserves mainly in gold, even had the Reichsbank Law permitted otherwise. It would have been inconceivable for the bank to hold its reserves mainly as claims on the central banks or money markets of Germany's former adversaries. In times of diplomatic tension gold serves the conflicting nations as cash serves criminals: it is anonymous and beholden to no one. The Reichsbank was willing to temper its policy in the interests of central bank co-operativeness: its discount-rate reduction of 12 January 1929 seems to have been a response to Norman's complaints about British gold losses. (Vogt, 1970: 207, 418–19). But even without Reichsbank

Law diplomatic considerations would surely have placed narrow limits on this willingness.

Germany's diplomatic position was a special one, and would not explain the peculiar note-reserve stipulations which tied up so much gold in the Bank of England, or the peculiar restrictions on currency creation by the Bank of France which stimulated the French demand for gold (Eichengreen, 1990*a*). In the world at large, the 'scramble for gold' seems to have been an avoidable irrationality. But apparent irrationality often signals the historian's misunderstanding of the true concerns of the time; and maybe monetary history needs to look more closely at the rationale of the inter-war demand for gold.

5. Eichengreen (1992: 6–10, 98, 207 ff., 285–6) maintains that the credibility of the international gold standard rested very largely on the readiness of international co-operation, and this so much the more in the 1920s, after wartime and post-war disruptions had exacerbated the adjustments needed to bring the 'real' economies into harmony with the parities, and when domestic political changes had reduced the ability to force through these adjustments. How much could better central bank co-operation have achieved in 1931? It is clear that suspicions, mainly of the French regarding the Germans, then of the British regarding the French (who had every reason to support sterling) limited the actual co-operation. But the deeper reflection is, that, even in the absence of these impediments to co-operation, the degree of international monetary and banking uncertainty would have made the size of the credits needed to recreate confidence extremely large—incomparably larger than, for example, in 1907. The scale required would surely have necessitated a degree of intergovernmental co-operation unnecessary in 1907, and impossible in 1931.

10. Conclusion: Monetary Conceptions and the Efficacy of Monetary Policy

> When we were young, we regarded the mechanism of the gold currency as an unimpeachable verity; today we recognize that it is no more than an episode, a more or less accidental happening.
>> An English conservative politician, summer, 1931
>> (Borchardt and Schötz, 1991: 71)

> They never told us we could do that.
>> Apocryphal, attributed to a Labour Party politician following the departure from gold (Williamson, 1984: 106, 183)

The first quotation above (uttered some weeks before the collapse of sterling) seems to capture the mood of the day in Britain better than the well-known second quotation. As far as Norman is concerned, the most deliberate and reflective articles of his belief were the virtues of central bank autonomy and central bank co-operation, beside which his commitment to the gold standard was rather inarticulate. Indeed, the impression of the literature of the time is that the practitioners accepted the intellectual hegemony of criticisms of the gold standard—and of arguments for a 'price stability' standard, but rather inarticulately felt that the alternatives were impracticable. It is perhaps significant, then, that in his reply to the Macmillan Committee's question 3, reproduced above, Sir Ernest Harvey tried, rather contortedly, to imply that a gold standard was a price-stability standard. Thus the gold standard was feebly defended in intellectual terms. And this may be why, when push came to shove, the gold standard fell, because, rather like the recent fall of the Soviet Communist Party, nobody was believed to have their heart in defending it. It is not clear that the more fundamental weaknesses of sterling really had a chance to operate.

Schacht's account of the Reichsbank's objectives, also reproduced above, was more robust and straightforward. But he was a pragmatist. In a well-known aside to the same committee he declared himself ready to follow any monetary theory with support in America and Britain (*Die Reichsbank*: 155). True words are spoken in jest. His *obiter dictum* may reveal that, diplomatic considerations apart, and given the simple monetary objective of maintaining the parity, what mainly mattered to him was market demand for the Reichsmark. This involved him in second-guessing what the market believed, and acting upon it. The argument has been advanced here that market's demand for Reichsmarks was founded, not on fashionable American theories, but on a thoroughly rational view of policy-related events, and that the rapidity of its reaction to such events forced the Reichsbank to pay the closest attention to market views. The recent history of the mark made policy-makers terrified to permit any weakening of public commitment to the parity; yet in the end Germany's political and diplomatic contradictions robbed this commitment of credibility, and the same uncertainties of external diplomacy (reparations) and of domestic fiscal control, which had generated Germany's first post-war monetary regime, destroyed her second.

References

Manuscript Sources

Bank of England Archives:
  G1/414, G1/416 (Governor's files)
  OV 34/81 (Germany)

Schäffer diary: Institut für Zeitgeschichte, Munich, ED 93 Hans Schaeffer Tagebuch, 14–18.

Published Works

Abramowski, G. (ed.) (1988), *Akten der Reichskanzlei: Die Kabinette Marx III u. IV*, Boppard am Rhein, 2 vols.,

Balderston, Theodore (1989), 'War Finance and Inflation in Britain and Germany 1914–1918', *Economic History Review*, 2nd Ser. 41: 222–44.

——— (1991), 'German Banking between the Wars', *Business History Review*, 66: 554–605.

——— (1993), *The Origins and Course of the German Economic Crisis: November 1923–May 1932* (Berlin).

——— (1994), 'The banks and the gold standard in the German financial crisis of 1931', *Financial History Review*, 1: 43–68.

Der Bankkredit (1930), Ausschuss zur Untersuchung der Erzeugungs- und Absatzbedingungen der deutschen Wirtschaft Unterausschuss V, vol. 2 (Berlin).

Die Bank. Periodical edited by Alfred Lansburgh (Berlin).

The Bankers', Insurance Managers' and Agents' Magazine, 129–132 (London).

Banking and Monetary Statistics (1943), (Board of Governors of the Federal Reserve System (Washington, DC).

Benning, Bernhard (1929), 'Der "schwarze Freitag". Eine Untersuchung des Börseneingriffs vom 13.5.27', in R. Gunzert, B. Benning, and E. Veesenmeyer, *Effektenbörse und Volkswirtschaft. Münchener Volkswirtschaftliche Studien*, NS 6 (Jena).

Bombach, Gottfried (ed.) (1976–81), *Der Keynesianismus*, 4 vols. (Berlin).

Borchardt, Knut (1991), 'Germany's Exchange-Rate Options during the Great Depression', in *id.*, *Perspectives on Modern German Economic History and Policy* (Cambridge).

——— and Schötz, Hans-Otto (eds.) (1991), *Wirtschaftspolitik in der Krise. Die (Geheim-) Konferenz der Friedrich-List Gesellschaft im September 1931 über Möglichkeiten und Folgen einer Kreditausweitung* (Baden-Baden).

Boyce, Robert (1987), *British Capitalism at the Crossroads 1919–1932: A Study in Politics, Economics and International Relations* (Cambridge).

Brown, William Adams (1940), *The International Gold Standard Reinterpreted 1914–1934*, 2 vols. (New York).

Capie, Forest, and Collins, Michael (1983), *The Interwar British Economy: A Statistical Abstract* (Manchester).

Cairncross, Alec, and Eichengreen, Barry (1983), *Sterling in Decline: The Devaluations of 1931, 1949, 1967* (Oxford).

Clay, Henry (1957), *Lord Norman* (London).

Eichengreen, Barry (1990*a*), 'The Bank of France and the Sterilization of Gold 1926–1932', in *id.*, *Elusive Stability: Essays in the History of International Finance 1919–1939* (Cambridge): 83–112.

——— (1990*b*), 'The Gold Exchange Standard and the Great Depression', repr. in id. (1990*a*): 239–270.

——— (1992), *Golden Fetters: The Gold Standard and the Great Depression* (New York).

—— Watson, M. W., and Grossman, R. S. (1990), 'Bank Rate Policy under the International Gold Standard', repr. in Barry Eichengreen, *Elusive Stability: Essays in the History of International Finance 1919–1939* (Cambridge): 57–82.

Feinstein, Charles H. (1972), *National Income, Output and Expenditure of the United Kingdom 1856–1972: Studies in the National Income and Expenditure of the United Kingdom*, vi (Cambridge).

Der Finanzausgleich (1931), *Der Finanzausgleich: Einzelschriften zur Statistik des Deutschen Reiches*, 16/17, 2 vols. (Berlin).

Garber, Peter (1982), 'The Transition from Inflation to Price Stability', in Karl H. Brunner and Allan Meltzer (eds.), *Monetary Regimes and Protectionism: Carnegie-Rochester Conference Series on Public Policy*, xvi (Amsterdam).

Gregory, Theodore E. (1926), *The First Year of the Gold Standard* (London).

Hardach, Gerd (1974), 'Die beiden Reichsbanken. Internationales Währungssystem und nationale Währungspolitik 1924–1931', in Hans Mommsen, D. Petzina, and B. Weisbrod (eds.), *Industrielles System und Politische Entwicklung in der Weimarer Republik* (Düsseldorf).

—— (1976), *Weltmarkorientierung und relative Stagnation. Währungspolitik in Deutschland 1924–1931* (Berlin).

—— (n.d.), 'Reichsbankpolitik unter dem Gold-Devisen Standard', unpublished manuscript.

Hawtrey, Ralph G. (1932), 'The Art of Central Banking', in *id., The Art of Central Banking* (London).

Hoffmann, Walther G., Grumbach, Franz, and Hesse, H. (1965), *Das Wachstum der deutschen Wirtschaft seit der Mitte des 19. Jahrhundert* (Berlin).

Holtfrerich, Carl-Ludwig (1986), *The German Inflation: Causes and Effects in International Perspective* (Berlin and New York).

Howson, Susan (1975), *Domestic Monetary Management in Britain* (University of Cambridge, Dept. of Applied Economics Occasional Paper 48, Cambridge).

James, Harold (1985a), *The Reichsbank and Public Finance in Germany, 1924–1933: A Study of the Politics of Economics during the Great Depression* (Frankfurt am Main).

—— (1985b), 'Did the Reichsbank draw the Right Conclusions from the Great Inflation?' in Gerald D. Feldman (ed.), *Die Nachwirkungen der Inflation auf die deutsche Geschichte* (Munich).

—— (1986), *The German Slump: Politics and Economics 1924–1936* (Oxford).

Kindleberger, Charles P. (1974), *The World in Depression* (London).

Konjunkturstatisches Handbuch des Instituts für Konjunkturforschung, (1936), 2nd edn., ed. Ernst Wagemann (Berlin).

Kunz, Diane B. (1987), *The Battle for Britain's Gold Standard in 1931* (London).

Lansburgh, Alfred (1928), 'Die Berliner Grossbanken im Jahre 1927', *Die Bank*: 205 ff.

Macmillan (1931b), *Minutes of Evidence taken before the Macmillan Committee on Finance and Industry*, 2 vols. (London).

Macmillan (1931a), *Report of the Macmillan Committee on Finance and Industry*, Cmnd. 3897 (London).

McNeil, William C. (1986), *American Money and the Weimar Republic: Politics and Economics on the Eve of the Great Depression* (New York).

Maurer, Ilse (1973), *Reichsfinanzen und grosse Koalition. Zur Geschichte des Reichs-kabinetts Müller 1928–1930* (Berne).

Moggridge, Donald E. (1969), *The Return to Gold, 1925* (Cambridge).

—— (1972), *British Monetary Policy 1924–31: The Norman Conquest of $4.86* (University of Cambridge, Department of Applied Economics Monograph 21, Cambridge).

Müller, F. (1934), 'Reichsbank, Stabilisierung und Sicherung der Währung', in *Untersuchung des Bankwesens 1933*, 2 vols. (Berlin).

Müller, Helmut (1972), *Die Reichsbank, eine Nebenregierung. Reichsbankpräsident Schacht als Politiker der Weimarer Republic* (Opladen).

Netzband, K.-B, and Widmaier, H.-P. (1964), *Währungs- und Finanzpolitik in der Ära Luther 1923–1925* (Basle).

Northrop, Mildred B. (1938), *Control Policies of the Reichsbank 1924–1933* (New York).

Die Reichsbank (1929), Ausschuss zur Untersuchung der Erzeugungs- und Absatzbe-dingungen der deutschen Wirtschaft Unterausschuss V, vol. i. (Berlin).

Sayers, Richard S. (1957), *Central Banking after Bagehot* (Oxford).

—— (1976), *The Bank of England 1890–1914*, 3 vols. (Cambridge).

Schuker, Stephen (1988) *American 'Reparations' to Germany 1919–1933: Implications for the Third-World Debt Crisis*, Princeton Studies in International Finance, 61 (Princeton, NJ).

Temin, Peter (1989), *Lessons from the Great Depression* (Cambridge, Mass.).

ten Cate, J. H. (1988), 'Reichsbank President Schacht and the Reparations Payments (1924–1930)', *German Yearbook on Business History* (Berlin).

Vogt, M. (ed.) (1970), *Akten der Reichskanzlei: Das Kabinett Müller II*, 2 vols. (Boppard am Rhein).

Webb, Steven B. (1988), *Hyperinflation and Stabilization in Weimar Germany* (New York).

Weber, Adolf (1927), *Hat Schacht Recht? Die Abhängigkeit der Deutschen Wirtschaft vom Ausland* (Munich).

Die Wirtschaftskurve, quarterly business periodical of the *Frankfurter Zeitung* (Frankfurt am Main).

Williamson, Philip (1984), 'Financiers, the Gold Standard and British Politics, 1925–1931', in John Turner (ed.), *Businessmen and Politics: Studies of Business Activity in British Politics 1900–1945* (London): 105–29.

Wrigley, Christopher J. (1990), *Lloyd George and the Challenge of Labour: The Postwar Coalition 1918–1922* (New York and London).

6

Exchange-Rate Policy and Macroeconomic Performance: A Comparison of French and Italian Experience between the Wars

JEAN-CHARLES ASSELAIN AND ALAIN PLESSIS

1. Summary of the Argument

The argument of this paper may be summarized as follows:

1. The monetary and economic histories of France and Italy from 1918 to 1934–6 present striking similarities, despite notable differences in foreign trade and in political systems.

2. Within an increasingly divided Europe, external affairs: monetary, financial, and commercial, continued to play a decisive role in the economic destiny of nations. To a large extent this explains the great overall shift which occurred during the period beginning with the 1920s and extending into the 1930s, and which was detrimental to both France and Italy.

3. The conventional view emphasizing the contrast between the stabilization of the franc by Poincaré and the revaluation of the lira by Mussolini must be qualified in certain respects. Starting from what were in effect widely different positions and developing along distinctly different lines by 1928, the two economies went down the same road in the process of adaptation. Both succeeded in refuelling their economies by turning to the domestic market, whilst preserving part of their previous gains on external markets.

4. In both countries, accidental factors, errors of understanding and submission to uncontrolled events in several cases determined monetary and economic policy.

5. However, Italy, under a Fascist regime, was able to impose more vigorous deflationary policies than France. The main difference was evident in the much more unfavourable evolution of wages in Italy, both in nominal and real terms.

6. The period from 1935 to 1939 merits special attention. The gulf between the two countries widened considerably, both quantitatively and qualitatively. Compared to the upturn in Italy, France's predicament worsened, showing that monetary imbalance had a negative impact on medium to long-term economic performance.

Following an overview of the period as a whole, we will turn our attention to two significant phases: (*a*) 1926–8, in the course of which the two countries opted for stabilization rather than revaluation of their currencies; and (*b*) 1934–8, during which France and Italy in succession went through a period of deflation, followed by devaluation.

2. An Overview

France and Italy are good candidates for a comparative study. The French franc and the Italian lira (together with the Belgian franc—see Chapter 7 by Cassiers) shared a common destiny during a major part of the twentieth century. The French and Italian economies were of similar size, and both remained in some sense semi-industrialized until the Second World War. Both had experienced a burst of industrialization during the 1920s, but were very severely hit by the Depression of the 1930s. However, the two countries differed markedly from the point of view of income levels, financial structures, and external relations, and their diametrically opposed political regimes inevitably had far-reaching consequences for their respective economic and monetary policies. So the Franco-Italian comparison shows both conspicuous similarities, and deep and growing divergences throughout the inter-war period.

Conspicuous similarities

The variations in the exchange rates of the French and Italian currencies (Fig. 6.1) remained strikingly synchronized from 1918 to 1936 (Falco and Storaci, 1975, 1977):

(*a*) The French franc and the lira depreciated rapidly in 1919–20, as soon as the financial solidarity of the Allies came to an end.

(*b*) The tendency to currency depreciation dominated the inflationary post-war years, especially in France, with a sudden acceleration around 1925–6. The 'exchange crisis' culminated in France in July 1926 and in Italy in August 1926.

(*c*) The French franc and the lira quickly and consistently recovered during the second half of 1926; the lira returned to gold in December 1927, the French franc in June 1928, after a prior *de facto* stabilization.

(*d*) The new parity of both currencies was maintained until the autumn of 1936, so that the variations of their effective exchange rates passively mirrored the devaluation of other currencies in 1931, 1933, and 1935.

(*e*) The French franc and the lira were eventually devalued at roughly the same time in September–October 1936, effectively bringing the gold bloc to an end.

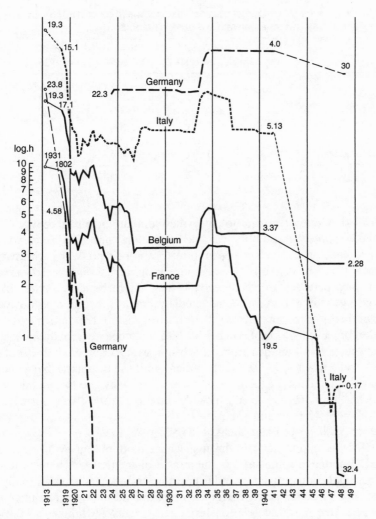

FIG. 6.1 Evolution of exchange rates to the dollar, 1919–1948

When the evolution of macroeconomic performance is related to the phases of their monetary history, the striking fact is that Italy and France both experienced strong economic growth during the years of recurrent inflation and currency depreciation until 1926, whereas the following decade of monetary stability was characterized by an abrupt deterioration of their performance, not only absolutely (under the impact of the world depression), but also in comparative terms (Table 6.1).

The three 'late stabilizers'—Italy, France, and Belgium—all improved their ranking in spite of heavy wartime destruction, and over the period

TABLE 6.1. *Manufacturing production per head, European countries,* 1881–5 to 1936–8 (annual percentage growth rate, with rank in brackets)

	1881–85 to 1911–13	1911–13 to 1926–29	1926–29 to 1936–38
Italy	4.0(2)	2.9(1)	0.1(4)
France	2.8(4)	2.1(2)	– 1.1(5)
Belgium	2.4(5)	1.5(4)	– 1.5(6)
Sweden	5.3(1)	1.7(3)	5.1(1)
Germany	3.2(3)	0.4(5)	1.7(3)
United Kingdom	0.8(6)	– 0.4(6)	2.5(2)

Source: League of Nations (1945).

1913–29 they outperformed not only the German and other central European economies affected by runaway inflation, but also England and Sweden, which had only succeeded in restoring their pre-war parities at the expense of severe deflation. Contemporary opinion was most reluctant to admit that some degree of monetary laxness might be more favourable to 'prosperity' than the sacrifices dictated by financial orthodoxy; but when Keynes in 1928 compared the British troubles to the 'much stronger' position achieved by the French who had 'offended so grossly against all sound principles of financing', his conclusion was: 'Assuredly it does not pay to be good' (Keynes, 1972). On the other hand, the traumatic experience of the post-war inflation explains to a large extent why the late stabilizers of the 1920s stubbornly rejected a new devaluation in the 1930s, forming the core of the gold bloc and suffering in turn all the costs of an overvalued currency (Eichengreen and Sachs, 1985).

One of the main channels through which economic growth was conditioned by monetary policies was the impact of the (real) exchange rates on international competitiveness and export performance. Whereas initially the adjustment of exchange rates tended to lag behind the domestic price rise, soon after the war the relationship was reversed (Aftalion, 1950). The expectation of further depreciation pushed the exchange rate of the inflationary currencies significantly below the purchasing-power parity level. This happened as early as 1920–1 for the lira and, to a lesser degree, for the French franc; but for the latter the gap tended to widen until summer 1926, as the depreciation of the French franc on exchange markets typically preceded the increase in the domestic price-level. The undervaluation of the lira and the French franc in comparison to the currencies restored to their pre-war parity persisted, albeit to a somewhat reduced extent, after the stabilizations of 1926–8 (cf. section 3). However, from 1931 to 1936 the refusal to embark on a new devaluation, together with the limited downward price flexibility (even in Italy), meant that the French franc and the lira tended to be overvalued in relation to their purchasing power parity *vis-à-vis* the newly devalued currencies. So, throughout the period, from 1920 onward, the real exchange rates typically varied in the same direction (although of course not to the same extent) as the nominal exchange rates.

TABLE 6.2. *Ratio of exports to GDP, Italy and France, 1920–1938 (per cent, at constant 1938 prices)*

	1920–2	1923–5	1926–8	1929	1930–2	1932–5	1936–8
Italy	10.4	13.4	12.9	12.5	10.3	6.8	6.9
France	9.1	10.8	12.1	11.5	9.0	7.7	7.5

Source: P. Ercolani, in Fua (1978).

The dynamics of French and Italian exports (see Tables 6.2 and 6.3), as well as the influence of real exchange rates, depended both on world tendencies and on structural factors specific to each country. Nevertheless, the contrasting phases of the evolution, as well as the simultaneous 'turning-points' in France and Italy, clearly suggest that the role of the variations in real exchange rates remained predominant at least until the mid-1930s.

TABLE 6.3. *Evolution of the relative position of France and Italy, 1913–1937*

	Share in European exports of manufactures (per cent)	Manufacturing exports per head (west European average[a] = 100)	Manufacturing production per head (west European average[a] = 100)
Italy			
1913	4.0	23	41
1929	5.5	29	44
1937	5.0	27	41
France			
1913	14.8	77	102
1929	16.1	85	111
1937	8.7	49	88

[a] Average for UK, Germany, France, Italy, Belgium, and Switzerland.

Source: Maizels (1963).

Two circumstances make the French and Italian export performance of the 1920s all the more remarkable. First, the general tendency in Europe, even before 1929, was already toward a decline in international trade. France was the sole country where the share of exports in GDP during the late 1920s significantly surpassed the pre-war figure. In the even more open Italian economy, the share of exports first increased markedly during the early 1920s, then was approximately stabilized at a fairly high level, near to the degree of openness reached before the war. Secondly, French and Italian market shares were growing in spite of their unfavourable specialization in export products such as textiles which represented a declining share of world trade. So, the export performance of the 1920s largely depended in both countries on the across-the-board advantage obtained for all export industries by currency depreciation (the 'exchange premium', that 'extraordinary piece of luck' as the managers of the French metallurgical firm Pont-à-Mousson frankly admitted; A. Baudant, quoted in Bouvier, 1986). This was independent of any specific effort of their own to improve productivity or adjust to foreign demand. But it was a double-edged advantage which would increase the vulnerability of the whole export sector in the event of a reappreciation of the real exchange rate. This eventually happened in two stages, first with the French and Italian stabilizations of 1926–8, then with the foreign devaluations of 1931–5. Hence the rather abrupt check to the export boom around 1928, and the dramatic reversal to the detriment of the French and Italian market shares during the 1930s.

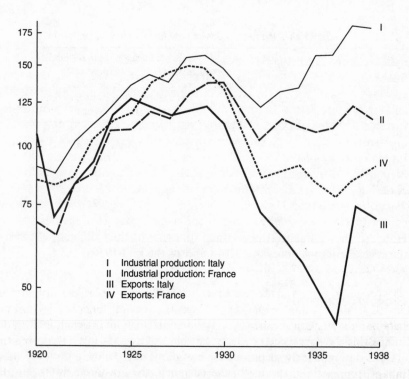

FIG. 6.2 Industrial production and exports, France and Italy, 1920–1938 (1913 = 100)

A comparison of the trends in the volume of exports and in industrial production (Fig. 6.2) aptly summarizes the main developments of the period. Four conclusions stand out:

1. A close parallelism between the developments in France and Italy persisted until around 1934.

2. In each country, the movement of exports and of industrial production also remained closely connected until 1933–4.

3. However, the variations in exports were of a larger magnitude, in both directions, than the variations in industrial production. Thus the dynamism of exports first acted as a driving force of economic growth during the 1920s, though Fig. 6.2 suggests that the phase of export-led growth proper was confined to 1922–5 in Italy, and lasted only one or two years more in France. The collapse of exports then pushed the two economies into the Great Depression.

4. The last four years (1934–8) stand out in several respects: they show the very different patterns of development, in which industry clearly recovered better in Italy than in France despite having the worse export performance.

On the whole, with the partial exception of the last subperiod, a common periodization, based on the turning-points of their exchange-rate policy, fits the inter-war economic experience of France and Italy reasonably well. A phase of inflationary growth, fostered by the depreciation of (nominal and real) exchange rates resulting in a strong export performance until 1926, was followed by the uncertainties of the stabilization (1926–9), then by a depression worsened by the effects of the overvaluation of the French franc and the lira, until their simultaneous devaluation in 1936. The exchange-rate variable at first sight explains more than could be expected in a world of ever-growing restrictions on international trade (even the late French and Italian devaluations in 1936 had more than trivial consequences). However, even if the story seems clear enough, the exchange-rate policy has to be placed in the more general framework of monetary, fiscal, and wage policies, where the similarities between France and Italy often gave way to outright contrasts. How were they affected by the different nature of the two regimes? How did they influence the eventual outcome of their different choices, in the crucial circumstances of 1926–8 and of the mid-1930s?

Growing divergences

In comparison with France, the Italian inter-war experience looks more successful in two respects.

Considering first the main objective of monetary policy in both countries, that is to preserve the value of the currency, the lira fared better than the French franc from 1922 to 1939. Starting from a greater depreciation just after the war (1 lira was worth 0.5 French franc around 1921), the lira appreciated *vis-à-vis* the French franc during the mid-1920s and was pushed to 1.34 French francs by the revaluation policy of 1926–7. Although the lira showed signs of weakness on several occasions, the official rate reached 2 francs a decade later, following the repeated French devaluations of 1937–8. The lira was, no doubt, somewhat overvalued at this rate. Nevertheless, it had also suffered a much smaller decline than the franc in terms of purchasing power, because the Italian development was consistently less inflationary than the French from 1922. Italian prices rose less than French until 1926, the downturn of retail prices occurred earlier in Italy (1926) than in France (1930), and the inflation of 1936–8 was significantly faster in France than in Italy. In 1938, Italian prices were at nearly the same level as in 1922, whereas French prices had more than doubled.

Italy was also ahead of France in the pace of economic growth, both before and after 1929. Both countries were late to emerge from the Great Depression of 1929–32, by comparison with those who devalued early, but from 1934 to 1938 the economic recovery in France was progressively outpaced by the growth in Italy (Fig. 6.2). The trade-off between monetary stability and economic growth did not seem to hold any more in those years, and the French performance, in particular, was equally disappointing in both respects.

Italy's growing advantage over France is hardly explained by structural factors. The relative 'backwardness' of the Italian industrialization, admittedly, left room for 'catching-up' effects; such was the case before 1914, though to a much lesser degree for Italy than for Sweden (Table 6.1). Comparison with the fast catching-up of Finland (still a semi-industrialized country around 1918), during the inter-war period, is even more unfavourable to Italy. Moreover, the growing disturbances in international capital markets hindered the development of all the economies depending on foreign capital, as Italy did. The quite different pattern of their external equilibrium was precisely the main structural contrast between France and Italy. France had been investing abroad for a long time, and its capital exports resumed in the 1920s; its balance of payments was usually positive, thanks to the returns on foreign investments, even when the balance of trade was negative. Italy on the other hand had a permanent trade deficit, and its external equilibrium was heavily dependent on such 'invisible' receipts as maritime freights, tourism, and the remittances of emigrants, and also on a permanent inflow of foreign capital.

All these items were immediately affected by the impact of the Great Depression, and Italy had to enforce a strict limitation of its imports and to apply stern pressures to bring its balance of payments back into equilibrium. France's gold reserves reached a level six times the amount of Italy's in 1929, fourteen times in 1936. The unequal abundance of capital typically resulted in significant interest differentials. Italy's domestic financial structures, characterized by the preponderance of mixed banks, also helped to make its economy more vulnerable in times of crisis (Ciocca and Toniolo, 1984; see also Chapter 10 by Toniolo).

While facing a stronger 'external constraint' than France, the dictatorship in Italy had a freer hand in imposing its will on the domestic scene. In France ministerial instability under the Third Republic more than once reached the point where no consistent policy could exist. The Banque de France jealously defended its independence, refusing for instance to engage its gold reserves to sustain the franc in 1926; and it did not hesitate to pass on occasion 'from covert hostility to open war' against a leftist government (Philippe, 1931). Even when the government's authority was not challenged, as under Poincaré, the decision processes in France remained fundamentally pluralistic. By contrast, Italy's rulers kept the central bank under control, in spite of a façade of measures adopted for the sake of international respectability. They were able to implement a forced consolidation of the debt without meeting significant opposition, to impose banking concentrations, to achieve 'rescue' operations in proper conditions of rapidity and secrecy, and ultimately to reorganize the whole financial and industrial structure. The radical contrast in the nature of the two regimes consistently showed itself in both the definition and the implementation of monetary

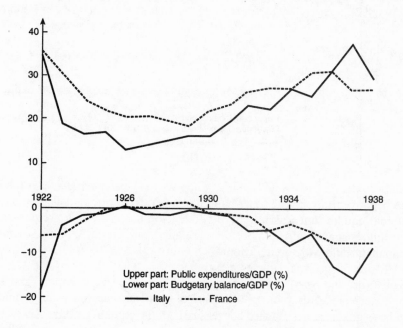

FIG. 6.3 Public expenditure and budgetary balance, France and Italy, 1922–1938

policy, as will be exemplified by the two main episodes studied below: the contrasted stabilizations of 1926–8 (section 3) and the enforcement of strong exchange controls by the Italian authorities in 1934, at a time when even the principle of such controls was rejected as 'totalitarian' by majority opinion in France (section 4).

French and Italian budgetary policies (Fig. 6.3) were at first sight much less contrasted. In both countries, they showed a distinctly contracyclical pattern throughout the period: the huge post-war deficits were gradually

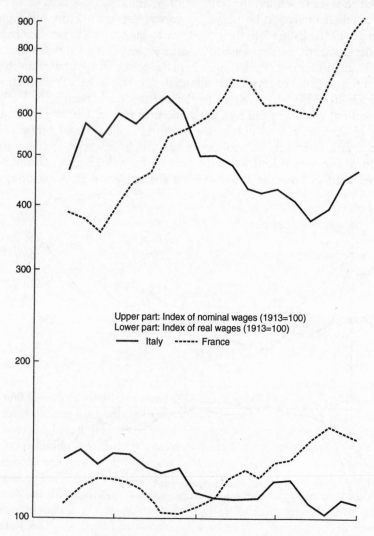

FIG. 6.4   Indices of nominal and real wages, France and Italy, 1913–1938

reduced during the 'prosperous' 1920s, equilibrium or surpluses were achieved around 1926, then growing deficits were experienced again during the 1930s. Yet the specificity of the Italian regime was evident in the harsh reduction of public expenditure during the first years of fascist rule (1923–4), and later in the magnitude of the public deficits connected with the Ethiopian war and rearmament policies (1934–8). Public revenues remained inelastic in both countries, but in France the distribution of the fiscal burden was at the centre of uncertain political struggles, especially under the Cartel des Gauches (1924–6).

The overwhelming contrast, however, concerned wage policy. The Fascist regime, after the prohibition of strikes in 1926, the dissolution of the CGL during the winter 1926–7, and the bringing to heel of Fascist trade unions, was able to enforce repeated wage cuts, which would in France have met insuperable resistance. The downward flexibility of nominal wages gave the Italian Government an 'additional degree of freedom' (Ciocca *et al.* in Ciocca and Toniolo, 1976) and made a crucial difference to the effectiveness of deflationary policies. Beyond controlling nominal variables, the Italian rulers succeeded in maintaining a consistent downward pressure on real wages throughout the decade 1926–36 (Fig. 6.4). In France, on the contrary, the share of wages in the national income showed the usual contracyclical tendency. The events of 1936 brought to a climax the contrast between the two countries.

Keeping in mind this particular mix of similarities and differences, we will now consider more precisely in what circumstances France and Italy embarked on definitely divergent paths. Should the end of the broad parallelism that had prevailed since the war be traced back to the monetary stabilizations of 1926–8 or only to the aftermath of the Great Depression?

3. Stabilization versus Revaluation, 1926–1928

According to the prevailing view (e.g., Kindleberger, 1983), the experience of monetary stabilization in France and Italy was entirely one of contrasts. Poincaré devalued the franc (to one-fifth of its pre-war parity: 'le franc de 4 sous'). Mussolini, driven by national pride, took the risk of revaluing the lira to *quota novanta* (90 lire per pound sterling: the rate prevailing at the end of 1922, when he seized power). Poincaré's reasonable choice is credited with the success of stopping French inflation (Poincaré's 'miracle'), at the expense of a minor temporary recession and with preserving the conditions of economic growth by a deliberate undervaluation of the franc (Sicsic, 1992). By contrast, the overvaluation of the lira, together with the accompanying deflationary policies, dealt a severe blow to the Italian economy. We will argue here in favour of a less one-sided analysis. The style of decision-making and the adjustment pattern were indeed quite different. But in both countries accidental factors, measures taken at cross-purposes, played a major part. At the same time, some of the mechanisms involved were common to France and Italy, and the final outcome shows much more convergence than could be expected.

Contrasted experiences

The model of export-led growth of the early 1920s in France and Italy, resting on a self-accelerating depreciation of the currency, was inherently unstable. Around 1926, the so-called 'virtuous circle' of inflationary growth looked exhausted (Toniolo, 1980). At the height of the exchange crisis (mid-1926), the cheapness of French, Italian, and Belgian exports, implying a considerable deterioration in the terms of trade, hardly counterbalanced the slow-down in world demand, and anyway the disorganizing effects on the domestic economy outweighed any possible advantage of further infla-tion. No sector of French or Italian opinion, including those who had benefited from the inflationary growth, questioned the urgency of overcom-ing the exchange crisis and stopping inflation: the restoration of monetary stability had become a national priority.

In several respects the conditions were now more favourable than a few years earlier. Most European currencies had already returned to gold and the 'late stabilizers' could apply to London and New York for a stabiliza-tion loan. Both governments had serious problems in rolling over the existing domestic debt, but current inflation was no longer fuelled by a significant budget deficit (Makinen and Woodward, 1989); the real burden of the debt had been reduced as a result of past inflation. 'Unconditional revaluationists' were more and more isolated, and monetary stabilization was no longer identified with the unrealistic objective of a full revaluation to the pre-war parity (Marconi, 1982). So, the French and Italian authorities faced basically the same problem: first, to stop the cumulative depreciation process, then to determine the 'proper' exchange-rate, amidst conflicting interests. The possible choices ranged from ratifying the very depreciated rates prevailing at the climax of the exchange crisis, to enforcing a significant though partial revaluation. Creditors, and especially the influen-tial category of the State's *rentiers* favoured the latter solution for obvious reasons. The interests of the borrowers pointed in the opposite direction; the export industries, such as textiles, were most concerned by the impact of an excessive revaluation on their competitiveness; the trade unions supported their warnings, stressing the risk of increasing unemployment. No clear-cut dividing line, however, existed between 'financial' and 'industrial' interests (Bouvier, 1986). The basic industries, for instance, might welcome the revaluation, as it automatically reduced the costs of their imported inputs. On the other hand, the disastrous impact on the economy of a protracted deflation, as exemplified by the British experience, was firmly denounced in advance by Demaria and del Vecchio in Italy, Rist and the Comité des Experts in France.

Poincaré, though he was initially 'heart and soul' (Wolfe, 1951) with the revaluers, listened to these warnings on two critical occasions. The first was in December 1926, when he stopped the spontaneous reappreciation of the French franc (according to his own testimony, the pressing intervention of the CGT unions leader, Jouhaux, was decisive) at a level meant to correspond to the French franc's purchasing-power parity. The second came in June 1928 when, under the threat of the resignation of Moreau (the governor of the Bank of France), he gave up any prospect of further revaluation and stabilized the franc at a gold parity corresponding to the exchange rate maintained since the end of 1926. Mussolini, in contrast, ignored (*a*) the protest of the textile manufacturers, stressing in December 1926 the 'catastrophic' consequences of any revaluation beyond *quota* 100 (100 lire per pound) and the anxiety of Italian workers in export trades confronted by growing unemployment; (*b*) the repeated warnings of the authorities of the Federal Reserve Bank of New York and of Governor Norman against the danger of choosing a grossly overvalued exchange rate; and (*c*) the advice of his own Finance Minister, Volpi. Stringher, the Governor of the Bank of Italy, was still more reluctant (Moreau, 1954). Yet Mussolini, after announcing in military terms that the currency was to be 'defended' at any cost (speech of Pesaro, August 1926), maintained a stern deflation policy until June 1927, when the lira had regained 75 per cent in comparison to July 1926.

Poincaré's stabilization was an unquestionable success. But it is worth recalling the conditions in which the French franc started its recovery. Before the announcement of any significant policy measure, the French franc had already appreciated by 20 per cent in six days (21–7 July 1926). Considerable progress toward the re-establishment of a balanced budget had already been achieved (in 1925, the deficit was almost negligible), although it remained unnoticed by French opinion. Following Péret's austerity programme (spring 1926), Poincaré's measures mainly affected the distribution of the fiscal burden (Prati, 1991) rather than the amount of public revenue or expenditure (the total impact did not reach one per cent of national income), and could hardly be interpreted as evidence of a 'new regime'. The much celebrated creation of the Caisse d'Amortissement was, admittedly, a novelty but its significance was essentially symbolic. Finally, the French franc was considerably undervalued in relation to its PPP from the end of 1925, in spite of a positive balance of payments. So 'Poincaré the magician' did not have to create an illusion: a political shock, restoring 'confidence' among business circles and ending the flight of capital, was enough to reverse the cumulative process of depreciation.

In contrast, when Mussolini committed himself at Pesaro to 'fight' for the lira, the immediate effect was only a slim appreciation of the lira by 2.7 per cent (18–27 August 1926). The conditions prevailing in Italy were less favourable for a sudden reversal: the lira was less undervalued than the French franc (the depreciation process had not reached the same degree of 'overshooting'), and the Italian balance of payment was much more precarious. So the Fascist regime had to embark on a full-fledged deflationary policy to push up the value of the lira, using the weapons available to a totalitarian State. The middle-term results, even though it was a Pyrrhic victory, costly in economic terms, were beyond the expectation of all foreign observers. After giving the Bank of Italy the monopoly of note issue (May 1926), the government in November 1926 suppressed the Autonomous Section of the Consortium for the Support of Industrial Values (in the operations of which a considerable part of the monetary creation had originated during the previous years), and eliminated three-quarters of the floating debt by imposing a forced consolidation (the 'Lictor loan') the same month. An extremely restrictive credit policy was abruptly enforced (it resulted in a panic run during the autumn of 1926) and maintained throughout 1927–8 (the discount rate, except during a few months, was held at 7 per cent, whereas the Bank of France was able to reduce its rate by steps to 3.5 per cent in February 1928).

However, the crucial characteristic of the Italian deflation was the effectiveness of the downward pressure on the level of wages, anticipating the decrease in retail prices. Employers were allowed to lengthen the working day from eight to nine hours for the same wage (June 1926). 'Spontaneous' wage-cuts were already widespread in the small firms of the export trades toward the end of 1926, and the fascist organizations worked throughout 1927 to generalize them (Salvemini, 1936). Finally a compulsory reduction of all wages by 10 to 20 per cent was decided in October 1927. The domestic deflation, however, had to be supplemented by a policy of massive borrowing abroad; the Volpi–Mellon settlement of the war-debts issue (November 1925), an uneasy step for the Fascist regime, had opened the way for American loans. Large electric companies and other private firms or public institutions were prompted to raise loans on the New York market. So the recovery of the lira in 1926–7 was directly dependent on the inflow of foreign capital, whereas Poincaré took pride in stabilizing the franc without any international loan.

Yet, the two 'miracles' showed some conspicuous similarities. In both countries, the reversal of expectations set up a sustained, self-amplifying process of appreciation, through short-term capital movements, and the major problem soon became to control both the impact on the monetary circulation and the excessive rise of the national currency. In both countries, the stabilization had to be a compromise between opposite interests (even though in Italy it was heavily biased against the workers). Moreover, the hurried circumstances of the *de facto* stabilization (December 1926 in France, June 1927 in Italy) predetermined the parities ultimately chosen for the franc and the lira, as the *de jure* stabilizations later merely confirmed the prevailing rates. Whereas Poincaré explicitly aimed at a purchasing-power–parity exchange-rate (Rueff, 1959), the previous undervaluation of the franc was reduced, but not eliminated (the downward adjustment of domestic prices subsequent to the reappreciation had been omitted from the calculations).

In the Italian case, various considerations, ranging from national pride (as the lira now surpassed the franc) to short-term concern for the price of imported food, not to speak of the hypothetical long-term plan for an inward reorientation of the Italian economy, combined with fortuitous circumstances (the un-coordinated issue of several major loans around 1927 even pushed up the lira beyond the 90 mark; Marconi, 1982) to generate a definite overshooting. But, most unexpectedly, the eventual impact on the real exchange rate was not so different from the French case.

Converging results?

The conventional approach sharply contrasting the 'stabilization' of the French franc and the 'revaluation' of the lira would lead one to expect a corresponding contrast in the respective behaviour of the two economies during the adjustment phase. The severity of the shock inflicted on the Italian economy by the *quota novanta* is seldom disputed. The issue of 'the economic consequences of the franc Poincaré' (Eichengreen and Wyplosz, 1990) is more controversial, but the relative mildness and brevity of the recession following the stabilization are usually emphasized: Poincaré's monetary success was nearly costless in economic terms (Sargent, 1983). As a matter of fact, no such dramatic opposition arises, at least in macroeconomic figures. As Table 6.4 indicates, the two recessions were of comparable intensity. In both countries, the 1926 production levels were already surpassed by 1928.

The interpretation should focus first on the export sector, which was most directly affected by the stabilization. France and Italy were facing the same

TABLE 6.4. *Comparison between the French and Italian recessions of 1927* (percentage change, 1926–7)

	Italy	France
GDP	– 2.5	– 1.2
Industrial production	– 4.0	– 5.0

Sources: GDP from Maddison (1982), industrial production from OEEC (1960).

problem: after several years of artificial boosting of their export performance by the overdepreciation of their currency (a very peculiar kind of 'export-led' growth), they had to achieve a 'soft landing', that is to preserve as much as possible their newly acquired position in foreign markets, while shifting to a more balanced, self-centred growth.

Not surprisingly, stabilization meant the end of the export boom, and several export industries, especially in Italy, suffered a severe rise in unemployment. Yet, these adjustment problems were in no way the cause of a general economic collapse. The French recession in 1927 was *not* due to a fall in the volume of exports, which kept growing and to some measure mitigated the effects of the slow-down in domestic demand. In 1928–9, the volume of French exports was stabilized on a high plateau, which was by no means a bad performance by international standards (although the period of export-led growth was now definitely over). The evolution of Italian exports was less favourable and more uneven; their growth was checked as early as the end of 1925 (that is, long before the *quota novanta*), but signs of a strong revival were perceptible in many cases around 1929 (Paradisi, 1976). Italy's share in the value of European exports was the same in 1929 as in 1925, and higher than in 1913. On the whole, both Italian and French exports had held their own through the adjustment process.

One explanation of this parallelism (Fig. 6.3) is that the choices concerning the parity at which the two currencies were stabilized had not been so different after all. As Table 6.5 shows, stabilization of the French franc fell midway between the lira and the Belgian franc.

The evolution of real exchange rates in Italy and France was still more convergent. In real terms, the franc appreciated more (+ 23 per cent) between 1925–6 and 1927–8 than the lira (+ 16 per cent). These averages, admittedly, conceal much more violent fluctuations in the Italian case: after a phase of abrupt revaluation until May 1927, the strong price deflation, facilitated by the repeated wage-cuts and by the decrease in the price of

TABLE 6.5. *Relative levels of stabilization in Italy, France, and Belgium*

	Lira	French franc	Belgian franc
Nominal exchange rate to the $, (as a percent of :			
(a) the lowest quotation			
(summer 1926)	166	196	118
(b) the average of 1926	135	121	85
(c) the average of 1923–6	126	87	67
(d) the pre-war parity	27	20	14

Source: Our elaboration from P. Einzig (1937).

imported goods, tended to restore the previous undervaluation of the lira. At the end of 1927, the lira was again undervalued in relation to its purchasing-power parity at retail prices, though not to the same degree as in 1925–6. Such was also the case for the franc. Moreover, in both countries, the export industries had to—and were able to—accept substantial sacrifices on their profit margins. While the downward flexibility of prices in general was less in France, the relative price of exported goods decreased even more in France than in Italy. As a result, the terms of trade were remarkably little affected by the stabilization in both countries.

In the medium term, however, the behaviour of French and Italian exports critically depended on increasing investments to modernize the old export industries, which had been relying for several years on exchange depreciation to maintain their competitiveness, and to develop new specializations. More generally, domestic investment had to replace exports as the main driving force of economic growth. The adjustment to a new growth path less dependent on foreign markets (and specially on declining industries, which had more than held their own during the depreciation years) was not yet completed in either country around 1929. But it was more advanced and better started in France (where certainly no 'great design' of economic strategy had inspired the stabilization) than in Italy.

An exceptional conjunction of factors concurred to generate the French investment boom of 1928–9. First, the political context: Poincaré had achieved a broad consensus, and any risk of confiscatory taxation was averted. Secondly, the financial and monetary conditions: high profits had been sustained for several years, while all borrowers had their debt burden lightened by past inflation; the restoration of a budget surplus ended the 'crowding out' of private investment (Eichengreen and Wyplosz, 1986; see also the chapter below by Cassiers); and the success of the monetary stabilization—particularly the repatriation of exported capital—permitted very low interest rates. Thirdly, consolidation of a high level of exports (even such an old export industry as textiles had the opportunity to modernize and increased its investments in 1928–9), together with rising domestic demand. The French balance of payments was in surplus, and the price of equities was booming.

The Italian economy, on the other hand, faced much more serious problems. The labour-intensive industries benefited around 1929 from the wage-cuts and at the same time increased their productivity through mass redundancies rather than by investment. The basic industries, producing mainly for the home market, showed a stronger dynamism; for them, the revaluation meant a decrease in the cost of imported inputs, and the regime gave first priority to their development. Yet the situation left little leeway for the Government's policy. On one hand, the precarious external equilibrium and permanent dependence on foreign capital imposed the maintenance of high interest rates through a protracted monetary deflation. At the same time, the Government had to sustain employment and the level of activity by increasing public expenditure while the financial institutions resumed their support to ailing industrial firms, leading to the 'monstrous Siamese twinning' (Marconi, 1982) of the 1930s. If the later divergences between Italy and France should be to some measure traced back to the late 1920s, that was due more to the various structural constraints facing Italy then than to the rash enforcement of the *quota novanta*.

4. Devaluation versus Deflation, 1934–1938

In the course of this period, Italy and France attempted in succession two contrasting monetary policies which clearly ended in failure. Both were members of the gold bloc, whose members were determined, initially, to preserve the value of their currencies. To this end, Italy and France at first set a deflationary course, after which, at almost the same time in 1936, they were forced to accept devaluation. But if these policies, which often resulted in similar technical measures, appeared to resemble one another to such an extent that they were referred to in identical terms, in reality their application varied considerably, acquiring in each case different characteristics.

Various roads to deflation

The two countries found themselves faced with grave problems due essentially to the overvaluation of their currencies. This was the mechanical outcome of the sharp devaluations of the pound sterling (1931), the dollar (1934 onwards), and the many currencies which had either followed, or even—in some cases—preceded, the Anglo-Saxon currencies down this road. As can be seen in Table 6.6, the overvaluation of the lira and the franc, made worse by the devaluation of the belga in April 1935, became apparent on the foreign-exchange market.

At the same time, the ratio of the pound sterling to the lira was lowered from the *quota novanta* to the *quota sexanta*. This revaluation led to an

TABLE 6.6. *Exchange rate of the French franc, 1930–1935*

	Pound Sterling	Dollar	Belgian franc (per 100)	Lira (per 100)
1930	123.9	25.5	71.6	133.6
1934	76.7	15.2	70.9	130.4
1935	74.3	15.15	55.9	125.0

Source: Sauvy (1984: 395).

increase in the ratio of French prices compared to English prices, which went from 0.89 in 1930 to 1.22 in 1935 (Sauvy, 1984), and more generally to a progression of the same proportion in the real exchange rate of the lira, as well as of the franc.

As a result France and Italy were no longer competitive on foreign markets; this penalized their exports and had repercussions on economic performance. At the same time, capital, attracted to the United Kingdom and above all the USA, tended to flee those countries which had not yet devalued and the gold reserves of their central banks were then exposed to strong attack.

Public opinion, the monetary authorities, and the public authorities reacted in the same way in both countries and agreed to combat any recourse to a devaluation, however effective this proved abroad. The fact was that France and Italy had already enacted sharp devaluations in 1927–8. French public opinion remained firmly attached to the gold standard of the Poincaré franc. Thus in June 1934, when Paul Reynaud proposed to devalue the franc as a means to end the crisis, he met with stiff resistance from the Banque de France, which was unanimously backed by the Chambers of Commerce. As for Italy, the Mussolini regime renewed a solemn undertaking, from the Pesaro discourse onwards (1927), to defend the gold parity of the lira, and this became for Mussolini a matter of national pride.

In France as in Italy, the governments were thus determined to maintain their exchange rate. From then onwards, only one policy was left them: in order to reduce their prices and thus stimulate their exports, and to keep foreign capital and balance the budget, they had no choice but to deflate. Deflation appeared, therefore, as the unique solution to emerge from a crisis which was blamed on excessive credit. On this point, analysts from the Banque de France and the Bank of Italy were agreed. For the former, recovery would become possible only after price reductions, which led to forced stock clearance and the elimination of marginal firms. Thus a monetary policy of restraint must be followed, and the market forces of supply and demand must be given free rein (Mouré, 1988). The Bank of Italy, an equally staunch advocate of orthodoxy in the area of finance, went on record as being opposed to a policy of expansion, which would only put a damper on those adjustment processes necessary to achieve an end to the crisis (Marconi, 1982).

The outcome of the two deflationary experiences was, however, quite different. First of all, in France the Government's powers and thus its scope for action were much more limited than in Italy, where an authoritarian regime controlled a large portion of the economy, namely the banking sector, and allowed producers and unions virtually no means to oppose its measures. Secondly, as late as 1934, France and Italy found themselves having to deal with monetary situations which were in sharp contrast to one another. The earlier undervaluation of the Poincaré franc and the international role of the Paris capital market resulted in a massive influx of funds in 1928, both the return of French capital and an inflow of foreign capital. This enabled the Banque de France to build up substantial gold reserves, which by the end of November 1932 reached a record figure of 83.341 billion francs. From then onwards, there was only a slight reversal of this trend, and at the end of 1934, gold reserves remained in excess of 82 billion francs (Sicsic, 1993). Thanks to this hoard, the franc remained quite solid, even though it could no longer be considered a monetary haven, and France was seen as the backbone of the gold bloc.

The lira, on the contrary, was an extremely vulnerable currency, which ever since its stabilization in 1927 had been seen to be overvalued. The inflow of risk capital came to a halt, and from then onwards Italy had to put up with the withdrawal of foreign deposits from its banks and the continuing erosion of national savings, thus aggravating the impact of a heavy balance of trade deficit. As a result, the Bank of Italy's reserves fell from over 12 billion liras at the end of 1927 to only 5.8 billion at the close of 1934, at which date they represented barely one-eleventh of the gold reserves of the Banque de France (Azzolini, 1937).

Two deflationary episodes ensued, at separate points in time. At first, France was reluctant to turn to a deflationary policy. Public spending grew as successive governments envisaged public-works schemes, however modest these may appear to us now. Loans were sought and secured from the Bank of France, as was credit from the banking sector in general, in order to cover Treasury needs. As a result, the mass of banknotes in circulation remained at its high level throughout 1934. Any attempt to hold down wages in the public sector or to reduce war pensions met with stiff resistance and there was no effective pressure on money wages. It was not until 1935, marked by increased speculation against the franc and the formation in June of the Laval Government invested with extraordinary powers, that the latter made effective use of the principal instruments of deflationary policy. The Banque de France lending rate, which had been at 2.5 per cent since the beginning of the year, was raised to 6 per cent. A series of decrees made it possible to increase fiscal pressure, and reduce public spending by 10 per cent through wage-cuts in the public sector and diminished returns on government stocks and bonds; prices were arbitrarily cut in certain areas. At the end of the year however, the deputies attempted to soften the effect of these decrees, and in January 1936 the Laval Government was forced to resign, thus signing the death-knell of a deflationary policy.

By 1932 Italy had already adopted a deflationary position and initially adhered to it. The Government tried to hold down the budgetary deficit, the central bank maintained its discount rate at one or two points above that of the Banque de France, and kept a tight rein on loans, with the result that the amount of money in circulation fell to 133 billion liras in 1934. This was 4 billion less than in 1929. Wages, which had been held down over a long period, continued to fall until 1934, at which time a campaign was launched to lower prices in an effort to bring them down from a factor of 4 to 3, compared to their pre-war level.

Italy's monetary policy, fundamentally different from that of France, further included setting up foreign-exchange controls. It would have been virtually impossible for a central bank with nearly depleted gold reserves to defend the gold parity of its currency within the free market! Thus foreign-exchange controls, which had existed in principle since 1931, were tightened during 1934. In May, a decree was passed which (*a*) forbade transactions on the foreign exchange without a real return; (*b*) forbade the purchase of foreign stocks and bonds; and (*c*) made it a treasonable offence to take liras out of the country (Toniolo, 1980). In December of the same year, the State laid claim to all foreign exchange obtained by exporters and a National Institute of Exchange was given a virtual monopoly on all foreign-exchange operations. This device was reinforced in 1935.

Having thus taken measures to protect its currency from possible fluctuations in the exchange rate provoked by adverse conditions beyond its frontiers, Italy was to experience a gradual but radical change of policy. As early as 1934, the conversion of consols paved the way for a fall in the cost of money and in March 1935 the discount rate of the Bank of Italy was reduced to 3.5 per cent. However, further pursuit of this policy was out of the question, due to the war in Ethiopia, which imposed a rise in this rate to 4.5–5 per cent. On the other hand, preparations for this same war (which began in October 1935), the cost of operations, and the consequences of sanctions imposed by the League of Nations forced the Government to change direction, without official acknowledgement. What was required at all cost, in lieu of the defence of the gold parity of the lira, was provision for the country's wartime priorities. The retreat from the deflationary drive can be deduced from three key indicators: First, there was a surge in public spending and, despite the tax increases, a soaring deficit which climbed from 2 to 13 billion liras for the following fiscal year. This amounts to deficit-spending the effects of which have not been clearly ascertained (Baudis, 1941; Toniolo, 1980). Next there was a sharp rise in the amount of money in circulation, which rose from 13 to 17 billion liras in 1935; this stemmed from the need to cover a part of the war costs by the growth of the money supply and an increase in lending by the Bank of Italy. Finally, prices rose by roughly 10 per cent between 1934 and 1935.

The policies followed by France as well as by Italy resulted in double failure. On the economic front, the contraction in exports was proportionally higher in Italy than in France, as a result of League of Nations sanctions. But in France deflation brought about a depression that was even deeper; industrial output declined by 22 per cent between 1929 and 1935. This was the result of several factors: a lack of competitivity; the decline in profitability as rising unit labour costs reflected the rise in real wages; and high real interest rates. As compared to France, Italy did better, maintaining industrial output, with an upturn in industry as austerity measures were dropped. However, the recovery was rather poor by comparison with the growth in Germany.

One can also speak of failure in the monetary area. This is obvious in Italy's case. It is true that the lira lost only 4.2 per cent on the money market, with respect to its official parity. Nevertheless, it became expedient to raise the market price of gold in liras by 18 per cent, to create a tourist lira which was depreciated by 25 per cent, and also to depreciate other liras. The gold parity of the lira had become fictitious and had fallen prey to surreptitious depreciation.

The franc, on the other hand, remained a strong currency and public opinion continued to counter any move to devaluate it. The situation of the franc was threatened in the end by a sharp increase in capital outflow: an estimate of the net figure for such 'invisible' outflows is 16 billion francs for 1935 (Sicsic, 1993).

Two cases of late devaluation

The devaluation of the franc and the lira did not reflect a sudden change of heart on the part of the monetary authorities, nor did it follow initial calculations of purchasing-power parities. In France, Leon Blum, the head of government, whilst promising a destruction of the deflationary measures of Laval and a revalorization of the purchasing power of the French, made an undertaking to maintain the integrity of the franc on foreign-exchange markets. Yet he was confronted with a massive flight of capital which doubled in the wake of elections, due to fears fuelled by social unrest and rumours of tax increases. The extent of this speculation rendered a devaluation inevitable, since from May to September the gold taken from the Banque de France vaults amounted to 10 billion francs. The devaluation took place on 26 September and the rate, which fell by between 25 and 34 per cent, was fixed in the course of negotiations between France, the USA, and England resulting in the tripartite agreement announced on the same day (see further Chapter 1 by Feinstein, Temin, and Toniolo).

The Fascist Government, in an attempt to save face, seized on the occasion provided by the French devaluation, proceeding on 5 October to 'align' its money. Devalued in the same proportion as the dollar in 1933–4, the value of the lira dropped down to its 1927 stabilization level, i.e. 19 liras per dollar and 90 liras (*quota novanta*) per pound sterling.

Devaluation, for those countries which had resorted to it in the early 1930s, on the whole provided beneficial results. Such an operation stimulated competitiveness in the goods market, increased business profitability, and paved the way for expansionist policies. Generally it led to an economic upturn. That none of these things took place following the devaluation of the franc and the lira can be ascribed to their late timing. The countries which were the first to opt for devaluation drew maximum benefits, and this was all the more detrimental to their rivals, whereas the latecomers succeeded only in eliminating a price differential which had by then inflicted grave damage upon them.

However, the degree of setback suffered by France and Italy differed considerably. Apart from the volume of exports, the comparison of which is somewhat uncertain—whilst French exports were rather poor, Italy's were adversely affected by a policy of self-sufficiency—Italy's overall economic performance during the period 1936–8, though mediocre when compared to that of Germany for the same period, was notably better than that of France. Thus industrial production rose by 14.9 per cent in Italy, while it stagnated in France, notwithstanding the upturn in the autumn of 1936, which proved to be short-lived. This depressed state coincided with a sharp rise in retail prices, and the situation in France at this point can be characterized by the (anachronistic) term of stagflation. Compared to Italy, France's inferior position became equally evident from the monetary point of view. Whereas the lira was officially stabilized until the war, it became necessary to intervene to readjust the franc in 1937 and again in 1938. From 1928 to 1938, the franc lost 60 per cent of its gold value, the lira 40 per cent only and Italy's leaders could pride themselves on the fact that one lira was officially worth nearly two French francs.

The difference in the extent of the devaluations of 1936 does not explain the fact that France's economic upturn failed to materialize. Doubtless the devaluation of the lira was deeper than that of the franc (40.94 per cent as opposed to 25–34 per cent), but one must take into account initial levels. As of 1927, the lira, in terms of purchasing power, was overvalued, whereas the Poincaré franc was vastly undervalued (Sicsic, 1992). In addition, with a marked increase in the depreciation of the franc in 1937–8, exceeding that of the lira, the economic performance of France did not overtake that of Italy.

Furthermore, compared to France, Italy enjoyed comparative advantages which enabled it to benefit to a greater degree from the devaluation. First of all, the latter was accompanied by drastic measures, albeit without a return to the harsh deflation of 1934. Certain prices were blocked for a two-year period (rents, gas, electricity), while others were placed under the control of local state and party organizations. Forced loans were implemented, based on real estate, new taxes were created (on dividends, then on corporation capital), thus holding down the growth of the money supply and of prices.

These were of the order of 20 per cent between 1936 and 1938, half the rate in France. Furthermore, while it was no longer possible to hold down wages, in view of the extent of the drop in living-standards, the increase was limited to 10 per cent, on two occasions. All this hindered the upturn in the private domestic sector, though activity was sustained through military orders. Although the competitiveness of Italian products failed to improve significantly, the conclusion of clearing agreements with Germany assured Italy of continued exports, in spite of everything. Finally, continuing stringent exchange controls protected the lira against speculation and above all made it possible to mask the extent of real depreciation: officially, Italian money lost only 4 per cent on the foreign-exchange market, but a depreciated tourist lira remained in existence and an exchange premium was instituted to encourage Italian workers to send funds abroad.

The policy adopted by France after the 1936 devaluation was decidedly unfortunate. What was required in principle to 'make a success' of a devaluation was the repatriation of capital, ongoing checks on prices, a clamp-down on wages, precluding any untoward display of generosity, and finally encouragment for industrial expansion. The Popular Front Government did just the opposite; its ill-advised intervention stemmed without doubt not so much from 'economic errors', denounced by Alfred Sauvy, as from contradictory constraints in the midst of which it struggled ineffectually.

First it preserved free trade, out of respect for the free-market economy and out of its determination to maintain good relations with the Anglo-Saxon democracies. Nevertheless at the same time, the social situation, fears of new taxes, and the threat of war prevented any lasting return of capital before the end of 1938 and in fact triggered fresh flights of capital. Due to the persistent crisis in confidence which hobbled the franc, the gold liquidity of the Banque de France continued to decline, and interest rates were relatively high (4 per cent for bank rate at the start of 1937, 6 per cent for the long-term rates).

Next, generous social measures whose postponement was politically hazardous (which even preceded the devaluation to a large extent) resulted in sharp wage rises, and so also wage costs. The net result was an unacceptable jump in prices which quite destroyed the competitive edge procured by the devaluation. But this increase, which was countered by controls that were more heavy-handed than effective, often remained insufficient to restore business profitability. Finally, a policy of stimulating internal demand by means of restoring purchasing power came up against the effects of a hasty and oversystematic application of the law limiting the working week to forty hours. A drop in the number of hours may have limited demand or production capacity (Villa, 1991), with the inevitable result of stagflation.

5. Conclusion

A comparison of the monetary policies of France and Italy between the two wars reveals first of all undeniable similarities and some evident synchronizations whose occurrence in fact reveals a significant shift in phase as well as quite real differences. Where France and Italy applied policies which can be designated by the same terms (stabilization, deflation, devaluation), the steps taken by the two countries frequently had neither the same impact nor the same significance. These divergences increased even further from 1934 onwards, as a result above all of the different political, economic, and social climate in each country.

The complexity of monetary phenomena derives from the fact that, from an historical perspective, they are not purely monetary. The choice of a foreign exchange-rate and the setting-up of an appropriate policy by the monetary authorities must be placed in their context. The decisions of the latter are not merely the fruit of their ideas. They are shaped to an equal degree by the pressure of public opinion which, for example in France, long deluded itself into believing in the restoration of the germinal franc, before becoming strongly attached to the Poincaré franc. They falter under the influence of the general policy of governments and of unforeseen events, such as the war in Ethiopia. They are also modified, above all where free trade is maintained, by mass movement of capital, reinforced by speculation.

Finally, the twofold experience of the franc and the lira between the two world wars shows that far from being neutral, currency is a variable which plays a considerable economic role. Hence the importance of monetary choices. But adjusting economic behaviour to evolving foreign exchange rates can be done in many ways. Thus the weakening of the franc on foreign-exchange markets had the immediate effect of stimulating exports and growth in France in the middle of the 1920s, whereas it did not have the same effect from 1936 onwards. Even in the long term, it is probable in the case of Italy and certain in the case of France, that the alternation of overvaluation and undervaluation of the currency had a negative impact on both economies, and helps to explain their mediocre performance throughout this period.

References

Aftalion, A. (1950; 2nd edn., 1958), *Monnaie, prix et change* (Paris: Sirey).
Azzolini, H. E. V. (1937), 'La Politique monetaire italienne', *The Banker* (trad. Archives de la Banque de France).

Baudis, P. (1941), *L'économie italienne et la lire* (Toulouse: Boisseau).

Bouvier, J. (1986), 'Presentazione' (to Emile Moreau), in *Memorie di un Governatore delle Banca di Francia* (Cariplo: Laterza).

Ciocca, P. (1976), 'L'economia Italiana nel Contesto Internazionale', in Ciocca and Toniolo (1976).

—— and Toniolo, G. (eds.) (1976), *L'economia Italiana nel Periodo Fascista* (Bologna: il Mulino).

—— —— (1984), 'Industry and Finance in Italy, 1918–1940', *Journal of European Economic History*, 13.

Eichengreen, B., and Sachs, J. (1985), 'Exchange Rates and Economic Recovery in the 1930s', *Journal of Economic History*, 45.

—— and Wyplosz, C. (1990), 'The Economic Consequences of the Franc Poincaré', in B. Eichengreen, *Elusive Stability* (Cambridge: Cambridge University Press).

Einzig, P. (1937), *The Theory of Forward Exchange Rates* (London: Macmillan).

Falco, G., and Storaci, M. (1975), 'Fluttuazioni monetarie alla meta degli anni 20: Belgio, Francia e Italia', *Studi Storici*, 16.

—— —— (1977), 'Il ritorno all'oro in Belgio, Francia et Italia (1926–1928)', *Italia Contemporanea*.

Fua, G. (ed.) (1978), *Lo Sviluppo economico in Italia*, 3 vols. (Milano: Franco Angli).

Keynes, J. M. (1972), *Collected Writings*, ix (London: Macmillan).

Kindleberger, C. (1983), *A Financial History of Western Europe* (London: Allen & Unwin).

League of Nations (1945), *Industrialization and Foreign Trade* (Geneva).

Maddison, A. (1981), *Les phases du développement capitaliste* (Paris: Economica).

Maizels, A. (1963), *Industrial Growth and World Trade* (Cambridge: Cambridge University Press).

Makinen, G. E., and Woodward, G. T. (1989), 'A Monetary Interpretation of the Poincaré Stabilization of 1926', *Southern Economic Journal*, 56.

Marconi, M. (1982), *La politica monetaria del fascismo* (Bologna: il Mulino).

Moreau, E. (1954), *Souvenirs d'un gouverneur de la Banque de France* (Paris: Médicis).

Moure, K. (1988), 'Une éventualité absolument exclue: French reluctance to devalue, 1933–1936', *French Historical Studies*.

OEEC (1960), *Industrial Statistics* (Paris: OEEC).

Paradisi, M. (1976), 'Il commercio estero e la struttura internazionale', in Ciocca, and Toniolo (1976).

Rueff, J. (1959), 'Sur un point d'histoire: le niveau de la stabilisation Poincaré', *Revue d'économie politique*, 69.

Salvemini, G. (1936), *Under the Axe of Fascism* (London: Gollancz).

Sargent, T. (1983), 'Stopping Moderate Inflations: The Methods of Poincaré and Thatcher', in R. Dornbusch and M. Simonsen (eds.), *Inflation, Debt and Indexation* (Cambridge, Mass.: MIT Press).

Sauvy, A. (1984), *Histoire économique de la France entre les deux guerres*, 3 vols. (Paris: Economica; 1st edn., 1965, 4 vols., Fayard).

Sicsic, P. (1992). 'Was the Franc Poincaré Deliberately Overvalued?', *Explorations in Economic History*, 29.

Sicsic, P. (1993), 'L'afflux d'or en France de 1928 à 1934', in *Du franc Poincaré à l'écu* (Paris: Ministère de l'Economie).

Toniolo, G. (1980), *L'economia dell 'Italia fascista* (Bari: Laterza).

Villa, P. (1991), 'Une explication des enchaînements macro-économiques sur l'entre-deux-guerres', *Le Mouvement social* (Jan.).

Wolfe, M. (1951), *The French Franc between the Wars, 1919–1939* (New York: Columbia University Press).

7

Managing the Franc in Belgium and France: The Economic Consequences of Exchange-Rate Policies, 1925–1936

ISABELLE CASSIERS

1. Introduction

Belgium and France, neighbours whose moneys shared the same name, had similar monetary histories between the wars. The period was marked, in Belgium as in France, by two major events: a monetary stabilization in the middle of the 1920s and a devaluation in the middle of the 1930s. The stabilization, which took place in 1926 in both countries, ended a period of floating currencies and exchange-rate depreciation. It buried any hopes of returning to the pre-war gold parity but permitted both countries to join the gold exchange standard. Belgium and France were to become, to differing degrees, among the last defenders of the link to gold. Belgium finally devalued its currency in 1935, followed by France in 1936.

The purpose of this chapter is to attempt a comparative study of these two monetary episodes. Although one striking feature is that Belgium took its decisions about exchange-rate policy in advance of France, the concern here is not with glorifying little Belgium as giving the lead to its large neighbour. Indeed the focus will not be on the making of policy but on its economic consequences. The role of monetary policy in the French economy between the wars is currently under revision. A closer look at the neighbouring Belgian experience lends support to this revisionist trend.

Most existing studies—by contemporaries and by historians, Belgian as well as French—see the late 1920s as a period of great economic prosperity in which exports, stimulated by undervalued exchange rates fixed at stabilization, were the main motor of growth in both countries. Such prosperity, it is argued, helped the French economy to resist the effects of the Great Depression.

The French version of this standard story has recently been challenged on two fronts. Eichengreen and Wyplosz (1990) have shown that French

The author would like to acknowledge her gratitude to Peter Solar, Herman Van der Wee, Michelangelo van Meerten, and Michel De Vroey for help in preparing this chapter. Special thanks go to Peter Solar for translating the text into English.

growth in the late 1920s rested more on the strength of investment, encouraged by a radical change in fiscal policy, than on the growth of exports stimulated by undervaluation of the franc Poincaré. An analysis at the sectoral level by Marseille (1980) has called into question the idea that prosperity was general and the notion that the franc Poincaré insulated France from the initial effects of the Depression.

In the case of Belgium Cassiers (1989) has shown that growth in the international sector, far from profiting from the stabilization, was diminishing in the late 1920s. Prosperity came to depend more on the growth of domestic activity and on a surge of financial activity increasingly unrelated to underlying industrial trends.

The aim of this chapter is to compare these national studies rejecting the traditional interpretation of the management of the franc (Belgian or French) under the gold exchange standard, and to suggest the essential similarities of the Belgian and French experiences. As analysis draws primarily on information in these three studies, it by no means exhausts the possibilities of comparison.

Section 2 gives an overview of the exchange-rate histories of Belgium and France between the wars. The stabilizations of the 1920s and the devaluations of the 1930s are set briefly in their economic and socio-political context. The analysis of the economic consequences of the stabilizations is taken up in the second section. The clear similarities of experience shown by the three studies cited above suggest that comparative analysis be continued into the 1930s, which is done in section 4 for the depression and deflation of the early 1930s and in section 5 for the devaluations of the Belgian franc (1935) and the French franc (1936).

2. The Belgian and French Francs between the Wars

The histories of the Belgian and French francs between the wars may be divided into four periods.

From 1919 to 1926[1] both currencies were floating. The financing of war and reconstruction led to inflation and exchange-rate depreciation. At the beginning of the 1920s both countries lived under the double illusion that Germany would pay reparations and that their currencies would return to pre-war gold parities. Both illusions were increasingly dispelled from 1924.

---

[1] Makinen and Woodward (1989) give a clear overview of this period, for Belgium as well as for France. For more detail, see Dupriez (1978) and Van der Wee and Tavernier (1975) on Belgium, and Sauvy (1984, vol. i) for France. It has not been possible to incorporate the results of Buissière (1992) and Levy-Leboyer *et al.* (1993) which were not available when this chapter was written.

The victory of the left in the French elections of May 1924 disquieted the financial community and the new Government was rapidly confronted with difficulties in renewing its loans. As nine Ministers of Finance followed one another over the next two years, the franc depreciated rapidly (Fig. 7.1). This downward pressure was communicated to the Belgian franc, which, since its origin, had been closely linked, economically and psychologically, to the French franc. Despite this link, the Belgian franc was stabilized *de facto* for six months in 1925. While this stabilization was the work of the Centre-Left Government that came to power following the triumph of the Socialists in the 1925 elections, the continued depreciation of the French franc under a left-wing Government undermined the confidence of banks and other financial institutions that the Belgian socialists would be able to maintain the value of the franc successfully. In May 1926 this lack of confidence resulted in a massive failure to refinance the public debt. The crisis led to a Government of national union, bringing parties of the Right into the coalition and Emile Francqui, a private banker, into the Government with the express task of stabilizing the franc. Francqui quickly did so, in September 1926, by means of drastic budgetary reforms and an explicit separation from the French franc.

In the meantime the Left in France was also compelled to share power in the interests of exchange-rate stability. In July 1926 Poincaré formed a Government of national union and succeeded in halting speculation against the franc (incidentally facilitating Francqui's job in Belgium). The French stabilization became effective from December 1926 and was closely related, as in Belgium, to draconian measures intended to return the public finances to balance.

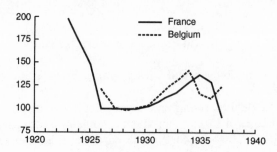

FIG. 7.1 Nominal effective exchange rates of the Belgian franc and the French franc, 1923–1937(1929 = 100)
Sources: Belgium: Hogg (1986); France: Eichengreen and Wyplosz (1990)

The laws of 25 October 1926 in Belgium and 24 June 1928 in France simply made official the earlier *de facto* stabilizations. Where both francs had exchanged at 25 francs per pound sterling before the war, they now traded at different values: Belgium had stabilized at 175 Belgian francs per £, France at 125 French francs per £. The larger depreciation in Belgium may be explained, in part, by the fact that it occurred first, at a time when the French franc traded at even less than the Belgian franc and before the sharp deflation of prices that occurred in France during the second half of 1926.[2] In any case, the rates at which both francs were stabilized seem to have been below those strictly justified by purchasing-power parities.[3] The adherence to these exchange rates in the context of the gold exchange standard marks the second period in the currencies' inter-war history, one which would last until September 1931 when Britain left gold.

The third period, lasting until 1935 in Belgium and 1936 in France, was characterized by these two countries' strict fidelity to gold parities in a world increasingly given over to floating currencies. When the USA abandoned gold in April 1933 France, Belgium, Italy, Switzerland, and the Netherlands decided to strengthen their allegiance to fixed exchange rates and formed the gold bloc. In order to defend their gold parities, these countries then undertook severe deflations. In effect, to remain competitive with countries in the sterling and dollar zones, the gold bloc sought to achieve by a fall in domestic prices what others obtained through exchange-rate depreciations. This deflation, carried out in Belgium as in France by Governments of the Right, prolonged the Depression.

Belgium entered the last period of its inter-war monetary history eighteen months before France. In March 1935 it devalued the franc by 28 per cent. The decision, taken by a new Government incorporating the Socialists and led by Paul van Zeeland, was intended to put paid to the policy of deflation that had reigned in all right-wing Governments since the beginning of the Depression. In France the Government of Léon Blum, after three months in office, abandoned the gold parity and devalued the franc in September 1936. Yet, in spite of the apparent similarities, it is in the period of the devaluations and after that the Belgian and French experiences differ the most. Whereas in Belgium the devaluation brought a certain degree of prosperity and calmed social tensions, France of the late 1930s was riven by internal conflict and faced continued depreciation of its currency.

This quick overview of the inter-war exchange-rate histories of Belgium and France brings out the central importance of the stabilizations of 1926. The exchange rates fixed at that time were maintained at all costs for almost ten years, in spite of the upheavals in the international monetary system. As will be seen, the stabilizations led to intersectoral disparities in the Belgian and French economies that would be accentuated by the Depression.

---

[2] 'Si l'on avait remis la stabilisation de deux mois, le taux de 125 eût aussi été atteint en Belgique, tandis que les devises rentraient', Dupriez (1978: 76).

[3] Commentators are unanimous on this point; see Dupriez (1978), Van der Wee and Tavernier (1975), Sauvy (1984: i. 70).

3. The Economic Consequences of the Stabilizations: The Convergence of Experience

France: a new view of prosperity and its causes

A devaluation—or stabilization at a favourable rate—can theoretically favour exports in two ways. If exporters maintain their prices in the domestic currency, then the fall in the exchange rate lowers prices expressed in foreign currency and increases their competitiveness. This is usually called the demand-side effect. But if exporters are price-takers on international markets and continue to sell their products at world prices, then their revenues in terms of domestic currency will rise. In so far as input prices do not rise or rise less than export prices, this will translate into an increase in profits. This is the supply-side effect, in that the increase in profits should stimulate the supply of export goods. If a currency stabilization is alleged to have encouraged a sustained expansion of exports, then it should be possible to observe one or the other—or a combination of—these effects.

But in the case of France Eichengreen and Wyplosz cannot find either effect after 1927. The stimulative effect of stabilization on the demand for exports did not last long:

Despite the real exchange rate's maintenance at peak levels through 1930, export volume fell in 1929, reflecting the decline in world incomes due to the onset of the Depression followed by imposition of trade restrictions abroad. The export share of GNP fell even earlier, in calendar year 1928. Although exchange-rate depreciation may have prevented exports from declining even more rapidly than this, the extent and the very fact of their decline suggests that the impact of real depreciation on export demand cannot by itself account for the persistence of French economic growth after 1928 (Eichengreen and Wyplosz, 1990: 158).

Sectorally disaggregated data collected by Marseille support this conclusion, although they offer a reminder of the limits of the aggregates employed by Eichengreen and Wyplosz. The French balance of trade, in surplus from 1924 to 1927, turned into deficit thereafter. French exports of manufactured goods began to decline slowly, though within this fall there were major differences among sectors. In some industries the fall in export volume between 1926 and 1929 was as high as 46 per cent (Marseille, 1980: 653–4).

As for the supply-side effect, the results are also negative. In order to judge the impact of the stabilization on the profitability of traded goods production, Eichengreen and Wyplosz look at the behaviour of domestic prices. Their results lend support to Marseille's argument that by halting the rise in wholesale prices accompanying the depreciation of the franc, the stabilization revealed to French exporters, too late, the tendency of world prices to fall and so put an end to a period of easy profits. The observed change in the movement of relative prices could have been behind the changes in sectoral growth:

The rise in the ratio of retail to wholesale prices after 1927 implies an increase in the relative price of nontraded goods that should have shifted resources out of the production of exportables and into the home goods sector. This explains how the French economy accommodated the fall in export demand associated with the onset of the Depression abroad without significantly reducing the level of economic activity. At approximately the same time as the onset of the Depression was reducing foreign demand for French exports, the rise in the relative price of nontraded goods at home was transferring resources out of the production of exportables and into the production of nontradables (Eichengreen and Wyplosz, 1990: 162).

While the company accounts analysed by Marseille show great variations in profitability across sectors, the pattern of variations is consistent with that revealed by the movements in production and exports:

There are indeed two sectors within French capitalism, a sheltered sector spared the weakening of the late 1920s and a sensitive, vulnerable sector tied to the markets for consumer goods and to transport, the profits of which stagnate and even crumble from the end of 1928, in some cases even earlier. It is as though the contraction of foreign markets, particularly noticeable from the end of 1927, was translated almost immediately into changes in the production, prices and profits of these sectors (Marseille, 1980: 658–9; author's translation).

This sectoral diversity seems to be a characteristic trait of the late 1920s. It is also to be found in the new issues of companies. Marseille found that the overall growth of 44 per cent in new issues in 1929 hid large sectoral differences, from − 46 per cent in textiles to + 72.5 per cent in electricity and 120.8 per cent for real estate and banking.

In France, then, two general phenomena stand out: (*a*) within industry, a contrast between the vigorous health of the sheltered sectors and the first signs of crisis in the exposed ones; and (*b*) a certain euphoria in banking, finance, and real estate, perceived at the time as a sign of great prosperity, but better seen as the augur of a financial crisis.

In sum, Eichengreen and Wyplosz's stimulating macroeconomic observations and Marseille's sectoral approach come together to form a new picture of the late 1920s in France. Far from stimulating exports, the stabilization revealed the underlying downward trend in world prices and opened the door to trouble for the exporting industries. The two works cited above do differ somewhat in their emphases. Eichengreen and Wyplosz insist on the role of investment in sustaining growth in the late 1920s. Marseille is more sceptical of this growth, proposing indicators that suggest an earlier reversal and emphasizing the contrast between the financial boom and the exhaustion of the factors underlying industrial growth. There is no need here to go further into the details of the French case. A look at Belgium will show the plausibility and the fruitfulness of this new interpretation of the French stabilization.

Belgium: difficulties in the international sector and financial boom [4]

To understand the consequences of exchange-rate changes on an economy so open as that of Belgium in the 1920s,[5] a sectoral analysis is even more essential than in the case of France. The justification and methods for dividing industrial activity into an international sector on one hand and a domestic sector on the other have been discussed in detail elsewhere,[6] so here the focus will be on the parallels to be drawn with France in the effects of stabilization.

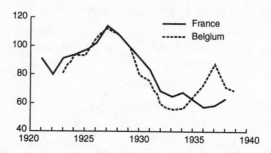

FIG. 7.2   Export performance in Belgium and France, 1921–1939 (exports as per cent of GNP, 1929 = 100)
Sources: Belgium: Mitchell (1975) and van Meerten et al. (forthcoming); France: Sauvy (1984) and Toutain (1987)

The depreciation of the Belgian franc during the early 1920s, as well as the strong demand generated by reconstruction for the standard goods in which Belgian industry specialized, produced a rapid growth in exports. The experience of Belgium in the years 1920–6 has all the hallmarks of export-led growth: rapid growth of trade, high profitability of tradable-goods producers, fast growth of employment in the international sector despite significant increases in productivity.

---

[4] This section is based on Cassiers (1989: esp. 140–54).
[5] Belgium was the most open of all the economies surveyed by Svennilson (1954). In 1938 its exports were 59% of production, as against 15% for France and 26% for the UK.
[6] Cassiers (1989: ch. 1). The international sector of the Belgian economy included the following industries: coal, coke, iron and steel, non-ferrous metals, quarrying, textiles (except clothing manufacture), chemicals, and glass. The domestic sector took in food-processing, construction and public works, gas and electricity, paper, and clothing.

The monetary stabilization of 1926 marked an end to these trends. To see that the growth of the late 1920s did not depend on exports stimulated by a favourable exchange rate consider, in turn, the demand and supply-side effects.

At the end of the 1920s the growth of Belgian exports slowed and their share in national product fell noticeably. The weakness of the notion that growth was export-led can be seen in Fig. 7.2. The falling export share in GNP did not mean that Belgium was losing its share in world markets, for the slow-down in trade was widespread, as the extraordinary growth in world production began to run up against a shortage of outlets (see Svennilson, 1954). In addition, the evidence suggests that Belgian firms behaved as price-takers[7] and that changes in the value of the franc were reflected almost completely in their profit margins. In the case of a small open economy specializing in standardized products, it is the supply-side effects that deserve the greatest attention.

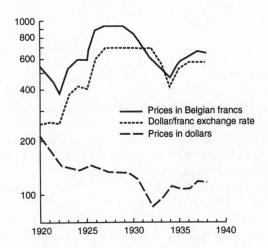

FIG. 7.3 World prices of manufactures, 1920–1938 (1913–14 = 100)
Source: Cassiers (1989)

As was the case in France, the return to a fixed exchange rate abruptly halted the growth in prices of tradables. Figure 7.3 shows clearly the change in the situation facing firms in the international sector from 1927.

The consequences of this reversal were all the more dramatic in that domestic prices did not move in the same way. As shown in Fig. 7.4, in Belgium relative price movements were similar to those highlighted by

---

[7] This hypothesis was tested on limited data available by ordinary least-squares regression and not rejected (Cassiers, 1989: 107).

TABLE 7.1. *Statistics of joint-stock companies in Belgium, 1927–1929* (1927=100)

	Banking	Finance	Industry	
			Domestic	International
Numbers of companies				
1927	100	100	100	100
1928	92	142	132	103
1929	91	163	141	110
Paid-up capital				
1927	100	100	100	100
1928	118	232	115	105
1929	144	402	154	150
Aggregate net profits				
1927	100	100	100	100
1928	132	223	106	72
1929	154	310	140	86
Distributed profits				
1927	100	100	100	100
1928	135	234	106	93
1929	163	300	143	108

Eichengreen and Wyplosz in the case of France, although the fall in the ratio of wholesale to retail prices was deeper and more prolonged in France.

This reversal, begun in 1927 with the stabilization, was at the root of a severe crisis in profitability in the international sector. A comparison of Figs. 7.5 and 7.6 shows this convincingly. The continuing fall in profits from 1927 to 1932 seems to have been closely associated with differences in the rates of growth of output prices and unit labour costs.

While the international sector was suffering from a slow-down in growth from 1927, and even more so from the very unfavourable change in the structure of prices, the domestic sector was doing much better. The vigorous growth in the real wage bill—+ 30.8 per cent between 1927 and 1929—cer-

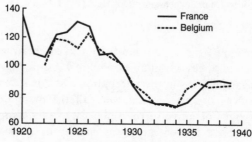

FIG. 7.4 Ratio of wholesale to retail prices in Belgium and France, 1920–1939 (1929 = 100)

Source: Mitchell (1975).

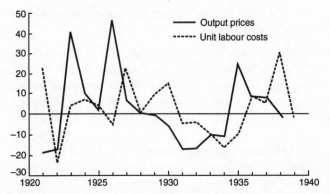

FIG. 7.5 Belgium: international sector, output prices and unit labour costs, 1921–1939
(annual rate of growth) (%)
Source: Cassiers (1989)

tainly had a favourable impact on the growth of final demand. Table 7.1
illustrates the contrast between the two industrial sectors. While net profits
in the international sector dropped by 14 per cent between 1927 and 1929,
those of the domestic sector rose by 40 per cent.

The same table also shows the extraordinary surge in banking and
financial activity. These statistics illustrate Van der Wee and Tavernier's
observation, recalling that the monetary stabilization was accompanied by
a reform of the National Bank widely perceived to have strengthened the
power of private banks:

The private banks were given a free hand and contributed thereafter to the feverish
expansion of the late 1920s. It was an impetuous enthusiasm not checked in time, an

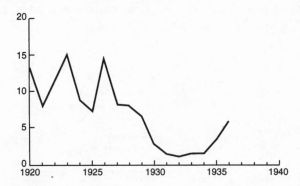

FIG. 7.6 Belgium: international sector, distributed profits relative to paid-up capital and
reserves, 1920–1936 (%)
Source: Cassiers (1989).

eruption of entrepreneurial spirits altogether too violent (Van der Wee and Tavernier, 1975: 208; author's translation).

It is strange that the feverish character of economic activity in the late 1920s has been emphasized so rarely. The financial agitation that reigned in Belgium seems to have masked to most observers the first signs that industrial activity in the international sector was weakening. Yet the signs of financial overheating were numerous (Cassiers, 1989 and Banque Nationale de Belgique).

(a) On the Brussels stock exchange prices rose by 246 per cent between August 1926 and May 1928, when the peak was reached.

(b) New issues of shares and bonds went from 2,656 million francs in 1926 to 14,966 million francs in 1929.

(c) In 1929 46 per cent of all new issues of shares and bonds were for banking and financial institutions, as against 19 per cent in 1927 and 17 per cent in 1930.

(d) The banks invested massively in financial companies: in 1929 62 per cent of their interventions in company capital formation concerned the financial sector, as against 18 per cent in 1927. This share would fall to 27 per cent in 1930.

(e) Dividends declared by all joint-stock companies grew by 45 per cent between 1927 and 1929, but their cash flow increased by only 7 per cent.

(f) The great divergence of experience among sectors shown in Table 7.1 deserves emphasis: while the profits distributed by financial companies tripled, the international sector reluctantly kept paying dividends at a time when its undistributed profits fell by 37 per cent.

These trends are certainly part of the 'turbulence dans les affaires' (Morsel, 1977: 174–9) observable in all Western countries at this time. Yet they seem particularly marked in Belgium, perhaps because of the inflow of capital that followed the monetary stabilization.

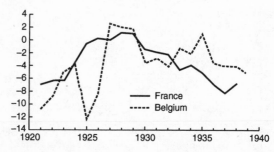

FIG. 7.7 Budget surplus as a share of GNP in Belgium and France, 1921–1939 (%)
Sources: Belgium: Moulard and Grauls (1954) and van Meerten *et al.* (forthcoming); France INSEE (1966) and Toutain (1987).

The fact that a large mass of capital in search of profitable investments could generate financial overheating also needs to be seen in the context of changes in public finance. Francqui could only stabilize the franc in Belgium through radical budgetary measures (Fig. 7.7). Within two years a deficit equivalent to more than 12 per cent of GNP gave way to a comfortable budgetary surplus. In so far as the available series may be believed,[8] the change in fiscal stance was much more pronounced in Belgium than in France. While Poincaré needed only to continue the fiscal restraint begun by his predecessors, Francqui had to bring definitively to an end the laxness apparent in 1925. By contrast with the French case, putting the Belgian public finances in order was not limited to cuts in expenditures. New taxes were levied, bringing an increase in the tax share in national income from 10.9 per cent in 1924 to 16.2 per cent in 1927.

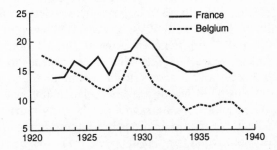

FIG. 7.8   Investment as a share of GNP in Belgium and France, 1921–1939 (%)
Sources: Belgium: van Meerten *et al.*; France: Eichengreen and Wyplosz (1990)

Although the pace of budgetary reform differed in the two countries, they both had repeated budget surpluses at the end of the 1920s. As in the case of France, for which Eichengreen and Wyplosz invoke the crowding-in effect of fiscal stabilization, the appearance of a government budgetary surplus coincided in Belgium with a strong surge in private investment (see Fig. 7.8). When sectoral data becomes available, a detailed analysis of Belgian investment across the two broad sectors should be instructive.[9] The rise in investment in the domestic sector can be easily explained by the growth in domestic demand, accompanied by still high profits at the end of the 1920s. The massive investments that appear to have been made in the

[8] Sauvy and Baudhuin both note the elements of fantasy in the budgetary figures of this period. Note, too, that the contrast between 1926 and 1927 was exaggerated somewhat by the exclusion from the government budget after July 1926 of the expenditures of the Belgian State Railways.

[9] Such an analysis will soon be possible, thanks to the forthcoming publication by van Meerten *et al.* of estimates for investment by sector.

international sector are less understandable, in that export demand was weakening and profits falling sharply. Did the combination of a brutal rise in wage costs and an abundant supply of capital lead firms to make labour-saving investments? In any case, the growth in investment demand in the late 1920s was not sufficient to protect the Belgian economy from the world crisis. Its degree of openness was far too high for it not to have been plunged immediately into distress. On this point, the Belgian case appears to differ from that of France. But perhaps it simply shows features that are more accentuated though fundamentally similar, a question to be taken up next.

4 Crisis and Deflation: The Propagation of the Depression

France is generally considered to have remained sheltered from the crisis longer than most countries. Eichengreen and Wyplosz offer a new sort of explanation for this remarkable resistance. They suggest that the good economic health of France until 1930, or even 1931, was 'due to the fact that the fiscal stabilization switched demand toward domestic scurces, namely, investment, reducing the economy's dependence on foreign demand and insulating the economy from the initial effects of the Great Depression'. But this good health was only relative, and when Marseille's many disaggregated indicators are examined, the early impact of the crisis on the more vulnerable sectors of French economy is apparent. In these sectors exports, production, and profits fell from the beginning of the international crisis.

As can be seen from the Belgian case, these two approaches are com-plementary. In Belgium the crisis hit the international sector very quickly and sent it into severe depression, while the domestic sector remained relatively prosperous, sustained by domestic demand. The sectoral differ-ences which appeared with the stabilization were accentuated by the Depression and reinforced year by year through the attachment to gold. Rigorous deflationary policy eventually broke domestic demand and gener-alized the depression.

In the 1930s the existence of sectoral differences caught the attention of some Belgian and French economists. In Belgium Dupriez (1934) refined his analysis of economic fluctuations by introducing a distinction between sheltered and non-sheltered industries and proposed the outline of a Scandinavian model thirty years ahead of its time. His work soon inspired Dessirier (1935), columnist of the *Revue d'économie politique*, to try to show how adherence to the pre-crisis parity led in France, as in Belgium, to disequilibrium in the domestic economy. Both authors helped prepare the ground theoretically for devaluations that would attempt to restore an equilibrium between the two sectors.

The presence of sectoral disequilibria in Belgium and France can be seen in Table 7.2. Although this table should be read with caution,[10] the disequilibrium appears to have been more severe in Belgium: the sheltered sector seems to have resisted more successfully, while the collapse of profits in the non-sheltered sector was more complete.

TABLE 7.2. *Index of profits distributed by joint-stock companies in France and Belgium,* 1931–33 (1928–9=100)

	France		Belgium	
	Sheltered sector	Non-sheltered sector	Sheltered sector	Non-sheltered sector
1931	96	48	147	63
1932	88	40	145	41
1933	89	40	141	33

Sources: Belgium: Cassiers (1989); France: Dessirier (1935)

The causes of such sectoral disequilibria can be seen in the figures presented earlier. The way in which the Depression spread in Belgium, it will be seen, resembles almost point for point the description by Caron and Bouvier of the French case (Caron and Bouvier, 1980: 656).

Figure 7.2 shows the dramatic contraction of external demand between 1929 and 1932. All industrialized countries saw their markets dry up, with the volume of European exports falling by 38 per cent in three years. But for Belgium and France sales abroad took place at lower and lower prices due to their adherence to the gold parity when their trading partners were devaluing. The continuous appreciation of the Belgian and French francs (Fig. 7.1) was a great burden for tradable-goods producers. In the Belgian case, where firms behaved as price-takers, the effect of overvaluation was absorbed almost completely by the profits of the international sector. Here again the consistency of the story told by Fig. 7.3, 7.4, and 7.5 is remarkable. Figure 7.3 shows how prices in Belgian francs failed to reflect the recovery of 1933–4 and continued their uninterrupted fall as a result of attachment to the gold parity. In the space of four years the prices received by Belgian exporters fell by 50 per cent. The resulting profitability crisis was all the more serious in that domestic prices resisted downward pressures. Figure 7.4 illustrates how much the ratio of wholesale to retail prices deteriorated. As wages tended to follow retail prices, unit labour costs rose relative to output prices until 1934. The collapse of profits distributed by the international sector (Fig. 7.6 and Table 7.2) is only a pale reflection of

---

[10] These figures are aggregates taken from separate Belgian and French sources. The definitions of the sectors and of profits may differ.

desperate situation faced by tradable-goods producers: from 1932 to 1935 this sector was in deficit (total profits minus total losses was negative).

Nothing so dramatic afflicted the domestic sector. But its good health was only relative. The fall in wholesale relative to retail prices should not deflect attention too much from the domestic deflation that was intended to compensate for the appreciation of the franc, though it never quite did so. The cost of living and nominal wages fell by 20 per cent; unemployment reduced domestic purchasing power; investments fell off in response to overcapacity and the fall in profits (Fig. 7.8); the government's new-found budgetary rectitude led to a further contraction of domestic demand from 1933 (Fig. 7.7).

The way in which Belgium, through its adherence to gold, fell into depression is perfectly consistent with the French experience as set out in detail by Mouré (1991):

From July 1933 the French economy declined while conditions in most of the rest of the world improved . . . Elimination of the budget deficit was the focus of government attention; this was believed essential to economic recovery and to preservation of the franc. But as revenue declined, successive governments were unable to raise taxes and cut expenditures sufficiently to balance the budget, and recurrent borrowing pushed up interest rates and weakened confidence. At the same time import quotas, subsidies, and prices supports, adopted for political reasons, rendered deflationary programs economically incoherent.[11]

5. The Devaluations: Divergent Experiences

According to Sauvy, Belgium and France faced much the same dilemma in the mid-1930s: deflation or devaluation. The essential difference in their experience lay in the existence in Belgium of an 'organisme de pensée et de réflexion', the school of economists around Dupriez in Louvain, which led that country to undertake 'une opération d'avant garde', a devaluation based on scientific calculation.

In the history of the interwar economy there are few examples of scientific reasoning dictating, in this fashion, a political decision . . . Thereafter Belgian policy would long be inspired by the Louvain Institute. The paths of Belgium and France became totally separate and, ironically but also logically, it would be Belgium that proved the model of monetary virtue, notably in 1945, whereas France, which had become allergic to deflation, went from adventure to adventure. . . . This striking event, which marked the victory of technique, emphasized once again France's problems.[12]

---

[11] Mouré (1991: 276). See also Caron and Bouvier (1980: 659–60). On the contradictions in Belgian deflationary policy, see Cassiers (1989: 162–4).

[12] Sauvy (1984: i.169) (author's translation). The pioneering nature of the Belgian devaluation is also underlined by Kindleberger.

That the Belgian devaluation was carefully calculated on the basis of the theory of purchasing-power parity deserves to be underlined, if only because it was so unlike the monetary confusion and improvised devaluations of the period. But it is perhaps a bit extreme to take this to be the essential difference between the Belgian and French experiences in the late 1930s. Two other differences are worth emphasizing.

A first difference: the relative weight of sectors

The monetary stabilizations in Belgium and France and the subsequent devaluations elsewhere had created great sectoral disparities in prices and profits. Firms in the international sector were severely tested; those in the domestic sector were, by comparison, in a reasonably good position. This was true of both countries. But the relative weights of the two sectors both in economic activity and in political decision-making differed. The sheltered sector in France was larger and more powerful than its counterpart in Belgium.[13] This could explain the *mildness of the depression* and the resistance to changes in economic policy, as Mouré has shown (Mouré, 1991: 277). In Belgium, on the other hand, the share of the international sector was so large that the Depression was fairly rapidly communicated to the sheltered sector.

Differences in the industrial structures of the sheltered sectors in the two economies also influenced their political leverage. The sheltered sector in France, as defined by Dessirier and Marseille, seems to have contained more large firms and cartelized industries than was the case in Belgium. Representatives of this sector argued publicly against devaluation, insisting, in effect, that exporting firms not be allowed to profit from another stroke of good fortune like that of the early 1920s (Dessirier, 1935: 1350; Marseille, 1980: 674). In Belgium, by contrast, the interests of the sheltered sector were relatively poorly defended, due to its small size and the prevalence of small firms within it. Another, perhaps more important factor in Belgium was the heavy involvement by banks in the large enterprises of the international sector. It is striking how the abandonment of deflation in favour of devaluation coincided with the threat of bank failures: as the result of financing the international sector's losses, the banks' own defences against deflation had been eroded.

The differences in industrial structure hidden behind the sectoral breakdown may then explain why France was less pressed to devalue. Although the devaluation of the Belgian franc in 1935 worsened the French situation,

---

[13] In order to analyse this point fully, it would be necessary to compare, first, the sectoral composition of the two economies. It would then be interesting to examine degrees of industrial concentration in these sectors and the extent to which banks were involved in industry.

the Popular Front Government that took power in June 1936 affirmed its devotion to the gold parity and

avoided devaluation until it could no longer be postponed. It was a coalition almost entirely opposed to devaluation, and its leaders would not decide to devalue as long as any freedom of choice remained. When it came, the devaluation was not so much a significant departure from previous policy as a necessary retreat, too long delayed, in an effort to recover the stability essential for a durable recovery (Mouré, 1991: 279–80).

A second difference: the socio-political context

The very different political contexts in which the decisions to devalue were taken certainly influenced subsequent divergences in monetary experience. It was noted above that the monetary stabilizations of the 1920s could only succeed, in Belgium as in France, if they gained the confidence of bankers and financiers. In the mid-1930s there is little doubt that the Van Zeeland Government, composed of all the major parties, had the confidence of holders of capital, whereas this group was legitimately upset by the decisions of the Popular Front—or rather, by the order in which these decisions were taken. A comparison of Belgian and French policies in the years 1935–7 shows that much the same economic and social measures were adopted, but in an order that was reversed.

The Popular Front that came to power in June 1936 started from the principle that an increase in purchasing power constituted in itself an alternative to deflation. As Mouré observes: 'The Socialists hoped to generate recovery by augmenting purchasing power, believing that prices would then fall because of higher production and tax revenue would rise to finance the growth in government spending' (Mouré, 1991: 237).

Accordingly, one of the first steps taken by Blum was a wage increase. This could only aggravate the sectoral disequilibria that had resulted from the increasing overvaluation of the franc since 1929. The direct increase in labour costs was almost doubled in practice by the introduction of the forty-hour week without a comparable reduction in wages. Of course, as Asselain (Asselain, 1974: 673) has observed, the reduction in working time was part of a programme designed to put the unemployed back to work and to stimulate final demand. But tradable-goods producers, who had already seen their profits cut to the bone, saw this measure above all as an increase in hourly wage costs. The forty-hour week came to be a symbol around which the hostility of the Right to the Popular Front was focused. The growing distrust by holders of capital brought on the most serious financial crises that France had known, according to Caron and Bouvier, and led to the devaluation. These authors hold that the devaluation, of between 25 and 34 per cent, was too little: 'it did not compensate for the gap that had resulted from the English and American devaluations and from the resulting increase in domestic prices that had taken place since July' (Caron and Bouvier, 1980: 661).

In February 1937 Blum was forced to call a halt to further changes in social policy. In December his successor let the franc depreciate even more (Fig. 7.1). Revision of the forty-hour week law was, in the end, the price that had to be paid to regain the confidence of wealth-holders.

In Belgium the socialists' opposition to deflationary policy, from 1933, coalesced around the *Plan du Travail* conceived by Henri De Man. The Plan proposed, as would the Popular Front, that economic activity be stimulated by a large increase in domestic purchasing power. The many social reforms that it contained were presented as the means to widen consumption demand and so come out of the Depression. Like their French counterparts, the Belgian socialists ignored the monetary implications of their policies and reaffirmed their attachment to the gold parity. The advocates of devaluation thus have to be sought in another quarter. They were the university economists whose perspicacity Sauvy has praised. Their influence on the Centre-Right Catholic Party produced a second force opposing deflationary policy. When, in March 1935, social unrest and the threat of a banking crisis combined to force a radical change in economic policy, the proponents of these two alternatives to deflation, in principle independent, found themselves associated in a government of national union.

The devaluation was the first act of the Van Zeeland Government which by its deft political presentation gained both the confidence of the financiers and the patience of the unions. The devaluation was carefully calculated to bring Belgian prices back into line with British and American prices and to restore the profits of the international sector. It was only afterward, when firms had been given a breath of life, that concessions to the Left were brought forward. The increase in wages, reduction in working hours, paid vacations, and many other measures that figured in De Man's *Plan du Travail* began to be implemented at a prudent speed and in a manner so as not to threaten profits. As against what took place in France, 'the social reform of 1936 was limited to what was possible for firms'. (L'experience Van Zeeland: 206; author's translation). It was thus fairly timid, certainly far short of the hopes of the socialists, but the gains made endured.

The consequences of the devaluation of the Belgian franc

The Belgian devaluation, worked out in this socio-political context and accompanied by measures to keep the growth in wages and domestic prices under control, corrected the sectoral disequilibria that had arisen in the period from 1926 to 1934 and relaunched a more balanced growth. The figures presented above illustrate the impact of the devaluation on the Belgian economy.

From 1935 tradable-goods producers finally began to benefit from the rise in world prices that had begun in 1933 (Fig. 7.3): after a fall of 50 per cent from 1927 to 1934, world prices of manufactures expressed in Belgian francs recovered by 43 per cent in the next three years. This increase was all the more advantageous to firms in the international sector in that wages were under control. In 1935 the large difference in the movements of output prices on the one hand and unit labour costs on the other explains the rise in the profits distributed by the international sector (Fig. 7.6). After an aggregate loss of 43 million francs in 1934 the sector's profits amounted to 717 million francs in 1935, 1,176 million in 1936, and 1,509 million in 1937.[14] Domestic prices were kept under control, so that, after the initial shock of the devaluation, relative prices stabilized at a level more favourable to the international sector (Fig. 7.4). The extent of the devaluation had taken account of an anticipated once-and-for-all increase in domestic prices.[15] Preventing further increases from undoing the effect of the devaluation was the task of several additional measures: customs duties were lowered; sanctions were threatened in the case of price increases judged to be excessive; wage increases were controlled through the *Conférence Nationale du Travail*, created in June 1936 to bring labour, business, and government together for collective bargaining at the national level.

There was a noticeable increase in purchasing power as a result of growth in real wages and the reduction in unemployment arising from an increase in activity. The rise in real labour income—23 per cent between 1935 and 1937—seems to have realized the expectations of the Left which, like the Popular Front, hoped to compensate for the apparently permanent contraction of international trade with a development of the domestic market. In Belgium, both Right and Left agreed that a rise in purchasing power would in the medium term permit a reorientation of the economy towards the domestic sector. This view was given its official statement by the *Commission d'Orientation Industrielle*, created in 1935 to advise the Government on economic policy.

The Belgian devaluation of 1935 was thus noteworthy for the set of policies which accompanied it. These measures were designed to promote a more balanced growth in the short term and to reorient industrial activity in the long term so as to make the economy less vulnerable to changes in world markets. This latter objective has, in fact, never been attained, but stronger and more balanced growth in the short term seems to have been achieved, to judge from the data currently available. The devaluation also

[14] Cassiers (1989: 236). Based on the Banque Nationale de Belgique's summary statistics drawn from company accounts.

[15] Dupriez had calculated, on the basis of purchasing power parities, that a devaluation of 25% was necessary to bring the Belgian franc back into line with the pound and the dollar. He added 3% to take account of higher import prices. See Dupriez (1978: 106–7).

left its legacy for policy-making, for subsequent exchange-rate operations have been planned so as to take account of sectoral differences along the lines of what is known today as the Scandinavian model.

6. Conclusions

This chapter has compared exchange-rate policy in Belgium and France between the wars, concentrating on the most striking lessons that can be drawn from the available literature. This explains the variety of approaches, from the investigation of the socio-political context of policy-making to the analysis of the consequences of monetary policy.

The similarity in the economic consequences of the stabilizations carried out in 1926 is astonishing and reinforces the recent scepticism about whether the boom of the late 1920s was export-led. In Belgium, as in France, the return to a fixed exchange rate, far from stimulating exports, heralded the first difficulties in the international sector and led to a shift in resources toward domestic activity. In both countries it was investment, not exports, that sustained demand at the end of the 1920s. At the same time the multiplication of financial activity concealed the early exhaustion of foreign trade and the incipient sectoral disparities.

The fidelity of the two francs to gold, together with the departures of the pound and the dollar, widened these disparities in the early 1930s and strangled the profitability of tradable-goods producers. The economic situation deteriorated more rapidly in Belgium as a result of its much greater openness, which contributed to the earlier devaluation of the Belgian franc.

The Belgian devaluation was part of a socio-political compromise that assured its success, whereas the devaluation of the French franc, along with the imposition of the forty-hour week, became a symbol of the Left's failure.

The Belgian devaluation of 1935 seems to have been the first time that monetary policy was linked explicitly to the internal distribution of incomes: not only the traditional distribution between wages and profits, but also the distribution of profits between sheltered and unsheltered sectors, a distinction newly introduced. Such questions of income distribution have figured prominently in recent monetary adjustments, notably the devaluation of the Belgian franc in 1982 and that of the French franc in 1986. On the eve of European monetary union it is salutary to rediscover how two of the partners to that arrangement learned that the management of the exchange rate could require painful compromises and could influence in the medium term their economic structures.

Appendix

TABLE 7.A1. Economic data for Belgium and France, 1920–1939

	(1) Exchange rate		(2) Exports			(3) Budget surplus		(4) Wholesale prices		(5) Cost of living		(6) Industrial production	
	B	F	B	F(a)	F(b)	B	F	B	F	B	F	B	F
1920	—	—	—	53.8	58.5	− 5 656	− 17 139	—	83	52.1	61	53.9	49.6
1921	—	—	—	39.4	56.5	− 2 885	− 9 275	43.0	57	45.5	53	46.8	43.9
1922	—	246.2	—	42.6	58.5	− 2 363	− 9 762	43.1	54	42.4	51	61.1	62.6
1923	—	197.0	30.5	61.6	70.1	− 1 527	− 11 806	58.4	69	49.6	57	69.4	70.7
1924	—	172.1	43.5	84.5	81.0	− 1 514	− 7 121	67.3	80	57.5	65	76.8	87.8
1925	—	147.2	46.4	91.3	84.4	− 5 192	− 1 507	65.6	90	61.1	69	74.2	87.0
1926	121.8	99.6	62.7	119.0	91.2	− 4 070	+ 1 088	87.4	115	73.4	90	85.7	101.6
1927	100.8	99.7	83.7	109.5	99.3	+ 1 675	+ 0 217	99.5	101	90.9	94	92.9	88.6
1928	99.5	99.4	94.6	102.5	100.7	+ 1 562	+ 3 929	99.1	102	94.2	94	99.4	102.4
1929	100.0	100.0	100.0	100.0	100.0	+ 1 523	+ 3 946	100.0	100	100.0	100	100.0	100.0
1930	101.6	101.7	82.1	85.4	89.1	− 2 721	− 4 918	87.4	87	102.7	101	89.3	100.0
1931	109.9	105.8	72.7	60.7	76.2	− 2 280	− 5 484	73.6	74	92.3	97	80.1	85.4
1932	121.9	112.5	47.4	39.3	57.8	− 2 627	− 6 148	62.5	65	83.2	88	69.1	74.0
1933	129.9	117.9	44.8	36.8	59.2	− 750	− 11 509	58.9	62	82.3	85	71.4	80.5
1934	142.0	128.2	43.3	35.6	61.2	− 1 323	− 8 813	55.6	59	79.1	82	73.0	74.8
1935	115.5	136.3	50.6	30.9	55.1	+ 0 724	− 10 383	63.1	56	79.5	75	83.0	71.5
1936	111.0	127.9	61.9	30.9	52.4	− 2 508	− 16 896	69.1	65	84.1	80	86.7	77.2
1937	125.0	90.2	80.0	47.7	57.1	− 3 043	− 28 308	80.4	90	95.5	101	97.2	81.3
1938	—	—	68.0	61.0	61.2	− 3 338	− 27 692	74.0	103	93.2	115	78.7	74.8
1939	—	—	68.8	63.0	67.4	− 4 381	− 86 762	76.3	108	92.3	122	83.3	—

(1) Nominal effective exchange rate of the franc, 1929 = 100. *Sources*: Belgium: Hogg (1986); France: Eichengreen and Wyplosz (1990).
(2) Exports 1929 = 100. Belgium and France (*a*): current values; France (*b*): volume. *Sources*: Belgium and France (*a*): Mitchell (1975); France (*a*) and (*b*): Sauvy (1984), vol. 3.
(3) Budget surplus (+) or deficit (−); millions of francs. *Sources*: Belgium: Moulard and Grauls (1954); France: INSEE (1966).
(4) Wholesale prices, 1929 = 100. *Sources*: Belgium: Cassiers (1989); France: Mitchell (1975).
(5) Cost of living, 1929 = 100. *Sources*: Belgium: Cassiers (1989); France: Mitchell (1975).
(6) Industrial production, 1929 = 100. *Sources*: Belgium: Cassiers (1989); France: Mitchell (1975).

References

Asselain, J. C. (1974), 'Une erreur de politique économique: la loi des quarante heures de 1936', *Revue économique*, 25 (July): 672–705.

Banque Nationale de Belgique (1919–28, 1929–40), *Statistiques économiques belges.* Special number of the Bulletin of Information and Documentation (Brussels: BNB).

Boyer, R. (ed.), (1991), 'Paradoxes français de la crise des années 1930', *Le Mouvement social*, 154 (Jan.–Mar.).

Buissière, E. (1992), *La France, la Belgique et l'organisation économique de l'Europe, 1918–1935* (Paris: Imprimerie Nationale).

Caron, F., and Bouvier, J. (1980), 'Guerre, crise, guerre', in F. Braudel and E. Labrousse (eds): *Histoire économique et sociale de la France* (Paris: PUF).

Cassiers, I. (1989), *Croissance, crise et régulation en économie ouverte. La Belgique entre les deux guerres* (Brussels: De Boeck Université).

Dessirier, J. (1935), 'Secteurs 'abrité' et 'non abrité' dans le déséquilibre actuel de l'économie française', *Revue d'économie politique*, 49/4: 1330–58.

Dupriez, L. H. (1934), 'La conjoncture de la Belgique et du Luxembourg', *Bulletin de l'Institut de Recherches Economiques*, 3: 219–37.

—— (1978), *Les réformes monétaires en Belgique* (Brussels: Office international de librairie).

Eichengreen, B., and Wyplosz, C. (1990), 'The Economic Consequences of the Franc Poincaré', in B. Eichengreen, *Elusive Stability: Essays in the History of International Finance, 1919–1939* (Cambridge: Cambridge University Press).

Hogg, R. L. (1986), *Structural Rigidities and Policy Inertia in Interwar Belgium*, Brussels: Royal Academy of Belgium, *Humanities*, 48/118.

—— (1987), 'Belgium, France, Switzerland and the End of the Gold Standard', in R. T. Griffiths (ed.), *The Netherlands and the Gold Standard, 1931–1936* (Amsterdam: Neha): 193–210.

INSEE (1966), *Annuaire statistique de la France: Résumé rétrospectif* (Paris: INSEE).

Levy-Leboyer, M., Aglietta, M. *et al.* (eds) (1993), *Du franc Poincaré à L'Ecu*. Actes du colloque tenu à Bercy. (Paris: Imprimerie Nationale).

Makinen, G. E., and Woodward, G. T. (1989), 'Funding Crises in the Aftermath of World War I', in R. Dornbusch and M. Draghi (eds.), *Public Debt Management: Theory and History.* (Cambridge University Press): 153–85.

Marseille, J. (1980), 'Les origines "inopportunes" de la crise de 1929 en France', *Revue économique*, 31/4: 648–84.

Mitchell, B. R. (1975), *European Historical Statistics, 1750–1970* (London: Macmillan).

Morsel, H. (1977), 'Conjoncture et structures économiques du monde jusqu'à la grande crise (1919–1929)', in P. Léon (ed.), *Histoire économique et sociale du monde*, v: *Guerres et crises, 1914–1947* (Paris: Colin): 145–88.

Moulard, E. and Grauls, J. (1954), 'Les résultats budgétaires de 1919 à 1939', in *Histoires des finances publiques en Belgique,* ii (Brussels: Bruylant): 269–90.

Mouré, K. (1991), *Managing the Franc Poincaré* (Cambridge: Cambridge University Press).

Sauvy, A. (1984), *Histoire économique de la France,* 3 vols. (Paris: Economica).

Svennilson, I. (1954), *Growth and Stagnation in the European Economy* (Geneva: UN).

Toutain, J. C. (1987), 'Le produit intérieur brut de la France de 1789 à 1982', *Economies et Sociétés, Cahiers de l'ISMEA,* 15.

Vandendriessche, S. (1977), 'Evolutie van de Belgische centrale overheidsuitgaven sinds 1919. Onderzoek naar de determinerende factoren', *Bulletin de documentation du Ministère des finances,* Nov.: 37–112; Dec.: 145–234 (Brussels: Ministry of Finance).

Van der Wee, H. and Tavernier, K. (1975), *La Banque nationale belge et l'histoire monétaire entre les deux guerres mondiales* (Brussels: Banque Nationale de Belgique).

van Meerten, M., Clement, P., and Nefors, P. (forthcoming), *Gross Capital Formation, Government Expenditure and Net Exports in Belgium during the Interwar Period 1920–1939* (Brussels and Leuven).

Villa, P. (1990). *Une analyse macroéconomique de l'économie française au 20ᵉ siècle* (Paris: INSEE, mimeo).

L'expérience Van Zeeland en Belgique (1940) (Lausanne: Payot).

8

Off Gold and Back again: Finnish and Swedish Monetary Policies 1914–1925

TARMO HAAVISTO AND LARS JONUNG

1. Introduction and Summary

Finnish and Swedish monetary policies during the years 1914–25 may be considered as laboratory experiments in economic policy. Both countries were exposed to large economic shocks pushing them off the gold standard and both eventually returned to gold; Sweden in 1924, as the first country in Europe[1]; and Finland in 1925. The years 1914–25 may be divided into three subperiods for both countries. First, the war years between 1914 and 1918, secondly, the years 1919–21 characterized by the post-war turmoil, thirdly, the 'stabilization' between 1922 and 1925. In both countries, stabilization was attained after the war by a return to the gold-standard system. However, the routes taken by these two countries differed sharply. Sweden went back to gold at the pre-war parity after a rapid deflation. Finland returned to gold at the going rate. The macroeconomic consequences of these two strategies were quite different; Sweden suffered from deflation and the international post-war contraction, while Finland was more or less unaffected.[2]

The focus of this chapter is on monetary disturbances and monetary policies. We bring together here consistently constructed data on money, prices, and exchange rates for both countries. In section 2, we present a short review of Finnish and Swedish economic development from the turn of the century to the outbreak of war in 1914. Section 3 highlights the behaviour of the money stock, exchange rates, and domestic price levels in the two countries.

We have received valuable comments from Michael D. Bordo, Barry Eichengreen, Klas Fregert, and Peter Temin.

[1] Sweden returned to gold, de jure, at the end of March 1924, followed by the Netherlands, Switzerland, and the UK one month later at the beginning of May. However, the pre-war par rate of the krona into gold had already been restored, de facto, in 1922. The return to convertibility of the Swedish currency was delayed by about two years, since the authorities disapproved of a unilateral Swedish return implying that the krona would be the only convertible currency in Europe.

[2] This conclusion is consistent with Eichengreen's (1991) study of inflation and recovery in the 1920s showing that policies affecting the price level had pronounced real economic effects.

Section 4 investigates economic policy issues, focusing on the role of monetary policy both during and after the First World War. The monetary expansion and corresponding price-level movements were not fully reflected by changes in the foreign value of the domestic currency. Although conditions were similar for both countries in the sense that their currencies were overvalued at the end of the war, there were also substantial differences. Most notably, the Finnish monetary expansion and inflation were considerably higher than in Sweden. Sweden returned to the old gold-parity rate in 1922. The deflation, necessary to restore the parity rate, was associated with a severe contraction of the domestic economy. Industrial production fell and unemployment increased sharply. Finland escaped such an adjustment by accepting the depreciation of its currency. This successful Finnish policy was determined by economic necessity—the Finnish central bank had no resources to support its currency—rather than by careful economic considerations on the part of the Finnish authorities.

Section 5 considers the economic debate. Monetary issues were eagerly discussed in Sweden by scholars and practitioners. The famous Swedish economists of the period, Gustav Cassel, Eli F. Heckscher, and Knut Wicksell, criticized the discount rate and exchange-rate policies of the Riksbank and claimed that the central bank had caused the rise in the price level. In Sweden, Knut Wicksell had a significant influence on post-war central bank policy. He strongly argued that Sweden ought to restore the pre-war price level for reasons of justice and fairness.[3] Both Gustav Cassel and, particularly, Eli Heckscher, also participated in the Finnish discussion concerning the goals of post-war economic policy. They were opposed to the policy recommended by Wicksell for Sweden and suggested that Finland should return to gold at the going rate. We should not, however, exaggerate the role of Heckscher and Cassel regarding the Finnish return to the gold standard. They were most likely used as foreign authorities in order to suppress the criticism of monetary reform by those Finnish experts who had already decided that the Finnish currency must remain devalued in terms of gold. Finally, section 6 examines briefly the subsequent inter-war record of monetary policy in Finland and Sweden.

2. The Finnish and Swedish Economies, 1914–1925

The background

Finland and Sweden share a long common history. Finland was joined to Sweden from the twelfth century, until it was annexed to the Russian

---

[3] This recommendation of Wicksell was never put into practice. The post-war deflation restored the pre-war gold rate of the krona, although the price level remained about 50 per cent above the pre-war level.

Empire as a result of the Napoleonic Wars in 1809. During the nineteenth century, Finland was an autonomous grand duchy of the Russian Tsar. During this period, up until 1917 when Finland declared its independence, the old Swedish Constitution, as well as fundamental parts of Finland's legal, administrative, and religious institutions that were in force under Swedish rule remained intact.[4] The autonomy of Finland was enforced by the maintenance of the Finnish central bank of its own currency, the markka. Fiscal policy, economic legislation, and the State finances remained under the control of the Finns.

Prior to the outbreak of the First World War, both Finland and Sweden participated in the classical gold-standard system. Sweden went on gold in 1873 and Finland followed suit in 1877–8. Their banking systems were well developed, their export sectors were relatively large and economic progress was rapid during the gold-standard period. Both countries could be described as small open economies. In 1913 exports represented about 20 per cent and 25 per cent of the Swedish and Finnish national products, respectively. Sweden had a population of 5.5 million and Finland of 3 million in that year.

The semi-independent status of Finland as a grand duchy of the Tsar prevented Finland, in contrast to Sweden, from maintaining its neutrality during the First World War. As Finland was a part of the Russian Empire, it became involved in the war. The Finns were exempted from military services and there were, as a rule, no Finns serving in the Russian army. Therefore, although Finland could not stay neutral during the war, the conduct of the war did not affect Finland directly. On the other hand, Russian troops were stationed in Finland. As the Russian military presence increased during the war, it contributed to a massive inflow of roubles. Two other factors, which contributed to the rouble inflow, were the Russian summer residences in south-eastern Finland as well as the large trade in the border districts. Wealthy Russians from St Petersburg had dwellings on the Finnish south coast. During the first years of the war those residences were used to escape from the discomforts of war in the capital of the Empire. Finnish exports to St Petersburg were largely a form of 'border trade'; the distance between the second largest city in Finland, Viborg, and St Petersburg, was only fifty miles, and a substantial trade in consumption goods, not included in the official trade statistics, took place.

After the outbreak of the war in 1914, Finnish foreign trade was completely dominated by exports to Russia, while Germany and the United Kingdom were the main trading partners for Sweden. The maintenance of

[4] At the turn of the century, Finnish autonomy was put under heavy pressure by the Russian authorities. Vital parts of the Finnish administration were threatened by the 'Slovophiles' among the Russian officials. However, the Finns managed to keep their legal, economic, and social institutions in operation until independence in 1917.

the convertibility of the rouble was a political issue and could not be decided by the officials at the Bank of Finland. The Finnish authorities and firms were obliged to accept payments made in roubles, and the Bank of Finland was obliged to exchange those rouble payments at a fixed rate. When the value of the Russian currency started to decline on the international exchange markets, the maintenance of convertibility at a fixed exchange-rate became a major burden for the Finnish central bank. After a while Finnish commercial banks were no longer allowed to trade roubles, although the Bank of Finland was forced to sustain the rouble exchange. As a result, the volume and share of rouble funds in the foreign reserves of the Bank of Finland increased rapidly.

The foreign-trade surplus that arose in both Finland and Sweden was an early effect of the war. Economic activity began to expand following a short depression which was part of the transition to a war economy. Both countries were able to sell their products to the war-participating countries, which resulted in positive net exports and increased foreign reserves. The Finnish trade surplus resulted in a monetary expansion and depreciation of the currency, when Russian funds were accumulated in Finland. In Sweden, the foreign-trade surplus was used for a huge capital export. The appreciated krona made foreign investment attractive, holdings of foreign funds included a speculative element in the sense that the appreciation of krona was seen as a temporary phenomenon caused by the war. Consequently, a return to the pre-war parity rates was expected to occur as a consequence of peace. To a large extent, the Swedish foreign-exchange reserves were denominated in reichsmarks. These claims as well as the Finnish rouble claims, turned out to be nearly worthless when the war was over. In this sense, the monetary expansion in both countries amounted to a deficit financing of the military expenditures of foreign countries. After the war, the governments in both countries were obliged to support their central banks. In Sweden, the central bank was able to use its own funds to compensate for the losses, but in Finland the rouble claims were transformed to government bonds in the balance sheet of the Bank of Finland.

The empirical picture

To investigate the macroeconomic development of Finland and Sweden in greater detail we use the framework of the quantity equation:

$$MV = Py \qquad (1)$$

where M is the money stock, M1, V, velocity, P, GDP deflator, and y, real income.

After taking logarithms and differentiating with respect to time, we obtain:

$$\frac{1}{M}\frac{dM}{dt} + \frac{1}{V}\frac{dV}{dt} = \frac{1}{P}\frac{dP}{dt} + \frac{1}{y}\frac{dy}{dt} \tag{2}$$

We use this breakdown in Table 8.1 to show the annual changes in money, velocity, prices, and real income. Changes in money and prices during the war years 1914–18 were clearly larger than changes in real income in both countries.[5] The income velocity fell substantially in both Finland and Sweden during each of the war years. Monetary growth exceeded the growth of the GDP deflator in each year until 1918. In 1918 the figures were about the same for money and prices. During the next two years, in 1919–20, the growth rate of nominal income was more rapid in both countries than the growth rate of the money stock.

TABLE 8.1. *Annual changes in the money supply* (M1), *velocity* (V), *price level* (P), *and real income* (y) *in Sweden and Finland* 1914–1925 (%)

	Sweden				Finland			
	M1	V	P	y	M1	V	P	y
1914	12.4	– 12.9	1.9	– 2.5	7.5	– 8.8	3.3	– 4.6
1915	23.6	– 7.1	12.8	3.6	27.8	– 19.8	13.3	– 5.4
1916	27.2	– 4.5	11.3	11.4	45.5	– 15.9	28.1	1.4
1917	30.6	– 19.6	20.5	– 9.5	47.2	– 20.6	45.7	– 19.1
1918	29.6	– 8.2	28.4	– 7.0	37.4	– 13.2	39.6	– 15.3
1919	11.5	4.2	13.4	2.2	13.4	27.9	24.1	17.2
1920	6.0	6.8	0.7	12.1	14.8	25.6	29.7	10.6
1921	– 10.6	– 19.8	– 16.9	– 13.5	11.3	4.2	12.3	3.2
1922	– 9.7	– 19.4	– 23.5	– 5.5	4.8	4.1	– 0.5	9.4
1923	– 6.3	6.5	– 7.5	7.7	11.7	– 4.9	– 0.1	6.9
1924	– 9.0	16	0.0	7.0	13.9	– 8.1	3.2	2.6
1925	– 11.6	22.1	1.7	8.7	– 2.9	10.3	2.0	5.3

Sources: Haavisto (1992), Hjerppe (1989), Jonung (1976), and Krantz and Nilsson (1975).

Velocity increased substantially in both countries, especially in Finland, although the adjustment was only partial in both countries compared to the heavy reduction during the war. In Finland, the growth of velocity continued until 1923. During the Swedish deflation in 1921–2, the money stock fell. However, the reduction of the price level and even real income was of

[5] In Finland, real income also declined in 1915 which contrasts with our discussion above of the war boom in both countries. The decline is, however, explained by the scattered pattern of the boom. According to Tudeer (1939: 32–4), a number of branches such as building and construction suffered heavily at the outbreak of the war, while others such as the manufacture of metals and textiles expanded. The total effect according to the measures provided by Table 8.1 led, however, to a negative growth of real income.

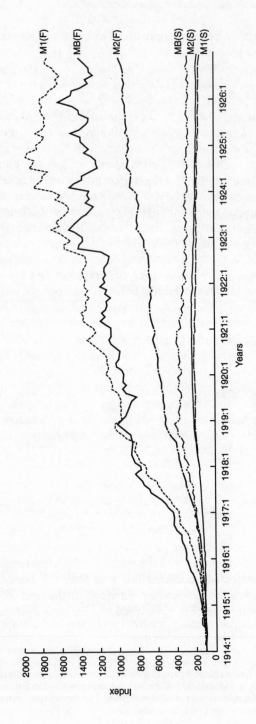

FIG. 8.1 Monetary expansion in Finland (F) and Sweden (S), 1914–1926 (1914 = 100)
Sources: Haavisto (1992); Jonung (1975).

a larger magnitude reflecting a velocity decline of 40 per cent during those two years. The monetary contraction also continued during the three subsequent years 1923–5. While the money stock declined, real income and the price level increased and, thus, velocity expanded sharply. Next, we proceed by examining the behaviour of money, prices, and exchange rates.

Money

Monthly data on the monetary base and the money stock (M1 and M2) for the period 1914–26 for Finland and Sweden are presented in Fig. 8.1. One significant feature of Fig. 8.1 is the monetary expansion in Finland. By the end of 1918, the monetary base was ten times the level of January 1914. During each of the five war years 1914–18, the Finnish monetary base nearly doubled. By the end of 1925, the volume was fourteen times the monetary base in January 1914.

Figure 8.1 suggests a close relationship between the monetary base and the narrow money stock, M1. This covariation appears to have been particularly strong in the early period. The growth rate of the M2-measure was lower and the fluctuations were more modest than those observed for M1. M2 shows a fairly stable trend without sharp declines or rapid expansions while M1 displays several periods of contraction.

The Swedish case differs from the Finnish one, although the initial monetary shock was of nearly the same size as in Finland. The annual growth of the monetary base in 1914 was more rapid in Sweden than in Finland.[6] While the Finnish monetary base continued to expand after 1914, the Swedish growth rate was more modest in 1915. A new phrase of expansion started in 1916 and continued until the end of the war. During the four and half years of war, the Swedish monetary base grew fourfold. A turning-point occurred in Sweden by 1918–19 and from then on until 1925, the monetary base was reduced by one-third.

The Swedish M1 and M2 followed each other initially. By the end of 1918, the money stock had doubled and M2 continued to expand until 1920–1. The decline of the Swedish money stock started in 1920, measured by M1, while the turning-point for M2 occurred one year later (measured by the monetary base, the decline had started already at the end of 1918). The magnitude of these declines was about the same for both aggregates; the reduction of the money stock was about one-third.

---

[6] The Swedish monetary base expanded rapidly in August 1914, while the response to the outbreak of war was smaller in Finland. By September, this expansion had ceased in Sweden, and the remaining part of the monetary expansion is explained by the seasonal component in December. For further discussion see next section.

Prices

The Finnish and Swedish inflation rates based on quarterly wholesale prices
are shown in Fig. 8.2. Immediately after the outbreak of the war, the Swedish
inflation rate was higher than in Finland. During 1915 the Finnish inflation
rate continued to rise, while the Swedish rate fell from 40 per cent to close
to 20 per cent. The inflation rate accelerated in both countries in 1917–18.
The wartime peak was reached in the spring of 1918; 97 per cent in Finland
and 45 per cent in Sweden. Thereafter, the rate of inflation fell rapidly in both
countries. The Swedish price level started to fall in 1919, although the sharp
decline of prices did not commence until 1921. The Finnish price level,
however, was not subject to a period of heavy deflation. Prices moved
roughly in a parallel fashion in the two countries during the whole period.

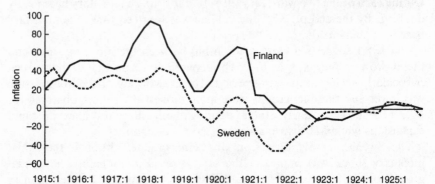

FIG. 8.2   Rates of inflation in Finland and Sweden, 1915–1925 (annual inflation based on
quarterly date; wholesale prices)
Sources: Heckscher (1926); Tudeer (1939).

By the end of 1920, the Finnish wholesale price level index was at 1402 (base
year 1913 = 100) while the Swedish price index had reached a value of 363 in
the third quarter of 1920. Between the third quarter of 1920 and the end of
1921, the Swedish price level was reduced by more than 50 per cent. By the last
quarter of 1921 the price index reached 174. The deflation continued until the
end of 1923, although the decline was moderate. In the fourth quarter of 1923,
the index reached 151. Finnish prices were also subject to a two-year-long
period of deflation. This deflation started later than in Sweden and was fairly
limited. The price level was reduced by nearly 20 per cent between the second
quarter of 1922 and the second quarter of 1924.

The covariation between prices and money in Finland is strong. In 1921
the monetary base had increased 12 times, M1 13.5, and prices 13.2 times
compared to the level of 1914. In Sweden the price index for 1921 was 174,

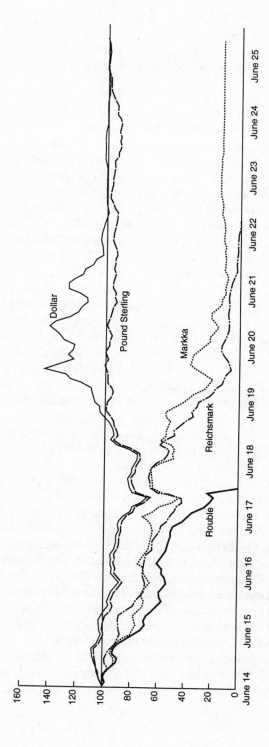

Fig. 8.3 Exchange-rate indices of krona, 1914–1926
Source: Sveriges Riksbank, 1914–26.

while M1 had increased 1.7 times. The Swedish price level declined by almost 50 per cent during 1921, and was stabilized thereafter. By the end of 1922, the price index was 155 and the index for M1 was 161. Thus, the indices are roughly the same in the Swedish case as well.

Exchange rates

During the classical gold standard prior to the First World War both Finland and Sweden maintained their currency convertibility into gold. At the outbreak of war both Finland and Sweden decided to abandon the gold-parity exchange rates. The initial effect of the war was that the Swedish krona depreciated against certain gold currencies such as the pound sterling, the Dutch florin, and the US dollar. After this initial depreciation, the war resulted in a continuous appreciation of the Swedish currency. This was in a sharp contrast to the Finnish markka, which followed the devaluation of the rouble against the leading currencies and against gold. Figure 8.3 displays the exchange rates (index series) of the Swedish krona in Finnish markka, reichsmark, rouble, pound sterling, and US dollar for June of each year.

By the end of 1917, the appreciation of the krona had stopped and was followed by a sharp depreciation, which continued during 1918–20 against leading currencies such as the pound and the dollar. However, currencies like the markka, the reichsmark, and the French franc depreciated faster than the krona and, thus, the krona appreciated against these currencies.

In the Finnish case, the excess demand for commodities after the war resulted in a trade deficit, which in turn caused an excess supply of markka in the exchange market. Although Sweden suffered from the same kind of monetary disequilibrium, the extent of the monetary disturbances was smaller. First, the Swedish inflation was modest compared to the Finnish one. Secondly, the large Swedish capital export facilitated the policy of the Riksbank to support the Swedish currency in exchange markets.

In Sweden the 'war-boom' was replaced during 1918 by a recession. However, in 1918 Swedish capital exports were still substantial although they had declined since 1916. Industrial production in 1918 was 25 per cent lower than in 1913, while the price level was still increasing. The Swedish krona had appreciated against the dollar until November 1917, but fluctuated heavily during 1918 and declined below its gold parity in 1919.

The monetary expansion continued during 1918, but in 1919 the monetary base started to decline. The price level fell during 1919, although the Swedish currency had still depreciated against the dollar. By the end of 1918, the krona was about 5 per cent over par to the dollar, but during 1919, the dollar exchange-rate was reduced by 25 per cent. This decline continued during 1920 and in March 1920, the krona was 35 per cent below gold parity.

The foreign-trade surplus turned into a deficit in 1919. Exports were further reduced by the heavy depreciation of the Finnish markka and the reichsmark. Although the value of the Swedish currency depreciated against the dollar, the krona was overvalued because of the rapid depreciation of other important currencies. The overvaluation of the krona put pressure on the Swedish economy. In Fig. 8.7 the rapid fall of Swedish exports to Germany reflected the overvalued Swedish krona against the reichsmark. At the same time, Germany's share of Finnish exports expanded; Sweden lost part of its export markets to Finland.

During 1919–21, the markka depreciated substantially. The gold par value of the Finnish currency–Swedish krona exchange rate was 138.9 markka to 100 kronor. In June 1919 the exchange rate was 287.6 (average value) and 1,307.6 in June 1921. From late 1921 to the end of 1923, the markka fluctuated against the krona. A new exchange rate was eventually established at a level of 1,060 markka equal to 100 kronor.

Industrial production and unemployment

The behaviour of real income is displayed in Table 8.1. The indices for industrial production are shown in Fig. 8.4, using industrial production in 1913 as the base. The war boom gave rise to a rapid growth of industrial production in Sweden, while production in Finland fell slightly. The turning-point in both countries occurred in 1917; in Sweden, production declined, but remained above the level of 1913. By 1921 Swedish industrial production had fallen below the level of 1913. However, a new

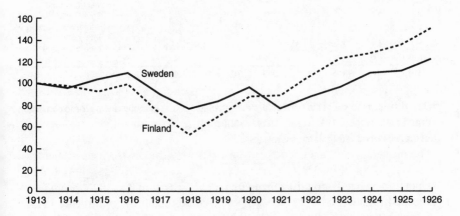

FIG. 8.4 Industrial production in Finland and Sweden, 1913–1926 (1913 = 100)
Sources: Hjerppe (1989); *Statistical Yearbook of Sweden*.

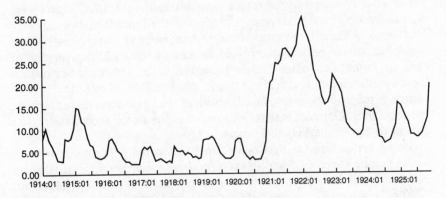

FIG. 8.5 Unemployment in Sweden, 1914–1925 (monthly data) (%)
Source: Statistical Yearbook of Sweden.

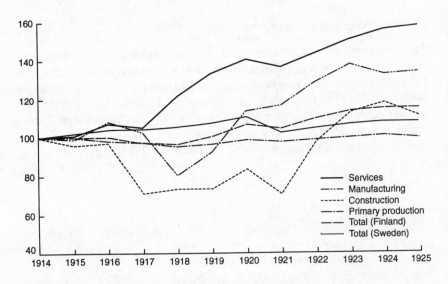

FIG. 8.6 Employment index numbers for selected sectors in Finland. Total employment in Finland and Sweden, 1914–1925 (1914 = 100)
Source: Hjerppe (1989); Johansson (1967).

expansion started already during the next year and by 1923 production exceeded the level of 1913.

The civil war caused a severe industrial contraction in Finland in 1917–18. The recovery started in 1919 and, with the exception of 1921, production continued to grow until 1925. By 1922 industrial production in Finland had exceeded its pre-war level, which was one year earlier than in Sweden. Finland retained this relative advantage over Sweden up to 1926.

The post-war recession was severe in Sweden as illustrated by the sharp rise of unemployment in Fig. 8.5. In Sweden, the rate of unemployment in the early 1920s exceeded the rate registered during the Depression of the 1930s (in contrast for example to the United Kingdom). The level of unemployment increased very sharply in 1921 and reached a level above 25 per cent according to Fig. 8.5. Although the decline of unemployment was rapid during 1923 and 1924, the level remained substantially above the pre-war level during the 1920s.

As far as we know, data on Finnish unemployment are not available. Instead in Fig. 8.6 we make use of employment indices for selected sectors of the Finnish economy. The sectors are primary production, manufacturing, construction, and services. According to Fig. 8.6, employment remained stable in 1914–16. Employment fell in both construction and manufacturing in 1917–18, remained fairly stable in agricultural production and increased sharply in the service sector. After 1920 employment expanded in all sectors with the exception of construction in 1921. These data confirm the pattern of expanding economic activity since 1919. Finland escaped the international Depression in 1921, employment in each sector exceeding 1913 levels as early as 1922, while in manufacturing, the contraction of 1921 was only reflected in a reduced growth rate.

3. Some Monetary Issues

Central bank response to the outbreak of war

The immediate monetary consequences of the outbreak of war were rather similar in Finland and Sweden. The first reaction was more dramatic in Sweden; a suspension of the gold convertibility on 2 August 1914. All commercial banks were closed from 3 to 5 August and a general moratorium was in force. This step was questioned by Swedish economists. In particular, the suspension of convertibility was considered to be an unconstitutional as well as an unnecessary action.

The reaction of the Finnish authorities was more modest. The board of the central bank suspended convertibility which was also against the law in Finland. However, the suspension first came into force in December 1914.[7]

---

[7] The Finnish suspension of convertibility can be defended by the fact that the Russian rouble was devalued after the outbreak of the war. The Finnish authorities were obliged to maintain convertibility with the rouble at the fixed pre-war exchange rate. Obviously, it was an impossible task to maintain convertibility of the national currency both into a certain weight of gold and into the rouble at a fixed exchange rate.

In both countries the central bank discount-rate was increased by two percentage points during the first days of August 1914. This rise was considered as a signal to reassure the financial market. No financial panics in terms of gold outflows or runs on banks occurred in either country. Deposits of the commercial banks were initially reduced as the public increased their holdings of notes, but that situation was met by support from the central bank.[8] The demand for gold did not increase substantially in either Finland or Sweden. In both countries, gold circulation had traditionally been very limited. The confidence of the public in the domestic currency was not altered by the outbreak of the war and of the domestic notes were not converted into gold in any considerable amounts. Therefore, the decision by the central banks to suspend the gold convertibility should be explained by excessive precautionary motives.

Exchange-rate policies and the purchasing-power parity delay

Both currencies thus depreciated against the gold currencies after the outbreak of the war. The depreciation of the Finnish currency could not be avoided because the exchange rate between the markka and the depreciating rouble was fixed. It was not until the collapse of the Russian Empire in 1917 that Finland was able to suspend convertibility between the Finnish and Russian currencies.

Swedish economists claimed that the main reason for the depreciation of the Swedish krona during the fall of 1914, was the composition of the foreign-reserve holdings of the Swedish central bank.[9] According to Östlind (1945: 32), a substantial (and disproportionately high) share of the foreign reserves of the Riksbank was held in the German currency, the reichsmark.[10] In those circumstances, the board of the Riksbank subordinated its exchange-rate policy to the profit motive of the bank, and acted to maintain the krona price of the German currency as high as possible. When the official central bank exchange-rate was held at an artificially high level and the Swedish krona followed the depreciation of the reichsmark, the announcement of the actual decline in the value of the central bank foreign reserves could be postponed.[11]

---

[8] The withdrawal of deposits was 21.6 million marrka from the commercial banks and 8 million from the savings banks during August. The volume of deposits held with the commercial banks was about 700 million in August 1914. Thus, the withdrawals represented only about 3 per cent of the stock of deposits. This reduction had already disappeared by September.

[9] Heckscher (1926) and Östlind (1945) suggested that the Swedish central bank manipulated the exchange rates to improve the profits of the Riksbank. The exchange-rate notations of the Riksbank were only indicative, nominal rates, and could differ from the actual market rates.

[10] Jonung (1984) shows that the reichsmark was the key currency of the Riksbank.

[11] The Swedish central bank concealed these losses until the end of the war. It appeared then that the losses were so substantial that all seigniorage profits caused by the monetary expansion during the war vanished when the losses were taken into account.

TABLE 8.2. *The Swedish PPP-indices against US and UK prices, 1914–1922 (annual data)*

	Wholesale price index (WPI)			Exchange rates		PPP-index	
	USA	UK	Sweden	$ US	£ sterling	US prices	UK prices
1914	98	100	108	3.8	18.46	100	100
1915	101	127	145	3.86	18.35	77	94
1916	127	160	185	3.5	16.6	69	83
1917	177	206	244	3.13	14.84	65	73
1918	194	227	339	3.09	14.64	51	57
1919	206	242	330	3.96	17.45	71	74
1920	226	295	347	4.92	17.93	92	89
1921	147	188	211	4.46	17.12	90	89
1922	149	154	162	3.83	16.93	102	94

Sources: Heckscher (1926); Friedman and Schwartz (1963).

The Swedish foreign-trade surplus resulted eventually in an appreciation of the Swedish currency. By the end of 1915, the convertibility of the krona was restored at the pre-war par rate. However, the export of gold was forbidden which implied that the value of the Swedish currency did not have downward limits.

In Table 8.2 the Swedish purchasing-power indices against UK and US prices are provided. We note two significant features. First, the Swedish currency was considerably overvalued during the war.[12] Secondly, the PPP-indices had almost returned to their pre-war level by 1922.

The relatively high Swedish inflation rate was thus combined with an appreciation of the foreign value of the krona. The result was an overvalued Swedish currency in 1918. The PPP-index had declined by nearly one-half against both US and UK prices compared to 1914, implying a rapid deterioration of the domestic purchasing power of the krona in terms of its foreign purchasing power; by 49 and 43 per cent against US and UK prices, respectively. The PPP-index can also be interpreted as a simple measure of the real exchange rate; in these terms, the Swedish currency was overvalued and the pre-war real exchange-rate of the krona was first restored in 1922.

In 1919, Sweden deflated, while inflation continued in the UK and USA. At the same time, the Swedish currency depreciated against sterling and the US dollar. According to Table 8.2, the Swedish currency was still over-valued in 1919 and, thus, the changes that took place in 1919 may be explained in terms of a lagged adjustment of the exchange rates during the

[12] The exchange rates in 1914 are regarded as the long-term purchasing-power parity rates.

war. The adjustment process continued during 1920, when the quotations moved closer to the pre-war PPP-rates.

The return to PPP-rates was completed in 1922 one year after the major deflation of 1921. This is consistent with the argument that the Swedish price level adjusted to the exchange rates, and not the other way around. The policy of deflation was designed in terms of exchange-rate targets, and the price level was subordinated to this target. In Sweden, the domestic currency was kept overvalued as long as was needed to restore the pre-war gold parity.

As mentioned earlier, the hands of the Finnish authorities were tied initially because of the free convertibility of the rouble into markka at a fixed exchange rate. Attempts were made to appreciate the Finnish currency in relation to the rouble, but the reaction of the Russian authorities was extremely negative. The Russians did not want to lose this channel of financing their war deficits, and any Finnish attempts to alter the exchange rates resulted in threats to their monetary autonomy. Under such political pressure, the Finnish authorities decided to keep the rouble exchange rate stable and allow the value of the Finnish currency to deteriorate against other currencies.

However, the depreciation of the Finnish currency against foreign currencies was incomplete judging from the differences in the monetary growth rates or price-level movements. The seemingly slow adjustment of the exchange rates may be explained by the circumstances of the war and by the fact that the Finnish economy became more isolated after the outbreak of war. Russia was the main trading partner before the Russian Revolution, and during the civil war years of 1917–18 commercial contacts with foreign countries were cut off almost completely.

The foreign price of the Swedish currency was fairly stable from July 1914 to June 1919. The exchange rate between the Swedish krona and the US dollar changed from 3.75 to 3.89, although during this period, the Swedish currency had appreciated against the dollar (and gold), and the value of krona had been as high as 2.55 for a dollar in November 1917.

As demonstrated in Table 8.2, the Swedish currency was heavily overvalued compared to both the pound sterling and the US dollar in 1917. The real exchange rate between markka and krona was fairly stable from 1914 to 1917 and, thus, measured by the real exchange rate, the Finnish currency followed the appreciation of the krona against the pound sterling and dollar.

In 1919, the Swedish currency was still overvalued against the pound and the dollar. The purchasing power between Finnish and Swedish currencies may be illustrated by the following exercise based on the purchasing-power parity approach. The Finnish cost of living index increased from 100 to 712 from July 1914 to June 1919. The corresponding Swedish price index

TABLE 8.3. *The purchasing-power parity between Finnish and Swedish currencies, 1914–1920*

Date	Prices indices		Estimated PPP: kronor per 1,000 markka	Actual exchange rate
	Swedish	Finnish		
July 1914	100	100	719[a]	719
June 1919	257	712	259	343
Dec. 1919	258	755	246	145
April 1920	265	850	224	254

[a] Assuming equilibrium in July 1914.

changed from 100 to 257. The exchange rates between the Finnish and Swedish currencies were 71.89 in July 1914 and 34.32 in June 1919. The estimated purchasing-power parity rate of krona per 1,000 markka is, assuming equilibrium in 1914, 259 while the actual exchange rate was 343. Thus, according to those exchange rates the Finnish markka was overvalued against the Swedish currency, which in turn was overvalued in terms of the pound and the dollar.

A rapid adjustment of exchange rates occurred during the latter half of 1919, when the markka depreciated from 34.32 in June to 14.48 in December 1919 and according to the estimated PPP exchange rates in Table 8.3, the Finnish currency became massively undervalued against the Swedish krona.

As a reaction to this rapid decline in the foreign value of the Finnish currency, exchange-rate regulations were introduced in Finland in January 1920. During the spring, the value of the Finnish currency temporarily appreciated. In April 1920, the exchange rate was 25.44, which in terms of the purchasing power of currencies meant that the quotation of the Finnish currency approximated the purchasing-power parity rate.

The overvalued Finnish currency immediately after the war resulted in a large deficit in Finnish foreign trade. As argued above, the subsequent rapid deterioriation of the Finnish currency should be regarded as a delayed reaction to the rapid inflation during the war. The Bank of Finland lacked funds to support its currency, with the exception of regulations on the flow of capital. As the effect of these regulations was insufficient, the heavy depreciation of the domestic currency could not be avoided.

According to Table 8.1, the major monetary disturbances occurred during the years 1915–18 in both countries. However in 1919, the monetary expansion was suddenly reduced to about one-third of the growth rate in 1918. The adjustment of prices and exchange rates to the monetary disturbances was delayed to the period immediately after the war. In Sweden, the rate of inflation was dramatically reduced in 1919, while in Finland the reduction was more moderate. During 1914–17, price fluctuations exceeded the fluctuations in exchange rates. This pattern was dramatically changed during the first year after the war. The large fluctuations in exchange rates outstripped changes in the price level and, consequently, fluctuations of real exchange rates were largely determined by changes in the nominal exchange rate.

Changes in the real exchange rate were moderate before 1917 relative to the period 1917–21. During 1914–15 the Finnish real exchange rate depreciated. This depreciation corresponded to the declining value of the markka (the markka followed the rouble), although the price movement was fairly similar in both countries. In 1917, the Finnish price level expanded rapidly and as the adjustment of nominal exchange rate was sluggish, the real exchange rate appreciated. In 1919–21, both fluctuations of nominal and real exchange rates exceeded price fluctuations and therefore the movements of real exchange rates were caused by changes in nominal exchange rates. Depreciation of the Finnish currency was followed by a rising price level with a lag of one or two quarters. To sum up, the turmoil of 1919–21 may be explained by a delayed adjustment of exchange rates to earlier monetary shocks and the subsequent price adjustment. Swedish exchange-rate policy had adopted the target of a return to pre-war parity rates. To reach this target, it was necessary to keep the krona overvalued in order to deflate the domestic price level (see Table 8.2).

In Finland, the targeting of the exchange rate was more complicated. A return to pre-war parity appeared to be impossible. After the war, the decline in the value of the Finnish currency could only be avoided by measures that would affect the trade balance (import regulations) or by major central bank interventions in the foreign-exchange market. The foreign reserves of the Finnish central bank had vanished during the war, and the rouble claims became totally worthless after the Russian Revolution in 1917. An adequate level of controls over foreign trade was difficult to accomplish, since exports were low and the demand for imported goods was large after the civil war. All actions to support the Finnish currency by selling foreign currencies on the market implied foreign borrowing. This was actually done, but not until January 1921.

In Sweden a deflation of the domestic price-level took place in order to depreciate the real exchange rates, while the Finnish adjustment of real exchange rates was carried out in terms of a heavy depreciation of the nominal foreign value of the Finnish markka with a stable domestic price-level. After nominal exchange-rate fluctuations were eliminated and new exchange rates were established in 1924, Finland returned to gold at the going rate.

Monetary expansion and monetary overhang

Monetary expansion was stronger in Sweden than in Finland during the first year of the war. One reason might be that hoarding was more prevalent in

Sweden than in Finland. According to Heckscher (1926), the outstanding stock of notes increased by 17.3 per cent during the first days of the war. The Swedish monetary base increased by 50 per cent during the first year of the war, while the money stock, both M1 and M2, remained unchanged. The Finnish monetary base expanded by 32 per cent and M1 by 22 per cent during 1914.

In contrast to the 'war boom', which started in 1915, the expansion of the Swedish monetary base in 1914 was not reflected in corresponding changes in foreign-exchange reserves. The expansion of the monetary base was instead caused by an expansion of central bank credit to the public. Both rediscounting of domestic trade bills and direct loans to the public contributed to the growth of the monetary base. In Finland, the modest monetary expansion in 1914 reflected the trade surplus to Russia and an expansion of the rouble claims in the central bank balance-sheet.

The rapid monetary expansion in Finland started in 1915, when the monetary base more than doubled, M1 almost doubled, and M2 increased by 25 per cent. The Swedish expansion was about 10 per cent in terms of base money, while M1 and M2 were nearly unchanged. Those measures reflected an important difference between the balance of payments of the two countries. While the Swedish export surplus was combined with a substantial capital export, the Finnish trade surplus with Russia resulted in a rapid expansion of the monetary base.[13]

According to Heckscher (1926), Swedish net capital exports during the period 1914–18 reached a value of 2,250 million kronor. For the years 1914–15, capital exports were estimated to be 360 million, and for the remaining three years the estimates were 670, 760, and 460 million, respectively. These figures suggest that net capital exports in 1916 and 1917 exceeded the stock of high-powered money during the same years, 432 and 602 million.[14] In fact, the Swedish monetary expansion should be regarded as rather modest in relation to its large trade surplus. In effect, Sweden repurchased its foreign debt in bonds at a considerable profit. It was this debt that had once been issued to finance Sweden's industrialization process during the classical gold standard. This was an extremely advantageous affair from a Swedish point of view.

In Fig. 8.7 we note that exports to Russia exceeded a share of 90 per cent of total Finnish exports. However, data on Finnish exports to Russia during these years are extremely deficient and it is not possible to estimate the trade

---

[13] Because of the convertibility of the rouble to markka, the Russians could pay for their imports from Finland by increasing their outstanding stock of roubles.

[14] Net capital exports in 1916 were more than one-third of the stock of money, M1, at the end of the same year. The growth of M1 during that year was 317 million, while the growth of the monetary base was 86 million, equivalent to a relative growth rate of 25 per cent. While the relative growth rate seems rather high, we must nevertheless conclude that the growth of the money base was rather limited when compared to the foreign surplus.

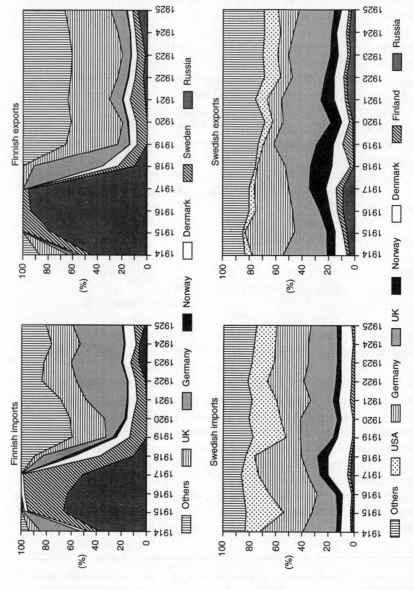

FIG. 8.7 Composition of foreign trade, Finland and Sweden, 1914–1925
Sources: Oksanen and Pinkala (1975); Pihkala (1968); *Statistical Yearbook of Sweden.*

surplus. The foreign claims of the Finnish central bank, i.e. the rouble claims of the bank, increased rapidly during 1914–17. The rouble inflow resulted in a rapid growth of the domestic money supply and the Finnish monetary base doubled during each of the years between 1915 and 1917. While the influence of the Swedish trade surplus was limited due to capital exports, the Finnish trade surplus resulted in an explosion of the monetary base.

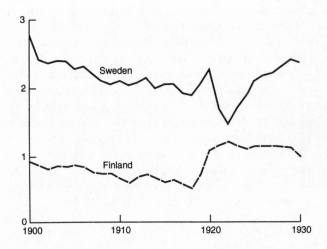

FIG. 8.8   The income velocity of money (M2) in Finland and Sweden, 1900–1930
Sources: Haavisto (1992); Jonung (1975); Krantz-Nilsson (1975).

The extent of the Finnish monetary disequilibrium is illustrated by the fact that the domestic money supply had by the end of 1918 increased to ten times its 1914 level (measured by the quantity of high-powered money or M1, about five times if we use M2). At the same time, the gross domestic product in current prices at the end of 1918 was about 3.5 times the level of 1914. This implies that the income velocity of money had fallen sharply in Finland. According to Dornbush (1990: 7) such a substantial decline in velocity reflects one of the key characteristics of a monetary overhang (assuming desired velocity to be constant). The monetary overhang in turn reflected an excess demand for commodities or, equivalently, excess supply of real money. In Fig. 8.8 such a substantial decline in velocity is noted for both countries. In Sweden, velocity (M2) declined from a value of 2.14 in 1913 to 1.88 in 1918, while the corresponding figures for Finland were 2.02 and 1.63, respectively.

In both countries, velocity increased sharply after the war, particularly in Finland. These changes in income velocities during 1919 and 1920 were partly a reaction to the monetary overhang caused by the war boom and the deficit financing. However, as shown by Fig. 8.8, the post-war Finnish income velocity reached a value far above the (declining) level of pre-war velocity. The Swedish income velocity also increased immediately after the war, declined during the deflationary recession, and increased rapidly after the deflation period 1922–5.

One possible explanation for the rise in velocity is a rapid rise in inflationary expectations.[15] Both in Finland and Sweden, the war boom was the first inflationary period that people had experienced for as long as anyone could remember; during the gold-standard period, price fluctuations were limited by the fixed gold value of the domestic currency. In contrast to the experience during the classical gold standard, the reduction of the purchasing power of money persisted as a permanent change. This deterioration of money as a store of value brought about by inflation might provide an explanation for the growth of the desired income velocity of money as well as the post-war discrepancy between velocities in the two countries. Immediately after the war, velocity expanded rapidly in both countries, but in Sweden the expansion was interrupted by the deflation. In Finland, the income velocity also remained high after the price level had been stabilized. The Finnish monetary reform implied that the pre-war gold value of domestic currency was suspended permanently.

5. The Economic Debate

The Finnish debate

After the outbreak of the war, when the Finnish war deliveries to Russia were started, warnings were raised against the consequences of the rouble inflow and the 'plethora of money'.[16] In August 1915, Emil Schybergson, an economist and the head of one of the commercial banks, suggested an emission of government bonds to withdraw Finnish currency from the market. The idea was that those funds, which were borrowed from the Finnish market by the Finnish authorities, would be forwarded to Russia to finance the Finnish war deliveries.[17] The aim was to prevent the

---

[15] Our measures of money include only commercial bank deposits. During this period the 'other banks', savings banks, co-op banks, and others, increased their share of deposits. Therefore, the growth of our measure of velocity is partly affected by the 'widening' of the empirical counterpart of money.

[16] See Rossi (1951: 292).

[17] The credibility of the Russian government in Finland was so low that it was impossible for the Russian State to borrow directly from the Finnish market. The incentive to borrow on the Finnish market was also reduced by the opportunity to finance the Finnish deliveries by simply printing new roubles.

monetary expansion which resulted from the rouble inflow. Emission of these 'exchange bonds' was first accomplished in late 1916. The effect of this borrowing was reduced because more than 75 per cent of the emission (305 million markka) ended up in the balance sheet of the Bank of Finland.[18] Therefore, the initial attempt to reduce the monetary expansion failed, and the major effect was to limit the foreign-exchange exposure of the central bank.

Rossi (1951: 95) emphasizes that the Bank of Finland was not particularly concerned about the monetary expansion. The plan of Schybergson to reduce the monetary expansion was not followed by the Bank of Finland. The exchange risk threatened the solvency of the central bank when the value of the rouble declined on the international exchange markets. However, as pointed out by Rossi, this borrowing opened up an opportunity for the Russian authorities to obtain funds directly in Finnish currency, and, thus, reduced the pressure on the Finnish central bank to sustain its high quotation of the rouble.

In 1917 the problem of superfluous banknotes and the threat of financial crisis attributed to an expected deflationary process and to the expected return to pre-war parity rates became urgent; see, for example, Korpisaari (1917). The severity of the Finnish situation was recognized by experts, contrary to public opinion which expected an automatic adjustment of the price level to its pre-war level as a consequence of peace and a normalization of market conditions. According to public opinion, the high price-level was due to the war and the extensive scarcity of products, rather than to the increase in the volume of means of payments. The Finnish experts, concerned with the monetary expansion, compared the case of Finland with countries like Germany or France. It was assumed that the deflationary process was feasible, but that it would take several years to complete. The idea of a return to the pre-war parity rates was still not questioned officially. The main target of the official policy was a 'price stabilization' to preserve confidence in the domestic notes.

However, in December 1917 the question of the devaluation of the Finnish currency was raised by the Finnish economist Tor von Wright. According to him, there were reasons to assume that the post-war value of the currency will 'be lower than it is at the moment [in 1917] and that the main aim is to stabilise it at a height, which corresponds to a price level several times higher than that of the middle of 1914'. Jucker-Fleetwood (1958: 72) refers to this statement and points out that von Wright was not

---

[18] Those domestic bonds implied great advantages for the Bank of Finland compared to the rouble-denominated funds when the future value of the rouble became more uncertain. Since they were redeemable in Finnish currency, the bonds reduced the central bank's exposure to rouble fluctuations and explains why the bonds were placed in the Bank of Finland. On the other hand, it reveals that concern about the domestic price level was of minor importance.

alone in his opinion. However, it took several years before the idea of a devaluation was widely accepted. The opinion of the monetary authorities was still 'that the most important task ... was to endeavour to raise the value of the Finnish currency' (A. Ramsay, chairman of the board of management of the Bank of Finland, as quoted by Jucker-Fleetwood, 1958).

In 1920, however, the statistical department of the Bank of Finland was instructed to investigate the earlier experiences of devaluation and the problem of subsequent price stabilization in other countries. This instruction confirmed the change of attitudes by the authorities; the acceptance of devaluation grew closer.

To convince public opinion of the necessity of permanent devaluation of the markka was a complicated task. The advocates of devaluation spread their opinion through speeches and newspaper articles; see Jucker-Fleetwood (1958: 75–8).[19] Swedish experts were also involved in this debate. The former chief of the Swedish central bank, Baron Langenskiöld, was already warning in 1917 of the consequences of forcing down the circulation of notes to restore the former level of purchasing power. Subsequently, both Gustav Cassel and Eli Heckscher became involved in the discussion. The latter Swedish experts were called upon by the advocates of the monetary reform to support their views. The return to the pre-war parity was seen as an impossible task, and the Swedish economists suggested a return at the current rate. A partial devaluation was not regarded as worth while in the prevailing uncertain circumstances. Measures such as increased taxes, which were necessary to put pressure on the domestic price level, were not popular and the Finns were warned about the expected, strong reaction from the public. Heckscher (1923) also noted that the exchange rates had already been stabilized at the lower rate and, therefore, there were no reasons to alter those rates. Both authors emphasized the importance of a rapid return to the gold standard. The main task was the return to gold, not the rate at which it was done. Heckscher's memorandum had a particularly significant role in influencing the public's acceptance of the return to gold at the new, lower parity rates.

The Swedish debate

The rapid movements in the Swedish price level, the inflation of 1914–20, and the subsequent deflation of 1920–3, gave rise to the most lively

---

[19] One should note that Finland was a newly independent nation. Traditionally, the threat against the value of the markka had come from Russia and, now, when Finland was emancipated from this threat, the country was obliged to accept a reduced value of its currency unit. In this situation it was not an easy task for the authorities to argue for the need for a permanent devaluation.

discussion of monetary matters that has ever taken place in Sweden. The leading economists of the day participated in this exchange of opinions: Gustav Cassel, David Davidson, Eli Heckscher, and Knut Wicksell, as well as the young Bertil Ohlin. Representatives of the Riksbank, of commercial banks, and of industry also took part in the debate. The opinions of the economists had a considerable impact, their views were sought after and they created an important platform for themselves. A number of monetary issues were dealt with such as the causes of inflation and the proper policy of the Riksbank.

During the period of inflation, the economists were fairly unanimous in criticizing the Riksbank for not preventing the rise of prices by increasing the discount rate. Wicksell was an articulate proponent of a return to the price level of 1914 and a stabilization of prices at this level for reasons of fairness and justice. In 1919 he argued:[20]

In my opinion we should try to return to the prewar price level. It is difficult to present any valid argument for stopping half-way. The means to do this is to maintain a high discount rate preferably combined with interest-bearing deposits with the Riksbank in order to reduce the stock of notes to the 1914 level. It is a very painful process, but it is probably better to do it now rather than to wait.

Wicksell exerted considerable influence due to his great reputation. Cassel and Heckscher were more critical of a deflationary policy. Cassel feared that it would create unemployment.

When the deflation of the early 1920s started, economists debated the proper strategy for monetary policy. Most economists wanted a return to the gold standard, many of them at the pre-war parity rate. The political parties were all in favour of a return to gold through deflation. The major opponents were found among industrialists and bankers, most prominently Ivar Kreuger. He stated in a debate in 1921 that 'the economic theories assumed an ability to adjust and a flexibility in the area of production which did not correspond to reality'.

In hindsight, it is safe to conclude that Kreuger made a more realistic assessment of the effects of deflation than the economists. However, they learned from the experience, as well. Heckscher and Cassel became critical of the workings of the gold standard in the 1920s. When Great Britain left gold in September 1931 and Sweden followed suit, Swedish economists recommended Knut Wicksell's norm of price stabilization as the norm for the policy of the Riksbank. Consequently, the Riksbank became the first central bank to adopt price stabilization as the guideline for its activities.

---

[20] For more detailed discussion, see Jonung (1979).

6. The Inter-War Era

The return to pre-war parity

Jucker-Fleetwood (1958) states that 'it is possible that more could have been done to create the conditions necessary to enforce a firm monetary policy in Finland in 1919–22 but it is debatable whether in the circumstances of the time anything really effective could have been done'. After the rapid inflation during the war, not much could be done in terms of a return to pre-war parity. Things were different in Sweden. The deterioration in the value of the krona was modest compared to the markka. Sweden followed several other countries in an downwards adjustment of the domestic price level in order to restore the pre-war parity against gold. This deflation, which occurred at the same time in several countries, caused an international recession. The severity of the Swedish recession was influenced by the fall in the value of the currencies of two of its important trading partners, Germany and Finland. The deflationary period in Sweden was short and Sweden was the first country in Europe to return to the old gold parity. However, it is probable that Sweden could have avoided the deflation and the sharp rise in unemployment that occurred in 1921–2 by pegging its currency to gold at the going rate.

Finland escaped the recession after the war. The permanent devaluation of the Finnish currency was one of the main factors behind the post-war Finnish boom. The passive central bank policy of the war period was replaced by more resolute actions. The monetary expansion was interrupted effectively and a return to the gold standard was accomplished in December 1925.

Swedish monetary policy in the 1930s

The world-wide Depression that started in the late 1920s first influenced Swedish exports which had already declined in 1928. The Depression made its impact felt on Swedish monetary policy in 1931. One week after the Bank of England left gold in September 1931, Sweden abandoned the gold standard as well. After Sweden had left the gold standard, price stabilization became the main goal of the Riksbank. Thus Knut Wicksell's price stabilization norm became the official goal for Swedish monetary policy some thirty years after he first presented it.[21]

---

[21] For further discussion, see Jonung (1979).

After the paper standard was introduced, the krona was permitted to fluctuate freely. The free floating was interrupted after only two months, when the Riksbank attempted to peg the pound rate. This experiment lasted only for three days, enough to exhaust the foreign reserves of the Riksbank. After this episode, the krona returned to a flexible exchange-rate system.

The price level remained practically stable in 1932. When the dollar started to appreciate in relation to the pound sterling, the Riksbank chose a 'middle course' between the dollar and the pound. Hence, the krona appreciated in relation to the pound and depreciated in terms of the dollar. The krona appreciated in relation to the pound by 6 per cent during the fall of 1932 and at the end of the year the pound rate reached the old gold-parity rate. The pound was the currency which dominated Swedish international trade and the appreciation of the krona influenced the domestic price level. In accordance with this appreciation, both wholesale and consumer prices fell slightly during the fall and winter of 1932–3.

In June 1933, the krona was again pegged to the pound at a rate which was 7 per cent above the gold parity. This return to a fixed exchange rate may be considered as a part of the price-stabilization policy. The fixed rate at around 19.40 resulted in a growing inflow of gold and foreign reserves.

According to the price-stabilization programme, the krona should have appreciated in 1936–7 in order to isolate the Swedish price level from the rise in the international price level.[22] The exchange rate remained, however, unchanged and the fixed pound rate was not abandoned until after the outbreak of the Second World War.

The Swedish monetary policy programme based on price stabilization was successful in the sense that the Swedish consumer price index was stable during the 1930s (during several years the index varied less than one per cent). Sweden avoided the international deflation during the first years of 1930s due to the depreciation of the krona. However, this depreciation could not prevent industrial production from falling when the demand for Swedish exports was reduced. Real national income was reduced by 12 per cent between 1930–2 and exports were 30 per cent lower in 1932 than in 1929.

The new Social Democratic Government, which came to power after the election of 1932, adopted an active fiscal policy to revive the domestic economy. However, as noted by Jonung (1979), the relative size of those fiscal measures was small compared to the expansion of the foreign trade that started. Changes in exports clearly dominated changes in public expenditure. Thus, both the Depression and the recovery are mainly explained by the behaviour of Swedish exports. The policy measure which

[22] Such appreciation was demanded by a number of economists, notably Gustav Cassel and Eli Heckscher. The Riksbank did not follow their recommendations.

most significantly influenced the rapid expansion of the Swedish economy during the 1930s was the depreciation of the krona.

The Finnish experience of the 1930s

The 1920s were a period of rapid economic growth in Finland that lasted almost the whole decade. The average growth rate exceeded 6 per cent between 1922 and 1928. The domestic boom was slowed down in 1928–9. This domestic recession was started by a slow-down of Finnish exports, but was also a consequence of a financial crisis that followed when the speculative boom in the Finnish building sector ended. One further reason was that the harvest in 1928 was very poor. Between 1929 and 1932 real GDP fell by nearly 5 per cent and nominal GDP by 22 per cent. However, the Depression of the 1930s did not have such a destructive effect on the Finnish economy as it did in many other countries. Between 1933 and 1938 annual real growth of the Finnish GDP exceeded 6 per cent.

The Finnish currency was devalued twice during this period. First after the First World War and secondly in 1931. At the end of October 1931, Finland went off gold as did many other European currencies after sterling left gold in September 1931. Both during the 1920s and the 1930s the value of the markka was stabilized soon after the devaluation. By 1933, the markka had already appreciated against many other currencies and in March 1933 its value was fixed against sterling. The new exchange rate was 17 per cent above the level during the inter-war gold standard and this exchange rate remained stable until the Second World War.

In Finland public expenditure increased during the Depression as well, but in contrast to Sweden, this increase was regarded as a serious policy failure. The goal of fiscal policy was that the annual revenues and expenditures of the central government should be balanced. Increasing expenditure during a recession endangered the budget balance.

One reason for the Finnish abandonment of the gold standard was that any defence of fixed exchange rates tightened liquidity in the Finnish money market and destabilized the banking system. In particular, the position of several Finnish commercial banks became critical. The rapid expansion of the savings banks had weakened Finnish commercial banks during the 1920s and several joint-stock provincial banks were near collapse. In this situation the Bank of Finland decided to support the commercial banks and guarantee the payment system. A comprehensive regulation of the Finnish financial markets took place. This regulatory system was initiated by the Finnish commercial banks in order to restore the existing banking structure by regulating deposit rates. Although the number of commercial banks was heavily reduced during these years, a banking crisis did not take place as happened in many other European countries. It seems probable that the regulation of deposit rates helped to avoid the banking crisis and temporarily increased the stability of the Finnish banking system. On the other hand, the regulatory system became a permanent part of the Finnish financial sector for several decades, a factor which was to put an effective drag on the development of financial markets in Finland.

Between October 1931 and March 1933, the Finnish markka depreciated substantially. In March 1933 the Finnish currency was pegged to the pound sterling. It is argued by several authors that the pegging rate implied an undervaluation of Finnish currency which supported Finnish competitiveness on foreign markets. During the 1930s, interest rates remained low, the price level was stable, and the pegged exchange-rate system remained unchanged. Thus, the Finnish experience confirms the conclusions from the Swedish record. Economic activity was supported by depreciation of the domestic currency. The undervalued currencies caused an export-led growth and the Depression was both short-lived and moderate in both countries relative to the experience of countries that remained on gold.

References

Dornbush, R., and Wolf, H. (1990), 'Monetary Overhang and Reforms in the 1940s' (Massachusetts Institute of Technology, Mimeo).

Eichengreen, B. (1991), *Elusive Stability: Essays in the History of International Finance, 1919–39* (Cambridge: Cambridge University Press).

Friedman, M., and Schwartz, A. (1963), *A Monetary History of the United States 1867–1960* (Princeton, NJ: Princeton University Press).

Haavisto, T. (1992), *Money and Economic Activity in Finland 1866–1985*, Ph.D. diss., Lund Economic Studies, 48, Dept. of Economics, Lund University.

Heckscher, E. (1923), *Nyordning av Finlands penningväsende* (Helsinki: Holger Schildts förlagsaktiebolag).

—— (1926), 'Penningväsende och penningpolitik', in E. Heckscher (ed.), *Bidrag till Sveriges ekonomiska och sociala historia under och efter världskriget*, ii (Stockholm: Norstedt).

Hjerppe, R. (1989), *The Finnish Economy 1860–1985, Growth and Structural Change* (Helsinki: Bank of Finland).

Johansson, Ö. (1967), *The Gross Domestic Product of Sweden and Its Composition 1861–1955*, Stockholm Economic Studies, NS 8. (Stockholm: Almqvist & Wiksell).

Jonung, L. (1975), *'Studies in the Monetary History of Sweden'*, unpublished Ph. D. diss., UCLA, Los Angeles.

Jonung, L. (1979), 'Knut Wicksell's Norm of Price Stabilisation and Swedish Monetary Policy in the 1930s', *Journal of Monetary Economics*, 5: 459–96.

Jonung, L. (1984), 'The Swedish Experience under the Classical Gold Standard, 1873–1914', in M. Bordo and A. Schwartz (eds.), *A Retrospective on the Classical Gold Standard, 1821–1931* (Chicago: University of Chicago Press).

Jucker-Fleetwood, E. (1958), *Economic Theory and Policy in Finland 1914–1925* (Oxford: Blackwell).

Krantz, O., and Nilsson, C.-A. (1975), *Swedish National Product 1861–1970, New Aspects on Methods and Measurement* (Lund: CWK Gleerup).

Korpisaari, P. (1917), 'Suomen rahan arvon aleneminen', *Yhteiskuntataloudellinen aikakauskirja*, 13 (Helsinki).

Oksanen, H., and Pihkala, E. (1975), *Finland's Foreign Trade 1917–1949* (Helsinki: Bank of Finland).

Östlind, A. (1945), *Svensk samhällsekonomi 1914–1922* (Stockholm: Svenska Bankföreningen).

Rossi, R. (1951), *Suomen pankin korkopolitiikka vuosina 1914–1938*, Institute of Economic Research, Series B. 12 (Helsinki: Bank of Finland).

Statistical Yearbook of Sweden, 1914–26 (Stockholm: National Central Bureau of Statistics).

Sveriges Riksbank, Yearbooks for selected years (Stockholm: Norstedt).

Tudeer, A. (1939), *Finland's Bank 1912–36* (Helsinki: Statsrådets Tryckeri).

PART III

Country Studies:
Banking, Money, and Financial Crises

9

Banking in Germany, 1918–1939

GERD HARDACH

Introduction

The German banking system was subject to considerable political and economic change during the inter-war period. The two decades between the November Revolution of 1918 and the beginning of the Second World War in September 1939 included the inflation from 1918 to 1923, a period of relative stability from 1924 to 1928, the Depression from 1929 to 1932, and the Nazi economy from 1933 to 1939. Political and economic change affected the banking system in many ways. Contemporary observers and economic historians were preoccupied by the short-term aspects; there are detailed studies on how the German banks coped with the vicissitudes of inflation and stabilization, crisis and Nazi rearmament. In this article, the focus is not on the short-term fluctuations but on the structural change in the banking system which occurred during the inter-war period. The foundations of a modern banking system were laid in imperial Germany from 1871 to 1914, when the 'universal bank' became the hallmark of German banking. The German universal banks were comprehensive in the range of financial products which they offered, but exclusive in their choice of customers. The majority of middle-class and working-class Germans were dependent on the rudimentary financial services offered by savings banks and co-operative banks. In the inter-war period, commercial banks, special banks, savings banks, and co-operative banks were amalgamated into a national banking system.

1. Structures

The German banking system of the early twentieth century was a conglomerate of quite different financial intermediaries: joint-stock banks, private banking firms, mortgage banks, state banks, savings banks, and credit co-operatives. The different bank types were defined by a combination of legal provisions, ownership, economic philosophy, and structure of business. The banking system was not a rational construct; it had gradually evolved during the nineteenth and early twentieth century.

The hub of the German banking system was the Reichsbank, which had been founded in 1875 as the central bank of the new empire. The function of the Reichsbank was the maintenance and management of the gold standard. Gradually the Reichsbank assumed the role of a monetary authority. The reason for the increase of central bank control was the general substitution of bank deposits for cash payments which happened at the time; Germany was in transition from a cash economy to a bank economy. As the banks piled a huge structure of debts and deposits on a relatively small basis of gold reserves, the whole system became extremely vulnerable to external shocks. In the Bank Inquiry of 1908, which was held after the banking crisis of 1907, the Reichsbank suggested that a modern monetary system should be established where the central bank would act as lender-of-last-resort by discounting bills or lending against collateral, but would also steer and control the banking system to maintain monetary stability (Bankenquete, 1908). Of the many regional note-issuing banks which had existed in the nineteenth century, only four remained on the eve of the First World War: the Badische Bank, the Bayerische Notenbank, the Sächsische Bank, and the Württembergische Bank. They maintained their note-issue privilege as a symbol of German federalism until 1935, but had no influence on monetary policy.

German commercial banks have been called 'universal banks' as they offered a wider range of financial services than banks in Britain, France, or the USA. They combined short-term banking, capital-market operations, broker services, and property management (Pohl, 1986). But German banks were not investment companies; their assets consisted almost exclusively of short-term advances, commercial bills, and bank drafts. Banks might hold securities to earn speculative profits, to influence stock and bond prices, or to exert economic control, but these assets were never substantial. Securities, excluding government bonds, amounted to 10 per cent of the total assets of metropolitan banks and major regional banks in 1913 (Deutsche Bundesbank, 1976: 78–81). The structure of assets and liabilities of modern German universal banks was therefore not substantially different from British or French commercial banks.

The investment business of the German universal banks relied on a close symbiosis between the banking system and the capital market. The expansion of banking was accompanied by the development of an efficient market for securities. Banks would assist company promotions, arrange acquisitions and mergers, underwrite stock and bond issues. Acting as intermediaries for both borrowers and investors, they also traded in securities and offered a full range of broker services (Hirsch, 1910; Schulze-Gävernitz, 1915). German banks derived substantial fee incomes from their investment and broker activities; in 1913 interest income contributed 55 per cent to the gross earnings of the metropolitan banks, charges for miscellaneous services 32 per cent, and dividends 13 per cent (Untersuchungsausschuss, 1934: 212–13).

German commercial banks maintained close links with the corporate sector; they provided short-term credit, traded in bills and bank drafts, financed foreign trade, and dominated the capital market. The mainstay of their power, however, was the trust vote (*Depotstimmrecht*). Shareholders could, and usually did delegate their votes to the bank which managed their portfolio; therefore the banks usually exerted majority control of joint-stock companies even without owning any stock. Rudolf Hilferding argued in his theory of 'finance capital', published in 1910, that the big metropolitan banks dominated the German economy; finance capital, in his definition, was capital applied in industry but provided and controlled by the banks (Hilferding, 1969).

There was a strong trend towards concentration in banking. The big metropolitan joint-stock banks controlled a great number of regional banks. Early in the century the metropolitan banks and the large provincial banks began to build networks of subsidiaries and branch offices. The individual banker was replaced by formal organizations with thousands of white-collar workers. The Deutsche Bank had 6,600 employees in 1913.[1] There were still many private banking firms in the early decades of the twentieth century, and some of them were quite important; but the age of private banking was over. According to a contemporary estimate, the nine metropolitan banks controlled 83 per cent of the assets of all commercial banks in 1913 (Grüger, 1933: 55).

Concentration fostered the rise of cartel arrangements in banking. The metropolitan banks organized in 1881 a cartel, the Berliner Stempelvereinigung. Originally formed to achieve uniform stamp duties, the agreement was soon extended to regulate interest rates, charges for miscellaneous services, and other conditions. With strong support from the Reichsbank, which was in favour of concentration and cartelization, this agreement was expanded in 1913 into a system of regional cartels which covered the whole market (Pilster, 1922).

Real estate credit was provided not by universal banks but by special banks, as mortgage banking had been legally separated from commercial banking since 1899. Mortgage banks were able to issue privileged bonds; in return, they were not permitted to engage in short-term commercial banking which was considered as more risky. Only a few commercial banks were allowed to continue their traditional mortgage business; the most important of these 'mixed banks' was the Bayerische Hypotheken-und Wechselbank.

[1] Geschäftsbericht der Deutschen Bank, 1913.

Mortgage banking was an expanding market as the rise of industry was accompanied by the growth of cities. Real estate credit was also provided by state banks and provincial banks, which had a different business ideology from either commercial banks or private mortgage banks; they were public-orientated rather than profit-orientated. Their main activities were long-term credit, especially for agriculture, and government finance. Some state banks and provincial banks issued the same kind of privileged bonds as private mortgage banks. The position of public banks was particularly strong in the agricultural mortgage market, where they provided 90 per cent of the credit volume in 1913 (Bente, 1933: 366).

Savings banks were regarded as non-profit organizations, ideologically opposed to the capitalist world of commercial banking. As a rule, savings banks were a part of the municipal administration and did not have a corporate identity of their own until 1931. The function of savings banks was to serve the interest of the general public, by accepting savings and investing them conservatively in mortgages or government credit. Their banking status was fairly recent. A new law on cheque payments provided in 1908 that savings banks might offer cheque accounts if the state governments under whose jurisdiction they fell were prepared to modify the regulations. Prussia was the first State to allow its savings banks in 1909 to open current accounts and participate in the cheque and giro system. As savings banks were restricted to their local financial markets, it was essential for them to develop forms of regional and national co-operation. Regional and national institutions were founded to facilitate giro and cheque trans-fers, to improve liquidity adjustment and to foster communication among member banks (Ashauer, 1991).

Co-operative banks were local institutions, going down to towns and districts and even to the small village. A bank co-operative, like any co-operative, emphasized solidity rather than profit; it required personal membership, often with unlimited liability; and while members might hold multiple shares in the capital of a co-operative, each member had only one vote in order to exclude the influence of wealth and power (Kluge, 1991). In international comparisons, the success of the co-operative bank is as much a German peculiarity as the universal bank. The rise of co-operative banking owes much to the traditional mentality of the German middle classes; the typical members were farmers, independent craftsmen, and shopkeepers who were reluctant to enter the capitalist market economy. Economic expansion gradually eroded the traditional values, but rural co-operatives, which were confined to the small world of their village were still very conservative. Friedrich Wilhelm Raiffeisen, the pioneer of the rural co-operative movement, was strongly in favour of decentralization. He had made it a rule that a co-operative should not expand its activities beyond the radius of the village church steeple (Raiffeisen, 1923). Hence the German countryside was dotted with thousands of rural co-operatives. Germany had 17,000 rural credit co-operatives in 1913; they contributed much to the modernization and commercialization of German agriculture (Deutsche Bundesbank, 1976: 122).

TABLE 9.1. *Banks in Germany, 1913–1936*

	1913	1925	1929	1938
Commercial banks	352	402	296	199
Private banking firms	1,221	1,406	1,100	491
Savings banks	3,332	3,262	3,235	2,558
Co-operative banks	18,557	20,977	21,499	19,076
Special banks	79	77	87	80
All banks	23,541	26,124	26,217	22,404

Sources: Deutsche Bundesbank (1976: 82, 121). Untersuchungsausschuss (1934: 9).

A comparison of the different bank groups shows that commercial banks, including private banking firms, controlled in 1913 less than one-third of the total assets of the banking system. This comparison certainly underrates the financial power of the commercial banks; neither the control of the commercial banks over the capital market, nor capital linkages with mortgage banks are reflected in the asset structure of the banking system. Nevertheless, it is obvious that Germany's economic growth was financed to a large extent not by universal banks, but by savings banks, co-operative banks, and special banks.

The success of savings and co-operative banks was facilitated by the conservatism of the commercial banks which concentrated on corporate finance, government lending, and wealthy individuals. Concentration in banking apparently increased this trend; in the pre-war years contemporary observers criticized the commercial banks for favouring the large industrial corporations and neglecting other sectors of the economy (Eschwege, 1908). Historical research has confirmed the bias of commercial banks in favour of big business and government loans (Tilly, 1986). Profit margins were higher and risks were easier to evaluate in big business and government finance, or at least so it seemed, than in transactions with small business and agriculture.

The rise of savings and co-operative banks showed the growth potential of an emerging financial mass market, which the commercial banks failed to grasp. Savings banks and co-operative banks filled a gap and captured large market segments. As they increased in importance, they moved away from the old ideologies of paternalism and charity and became 'middle-class banks' (Kruse, 1941). Commercial banks did not see either savings banks or co-operative banks as competitors; hence no attempt was made to include these institutions in the cartel agreements (Pilster, 1922).

TABLE 9.2. *The structure of banking in Germany, 1913–1938 (% of total assets)*

	1913	1925	1929	1938
Commercial banks	31	49	33	15
Special banks	27	17	26	29
Savings banks	33	19	31	45
Co-operative banks	9	15	10	11

Sources: Deutsche Bundesbank, 1976; Statistisches Reichsamt, 1927.

In the years before the First World War German banking had reached an impressive level. There were 23,544 banks and 25,500 bank units, either a bank or a branch office, in 1913, including savings banks and thousands of small credit co-operatives. The total assets of the banking system were approximately 71 billion marks in 1913. Commercial banks were not yet the ubiquitous national organizations we know today; but savings banks and credit co-operatives brought banking facilities to small towns and villages. There was, on average, one bank unit for 2,600 inhabitants in 1913. In addition, there was the giro system of the Reichspost which made cashless payments easily accessible in every town and village (Deutsche Bundesbank, 1976: 102, 122; Statistisches Bundesamt, 1972: 90).

2. Inflation

The Treaty of Versailles reduced Germany's territory by 13 per cent. To some extent, therefore, local commercial banks, savings banks, and co-operative banks came under the sovereignty of neighbouring States. But neither the Peace Treaty, nor the revolution of 1918–19 affected the banking sector very much; there was a strong continuity in banking from imperial Germany to the Weimar Republic.

The early years of the Weimar Republic were characterized by a strong inflation. The inflation was inherited from the war economy, but accelerated as a consequence of inadequate fiscal and monetary policies. There was a brief attempt to stabilize the mark in 1920–1. It was supported by the optimism of foreign speculators who invested in mark assets, in expectation of a revaluation which was never to happen. In the summer of 1921 inflation gained momentum again, and the hyperinflation of 1922–3 virtually destroyed the currency (Holtfrerich, 1980; Webb, 1989). When the mark was stabilized in November 1923, the dollar parity, which had been 4.2 marks for one dollar under the pre-war gold standard, had climbed to the impressive rate of 4.2 million million marks for one dollar.

An inflation of these dimensions was without historical precedent, and experience provided no guide to how to cope with the situation. The

German banks followed essentially a strategy of adaptation, increasing their business as fast as possible in order to keep pace with inflation. Banks defined their business objectives in nominal values, rather than real values. However, the efforts of the financial intermediaries to keep up with the inflation were unsuccessful. As prices soared, the real demand for financial assets plummeted. Banks and the public emphasized maturity shortening; the long-term capital market practically ceased to exist and savings declined (Grüger, 1933; Holtfrerich, 1985; Pohl, 1978). As the real value of many transactions became insignificant, the large commercial banks tried to get rid of the small accounts (Deutsche Bank, 1922). It was a policy which the banks would regret after the currency reform, when commercial banks and savings banks competed for deposits.

Commercial banks, which concentrated on short-term business, were better equipped than other financial intermediaries to cope with the depreciation of the currency. They turned increasingly from the traditional credit activities to stock-exchange speculation and foreign-exchange speculation, both on their own account and for their customers. The metropolitan banks and the large regional banks continued to expand. There were eight metropolitan banks in 1919, the Berliner Handels-Gesellschaft, Commerz- und DiscontoBank, Darmstädter Bank, Deutsche Bank, Disconto-Gesellschaft, Dresdner Bank, Mitteldeutsche Creditbank, and National-bank. The Darmstädter Bank merged in 1922 with the Nationalbank to form the Darmstädter und Nationalbank, whose collapse would trigger off the banking crisis. Altogether, the commercial banks took over more than 150 banks from 1919 to 1923 (Centralverband, 1933: 105). Many of these regional banks became branch offices. In 1925 the largest five metropolitan banks national banks had an average of 104 branches, the provincial banks eleven branches (Untersuchungsausschuss, 1934: 9–11). A vast labour force was recruited during the inflation to fill the expanding organizations and handle the excessive paperwork. The Deutsche Bank had 26,000 employees in 1922 and 40,000 employees in 1923; the Dresdner Bank had 19,000 employees in 1922.[2] At the same time, however, new joint-stock banks and private banking houses entered the market in great numbers. A contemporary observer compared the inflation to the boom years of 1871–3 (Pilster, 1922: 72–3). The new banks derived their profits from speculation in shares and foreign exchange, rather than from credit activities (Weber, 1938: 147; Grüger, 1933: 54–5).

Savings banks with their heavy emphasis on long-term deposits and credits found it difficult to adapt to the inflation. Few people were inclined to put their money into savings deposits where they could only lose. In 1913

---

[2] Geschäftsberichte der Deutschen Bank, 1922, 1925; Geschäftsbericht der Dresdner Bank, 1922.

savings deposits and savings bonds had accounted for 64 per cent of the total liabilities of savings banks, sight and time deposits for 13 per cent. At the end of 1924, savings deposits and savings bonds were only 11 per cent of total liabilities, while the share of sight and time deposits had increased to 55 per cent (Deutsche Bundesbank, 1976: 74–5). The assets of the savings banks, especially real estate credit and local government loans, which had always been regarded as a safe investment, were heavily devalued as prices soared. The savings banks had to turn from long-term to short-term business in order to survive. In 1921 the Government lifted most of the remaining restrictions on savings banks, so that they could offer almost the full range of banking services. This was an important step in the transformation of savings banks into local universal banks. Co-operative banks were not as versatile as commercial banks, but more flexible in their business than savings banks. Many co-operatives engaged in broker services and security speculation to offset the decline of their traditional business (Kluge, 1991: 218–19). Mortgage banks were the most disadvantaged financial intermediaries, as the capital market was virtually destroyed by the inflation.

The inflation sheltered Germany from the world economic crisis of 1920–1; production and employment were relatively stable during these years. Real per capita income attained 89 per cent of the pre-war level of 1913 in 1922 (Witt, 1982). But the inflationary boom was short-lived; the hyperinflation of 1923 and the following stabilization threw the German economy into a deep crisis. In January 1924 the production of basic industrial materials dropped to 54 per cent of the 1913 level, and three million people were out of work (Hardach, 1976: 29). The monetary expansion of the inflation years had financed a bubble economy.

3. Financial reconstruction

With the stabilization of the currency in 1923, and the return to the gold standard in 1924, the Weimar Republic entered into a period of relative economic stability. The banking system entered the new era with a serious disequilibrium (Balderston, 1991). The Weimar Republic had more banks in 1925 than the German Empire in 1913. The number of savings banks was smaller, due to the contraction of the German territory, but in all other bank groups the number of firms had increased. There were 26,130 banks and 32,900 bank units with, on average, one bank unit for 1,900 inhabitants in 1925 (Deutsche Bundesbank, 1976: 102, 122; Statistisches Bundesamt 1972: 90). The volume of business, however, had been sharply reduced by the inflation. At the end of 1924 the total assets of the banking system were in current Reichsmark 21 per cent of the 1913 level, and only 17 per cent of the pre-war level when the nominal value is deflated by the wholesale price index (Deutsche Bundesbank, 1976: 74; *Statistisches Jahrbuch*, 1924–5: 264).

It was an accepted opinion at the time that the banking system was too large for the reduced volume of business (Walb, 1933). In commercial banking, there was only one important newcomer, the state-owned Reichs-kreditgesellschaft which was founded in 1924. Mergers reduced the number of firms considerably. Within four years, 106 joint-stock banks and 306 private banking firms disappeared. Two important mergers took place in 1929, when the Deutsche Bank merged with the Disconto-Gesellschaft, and the Commerzbank with the Mitteldeutsche Creditanstalt. This left four metropolitan banks with branches on the eve of the great depression: the Commerz- und Privatbank, Darmstädter und Nationalbank, Deutsche Bank und Discontogesellschaft, and Dresdner Bank. Two metropolitan banks, Berliner Handels-Gesellschaft and Reichskreditgesellschaft, did not establish branches outside Berlin. Mergers and acquisitions did not necess-arily reduce the number of bank units, as regional banks and private banking firms which were taken over by other banks were often turned into branches. The reason must be sought in the high degree of concentration and cartelization. As interest rates and charges for miscellaneous services were virtually frozen by the various cartel agreements, the availability of bank services was almost the only means for banks to increase their market share. Employment was severely reduced, however, and thousands of bank employees joined the army of the unemployed. The Deutsche Bank reduced its staff to 16,000 employees in 1925, the Dresdner Bank had 8,600 employees in 1926, and the Commerzbank had 8,114 employees in 1931.[3] Few savings banks disappeared, and the number of co-operative banks actually increased. Savings banks were incorporated into the structure of local government, and as a kind of public service they did not depend on the volume of business. Urban and rural co-operative banks were backed by their local membership; many of the small rural co-operatives were managed by part-time staff at little cost. Altogether there was a slight increase in firms and a decline in bank units, with 26,221 banks and 32,500 bank units in 1929. As the German population increased, one bank unit served on average 2,000 inhabitants in 1929 (Deutsche Bundesbank, 1976: 102, 122; Statistisches Bundesamt 1972: 90).

As there was not much scope for removing the disequilibrium between too many banks and a reduced market by a reduction in the number of suppliers, financial reconstruction became the overriding objective in bank-ing strategy. Commercial banks, savings banks, co-operative banks, and mortgage banks strove frantically to rebuild their assets. Competition

---

[3] Geschäftsbericht der Commerz- und Privatbank, 1932; Geschäftsbericht der Deutschen Bank, 1925; Geschäftsbericht der Dresdner Bank, 1926.

between different types of bank was keener than before the war, and traditional demarcation lines between the various bank types and their markets diminished in importance (Dickhaus, 1991).

The economic environment in which the banks operated was drastically changed by the stabilization and the return to gold. For most of the time, except for two episodes of falling interest rates in early 1926 and in early 1927, the Reichsbank pursued a deflationary policy to defend the gold parity of the mark. The average bank rate from 1924 to 1928 was 8 per cent (Hardach, 1976; James, 1985). The Dawes Plan and the return to gold restored international confidence in the German economy, and the high interest rates attracted considerable capital imports, especially from the USA (McNeil 1986). By the end of 1930, Germany had accumulated a foreign indebtness of RM 25.3 to RM 25.8 billion, of which RM 14.5–15 billion were short-term debts (Untersuchungsausschuss, 1934: 462–3).

A large part of these capital imports was used for reparation transfers. In fact, foreign credits were indispensable for the fulfilment of the Dawes Plan and later the Young Plan.[4] From 1924 to 1931 Germany had net capital imports of RM 14.7 billion, while reparation transfers were RM 11.1 billion (Statistisches Reichsamt 1934). Germany was 'borrowing from Peter to pay Paul', as the American banker James Warburg remarked in retrospect (Warburg, 1964: 87). That this was a dangerous system was perceived early on both sides of the Atlantic. Governor Benjamin Strong of the Federal Reserve Bank of New York feared in 1925 that foreign credits to Germany meant 'simply pouring money into a rat hole', as the foreign exchange would be used for reparation payments to France and England.[5] Hjalmar Schacht, who was president of the Reichsbank from 1924 to 1930, warned in 1925 that a withdrawal of the foreign credits would lead to a collapse of the German monetary system; Germany must therefore seek stability in its international relations.[6] There were some attempts, both in the USA and in Germany, to discourage excessive loans, but international capital movements were inherent in the gold standard and could not really be brought under control.[7]

The inflation had thoroughly changed the structure of the banking system. Commercial banks and co-operative banks had vastly increased their market shares, whereas savings banks and mortgage banks had lost ground. The new environment of a substantial economic recovery, monetary restrictions, and an internationalization of financial markets shifted again the competitive position of the different bank groups.

[4] Cabinet meeting with Schacht, 7 Oct. 1927. Akten zur deutschen auswärtigen Politik 1918–1945, Series B, vii. 70–1.

[5] Strong to Jay, 20 July 1925. Federal Reserve Bank of New York (FRBNY), Strong Papers.

[6] Cabinet meeting with Schacht, 14 Aug. 1925. Bundesarchiv Koblenz (BA), R 43 I/634.

[7] Strong to G. E. Winston, Under-Secretary of the Treasury, 19 Nov. 1925. FRBNY, Germany 1924–8.

Commercial banks participated eagerly in the internationalization of financial markets, both as importers and as exporters of capital. Capital imports took the form of foreign deposits with German banks, or the intermediation of foreign credits for German borrowers. Foreign deposits amounted to 40 per cent of all deposits with German credit banks in 1929. The interbank deposits were either advances on current account, or bank acceptances (Ausschuss 1930: 80–105; Fischer, 1933: 512). German banks considered their international business not as a temporary solution, but as a transition towards an internationalization of money and banking. They maintained close relations with foreign banks and were not only importers, but also exporters of capital. In 1930 the foreign short-term assets of the German commercial banks amounted to 40 per cent of their foreign liabilities (Ausschuss, 1930: 81). In 1930 the internationalization of banking was still regarded as a definite advantage. German banks received praise for their efficiency in providing the economy with cheap foreign credits, and it was asserted that the liquidity of the banking system was secured by its considerable foreign assets (Wegner, 1930: 1745–7).

In the international business foreign banks competed with German banks, offering short-term credits and loans to business, state governments and cities in Germany. 'I am conscious of the fact that Germany has been somewhat overrun with representatives of American banks eagerly seeking and competing for business,' wrote Governor Strong in 1925 to Parker Gilbert, the Agent-General for Reparation Payments in Berlin.[8] Thus foreign banks were able to gain a share of the German credit market (Balderston, 1989). But competition was moderate; the market was so large that both German and foreign banks could increase their volume of business.

The internationalization of finance accelerated concentration in commercial banking. Only the metropolitan banks and a few prestigious private banking firms had access to foreign capital markets. Smaller banks usually lacked the reputation, the funds, and the expertise that were required for international transactions. Regional banks were squeezed between the international resources of metropolitan banking, and a vigorous expansion of the savings banks on the domestic market.

Capital imports were paralleled by a substantial recovery of the domestic capital market. From 1925 to 1931 the average annual volume of new issues of shares and bonds was RM 2.9 billion. This was quite impressive; from from 1901 to 1913 the annual volume had been much lower with RM 2.0 billion (Centralverband, 45). The background of the frequent contemporary complaints about a credit shortage was not an inadequate supply, but rather the huge liquidity gap which the inflation had left not only in banking, but

---

[8] Strong to Gilbert, 30 Sept. 1925. FRBNY, Strong Papers.

also in industry, agriculture, and commerce. As the capital market was reconstructed, the commercial banks could resume their role as intermediators of domestic credit. International and domestic transactions together boosted the fee income of the commercial banks. In 1929 interests contributed 47 per cent to the profits of the metropolitan banks, charges for miscellaneous services 51 per cent, and dividends 2 per cent (Untersuchungsausschuss, 1934: 232–3).

TABLE 9.3. *The structure of commercial banking, 1913–1938* (% of total assets)

	1913	1925	1930	1938
Metropolitan banks	39	50	70	77
Regional banks	37	36	11	12
Private bankers	24	13	19	11

Source: Deutsche Bundesbank (1976: 67–121).

Savings banks experienced an impressive recovery during the stabilization period. Their financial reconstruction was based on a surprising renaissance of popular saving. The return to the gold standard restored not only the confidence of international investors, but also the confidence of the general public. The savings deposits with the German banking system, which had been reduced by war and inflation from 23.8 billion marks in 1913 to RM 0.8 billion in 1924, recovered within five years to RM 12.5 billion in 1929 (Deutsche Bundesbank, 1976: 774). The savings banks were rooted in the local economy and were therefore able to win the largest share of this expanding market. Savings banks carried on their general banking activities which they had started in 1921, and attracted short-term deposits in addition to savings. On the other side of the balance sheet, the transformation of the savings banks into local universal banks began to change their assets. The decline in mortgages was partly compensated by a strong increase in current account advances (Deutsche Bundesbank 1976: 102–3).

The competition between commercial banks, savings banks, and co-operative banks received much attention at the time. Commercial banks increased the range of their financial services and tried to attract new customers beyond their traditional clientele. They began in 1927 to accept savings deposits, in competition with the savings banks; but they were not yet very successful in that particular market (Ausschuss, 1930: 41). After a few years of ideological warfare, commercial banks and savings banks settled in 1928 for a cartel agreement between the two bank groups.

While the large commercial banks extended their branch networks into the domains of regional and local banking, savings banks and co-operative banks strengthened their central institutions to compete on regional and national levels. These institutions fulfilled the important service functions of interregional payments and liquidity clearing for the members of their group, but they also entered into regular banking operations of their own when financial transactions were too large for individual savings banks or credit co-operatives.

Mortgage banks and state banks could also reap some benefits from the restoration of the capital market and recovered some of the ground which they had lost during war and inflation. In addition, the market share of the special banks group was increased by government intervention, which led to the creation of new financial intermediaries (Preiss, 1933). Special banks were also founded by interest groups and some industrial corporations. The result of structural change and competitive adjustment was that the banking groups re-established more or less the pre-war structure of the financial sector, with some gains for savings banks and credit co-operatives at the expense of commercial banks and special banks.

TABLE 9.4. *Central institutions of savings banks and co-operative banks in Germany,* 1913–1938 (% of total assets within each group)

	1913	1925	1930	1938
Savings banks	92	63	65	70
Central institutions	8	37	35	30
Credit co-operatives	89	47	77	74
Central institutions	11	53	23	26

Source: Deutsche Bundesbank (1976: 67–121).

The huge liquidity gap which the inflation had created by annihilating the monetary assets of the economy was gradually filled; the banking system increased its total assets from 1925 to 1930 at a stupendous rate of 30 per cent per year. Too soon, however, the Depression of 1929 interrupted the process of financial reconstruction. In 1929 the total assets of the banking system attained RM 64 billion, or 89 per cent of the pre-war level of 1913; as the Reichsmark prices of 1929 were much higher than the mark prices of 1913, however, the real volume of banking assets was only 58 per cent of the pre-war level.

The growth of financial assets was not excessive, but many banks neglected traditional security standards in the drive for financial reconstruction. They reduced their liquidity in favour of less liquid, but more remunerative assets (Henning, 1973). Commercial banks reduced their ratio of cash and Reichsbank balances to deposits from 7.3 per cent in 1913 to 3.8 per cent in 1929. The ratio of capital and reserves to total assets declined during the same time from 22 per cent to 7 per cent (Untersuchungsausschuss, 1934: 88–91). Banks relied essentially on their portfolios of commercial bills as a liquidity reserve; they were confident that in times of need they could rediscount bills at the Reichsbank to obtain additional liquidity

(Ausschuss, 1929). The deterioration of cash liquidity made the banking system more dependent upon the Reichsbank as a lender-of-last-resort, and the reduction of reserves made the banks extremely vulnerable when the crisis set in. The increasing dependence of the banking system upon the Reichsbank was particularly dangerous as international agreements obliged the Reichsbank to give priority to the defence of the gold standard.

TABLE 9.5. *Financial contraction and reconstruction in Germany, 1913–1938*

	1913	1925	1929	1938
Nominal assets	100	35	89	111
Real assets	100	24	58	92
Nominal NNP	100	128	152	187
Real NNP	100	89	99	155

Sources: Deutsche Bundesbank (1976: 74–5, 118); Hoffmann, *et al.* (1965: 598–601, 825–828).

The rapid financial reconstruction of the late 1920s was essential for the banking industry, but it was also essential for the economy at large. Credit was expensive in the stabilization years. Immediately after the currency reform interest rates were extremely high as banks raised the profit margin to restore their reserves; in 1924 the rate for current advances was 19 per cent. These were extraordinary conditions, and in the following years the financial reconstruction brought the interest rate down to 10 per cent in 1928. Average bond yields were 8.2 per cent from 1925 to 1928 (Deutsche Bundesbank, 1976: 278). This was a very high level by pre-war standards.

After the long stagnation which was a consequence of the war and the inflation, the German banking system in the late 1920s resumed its role as an agent of economic growth. Net social product per head at constant prices reached in 1927 its pre-war level of 1913, and it was 7 per cent above the pre-war level when the boom came to an end in 1928 (Hoffmann *et al.*, 1965: 172–4, 827–8). Yet growth was uneven, and unemployment was high during the recovery. Monetary restrictions and high interest rates contributed to the recessions in 1924, 1926, and 1928, as well as to the high level of unemployment. Monetary restraints, rather than collective bargaining, wages, and government spending, were the primordial issue (Kruedener, 1990). A slower pace of financial reconstruction, or an effective control of capital imports, would have further aggravated the economic problems of the Weimar Republic. In Germany as in other countries, the return to gold imposed a heavy burden on the economy, as fiscal, monetary, and economic policies had to be adjusted to the objective of international competitiveness (Eichengreen, 1992).

4. The crisis

Economic growth slowed down in 1928, and in 1929 there was a decline in real national product. The German economy entered the Great Depression, which resulted in an unprecedented fall in production and employment. In 1932 real per capita income was 18 to 24 per cent lower than in 1928, depending on the estimates (Statistisches Bundesamt, 1972: 261; Hoffmann *et al.*, 1965: 827–8). On average, 31 per cent of the labour force were either unemployed or working short hours in 1932, and in January 1933 there were more than 6 million unemployed (Gleitze, 1960: 45; *Konjunkturstatistisches Handbuch*, 1936: 16). The crisis management by the Government and the Reichsbank was woefully inadequate. This was to some extent due to economic constraints, but even more to deliberate choice. As the crisis discredited the liberal promise of economic growth in a stable economic environment, government, business and a large part of the electorate opted for an authoritarian State and economic nationalism (Meister, 1991).

The crisis caught the banks half-way in their reconstruction process. Any plans for expansion and growth were frustrated. Investments which had seemed sound and profitable were caught in a quagmire of declining demand, sinking profits, and business failures. The banking system did not collapse under the first blow, but struggled for two years against the heavy odds of inadequate reserves, low liquidity, and dependence on foreign capital.

American credits were withdrawn from 1928, but were replaced by credits from European countries. Germany's foreign indebtedness had become a serious problem, but the balance of trade improved from 1928, and there was reason to expect that a consolidation and ultimately repayment of the debt was feasible. T. W. Lamont of the Morgan bank recommended in 1929 that the Morgan group should 'stand sturdily for continued confidence' in its German engagements.[9] Consolidation, however, required economic and political stability. It was the political uncertainty, not the economic instability which undermined Germany's creditworthiness. The sequence of credit withdrawals began in April 1929, when German intransigence almost wrecked the Paris reparations conference.

The political vicissitudes of 1929–30 were compounded by the precarious situation of government finance. Government expenditure had been severely cut during the stabilization of 1923–4. But it rose during the following years, and tax income did not keep pace with expenditure. From 1925–6 to 1928–9, government spending increased from RM 15 billion to RM 21 billion, and

---

[9] Lamont telegram from Paris to Morgan New York, 29 Apr. 1929. Harvard University, Baker Library, Lamont Papers.

the deficit rose from RM 1.5 billion to RM 2.7 billion (Statistisches Reichsamt, 1936: 42–3). Reichsbank President Schacht was a severe critic of public expenditure. In 1929 he enforced fiscal stabilization measures which his critics considered an abuse of central bank power (James, 1987; Witt, 1985). The transition from expansion to recession was certainly an untimely moment for fiscal austerity. But the situation was in fact difficult as the inflation and the currency reform of 1923–4 had demonstrated the close interrelation between fiscal and monetary stability. The stability of the international system depended not only on the confidence of foreign investors, but also on German expectations. The possibility of a fall in the Reichsmark exchange rate, or fear of exchange controls, might easily conjure the spectre of inflation and lead to massive capital flight (Balderston, 1991: 585–8). Schacht, who anticipated the impending collapse of the currency but felt unable to prevent it, left the Reichsbank in 1930 and was replaced by the former Finance Minister and Chancellor Hans Luther.

The brief respite which the banking system had enjoyed since the beginning of the Depression was over in 1931. The crisis had eroded the liquidity of several banks, and the Reichsbank, paralysed by credit withdrawals and capital flight, refused to act as a lender-of-last-resort. On Saturday, 11 July 1931 Jakob Goldschmidt of the Darmstädter Bank went to Chancellor Brüning to declare that his bank had to suspend payments. On Monday, 13 July the Darmstädter Bank was closed.[10] The collapse of one of the prominent metropolitan banks led to a general panic and a run on all banks; people rushed to withdraw their deposits. The crisis spread rapidly; the Dresdner Bank was on the verge of collapse, other metropolitan banks were seriously impaired, and several provincial banks, savings banks, and co-operative banks suspended cash payments. In many cases there was only a temporary illiquidity, when assets were frozen but basically sound; this was the typical problem of savings banks and other public banks, which were eventually guaranteed by the taxpayers. In the more serious cases, which included many commercial banks of any size from the Darmstädter Bank to small regional banks, the depreciation of assets had completely exhausted capital and reserves. On 14 July 1931 a general bank moratorium was declared. The gold standard, which the Reichsbank had sought to defend at the expense of the banking system, survived the collapse of the banks by only one day; foreign-exchange controls were introduced on 15 July 1931. They were gradually expanded, and after 1933 became an integral part of Nazi economic policy.

The cause of the banking crisis was a conjunction of structural problems, management errors, and inadequate policy. The crisis was not inherent in

[10] Entwicklung der Bankkrise. Reichsbank Memorandum, 12 Oct. 1931. Schäffer Diary, 11 July 1931. Institut für Zeitgeschichte München ED 93.

the combination of commercial banking and investment banking which was typical for the German universal bank. When the Government, in August 1931, discussed strategies to overcome the banking crisis, Reichsbank President Luther suggested that commercial banking and investment banking should be separated; but other experts opposed the suggestion and defended the universal bank.[11] According to contemporary critics, the fundamental flaw of the German banking system was not the combination of short-term and long-term banking, but the monopolistic strategy of the commercial banks. Too often the banks preferred large credits to individual corporations, instead of decentralizing the risk by a greater number of smaller credits. This policy made many banks dependent on a particular company; the Darmstädter Bank had linked its fate to the Norddeutsche Wollkämmerei, the prestigious Hamburg banking firm of M. M. Warburg to the Karstadt department store. Warburg was supported by the American branch of the family, Paul Warburg and Felix Warburg, with a fabulous amount of money. 'Still, it is the right thing to do. What good does money do us if we lose our good name and desert those we love,' wrote Paul Warburg to his son James whom he had sent in haste to Germany as crisis manager.[12] But this was an exception; many banks were ruined by the default of big debtors.

The situation in the savings banks sector was different. As an integral part of the municipal administration savings banks were protected against failure. But savings banks and their central institutions were still primarily engaged in long-term credits to house owners and government, and found it difficult to procure sufficient liquidity when deposits were withdrawn on a large scale; nor could the municipalities, which were themselves in financial straits, offer immediate help. Local savings banks drew heavily on their liquidity reserves in central institutions, and thus multiplied the problem (Ashauer, 1991: 246–51).

On 13 July 1931 the Government guaranteed the liabilities of the Dresdner Bank. At the end of July 1931 the Akzept- und Garantiebank was founded jointly by the Government and a bank consortium. It underwrote bank drafts, which made these drafts eligible for Reichsbank discount. The Akzeptbank thus provided new liquidity for commercial banks, savings banks, and co-operative banks with frozen or depreciated assets. The banks opened after a moratorium of two days to pay out cash for wages, taxes, and other essential transactions, and normal operations were resumed on 5 August 1931.

As private investors were unwilling to reconstruct the depleted capital and reserves of the banking system and provide liquidity for new investment, the

[11] Cabinet meeting, 18 Aug. 1931. BA R 43 I/647.
[12] Paul Warburg to James Warburg, 16 June 1931. John F. Kennedy Library, Warburg Papers, box 1.

Government and the Reichsbank took upon themselves the burden of financial reconstruction. They purchased new shares of the national banks and other banks that were defined as essential for the economy, granted subsidies, and infused new liquidity. The Darmstädter Bank, which had triggered off the crisis, was merged in March 1932 with the Dresdner Bank. As a consequence of the intervention the leading commercial banks came under public control. The Reich, together with the Deutsche Golddiskont-bank, a subsidiary of the Reichsbank, and some state governments, held 91 per cent of the capital of the Dresdner Bank, 70 per cent of the Commerz-bank, 70 per cent of the Allgemeine Deutsche Credit-Anstalt, an important regional bank, 67 per cent of the Norddeutsche Kreditbank, and 35 per cent of the Deutsche Bank (Bente, 1933).

Contemporary critics pointed out the arbitrariness of government inter-vention. The metropolitan banks and a few important regional banks were subsidized, while all the other banks were denied government support.[13] Within three years, from 1929 to 1932, the number of commercial banks declined from 298 to 220, the number of private banking firms from 1,100 to 709 (Untersuchungsausschuss, 1934: 9). Government intervention created a privileged state-guaranteed sector within the commercial bank sector.

Brüning declared in August 1931 that the intervention in favour of the banking system entailed new responsibilities for the government; the bank-ing system must be thoroughly reformed.[14] The Chancellor acted under political pressure; the huge subsidies for the banking establishment were ill-received by the public at a time when the Government put the civil service on a fasting diet, asked sacrifices from every citizen, and dismantled the social security system because of a pretended shortage of funds. Several directors of the Darmstädter, Dresdner, and other subsidized banks were dismissed. Government control over banking was reinforced. A government commissioner on banking (Reichskommissar für das Bankgewerbe) was appointed in September 1931, who acted under the supervision of a committee with delegates from the Government and the Reichsbank.[15] The savings banks obtained in August 1931 their own legal identity, which strengthened their position against the credits demands from local govern-ments. In December 1931 a general cartel on interest rates and charges for misscellaneous services was established which included all bank groups.

The Brüning Government regarded the public ownership of the commer-cial banks as a temporary measure; no attempt was made to interfere in the business of the banks. Nevertheless the banking establishment was weary of

[13] Vereinigung privater Mittelstands-Aktienbanken Westdeutschlands to Brüning, 26 Feb. 1932. BA R 43 I/648.

[14] Cabinet meeting, 18 Aug. 1931. BA R 43 I/647.

[15] Notverordnung vom 19 Sept. 1931. Reichsgesetzblatt 1931 I. 493–503. Ernst appointment, 23 Sept. 1931. BA R 43 I/647.

state control. The big commercial banks had successfully substituted government finance for the languishing capital market but were not prepared to share their power. They denied any need for structural reforms.[16] The Centralverband des Deutschen Bank-und Bankiergewerbes, which represented the commercial banks, supported in September 1932 the recovery programme of the Papen Government but emphasized at the time that government interference in banking should be kept to a minimum.[17] In a memorandum to the Schleicher Government in December 1932 the bankers renewed their plea for continuity; the universal bank should be maintained, private initiative should be restored, and state holdings in commercial banks should be sold to private investors once the economy recovered from the slump.[18] When the Weimar Republic ended, bank reform was still an unfinished business.

From December 1931 the recalcitrant Reichsbank was gradually brought to abandon its deflationary policy, and to supply the desperately needed liquidity.[19] But Luther was orthodox in his views on fiscal and monetary policy, and he still hoped to restore the gold standard. When Chancellor von Papen succeeded the hapless Brüning in June 1932 and embarked immediately on an employment programme, Luther warned repeatedly against inflation.[20] The contraction of banking assets continued in 1932. The Akzeptbank complained that the banks were too restrictive and discouraged investors.[21] It sought a more active role and offered not only short-term credits to banks, but also direct credits to industrial and commercial corporations.[22] To revive banking activities, two new financial intermediaries were founded in December 1932, the Deutsches Finanzierungsinstitut AG (FINAG) and the Tilgungskasse für gewerbliche Kredite (TILKA). They accepted illiquid or depreciated bank assets as collateral for credits, so that the banks could finance new investment.

5. Rearmament and War

The Nazi seizure of power in January 1933 interrupted the banking reform which Brüning had initiated in July 1931. The future of the banking system

---

[16] Dernburg memorandum, 9 Sept. 1931. BA R 43 I/648.
[17] Sitzung des Vorstandes und Ausschusses des Centralverbandes des Deutschen Bank- und Bankiergewerbes, 29 Sept. 1932, in Bank-Archiv, 32 (1932–3).
[18] Centralverband des Deutschen Bank- und Bankiergewerbes, Memorandum zur Frage der Reform des Depositenbankenwesens, 28 Dec. 1932. BA R 43 I/649.
[19] Verwaltungsbericht der Reichsbank, 1932.
[20] Cabinet meetings, 26 Aug. 1932 and 31 Aug. 1932. BAK R 43 I/1457.
[21] Akzeptbank to Reichsfinanzministerium, 1 Aug. 1932. BA R 2/13607.
[22] Akzeptbank Generalversammlung, 8 Mar. 1932. BA R 2/13006. Akzeptbank, Geschäftsbericht 1932–3.

seemed to be uncertain. The Nazi Party programme of 1920 had requested the 'breaking of interest slavery' (Kühnl, 1977: 161–8). Gottfried Feder, the author of that slogan, and other members of the Nazi movement demanded that the temporary state ownership and control which was a result of the 1931 crisis should be turned into complete and permanent nationalization of banking. Feder argued that the savings banks represented the genuine 'national' tradition in banking, as opposed to the 'internationalist' tendencies and the Jewish influence in commercial banking (Barkai, 1977; Hardach, 1984: 228–30).

The Hitler Government called Schacht back to the Reichsbank in March 1933, much to the chagrin of traditional Nazis like Feder who criticized the 'liberal-capitalistic' inclinations of the old and new President.[23] Schacht enjoyed considerable prestige within the Nazi regime as long as his expertise and international reputation were needed. But there was no question of central bank autonomy; the Reichsbank became an instrument of government finance. The privileges of the regional note-issuing banks were abolished in 1935. When Schacht criticized excessive military spending and requested a restoration of sound monetary policy, he was removed from the Reichsbank in 1939 and replaced by the more docile Walther Funk.[24]

In the dispute over the future of the banking system in 1933–4, Schacht became the chief opponent of nationalization; he convinced the Government that the commercial banks were indispensable for economic recovery and national strength. The controversial issue of bank reform was transferred in September 1933 from the public debate to the closed discussions of a Bank Inquiry Commission (Untersuchungsausschuss, 1933, 1934). Feder, who was still influential enough to become a member of the commission, argued for nationalization; the savings banks should become the core of a new national-socialist banking system based on public ownership. But the majority of the Inquiry Commission decided to maintain the existing banking system; and when Feder tried to rally political support for his plan he was excluded from the commission.[25] In October 1934 the Inquiry Commission submitted its final report together with a draft law on banking. The report asserted that the structure of the German banking system was sound. In an explanation which conformed to the xenophobic Nazi ideology, the Inquiry Commission put the blame for the banking crisis of 1931 on the international community; the Versailles dictate and insensate reparation claims had destroyed German capital formation and had led to an excessive influx of short-term credits. Other causes which the report mentioned were the preference of commercial banks for big business, the

[23] Reichsfinanzministerium, 25 Jan. 1934. BA R 2/13683.
[24] Reichsbank-Direktorium memorandum for Hitler, 7 Jan. 1939. BA R 43 II 234. Hitler to Funk, 19 Jan. 1939. BA R 43 II 234.
[25] Report by C. O. Fischer on the Bank Inquiry, 7 Dec. 1933. BA R 13 I/106.

low liquidity of the banking system, and the great number of banks especially in the public sector.[26] Foreign observers remarked with some surprise that the report seemed to be moderate. *The Economist* commented on the final report of the Bank Inquiry Commission that 'Nazi plans and promises have been rejected or ignored by the Committee. There is, however, a marked tendency towards closer state control and towards an increase in the power of the Reichsbank.'[27]

The draft law which the Inquiry Commission had worked out was approved and enacted by the Hitler Government in December 1934. The Banking Law acknowledged the differentiated banking system of commercial banks, special banks, savings banks, and co-operative banks. The transformation of savings banks into local universal banks, which began after the Bank Inquiry of 1908, was now legally confirmed. Public control over the banking system was extended; it was exercised by the Reichsbank, the banking commissioner and a new bank control board (Aufsichtsamt für das Kreditwesen). New liquidity rules and reserve requirements were introduced to enhance the stability of the banking system. Competition in banking was suppressed; new banks or subsidiaries could only be established with government approval, and the government was entitled to fix interest rates and provision.[28] The Banking Law of 1934 combined modern and conservative aspects. State supervision and liquidity rules were a necessary reaction to the banking crisis of 1931; if the State was expected to warrant the stability of the banking system, some kind of public control was inevitable. Several rules which were introduced by the Banking Law of 1934 outlasted the Nazi era and are still in force in the Federal Republic of Germany. But these functional regulations were cast into a reactionary form. The monopolistic tradition in banking, and the Nazi claim to supreme control, combined to create a stationary model of banking.

The Nazi regime confirmed its confidence in the existing differentiated German banking system a few years later, when it returned in 1936–7 the commercial banks which had come under public control during the banking crisis to private ownership.[29] Nazi ideology fell with a vengeance, however, on bankers and bank managers of Jewish descent. Traditional private banking firms whose owners were of Jewish origin were either dissolved, or taken over by non-Jewish owners; prominent bank directors had to retire (Barkai, 1987; Genschel, 1966).

---

[26] Bericht des Untersuchungsausschusses für das Bankwesen mit dem Entwurf eines Reichsgesetzes über das Kreditwesen, 23 Oct. 1934. BA R 43 II/237.

[27] *The Economist*, 8 Dec. 1934.

[28] Reichsgesetz über das Kreditwesen, 5 Dec. 1934. Reichsgesetzblatt 1934 I. 1203–1214.

[29] Commerzbank-privat, in *Die Bank*, 4 Nov. 1936. Der Schlusstrich, in *Die Bank*, 6 Oct. 1937.

The powers and instruments which the Banking Law of 1934 conferred on the government were sufficient to subordinate the banking system to the objectives of the Nazi economy. During the early years the Government sought to stimulate economic recovery with employment programmes. With the Four-Year Plan of 1936, however, preparations for war became dominant. A vast rearmament programme and a systematic autarky policy transformed the German economy. Taxes lagged behind rising expenditure, and deficits became a standing fixture in German fiscal policy. Government expenditure increased from RM 9 billion in 1933–4 to RM 33 billion in 1938–9, and the current deficit increased from RM 2 billion in 1933–4 to RM 15 billion in 1938–9 (Overy, 1982: 46). The share of government expenditure in the net social product increased from 14 per cent in 1925–9 to 26 per cent in 1935–8 (Hoffmann et al., 1965: 108).

The armament boom created an almost self-contained investment cycle which benefited the corporate sector. Government deficit-spending created considerable liquidity, especially in the industries which were connected with armament and autarky. A rigid income policy kept wages at the low depression level, while profits were allowed to rise, with the intention to encourage investment and to limit consumer expenditure. In 1938 total wages were 3 per cent lower and profits 105 per cent higher than in 1928 (Hoffmann et al., 1965: 506–9). Corporate savings were further encouraged by a limit on dividends. Much of the increase in industrial capital from 1933 to 1938 was financed from retained profits, which contributed RM 7 billion, while the issue of new shares brought RM 4 billion. The new shares, which resulted mainly from the investment programmes of the Four-Year Plan, were not placed on the capital market but were taken over by other industrial corporations (Reinhard and von Zabern, 1942). There was a trend, according to Wagemann, towards a 'financial autarky' of industry (Wagemann, 1936–7: 388). Industrial corporations obtained sufficient liquidity from government contracts and subsidies. They invested their excess liquidity in government bonds, treasury bills, or inter-industry loans rather than bank deposits. Insurance companies circumvented the banking system and negotiated credits directly with industrial investors (Bötzkes and Krebs, 1942).

The close co-operation between government and industry forced the banking system into a passive role. After years of credit shortage, banks collected more funds than they could profitably invest in industry and commerce. The Akzeptbank, which had been founded in 1931 to provide additional bank liquidity, became redundant and was closed in 1936.[30] Bond yields fell to 4.5 per cent in 1936–8 (Deutsche Bundesbank, 1976: 278). The banks became essentially intermediaries between the government and private investors. A part of the government debt was placed on the capital

[30] Akzeptbank Generalversammlung, 20 May 1936. BA R 2/13609.

market. But these loans were ill-received by the public; apparently the depreciation of the war loans of 1914–18 had not been forgotten. The 1938 loan was an outright fiasco, in spite of a strong propaganda effort.[31] To avoid a loss of prestige the government preferred the 'noiseless' consolidation of the deficit with the banking system.

The predominance of government finance changed the structure of the banking system. The commercial banks had successfully defended their position in the political debate of 1933–4, but lost in the market. The recovery of 1933 brought no revival in commercial banking; on the contrary, the contraction of business continued until 1935. It was only with the Four-Year Plan of 1936 and the acceleration of the armament boom that the business of the commercial banks recovered (Balderston, 1991: 600–3). But the 'financial autarky' of industry meant that the banks lost much of their corporate business. A considerable part of the bank's funds were invested in Treasury bills; Schacht had invented an ingenious device to give these bills the appearance of regular commercial paper (*Mefo-Wechsel*). The share of the commercial banks in the total assets of the banking system was lower than in any previous period. Contrary to the Nazi middle-class propaganda, concentration in banking proceeded. The share of the big metropolitan banks in the total assets of the banking system increased to 77 per cent in 1938; regional banks and private banking firms were being marginalized (Deutsche Bundesbank, 1976: 67–121).

Savings banks had a competitive edge as they attracted the savings of the middle and working classes. The wage rate was frozen, but the expansion of employment during the armament boom led to an increase in monthly wages. Savings banks invested their funds mainly in government savings bonds. The share of savings banks in the total assets of the banking system reached an all-time high in the 1930s. Co-operative banks and special banks maintained their relative market shares.

Economic concentration and political oppression reduced the number of banks in Germany; there were 22,404 banks in 1938 before the annexation of Austria. The reconstruction of the banking system lagged behind the general economic expansion. Boosted by the armament programme, German net national product at constant prices increased on the eve of the Second World War in 1938 to 155 per cent of the level of 1913. The total assets of the banking system attained RM 79 billion in 1938 before the occupation of Austria; this corresponded to 111 per cent of the 1913 level in current prices, but only 92 per cent in real terms (Deutsche Bundesbank, 1976: 74–5).

In retrospect, the inter-war years left a contradictory heritage. The Weimar Republic had created a differentiated system of commercial banks,

---

[31] Schacht telegram to Hitler, 11 Jan. 1938. BA R 43 II 234.

savings banks, co-operative banks, and special banks. Concentration in commercial banking and regional specialization in other bank groups suppressed competition within the bank groups, but competition between bank groups increased as traditional demarcation lines lost significance. The stability of the banking system depended on the Reichsbank, which acted as monetary authority and lender-of-last-resort. This corporatist system, which had been established after the Bank Inquiry of 1908, collapsed in the banking crisis of 1931. As the corporatist model failed, the responsibility for the stability of the banking system was transferred to the government. The Banking Law of 1934 reorganized the banking system as a monopolistic structure under strict government surveillance. It fitted the Nazi system of armament and autarky, but was not an adequate model for a modern banking system in an expanding world economy. In the Federal Republic of Germany the tightly controlled banking system was thoroughly changed during the years of deregulation and financial expansion from 1958 to 1982, when commercial banks, special banks, savings banks, and co-operative banks entered a new era of mass consumption of financial services and international competition.

References

Ashauer, Günter, (1991), *Von der Ersparungscasse zur Sparkassen-Finanz-gruppe* (Stuttgart).
Ausschuss zur Untersuchung der Erzeugungs- und Absatzbedingungen der deutschen Wirtschaft (1929), Die Reichsbank (Berlin).
Ausschuss zur Untersuchung der Erzeugungs- und Absatzbedingungen der deutschen Wirtschaft (1930), Der Bankkredit (Berlin).
Balderston, Theo (1991), 'German banking between the wars: The crisis of the credit banks', in *Business History Review*, 65.
—— (1993), *The Origins and Course of the German Economic Crisis* (Berlin).
Bankenquete 1908, (1909–10), *Stenographische Berichte*, 2 vols. (Berlin 1909–10).
Barkai, Avraham (1977), *Das Wirtschaftssystem des Nationalsozialismus* (Köln).
—— (1987), *Vom Boykott zur 'Entjudung': Der wirtschaftliche Existenzkampf der Juden im Dritten Reich 1933–1943* (Frankfurt am Main).
Bente, Hermann (1933), 'Das Eindringen des Staates und der Kommunen in das Bankwesen', in *Untersuchung des Bankwesens*, p. 1 (Berlin), i. 36.
Bötzkes, W., and K. Krebs (1942), 'Fragen der Industriefinanzierung', in Deutsches Institut für Bankwissenschaft und Bankwesen, ed., *Probleme und Aufgaben des deutschen Geld- und Kreditwesens* (Berlin).
Borchardt, Knut (1987), ' "Das hat historische Gründe". Zu Determinanten der Struktur des deutschen Kreditwesens unter besonderer Berücksichtigung der Rolle der Sparkassen', in Hansjoachim Henning *et al.* (eds.), *Wirtschafts-und sozialge-schichtliche Forschungen und Probleme* (St Katharinen).

Born, Karl Erich (1967), *Die deutsche Bankenkrise 1931* (Munich).

—— (1983), 'Vom Beginn des Ersten Weltkrieges bis zum Ende der Weimarer Republik (1914–1933)', in *Deutsche Bankengeschichte*, iii (Frankfurt am Main).

Centralverband des deutschen Bank- und Bankiergewerbes (1933), *Materialien zur Vorbereitung der Banken-Enquete 1933* (Berlin).

Deutsche Bundesbank (1976), 'Deutsches Geld- und Bankwesen in Zahlen 1876–1975' (Frankfurt am Main).

Dickhaus, Monika (1991), 'Innovationen im deutschen Bankwesen 1918–1931', in *Scripta Mercaturae*, 25.

Eichengreen, Barry (1992), *Golden Fetters. The Gold Standard and the Great Depression, 1919–1939* (New York).

Eschwege, L. (1908), 'Hochfinanz und Mittelstand', in *Die Bank* (May).

Fischer, O. C. (1933), 'Die fehlerhafte Kreditpolitik', in *Untersuchung des Bankwesens 1933*, p. 1, i. (Berlin).

Flaskamp, Jürgen (1986), *Aufgaben und Wirkungen der Reichsbank in der Zeit der Zeit des Dawes-Planes*, (Köln).

Fritz, M. (1927), *Der Kampf zwischen den Sparkassen und den Banken* (Berlin).

Gehr, M. (1959), 'Das Verhältnis zwischen Banken und Industrie in Deutschland seit der Mitte des 19. Jahrhunderts bis zur Bankenkrise 1931' Diss., Tübingen.

Genschel, Helmut (1966), *Die Verdrängung der Juden aus der Wirtschaft im Dritten Reich* (Göttingen).

Gleitze, Bruno (ed.) (1960), *Wirtschafts- und sozialstatistisches Handbuch* (Cologne).

Goldschmidt, Raimund W. (1927), *Das deutsche Grossbankkapital in seiner neueren Entwicklung* (Berlin).

Gossweiler, Kurt (1971) *Großbanken, Industriemonopole, Staat* (Berlin).

Grüger, F. (1933), 'Die Wirkungen des Krieges und der Kriegsfolgen auf das deutsche Bankwesen mit einem Rückblick auf die Vorkriegszeit' in *Untersuchung des Bankwesens*, p 1, i (Berlin).

Hagemann, W. (1930), 'Das Verhältnis der deutschen Großbanken zur Industrie', Diss., Berlin.

Hardach, Gerd (1973), 'Währungskrise 1931: Das Ende des Goldstandards in Deutschland', in H. Winkel (ed.), *Währungs- und finanzpolitische Probleme der Zwischenkriegszeit* (Berlin).

—— (1976), *Weltmarktorientierung und relative Stagnation. Währungspolitik in Deutschland 1924–1931* (Berlin).

—— (1984), 'Banking and industry in Germany in the interwar period 1919–1939', in *Journal of European Economic History*, 13.

Henning, Friedrich-Wilhelm (1973), 'Die Liquidität der Banken in der Weimarer Republik', in H. Winkel (ed.), *Währungs- und finanzpolitische Fragen der Zwischenkriegszeit* (Berlin).

Hilferding, Rudolf (1969), *Das Finanzkapital. Eine Studie über die jüngste Entwicklung des Kapitalismus* (1910) (Frankfurt am Main).

Hirsch, S. (1910), *Die Bank, ihre Geschäftszweige und Einrichtungen* (Berlin).

Hoffmann, W. G., Grumbach, F., Hesse, H. (1965), *Das Wachstum der deutschen Wirtschaft seit der Mitte des 19. Jahrhunderts* (Berlin).

Holtfrerich, Carl-Ludwig (1980) *Die deutsche Inflation 1914–1923* (Berlin).

Holtfrerich, Carl-Ludwig (1985), 'Auswirkungen der Inflation auf die Struktur des deutschen Kreditgewerbes', in Gerald D. Feldman and Elisabeth Müller-Luckner (eds.) *Die Nachwirkungen der Inflation auf die deutsche Geschichte* (Munich).

James, Harold (1984), 'The causes of the German banking crisis of 1931', *Economic History Review*, 37.

—— (1985), *The Reichsbank and Public Finance in Germany 1924–1933* (Frankfurt am Main).

—— (1986), *The German Slump: Politics and Economics 1924–1936* (Oxford).

Kluge, Arnd Holger (1991), *Geschichte der deutschen Kreditgenossenschaften* (Frankfurt am Main).

Konjunkturstatistisches Handbuch (1936) (Berlin).

von Kruedener, Jürgen (ed.) (1990), *Economic Crisis and Political Collapse of the Weimar Republik 1924–1933* (New York).

Kruse, Alfred (1941), *Der Mittelstandskredit* (Berlin).

Kühnl, Reinhard (ed.) (1977), *Der deutsche Faschismus in Quellen und Dokumenten* (Cologne).

McNeil, William C. (1986), *American Money and the Weimar Republic* (New York).

Meister, Rainer (1991), *Die große Depression: Zwangslagen und Handlungsspielräume der Wirtschafts- und Finanzpolitik in Deutschland 1929–1932* (Regensburg).

Overy, R. J. (1982), *The Nazi Economic Recovery 1932–1938* (London).

Pilster, Rolf (1922), *Die Kartellierung der Geschäfts-Bedingungen im deutschen Bankwesen* (Berlin).

Pohl, Manfred (1978), 'Die Situation der Banken in der Inflationszeit', in O. Büsch and G. D. Feldman, (eds.), *Historische Prozesse der deutschen Inflation 1914 bis 1924* (Berlin).

—— (1982), *Die Konzentration im deutschen Bankwesen (1848–1980)* (Frankfurt am Main).

—— (1986), *Entstehung und Entwicklung des Universalbankensystems* (Frankfurt am Main).

Preiss, Kurt (1933), 'Die öffentlichen Kreditinstitute', in *Untersuchung des Bankwesens 1933*, p. 1, i (Berlin).

Raiffeisen, Friedrich Wilhelm (1923), *Die Darlehenskassen-Vereine* (1866) (Neuwied).

Reinhart, F., and von Zabern, M. (1942), 'Die Eigenkapitalbildung gewerblicher Unternehmungen', in Deutsches Institut für Bankwissenschaft und Bankwesen (ed.), *Probleme und Aufgaben des deutschen Geld- und Kreditwesens* (Berlin).

Riesser, Jacob (1912), *Die deutschen Großbanken und ihre Konzentration im Zusammenhange mit der Entwicklung der Gesamtwirtschaft* (1905), (Jena).

Rummel, H. (1933), 'Die Rentabilitätsfrage der Banken, ihre Unkosten und ihre Kalkulation', in *Untersuchung des Bankwesens* 1933, p. 1, i (Berlin).

von Schulze-Gävernitz, G. (1915), *Die deutsche Kreditbank* (Tübingen).

Shuker, Stephen A. (1988), *American 'Reparations' to Germany, 1919–1933: Implications for the Third-World Debt Crisis* (Princeton).

Statistisches Bundesamt (1972), Bevölkerung und Wirtschaft 1872–1972, Stuttgart and Mainz 1972.

Statistisches Reichsamt (1927), 'Die deutschen Banken 1924–1926' *Einzelschriften zur Statistik des Deutschen Reichs*, 3.

Statistisches Reichsamt (1934), 'Die deutsche Zahlungsbilanz der Jahre 1924–1931', *Wirtschaft und Statistik*, 14.

Statistisches Reichsamt (1936), 'Die, Finanzwirtschaft der öffentlichen Verwaltung im Deutschen Reich', *Statistik des Deutschen Reiches*, 475.

Strauss, Willi (1928), *Die Konzentrationsbewegung im deutschen Bankgewerbe, mit besonderer Berücksichtigung der Nachkriegszeit* (Berlin).

Strucken, Rudolf, (1964), *Deutsche Geld- und Kreditpolitik 1914–1963* (Tübingen).

Tilly, Richard (1986), 'German banking 1850–1914: Development assistance for the strong', *Journal of European Economic History*, 15.

Untersuchungsausschuss für das Bankwesen (1933–4), *Untersuchung des Bankwesens 1933*, pt 1 (Berlin 1933); pt 2 (Berlin 1934).

Wagemann, Ernst (1936–7), 'Bankenliquidität und öffentliche Kurzkredite', *Vierteljahrshefte zur Konjunkturforschung*, 11.

Walb, Ernst (1933), 'Übersetzung und Konkurrenz im deutschen Kreditapparat', in *Untersuchung des Bankwesens 1933*, pt 1, i (Berlin).

Wandel, Eckhard (1983), 'Das deutsche Bankwesen im Dritten Reich', *Deutsche Bankengeschichte*, 3 (Frankfurt).

Warburg, James P. (1964), *The Long Road Home: The Autobiography of a Maverick* (Garden City, NY).

Webb, Steven B. (1989), *Hyperinflation and Stabilization in Weimar Germany* (New York).

Weber, Adolf (1938), *Depositenbanken und Spekulationsbanken* (1902), (Munich).

Wegner (1930), 'Die Bankkritik des Enquete-Ausschusses', *Der Deutsche Ökonomist*, 48.

Whale, P. Barrett (1930) *Joint Stock Banking in Germany* (London).

Witt, Peter-Christian (1982), 'Staatliche Wirtschaftspolitik in Deutschland 1918–1923', in G. D. Feldman et al. (eds.), *Die deutsche Inflation: Eine Zwischenbilanz* (Berlin).

—— (1985), 'Die Auswirkungen der Inflation auf die Finanzpolitik des Deutschen Reiches 1924–1935', in Gerald D. Feldman and Elisabeth Müller-Luckner (eds.), *Die Nachwirkungen der deutschen Inflation auf die deutsche Geschichte 1924–1933* (Munich).

10

Italian Banking, 1919–1936

GIANNI TONIOLO

In the summer of 1992, the Italian Government launched a major programme for the privatization of its stakes in manufacturing, utilities, and banking. The outcome of what is likely to be a long process cannot be anticipated. However, the potentially explosive situation of Italy's public finances provides little alternative to the government's privatization plan. In the 1920s and 1930s, state ownership in industry originated as a response to the banking and industrial crises; its dismantling will mature, if at all, out of another emergency: the fiscal crisis of the 1990s.

The history of Italian banking in the inter-war years and that of the creation of state enterprises are largely overlapping. They cannot be separately understood. Therefore, this chapter will devote considerable attention to the behaviour of the so-called 'mixed banks' and to the operations of lending-of-last-resort which resulted in the large state involvement in industry. The overall evolution of the banking industry, however, cannot be neglected since the changes that took place between the wars led to a far-reaching reorganization, which outlived Fascism and remained in place, with minor adjustments, possibly until the present day and certainly throughout the 1970s.

The chapter takes a chronological approach not only because its main purpose is merely narrative but also because there appear to be fairly consistent cause–effect links between the main events in this story as they unfold over time.

1. The Evolution of Italy's Banking System to the End of the First World War

If there is one peculiarity the Italian economy shares with the Japanese, it is the overwhelming importance banks retained within the financial intermediation system, at least up to the 1960s. While 'financial deepening'—as measured by Goldsmith's financial intermediation ratio (FIR)—showed a secular trend similar to that of countries at comparable levels of economic

I am grateful to Charles Feinstein and Peter Temin for comments, on an earlier draft of this chapter.

development, the share of total financial liabilities held by banks did not fall—contrary to Goldsmith's expectations—as markets became more sophisticated and diversified.[1]

For a long period of time, coinciding with Italy's rapid industrialization up to the 1970s, banks remained the most important providers of financial services of all kinds: short- and long-term lending, security dealing, underwriting, foreign-exchange operations, and—almost as a matter of course—advising on mergers, acquisitions, and industrial restructuring. Together with state bonds, bank deposits were virtually the only financial assets held by the average Italian family.

From the time of the political unification of the country in 1861 to the banking crisis of 1893, nation-wide branch-banking was conducted by six banks of issue, which the new kingdom inherited from the states into which the peninsula had previously been divided, and by two large commercial banks. One of the latter, the Credito Mobiliare, was created by the Peréire brothers in 1863. Other smaller commercial banks operated on a regional or local basis. Savings banks, the first of which was established in 1822, developed fairly rapidly, particularly in the north, as public institutions (usually owned by local bodies such as municipalities and provinces). Most of them specialized in the collection of small deposits, which they employed in short-term lending and state bonds. In the last part of the century, small co-operative banks were established, again mostly in the northern part of the country, according to the model of the German Reiffeisenkasse; their development followed the expansion of the Social Catholic and Socialist influence in the regions of northern and central Italy.

As a result of a severe financial crisis, the banking system was reorganized in 1893–5. Four banks of issue were merged to create the Bank of Italy which was then granted the virtual monopoly of note issue, sharing a small portion of it with two southern banks.[2] At the same time the two largest commercial banks were liquidated, together with a number of smaller ones, thereby bringing to an end the era of 'French-type' banking in Italy. The vacuum was soon filled by German capital and managers with the establishment of the Banca Commerciale and the Credito Italiano in 1894 and 1895.

The years 1893–5 mark a true watershed in Italian banking history. According to a well-known interpretation, the crisis made possible the importation 'of the great economic innovation of German banking in its most developed and mature form' (Gerschenkron, 1962: 88). At the same

---

[1] Between 1881 and 1971 Italy's FIR grew from 0.4 to 1.0. The financial assets issued by the banking system as a share of those issued by all financial intermediaries declined very slowly from 89% in 1913, to 87% in 1929 and 81% in 1951 (Biscaini-Ciocca, 1979).

[2] Roughly three-quarters of note circulation was allocated by law to the Bank of Italy, the Banco di Napoli retained about 20%, and the Banco di Sicilia the remaining share.

time, one could argue that the creation of the Bank of Italy itself proved to be one of the most fortunate in the economic history of modern Italy. During the so-called 'Giolittian era', the Bank's monetary policies were responsible for some of the conditions that made rapid growth possible (Toniolo, 1990a). Moreover, by developing its skills as a lender-of-last-resort, it created a more stable financial environment, therefore enabling German-type banks to make their best contribution to the industrialization process.

The war accelerated the Bank of Italy's acquisition of a fully-fledged central bank profile while, at the same time, creating circumstances that made closer collaboration with the main banks necessary.[3] In 1914, a *parvenu* to the large banking business was born and immediately acquired the status of 'third big bank' and a good slice of the market. The Banca Italiana di Sconto differed in one important respect from the two German-type banks, by then almost entirely in Italian hands: it had been created by a large industrial group (Ansaldo) almost exclusively to serve the latter's own financial needs.

2. The Banking Crisis of 1921–1922

Poorly managed from the beginning (Toniolo, 1989), The Banca Italiana di Sconto soon turned out to be a menace to the stability of the system. However, the abundant wartime liquidity maintained financial stability until the end of hostilities.

As the war drew to an end, it became clear that large credit provisions would be needed to convert industry to peacetime production while state grants and subsidies would dry up. Due to wartime forced savings by the public and less-than-normal industrial lending, the two large German banks looked like an attractive liquidity coffer, which prompted the attempt by industrial groups to gain control of them in March 1918. The Agnelli-Feltrinelli group acquired enough shares in the Credito Italiano to be able to make a deal with the existing shareholders' majority by which the two groups would jointly manage the bank. The Banca Commerciale, on the other hand, repelled the assault and continued to be run, as before, by professional managers coming from the bank's own rank and file.

As is often the case, soon after the armistice, wartime pent-up liquidity created a brief demand boom for consumer goods which the industrial

---

[3] The underwriting and marketing of state bonds required the creation of consortia, led by the Bank of Italy, as well as the opening of special discount windows for Treasury bills and bonds. Foreign-exchange markets provided another area where co-operation was mutually advantageous. Finally, the Bank of Italy acted as a go-between for the Government and banks, a function which the latter came to appreciate (Toniolo, 1989).

sector could not meet at existing prices: excess capacity in war-related industry was coupled with bottlenecks in the consumer-goods sectors. Hence the balance of payments deficit, exchange-rate devaluation, and inflation. The latter eroded the purchasing power of the wartime savings accumulated by the public. By mid-1920 it was clear that the economy was in recession. The crisis was not as deep as that in other countries, notably the UK. Unemployment, however, contrasted with the hopes of those who had returned to civil life after four years of almost inhuman military service. Unfulfilled expectations fuelled social unrest in the so-called 'red biennium' which saw workers taking control of such industrial concerns as Fiat, and the scared middle class taking refuge in the Fascists' arms. Eventually, Mussolini 'marched on Rome' and was appointed Prime Minister by the King in October 1922.

During 1921–2, a major banking crisis developed. The Banca Italiana di Sconto was severely hit by the fall in demand for the products of Ansaldo, both its main shareholder and its principal client (Doria, 1989; Falchero, 1990). This metalmaking and engineering concern had grown disproportionately large during the war. Conversion to peacetime production required large financial capital. Hence a second attempt by the owners of Ansaldo and the Banca Italiana di Sconto to gain the majority stake in the largest bank of the country, the Banca Commerciale Italiana. A group of the latter's majority shareholders, however, organized themselves into a syndicate under the leadership of Toeplitz, the Russian-born head of the bank, and were able to remain in control. The failure to get control of the Commerciale's liquidity made the difficulties of the Banca Italiana di Sconto much more acute. At that point, Ansaldo, one of the largest industrial concerns of the country, could only be saved by turning to the Bank of Italy for lending-of-last-resort.

In the summer of 1920 the head of the central bank was, therefore, faced with a dilemma. Inflation, high public debt, and a depreciating exchange-rate postulated prudent management of the money supply. At the same time, Ansaldo was urgently seeking advances for 'payments of wages and coal' (Guarino and Toniolo, 1993). A refusal to meet Ansaldo's requests would have created large unemployment in the area of Genoa at a time when social unrest was at its peak and workers were taking control of factories. The required advance was granted.

In the following months, the Bank of Italy not only provided increasing amounts of credit to Ansaldo and to the Banca Italiana di Sconto but got indirectly involved in the management of the former. In the autumn of 1921, the Banca Commerciale and the Credito Italiano were reluctantly drawn into a consortium created as a last attempt at saving the third largest bank in the country. This measure failed to produce the desired results, for a number of reasons: they can be summarized by saying that there was not enough co-operation between the Government, the Bank of Italy, and the largest commercial banks. In the last days of 1921, a moratorium was decreed for the Banca Italiana di Sconto in preparation for its liquidation. It was decided, however, that the Ansaldo concern could not be left to its own destiny. Some of its subsidiary companies were sold or liquidated but the bulk of its steelworks, shipbuilding, automobile, and other engineering activities were saved: the necessary capital was provided by the State through the Bank of Italy. It is in this way that the Government came to own its first large manufacturing company.

During 1922, another ailing bank, the Banco di Roma, required large assistance from the Bank of Italy (De Rosa and De Rosa, 1981). This time, the fourth largest bank in the country was allowed to survive. The central bank's action was mainly prompted by the consideration that the whole banking system could be severely hit by a confidence crisis if another of the 'big four' had to be liquidated so shortly after the fall of the Sconto. This concern was made more acute by the fact that Banco di Roma was the centre of the financial web of a large number of small Catholic banks (De Rosa, 1990; Caroleo, 1976; Rossini, 1966). As for the newly elected Fascist Government, its willingness to lend a benevolent ear to the demands of the Banco di Roma depended on its need of the Popular Party's (Catholic) vote in Parliament.[4] As a result of this other lending-of-last-resort operation, some of the industrial enterprises hitherto controlled by the Banco di Roma came under indirect state ownership.

3. Overtrading in the 1920s

Table 10.1 provides an overview of some trends in the banking industry during the inter-war years.[5]

Figures in Table 10.1 show the impact of the war and the banking crisis of 1920–2 on bank assets, particularly on those of commercial banks as a result of: (*a*) self-financing by industrial enterprises due to the organization of the war economy and to inflation, (*b*) the slump of 1920–2, and (*c*) the destruction or reallocation of assets outside the banking system during the crisis, as described above.

From 1922 onward the banking industry saw an unprecedented boom. Bank assets rose dramatically as a percentage of GDP. Between 1919 and

---

[4] The first Fascist Government's banking policy is still the subject of disagreement among Italian historians. Some (e.g. De Stefani, 1960) find that it was much too benevolent to Catholic banks, others (e.g. De Rosa, 1990) argue just the opposite.

[5] Figures in Table 10.1 should be taken as provisional: the forthcoming publication by the Bank of Italy of a major reconstruction of monetary and banking statistics might considerably alter the picture given here.

TABLE 10.1. *Italy's banking system, 1913–1936*

Year	Total bank assets[a]	Bank assets as % of GDP	Commercial bank assets as % of total assets	No. of commercial banks
1913	52,567	45.0	32.5	39
1919	42,946	30.7	62.4	n.a.
1922	37,075	27.3	46.7	209
1925	56,247	38.7	61.4	259
1929	96,354	58.8	47.4	278
1932	114,103	68.9	41.0	200
1936	108,266	57.6	33.9	n.a.

[a] Lire (million) at constant 1938 prices (GDP deflator)

Sources: Bank assets: De Mattia (1967); no. of Banks: Associazione fra le Società italiane per Azioni (1933); GDP and price deflator: Rossi, *et al.* (1992).

1926 the number of banks increased by 30 per cent (from 3,601 to 4,657) and that of bank branches almost doubled. The number of bank employees grew by 45 per cent (Biscaini and Ciocca, 1979).

In particular, between 1922 and 1925, the annual rate of growth of bank deposits was 14.4 per cent, that of bank lending to the private sector 23.7 per cent. A rapid expansion of the real economy—particularly in the investment and export sectors—high savings ratios, and crowding-in induced by fiscal policy all created excellent profit opportunities for financial intermediaries. This short period of hectic, at times even wildcat, banking activity was characterized by (*a*) an increasing weight of *banking* intermediation, (*b*) a rising relative importance of mixed (German-type) banks, and (*c*) a lively stock-exchange market for industrial securities (Ciocca and Toniolo, 1984).

During the same period (1922–5) the total net profits of joint-stock (commercial) banks doubled. The development of the real and the financial sectors of the economy was particularly favourable to German-type banking. Their high-interest deposits provided small savers with an alternative to their traditional investment in state consols when real yields on the latter declined as a result of the shrinking budget deficit. The rapid growth of industrial investment (over 10 per cent a year in real terms) increased the demand for bank finance by traditional borrowers. Moreover, even firms traditionally self-financing, such as those in the textile sector, could not meet their entire investment needs by retained profits alone and had to turn to banks. The practice of universal (German-type) banking spread to most joint-stock banks, even small ones. The stock-market boom not only made industrial stocks readily acceptable as collateral for loans, but induced bank lending to speculators and even direct stock-market speculation by banks themselves. The latter could not be regulated by public authorities since no official supervision of banking activity by monetary authorities was possible under Italian law until 1926.[6]

With their two main competitors either out of the way or severely crippled, the Banca Commerciale and the Credito Italiano were able to expand their lending to industrial enterprises at an unprecedented speed. Their portfolio of industrial stocks rose substantially, as a result both of the policy of welcoming stocks as securities for loans and of the banks' direct forward stock-market operations. Having successfully repelled the hostile take-over attempts of the early 1920s, the two largest banks held a dominant position in the commercial bank market. Expansion went on unchecked until 1925. Admittedly, some of the assets were becoming increasingly illiquid, others—such as those in steelmaking and shipbuilding—were performing poorly, others again required continuous injections of fresh cash. But the situation looked rosy on at least three grounds: the real economy was expanding rapidly, deposits were coming in at a fast pace, and the State was implicitly assumed to guarantee most of the loans made, at times under some government pressure, to steelmakers and shipbuilders soon after the war and as a result of the collapse of the Banca Italiana di Sconto.

4. The Banking Act of 1926

Free (i.e. unregulated) banking prevailed in Italy until the mid-1920s: the Commercial Code of 1882 made it compulsory for companies operating in the credit business to disclose their monthly accounts; other than that, the law did not distinguish between banking and other businesses. However, banks of issue and saving banks were subject to some regulation and state supervision.

The banking crises of 1921–3 provided new arguments for those who favoured bank regulation but it was not until 1926 that political conditions for the introduction of a banking act could be met. By then, Mussolini had acquired full dictatorial powers: this time the powerful banking lobby did not have the strength to stop banking legislation from being passed, once the head of the Government had thrown his political weight in its favour. This happened when Mussolini and Volpi, the new Minister of Finance, gave full priority to monetary policies aimed at a revaluation of the exchange rate of the lira with a view to a return to gold. To that end, it was thought advisable on the one hand to give the Bank of Italy full control of money supply and, on the other, to create an institutional setting in which bank failures, with the attendant lending-of-last-resort and monetary expansion, would be less likely than before.

[6] The Commercial Code of 1885 did not make banks a special category of business activity.

Effective from the beginning of July 1926, the Bank of Italy was granted the monopoly of note issue. In September, a banking act was passed regulating the credit sector and granting the Bank of Italy supervisory powers. The establishment and merger of banks was to be authorized; a minimum capital according to the type of bank and area of operation was required, together with ratios of capital and reserves to deposits; and a limit to risk concentration was set.

While marking an ideological and political departure from 'free banking', the Act of 1926 did not prove effective in achieving its major aim, that of preventing banking crises, as the events of 1931 would shortly prove. This was partly due to three technical reasons: (*a*) effective bank supervision could not be established overnight: it required a long period of learning-by-doing; (*b*) co-operation between the Government, which retained regulatory powers over savings banks, and the bank of issue was not easy due to lack of co-ordination and some misunderstandings; and (*c*) the number and size of economic interests rotating around the two largest 'mixed banks' were such as to make it impossible for the Bank of Italy to exercise any meaningful form of supervision over them. One can doubt, however, that even superbly managed bank supervision would have been able to offset the effects on credit institutions and on industrial companies of the 1930–1 slump, given the magnitude, nature, and international diffusion of the latter.

5. From Mixed Banks to Industrial Holding Companies

The stock-market boom came to an abrupt end in the spring of 1925. De Stefani's[7] restrictions on forward operations aimed at checking speculation were held responsible for the downturn. Such measures were probably technically ill-advised but it is difficult to conceive that the rise in stock prices, which had already gone far beyond all previous records, could have continued much longer. Real growth was slowing down, expected inflation and exchange-rate depreciation were rising, and uncertainty prevailed as to future economic policies after Britain's return to gold. The most far-sighted stock-market investors took their gains and quit. The large banks could not do the same, given the size of their own holdings of industrial stocks. They decided to sail against the tide and buy in order to protect the value of their own portfolios and, in fact, of their entire balance sheet. This strategy met with the approval of the Bank of Italy, which advanced 500 million lire to a three-bank[8] consortium hastily organized to sustain the price of the most important 'blue chips' in the banks' portfolios. The sum, however, was

[7] A. De Stefani was Minister of Finance in the first Mussolini cabinet, between Oct. 1922 and July 1925.

[8] The Banca Commerciale, the Credito Italiano, and the Banco di Roma.

rapidly exhausted with no tangible results except that of increasing the amount of industrial stocks held by the large banks.

The consortium was put to sleep but each bank individually continued to use depositors' money to buy stocks on the market. This policy included substantial purchases of the banks' own shares, an operation strictly forbidden by the law, in order to keep their price at a level that would signal to the markets that the banks were perfectly sound.

This defensive stock-market policy is one of the reasons behind the massive acquisition of industrial stocks by the largest banks that took place from 1925 to 1930. The second reason is to be found in the effects of the lending policy of the early 1920s once a deflationary environment had set in, after the summer of 1926. A number of companies had used bank loans to expand their productive capacity. Some of these investments were still in the making when the slow-down in demand and prices occurred as a result of a normal investment cycle coupled with the tight monetary policy undertaken to create conditions for the resumption of gold convertibility. Securities backing industrial loans consisted either of the firm's own stocks or of some forms of mortgage on their plants, equipment, and buildings. In either case, the major hope for the bank to receive regular interest payments on its loans and, eventually, to be paid back lay in the firm's medium-and long-term profitability. After 1926, this meant the continuation, or expansion, of industrial lending in order either to make the completion of ongoing investment possible or simply to help the survival of those enterprises which had accumulated large outstanding liabilities to the banks. The assumption being, in both cases, that aggregate demand would resume its pre-1926 buoyancy once incomes and prices had settled to the new post-revaluation equilibrium.

As a result of the 'overtrading' of the early 1920s and of the strategy followed after 1926—for which, given the circumstances, there was probably little alternative—the banks ended up not only with risky and illiquid portfolios but also with majority holdings in several large industrial enterprises, particularly in the electric-power, steelmaking, heavy-machinery, shipbuilding, telephone, and maritime transport industries. Moreover, they held the majority of their own shares.

According to Saraceno, the end-result of the lending policy of the 1920s was the transformation of the very nature of the Banca Commerciale and the Credito Italiano from 'mixed' or 'universal' *banks* into 'industrial *holdings*'. Hence their concern with the market share, and eventually with the survival, of their 'industrial empires' rather than with profit-maximizing in the banking business.

The situation of the two 'German banks', however, was not identical. Short-term banking operations had retained an important role in the business of the Credito Italiano, which had not neglected its viable branch network (and that of its subsidiary, the Banca Nazionale di Credito) and somehow managed to keep some liquid assets in its portfolio. A group of shareholders, which included some of the best names in Italian industry, were in control of the bank and entertained good and frequent relations with the Government and the Fascist Party.

The Banca Commerciale, by far the largest of the two, was potentially less stable. Its industrial portfolio was larger, less diversified, and definitely less liquid than that of the Credito Italiano. Moreover, being the only multi-national bank in the system, a substantial part of its liabilities consisted of foreign short-term deposits. Last but not least, the Banca Commerciale was entirely controlled by its own management, with Toeplitz standing at the top of the pyramid as unchallenged ruler.[9] Either directly or indirectly, the bank owned the overwhelming majority of its own shares.

6. Monetary Policy and the Banking Sector, 1926–1930

While, as we have seen, in the second half of the 1920s the major banks in the system managed to retrench and postpone their crisis, tight money and a slow-down in industrial demand had a severe impact on the weakest among the small and medium-sized banks. In some cases it led to liquidation, in others to either overt or disguised state intervention.

A new bank policy stance was announced. Pre-1926 inflation and exchange-rate devaluation were blamed on the war and on pre-Fascist liberal governments. Given the situation of 1922–3, state intervention to bail out ailing banks or large firms was said to be justified as an emergency measure which, however, had no reason to continue. The Government made it clear that it did not consider the new monetary order created by Fascism and crowned by the return to gold to be compatible with easy lending-of-last-resort.

The Bank of Italy took the Government's stance at its face value and was even prepared to allow a number of banks to fail. This approach to banking policy was to some extent new: the Bank of Italy had hitherto been very sensitive to the issue of bank liquidations on the assumption that the weak economic and social fabric of the country could not tolerate confidence crises, a sudden rise in unemployment even in small areas, or the scramble for liquidity among powerful capitalist groups. At the time, however, it apparently believed that none of the above dangers was in sight: after all, large banks were not in peril and Fascism had managed to force 'social peace' not only on worker–capitalist relations but between conflicting

[9] On the life of this important figure in Italy's inter-war economic history see the biography written by his son (Toeplitz, 1963).

groups of capitalists as well. After the years of 'wildcat banking', the Bank of Italy thought it advisable to take advantage of calmer times to induce—in some cases to force—a reduction in the number of banks through mergers, acquisitions, and even liquidations. In this context, the failure of some small, poorly managed banks came to be seen almost with favour: as Marshal Foch used to say during the war, 'il faut fusiller quelqu'un pour encourager les autres'.

It was natural too for this sound central banking policy to be met with heavy opposition; less natural was the fact that it should be resisted by the Government itself. This is, however, what happened more than once. Some small banks were in fact allowed to fail but some were saved thanks to the direct intervention of the Treasury or of Mussolini himself upon the instigation of powerful politicians, who were popularly nicknamed *ras*, after the Abyssinian local lords. Needless to say, even an established dictatorship needs to keep a balance of power among its supporters and, more generally, prefers to create consensus rather than ruling by force.

If petty interests were allowed to interfere with banking policy, at least in one instance it was policy with a capital P that stood in the way. This was the case of the Catholic banks. These were mostly small or medium-sized banks, organized around a Federation which at times acted as provider of last-resort liquidity for its members. The Banco di Roma, the third largest bank in the country, traditionally very close to the Vatican, kept close links with the smaller Catholic banks. When a number of such banks ran into problems, often due to incompetent and at times even fraudulent manage-ment, the Banco di Roma could not come to their help, being itself still ailing. Moreover, as a result of the 1922–3 crisis, the Bank of Italy had been able, not without difficulties, to appoint a new, more competent and independent management to the Banco. Without the latter's help, the Catholic banks could only turn to the Bank of Italy which, however, showed a very lukewarm attitude to their problems. At first, the government backed the position of the Bank of Italy. In 1928, however it came under heavy pressure from the bishops and the Vatican itself to soften its position. At the time negotiations that would shortly lead to the Lateran Pacts (Con-cordat) between the Italian State and the Holy See were in the final stage. For Mussolini much was at stake: a large popular consensus to his regime was expected once the benevolence or at least the neutrality of the Catholic Church could be gained. The Bank of Italy had to bend to such over-whelming political reasons: in 1929 some liquidity was granted to Catholic banks, mergers and painless liquidations were favoured. The reorganization of this group of banks with the help of the State and of the Bank of Italy continued into the 1930s.

In another instance it was the central bank itself which decided to allow an exception in its own policy stance. This was the case of the fairly large

Banca Agricola Italiana which found itself in major difficulties because of the accumulation of excess capacity by its main shareholder and client, Snia Viscosa, Europe's largest producer of 'artificial silk' (rayon). In this case, the relation between a single industrial company and a bank was particularly unsound, and similar to that which had led to the liquidation of the Banca Italiana di Sconto. The outcome was also similar. After a period of time (1928–30) during which the Banca Agricola Italiana was kept alive by continuous injections of liquidity from the Bank of Italy, it became clear that such efforts would lead to nothing; a liquidation was arranged in 1930–1 which saved depositors from losses, through the sale of branches to various banks, the State however having to bear most of the industrial losses itself. As a small consolation, the Bank of Italy acquired one of the finest private art collections in the country which had been given by the main shareholder of the Banca Agricola Italiana as collateral for the central bank's loans. The episode shows that the reaction of the Bank of Italy to the difficulties of a *large* bank had remained the same; while it was ready to see small credit institutions go bankrupt, this was not the case when larger ones were in danger.

7. The Banking Crisis that did not Surface (or the Bailing-Out of the Two Largest Banks), 1931–1933

Given the composition of the balance sheet of the major banks and the magnitude of the slump in industrial demand and production, it is not surprising that Italy experienced a major banking crisis in 1931. Very surprising, on the other hand, is the fact that while such a crisis unfolded the public remained almost unaware of it, so much so that it was subsequently overlooked by most historians. There were no panics, no runs on deposits, no bank holidays. The transmission of the financial crisis to the real sector of the economy is likely to have been much less disruptive than in the case of Central European countries. These peculiar circumstances are due to the swift and almost secret lending-of-last-resort operation undertaken by the Government and the Bank of Italy. This eventually resulted in the end of universal German-type banking, in the creation of IRI (Istituto per la Ricostruzione Industriale), and in the overall reshaping of the country's financial structure culminating with the Banking Act of 1936.[10]

The first signs of distress of one of the two largest banks began to surface in 1930 when the management of the Credito Italiano became aware that the weight of illiquid assets (mostly industrial stocks) made the bank vulnerable to a decline in deposits, not to mention to withdrawals. The

[10] On the banking crisis of the 1930s see Cianci (1977) and Toniolo (1978, 1980).

situation was made known in Rome which gave its (fiscal) blessing to a reorganization of the bank's structure based on the separation of normal banking operations from those of an 'industrial holding company'. In order to restructure the banking side, the Credito Italiano merged with its affiliate the Banca Nazionale di Credito. At the same time, most of the industrial stocks in the portfolio of both banks were passed on to a newly created holding company.[11] The balance sheet of the Credito Italiano was therefore cleared of industrial stocks, substituted by a credit to the holding company.

However, industrial demand continued to decline during 1930. Hopes were that a swift revival in profits would make firms controlled by the new holding company less dependent on credit from the Credito Italiano. By the autumn, it was clear to the management that some sort of outside help in the form of cheap liquidity was needed. The Government was secretly approached[12] and a 'rescue operation' agreed upon. The necessary decrees were not published in *Gazzetta Ufficiale* as required by Italian law. In February 1931, an agreement (*Convenzione*) was signed between the Credito Italiano on the one side and the Treasury and the Bank of Italy on the other, which provided for a 330-million lira loan to the distressed bank. This too was kept secret.

Previous banking crises had been solved by lending-of-last-resort and/or bank failures. The latter option being ruled out on account of the 'too-large-to-fail' doctrine, the authorities were this time determined at least to take the opportunity to reduce the likelihood of crises in the future. Separation of short-term from long-term lending financial institutions seemed to be the right solution. Therefore, the grant of 330 million lire to the Credito Italian was made conditional upon the bank: (*a*) conferring all its industrial stocks on a new holding company (Societa' Finanziaria Italiana or SFI), the directors of which would be appointed by the Bank of Italy; and (*b*) pledging itself to confine future business to short-term banking only.

In May 1931, the problems of the Creditanstalt became known to the public and triggered the most serious banking crisis in the history of Central Europe. At that time, a crisis of larger dimensions in the second largest Italian bank had been secretly and effectively put on track for a positive solution.

The Italian banking crisis itself, however, was only beginning. The Banca Commerciale tried, in Toeplitz's words, to stand alone in weathering the storm (Conti, 1986). Its top management was more isolated from the political power than that of its smaller sister[13] and less willing to jeopardize the

[11] The Banca Nazionale di Credito *Nuova*.

[12] Secrecy was indeed one of the keys to success. Negotiations were conducted by two or three persons only, the Bank's board of directors being kept almost in the dark throughout (Toniolo, 1990*b*).

[13] Toeplitz prided himself on never having met Mussolini.

Commerciale's status in high banking.[14] During the summer, however, the German crisis did not precisely boost expectations about the future of the largest Italian universal bank and large amounts of foreign deposits were withdrawn; the Bank of Italy had to supply the needed foreign exchange. At the same time the situation of most industrial firms under the bank's control continued to deteriorate, and they were forced to apply for fresh loans, often simply in order to pay wages and salaries. By September, it became clear that the bank could not survive long without substantial help from the State. Mattioli, the young rising star within the top management, convinced the aged Toeplitz first to meet secretly with Azzolini, the new Governor of the Bank of Italy, in the Florentine Basilica of Santa Croce and then to walk up the stairs of Palazzo Venezia, Mussolini's office.

A secret agreement was signed in October 1931 between the Banca Commerciale, the Treasury, and the Bank of Italy. Its provisions were similar to those agreed upon in the case of the Credito Italiano. The cash advance to the Banca Commerciale, however, was three times larger: one billion lira.[15] The bank's industrial stocks were sold to a holding company (Sofinfit), which received an advance from the Bank of Italy to pay Banca Commerciale's industrial shares: their value[16] was set equal to the amount of cash needed by the Banca Commerciale to reorganize and start a new life as a commercial bank pledged to undertake short-term operations only.

The two agreements of 1931 proved to be the first step in a long process. They were successful in providing enough immediate relief to avoid an outcome similar to that of Austria and Germany, and certainly spared the Italian economy much of the economic distress that the collapse of mixed (German-type) banks brought about in those countries. But costs were high. The difficulties of the largest companies were exacerbated when they found their close ties with the 'holding banks' severed overnight. Reorganization of financial channels was not immediate, even if the Commerciale and the Credito Italiano were eventually allowed to help. The Bank of Italy was put in the most uncomfortable situation of almost window-dressing its balance sheet: since central bank loans could by law be only short term, the 'rescue' lending to the two big banks had to be backed by three-month maturity bills endorsed by the new industrial holding companies and by the banks, the understanding being that such bills would be renewed indefinitely. In practice, however, almost 50 per cent of the bank's assets were definitely

---

[14] Toeplitz candidly claimed that its large industrial stakes were the Commerciale's only *raison d'être* (Toeplitz, 1963).

[15] At the exchange rate of the time, this first injection of liquidity amounted to $200 million.

[16] It was obviously difficult to evaluate the market price of such a large amount of shares at a time of falling prices and heavy losses of the firms in which the bank held a majority stake. At the same time, it was obvious that without at least a billion lire in fresh cash, the Banca Commerciale simply could not survive. The entire operation was clearly one of lending-of-last-resort with some important conditions attached to it.

illiquid, a most awkward position for a central bank which thereby lost much of the necessary freedom of action in its discount and advance policy.

Other emergency measures had to be taken in 1932, while a permanent solution was being worked out.

8. Lending-of-Last-Resort and the Gold Standard: Speculations on Monetary Policy and Credit Crunch

During 1931–3, the three largest Italian banks[17] were granted last-resort credit for amounts equal to 54 per cent of the Bank of Italy's outstanding note-circulation. How could such a policy be consistent with strict adherence to the rules of the gold standard?[18] In spite of the relevance of the question no comprehensive analysis of monetary and banking policy exists on which to base a definite answer. We can, therefore, resort only to educated guesses.

During 1931, the Bank of Italy held reserves (in gold and convertible currencies) for an amount exceeding 50 per cent of note circulation, as against a legal requirement of 40 per cent. Although the ratio was falling due to the current-account deficit, it was possible moderately to expand nominal money supply during the last part of the year and throughout 1932 without hitting the floor set by the legal currency-reserve ratio. In this way, however, the Bank of Italy could supply only less than half of the liquidity required to 'rescue' the big banks. The source of the remaining part of the last-resort credit they were granted must, therefore, be accounted for. Since the bank's balance sheets are of no help in solving the puzzle, we must resort to speculation.

A likely hypothesis is that the Bank of Italy diverted a large part of the resources available for discounts and advances from the banking sector at large to the two ailing banks. Since bank operations were typically short term, there seems to be no time-inconsistency in this explanation, which, however, entails a rationing of central bank credit to small and medium-sized banks. Do we find evidence of that? The number of commercial banks that went out of business increased in 1931 to 12 per cent of the total, up from 7 per cent in 1929.[19] During 1932–3 mergers and acquisitions reduced the number of commercial banks from 457 (1931) to 266 (1933). These figures are consistent with, but do not prove, credit rationing by the Bank of Italy. If, however, we assume that such was the case, this policy doesn't seem to have been terribly detrimental to the banking sector: the less

[17] The Banco di Roma too ended up in need of some help.

[18] The lira was not devalued with the pound in Sept. 1931. In fact, Italy later became one of the members of the 'gold bloc' created in 1933 on the initiative of France and went officially off gold only in Oct. 1936, although convertibility had been suspended *de facto* at least one year earlier.

[19] Data for 1932 are, unfortunately, not available.

efficient banks were forced out of business, the others were forced to retrench and reorganize. The resilience of small and medium-sized banks was probably derived both from the asset and the liability sides of their balance sheets. On the one hand, they took advantage of the fact that nominal deposits fell less than nominal incomes thereby easing the squeeze on liquidity created by the Bank of Italy. On the other, hand, some evidence exists (Ferri, 1993) that small and medium-sized banks were better able than large ones to shift the composition of their portfolios to more liquid assets.

According to Ferri (1993), investment by small banks was shifted to security-backed assets and state bonds; the spread between interest rates on loans and those on deposits widened; credit was rationed. Small business, the main clients of medium-sized commercial, savings, and co-operative banks suffered from a severe credit crunch, given the sharp segmentation of Italy's credit market.[20] Given asymmetric information an average interest rate was charged to all bank customers, with likely adverse selection results: good clients did not get all the loans their projects deserved, bad ones got more than their fair share with an overall deflationary effect on the real sector of the economy. The latter are evident in a sharp increase in bankruptcies.

Further research is needed on the above-mentioned hypothesis. Should it be confirmed, we would have a more complete picture of Italy's banking crisis on the following lines: while it remains true that swift and secret central bank lending to the major banks avoided panics and open runs on deposits, thereby sparing the country the most severe real effects of the financial crisis, the crisis was partly transferred onto smaller intermediaries. Ultimately, financial instability had real deflationary (and allocative) effects although milder than in the case of, say, Germany, Austria, and Hungary.

9. The End Result: IRI and the Banking Act of 1936

In January 1933, the creation of the IRI (Istituto per la Ricostruzione Industriale) provided a solution to the problems both of long-term industrial finance and of the Bank of Italy. The IRI was a holding company entirely owned by the Government but incorporated under *private* law. It acquired the entire portfolio of industrial shares of the two holding companies created as a result of the 1931 agreements. In practice, as a result of the state intervention to rescue the two largest Italian banks, the State pooled all the industrial shares previously owned by the former German-type banks under its own control. The value of the shares was equal to half

---

[20] A *de facto* segmentation was created by the credit policy of the large banks themselves. By imposing rules on collaterals and fixed fees they deliberately discriminated against small clients.

the total of those of public (limited liability) companies listed on the Stock Exchange.

For all practical purposes, the IRI became the industrial substitute for the 'mixed banks': it took responsibility for choosing and supervising corporate management and for providing long-term finance to enterprises under its control. The latter task could be performed more stably than under 'German-type' banking. To do so, a problem had to be solved: that of the endemic lack of risk capital, given the aversion to investment in industrial shares by the average Italian saver. This was done by granting IRI-issued bonds all the privileges of state bonds[21] and, therefore, making them immediately appealing to small savers, savings banks, insurance companies, and other financial institutions.

Taking immediate advantage of such privileges, the IRI issued a large loan, the proceeds of which were designed to reimburse the Bank of Italy for part of its advances to the holding companies (but ultimately to the banks). Further payments followed. The central bank's balance sheet was again able to show liquid assets as required both by law and by good banking practice.

Bonds were also issued to provide for the medium- and long-term financial needs of the enterprises controlled by the IRI. By using its market power, the State was able to create a viable substitute for the German-type banks in providing long-term credit to Italian industry. As a result of the collapse of the largest banks in the country, the State found itself at the heart of Italy's financial intermediation system. The public-sector area in the credit business was further enlarged due to the fact that small-bank failure had been concentrated in the private sector while savings banks, themselves public institutions, not only managed to survive but emerged from the Depression endowed with a larger share of the country's deposits. A state-owned bank, the Banca Nazionale del Lavoro, rapidly acquired the 'big bank' status by managing substantial government funds. Special institutions for long-term credit were established or reinforced, within the public sector. In 1934, the Banca Commerciale and the Credito Italiano (together with the Banco di Roma) were no longer allowed to own their own shares and came under the control of the IRI.

The reorganization of the banking system which resulted from the Depression was formally sanctioned by the Banking Act of 1936 (and, in fact, by others that followed up to 1947, incorporating changes suggested by experience). The Bank of Italy became a public institution whose shares were owned by savings banks. It enjoyed considerable independence from the Government and was granted larger supervisory powers over the

---

[21] Mainly full state guarantee on principal and interest; but also full exemption from tax payments (e.g. income tax on interest, death duties on principal).

banking system which was more precisely regulated. Banks were required not to hold industrial shares in excess of 10 per cent of their capital, unless authorized to do so. In no case could they make loans to their main shareholders. Some separation between long- and short-term credit institutions was introduced.

In spite of large state involvement in financial intermediation, individual banks were in practice allowed considerable independence. This was particularly the case of the Banca Commerciale and the Credito Italiano: they reorganized themselves as large deposit institutions, their new management came entirely from the banks' rank and file. In both cases, they retained a large degree of independence from the IRI, their new owner. Immediately after the war, the former 'German-type' banks created the Mediobanca, a special institution for long-term industrial finance which they owned and managed without government interference, using part of the managerial expertise and foreign connections inherited from their experience as universal banks.

Post factum, it can be plausibly argued that the structure of the banking system which emerged from the Great Depression—as a result both of the bailing-out of the large banks and of the Banking Act of 1936—proved to be well designed and, therefore, long-lasting. It served the country well during the post-war period of rapid growth (Caranza *et al.*, 1987) and guaranteed financial stability during the following unstable decade. This was not a minor achievement for a set of 'emergency measures'.

References

Associazione fra le Società Italiane per Azioni (1933), *Società italiane per azioni. Notizie statistiche* (Rome).

Biscaini A. M., and Ciocca, P. (1979), 'Le strutture finanziarie: aspetti quantitativi di lungo periodo (1870–1970)', in F. Vicarelli, (ed.), *Capitale industriale e capitale finanziario: il caso italiano* (Bologna: Il Mulino).

Caranza, C., Frasca, F., and Toniolo, G. (1987), 'Cinquant 'anni di legge bancaria in Italia: alcune considerazioni economiche', in Associazione Bancaria Italiana, *Quaderni di Ricerche e Documentazione*, 9 (Rome).

Caroleo, A. (1976), *Le Banche Cattoliche dalla prima guerra mondiale al fascismo* (Milan: Feltrinelli).

Cianci, E. (1977), *Nascita dello stato imprenditore in Italia*, (Milan: Mursia).

Ciocca, P. L. and Toniolo, G. (1984), 'Industry and Finance in Italy 1918–1940', *Journal of European Economic History*, 13/1: 113–36.

Conti, E. (1986), *Dal taccuino di un borghese* (Bologna: Il Mulino).

De Mattia, R. (ed.) (1967), *I bilanci degli istituti di emissione italiani, 1845–1936* (Rome: Banca d'Italia).

De Rosa, G. (1990), *Una banca cattolica fra cooperazione e capitalismo. La Banca Cattolica del Veneto* (Rome and Bari: Laterza).

De Rosa, L., and De Rosa, G. (1981), *Storia del Banco di Roma*, 2 vols. (Rome: Banco di Roma).

De Stefani, A. (1960), *Baraonda bancaria* (Milan: Le edizioni del Borghese).

Doria, M. (1989), *Ansaldo. L'impresa e lo stato* (Milan: Angeli).

Falchero, A. M. (1990), *La Banca Italiana di Sconto 1914–1921* (Milan: Angeli).

Ferri, G. (1993), ' On the Effects of Financial Instability during the Great Depression in Italy', *Rivista di Storia Economica*, 2: 209–43.

Gerschenkron, A. (1962), *Economic Backwardness in Historical Perspective* (Cambridge, Mass.: Belknap Press).

Guarino, G., and Toniolo, G. (1993), *La Banca d'Italia e il sistema bancario, 1919–1936* (Roma: Laterza).

Rossi, N., Sorgato, A., and Toniolo, G. (1992), 'Italian Historical Statistics, 1890–1990', Dept. of Economic Science, University of Venice, Working paper n. 18 (Venice).

Rossini, G. (1966), 'Banche cattoliche sotto il fascismo', *Il Nuovo Osservatore*, 56 and 57: 905–51.

Toeplitz, L. (1963), *Il banchiere*, (Milan: Ed. Milano Nuova).

Toniolo, G. (1978), 'Crisi economica e smobilizzo pubblico delle banche miste (1930–34)', in G. Toniolo (ed.), *Industria e banca nella grande crisi, 1929–1934*, (Milan: Etas Libri).

—— (1980), *L'economia dell'Italia fascista* (Roma: Laterza).

—— (1989), *La Banca d'Italia e l'economia di guerra, 1914–1919*, (Roma: Laterza).

—— (1990*a*), *An Economic History of Liberal Italy, 1850–1918* (London: Routledge).

—— (1990*b*), 'Crisi bancarie e salvataggi: il Credito Italiano dal 1930 al 1934', in *Il Credito Italiano e la fondazione dell'IRI*, (Milan: Scheiwiller): 115–42.

11

Banking in France in the Inter-War Period

MICHEL LESCURE

1. The Inherited Structures

Even though a lot of criticisms were levelled at the French banks, it can be argued that on the eve of the First World War they were on the way to success in their process of economic integration.

With a money supply (M1) growing on average by 3 per cent a year between 1890 and 1913, the French economy ceased to be the sub-monetized economy that it had been during the nineteenth century. The ratio of M1 to national income rose from 0.66 in 1880 and 1900 to 0.77 in 1910 (Saint-Marc, 1983; Lévy-Leboyer and Bourguignon, 1985). In this process of monetization, the banks' policy, coupled with the progress of urbanization and industrialization, operated as a driving force. In 1890 the bank deposits stood at 2.9 milliard (thousand million) francs; in 1913 they had increased over fourfold, to 12.3 milliard. The growth accounts for 69 per cent of the overall increase in the money supply.

The take-off of the banks' deposits dated back to the mid-1890s, when large banks, followed in step by regional banks, decided to extend their branch network. In the expansion of 1890–1913, 1,261 offices were opened by the three largest banks (Crédit Lyonnais, Société Générale, Comptoir d'Escompte). The total of their branches was 1,519 in 1912 compared with 258 in 1890 and 195 in 1880.

Admittedly, this progression should not be overestimated. With a total number of 6,000 offices (one per 1,800 households), France stood far behind countries like Britain. Furthermore, the growth in the number of customers (at Crédit Lyonnais the number of accounts jumped from 95,273 in 1887 to 693,288 in 1914) did not bring about a wide social diffusion of bank money (Lévy-Leboyer, 1976; Bouvier, 1979). By 1914 most of the banks' customers continued to be recruited from the ranks of large or medium-sized enterprises, and from those of the urban upper and middle classes, when in fact 58 per cent of industry consisted of small firms employing fewer than ten wage-earners, and 55.8 per cent of the population were living in rural areas. In the Vaucluse region for instance, a rural but rather speculative agricultural area, bank deposits were found in only 2 per cent of the inheritances (Mesliand, 1967).

This is less to deny that commercial banks played a role in the process of monetization than to help to specify this role. In France, the monetization of the population came not so much from the use of bank facilities as from the spread of notes issued by the Banque de France. It must be recalled that this semi-public institution had been founded in 1800 to provide facilities to tradesmen and manufacturers, especially by discounting short-term bills guaranteed by three signatures. Advances to the State and the purchase of gold were further transactions that resulted in the issuing of banknotes. The extent to which the Banque de France was allowed to make a fiduciary issue was decided by the State without strict reference to the bullion reserve. Its amount rose from 1,800 million francs in 1870 to 6,800 million in 1914. As a result, the ratio fiduciary currency/national income increased twofold, from 8.2 per cent in 1870 to 16.4 in 1910. In the same period when banknotes tended to replace coin in the money supply, bank deposits tended to replace bills of exchange, an important monetary substitute amounting to 13.2 milliard francs in 1913 (equivalent to half the official money supply), and still held in a proportion of 40 per cent outside the banking system (Lévy-Leboyer and Bourguignon, 1985). The result of this process is shown in Table 11.1.

Even though the composition of the money supply remained to some extent that of a backward and rural country (with coins representing 34.8 per cent of the supply), the share of bank deposits, which had been less than 22 per cent in 1890, reached 43.2 in 1910. Similar progress was recorded on the other side of the banks' balance sheet. Loans and advances granted by the banks to metropolitan enterprises rose from 15 per cent of national income in 1890 to 30.1 per cent in 1913 (Teneul, 1960).

The growing importance of the banks in the economy implied important changes in the French banking system. The first of these was the growth of the corporate sector and the relative decline of the private banks. The number of joint-stock banks in operation rose from 42 in 1891 to 132 by

TABLE 11.1. *Composition of the French money supply* (M1), 1880–1939 (%)

	Coin	Banknotes	Bank deposits
1880	65.7	17.2	17.2
1890	56.3	22.2	21.5
1900	42.1	26.5	31.4
1910	34.8	22.0	43.2
1920	1.5	56.7	41.8
1925	2.2	48.4	49.4
1930	0.6	43.6	55.8
1935	1.9	54.4	43.7
1939	3.0	52.6	44.4

Sources: Saint-Marc (1983); INSEE (1966).

1913 (with total assets amounting successively to 14.6 and 38.4 per cent of national income). The second change was a new division of banking activity. In the period running from 1880 to 1914, the large banks that had been launched during the Second Empire tended to give up their role as universal banks, and to become specialized financial institutions. As a result of both the disappointing performances of the French economy in the 1880s, and the extension of their branch network from the 1890s (with what was now a metropolitan management guiding banking practice through rule books), most of the large banks followed the path pioneered by the Crédit Lyonnais and became deposit banks. They curtailed their illiquid transactions and made giving of discounts, a very short-term self-liquidating credit, their most important operation. On the eve of the war the commercial portfolio of the three largest deposit banks represented 46.7 per cent of their total assets compared with 37.6 in 1890 (Plessis, 1991). More significant industrial commitments were left to the 'Old Banks' and to new financial corporations (investment banks) specially designed to provide long-term loans and to control industrial operations through shareholdings and 'participations' in other firms.

At the national level, there were few exceptions to the growing tendency for banks to specialize. They came from the youngest deposit banks, the Crédit Commercial de France and the Banque Nationale de Crédit (Daviet and Germain, 1994; Bonin, 1978) for which some degree of industrial commitment was the only way to face competition from the old established banks. It must be added that, given the role played by Swiss and German banks in their creation, these banks were likely to be influenced by the universal bank pattern.

At the regional level things were quite different. By contrast with the decline of the local unit banks in the opening decade of the century (Plessis, 1985), regional banks experienced a rapid growth on the eve of the war. Even though there was a great variety of country banks, most of them were shaped on the model of the universal banks. In fact, the basic nature of the regional banks was not the addition of industrial initiative to discounting. In 1913, their investment portfolio never exceeded 10 per cent of their assets and the ratio of advances to the commercial portfolio was 1.4 in the north of the country, 1.7 in the south, 10 in some eastern banks (compared with 0.76 at the four big deposit banks). The special characteristic of the country banks was the rolling-over of formerly short-term industrial credits so that overdrafts, most of them without any security, and loans were in fact often long-term credits (Lescure, 1985a; Lévy-Leboyer and Lescure, 1991). When designed to serve new investments, credits were usually coupled with further securities issues.

The strategy of the regional banks, made possible by the close relationship which existed between bankers and small and medium-sized local enterprises, was the consequence of the growing worry of the large banks over their liquidity and that of the policy of the Banque de France. Just like the regional banks, the Banque de France faced serious competition for discounting from large deposit banks. The growing amount of their deposits made these banks more reluctant than before to discount their bills at the 'banker's bank'. From 1880 to 1913 the commercial portfolio of the four largest banks rose from 451 to 3,598 million, while that of the Banque de France grew only from 751 to 1,645 million. In order to overcome this decline in traditional business, the Banque de France decided to discount bills directly issued by merchants and manufacturers (by admitting as the third signature a simple endorsement) and concomitantly it turned to the country banks. By discounting their bills (some of them issued for long-term purposes) the Banque de France enabled regional banks to extend their long-term current-account credits without their liquidity being threatened. Thus, through a new division of banking activity (now a technical division rather than a geographical one), the French banking system kept a dualistic structure.

As a general rule it seems that a high degree of competition existed between each kind of bank. However, many types of relationship could be observed from one category of bank to another, most of them related to the central position occupied in banking business by the flotation of French and foreign securities. Because of their lack of connection with the savers, investment banks had relations both with deposit banks and with country banks. Paribas, for instance, had connections with the Société Générale since 1905 and during the war it made contact with the Crédit Lyonnais. In the inter-war period, investment banks were to greatly extend their strategy of collaboration with regional banks; it enabled them not to be too dependent on deposit banks, while allowing country banks to share in the large operations of securities issues. The BUP, for instance, a bank which had close relations with the CNEP and the CCF was connected with many regional banks.

Although it remained modest, the role played by the banks on the eve of the war reached a peak that in some respects was not to be much exceeded until the 1950s. The subsequent inter-war period can be described as a period of decay for French banks.

2. The Inflationary Years, 1918–1926

This decay was particularly obvious during the inflationary boom 1914–1926. In 1926 the ratio of total assets to national income was only 54 per cent of its pre-war level for the six largest deposit and universal banks, 50 per cent for the two largest investment banks. Never during the twentieth century was a lower figure reached (Bouvier, 1977).

The efforts made by the financial intermediaries to keep pace with inflation appeared to be relatively unsuccessful. From 1913 to 1926 the nominal value of the banks' deposits increased over fourfold, but adjusted for the growth in prices the contraction was 30 per cent (20 per cent according to another estimate); see Fig. 11.1. The upward movement in banks' deposits from 1919 onwards was not sufficient to compensate for the wartime slump, and during the years of hyperinflation 1923, 1924 and 1926 the trend in real terms turned down.

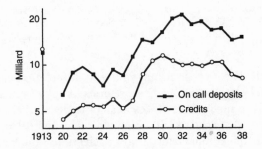

FIG. 11.1   Deposits and banking credits to metropolitan enterprises, France, 1920–1938 (in constant 1913 francs)
Sources: Saint-marc (1983); Teneul (1960).

Even though there was some degree of co-ordination in the policy of the banks (with minimum interest rates to be charged now to depositors set by the Union of the Bankers), not all kinds of bank were affected by inflation to the same extent (Table 11.2). Universal banks, whether they were national or regional, experienced the fastest growth. In real terms their deposits grew on average by 9.6 per cent a year for BNC and CCF between 1913 and 1927, 4.4 per cent for five regional banks. For the large specialized banks, the rate of growth was negative: – 0.6 per cent for investment banks, – 1.4 per cent for deposit banks.

It was during the first years of inflation that the universal banks appeared to be the most successful in their attempt to overcome the erosion of their deposits. By contrast with the strategy followed by most of the large deposit and investment banks such as the CNEP or Paribas (Bussière, 1992a, 1992b; Bonin, 1992), many universal banks developed an aggressive strategy of

TABLE 11.2. *Coefficient of growth in 'on call' bank deposits*, 1913–1929 (current prices)

	1913–23	1923–7	1913–27	1927–9
Four largest deposit banks (CL, SG, CNEP, CIC)	2.7	1.8	4.8	1.24
Two largest investment banks (PB, BUP)	4.4	1.2	5.4	1.07
Two largest metropolitan universal banks (CCF, BNC)	14.8	1.4	21.2	1.06
Total metropolitan banks	3.4	1.6	5.6	1.20
Five large regional universal banks (CN, SNCIC, SLD, BP, SMC)	6.9	1.6	10.7	1.05
Prices (average retail and wholesale)	3.8	1.6	5.8	1.02

Notes: CL = Crédit Lyonnais; SG = Société Générale; CNEP = Comptoir National d'Escompte de Paris; CIC = Crédit Industriel et Commercial; PB = Banque de Paris et des Pays-Bas; BUP = Banque de l'Union Parisienne; CCF = Crédit Commercial de France, BNC = Banque Nationale de Crédit; CN = Crédit du Nord; SNCIC = Société Nancéienne de Crédit; SLD = Société Lyonnaise des Dépôts; BP = Banque Privée; SMC = Société Marseillaise de Crédit.

Source: *Revue d'économie politique*.

external growth. Through amalgamations and the creation of new offices the branch network of the eight largest regional banks in the north of the country rose from ninety-nine offices in 1914 to 364 in 1923 (Laloux, 1924; Pouchain, 1986; Bergeron, 1989). Between 1913 and 1930, the BNC absorbed 39 local and regional banks (most of them, like the Banque Française pour le Commerce et l'Industrie, before 1925) and the number of its offices increased over eightfold (from 89 to 748). At the Crédit Lyonnais, the largest French bank in 1913, the 1920s also experienced a considerable extension of the branch network, but the total number of offices increased only two and a half times (from 374 in 1913 to 1,000 in 1928). A borderline case is provided by the CIC, a bank without a branch network in the country, which decided to grow only by taking 'participations' in regional banks; between 1913 and 1930 its investment portfolio was multiplied by 10 but the amount of its deposits by only 5.5.

These developments, coupled with the growing number of joint-stock banks (the number of banks publishing balance sheets rose from 132 to 265), explain why the share of the four big deposit banks in total bank deposits dropped from 59.2 per cent in 1913 to 37.5 per cent in 1926. During the same period the share of the fifteen largest universal banks (most of them regional banks) rose from 12.7 to 19.5 per cent (with a peak of 23.2 per cent in 1921).

In spite of the early reaction of the universal banks, and the ensuing attempt of the deposit banks to increase their resources, it was not until 1928 that the overall amount of bank deposits regained its pre-war level in real terms (Fig. 11.1). This decline in bank deposits had important monetary and economic consequences. As shown by Table 11.1, the rise in the share of bank deposits in the total money supply came to a sudden stop in 1914. The reconversion of industrial capacity during 1914–16, with its negative effects on prices, and the growing scale of the Banque de France's advances to the State (rising from 200 million francs in 1913 to 30,000 million in 1920), brought about an increase in the fiduciary issue of 567 per cent between 1913 and 1920. Banknotes, which had accounted for 21 per cent of the money supply in 1913, accounted for 56.7 per cent in 1920. Until 1924 bank deposits as a percentage of M1 were below their pre-war level.

The contraction in lending was both a consequence and a factor of the decline in bank deposits. Total lending fell from 33.4 per cent of national income in 1913 to 18.6 per cent in 1926. With regard to the advances in metropolitan enterprises, the fall was still more important, from 30.1 per cent to 11.6 per cent. In 'real terms' the contraction was 58 per cent. Against a fall in deposits of only 20 or 30 per cent, this implied that other factors had led French banks away from significant economic commitment.

TABLE 11.3. *Distribution of assets and resources of the French banks, 1913–1938* (average of the annual rates, percentage)

	1913	1920–6	1927–31	1932–5	1936–8
Six largest deposit and universal banks					
ASSETS					
Cash, banks, correspondents	7.7	12.9	18.8	19.7	19.3
Investment portfolio	2.0	1.0	0.6		
Advances	88.5	84.5	79.8	78.8	77.3
(Ratio: portfolio of private and public bills/loans and overdrafts)	59.6/40.4	73.2/26.8	65.5/34.5	67.4/32.6	69.9/30.1
RESOURCES					
Deposits	75.4	89.3	90.0	89.5	88.0
Capital funds	14.9	7.1	6.0	8.1	8.2
Two largest investment banks					
ASSETS					
Cash, banks, correspondents	5.2	18.2	24.1	19.1	26.5
Investment portfolio	24.1	13.1	13.5	22.0	17.0
Advances	62.6	62.5	56.0	49.1	45.2
(Ratio: portfolio of private and public bills/loans and overdrafts)	34.0/66.0	50.5/49.5	40.0/60.0	53.2/46.8	65.1/34.9
RESOURCES					
Deposits	58.3	70.3	78.1	71.7	74.8
Capital funds	31.7	18.7	13.7	22.4	18.1

Sources: Revue d'economie politique; Bouvier (1977); Pose (1942); Teneul (1960).

The first of these factors was the difficulty encountered by the banks in halting the downward slide in their capital funds. For the six big banks, the fall was 76 per cent in real terms between 1913 and 1926. In 1913, paid-up capital and total reserves of these banks represented 14.9 per cent of their total resources. By 1928 the ratio had plummeted to 4.1 per cent. Given the disappointing circumstances on the capital market, banks were not likely to raise the ratio to a level more in keeping with the scale of their business.

The second type of factor involved the tendency for banks to reduce the share of their resources devoted to loans and credits to enterprises (Table 11.3). As a result of inflation and state deficits, several unproductive items became a larger proportion of the banks' assets. For the six big banks, cash reserves rose from 6.5 per cent of assets in 1913 to 11.7 per cent in 1927. The growth of the item 'banks and correspondents' was still more important. At Paribas and BUP, for instance, it rose from 3.8 to 21.8 per cent of assets between 1914 and 1928. The growth in the short-term interbank transactions reflected the tendency for the banks to protect themselves against the fluctuations in the value of the franc. But the net result of the increase in these two items was to swell the liquidity of the banks. At the four big deposit banks the share of deposits represented by liquid assets rose from 12 per cent in December 1913 to 23 per cent in December 1927 (with a peak at 40 per cent in June 1927); at the other banks, it rose from 12 to 20 per cent.

The fall in the investment portfolio of the banks, and the shift in the distribution of their advances, confirm the view that the search for liquidity was gaining ground during these years. As early as 1913, shareholdings and 'participations' represented less than 2 per cent of the assets of the four big deposit banks; from 1924 onwards the ratio fell below 1 per cent. On the side of business banks, the investment portfolio declined from 24.1 per cent in 1913 to 10 per cent in 1927. As a percentage of total assets the retreat was more pronounced at Paribas than at BUP, so that it was now the latter which was the most committed to this kind of immobilization. However, in spite of the high profitability of this item, its share in the BUP assets (15.7 per cent between 1919 and 1931) remained below its 1904–13 level of 20.5 per cent (Rebotier, 1935; Bussière, 1979, 1992b).

The shift in the composition of advances reflected the same tendency. By contrast with the pre-war period the commercial portfolio of the banks grew faster in nominal value than loans and overdrafts. At constant prices, the latter dropped by 58 per cent from 1913 to 1926, compared with a fall of 22 per cent for the former. In addition to factors already discussed, this development produced a loosening of the links between the banks and the economy. Small and medium-sized enterprises were probably the most affected by this evolution, because current account loans were the most suitable kind of credit for them.

As shown through the ratio of loans and current accounts to the commercial portfolio, the extent to which banks were involved in the evolution differed from one group to another (Table 11.4). For investment banks the contraction was modest; nevertheless the growth of the commercial portfolio implied some decrease in the specialization of these banks. Even though the degree of commitment of the universal banks remained slightly above that of the deposit banks, their ratio was divided by 2.5 between 1913 and 1926. In part, this was the consequence of the rapid extension of the branch network of these banks.

TABLE 11.4. *Ratio of secured loans and overdrawn current accounts to the commercial portfolio,* 1913–1930

	Four largest deposit banks	Two largest investment banks	Universal banks
1913	0.76	1.94	1.3[a]
1926	0.34	1.36	0.53[a]
1930	0.57	1.37	0.82[b]

[a] 15 metropolitan and regional banks.
[b] 2 metropolitan banks.

Sources: *Revue d'economie politique*; Pose (1942); Teneul (1960).

For the banks as a whole the shift in the composition of the advances reflected more fundamental changes that led to a further reduction in the efficiency of French banks. Not only did the banks tend to give greater importance to the less productive of their credits (their commercial portfolio accounted for 60.8 and 36.7 per cent of the assets of the deposit and investment banks against 47 and 22.5 per cent in 1913) (Bouvier, 1984), but inside the commercial portfolio it was now Treasury bills rather than bills of exchange that occupied the dominant place (see below, Table 11.10). In 1921–3 Treasury bills represented 87 per cent of the commercial portfolio of the deposit banks. As bankers explained: 'high-quality bills of exchange were lacking' in the early 1920s (quoted in Pose, 1942). Furthermore, during the periods of monetary crises (as in 1924) the banks were required by the Banque de France to cut down their discount credits (Daviet and Germain, 1994). In these disturbed circumstances, the purchase of Treasury bills could be considered as a quite secure and liquid investment; they could be rediscounted by the Banque de France without any restriction, and in 1921 the return on state funds and bills accounted for 42.9 per cent of the gross profits of the nine largest banks (Debeir, 1980).

In the same period, when Treasury bills made a large share of the commercial banks' resources unproductive from the point of view of the economy, direct advances to the State made a growing part of the business of the Banque de France unproductive (Table 11.5). As a ratio of Banque

M. Lescure

de France assets, credits to enterprises through discounts and advances dropped from one-third to 10.8 between 1913 and 1926. In real terms the contraction was 52 per cent against 38 per cent for the commercial banks. By contrast with its growing role in the money supply, the Banque de France was losing ground as supplier of credits (Table 11.6).

TABLE 11.5. *Structure of Banque de France assets, 1913–1938 (as per cent of total assets, average of the annual rates)*

	Gold and currency reserves	Credits to enterprises	Advances to the State
1913	59.4	32.5	5.9
1918–26	13.1	11.6	67.4
1927–31	69.3	9.0	13.0
1932–5	77.0	8.1	3.2
1936–8	57.6	10.9	22.1

Source: Banque de France.

TABLE 11.6. *Share of the nine largest commercial banks and the Banque de France in total lending, 1913–1938 (average of the annual rates, percentage)*

	Nine commercial banks	Banque de France
1913	76.7	23.3
1920–6	78.4	21.6
1927–31	82.5	17.5
1932–5	80.8	19.2
1936–8	72.8	27.2

Source: Teneul (1960).

The loosening of the links between banks and the economy was a rather unexpected issue. The instability of the franc, coupled with the legal restrictions placed on the export of capital between 1918 and 1928, made it more difficult for the banks to operate on foreign markets. In 1930 the accumulation of foreign investment can be estimated at 16 milliard in 1913 francs, compared to 45 milliard in 1913. During the years 1919–28 capital outflows from France did not exceed 2 milliard (3 milliard if we include French colonies). Except for the peak years 1928–30, the inter-war period is characterized by a tendency for long-term foreign investment to be replaced by speculative outflows of short-term capital. Domestic and colonial markets were the main beneficiaries of the redeployment of the banks' activity. At BUP and Paribas, two banks which held important foreign interests, particularly in Eastern and Danubian Europe, the share of domestic securities in the investment portfolio rose from 26.6 to 36.3 per cent for the former (between 1914 and 1931), and from 23.3 to 41 per cent for the latter (between 1914 and 1928). The fast growth that the French economy experienced during the 1920s was a second development that ought to have strengthened the links between banks and enterprises (Table 11.7).

TABLE 11.7. *Growth rate of output and investment rate in France, 1896–1938*

	Growth rate of GDP (% increase per annum at constant prices)		Investment rate (total investments as % of GDP)
1896–1913	1.9	1913	16.8
1920–5	6.1	1925	15.2
1925–30	2.2	1930	20.8
1930–5	– 1.6	1935	14.7
1935–38	2.5	1938	13.4

Source: Carré *et al.*, (1977).

In order to meet their increasing needs for cash and to finance new capital formation, French enterprises were not likely to turn to the capital market. Inflation prevented new funds from being accumulated; and public issues took 69.6 per cent of the limited funds available (see Table 11.10 below). The consequence was that private security issues dropped by 71.5 per cent in 'real terms' between 1913 and 1926; as a ratio of GDP the fall was from 5.5 per cent in 1913 to 4.5 per cent in 1924. Admittedly, the influence of these adverse circumstances should not be overestimated. Only some top-ranking firms resorted to the stock market. In 1913 self-financing through retained profits accounted for 65 per cent of the financing of French firms. However the rate of self-financing was decreasing on the eve of the war. In the following period, a sharp rise in the rate of profit enabled firms to maintain a high rate of self-financing up to 1927. But one condition for this achievement was a record rate of undistributed profit: from 1921 to 1926 the rate was 51.1 per cent (60.6 per cent in 1922–3) compared with 36 per cent in the years 1927–30 and 30.6 per cent in the 1930s (Malissen, 1953; Caron, 1976; Biriotti *et al.*, 1976).

Given the imbalance between the need for and the availability of funds, enterprises were more likely than before to turn to banks. In the car industry, for instance, shortages of liquid funds during the crisis of 1921, and the growing requirement of cash in hand and long-term capital in the years 1922–6, made car manufacturers less reluctant than before to ask for bank facilities. The setting up of their own consumer-credit agencies (DIAC for Renault in 1924, SOVAC for Citroën in 1926, DIN for Peugeot in 1928) made this collaboration still more necessary. Actually, the role of the banks increased in the car industry and many bankers joined the boards of automobile companies. However one can doubt whether this role was sufficient. In the early post-war years, it seems that it was 'Old Banks' (such as Mirabaud at Renault) and young investment banks (such as the BUP at Citroën) that played the leading part. By contrast, the role played by the large deposit banks looked modest. Berliet and Renault benefited by important facilities from the Crédit Lyonnais but, probably because of their overcommitment to public funds, it was not until the end of the decade that the big deposit banks enlarged their position as bankers to the car industry. Citroën, for instance, a fast-growing firm during these years, had no relation with this group of banks, so that its course was interrupted by recurrent financial crises (Fridenson, 1972; Bonin, 1985; Schweitzer, 1992).

The investment banks provide a good illustration of the opposite pattern (a greater willingness but also a greater inability to finance domestic enterprises) that characterized French banks as a whole. During the war and the early 1920s, Paribas, for instance, developed ambitious industrial strategies, most of them related to state plans. As an attempt to overcome German industrial hegemony, the bank promoted several corporations located in strategic sectors like chemicals, electrical industries, and steel metallurgy. But the financial capacity of the bank was not equal to the scope of these operations, so that Paribas disengaged from 1925 onwards. At the same time, BUP, its main competitor, was still more committed to industrial investments. At the end of the decade, non-financial securities represented 68 per cent of its investment portfolio, against 54.4 per cent at Paribas; similarly, manufacturers accounted for 22 per cent of its board of directors against 9.4 at Paribas. However the industrial strategy of the bank was careful and, as shown through the example of Citroën, the assistance it could provide to firms remained modest. The prosperity of the bank tended now to depend on the profits drawn from the transactions in share packages on the Stock Exchange rather than those coming from interest and dividends (Bussière, 1979, 1992a).

The deficiencies in the banking system explain why the classical relationship between industry and banks, in which the latter are described as controlling the former, tended to be reversed. Several banks and financial branches were launched by large industrial corporations during the 1920s (Union des Mines by Colliars in 1923, Electro-Crédit by the Compagnie Générale d'Electricité in 1928). Most of them were designed to provide financial facilities to their parent firm and to other subsidiaries of the group. In the electrical-machinery industry, for instance, a sector characterized by very heavy investment requirements, large corporations set up financial branches (Société Financière Electrique for Thomson group, Union Financière et Electrique for CGE) to pool the surplus resources of member firms and to raise extra capital on domestic and foreign markets. The result was that in the inter-war period the electrical industry tended to be independent of the banks; in 1937–9, bankers accounted for 8.9 per cent of the board of directors of the large corporations of this sector, against 15.6 per cent in 1911–13 (Lévy-Leboyer, 1980; Lanthier, 1987).

3. The Recovery Years, 1927–1930/1

It was not until the late 1920s that the banking system was to experience a marked recovery. Although it was rising from 1927 onwards, the ratio of total banking assets to national income did not regain its pre-war level. But at constant prices, banking assets increased by 15 per cent a year between 1926 and 1930. The growth reflected the new financial and monetary conditions brought about by the stabilization of the franc by Poincaré in 1926–8. The end of inflation encouraged the formation of new savings, while the influx of foreign capital swelled the general liquidity of the economy.

The boom that the stock market experienced in the years 1928–30 enabled the banks to check the erosion of their capital funds. In 1929, a record year for the reorganization of banks' capital, the issue of fresh shares by the banks amounted to more than one milliard, and their total reserves more than doubled. As a ratio of total resources, the capital funds of the six big banks stood at 7.4 per cent in 1930 against 4.1 per cent in 1928. In relation to liabilities they rose from 4.5 per cent to 8.4 per cent (compared with 19.8 per cent in 1913). However, this growth in capital funds should not lead one to underestimate the stimulus that banks were to receive from the increase in their deposits. To a large extent this growth was the consequence of the flow of foreign capital and the re-entry of domestic capital exported between 1921 and August 1926. During the period running from December 1926 to June 1928, when the franc was stabilized *de facto* but its return to gold convertibility was still under discussion, the Banque de France bought gold and foreign currency on a massive scale in order to prevent an excessive revaluation of the franc. Gold and foreign currency accounted for 77.3 per cent of the assets of the Banque, compared with 9.6 per cent in 1926. The net result of the creation of money by the Banque de France was that in 1928 the volume of bank deposits exceeded its pre-war level. As a proportion of M1 they reached the highest ratio of the inter-war period (58.3 per cent). Furthermore, fixed-term deposits now accounted for 5.6 per cent of total deposits, compared with 3 per cent in 1925.

Banks did not all share to the same extent in the general growth. By contrast with their rapid development during the previous period, the deposits of regional banks were now growing more slowly than those of metropolitan banks (see Table 11.2 above). Even though a great diversity characterized the growth of the latter, with the BNC and the Société Générale lagging from 1926 to 1929 while CCF, the Crédit Lyonnais, and the CNEP took the lead, it was the relatively fast growth of this group (more particularly that of the large deposit banks), coupled with the stable number of banks publishing their balance sheet, that initiated the process of banking concentration (Table 11.8).

The counterpart of the increase in banks' resources was the growth in lending. This growth was all the more important as the banks' unproductive assets declined. With the return to balance in the national budget, and the solution to the problem of the national debt, the share of the 'commercial portfolio' devoted to the holding of Treasury bills fell from 60 to 33 per cent. As a ratio of national income, banks' advances to metropolitan enterprises rose from 11.6 per cent in 1926 to 19.2 per cent in 1930. It was well below the proportion reached in 1913 (30.1 per cent), but at constant prices the volume of advances increased by 21 per cent a year.

TABLE 11.8. *Deposits in the four big deposit banks as a percentage of total deposits in banks publishing their balance sheet, 1913–1937*

	1913	1921	1926	1929	1931	1935	1937
	59.2	41.5	37.5	37.7	51.2	50.2	45.1
N^a	132	182	265	276	226	187	187

[a] Number of banks publishing their balance sheet.

Source: Laufenberger (1940).

The growing commitment of the banks to enterprises was not only quantitative in nature. As shown through the introduction of acceptance credits, banks strove to diversify the facilities they offered to firms. Moreover, by contrast with the previous period, secured loans and overdrawn current accounts, two low-rated advances in terms of liquidity, enlarged their position in total lending. The ratio of loans and overdrawn current accounts to commercial portfolio, which had dropped from 0.79 to 0.43 between 1913 and 1926 stood at 0.7 in 1930. Because of their close relationship with some large enterprises (the Vincent group for instance with the BNC), investment and universal banks remained the most involved with this type of credit (see Table 11.4 above). But conspicuous progress was also recorded on the side of the big deposit banks. Not only had the ratio already quoted tended to increase, but within the item 'loans and current accounts' it was the latter that enlarged their share. At the Crédit Lyonnais, for instance, a bank often described as a very cautious lender, the ratio rose from 0.44 in 1920 to 0.6 in 1930 (the highest ratio with the Société Générale among the deposit banks). At this ultimate date, overdrafts accounted for 92 per cent in the numerator against 67.6 per cent in 1913; at the Société Générale, the figures were 84 and 56 per cent.

The shift in the composition of advances was linked to several factors. The first was the imbalance between the growth in deposits and the creation of bills of exchange (particularly in 1927, when production turned down). Secondly, there was the high profitability of loans and overdrafts in a context of a falling tendency in interest rates (at Paribas for instance the return on loans and current accounts was 5.4 per cent in 1928 against 3.27 per cent for discount). The third was the requirements of the firms, because the increase in real wages and taxes in 1929 had resulted in severe shortages of liquid funds. Finally, the readjustment of the banking resources enabled the banks to support some degree of illiquidity. In order to go further in this direction, most of the large banks launched financial subsidiaries specially designed to provide medium-term loans to enterprises. The first of these intermediaries (UCINA) had been founded in 1919 by the CNEP and the Crédit Lyonnais. In the late 1920s the CALIF came into being (created by the Société Générale together with the CCF, the BNC, and the BUP), followed by the Union des Banques Regionales (launched by the CIC and its group). In 1930 the credits granted by this group of banks amounted to 1,000 million francs compared with 92 million in 1926. The growing share of the banks' credits in the total debts of French enterprises provides a good illustration of the new ability of the banks to keep up with demand (Table 11.9).

However it must be emphasized that the growing involvement of the banks with trade and industry was achieved without their liquidity being threatened. According to Truptil (1934) the liquidity of French banks equalled that of the big five English banks. Although it had been decreasing since 1926, the share of deposits represented by the items 'cash, banks, and correspondents' stood at 18.7 per cent in 1930 compared to 10 per cent in 1913. Symmetrically, secured loans and current accounts as a ratio of deposits rose from 23.7 per cent in 1926 to 35.8 per cent in 1930, but in 1913 the figure had been 43.2 per cent. Compared with English banks, large French banks continued to use a considerable proportion of their funds for discounting, 48.6 per cent of their assets in 1930 against 48.1 in 1913. To some extent this high liquidity reflected the great instability of deposits in France, not only those generated by hot money. In the following period this

TABLE 11.9. *Share of financial intermediaries in the total debts of industrial enterprises, 1926 and 1929 (%)*

	Averaged rate		Average of the rates		Median rate	
	1926	1929	1926	1929	1926	1929
Number of wage-earners						
100 and under	19.0	27.4	18.9	28.5	10.7	25.5
More than than 100	30.1	37.1	29.3	35.3	20.6	36.2
TOTAL	25.1	31.0	21.9	28.8	13.9	26.1

Note: The survey deals with all the industrial enterprises (336 cases) which asked for a loan at Crédit National in 1927 and 1930.

Source: Lescure (1992).

factor was to be of great influence on the extent to which banks were to be affected by the economic crisis.

4. The Banking Crisis and the New Orientations of the French Banking System, 1930–1939

The chronology of the French banking crisis complies with the general pattern of the countries that delayed leaving the gold standard (see chapter 2 by Jonker and van Zanden). A first crisis occurred in 1930–1, with two peaks in October 1930 and September 1931; 230 banks went bankrupt, among them the Bank Adam at Boulogne and the Banque d'Alsace-Lorraine. After a lull in the years 1932–3, the crisis recurred in 1934 in relation to a second deflationary shock; the number of failures rose from 67 to 106. However the French banking crisis remained far milder than those experienced by most of the other countries. In fact the crisis was very selective. Among the 670 banks which went bankrupt from October 1929 to September 1937 there were only 276 joint-stock banks. Half the failures concerned country banks; this group included some long-standing regional banks (such as the Banque Renauld at Nancy and the Banque Charpenay at Grenoble) and a mass of small bankers in personal partnership. Only one large bank, the BNC (because of its overcommitment with the Vincent group) was affected. The State and the Banque de France intervened to refloat this bank—more than they did for most of the regional banks—but in 1932 it was put into liquidation and replaced by a new bank, the Banque Nationale pour le Commerce et l'Industrie.

The fact that it was the universal banks which were the most affected by the crisis underlines the difficulty encountered by these banks in matching the two sides of their balance sheet, especially when production turned down. Large specialized banks were not concerned with this kind of problem so that 'the banking structure as a whole emerged from the crisis in a "healthier" and more concentrated state' (Bouvier, 1984).

Admittedly these banks were not spared from certain shocks, such as a run on cash, the failure of some large customers, or a stock-market crash; but usually their liquidity and solvency, coupled with the large financial support they could get, enabled them to absorb these shocks. The BUP, for instance, recorded considerable losses on its investment portfolio and on its credits, most of them related to its special interest in Danubian Europe, where banking and monetary crises were particularly acute. A misguided financial policy added further difficulties, since illiquid assets exceeded capital funds by 140 million in December 1931 (by 220 million with bad debts). However, at the expense of a broad reorganization of the bank (including its amalgamation with the Crédit Mobilier, the reduction of its capital, and the changing of its directors) and with the massive assistance of the Banque de France (in March 1932 it was the largest debtor of the Banque), the BUP got on its feet again.

The second reason for the solidity of the large banks was the long stability of their resources, which contrasted with the early outflow of capital experienced by banks in several other Western countries. While the total amount of deposits in banks publishing their balance sheet slid from 90.5 to 74.6 milliard francs between 1929 and 1931, those in the four big deposit banks rose from 34 to 38.2 milliard. From the peak of June 1931 to December 1932 they stood above 37 milliard and in July 1933 they still exceeded their 1929 level. In addition to probable transfers of deposits from small banks, large banks benefited from the flow of hot money towards Paris. In the international context of economic and monetary crises, the stabilized franc, coupled with French prosperity up to 1930, attracted foreign capital. From December 1928 to August 1930 the gold reserves rose from 31.8 to 45 milliard francs. This represented 51 per cent of the banknotes and credit current accounts of the Banque de France, while the legal rate of representation fixed by the monetary law of June 1928 was 35 per cent. Together with foreign currency reserves (between 1926 and 1931 the Banque de France was on a gold-exchange standard system) gold covered 100 per cent of the banknotes in circulation. These developments strengthened confidence in the franc, so that in 1933 gold reserves, now the sole item among the 'monetary guarantees', equalled the amount of fiduciary issue (81 milliard francs against 83).

Thus, for the large banks, the first stage of the crisis was dominated by the concern to find some return to their abundant resources. On two occasions in the recent past, banks had turned to the Banque de France for the rediscounting of their bills: during the first nine months of 1929, when the hot money flowed back for a short while, and at the end of the year 1930 and in 1931, when the banking crisis occurred. In 1932–3 they reversed their policy. Given the size of their deposits and the liquidity of the market (which made it easier for them to refinance in the market *hors banque*), the banks reduced their resort to the Banque de France. As a result, the portfolio of the central bank (of which two-thirds were rediscounts and one-third direct discounts in March 1932), fell from 6.8 to 3.3 milliard francs. Because of this, the Banque de France lost its control over the monetary market.

The slow-down of business limited the effects of this policy. Between 1930 and 1933, the volume of the deposits in the eight largest banks decreased by 6.5 per cent, while that of their advances to metropolitan enterprises slumped by 12.2 per cent. Fortunately the return to the budget deficits from 1931 onwards was to provide further opportunities to the banks (Table 11.10).

TABLE 11.10. *The financial weight of the State, 1913–1938*

	Financial needs of the state as per cent of GDP	Public issues as per cent of total issues	Percentage of the 'commercial portfolio' of the banks devoted to Treasury bills	Deposits in public financial institutions as per cent of total bank deposits
1905–13	+ 0.13	20.4[a]		35.6[b]
1920–5	– 6.07	69.6	60.3	32.0
1926–30	+ 3.37	44.7	33.1	37.4
1931–5	– 1.97	76.3	36.0	56.8
1936–8	– 7.26	94.9[c]	28.0	55.7

[a] average of the years 1910–13; [b] 1913; [c] 1936.

Sources: Fontvielle (1977); Dieterlen (1939); Teneul (1960); Lescure (1991).

The share of Treasury bills in the 'commercial portfolio' of the banks rose from 44 per cent in December 1931 to 69 in December 1933 (Plessis, 1991). All together, the various facilities provided by the banks to the State help to explain why the contraction in the volume of the banks' profits was only 3.5 per cent between 1931 and 1935. However, the main result of the imbalance between the movement of the advances and that of the deposits was an increase in cash reserves; the liquidity ratio averaged 25.4 per cent from 1931 to 1933, compared with 18.7 per cent in 1930.

This high liquidity was to be helpful during the second stage of the banking crisis, when deposits went down. Between July 1933 and August 1936 the deposits in the four big banks slumped from 35 milliard francs to less than 25 milliard. The decline in the role of the bank deposits in the money supply was general; as a proportion of M1, banks' deposits dropped from 56 per cent in 1929–30 to 43.7 per cent in 1935. In addition to the direct consequences of the Depression, the main reason for such a retreat was the growing lack of confidence in the franc. The reflux of hot money increased from September 1933 onwards, while private hoarding of gold and foreign currencies gained ground. The outflow of foreign and domestic capital was to last up to 1938.

Further difficulties came from the cut-throat competition that commercial banks had to face from public financial institutions. Several public and semi-public institutions came into being in the inter-war period, most of them designed to provide loans to special kinds of customers that suffered a lack of banking facilities (farmers, craftsmen, SMIs). Although the role of these new intermediaries increased sharply in the 1930s (Lescure, 1985*b*) the volume of their resources remained modest. In total, the postal cheques centres and the deposits in the co-operative sector (the Banque Populaires, the Crédit Agricole), two kinds of institutions that had been launched or reorganized at the end of the war, accounted only for 7.5 per cent of M1 in

1938 (Gueslin, 1991). The competition with the dense and well-established network of the saving banks (*caisses d'épargne*) was much more acute. Between 1926 and 1936, deposits in the saving banks, whether they were private *caisses d'épargne* or postal ones, were multiplied by 3.8, while those in the private commercial banks increased only 1.3 times. With 27,000 outlets (including 16,800 post offices for the CCP and the Caisse Nationale d'Épargne) against 9,057 banking offices in 1938, public and semi-public channels tended to take over the collection of savings from the private banks (Table 11.10).

Because the deposits of the *caisses* were recycled by the *caisse des dépôts* and used to buy *rentes*, the holding of a passbook was a secured and profitable investment. Between 1926 and January 1931 the rates paid by the banks slid from 3 or 4 per cent to 1 per cent while that of the *caisses d'épargne* remained stable at 3.5 per cent. In 1933 the rates were 0.25–0.5 per cent for the former, 3 per cent for the latter. Furthermore the ceiling of the passbooks was raised from 7,500 francs in 1925 to 20,000 francs in 1931. In addition to various advantages offered to the depositors, these conditions drew towards the *caisses* a wider range of customers than they were expected to receive; the number of passbooks rose from 15.5 million in 1920 to 20 million in 1935, one for every two inhabitants (Priouret, 1966).

As their deposits vanished, the large banks reduced the volume of their credits, and from 1934 onwards they again turned to the central bank for the rediscounting of their bills. They also gave away a part of their cash reserve. However, their liquidity remained at a high level during the ultimate years of the period; the liquidity ratio for the six largest deposit banks stood at 20.4 per cent in 1935–6 and 22.6 per cent in 1937–8. From 1935 onwards the revival of advances by the Banque de France to the State brought in its wake a further upsurge in the money supply. Although they were growing in nominal value from 1936 to 1938, the banks' deposits fluctuated to the beat of internal and external events, so that they could not rely on stable resources. It must be recalled that three devaluations of the franc occurred between September 1936 and May 1938, and that gold convertibility was abolished. This liquidity gave considerable security to the banks; by contrast with 1914 no moratorium was decreed in 1939–40.

But, as suggested by the Brunet report of 1936, the extent to which the search for liquidity acted as a brake upon expansion must be questioned. From 1931 to 1938 the volume of the banks' credits to metropolitan enterprises decreased by 23.4 per cent, and within total lending the ratio of loans and current accounts to 'commercial portfolio' slumped from 0.66 to 0.36. As proved true in the case of aeronautical industries, the reluctance of the banks to finance certain kinds of operations, like public markets, may have checked the growth in some sectors (Frankenstein, 1982). However, the lack of historical studies does not allow generalization.

The unsuccessful policy tried by Chautemps in 1937 in order to boost the economy through a stimulation of credit suggests that the need for funds was not a central issue for firms. By contrast with the reform of the Banque de France by Blum in 1936, which was political in nature, the reforms undertaken by Chautemps were economic; they included a better organization of the distribution of medium-term credit (with the Banque de France now authorized to rediscount the bills that the *caisse des dépôts* had received since 1931 from the banks as a counterpart of medium-term loans), a fall in the interest rates (with a part of this rate borne by the State) and the end of the financial gap supported by the SMIs (with the reorganization of the Crédit Hôtelier). Given the bad expectations of the entrepreneurs it was not until the take-off of the war industries gave a boost to the economy as a whole—from November 1938 onwards—that these measures were to bear fruit (Lescure, 1987).

Undoubtedly the sharp inflation of the 1920s and the Depression of the 1930s had increased the traditional weakness of the French banking system. In 1936 the deposits at the Crédit Lyonnais equalled 19 per cent of those at the Midland Bank; in 1911 the figure had been 89 per cent. At the end of 1937 the average amount of deposits per inhabitant was 1,700 francs in France against 10,100 francs in England, and 12,000 in the USA. The decline affected all kinds of banks' functions. As a proportion of M1 the share of deposits in the pure commercial banks and at the Banque de France was 41.5 per cent in 1938 against 44.3 per cent in 1913. As a ratio to national income the banks' advances to metropolitan enterprises never exceeded 64 per cent of their pre-war level.

Coming after a long period during which large banks went to great pains to prove their economic usefulness, this disappointing performance explains the bad opinion that French people had of their banks. The nationalization of the large deposit banks that occurred in 1945 was not independent of these developments.

References

Bergeron, L. (1989), 'Les espaces du capital', in J. Revel (ed.), *Histoire de la France* (Paris: Seuil).

Biriotti, A., *et al.* (1976), 'Le taux de profit sur longue période et l'évolution de l'économie française aux XIXe et XXe siècles' (INSEE, mimeographed note).

Bonin, H. (1978), 'La Banque Nationale de Crédit: Evolution et rôle éonomique de 1913 à 1932', unpublished Ph.D. dissertation, Université Paris-X.

Bonin, H. (1985), 'Les banques face au cas Citroën (1919–1930)', *Revue d'histoire moderne et contemporaine* 1.

—— (1992), 'Une grande entreprise bancaire: le CNEP dans l'entre-deux-guerres', *Études et Documents Comité pour l'histoire économique et financière* 4.

Bouvier, J. (1977), 'Système bancaire et inflation au XXe siècle: de 1913 à la seconde guerre mondiale', *Recherches et Travaux de l'IHES* 6.

—— (1979), 'L'extension des réseaux de circulation de la monnaie et de l'épargne', in F. Braudel and E. Labrousse (eds.), *Histoire économique et sociale de la France, 1789-années 1880* (Paris: PUF).

—— (1984), 'The French Banks, Inflation and the Economic Crisis, 1919–1939', *Journal of European Economic History*, 13/2.

Bussière, E. (1979), 'La Banque de l'Union Parisienne 1919–1931', unpublished diss., Université de Paris-IV.

—— (1992*a*), *Paribas, l'Europe et le monde 1872–1992* (Paris: Fonds Mercator).

—— (1992*b*), 'La stratégie industrielle de Paribas: 1900–1930', *Entreprises et Histoire*, 2.

Caron, F. (1976), 'La stratégie des investissements en France aux XIXe et XXe siècles', *Revue d'histoire économique et sociale*, 1.

Carré, J. J., Dubois, P., and Malinvaud, E. (1977), *La croissance française, un essai d'analyse économique causale de l'après-guerre* (Paris: Seuil).

Daviet, J. P. and Germain, M. (1994), *Le Crédit Commercial de France, une banque dans le siécle* (Paris: Textuel).

Debeir, J. C. (1980), 'Inflation et stabilisation en France, 1919–1928', *Revue économique*, 4.

Dieterlen, P. (1939), 'l'Épargne', *Revue d'économie politique*, no special.

Fontvieille, L. (1977), 'Evolution et croissance de l'État français: 1815–1969', *Cahiers de l'ISMEA*, AF 13.

Frankenstein, R. (1982), *Le prix du réarmement français (1935–1939)* (Paris: Publications de la Sorbonne).

Fridenson, P. (1972), *Histoire des usines Renault* (Paris: Seuil).

Gueslin, A. (1991), 'Banks and State in France from the 1880s to the 1930s: The Impossible Advance of the Banks', in Y. Cassis (ed.), *Finance and Financiers in European History 1880–1960* (Cambridge: Cambridge University Press).

INSEE (1966), *Annuaire statistique de la France, resumé rétrospectif* (Paris).

Laufenberger, H. (1940), *Enquête sur les changements de structure du crédit et de la banque, 1914–1938. Les Banques françaises* (Paris: Sirey).

Laloux, J. (1924), *Le rôle des banques locales et régionales du Nord de la France dans le développement industriel et commercial* (Paris: Giard).

Lanthier, P. (1987), *Les constructions électriques en France, 1880–1940*, unpublished Ph.D. dissertation, Université de Paris-X.

Lescure, M. (1985*a*), 'Banques régionales et croissance économique au XIXe siècle: l'exemple de la Société Marseillaise de Crédit', in *Banque et investissements en Méditerranée à l'époque contemporaine* (Marseilles: Publications de la Chambre de Commerce et d'Industrie de Marseille).

—— (1985*b*), 'La concurrence des secteurs bancaires publics et privés dans la France de l'entre-deux-guerres: l'exemple du Crédit National', in *États, fiscalités, économies* (Paris: Publications de la Sorbonne).

Lescure, M. (1987), 'L'État, l'investissement et la petite entreprise: l'expérience des bonifications d'intérêts (1937–1939), in P. Fridenson and A. Straus (eds.), *Le capitalisme français 19ᵉ–20ᵉ siècle* (Paris: Fayard).

—— (1991), 'L'Intervention de l'État: le manque de resources (1880–1935)', in M. Lévy-Leboyer and J. C. Casanova (eds.), *Entre l'Etat et le marché: l'économie française des années 1880 à nos jours* (Paris: Editions Gallimard).

—— (1992), 'Les banques et le financement des PME dans la France des années 1920', *Entreprises et histoire*, 2.

Lévy-Leboyer, M. (1976), 'Le crédit et la monnaie: l'apprentissage du marché', in F. Braudel and E. Labrousse (eds.), *Histoire économique et sociale de la France, 1789-années 1880* (Paris: PUF).

—— (1980), 'The Large Corporation in Modern France', in A. D. Chandler and H. Deams (eds.), *Managerial Hierarchies: Comparative Perspectives on the Rise of the Modern Industrial Enterprise* (Cambridge, Mass.: Harvard University Press).

—— and Bourguignon, F. (1985), *L'économie française au XIXᵉ siècle. Analyse macroéconomique* (Paris: Economica).

—— and Lescure, M. (1991), 'France', in R. Sylla and G. Toniolo (eds.), *Patterns of European Industrialization: The Nineteenth Century* (London: Routledge).

Malissen, M. (1953), *L'autofinancement des sociétés en France et aux États-Unis* (Paris: Dalloz).

Mesliand, C. (1967), 'La fortune paysanne dans le Vaucluse (1900–1938)', *Annales ESC* 1.

Pose, A. (1942), *La Monnaie et ses institutions* (Paris: PUF).

Plessis, A. (1985), 'Les concours de la Banque de France à l'économie (1842–1914)', in *Etats, Fiscalités, Economies* (Paris: Publications de la Sorbonne).

Plessis, A. (1991), 'Les Banques, le crédit et l'économie', in M. Lévy-leboyer and J. C. Casanova (eds.), *Entre l'État et le marché, l'économie française des années 1880 à nos jours* (Paris: Éditions Gallimard).

Pouchain, P. (1986), 'Banque et crédit à Lille de 1800 à 1939', *Revue du nord*, 270.

Priouret, R. (1966), *La Caisse des dépôts, cent cinquante ans d'histoire financière* (Paris: PUF)

Rebotier, M. (1935), *Les participations bancaires à l'industrie* (Paris: Sirey).

Saint-Marc, M. (1983), *Histoire monétaire de la France, 1800–1980* (Paris: PUF).

Schweitzer, S. (1992), *André Citroën* (Paris: Fayard).

Teneul, G. F. (1960), *Contribution à l'histoire du financement des entreprises en France depuis la fin du XIXᵉ siècle* (Paris: LGDJ).

Truptil, R. J. (1934), *Le Système bancaire anglais et la place de Londres* (Paris: Sirey).

12

From Imperial to Regional Banking: The Austrian Banking System, 1918–1938

FRITZ WEBER

1. Introduction

On the eve of the First World War Vienna was still the unchallenged financial centre of the Habsburg monarchy and the domicile of ten big joint-stock banks comprising two-thirds of the overall bank share capital of the western ('Cisleithanian') part of the Austro-Hungarian monarchy. By 1937 there were only three major banks and one holding company (the successor of a bank closed in 1934) left, each of them dominated either by the Austrian State or by foreign capital. The then biggest Viennese bank, the *Österreichische Creditanstalt-Wiener Bankverein* (CA-BV), was in a quasi-monopolistic position, comprising about 57 per cent of the overall accounts receivable of the Austrian banking community.

Six of the ten major banks of Imperial Vienna had been—directly or indirectly—incorporated in the CA-BV by amalgamation (see Fig. 12.1). One bank, the Allgemeine Depositenbank, had closed its counters in 1924; the former Länderbank had been transformed into the Viennese branch of the Banque des Pays de l'Europe Centrale in 1921. And the Mercurbank was, in 1937, hardly more than an affiliation of the Dresdener Bank in Berlin, which controlled more than 90 per cent of its share capital.

Rather crude figures of that kind may perhaps tell the foreigner more about the fate of the Austrian banking sector during the inter-war years than any lengthy introduction. They reflect a process of contraction rather than of concentration which had no parallel in the post-1918 financial history of other countries, not even in Germany or Italy. As for the whole Austrian economy, for the Viennese banks the 'Roaring Twenties' were a period of persistent creeping crisis, which developed into an open catastrophe at the end. In autumn 1929, the Boden-Credit-Anstalt was finished and had to be amalgamated with the Austrian Creditanstalt; in spring 1931, the Creditanstalt itself had to ask for state support, and finally, in 1934, another emergency amalgamation led to the formation of the Austrian Creditanstalt-Viennese Bankverein, the name of which was altered to Creditanstalt-Bankverein during the Nazi period.

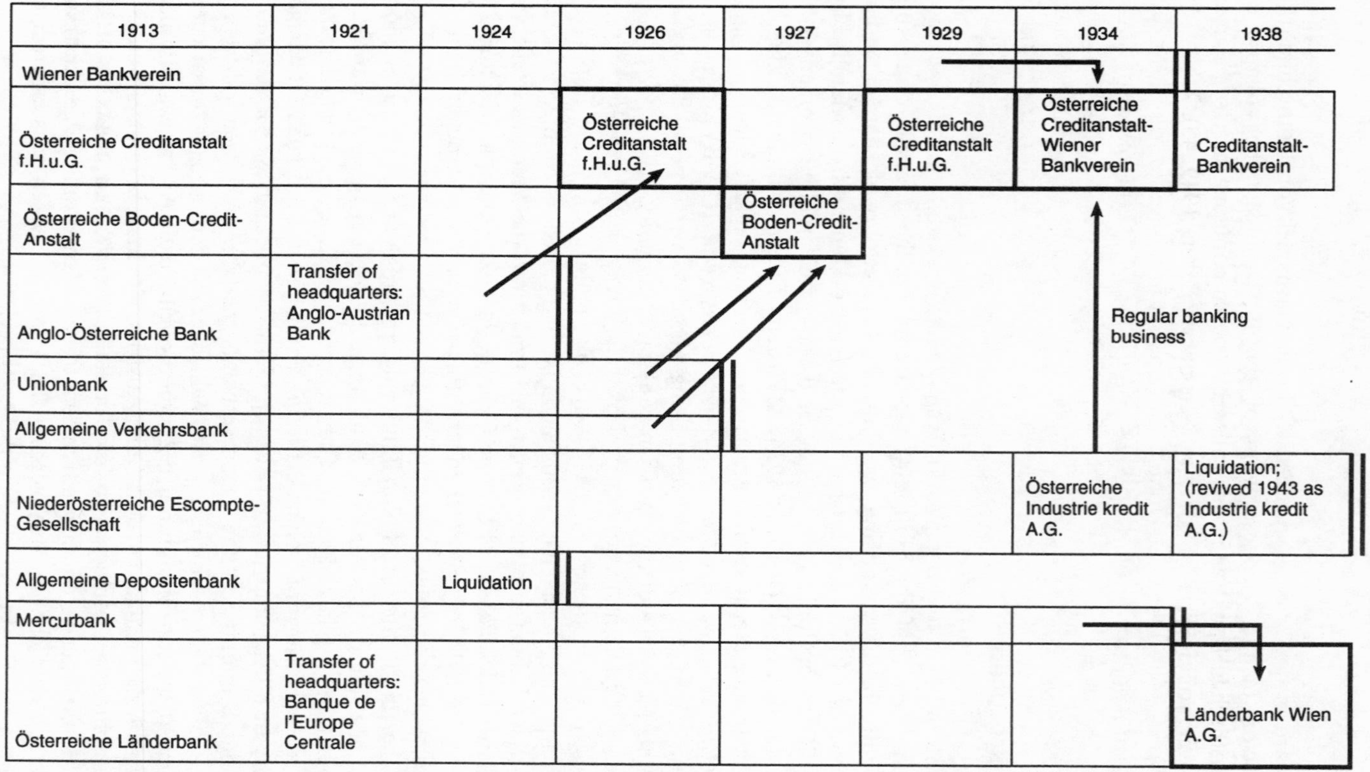

	1913	1921	1924	1926	1927	1929	1934	1938
Wiener Bankverein								
Österreiche Creditanstalt f.H.u.G.				Österreiche Creditanstalt f.H.u.G.		Österreiche Creditanstalt f.H.u.G.	Österreiche Creditanstalt-Wiener Bankverein	Creditanstalt-Bankverein
Österreiche Boden-Credit-Anstalt					Österreiche Boden-Credit-Anstalt			
Anglo-Österreiche Bank		Transfer of headquarters: Anglo-Austrian Bank						
Unionbank								
Allgemeine Verkehrsbank								
Niederösterreiche Escompte-Gesellschaft						Österreiche Industrie kredit A.G.	Liquidation; (revived 1943 as Industrie kredit A.G.)	
Allgemeine Depositenbank			Liquidation					
Mercurbank		Transfer of headquarters: Banque de l'Europe Centrale						
Österreiche Länderbank							Länderbank Wien A.G.	

Regular banking business

FIG. 12.1 The concentration process within the Viennese banks, 1918–1938.

The *Creditanstalt* was not just a bank in 1931: it was *the* bank of the Danubian area, its balance sheet equalling the budget of the Austrian State. Its board of directors was headed by Louis Nathaniel von Rothschild, the last scion of the Viennese wing of the Rothschilds. The collapse of the Rothschild Bank (as it was called by contemporaries) therefore started 'the stone rolling'—as a foreign scholar put it (Beyen, 1949: 45).

The stone, or rather, the stone avalanche, set in motion in May 1931 was a run on liquidity, which affected not only Austria and the successor States of the Habsburg monarchy but shattered the fragile international financial market as a whole. In July, two months after the outbreak of the Creditanstalt crisis, a banking moratorium had to be declared in Germany, and in September the Bank of England saw no alternative to devaluation of the pound sterling.

TABLE 12.1. *Capital resources and overall balance sheet of the major Viennese banks,* 1913–1936 (million AS)

Year	Number	Capital resources	Total balance sheet
1913	8[a]	1,369.0	6,640.1
1925[b]	7	306.0	1,875.4
1927	5	364.9	2,926.7
1929	4	336.0	2,589.3[c]
1932	4	221.1	1,647.8
1934	3[d]	193.7	1,192.6
1936	3[d]	129.3	1,092.1

[a] Without Länderbank and Anglobank, which became foreign banks in 1921.

[b] Gold balance sheets of 1 Jan. 1925, by which the banks were allowed to revalue their assets and liabilities after the end of hyperinflation.

[c] Figures of the Boden-Credit-Anstalt (BCA) are included in the balance sheet of the CA with a small flat sum only.

[d] Including Österreichische Industriekredit AG, a holding company emerging from one of the big banks, the Niederösterreichische Escompte-Gesellschaft in 1934.

Sources: Compass, 1915; Benedikt Kautsky, 'Die Bankbilanzen des Jahres 1925', *Arbeit und Wirtschaft,* 1 (1926): 16–20; *Der Österreichische Volkswirt* (ÖVW), several vols.

The decay of the Viennese banks can be seen in Table 12.1, which shows that by 1936 the overall balance sheet of the major institutions came to only one-sixth of their 1913 level; the share capital had dwindled even more and amounted to only one-tenth of the pre-war value.

The permanent problems of the banking sector were also reflected in changes in ownership. Before the First World War the share capital of the Viennese banks had been in the hands of Austrian private bankers, industrialists, and what were called 'private capitalists', i.e. members of the wealthy middle classes. The foreign share amounted to only 10 per cent. In the late 1930s private bankers no longer played a role in the board of directors of the great commercial banks. The shares were either held by foreigners (Länderbank, Mercurbank) or by the State and the Nationalbank, which owned the majority of shares of the CA-BV and the Österreichische Industriekredit AG. Public ownership can be regarded as a compensation for the socialization of losses accepted during the years 1931–4. The total losses came to more than 1 billion Austrian Schillings (AS) (Stiefel, 1989: 230–1), and equalled 10 percent of the Austrian GNP in 1931; 850 million had to be covered by the public authorities.

The reasons for the downfall of the Viennese banks after 1918 must be attributed to three main 'objective' causes (and, of course, to management failures, i.e. wrong responses to these structural challenges): (a) the dissolution of the Habsburg monarchy; (b) post-war inflation, and (c) the adverse performance of the Austrian economy.

2. Austrification or Multinationalization?

The orientation of the Viennese banks had been—since the inception of the modern banking system in the second half of the nineteenth century—multinational, in so far as their business had been conducted within the multinational framework of the Habsburg monarchy. They were central European rather than Austrian institutions. The centre of gravity of their activities was not to be found within the confines of the later Austrian republic; the most important branches were situated in Budapest, Trieste, and—above all—in the Czech lands—in short in those regions where the industrial centres of the monarchy were located.

On the eve of the war the ten major banks operated 149 branches outside Vienna; 114 of them were located in the later successor States (*Compass*, 1915). Among their customers were the Skoda works and other important firms of the Czechoslovakian mechanical engineering industry as well as the leading Hungarian mining and metallurgic company, the Rimamurany iron works, and the Trifail coalmines in Slovenia, the Galician oil companies and the Stabilimento Tecnico Triestino, the biggest shipyard of the monarchy. Of eighty-five industrial combines forming the *Konzern* of the Creditanstalt in 1913, fifty-seven were situated outside the borders of later Austria (März, 1984: 63–80, 544–6).

After the break-up of the monarchy a wave of nationalism swept over the new States, and the political élites in Prague, Belgrade, and Warsaw tried to break the economic influence of 'Vienna', i.e. mainly the Viennese banks, which were considered—if not as imperialistic—at least as Imperial institutions. What was called 'nationalization' of the economy then, meant the take-over of branches, affiliates, and conglomerates of the Austrian banks by 'national' capital groups, often with the support of Western European business friends.

To that challenge two possible responses could be given by the Viennese banks:

1. *Austrification*: a general 'retreat' from the Danube basin, the sale of assets, and concentration on the small, national Austrian business. This policy, which was favoured by a very small group of economic experts, would have implied a quick shrinking of the Viennese banking apparatus.

2. *Multinationalization*: the attempt to defend the traditional spheres of influence in the Danubian States, which meant more than just continuing with 'business as usual', since the funds necessary for expansion (or at least maintaining relations abroad) could not be raised on the home market.

The Viennese bankers decided in favour of the latter alternative. They believed—as one of their strongest supporters, the well-known economist (and Austrian Minister of Finance in 1919) Joseph A. Schumpeter put it (cited in März, 1984: 330)—that Vienna would in any case remain the financial centre of the Danubian area and that 'political separation [would] affect only marginally the purely economic relations' between the successor States, in short that 'business as usual' could be continued even within the drastically altered post-war political framework.

This decision was widely supported by Austrian politicians and economic experts as well as by foreign authorities like Montagu Norman, the governor of the Bank of England (cf. März, 1984: 459–60; Cottrell, 1983: 330–2; Teichova, 1979: 368–79). It was only *a posteriori*, when it was clear that the Danubian strategy had failed, that everybody hurried to join the side of the critics. Most historians have followed along these lines (Stiefel, 1989: 97–100; Ausch, 1968: 312–13, 344–68; Bachinger, 1981: 958–975). But could the Great Depression of the 1930s really have been foreseen in 1919 or even in 1925?

The transnational orientation of the Viennese banks had some fatal consequences:

1. The banks tended to 'hoard' employees, anticipating better times for their multinational business.

2. They tried to protect their spheres of influence in the successor States by either transforming subsidiaries into new banks or by inserting them into already existing 'national' banks. As a result, of 143 foreign branches owned by the ten major Viennese banks in 1918 only nine were left in 1923. The banks in the successor States, however, could not be controlled from Vienna.

3. Until 1918 the Viennese banks had at their disposal the savings of the whole Austrian (i.e. western) parts of the monarchy and had thus been able to reinvest them among all regions of Austria-Hungary. By giving up their foreign branches they lost their most powerful customers, the deposits of which had to be replaced by credits of Western banks.

4. The need to attract foreign money led to a change in the composition of the shareholders of the Viennese banks: the foreign quota in the share capital of the major Austrian banks rose from 10 per cent in 1913 to 30 per cent in 1923 and seems to have remained stable until the outbreak of the

1931 crisis. In May 1931 one-third of the Creditanstalt shares were in foreign hands (Weber and Haas, 1978: 186; Weber, 1991: 570).

3. The Failure of the Danubian Strategy

The degree to which the Viennese banks were able to maintain their foreign empires after 1918 has been considerably overestimated by contemporaries as well as by historians, who tended to look at the colourful façades, so carefully cultivated by the banks, rather than at the hidden facts. The harsh reality was that the foreign business of the banks had dwindled to an amount very much below the pre-war level. As calculated elsewhere (Weber, 1985: 330–1), this came—at the height of the transnational activity of the Viennese banks in 1928–9—to only one-fifth of the 1913 level. And it had also changed its character: whereas in 1913 the banks had granted credits directly to industrial customers throughout the monarchy, in 1928 about one-third of the foreign advances consisted of loans to those banks in the successor States, in which the Austrian banks had acquired shares after 1918.

In 1918 the Austrian banks held a considerable number of shares of enterprises located in the later successor States. (There are various contemporary calculations about these assets. Unfortunately they vary widely and none of them can be regarded as reliable. It would therefore be unwise to refer to these figures.) In subsequent years a considerable part of these stocks was sold to citizens of the new States as well as to western firms eager to replace the Austrian shareholders. The most spectacular case was certainly that of the Skoda works, where the Viennese banks were out-manœuvred by the French Schneider-Creuzot dynasty.

It should be understood, however, that ownership of shares must not be regarded as identical with influence: during the immediate post-war period the Viennese banks were holding (and hoarding) shares of their clientele in the successor States without being able to act as a bank to them, i.e. without being able to grant credits, since both the loss of deposits and the depreciation of the Austrian currency rendered it impossible to invest money abroad any longer. In this period the influence of the Austrian banks *vis-à-vis* foreign firms was, as the chief editor of a well-reputed Central European economic review wrote, only 'a personal one of the Viennese bank managers' (Federn, 1932: 412).

When the banks were able to resume their foreign business along normal lines with a certain time-lag after the stabilization of the Austrian crown (which took place in the autumn of 1922), in many cases only the bad debtors had been left to them. Only between 1925 and 1928 were the Viennese banks able to fulfil transnational functions, failing however to meet what customers would expect from an intermediary financial centre. Instead of reducing the price of foreign credits for the Danubian economies, they increased the credit costs by passing on their own high expenses to their clients through various additional charges and commissions (Kernbauer and Weber, 1986).

Moreover, the foreign activities of the Viennese banks were not distributed equally over the successor States. Their main business was directed to Yugoslavia and Poland, where the banking sector had been underdeveloped prior to 1918. In Czechoslovakia they had already lost their privileged position in the immediate post-war years. There were only a few cases in which strong ties survived between Czechoslovakian firms and Viennese banks. The most famous (because disastrous) example was perhaps that of the Mautner textile works. The Mautner works were the source of heavy losses for the Boden-Credit-Anstalt (BCA) as well as (after the amalgamation of 1929) for the Creditanstalt (Weber, 1991: 450–6, 504–6).

As a rule, foreign credits to Hungary and Czechoslovakia were granted directly by Western banks; the intermediary role of Vienna was reduced to what we could call 'moral backing': The Bohemian Bank-Verein (BBV) received loans from the foreign shareholders of the Wiener Bankverein (WBV), which were, at the same time, shareholders of the BBV. The Creditanstalt acted as guarantor with regard to Western credits raised by the Bohemian Escompte and Credit-Bank (BEBKA), a bank in which it held a minority interest of 25 per cent. Of the Viennese banks only the Creditanstalt succeeded in creating—together with the Austrian Rothschilds and Dutch bankers—an affiliate in Western Europe, the Amstelbank in Amsterdam, which was designed to mobilize Western money to be allocated all over the Danube region. This bank, founded in 1920, ran into trouble in 1931 and had to be liquidated.

Undoubtedly, the attempt to regain a strong position within the Danubian economies contributed—to a considerable extent—to the difficulties of the Austrian banking sector throughout the 1920s. After the events of 1931, of course, it was evident that it would have been wiser to sound the retreat earlier. A rational policy of that kind would have allowed the planned relinquishment of all those footholds which had to be given up after 1931 hurriedly, under pressure, and accompanied by great losses.

But was there any point of return for the Viennese bankers prior to 1931 after the wrong decision had been made in 1918–19? Until 1923 economic conditions must have appeared quite anomalous in any case. After a waiting period the banks started granting loans to Eastern Europe on a greater, but still modest scale not earlier than in 1925. In 1927 a general upswing began, which must have been interpreted as the final return to normality. At the earliest, the outbreak of the Great Depression in 1929 must be regarded as the point at which to correct the wrong strategy.

It may be that as early as 1919 a very conservative banker would have opposed a policy which implied investing foreign credits in foreign loans. But would this argument not have had the same bad smell of autarkic backwardness, which distinguished those politicians from the Austrian provinces, who advocated—precisely in 1919—the idea that Styrian savings should be invested only in Styria?

4. The General Difficulties of the Austrian Banks in the 1920s

The strategy of multinationalization undoubtedly increased the problems of the Viennese banks in the long run, not only because of the dependence on foreign short-term credits (which were, by the way, not mere transitory items for the Austrian economy, but were also used to grant loans to domestic firms). The banks had to show profits (which they usually had not earned) to satisfy their new Western shareholders. The non-profitability of the Austrian banking business, however, was home-made rather than caused by activities abroad. It is notorious today that the Boden-Credit-Anstalt crisis (in 1929) as well as the crisis of the Creditanstalt (in 1931) were not created by the sudden withdrawal of foreign credits. They were caused mainly by lack of liquidity and losses emerging from a rather small number of big industrial debtors, and—in the second place—by the depreciation of equities held in the portfolios of the banks.

To understand the nature of these losses one has to take into consideration the bad performance of the Austrian economy in the 'golden' 1920s. Not even in 1929 did industrial production reach the pre-war level; GNP came to 105 per cent. In this extremely adverse context any wrong decisions by bankers were of greater weight than under conditions of 'normal' economic growth.

Many bank problems had their origins in inflation or in later consequences, which can be related to the period of monetary disturbances:

1. The over-accumulation of industrial shares, which started during inflation, when the banks tried to 'hoard' equities in order to escape inflation and to secure their capital funds.

2. The Stock Exchange boom (1923) and crash (spring 1924), and the subsequent paralysis of the Austrian capital market.

3. The loss of working capital suffered by industrial firms during inflation, which drastically increased the demand for bank credit after 1922 and—given the high interest rates resulting from the great demand for money—reduced the profitability of the industrial sector.

The symbiosis between banks and industry—seen as a source of power and influence for 'finance capital' prior to 1914—turned out to be the cause of great and chronic losses for the banks in the inter-war period. As opposed to Germany, where industrial enterprises became more independent of the banks during post-war inflation (Born, 1979), the ties between credit institutions and industry were tightened in Austria. On the one hand, the demand for credit rose steadily; on the other hand, the banks tried to limit the risks of credit-granting[1] by transforming loans into equity participations (*Veraktionierung*).

The strategy of accumulating (or, better, hoarding) real assets, however, proved to be detrimental in the long run, because after the Stock Exchange crash of 1924 the banks were unable to sell the huge packages of shares they had acquired. Moreover, between 1924 and 1929 the banks were forced to

TABLE 12.2. *Investment as a percentage of the capital funds of four big Austrian banks, 1913 and 1925 (equity portfolio plus syndicate holdings as a percentage of share capital plus published reserve funds)*

Bank	1913	Gold balance sheets 1925
CA	54	89
BCA	20[a]	117
WBV	49	49
NEG	57	71

[a] Holdings in a syndicate listed as debtors.

Sources: *Compass*, 1915; Mitteilungen des Direktoriums der Österreichischen Nationalbank July 1926.

grant industrial credits to a dangerously high extent because their clientele proved to be unable to raise new share issues on the languishing Viennese capital market. And—what made things even worse—they used even short-term foreign deposits to meet the urgent demand for investment credits.

Those banks suffered most which sinned most and—by taking over other banks (see Fig. 12.1)—excessively increased their industrial holdings: the Boden-Credit-Anstalt and the Creditanstalt. Since practically every bank was affected by creeping illiquidity every merger meant the taking-over of one unsound institution by another weak one. Moreover, amalgamation not only involved growing problems in meeting the financial needs of an enlarging *Konzern*, it also overstrained the organizational apparatus of the banks.

Presentiments of the questionable ingenuity and the future dangers of such action can be found in the minutes of the banks. When the

---

[1] Stable-value clauses which would have added the rate of inflation to the interest rate were unknown then in Austria (as well as in Germany). At a time when the rate of inflation amounted to 100% the credit costs charged by the banks were about 20% (including commissions). Credits in foreign currency came into general practice only during the very last stage of hyperinflation.

TABLE 12.3. *Share capital and declared reserves of four Viennese banks, 1913* (including increase 1914–24) *and* 1925 (gold balance sheets) (million AS)

Bank	1913	1925	1925 as % of 1913
CA	452.5	70.0	15.7
BCA	308.4	50.0	16.2
WBV	389.0	60.0	15.4
NEG	222.0	50.0	22.5
7 biggest banks	1,860.0	296.0	15.9

Source: *Wirtschaftsstatistisches Jahrbuch der Arbeiterkammer 1926.*

Boden-Credit-Anstalt acquired a majority interest in the Verkehrsbank in 1925, one of its managers pointed to the danger of an 'immobilization' caused by the 'financial needs of such a great number of additional industries' (C-B, Enclosure to MMB-BCA, 9 July 1925). And some years later, when the bank had formally carried out the merger with both Unionbank and Verkehrsbank, Baron Schröder, one of the English shareholders of the Boden-Credit-Anstalt, noticed a conspicious 'great strain' in the half-yearly balance sheet (C-B, Enclosure to MMB-BCA, 20 February 1928).

Maybe, in that situation, the consciously planned merger of several medium-sized banks would have been an alternative to the affiliation of smaller institutions to big ones. But the Austrian government restricted interventions to the clear field of provincial banking, where it supported—for political reasons—several mergers and reconstruction plans.[2] However, more significant banking decisions were voluntarily left to a small and exclusive circle of banking experts, i.e. to representatives of private banking and to central bankers, who usually were former conservative members of the high state bureaucracy or former private bankers, like the powerful president of the Austrian Nationalbank, Richard Reisch, who had been a member of the managing board of the Boden-Credit-Anstalt. The Viennese Christian Socialists even killed an initiative aiming at Austrification, which had been raised by Styrian Conservatives in 1925 (Kernbauer, 1991: 247–54).

Already in 1914, the balance sheets of the Viennese banks showed a characteristic tendency towards illiquidity, since the bigger part of their capital funds was frozen in industrial shares than was the case in Germany (Federn, 1914). The gold balance sheets of 1925, by which the Austrian banks were called to reassess their assets and liabilities after eight years of inflation,[3] clearly show that this danger had been further aggravated (see Table 12.2).

[2] Many conservative politicians and representatives of peasant organizations had involved themselves in banking matters at a provincial level after 1918; in order to shield political friends these interventions were supported by politicians who in general favoured a course of non-intervention in banking matters.
[3] At the end of inflation 1 gold crown amounted to 14.400 paper crowns. In 1925 the Austrian schilling (AS) was introduced as a new currency, 10,000 crowns equalled 1 AS.

TABLE 12.4. *Credit costs in Austria and other European countries, 1924–1929 (annual averages)*

	Austria	Germany	Switzerland	Great Britain
1924	17.8	20.0	7.0	5.8
1928	13.5	10.0	6.5	6.3
1929	14.9	9.5	6.5	6.3

Sources: *Wirtschaftsstatistisches Jahrbuch 1924, 1930/31*; KOFO-Monatsbericht June 1938: 140.

Moreover, the banks had lost a considerable part of their own capital during inflation. If we also take into consideration the amounts of capital injected between 1913 and 1924, the losses were even higher (see Table 12.3). The Viennese banks had—as everywhere in Europe—to conduct their business with less strong backing by capital resources after the First World War. Whereas the capital / assets ratio of the Creditanstalt had been 1 : 3.6 in 1913, it ranged from 1 : 7 to 1 : 9 in the second half of the 1920s. In Berlin

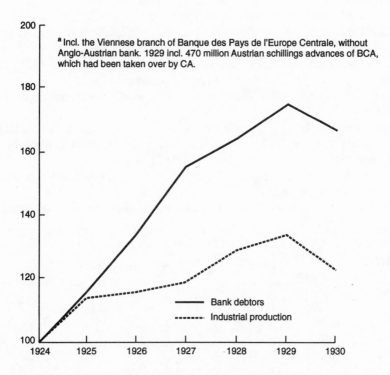

FIG. 12.2   Bank debtors[a] and industrial production, Austria, 1924–1930 (1924 = 100)

this ratio was even more unfavourable, varying from $1:9$ to $1:20$, according to calculations reported by the general manager of the Creditanstalt after 1932, Adrianus van Hengel (Country Court of Vienna, 1932).

As Fig. 12.2 shows, the increase in advances granted to bank customers in the 1920s exceeded by far the growth of the Austrian economy. This phenomenon can only to a small extent be attributed to capital exports into the Danubian basin (Kernbauer and Weber, 1986: 193–4). Rather, the figures reflect the fact that the Viennese banks financed investments in anticipation to prepare the firms in their industrial conglomerates for a boom which they confidently expected. (We must not forget that the generation of bank managers acting in the 1920s had passed through their formative years during the boom period preceding the First World War, and therefore could hardly comprehend the overall change in growth patterns after 1918. It is against that background that we have to see their post-war failures.)

To be sure, this anti-cyclical credit policy, as we may call it with reference to Ludwig von Mises's theory of the business cycle (von Mises, 1928, 1931), was not part of any rational or voluntary strategy. The banks took over entrepreneurial risks because they had become the main shareholders of industry. If they wanted to have a chance ever to sell the shares, they *had* to grant ever-increasing amounts of credit to their industrial clients with the argument 'not to endanger the international credit of the firm and to secure future share issues' (C-B, Enclosure to, MMB-BCA, 24 January 1924). It is clear that a strategy which only postponed problems instead of solving them could not be continued indefinitely, particularly in stormy economic weather.

Moreover, this form of financing investments was as dangerous for the banks as it was expensive for the borrowers, who had to pay fantastically high interest rates compared to Western standards (Table 12.4).

Of course, large enterprises had access to less expensive credit facilities in foreign currency through the good offices of their patron banks (Layton and Rist, 1925: 19–20). For the majority of industrialists however—the average

TABLE 12.5. *Regional distribution of the industrial conglomerate of the Creditanstalt, 1913–1931* (no. of firms)

Year	Austria	Foreign countries	Total
1913	28	57	85
1923	36	64	100
1929[a]	147[b]	68	215
1931	192	95	287

[a] Prior to amalgamation with BCA.

[b] 41 companies added by merger with Anglobank in 1926.

Sources: Various.

Austrian enterprise was small or medium-sized—the dear money policy aggravated the problem of 'capital shortage' inherited from inflation; and passing on the costs of swollen banking apparatus by means of cartelization rendered it impossible for industrial firms to earn profits high enough to pay off bank loans, distribute dividends, and accumulate savings for further investment.

Austrian industry was certainly not only the victim of monopolistic banking practices, it was also a source of (potential as well as actual) losses to the banks, and the high credit costs should also be interpreted as including a premium for risky transactions.

On the other hand, it would certainly have been wiser, in the long run, to bear the consequences of higher operating losses during the deflationary years 1924–6; a course which would have been facilitated by courageously sounding the retreat from the shaky and beleaguered outposts in the successor States.

Even though the banks tried to ignore the consequences of the war, the centre of gravity of their conglomerates gradually shifted to Austria after 1918 (see Table 12.5). Since this development was not consciously carried through and was interpreted as only transitory, the Austrian clientele of the banks were compelled to continuously subsidize an overgrown banking apparatus.

At the end of these considerations we have to ask what other alternatives were left to the banks after the Stock Exchange disaster of spring 1924, taking into account the general performance of Austrian industry, its need for investment credits to compete in foreign markets, and the given structure of ownership in joint-stock companies after 1923.

An alternative always open in times of crisis or/and overexpansion is conservative banking. It would have meant (besides Austrification) pursuing a selective and cautious credit policy, minimizing risks by forming credit syndicates with Western banks, and separation from enterprises in branches with the most severe structural problems. Elements of that policy can be found in the Viennese Bankverein (BV) and the Austrian branch of the Banque des Pays de l'Europe Centrale.

The more radical solution of the Austrian banking problem was demonstrated by the Anglo-Austrian Bank, which gave up its Viennese branch in 1926, selling it lock, stock, and barrel to the Creditanstalt. However, liquidating banking activities was a way of solving the problem open only to one player in the game. While the representatives of the British bank seemed glad that they could 'now operate through first-class local banks such as the Österreichische Creditanstalt instead of directly financing Continental industries' (PRO, FO 371/11213–82091), the management of the Creditanstalt emphasized the idea of 'rendering Austrian industry a good service' by taking over the affiliate, and wanted to 'secure the survival of the industrial conglomerate of the Anglo-Austrian Bank' (C-B, Enclosure to CA-MBD, 22 June 1926).

The two protagonists of the transaction also represented different ways of perceiving reality: the British bankers referred to 'proper caution . . . with regard to so unstable an element as Central Europe still represents today'; their Austrian colleagues were much more optimistic with regard to the future prospects of the region. It was the functional optimism of people who tried to continue business as usual in an unstable world.

5.   The Silent Accumulation of Losses during the 1920s

Even under 'natural' conditions the balance sheets of banks have a strong tendency not to show the real swings of business, but to tone them down. The range of window-dressing, however, is limited by the existing banking law. The Austrian regulations were—until 1989—quite liberal, leaving a wide margin for vague figures, which veiled the real state of the banks. Until the outbreak of any crisis, the afflicted institutions therefore seemed to be sound; the only harbinger of future dangers was usually the indebtedness *vis-à-vis* the central bank.

Four stages of crisis can be identified in the Austrian banking system during the 1920s. (We may assume that the surviving banks, too, underwent—but were able to overcome—each of the subsequent stage of difficulties.)

First stage: the bursting of the speculative bubble.

After 1918 the number of banks increased sharply due to the speculative inflationary boom and the gambling spirit of the Stock Exchange. After the crash of 1924 a great number of the newly founded institutions disappeared again (see Table 12.6). The only bank of good reputation affected by these events was the Depositenbank, which had to close its counters because of speculative losses caused by its main shareholders.

Although the government was in a legal position to control the placing of bank concessions, it refused to intervene in the banking sector during inflation. The new Banking Act of 1924, enacted after some financial

TABLE 12.6.   *Number of banks in Austria, 1913–1926*

Year	Joint-stock banks	Private banks
1913	27	194
1920	36	367
1923	76	377[a]
1926	36[b]	236

[a] 1924.

[b] Increase as against 1913 caused by the foundation of provincial banks.

Sources: *Compass*, 1915–28; *Statistisches Handbuch der Republik Österreich*, vols. 1–9.

scandals had frightened the public, did not fundamentally change the control mechanism.

Second stage: too many banks, diminishing deposits, and the shrinking of the 'natural' field of activity after the dissolution of the Habsburg monarchy.

The shrinking of the number of domestic creditors by the reduction of the state territory and the loss of branches in the successor States brought about, together with inflation, a maladjustment between creditors and debtors. The loss of deposits surpassed the shrinking of foreign assets, since the domestic demand for credit was steadily growing during inflation as well as during the deflationary crisis of 1924–5. Victims of the crisis were two of the three medium-sized banks: the Unionbank and the Verkehrsbank, which were both amalgamated with the Boden-Credit-Anstalt. (The third one, the Mercur-bank, was able to overcome the crisis thanks to the assistance of its German shareholder, the Danatbank.)

Third stage: illiquidity after eating too much.

The problem of financing the huge Austrian conglomerates of the two disappearing banks was inherited by the *Boden-Credit- Anstalt*, which had to procure ever-increasing financial means after 1926. The BCA—similar to the Danatbank in Berlin—pursued the most expansive course in the 1920s. Its business had been conducted in a strongly centralized manner—there was not a single branch—until 1918. Afterwards the bank undertook a hasty expansion into the Austrian provinces (by means of buying up or founding provincial banks). By taking over the Unionbank and the Verkehrsbank in Vienna, it acquired a network of branches and considerably enlarged its *Konzern*, mainly in the investment goods sector.

From 1927 on, the accounts of the BCA *vis-à-vis* the central bank rose steadily, and the bills discounted by the Nationalbank contained a significantly large share of finance bills. In summer 1929, when political tensions led to the flight of domestic capital, the liquidity problem could no longer be concealed, and the bank had to draw in excess of its credit limits at the

TABLE 12.7. *Share of the Creditanstalt in the sum total of accounts receivable of Austrian joint-stock banks, 1925–1929*

Year	Sum total (million AS)	Credit-anstalt	The Share of CA as % of total
1925	1,609	484	30.1
1926	1,867	742	39.7[a]
1928	2,265	915	40.4
1929	2,402	1,543	64.2[b]

[a] After taking over the Viennese branch of the Anglo-Austrian Bank.
[b] Including 470 million AS debts taken over from BCA.

Sources: KOFO-Monatsbericht June 1938: 138; Annual reports of the Creditanstalt.

Nationalbank. In the end, the lender-of-last-resort refused to continue granting uncovered advances, and—persuaded by the Austrian government—the management of the Creditanstalt took over its sinking sister-ship.

Political interventions of that type seem to have copied the model invented by the conservative governments in the years 1924–6, when several provincial banks had been 'soundlessly' saved for political reasons. It may not be surprising to hear that the president of the Boden-Credit-Anstalt, too, was a partisan of the Christian Socialist movement.

Village-pump politics never provide far-sighted solutions. The difference between this case and the provincial model was one of scale: The amalgamation of 1929 was a marriage of two giants, joining a single bank which controlled a great share of the credit sector in Austria (see Tables 12.5 and 12.7). Moreover, the further extension of the industrial combine played a similarly fatal role for the Creditanstalt as it had done for the other banks. When the CA took over the Boden-Credit-Anstalt, the Bank of the Rothschilds (as it was known all over Europe) was itself anything but sound. And the amalgamation of two weak banks led to more than just a mechanical addition of bad debts; it meant a multiplication of problems.

Fourth stage: the necessity to confess the hidden losses accumulated throughout the 1920s.

The crisis of 1931 was not caused by an acute liquidity crisis; in contrast to the BCA, the Creditanstalt was not forced to ask for the help of the central bank prior to May 1931, and the call on foreign credits, too, was only the consequence of the crisis. However, a loss of 140 million AS, as announced in May 1931, could not have occurred during a one- or two-year period. It was substantially higher than the accumulated net profits published 1923–9 (58.4 million AS).

How did the bank manage to hide the truth for years? The internal balance sheets of the Creditanstalt—and several hints we have for the other banks—indicate that there was no 'normal' year between 1924 and 1929. The profits of the Creditanstalt had been artificially created by revaluation of so-called 'internal' or 'hidden' reserves, i.e. the book value of equities (März and Weber, 1983: 515).

The margin between the book and the market value of equities, however, was of a very fictitious character in the 1920s. For many of the shares in question the quantity owned by the bank was too large to render possible an inconspicuous sale without substantial losses; and finally, the alleged value of many shares did not reflect the market's valuations, but only the secret price manipulation by the bank itself. In other words, the Creditanstalt systematically overestimated the amount of hidden reserves to which it took recourse in order to distribute dividends.

Such 'accounting with considerable blemishes', as one of the Creditanstalt managers put it (Country Court of Vienna, OZ 9), also included the (conscious or unconscious) underestimation of dubious assets: the bank invented new instruments to activate dubious loans, like the so-called 'bills of betterment', by which industrial clients promised to pay interest later, in a hoped-for prosperous future.

Other banks, too, with the exception of the Viennese Bankverein and the Banque des Pays de l'Europe Centrale, had prepared overoptimistic balance sheets prior to 1931. Although the losses of the Niederösterreichische Escompte-Gesellschaft (NEG) were far lower than those of the CA, it had—after an abortive attempt at reorganization in 1933—to be disbanded as a commercial bank in 1934. The Bankverein was formally amalgamated with the Creditanstalt all in one go, although its management had carried out its task quite well.

6. The Case of the Creditanstalt: A Revision of Some Myths

The first calculations the Creditanstalt management presented to the Government in May 1931, attributed 60 million of a total loss of 140 million AS to the heritage of the Boden-Credit-Anstalt, 30 million to the depreciation of equities, and 50 million to the necessity of writing down industrial loans (CB, MMB-CA, 15 May 1931). It soon appeared, however, that a radical solution of the bad debt problem would require much higher amounts. In autumn 1931 estimates of that kind came to more than 500 million AS; in the end, the second reconstruction plan of 1933 fixed the loss caused by depreciation of outstanding loans at 602.3 million AS.

TABLE 12.8. *Geographical distribution of the debtors of the Creditanstalt at 31 May 1931 (%)*

	Domestic	Foreign
Over 1 million AS	56.7	43.3
Over 5 million AS	66.9	33.1

Sources: Country Court Vienna, OZ 17; CB, Inheritance Georg Stern.

Later, this radical writing down was considered as over-reconstruction. This is particularly true with regard to the foreign assets of the bank. The Creditanstalt had invested about one-third of its assets (accounts receivable) abroad. Whereas the overwhelming majority of its small debtors were Austrian, the share of foreign clients was considerably high in medium-sized credits, but smaller again in the biggest ones (see Table 12.8).

Since the necessity for depreciation was clearly correlated with the size of the debt (see Table 12.9), the abnormally high losses from foreign business have to be doubted. I also would disagree with the argument that

TABLE 12.9. *Percentage depreciation of advances of the Creditanstalt in 1931*

Average all loans	Loans over 1 million AS as a whole	Ten biggest debts	Remaining debts over 1 million AS	Loans smaller than 1 million AS
32	40	58	24	9

Sources: C-B Archives; various records.

managerial 'loss of control over things' was responsible for the crisis of 1931 (Stiefel, 1989: 106–22). Although there were severe organizational imperfections with the Creditanstalt as well as with other banks, it was not the wide range of activities which brought the banks to the verge of ruin, but only a very small number of bad clients. The ten biggest debtors caused the CA to write down about 40 per cent of the total losses, according to the calculation made in autumn 1931. The case of the Boden-Credit-Anstalt shows the trend even more clearly: its biggest debtor, the Steyr works (an automobile company), was in the red to the extent of 106 million AS *vis-à-vis* the patron bank in 1929, an amount exceeding the capital funds of the bank (C-B, MMB-CA, 22 Nov. 1929).

7. The End of the Story: The Crisis of 1931 and its Consequences

When the Austrian government decided in favour of the reconstruction of the Creditanstalt in mid-May 1931, the impression left with contemporaries was that of a decisive action. But the more the politicians began to realize that what had been initiated went beyond a mere excursion into the land of business, the more a delaying attitude came to the fore. The government was anxious not to take over the responsibility for the bank (Stiefel, 1989).

A bank in difficulties without a determined leader, however, is worse than just a bank in difficulties. The Creditanstalt desperately tried to sell off shares to increase its liquidity; the result was meagre. Efforts to redeem industrial loans on a large scale failed, too. The bank managers themselves calculated that, at the best, they would be able to mobilize an amount of 70 million AS or only 5 per cent of the outstanding loans (C-B Archives, 30 November 1931). Moreover, the incentive to strive for liquidity was not strong in 1931, since the Austrian Nationalbank continued to discount the bills of the Creditanstalt until the end of 1931, the amount of which increased from 81 million AS (9 May 1931) to 677 million (2 January 1932). Deflation started only in February 1932, when the general manager of the Nationalbank, Richard Reisch, the advocate of an 'inflationary' course, was replaced by Victor Kienböck, a man, who had—as the minister of finance— already executed the restrictive Geneva reform scheme imposed on Austria by the League of Nations in 1923–4.

At the same time the Dutch banker Adrianus van Hengel took over the seat of Alexander Spitzmüller, an elderly man, who had been designated in summer 1931, as the head of the Creditanstalt. The new chairman was a confidant of the foreign creditors of the bank, and was regarded as just the tough trouble-shooter necessary for carrying through the bitter reconstruction of the still-sinking flagship of the Austrian credit sector.

Particularly during the first months of his (and Mr Kienböck's) reign, the Creditanstalt had to face days, when—according to van Hengel—'the cash holdings were so low, that it seemed uncertain, if we could keep the counters open' (Ministry of Finance Archives, Vienna, 77, 685/1832: Report of A. van Hengel to the foreign creditors of the Creditanstalt, November 1932.) In other words the Creditanstalt was anything but a living financial body; it had lost the greatest part of its deposits, had completely ceased lending, and reduced its activities to a rigorous collecting of outstanding loans. Only after an agreement between the Creditanstalt and the Austrian Government, by which the State took over the debt of the bank *vis-à-vis* the Nationalbank in 1932, was the bank put back into a position where it could fulfil 'normal' banking functions.

Backed by the agreement, the first attempts were directed towards reorganizing the heavily indebted industrial combine of the bank. From 1933 onwards the CA systematically wrote down assets (equities as well as advances) and participated in reconstructing the capital funds of the firms. The easements the Creditanstalt was able to offer were, however, very limited in scope. After the experience of the 1920s the bank—which from 1934 practically held a monopolistic position in the Austrian banking sector—refused to grant investment credits to its industrial clients and limited itself to the realm of short-term banking transactions. It was van Hengel's idea to make the Creditanstalt act according to Western banking principles. Although this tendency was tempered somewhat after his unexpected death in 1936, the restrictive course remained unchanged—as can be seen in Table 12.10—until the Anschluss of 1938.

The idea of founding a common holding company for the industrial combines of all Austrian banks, favoured by van Hengel in 1933–4, was not carried out. Nor was there any attempt to take advantage of the Creditanstalt as a means of stimulating the economy. However, within the

TABLE 12.10. *Accounts receivable of the Creditanstalt-Bankverein, 1934–1937 (million AS)*

Year	Loans
1934	497.6
1935	425.6
1936	391.1
1937	371.9

Sources: Annual reports of the C-B.

supply-side-orientated strategy of the government the cancellation of industrial debts made some sense, because it could be regarded as an important element in decreasing the costs of production. On the other hand, it cannot be denied that the restrictive credit policy of the bank contributed to the persistent economic stagnation in Austria even after 1933.

With regard to activities abroad, the Creditanstalt had suspended them already in 1931 and had started selling off parts of its conglomerate, equities as well as whole packages of assets including outstanding loans, to national groups. The other big Viennese banks—Escompte-Gesellschaft and Bankverein—tried to maintain their position as shareholders and creditors in the Danubian area, despite the transfer moratoria and exchange controls introduced by the successor States. Immediately after the amalgamation of 1934, the Creditanstalt got rid of the Czechoslovakian assets it had inherited, and retained only the Budapest branch and the banking affiliates of the Bankverein in Yugoslavia and Poland.

Thus in the end, the Austrian banking community had by force been pushed back to those limits which it had been unwilling to accept fifteen years earlier. Only after 1938, when the Creditanstalt had been degraded to a mere junior partner of the Deutsche Bank, a new but short-lived expansion to the south-east was started, which, however, came to a sudden end with the retreat and, finally, defeat of the German Reich in 1945.

References

Ausch, K. (1968), *Als die Banken fielen* (Vienna).

Bachinger, K. (1981), *Umbruch und Desintegration nach dem 1. Weltkrieg. Österreichs wirtschaftliche und soziale Ausgangssituation in ihren Folgewirkungen auf die Erste Republik*, unpubl. diss., Vienna.

Beyen, J. W. (1949), *Money in a Maelstrom* (London).

Born, K. E. (1979), 'Die Deutsche Bank in der Inflation nach dem Ersten Weltkrieg', *Beiträge zu Wirtschafts- und Währungsfragen und zur Bankengeschichte*, 17.

Compass. Finanzielles Jahrbuch, various vols. (Vienna).

Cottrell, P. L. (1983), 'Aspects of Western Equity Investment in the Banking Systems of East Central Europe', in A. Teichova, and P. L. Cottrell (eds.), *International Business in Central Europe, 1918–1939* (Leicester).

Country Court of Vienna 26 d Vr. 6373/31–37. OZ 9: Examination Otto Deutsch; OZ 253: A. van Hengel, *Aide-mémoire* (1932).

Creditanstalt–Bankverein (C-B) Archives: Minutes of Managing Board (MMB), of the Board of Directors (MBD) of Boden-Credit-Anstalt (BCA), Creditanstalt (CA), and Bankverein (BV).

Federn, W. (1914), 'Die Kapitalserhöhungen der Banken', *Der Österreichische Volkswirt* 21 Feb.

—— (1932), 'Der Zusammenbruch der Österreichischen Kreditanstalt', *Archiv für Sozialwissenschaft und Sozialpolitik*, 67.

Kernbauer, H. (1991), *Währungspolitik in der Zwischenkriegszeit* (Vienna).

—— and Weber, F. (1986), 'Multinational Banking in the Danube Basin: The Business Strategy of the Viennese Banks after the Collapse of the Habsburg Monarchy', in A. Teichova, M. Lévy-Leboyer, and H. Nussbaum (eds.), *Multinational Enterprise in Historical Perspective* (Cambridge: Cambridge University Press).

Layton, W. T. and Rist, C. (1925), *Die Wirtschaftslage Österreichs* (Vienna)

März, E. (1984), *Austrian Banking and Financial Policy: Creditanstalt at a Turning-Point, 1913–1923* (London).

—— and Weber, F. (1983), 'The Antecedents of the Austrian Financial Crash of 1931', *Zeitschrift für Wirtschafts- und Sozialwissenschaften*, 5.

Stiefel, D. (1989), *Finanzdiplomatie und Weltwirtschaftskrise. Die Krise der Credit-Anstalt für Handel und Gewerbe 1931* (Frankfurt-am-Main).

Teichova, A. (1979), 'Versailles and the Expansion of the Bank of England into Central Europe' in N. Horn and J. Kocka (eds.), *Recht und Entwicklung der Grossunternehmen im 19. und 20. Jahrhundert* (Göttingen).

Von Mises, L. (1928), *Geldwertstabilisierung und Konjunkturpolitik* (Jena).

—— (1931), *Die Ursachen der Wirtschaftskrise* (Tübingen).

Weber, F. (1985), 'Die Österreichischen Banken in der Zwischenkriegszeit', *Christliche Demokratie*, 4.

—— (1991), *Vor dem grossen Krach. Die Krise des Österreichischen Bankwesens in den zwanziger Jahren*. Unpubl. diss., Vienna.

—— and Haas, K. (1978), 'Deutsches Kapital in Österreich', *Jahrbuch für Zeitgeschichte* (Vienna).

13

Polish Banking in the Inter-War Period

ZBIGNIEW LANDAU and WOJCIECH MORAWSKI

1. The Development of Polish Banking in the 1920s

The general trend in the development of Polish banking in the inter-war period was towards a gradual decrease in the importance of private banking and a rise in the importance of the state banks. This process was not the result of the deliberate policy of succeeding governments but of the weakness of private Polish capital and of concern of foreign capital about making large investments in a country situated between Germany and the Soviet Union.

Before the First World War private banking was most fully developed in the territory under Russian control. There were twelve joint-stock banks owning 69.8 per cent of the total capital invested in the private sector. Nine private banks in Galicia (the Austrian-held part) owned 21.7 per cent. Private banking was weakest in the Prussian-held part, with nine banks owning only 8.5 per cent of the total capital (Nowak, 1932: 357). German banking law was the most liberal. It did not demand concessions for banking—registration was sufficient. Banks could participate in the launching of business enterprises and get directly involved in industry. Russian law was at the opposite extreme—banking was subject to very strict conditions, and any links with industry other than the provision of credit were forbidden. Austrian banking law lay between those extremes. The functions of note issue were performed by central banks of the partitioning powers; their currencies were also in circulation in their particular areas. The origins of Polish banking emerged in Galicia as the Bank Krajowy, founded in 1883 and subordinated to the Galician regional authorities.

The years of the First World War turned out to be most destructive for banks in the Russian-held part. In 1915 they lost their connections with the Russian financial market. For the Galician banks the worst was the first year of the war, when the major part of Galicia fell under temporary Russian occupation. On the other hand, banks of the Prussian-held part grew in importance from 1915 when they started to extend their activity in to the area of the kingdom of Poland. In Galicia three banks existed—the Bank Krajowy and two new smaller banks, also subordinated to the regional authorities. In 1916 the Germans resolved to found a new institution in the occupied kingdom of Poland, the Polska Krajowa Kasa Po życzkowa, to issue Polish marks. The exchange of these marks against German marks at the rate of 1 : 1 after the end of war was guaranteed by the government of the Reich. That bank was subordinated to the authorities in occupation (Czapska, 1988: 23).

The system of long-term credit was based on land credit associations existing in the three areas which had been subject to partition (in the Prussian-held area since the eighteenth century, in the Russian since 1825, and in the Austrian since 1841). In the Russian-held area urban credit associations were also in operation (from 1841), and in Galicia there were three specialized mortgage banks. Communal savings banks existed in the Prussian and Austrian partitions.

Within the first years after Poland gained independence there was inflation, which in 1923 turned into hyperinflation. The inflation was initially brought about by the war waged on the eastern frontier until 1921, and then by the need to rebuild the country.

The increase in the money-issue was smaller than the budget deficit until the end of 1920 but then, from 1921, it increased more rapidly than the deficit and inflation became an instrument of interventionism. The functions of issue were still performed by the Polska Krajowa Kasa Pożyczkowa (PKKP), taken over in November 1918 by the Polish authorities. It was a state bank and issued Polish marks different in appearance from those issued by the occupying authorities. The PKKP worked for restoration of the country and for state intervention in economic development by granting credits to industrial enterprises, by rediscount credits to commercial banks, and by keeping the bank rate at a level well below the rate of inflation. As a result, within the whole period of inflation there was, in fact, a negative real interest rate (Nowak, 1932: 257–65), which allowed the bank's debtors to make remarkable profits.

Beside the PKKP, the state banking sector at that time consisted of the Bank Krajowy, which moved in November 1920 to Warsaw; and two smaller state-owned banks in Galicia: the Państwowy Bank Rolny, formerly the Polski Państwowy Bank Rolny, and the Pocztowa Kasa Oszczędności, both founded in February 1919 (Nowak, 1988: 17–24; Landau, 1989: 6–7). However, in the period of inflation these institutions did not yet operate on a large scale. The State also participated on some occasions in founding banks together with private capital (e.g. the Syndykat Przekazowy Banków Polskich SA), but those ventures were not successful.

For private banks inflation meant, on the one hand, rapid quantitative and organizational expansion and relative comfort caused by the absence of bankruptcies; on the other hand it reduced capital and decreased real financial potential. The number of joint-stock banks grew from twenty-eight at the end of 1918 to 111 at the end of 1923; the number of branches from

208 in 1920 (earlier data are not available) to 655 in 1923 (Landau and Tomaszewski, 1967: 296; Broniewski, 1939: 133). Fairly often, however, establishing numerous new branches was just a pretext for purchasing property. The banks which resisted such temptation (e.g. the Bank Dyskontowy Warszawski SA) coped better with the post-inflation crisis. The largest number of new banks, thirty-two, was founded in 1921, and in the period 1918–23 not even one bank insolvency was declared.

At the same time, however, the real value of banks' turnovers was getting smaller. The average balance sheet per bank (in million zlotys at the parity from 1927) decreased from 107.0 in 1913 to 2.68 in 1923. The capital invested in all Polish private banking, which in 1913 amounted to 708.2 million zlotys (at the parity from 1927) was worth only 0.7 million zlotys in 1923 (Nowak, 1932: 292). There were three basic ways of gaining protection—against the depreciation of capital: investment in property, shares in enterprises, and speculation in foreign currencies. The latter was economically the safest but frequently changing foreign-currency regulations made it illegal. The first two alternatives were efficient during inflation but once it was suppressed they often turned out to be traps because they did not secure the necessary liquidity of capital.

Polish banking law, which was created at that time, followed the Russian law in respect of the rules of bank licensing, but followed the German pattern with respect to connections with industry, with the banks participating in launching of business enterprises on a grand scale.

The negative real bank-rate led to a fall in deposits, the real value of which was diminishing under the pressure of inflation. In 1913 they represented 39.4 per cent of total liabilities, compared with only 17.2 per cent in 1923. Time-deposits accounted for 44.8 per cent of all deposits in 1913 but only 4 per cent in 1923 (Nowak, 1932: 299). With such changes in the structure of deposits there was an increase in cash in hand and this reduced the ability of the banks to grant credits. On the assets side, current accounts loans became more important as banks willingly shifted to this way of granting credits to friendly enterprises. The importance of pawn credit was getting smaller and mortgage credit dwindled to nothing.

In the period of inflation the importance of profits from normal bank operations was declining, while the importance of profits from shares in enterprises and from speculation in foreign currencies was rising. Organizational expansion of banking caused a remarkable increase in commercial costs, from 1.2 per cent of circulating capital in 1913 to 13.4 per cent in 1923.

In 1920 the private banks of the former Russian and Austrian partitions combined in the Zwiazek Banków w Polsce (ZBwP, Union of Banks in Poland). The banks of the former Prussian-held area established their own

Zwiazek Banków Polski Zachodniej (Union of Banks of Western Poland) which joined the ZBwP only in autumn 1923. The Union acted on behalf of banking in relation to the government. It was not a cartel agreement because usually, apart from some exceptional cases, it did not try to standardize the level of bank rate. During inflation the Union started to prevent the 'invasion' of new, weak, and often shady firms. It protected its exclusive position by eliminating unreliable banks and pressing the government to restrict the granting of concessions.

The controversy, which emerged during the first years of independence, between the adherents of the British type of banking (though in Poland it should be called rather the 'Russian type'), that is strictly discount banking, and the German type, founding and closely connected with industry, was at the time of inflation spontaneously and decidedly resolved in favour of the latter. The question reappeared after the crisis of 1925 but it did not change the shape of Polish banking. A specific form was applied to so-called branch banks which were connected with particular sectors of economy. Only two, out of about a dozen, proved to be solid (the Bank Cukrownictwa SA in Poznań and the Bank Naftowy in Lvov).

In the territory of the former Austrian-held territory new banks were often founded by Polish branches gaining independence from Viennese banks. The firms so created kept their specific relationships with their former headquarters (e.g. the Bank Unii w Polsce SA consisting of branches of the Viennese Union Bank; the Powszechny Bank Zwiazkowy w Polsce SA consisting of branches of the Wiener Bank Verein). The German banks dissolved their branches in Poland instead creating a network of four banks serving the German national minority. Danziger-Privat-Aktion-Bank was an important intermediary between German banks in Poland and their base in the Reich. The situation in Upper Silesia was slightly different. The convention dividing this territory between Poland and Germany from 1922 allowed the German banks to keep their branches there. Besides, banking in Silesia was not regulated by concessions. Therefore, the banks there were reluctant to establish branches outside the Silesian province because they would have had to apply for concessions.

French capital had already appeared in Polish banking in 1913 (the Bank dla Handlu i Przemystu w Warszawie SA) and in the period of inflation it took over two banks in Lvov (the Polski Bank Przemyslowy SA and the Powszechny Bank Kredytowy SA). It also participated, together with the Polish Government, in founding the Bank Ślaski SA in Katowice. British capital appeared on a bigger scale in 1920 when the Bank Angielsko-Polski S.A. was founded with over 50 per cent of stock belonging to the British Overseas Bank. Italian capital participated in two small banks (the Bank Zjednoczonych Ziem Polskich w Warszawie SA and the Polski Powszechny Bank Kredytowy w Katowicach SA). The following foreign capital was engaged in single banks: Czech (Polski Akcyjny Bank Komercyjny SA), American (Syndykat Przekazowy Banków Polskich SA), Latvian (Polski Akcyjny Bank Komercyjny SA), and the American Jewish Joint Distribution Committee (Bank dla Spółdzielni SA). Because of the poor quality of the numerical data for the period of inflation it is easier to say something about the trends in foreign capital investing in Polish banks at that time than about its volume.

In the second half of 1923 inflation turned into hyperinflation and reached, in October, a rate of 360 per cent per month. Industrial production had been decreasing since March, and the benefits of inflation had diminished. In these circumstances, at the beginning of 1924, the government led by Władysław Grabski carried out two reforms: fiscal and monetary. The former, by making economies in administration, cutting subsidies for railways, valorizing taxes, and introducing a new property tax, enabled a temporary balanced budget and the cessation of money issue for fiscal purposes (Tomaszewski, 1961).

Monetary reform included, after the stabilization of the Polish mark, closing down the Polska Krajowa Kasa Pożyczkowa and founding the Bank Polski SA as a bank of issue. The central bank was made a private joint-stock company in order to make it independent of the government. It was to issue a new currency, the zloty, which would have 30 per cent cover in gold, foreign currencies, and foreign exchanges (i.e. it was a gold-exchange standard). The issue of token coins and silver coins (in total up to 9.5 zlotys per capita, later raised to 12 zlotys) as well as of Treasury notes (up to 150 million zlotys) was the responsibility of the State. The Bank Polski SA started work on 28 April 1924. The parity of the zloty was settled at the level of the franc germinal, i.e. one dollar equalled 5.18 zlotys.

Although the government decided to have a private central bank it maintained three powerful institutions in the state-owned sector. In May 1924 the former Bank Krajowy, from 1922 called the Polski Bank Krajowy, was joined by two smaller Galician banks, which resulted in the foundation of the Bank Gospodarstwa Krajowego (Górecki, 1928: 5). In the situation of monetary stabilization the activities of the Pocztowa Kasa Oszczędności and the Państwowy Bank Rolny became more vigorous.

In the summer of 1925 the so-called second inflation occurred, and the zloty became unstable. There was no possibility of a return to the previous parity. In spite of that Prime Minister Grabski insisted that the Bank Polski should intervene on the Stock Exchange in order to support the currency. When the president of the bank, Stanisław Karpiński, refused, the government resigned (in November 1925). After that event the position of the Bank Polski in relation to the government was never so strong. Depreciation of the zloty was in some sense profitable, however, for it started the revival. In the spring of 1926 the zloty was stabilized at a level about 40 per cent below the previous parity, and in October 1927 official devaluation to that level was carried out, together with the extension of cover to 40 per cent and the shift to the gold-bullion standard (Landau, 1963: 176–180).

After the initial monetary stabilization in 1924 it became clear that the Polish banking network was too extended and that many weak banks would not be able to function in a normal (non-inflationary) situation. The process of liquidation of private banks was therefore inevitable. However, while Grabski thought it should happen by closing down weak firms, the banking circles saw the process as a series of fusions (Grabski, 1927: 207). The government's restrictive policy towards private banking was revealed through the Banking Law enforced by the president's decree from 27 December 1924. It evidently followed the Russian law, strengthening the system of concessions, the necessity to have a definite minimum foundation capital, division between long-term and short-term loan operations, and state control over banking.

Meanwhile, the success of Grabski's reforms in 1924 built up the atmosphere of optimism and confidence in the new currency. This was reflected, among other ways, by the increase in bank deposits. On 31 March 1924 deposits in private banks amounted to 37 million zlotys, of which time-deposits were 8.9 per cent; while on 31 December 1924 they had increased to 157.6 million zlotys, of which time-deposits were 19 per cent (RSRP, 1929: 155); and on 31 July 1925 to 212.3 million zlotys, with time-deposits accounting for 48.0 per cent (RMS, 1928: 607). Those positive trends diminished the banks' vigilance and slowed down the processes of concentration. In the course of 1924 the number of banks fell by only four and the number of branches by 125 (Landau and Tomaszewski, 1971: 235). The bank rate was being gradually normalized although, as a result of the inflationary habits and low capitalization, it was still very high. The discount rate of the Bank Polski, fixed in the spring of 1924 at 12 per cent, was lowered in November 1924 to 10 per cent. In July 1924, by the terms of the ordinance against usury, the maximum bank rate was fixed at 24 per cent (Sołowij, 1939: 89, 90) but it was not kept. On the non-bank market the rate often reached, even in short-term loans, 90 per cent yearly.

The disaster came in summer 1925 as a result of the slump in the zloty and the sudden decrease of farmer-debtors' solvency caused by a good harvest and a fall in farm prices. In September 1925 the run on the banks started. Between August and October 1925 the banks lost 44.0 per cent of their sight deposits and 36.6 per cent of time-deposits. The crisis of 1925 brought about the bankruptcy of 58 per cent of private banks in Poland. It occurred more often among new banks founded in the years of inflation (66 per cent) than among the old ones (26 per cent, Morawski, 1991: 45).

The government and the central bank faced a very difficult dilemma: whether to maintain the rate of the zloty by, among other steps, credit restrictions, lowering rediscount and raising discount rate, or to save banks by easing credit at the cost of further depreciation of the currency. The former policy was chosen. The crisis had a positive aspect in that it eliminated a lot of financial institutions which, from an economic point of view, were redundant. In order to maintain those which the Government considered worth saving, funds were obtained by the issue of Treasury notes. At first, in September 1925, Grabski estimated the needs of private banking at 25–8 million zlotys.

On 28 November 1925 the state Fundusz Pomocy Instytucjom Kredytowym (the fund supporting credit institutions) was established, with 65 million zlotys at its disposal. The biggest sum, 20 million zlotys, was assigned to the Bank Handlowy SA in Warsaw. Among big banks, apart from the Bank Zwiazku Spółek Zarobkowych SA in Poznań which survived unaided, those that received financial aid from the Government or foreign capital were maintained. The crisis of 1925 made private banking dependent on the State and on foreign capital. It also weakened public confidence in private banks. That trauma persisted and became one of the premisses of étatisme in banking in the following period.

Bank deposits had already started to increase again in the first months of 1926, mainly as a result of the rapid improvement in the economic situation. In May and June deposits decreased, but this was for political reasons (the coup d'état). Normal expansion resumed in July 1926. In the period 1926–9 deposits in private banks increased from 459 to 908 million zlotys, and short-term credits from 486 to 1,220 million zlotys. The ratio of deposits in private banks to the total sum of deposits in Polish banking fell within the same period from 38.5 per cent to 33.1 per cent, whereas the ratio of short-term credits rose from 35.1 per cent to 40.4 per cent (Żyta, 1931: 655). The total liabilities of private banks rose from 1,109 to 2,137 million zlotys, but their ratio to the total in Polish banking fell from 36.1 per cent to 29.7 per cent. In the period under discussion the reconstruction of long-term credit was undertaken, but in 1929 it amounted only to 27 per cent of the level in 1913 (Landau and Tomaszewski, 1971: 238).

The network of banks was considerably reduced: at the end of 1926 there were seventy-one banks with 218 branches, but at the end of 1929 only fifty-one banks and 164 branches. Only one new bank was founded in that time: the Bank Amerykański w Polsce S.A., belonging to the Swedish-American syndicate of Ivar Kreuger. The system of links with foreign capital underwent certain changes. The ties with Czech and Latvian capital were cut and the position of French capital weakened. Austrian and Italian capital became stronger in Polish banking. Belgian, Swedish, and Swiss capital were involved only with single banks.

The State's growing importance in relation to banking was manifested in the new banking law enforced by the president's ordinance of 17 March 1928. This strengthened the Treasury Ministry's control over the banks.

2. The Banks in the Economic Crisis

The great economic crisis lasted longer in Poland than in many other countries, starting in autumn 1929 and continuing until 1935. The main factor prolonging the crisis was the deepening economic recession in Polish agriculture, on which the majority of population depended, and which produced more than half the national income. The crisis affected both production and the system of banking and credit. The situation of the private banks was much more difficult than that of those in the state sector. The private banks encountered serious problems in withdrawing credits granted before the crisis, and this made it impossible for them to repay their depositors on time. That, in turn, caused uneasiness among savers. Fearing the possible insolvency of the banks they withdrew their deposits and investments in order, in many cases, to place them in the state-owned banks which were regarded as more secure.

It is difficult to present an exact account of the contraction of deposits in the private banks because the data provided by various sources differ to a high degree. The decrease had already started in the second term of 1931. It was probably connected with the bankruptcy of a medium-sized bank, the M. Stadthagen S.A. in Bydgoszcz and of the well-known Bank Handlowy SA in Łódz. In May 1931 the collapse of the Österreichische Credit Anstalt and of Amstelbank caused real panic. At first, depositors began withdrawing funds from the banks connected with Austrian capital. Bankruptcies of several German banks strengthened the tendency. According to the data of the Chief Bureau of Statistics, deposits in private banks decreased in 1931 by 428 million zlotys, or 39 per cent (MRS, 1936: 144), whereas the Union of Banks in Poland put the decline at 50 per cent (SZBP, 1932: 9).

In 1932 the situation eased to some extent, although the outflow of deposits continued and, according to official data, amounted to about 160 million zlotys (Landau and Tomaszewski, 1982: 289). In 1933 deposits decreased by 100 million zlotys. However, according to the Ministry of Treasury's estimates, in period 1931–3 the private banks lost 588 million zlotys in domestic deposits and 330 million in foreign credits (Uzasadnienie, 1925: 26). Deposits decreased in 1933 by 54 per cent when compared with 1930. That situation remained unchanged until 1935.

The circulating capitals of the private banks decreased in similar measure. In 1930 they amounted to 2,366 million zlotys, while in 1934 this had halved to only 1,200 million zlotys. At the same time, however, the deposits in public banks (owned by the State and by local governments) increase by 52 per cent from 1,301 million zlotys in 1930 to 1,976 million in 1935 (SZBP, 1935: 9). In consequence, while the private institutions held 38.5 per cent of deposits and investments at the end of 1926, this had fallen to only 18 per cent by the middle of 1934 and 29 per cent in 1935.

The more favourable situation of the public banks was explained by the greater confidence of savers and, more significantly, by substantial help from the Government. First of all, within the period of the crisis, the Government increased its investments in the state-owned banks from 950 million zlotys in 1929 to 1,269 million in 1935. In addition, these banks had various kinds of legal privileges, such as dispensation from most taxes, dispensation from income tax for deposits in the state-owned Pocztowa Kasa Oszczedności SA, and also some privileges concerning execution of dues, etc.

The central bank also gave more help to state-owned banks than to the private ones, reflected, for example, in the higher rate of rediscounted credits. In the private banks rediscount at the Bank Polski amounted to 47 per cent of the credits granted in 1935, while in the state-owned banks it was 74 per cent (Knakiewicz, 1967: 186). The development of the activities of the state banks, especially of the Bank Gospodarstwa Krajowego, created a situation in which many of the credits which the bank granted to private enterprises were not repaid. Those credits were usually granted by order of the state authorities who wanted to support some enterprises important to the country for military, economic, or social reasons. Thus, the bank took those enterprises under its direct management, building up the so-called syndicate of the Bank Gospodarstwa Krajowego. By 1935 the BGK's share in the joint-stock capital of the private joint-stock companies amounted to 39 million zlotys (Konderski, 1962: 69). During the crisis two new joint-stock banks owned by the State were founded. The Bank Polska Kasa Opieki SA was established at the end of 1929, and its main objective was to take care of the savings of Polish economic emigrants. In May 1933 the Bank Akceptacyjny SA was founded with the aim of helping credit institutions which carried out conversion of credits for agriculture together with lowering the bank rate and prolongation of repayment.

In supporting its sector the State did not intend to eliminate private banking; its approach was actually hostile to economic *étatisme*. The development of the public sector in banking resulted mainly from the necessity of filling certain gaps in the credit market which threatened the economic system of the country. It was for this reason that the Government considered it important to help private credit institutions. The Minister of Treasury, in one of his conclusions at a meeting of the Economic Committee of Ministers, stated directly (Uzasadnienie, 1935: 26) that

help for private credit institutions in Poland from the State is necessary not only in order to support private banking, but also for some other reasons of a more general nature. The task is to keep the entire credit market stable and to maintain our structure of credits as a whole. Serious destablization of private banking may bring about inestimable consequences for the whole banking system, including the State and public credit institutions.

However, because of the Treasury's lack of adequate financial means the government decided—for example, in 1925—to save the big private banks first of all, leaving the small ones to look after themselves.

On 17 March 1931 a regulation was enforced which furnished the Government with the right to support private credit institutions financially up to 20 million zlotys. This sum turned out to be insufficient, and on 27 October 1932 an ordinance of the president of the Polish Republic regarding financial support for credit institutions was put into force. It provided that the support could be given in the form of loans, partial or total take-over of the joint-stock capital, giving a state guarantee, remission of debts, or relief from other obligations. On the basis of these regulations the private banks had by 1934 received financial support of 140 million zlotys, and in 1935 the Government assigned another 18 million zlotys for the reform of one of the biggest private banks—the Bank Handlowy SA in Warsaw (Landau and Tomaszewski, 1970: 96–9).

Through support for private credit institutions the State increased its share in the private banking sector. For example, when the Bank Zwiazku Spółek Zarobkowych w Poznaniu SA (one of the biggest private credit institutions) was being reformed, the State became the owner of 78 per cent of the joint-stock capital, sufficient to enable it to exercise full control over the institution. The Bank Handlowy w Warszawie SA also became highly dependent on the government which, however, owned none of the bank's capital. As a result of the changes which occurred at this time the predominantly private banks were compelled to reduce their share capital. For example, the capital of the Bank Handlowy w Warszawie SA was reduced by 50 per cent (from 30 to 15 million zlotys), and that of the Bank Zwiazku Spolek Zarobkowych w Poznaniu SA by 75 per cent (from 20 to 5 million zlotys).

As the Government's support was directed mainly at the most important private banks, the smaller ones went bankrupt during the crisis. Some of them declared insolvency, others united with stronger banks. As a result, the number of private banks fell from fifty-seven in 1930 to thirty-three in 1935, and their branches decreased from 136 to eighty-four. The reduction in the branches of foreign banks in Poland—from thirteen to ten—was less serious (MRS, 1931: 79; 1936: 136). Overall, the total assets of private banks decreased by 63 per cent in the period 1929–35. For comparison it should be mentioned that over the same period the total assets of the state-owned banks increased considerably. The Pocztowa Kasa Oszczędności expanded by 101 per cent, from 505 to 1,016 million zlotys; the Bank Gospodarstwa

Krajowego by 27 per cent, from 1,778 to 2,254 million zlotys; and the Państowowy Bank Rolny by 14 per cent, from 744 to 846 million zlotys.

The position of the central bank was much worse. Its balance sheet decreased by 20 per cent, from 2,256 to 1,818 million zlotys. Formally, the Bank Polski SA was still a private joint- stock company, but its dependence on the government became stronger during the crisis. The reasons were political rather than economic in nature. The group then ruling Poland wanted to introduce an authoritarian regime. Therefore, their aim was to subordinate not only political and administrative institutions, but also the most important economic institutions. This policy was made easier by the appointment of Wladyslaw Wroblewski as president of the Bank Polksi SA in 1929. He was a former ambassador in Washington and had no knowledge of banking or finance. As Zygmunt Karpiński, an expert in the history of the Bank Polski SA and its former director, wrote: 'not expressing his own opinions in important matters concerning the bank, [Wróblewski] became rather an executor of the wishes of the Government and the Minister of Treasury, the exponent of which was commissioner of the bank' (Karpiński, 1958: 210–11).

It has already been mentioned that foreign credits were being withdrawn from Polish banks during the great crisis. The outflow of investments and credits was one of the important causes of the difficult situation of private banking at that time. Foreign capital was invested in Polish credit institutions in short-term renewable credits rather than by buying shares. Therefore, it is very difficult to determine the degree to which foreign participation in Polish banking changed within the period 1930–5; the more so because the granting of foreign credit and the acquisition of share was often undertaken, not directly by foreign institutions, but formally by Polish institutions in which, however, foreign capital was of primary importance. At the end of 1931 it was estimated that twenty-five private banks with foreign connections possessed 54 per cent of all private banks' own capital funds and 58 per cent of deposits. Of this 30 per cent fell to the share of six banks under the influence of Austrian banks and having connections with Austrian capital (for example, the Bank Dyskontowy SA w Warszawie, the Akcyjny Bank Hipoteczny we Lwowie, the Ślaski Zakład Kredytowy SA w Bielsku, the Powszechny Bank Zwiazkowy SA, and the Powszechny Bank Kredytowy SA). In the second place there were nine banks connected with German capital (among them the Poznański Bank dla Handlu i Przemysłu SA, the Górnośląski Bank Dyskontowy SA, and the Bank Komercjalny SA w Krakowie). Belgian, British, and Swedish capital also had shares in Polish banking (Smerek, 1933: 40–3).

As a result of the weakened position of the private banks the volume of short-term credit granted by them decreased by 57 per cent in the years 1929–5, whereas in the state-owned banks the reduction was only 10 per cent, and in the Bank Polski SA there was an increase of 11 per cent. Since, however, from 1928 it had been mainly the private banks which granted short-term credits, the overall level dropped by 26 per cent (MRS, 1937: 203). At the same time the volume of long-term credits, being mainly managed by the state-owned banks was increasing. The share of the state banks in the total of those credits increased from 92 per cent in 1929 to 96 per cent in 1935 (Breit, 1935: 95). That increase, however, was to some extent apparent as a result of difficulties in paying off short-term debts which were thus converted into long-term ones. For example, new issues of mortgage bonds, which in 1928 amounted to 150 million zlotys, by 1933 were only 0.7 million zlotys, recovering to 4.8 million in 1934 and 16.2 million in 1935. Those sums were very small, though in the period 1929–35 the ratio of long-term credit to all credits granted by Polish credit system also increased from 36 per cent to 61 per cent (Zalewski, 1938: 144).

3. Recovery and War, 1935–1939

In autumn 1935 the beginnings of prosperity could be noticed. This was connected, among other things, with the shift to the policy of interventionism through intensification of the public- sector's financial investments. At the same time, the situation of banking, both state-owned and private, also improved, although the former—and the banks depending on it—were still in a better condition than the latter.

It is difficult to determine the extent to which the position of the private banks improved because different sources provided conflicting data. For example, deposits in private banks in 1938 were estimated as 712 million zlotys in the *Concise Statistical Year-Book of Poland* published by the Chief Bureau of Statistics; as 1,001 million in the report of the Union of Banks in Poland; as 682 million in the report of the Bank Polski SA; and as 725 million in the report of the Bank Gospodarstwa Krajowego (Landau and Tomaszewski, 1989: 394). Therefore, there were corresponding differences in the estimates of the participation of private banks in all deposits and investments placed in credit institutions. For example, for 1936–8 it was 18–19 per cent according to the Bank Gospodarstwa Krajowego, whereas according to the Union of Banks in Poland it was 20–7 per cent (SBGK, 1936: 15; 1938: 11).

However, no matter which data we consider more reliable, it appears that the importance of private banking, although growing slightly in the post-crisis period, was still definitely less than that of the state banks. Moreover, the data for the end of the year do not reflect great changes within particular years. In some periods banks were subject to sudden withdrawals of deposits by uneasy savers. The first outflow of deposits in this period was caused by the uncertainty

about the Polish Government's views on monetary policy, especially after
the imposition of some exchange controls in 1936, although the convertibility of the zlotys was not formally suspended. At that point the disturbed
clients withdrew 21 million zlotys from the private banks. As a result of the
Anschluss and, almost at the same time, of the deterioration in Polish–
Lithuanian relationships a further sum of approximately 100 million zlotys was
withdrawn from banks. Another surge of withdrawals was connected with the
Reich's preparations for the capture of Czechoslovakia, which cost the private
banks 58 million zlotys and the banking system as a whole about 300 million
zlotys (about 10 per cent of all deposits). Usually, after the political situation
eased, the deposits returned to banks.

In March 1939, after the German invasion of Czechoslovakia, 500 million
zlotys were withdrawn; and this situation continued for several months
because of fears about the outbreak of a German–Polish war. This greatly
aggravated the position of the private banks and forced them look for help
to the Bank Polski SA. The latter, too, faced some difficulties, and finally
agreed to the Government's demand to relax temporarily the requirement
that issues of the zloty should be based on the reserves of gold and foreign
currencies. In February 1939 the statute of the Bank Polski S.A. was
modified to authorize it to issue 800 million zlotys without cover, with the
possibility of raising this sum to 1.2 billion zlotys. To underline the
importance of that amount it should be added that the total banknote
circulation on 31 December 1938 was 1.406 billion zlotys (SBP, 1938: 22, 29,
33). The funds from the fiduciary issue were to be used both for financing
Poland's preparations for war and for providing the banking system with the
money necessary for payment of the withdrawn deposits. The Bank Polski
SA was becoming more dependent on the Treasury Minister, and was
compelled to carry out the policies imposed on it. This was often done
unwillingly, and sometimes the Bank's authorities tried to argue against the
Government's demands, but their position had already been undermined.

In total, the deposits in the banking system increased from 2,483 to 3,660
million zlotys (by 47 per cent) in the years 1935–8. In 1938, 27 per cent of
deposits were held by the private banks and 73 per cent by the state and
municipal banks. The level of deposits in the private banks was only 92 per
cent of what it had been in 1930 before the crisis. Over the same time
deposits in the state and municipal banks increased by 104 per cent. There
was keen competition for deposits between the two sectors, pushing the
private banks into a defensive position. Thus, although the number of
private banks was still decreasing (from thirty-three in 1935 to twenty-six in
1936), the number of branches remained constant at eight-four. The number
of branches of foreign banks in Poland decreased from ten to nine.

The total assets of the private banks was still behind that of the Bank
Polski SA and the Bank Gospodarstwa Krajowego, but it moved ahead of

the Pocztowa Kasa Oszczędności and the Państwowy Bank Rolny. In the years 1935–8 the assets of the private banks increased by 12 per cent, of the Bank Gospodarstwa Krajowego by 22 per cent, of the Pocztowa Kasa Oszczędności by 21 per cent, of the Bank Polski SA and the Państwowy Bank Rolny by 10 per cent. This reflected a considerable reduction in the disparity in the rates of growth of the two sectors.

It should be remembered, however, that joint-stock banks in which there was significant state participation (for example, the Bank Zwiazku Spółek Zarobkowych SA w Poznaniu), as well as those that depended on the State indirectly, such as the Bank Handlowy w Warszawie, were included among the private banks. The State did not participate in the share capital of the Bank Handlowy w Warszawie SA but controlled it through granting special credit to a group of west Polish sugar mills which thus became very influential in relation to the bank. The influence of the State on the Bank Handlowy w Warszawie strengthened when the former president of the Bank Polski SA, Adam Koc, became a member of the board and a former officer of the Treasury Ministry was made a member of the management (Landau and Tomaszewski, 1970: 76–79).

The outflow of deposits and foreign credits granted to the private banks continued, although on a lesser scale. In 1939 they were estimated at 100 million zlotys, whereas in 1929 they had been 700 million zlotys. However, in the years 1935–7 foreign participation in the share capital of the private banks was growing (from 39 to 47 per cent; data for the following years are not available) (MRS, 1937: 95, 108). Nevertheless, the growth of participation in the share capital did not mean a financial inflow but only the taking-over of the shares of some credit institutions which were unable to clear their debts. The decrease in the foreign liabilities of the banks had, on the one hand, a positive effect because it loosened their strong dependence on foreign creditors and allowed a reduction in the transfer of foreign exchange for debt payments. On the other hand, it reduced the funds at the banks' disposal. With domestic capitalization progressing relatively slowly it was quite difficult to replace the credits withdrawn from other sources.

The poor condition of the private banks every now and again set new tasks for the state banks, especially in the sphere of financing state investments and granting long-term credits for private economic initiatives. Thus, the state-owned banks did not aim at gaining higher profits; their highest priority was to support the economic policy of the State. Long-term credits increased considerably in 1935–8, that is by 25 per cent (from 2,113 to 2,634 million zlotys). Within the same period short-term credits increased by only 17 per cent (from 2,831 to 3,305 million zlotys). However, if we take the pre-crisis year 1928 as the base for comparison, the level of short-term credits is still 13 per cent lower, while long-term credits are 138 per cent higher. The main reasons for this were discussed earlier in this chapter, but the additional cause in 1936–8 was the financing of the Government's programme of investments by the state-owned and municipal banks.

Despite the gradual reduction of the discount rate of the Bank Polski SA (from 5 per cent in 1933–7 to 4.5 per cent) (Sołowij, 1939: 87–8), it was still higher than in many other European countries. The relatively high discount rate of the central bank resulted in a relatively higher cost of credit. The rate could not be lowered because this would require, at the same time, a reduction in the interest on deposits and savings investments, which in turn might discourage the savers from placing their funds with domestic credit institutions. Higher rates of interest on deposits in Poland could counter-act—although not always efficiently—the transfer of capital abroad to make more profitable or more secure investments there. From the formal point of view it was illegal (from 1936), but not everybody obeyed that ban.

Summing up, it may be stated that the primary feature of the development of the banking system in Poland was the gradual increase in the influence of the State. It affected the private banks as well as the central bank founded in 1924, and it should be stated clearly that it was not the result of any ideological or theoretical conception but of the necessity for the State to fill a certain gap in the credit system. Another feature of the Polish banking system was the dependence of private banks on foreign funds, developing until the great crisis. That development was carried out, not through investments in the share capital of credit institutions but through the granting of short-term credits. The great crisis started the process of withdrawal of those deposits, which was simultaneous with the increase in foreign participation in the share capital of the banks. It resulted from taking over a part of the shares in return for unpaid loans. It should be kept in mind that Polish statistics of the participation of foreign capital in the share capital of the banks were highly inexact because of the difficulty of ascertaining the true position where bank shares were owned by institutions which were formally Polish but which were themselves effectively dependent on foreign capital. The rapid outflow of foreign credits was one of the important factors weakening the private banks and forcing the government to participate directly in the credit market.

References

Archival Sources

Uzasadnienie do scisle tajnego wniosku Ministra Skarbu . . . z 12 lutego 1935 (abbr. Uzasadnienie (1935), in *Archiwum Akt Nowych* (Warsaw: fond: Komitet Ekonomiczny Ministrów, vol. 1258.

Official and Statistical Sources

Mały Rocznik Statystyczny (MRS) (1931; 1936; 1937; 1939) (Warsaw: GUS Press).
Rocznik Ministerstwa Skarbu (RMS) (1928) (Warsaw).
Rocznik Statyki Rzeczypospolitej Polskiej (RSRP) (1924) (Warsaw: GUS Press).
Sprawozdanie Banku Gospodarstwa Krajowego (SBGK) (1936; 1938) (Warsaw).
Sprawozdanie Banku Polskiego (SBP) (1938) (Warsaw).
Sprawozdanie Zwiazku Banków w Polsce (SZBP) (1932; 1935) (Warsaw).

Books and Articles

Breit, M. (1935), 'Koniunkturalny rozwoj kredytu długoterminowego w Polsce', *Prace Instytutu Badania Koniunktur i Cen*, 1.
Broniewski, W. (1939), 'Banking in Poland', *The Banker*, 1: 132–6.
Czapska, E. (1988), 'Polska Krajowa Kasa Pożyczkowa', *Bank i Kredyt*, 5–6: 21–30.
Górecki R. (1928), *The Activity of the National Economic Bank* (Warsaw: BGK Press).
Grabski, W. (1927), *Dwa lata pracy u podstaw państwowoś naszej (1924–1925)* (Warsaw: F. Hoesick Press).
Karpinski, Z. (1958), *Bank Polski 1924–1939* (Warsaw: PWG Press).
Knakiewicz, Z. (1967), *Deflacja polska 1930–1935* (Warsaw: PWE Press).
Konderski, W. (1962), *Z dziatalności banków polskich w latach 1928–1935* (Warsaw: KiW Press).
Landau, Z. (1963), *Plan stabilizacyjny 1927–1930. Geneza, zatożenia, wyniki* (Warsaw: KiW Press).
—— (1989), 'Powstanie Pocztowej Kasy Oszczędności na tle istniejacych warunków politycznych i sytuacji gospodarczej Polski', *Bank i Kredyt*, 4–5: 6–11.
—— and Tomaszewski, J. (1967), *W dobie inflacji 1918–1923* (Warsaw: KiW Press).
—— (1970), *Bank Handlowy w Warszawie SA Historia i rozwódj 1870–1970* (Warsaw).
—— —— (1971), *Od Grabskiego do Pilsudskiego. Okres kryzysu poinflacyjnego i ożywienia koniunktury 1924–1929* (Warsaw: KiW Press).
—— —— (1982), *Wielki kryzys gospodarczy 1930–1935* (Warsaw: KiW Press).
—— —— (1989), *Lata interwencjonizmi panstwowego 1936–1939* (Warsaw: KiW Press).
Morawski, W. (1991) 'Polska bankowość prywatna w okresie inflacji 1918–1923', *Bank i Kredyt*, 5–6: 40–6.
Nowak, H. (1932), *Bankowosc w Polsce* (Warsaw: Bank Polski Press)
Nowak, M. (1988), *Panstwowy Bank Rolny w Drugiej Rzeczypospolitej* (Kraków: Jagiellonian University Press).
Smerek, M. (1933), 'Kapitaly zagraniczne w bankowosci polskiej', *Bank*, 1: 10–17; 2: 39–49.
Sołowij, T. (1939), *Rynek pieniężny i stopa procentowa w Polsce* (Warsaw).
Tomaszewski, J. (1961), *Stabilizacja waluty w Polsce 1924–1925. Z badan nad polityka gospodarcza rządu polskiego przed przewrotem majowym* (Warsaw: KiW Press).
Zalewski, S. (1938), *Ewolucja kredytu dlugoterminowego w Polsce* (Warsaw).
Żyła, K. (1931), 'Banki prywatne w latach 1926–1930', in S. Starzynski (ed.), *Pięć lat na froncie gospodarczym*, i (Warsaw: Droga Press): 652–69.

14

Budgetary Policy, Money Supply, and Banking in Bulgaria between the Wars

LJUBEN BEROV

1. Introduction

Analysis of inter-war economic policy and of the main economic indicators in the former socialist countries of Eastern Europe is not only a question of the history of the past. It is closely linked to the current economic situation and policy of these countries because the main task of the economic reforms following the collapse of the communist regimes is to change the economic and political system. This requires the replacement of the discredited socialist system (based on state property and a centrally planned command economy) with a market-oriented or capitalist economy. This is a return to capitalism as it existed in these countries before the Second World War. In some cases, the historical experience of this type of economy in individual East European countries between the two world wars may give some indication of the direction economic reforms should take.

The period between the two world wars was one of significant change in the economy of all European countries, and especially in Bulgaria. There were drastic changes in prices and in the exchange rate of the national currency (the Bulgarian lev), and also changes in the general orientation of the economic policy of the State. After a period of very liberal economic policy Bulgaria turned in the 1930s toward intensive state intervention in many fields, including credit, industrial production, trade in agricultural products, labour relations, foreign trade, and the currency regime. After headlong inflation during and immediately after the war, the free convertibility of the former golden Bulgarian lev was replaced by a partially convertible paper currency with many restrictions. Of course, it would be incorrect to comment on the 1920s and the 1930s as a whole because the situation was not the same. There is also a significant difference between the two parts of the 1920s—the subperiods 1919–23 and 1924–9.

During the years immediately after the First World War, and until the summer of 1923, prices in Bulgaria rose dramatically. In 1918 the average level of prices was only six times the pre-war level (1912), but by 1923 it had risen thirty times (see Table 14.1). The rate of exchange between the Bulgarian lev and the relatively stable Swiss franc rose at a slightly slower pace: by 1923 it was only twenty-two times the 1912 level because of the state monopoly of the trade in foreign currency introduced immediately after the war (Hadginikolov and Berov, 1982: 541–2). After the *coup d'état* and the end of the regime of Al. Stambolisky (the leader of the Bulgarian Agrarian Union) in June 1923 further inflation was almost eliminated, and prices increased very slowly till the autumn of 1929, with some variation.

The economic crisis of 1929–33 brought a sharp fall in all prices in Bulgaria (about three times as an average for agricultural commodities, and about two for industrial commodities). After this crisis economic conditions changed in 1934 and there was a cyclical revival during the second half of the 1930s. During this period prices rose again, but slowly and without regaining the 1929 level.

The main reason for all these changes in the level of prices is to be found in the budget policy and in the money supply. Of course, other (real) factors should also be also mentioned, for example, changes in the volume of the industrial and agricultural production, in the balance of payments, and in the export and import of commodities for private consumption; changes in savings; the influence of prices in world trade (reflected through the current rate of exchange); and the inflow or withdrawal of foreign capital. So the degree of correlation between budgetary policy, money supply, and level of prices must be carefully analysed.

TABLE 14.1. *Index of prices and rate of exchange in Bulgaria, 1912–1923*

	General index of retail prices (1912 = 100) (1)	Rate of exchange for the Swiss franc (leva for 100 francs) (2)
1912	100	100
1915	125	107
1916	201	136
1917	360	173
1918	697	166
1919	1,315	433
1920	2,460	1,054
1921	2,272	1,958
1922	2,756	2,846
1923	3,045	2,281

Source: Ekon. Bulg. (1969: 494).

The statistical data

Detailed investigation of these factors during the 1920s, and especially in 1919–23, is made very difficult by the large gaps in Bulgarian statistics. Although Bulgaria stood out among the capitalist countries for having rather well-organized economic statistics, the development of statistics covering the banking system were less satisfactory (*Stat. god.* 1925: 290–5). Data on the basic indices for private banks were not officially published in statistical annuals until 1929. For the 1911–28 period, a similar statistical surveillance was carried out by the department of financial studies of the Bulgarian National Bank, but publication of the data was restricted. For similar reasons, more detailed data on Bulgaria's balance of payments are also lacking until 1924. Information about Bulgaria's national income (based on the investigations of A. Chakalov) is available only for the period after 1924.

During the 1920s more detailed annual statistics for the basic indices of the country's industrial output are also lacking, except for the 1921 data covering all industrial enterprises with more than ten workers. Official annual publication of statistical data in the field of industry only started to appear in specialized statistical works and in the general statistical annuals in 1929. Until that year the annuals contained irregular and limited information about some branches of industrial production under the fiscal supervision of the State, such as the production of sugar, salt, and tobacco products. Indeed, at that time all large industrial enterprises employing more than ten workers regularly submitted annual statistical reports to the Ministry of Trade, Industry, and Labour, but those reports were statistically summarized only with respect to a number of general indices, and referred exclusively to the 1911–12 and 1923–9 periods. This marks the beginning of detailed annual industrial statistics.

Up to the First World War there were no statistical data on the development of stockbreeding output in the country—there is only incomplete information on cattle slaughtered at the slaughter-houses and a single representative inquiry into agrarian output in 1933–4. No statistics are available on unemployment up to 1935. Even after that the existing information provides data only about the number of people seeking jobs through specially established employment offices, and the number of those employed; it does not cover the total number of the unemployed in the country or their ratio to the whole 'working class'. The inadequate coverage is due to the existence of a great number of semi-proletarian poor farmers or younger members of their families who, without completely joining the working class were constantly migrating between urban and rural areas in accordance with fluctuations in employment; if unemployed in the town, they temporarily went back to the village.

2. Money and Prices

Changes from the war to 1923

Because of the gaps in the statistical information for the period before 1923 a separate analysis of the situation before and after 1923 is necessary.

During the First World War the budget policy of the Government was characterized by large annual deficits (Berov, 1985): the State financed the war mainly by printing new paper money. After the war, budget deficits continued to be significant until 1923. The main reason for this was the extraordinary expenditures made to comply with the Neuilly-sur-Seine Peace Treaty, and the belated payment made from 1919 for the livestock, vehicles, grain, etc. commandeered during the war. For the fiscal year 1919–20 the deficit amounted to 469 million leva, and for 1921–2 to 1,043 million leva. As a result, the amount of money in circulation rose repeatedly (only after 1924 was it kept relatively stable, with variations of not more than ± 12 per cent). The results of this budget policy can be seen in the abrupt increase in the amount of the money in circulation, and in the size of the unconsolidated debt of the Treasury to the Bulgarian National Bank (see Table 14.2).

Analysis of the Treasury's debt for each year until 1923 shows no strict interrelation between this index and variations in the general price index.

TABLE 14.2. *Prices, debt of the state treasury and money in circulation, 1912–1923*

	Index of 'market' (retail) prices	Unconsolidated debt of the State Treasury to the Bulgarian National Bank	Amount of money in circulation (yearly average)	
	(1912 = 100) (1)	(m. leva at 1 Jan.) (2)	m. leva (3)	(1912 = 100) (4)
1912	100	—	132	100
1913	110	7	188	142
1914	112	146	195	148
1915	125	134	269	204
1916	201	146	569	433
1917	360	260	1,148	873
1918	697	612	1,884	1,433
1919	1,315	839	2,509	1,911
1920	2,460	1,742	3,266	2,480
1921	2,272	2,891	3,301	2,502
1922	2,756	3,667	3,789	2,881
1923	3,045	4,600	3,863	2,928

Budget deficits were not always formulated as officially declared debt of the State to the National Bank. They were often partially covered by funds belonging to other public institutions or hidden in other balances of the State Bank. Hence, a direct statistical connection between increases in the state debt to the National Bank and in the amount of paper circulation in the country are not to be expected.

There is a much closer parallel between the average annual amount of paper money in circulation and the increase in the general price index (see Table 14.2), but this cannot be regarded as the only causal relationship. For example, by 1917 the general price index reached 3.6 times the 1912 level, whereas the volume of paper circulation had increased 8.7 times over the same period. For 1919 the corresponding levels are 13.1 against 19.1, and for 1921 22.7 and 25.0. The apparently lower rate of increase of the official price index during and immediately after the First World War can be partly explained by the existing system of ration coupons under which goods were supplied at artificially low prices fixed by the State, while 'black market' sales at considerably higher prices were excluded from the official price index. By the end of 1919, however, ration coupons and the policy of fixed prices were almost completely abolished. Nevertheless, even under the conditions of a more liberal economic policy, the difference between the two indices did not diminish until 1922–3.

The presence of an insufficiently strong parallel relationship between the movements of the price index, and of the average annual volume of money in circulation (M1), shows the extent to which the rate of inflation depended on other factors. The most important of these was the deposits in credit

TABLE 14.3. *Bank deposits and general amount of potential purchasing-capacity of the population of Bulgaria, 1912–1923*

	Bank deposits (million leva) in				Potential purchasing capacity of the population (bank deposits and money in circulation)	
	Private	Bulgarian Agricultural Bank and Bulgarian Central Co-operative Bank	Postal Savings Bank	Credit co-operatives and 'Popular banks'		
					m. leva	Index (1912 = 100)
	(1)	(2)	(3)	(4)	(5)	(6)
1912	63	75	—	5	275	100
1918	547	283	141	20	2,875	1,047
1919	839	291	110	40	3,789	1,380
1920	1,072	400	98	200	5,036	1,833
1921	1,384	601	97	400	5,783	2,105
1922	1,287	885	96	600	6,657	2,423
1923	1,550	1,290	79	831	7,613	2,775

institutions (private joint-stock banks, some state banks, popular co-operative banks, and agricultural credit co-operatives). The amount of these deposits, together with the funds in possession of the public (the amount of money in circulation) gives M2, equivalent to the overall amount of the potential purchasing capacity of individuals and capitalist enterprises. Its movement does not always run completely parallel to the amount of money circulation itself, since households and firms could, to a different degree, spend or save their current incomes (they could, also to a varying degree, keep the income saved either in ready money or in deposits with the banks). In Table 14.3 an attempt is made, despite the shortage of statistical information noted above, to provide a general picture of deposit movement in Bulgaria during the first stage of inflation from the end of the war to 1923.

In this connection, however, one should bear in mind that the extent of the price movement depended not only on the demand from consumers and businesses but also on changes on the supply side in the volume of material goods and services available on the home market. Clearly, it is possible for prices not to increase, even after a considerable rise in the volume of money circulation, when this is accompanied by a matching or greater increase in production and in the quantity of imported commodities. For this reason, an attempt has been made in Table 14.4 to present an overall evaluation of the changes in agricultural and industrial output (the changes in other branches, such as handicrafts, construction, transport, etc., are assumed to have moved along approximately the same lines). This index can be provisionally accepted as an approximate indicator of the growth of the aggregate material product at constant prices.

When considering changes in the supply of goods relative to the potential purchasing capacity of the population (or M2), account should also be taken

TABLE 14.4. *Gross national product in Bulgaria, 1912–1923*

	Index of agricultural production (1912 = 100)	Index of stock-breeding production (1910 = 100)	Index of industrial production (1911 = 100)	General index of gross product in main branches of material production (1911–12 = 100)	Index of potential purchasing power divided into index of GNP (1912 = 100)
	(1)	(2)	(3)	(4)	(5)
1912	100	—	101	100	100
1919	81	90	80	83	1,662
1920	75	102	100	83	2,215
1921	78	104	123	88	2,393
1922	77	107	138	90	2,696
1923	85	110	153	97	2,860

of the flow of goods to or from the country. In reality, however, this could not lead to more accurate results since the Bulgarian foreign-trade statistics for the inter-war period—especially for the years 1919–28—did not cover either actual export prices for some significant items, for example, tobacco; or exports by firms working with foreign capital. It is not certain how completely they recorded on their customs declarations at the Bulgarian border the real selling-prices for the tobacco exported. The matter is further complicated because occasionally (especially in the early 1920s) the export or import of certain items was registered by Bulgarian statistics at a later date, so that the commodity in question was only included in the statistics in the year following the actual exports. Due to these factors the active or passive balance of trade is not taken into consideration. An additional reason for statistical uncertainty is that it is not possible to establish the degree to which the inflow of foreign goods during a passive trade balance was due to goods imported on consignment or against long- or short-term trade credits in foreign currencies.

Division of the index of the potential purchasing capacity on the home market (col. (6) of Table 14.3) by the aggregate material product (col. (4) of Table 14.4) results in a combined index reflecting the activity of the basic economic factors (*Stopanska Istoria*, 1981: 333–5). Comparing the alterations in that index (col. (5) of Table 14.4) and those in the common price index in column (1) of Table 14.1 shows a higher degree of parallelism than that obtained when tracing the amount of money circulation only. The extent of the deviations between the level of the price index for a given year and the combined index as shown in Table 14.4 for the period 1919–23 is 12 per cent less than that obtained by comparing the price index with the money-circulation index.

As can be seen, the initial increase in prices was due to a combination of a large increase in money in circulation and deposits with a diminished supply of goods and services (compared to pre-war levels) during the post-war economic crisis, which lasted until 1923 (Berov, 1983).

Stabilization, 1924–1929

It was only from 1924 that the Bulgarian National Bank managed to end the rapid expansion of the volume of money in circulation, and thus keep prices from shooting up (*Stat god.*, 1942: 604–5). It was not, however able to avoid two further weak, short-lived increases in prices, in 1925 and 1928–9 (see Table 14.5). The available statistical data show that the second of these two waves was weaker than the first. The series of 'market price statistics' (the actual statistics covering retail prices in urban areas) shows that prices rose by 7 per cent in 1925, while in 1929 the annual increase was 11 per cent. However, according to the new—and more reliable—retail price index begun in 1926 and covering an expanded range of commodities, the cost of living rose by only 1 per cent in 1929. More important, it is clear that the temporary forcing up of prices during the late 1920s does not match the rate of inflation in the earlier part of the decade.

1924–9 thus marked a new stage in the post-war development of Bulgaria, characterized by a slight and unsteady further increase of the price level without any really pressing attempts at partial deflation policy to reduce the volume of money in circulation through external state loans. There were still budget deficits in some years of the period. For the fiscal year 1923–4, the deficit amounted to 116 million leva; in 1925–6 it soared to 1,112 million leva. It did not, however, lead to an increase in the average annual amount of money in circulation as a clearing-house was set up in 1925, registering and partially or completely compensating for mutual payments between the banks, insurance companies, and some other enterprises, thus speeding up the velocity of circulation. Another factor helping the reduction of money in circulation in the ensuing years was the use of part of the funds, free after the official stabilization loan contracted with West European and American banks

TABLE 14.5. *Main statistical indicators of prices and money supply in Bulgaria, 1924–1939*

	General index of prices (1935 = 100)		Money in circulation		Bank deposits (million leva) at 31 December	General amount of potential purchasing capacity	
	retail prices[a] (1)	whole-sale prices (2)	million leva[b] (3)	Index (1935 = 100) (4)	(5)	million leva (6)	Index (1935 = 100) (7)
1924	— (175)	—	4,220	123	5,959	10,179	62
1925	— (187)	—	4,215	123	7,263	11,478	70
1926	176 (176)	164	3,677	107	7,764	11,441	70
1927	171 (170)	164	3,796	110	9,281	13,077	80
1928	188 (174)	177	4,126	120	12,435	16,563	102
1929	190 (193)	182	4,116	120	14,027	18,143	112
1930	149 (159)	148	3,595	105	13,759	17,354	106
1931	119 (130)	122	3,553	104	12,646	16,199	99
1932	104 (109)	107	3,495	102	12,394	15,889	98
1933	93	95	3,556	104	11,420	14,976	92
1934	99	99	3,630	105	12,026	15,656	96
1935	100	100	3,423	100	12,791	16,214	100
1936	99	102	3,586	105	13,555	17,141	105
1937	108	115	3,876	107	14,685	18,561	114
1938	116	119	3,886	113	16,298	20,184	124
1939	116	121	4,813	140	17,567	22,380	138

[a] The index in brackets is the previous series of 'market' retail prices recalculated with 1935 = 100.

[b] Yearly average.

in 1928, to meet a portion of the Treasury debt to the Bulgarian National Bank. Owing to this loan the state budget for the fiscal year 1928–9 ended with a surplus of 502 million leva, thus influencing the money in circulation.

The policy of restricting the state budget was pursued more distinctly in the period 1926–9, when the amount of state expenditures was fixed at about 6.2–6.4 billion leva per annum, bringing about a balance in the state budget. This policy was backed up by the obligation (supported by proper fiscal control), assumed by the Bulgarian Government under the agreements concluded under the wardship of the financial committee of the League of Nations for two substantial foreign loans in 1926 and 1928. This required that the Treasury should effect payment only within the framework of its own current receipts from taxes and revenues, without recourse to credits granted by the Bulgarian National Bank and correspondingly increases in the state debt to the bank. The importance of this policy should not, however, be exaggerated, as in spite of the control, infringements sometimes occurred. In 1926–7, for example, a small deficit was allowed, only 3 per cent of state expenditures.

The juxtaposition of the price index and the average annual amount of money in circulation, for the years 1924–9 (*Stat. god.*, 1942: 602; see Table 14.5 above), reveals the absence of any close relationship between these indices. This applies also to the relationship between the indices of retail (consumer) prices and of potential purchasing capacity; (the level of deposits went up abruptly during the second half of the 1920s because of the upsurge in the economy). At first glance this seems to deny the decisive role of the scale of money in circulation, and of M2 or the money supply (including savings), in determining the movement of prices in Bulgaria. In order to understand this it is necessary to include in our analysis the positive and negative changes on the supply side as a result of the movements in industrial and agricultural production, handicrafts, etc.

An index for this (roughly equivalent to the national material product) is given in column (4) of Table 14.6. It is calculated from data about the 'primary' national income in the study by Chakalov (1946) of national income and expenditure in Bulgaria from 1924 to 1945 (the secondary incomes of employees and other social strata are not included). Only the combined analyses of the changes in the money supply (including money in circulation and savings or M2) and the commodity supply can explain the variations in the level of prices in Bulgaria.

The results in Table 14.6 shows that the correlation between the changes in these three indices for 1925 is broadly consistent with this approach. At first sight it seems that the increase in prices of 12 is inconsistent with an increase in potential purchasing capacity of 8 offset by a rise in output of 3 points. However, that latter figure is incorrect. The apparent increase in material production is due to the fact that in 1925 Bulgaria had a very good crop of export tobacco but could not realize it on the international market because of a deep crisis in the European tobacco trade; this is not taken into account in Chakalov's national income data. The correct figure for the index of the material product for that year should be about 67, making a fall in supply of 2 percentage points rather than an increase of 3.

In 1926, the fall of 11 points in retail prices (see column (1) of Table 14.6) is consistent with the large increase in the national material product, linked to a static money supply. Similarly, in the three following years, an approximate relationship between the three indices is again apparent, and discrepancies are partly accounted for by the deficiencies of the statistical data, especially the estimate of national material product.

The crisis of 1929–1933

The same conclusion can be drawn from analysis of the corresponding data for the 1930s (Tables 14.5 and 14.6). This stage of the inter-war development is characterized by frequent, though not substantial, state budget deficits until 1936. Those deficits, however, did not affect the direction of increase of money in circulation during the first half of the 1930s, largely because of

TABLE 14.6. *Annual change in prices, potential purchasing-capacity, and national material product*, 1924–1939 (percentage points)

	Change in index of retail prices	Change in index of potential purchasing capacity	Index of national material product[a]	
			Change	Index (1935 = 100)
	(1)	(2)	(3)	(4)
1924	—	—	—	69
1925	+ 12	+ 8	+ 3	72
1926	− 11	=	+ 17	89
1927	− 5	+ 10	+ 8	97
1928	+ 17	+ 22	− 1	96
1929	+ 2	+ 10	− 4	92
1930	− 41	− 6	+ 7	99
1931	− 30	− 7	+ 14	113
1932	− 15	− 1	− 3	110
1933	− 11	− 6	+ 2	112
1934	+ 6	+ 4	− 9	103
1935	+ 1	+ 4	− 3	100
1936	− 1	+ 5	+ 23	123
1937	+ 9	+ 9	+ 10	133
1938	+ 8	+ 10	= 4	137
1939	=	+ 14	+ 1	138

[a] At constant prices; changes in the import and export of consumer goods are not taken into account.

the abrupt drop in commodity prices following the great economic crises of 1929–33. The 1930s are also characterized by a moderate rate of growth of deposits, but this did not lead to a corresponding rise in prices because of the almost uninterrupted growth of the country's agricultural and industrial production (Berov, 1981). As a result, the price level towards the end of the 1930s remained approximately 33–7 per cent lower than in 1929.

Analysis of the results in Table 14.6 shows that the number of years in which the changes in the three indices are not consistent was greater during the 1930s than in the late 1920s. This is to be explained by the intervention of the State to fix the prices of some grain products and industrial commodities after the creation of the state monopoly enterprise 'Hranois-nos' in December 1930, and by some cases of normal prices after the law on cartels in 1931. This intervention, in parallel with the increasing intervention in the exchange regime and in foreign trade, partially hampered prices from moving as they would have done in a really free-market economy.

Finally, to conclude these comments on the role of the state budget and monetary policy, it can be stated that after 1923 they stand out as important stabilizing factors in the inter-war Bulgarian economy, despite the outside pressure on Bulgaria (especially in 1924–9) to pay some reparations and other financial obligations under the Neuilly Treaty. The stabilization of the state budget was mainly due to the introduction of some new direct or indirect taxes (tax on the general yearly income, additional income tax, turnover tax, higher customs duties after 1926, etc.), the improvement in the collection of state budget incomes after the reorganization of the tax service, and the creation of a severe Financial Revision Department in the Ministry of Finance.

The issue of banknotes remained the monopoly of the Bulgarian National Bank (the bank was fully independent of the Government), and was used very carefully, in spite of the pressure on the active balance of the German–Bulgarian Clearing Agreement. In this connection it may also be noted that the relative amount of money in circulation per capita (recalculated in Swiss francs) in 1930 was 22 francs in Bulgaria against, for instance, 36 francs in Romania and 189 in the USA (including Treasury bonds). In 1939 the figure was 29, against 58 and 239 respectively. This difference was partially due also to the smaller degree of commercialization of Bulgarian agriculture. It should also be noted that the National Bank of Romania held more assets in gold and sound foreign currencies than the Bulgarian National Bank.

The foreign-exchange regime

The new foreign-currency regime was introduced in Bulgaria immediately after the end of the war in 1918 (Vladikin, 1931–2). This too can be regarded as a stabilizing factor in the 1920s and the 1930s. Bulgaria abandoned the Latin Monetary Union; the lev ceased to be convertible; and trade in foreign currency was declared a state monopoly of the Bulgarian National Bank. All exporters and other recipients of foreign currency were obliged to sell to the National Bank almost the entire currency realized. All importers, Bulgarian students abroad, etc. had to ask the National Bank to sell them the necessary foreign currency; banks with foreign capital in Bulgaria could leave to their customers credits in foreign currency, but only from their own currency resources received from their parent companies abroad. So floating exchange rates occurred under the direct control and regulating intervention of the National Bank.

This regime was temporarily liberalized after 1928 (after the official devaluation of the gold content of the lev) under the pressure of some big European banks, who gave money for a state loan to stabilize the Bulgarian currency. In October 1931 the old currency regime was restored with more restrictions than there had been before 1928. In effect, the Bulgarian National Bank determined the rates of exchange of the lev (especially for countries within the clearing regime). A complex system of currency 'premiums' was introduced in 1934 for all hard currencies, such as the US dollar, the French franc, the Swiss franc, and the pound sterling. Every exporter of commodities which were explicitly considered under the 1934 law to be important for the national balance of payments was obliged to sell the greater part of the currency acquired to the National Bank at a fixed rate. However, they had the right to sell the remainder of the currency on the free market at a premium over the current official rate. This regime was introduced to hide the incorrectness of the official rate of exchange. The premiums were allowed to float in accordance with the demand for, and supply of, particular foreign currencies on the Bulgarian market, but a 35 per cent ceiling to the premiums was established by the law.

Under this exchange regime, the Bulgarian lev was as a rule overvalued with the help of the state intervention. This overvalued rate was favourable both for Bulgarian exporters and for home producers (although that was never acknowledged in the national economic literature at the time). In this situation the Bulgarian exporter of agricultural products could easily pay a reasonable price to the home farmer and at the same time could be competitive on the European market. For the home producers of industrial goods the system signified protectionism because of the higher uncompetitive prices in leva for all imported industrial commodities.

3. The Banking System

In broad terms the inter-war banking system was also a factor assisting the relative stability of the national economy. The main changes in the structure of the banks are shown in Table 14.7. These data demonstrate that there was a significant expansion of the banking system after the First World War. The general number of the banks in the country in 1939 was thirty-one times greater than in 1911 (Popov, 1916: 400–3). But it was not until 1939 that the real value of deposits and current credit accounts (with the pre-war Bulgarian golden lev recalculated in post-war paper leva by means of the general index of prices) exceeded the 1911 level. This reflected the diminished confidence of the population in the stability of the national currency after the transition to the paper lev. The situation of the banks was especially delicate in 1919–23. At that time Bulgarian capital fled from money in order to avoid the inflationary effects of the devaluation, turning instead to investments in industry or trade but not in credits or deposits (*Ekon. Bulg.*, 1969: 500–3); savings in bank deposits or current credit accounts fell relatively to the national income.

Table 14.7 also shows the extent to which the ratio between state, co-operative, and private banks changed. The big state banks roughly maintained or reinforced their positions in the second half of the 1930s. The number of these state banks remained the same until 1934 (Bulgarian National Bank, Bulgarian Agricultural Bank, and Bulgarian Central Co-operative Bank). Only in 1934 was it reduced to two after the merger between the Bulgarian Central Co-operative Bank and the Bulgarian Agricultural Bank, creating the new Bulgarian Agricultural and Co-operative Bank.

The emergence of a central bank

The Bulgarian National Bank, founded in 1879, occupied the leading position in the country as the central bank. In the beginning it was a state commercial-deposit bank, not large in size (the capital was 2 million gold leva equal to 2 million gold francs). The task of this bank at the end of the nineteenth century was to provide short-term credit for the home trade in

TABLE 14.7. *Main indicators of the banking system in Bulgaria, 1911–1939 (state, co-operative, and private banks)*

	No. of banks			Paid-up capital and reserves (m. leva)			Bills and current debit accounts (m. leva)			Deposits and current credit accounts (m. leva)			National income[a] (bn. leva)
	(1)			(2)			(3)			(4)			(5)
	State	Co-op.	Pvt	State	Co-op.	Pvt	State	Co-op.	Pvt	State	Co-op.	Pvt	
1911	3	17	58	71	111	45	186	983	208	333	345	385	1.6
1929	3	1,707	137	775	1,118	1,498	5,130	3,609	7,407	5,610	3,259	7,247	56.2
1939	2	2,386	89	1,223	4,303	4,908	11,589	5,524	3,778	12,927	4,303	4,908	59.4

[a] Estimates of Kiril Popov.

the towns, long-term credit for town communities for public services, and cash to meet the needs of the state budget. The discount rate of interest of the bank fluctuated in 1879–90 between 7.5 and 9 per cent, but in 1900–11 came down to 6–8 per cent. At first the Bulgarian National Bank had only a central office in Sofia, but in 1884–6 it created its first three branches in the largest towns in the country. By 1911 it already had fifteen branches in the bigger towns and sixty-three agencies in smaller towns.

After the Law of 1885 the Bulgarian National Bank began gradually to pay more attention to its role as an issuing bank. In that year it began to issue banknotes against one-third gold backing. But in the second half of the 1880s and in the 1890s the bank preserved a variety of functions because until 1905 it continued to be the only significant credit institution in the country. (The first three really large private banks with foreign capital only appeared in 1905.) In 1885 the amount of the capital was raised to 10 million gold leva and in 1911 to 20 million leva (Berov, 1991).

After the economic crisis in 1898–9, and especially after 1902, the operations of the bank started to grow rapidly in response to an economic upswing. The bank continued to provide credits mainly for exporters and industrialists, but after 1905 it initiated its role as a 'bank of the banks' parallel with the increase in the quantity of banknotes issued (freely negotiable in gold and silver) from 1.5 million leva in 1890 to 131.9 million in 1911. The rediscounting of a considerable part of the portfolio of the private banks increased. As a source of funds, deposit accounts proved to be increasingly expensive for the bank, and it began to redirect them to the big private banks by lowering its rate of interest on deposit below those of the private banks. In 1890 the bank's deposit rate was 5–7 per cent, but after 1897 it was lowered to 4–6 per cent. During 1892–1900 the deposits constituted on average 36 per cent of all liabilities of the bank, but later this percentage decreased significantly.

During the inter-war period the role of the Bulgarian National Bank changed considerably. Its capital was raised in 1919 and 1922 to 200 million leva plus 50 million 'stand-by' capital. In real terms that was less than half the pre-war level (250 million leva during the inflationary year 1922 represented only 9.8 million pre-war gold leva).

Already at the beginning of the 1920s the tendency was towards a real decrease in the amount of the credits distributed by the Bulgarian National Bank because of its policy of transferring this activity to the private banks. The bank's resources from current deposit and current credit accounts decreased in parallel. The private banks also experienced a reduction in their deposits as a result of the diminished confidence of the population in the Bulgarian lev, but in contrast to these private banks the Bulgarian National Bank did not in general try to counteract this tendency. In 1922 the amount of the current deposits and the current credit accounts in the Bulgarian

National Bank reached 1.47 billion leva. This amount in real value was 2.5 times below the level on the eve of the Balkan War.

The debt of the state Treasury to the bank ceased to grow, and in 1924–9 it ranged between 4.19 and 4.47 billion leva. The law on stabilization of the lev reduced the theoretical gold content of the currency from 0.290326 to 0.010870 grammes. This decrease at the rate of 26.7 times did not exactly reflect the degree of price increase, and corresponding devaluation of the lev on the home market in comparison with the pre-war level, but it was close to the reality. In 1924 a Clearing Chamber was created (as an appendage to the Bulgarian National Bank), as an office for mutual compensation of the payments between the banks in Sofia.

In the period 1924–9 the nominal amount of credits given by the Bulgarian National Bank to private industry and trade increased, but in reality it was several times below the pre-war level of current accounts and discounted bills of exchange in gold leva (*Stat. god.* 1942: 610–11). The policy of the bank continued to be directed towards gradual assignment of this kind of activity to the private banks. The Bulgarian National Bank also ceased to give mortgage credits. After the Law on the Bank in 1924 its capital was nominally raised to 500 million leva, but in real equivalent this still lagged behind the pre-war level. The bank continued to be a state institution, but the law in 1924 consolidated its autonomy. The board of managers acquired more independence and competence, though the State preserved its right to control the activity of the bank through the participation of one governmental delegate in the meetings of the board. The State also preserved the right to receive credits from the bank to the amount of 300 million leva, given against Treasury bonds. In addition, the State continued to receive a part of the profits of the bank, and the bank provided the cash service of the state budget without charge.

After the reform of January 1927 the bank freed itself from all long-term credit operations, and became purely a bank of issue. The short-term credit activity of the bank was limited following the gradual liquidation of certain kinds of loans. The rediscounting of part of the portfolio of the private banks was, however, reinforced.

The transformation of the Bulgarian National Bank to a purely issuing bank and a regulator of the banknote currency was finally confirmed with the new law of 1928. The maximum credit for the state budget was slightly raised, and fixed at 400 million leva. After the contraction of the Stabilization Loan in 1928 the greater part of the state debt to the bank was redeemed, and the bank's room for manoeuvre was increased.

During the 1920s the discount rate of interest of the Bulgarian National Bank increased from 6.5 per cent until July 1922 and 7 per cent in July 1923 to 9 per cent after 1923 and 10 per cent after August 1924. This raising of the discount rate of interest was due to the significant difference between the bank's rate and the rate on the free money market (where a rate of interest from 18 to 30 per cent was a frequent, even customary, phenomenon). In 1927, however, after increasing competition, the private discount rate was reduced to 14 per cent and in 1928 to 11–13 per cent (later 8–10 per cent).

Thus, in a few decades after the initially difficult conditions of work in a backward country, the Bulgarian National Bank had by 1928 succeeded in making the transformation from a relatively small commercial-deposit bank to a modern (by contemporary standards) issuing bank. In this role it coped very well with its nation-wide tasks of regulating the banknote currency and the general lines of the credit activity in the country.

After the crisis in 1929–33 the amount of banknotes in circulation decreased considerably. This was a spontaneous development, not the result of a deliberate policy on the part of the bank; and was caused by the sharp fall in prices, on average by 39–48 per cent from the 1929 level. The rates of exchange of the Bulgarian lev against the 'hard' currencies had been stabilized since the second half of the 1920s, and this continued until the end the 1930s, but after 1931–2 a hidden premium of 35 per cent appeared in barter transactions. These premiums, together with the complex system of controls over foreign trade and the balance of payments marked the acknowledgement of the unreality of the official exchange rates. Because of the crisis, and a sharp decrease in the returns of foreign currency, the Bulgarian National Bank was forced in October 1931 to re-establish in a rather more severe form the regime of state intervention in trade in foreign currency which had been temporarily abolished in 1928–31. The bank was the main buyer and seller of foreign currency.

In the 1930s the level of credits in the balance sheet of BNB decreased considerably, because of the general policy of concentrating on the note issue, and the difficulties caused by the economic crisis. In 1933 the credits amounted to only 262 million leva (410 million in 1938) against 1,423 million leva in 1929. The discount rate of the bank during these years decreased from 10 per cent to 6–8 per cent with a tendency towards diminution.

The dependence of the Bulgarian National Bank on the State increased in the second half of the 1930s. After the decree of 8 February 1937 the profit of the bank (after deduction of sums for different funds) was to be deposited as revenue of the state budget. The bank was forced to take part in the capital of certain state enterprises, created after special laws. It was also required to participate in the capital of the Bulgarian Central Co-operative Bank, the bank Bulgarski Credit (Bulgarian Credit), and the hydro-electric station Vucha. The bank also played an active part in the granting of credit for the big barter compensation with Bulgarian tobacco in 1934. The state debt in the balance sheets of the bank began again to increase, and reached 3.44 billion leva in 1938. That all diminished the manoeuvring capacity of the bank, and limited its scope for regulating the currency and credit activity.

Another big state bank was the Bulgarian Agricultural Bank which provided credit for the farmers (Janchulev, 1939). The state-owned Post Office Savings Bank and the Central Co-operative Bank (which gave credits to the different kinds of co-operative organization) were also very important. In 1930 the State tried to save the deposits in nineteen private banks which had failed, and used new money from the state budget (together with the remaining assets of these nineteen banks) to create a new bank, Bulgarian Credit, with 95 per cent of the capital held by the State (Karamikhailov, 1939).

The private banks

The relative importance of the private banks rose significantly until the end of the 1920s. This was due mainly to the creation of some big new private commercial banks with foreign capital (for example, the Bulgarian–Italian Commercial Bank, the Anglo–Pragian Bank, and the Franco–Belgian Bank) and the reconstruction of some large private banks with Bulgarian capital as the Bulgarian Commercial Bank (Kemilev, 1939).

At the beginning of the 1920s these banks attempted to combine commercial-deposit banking with the German type of universal bank, taking shares in many related or 'daughter' enterprises. This temporary activity of the Bulgarian commercial banks led to the commitment of a considerable part (sometimes more than 40 per cent) of all their available resources in shareholdings. That was not so much a question of their own preferences, but a consequence of a practice which gained recognition during the period of inflation at the beginning of the 1920s, and continued at a lower tempo in the second half of the decade. Its main feature was the transformation of short-term (three- or six-month) credits into shares of the indebted enterprise. Sometimes these enterprises were forced to increase their capital and transfer the proceeds of the new issues to their bank creditors (in Germany, this practice was known as *Veraktionierung*).

As a result of this tendency each of these big private banks also created a financial group, consisting of seven to thirty affiliated companies in industry, trade, insurance, etc. (Natan and Berov, 1958; Berov, 1965). In this way the private banks expanded their role as organizational centres of the economy. Until 1929 the big banks with foreign capital received from their 'mother' banks in France, Belgium, Germany, and other foreign centres substantial short-term credits in foreign currency. This facilitated the development of industry and trade at that time, but became a destabilizing factor in the crisis years of 1929–33, when the parent concerns were hit by the Depression and the credits were rapidly withdrawn.

Another reason for the sharp fall in the relative share of the big private banks in credit activity was the fact that some of these banks suffered heavy losses because of jobbery with Bulgarian export tobaccos in 1928–30, or because a great number of debtors went bankrupt. There were two main reasons for these bankruptcies. The first was the inadequate investigation of the financial situation of the debtors (especially the larger ones). The investigation usually consisted of a very formal review of the balance sheets, with no examination of the commercial and technical aspects of the debtors' investment projects. The second reason was the spontaneous transformation into long-term investment credits of a large part of the short-term credits granted by the banks. This also happened to a substantial part of the short-term credits in foreign currency received from their 'mother-banks' abroad at the end of the 1920s by the large Bulgarian banks with foreign capital: they were effectively transformed into long-term loans to Bulgarian industrial enterprises for investments in machinery, new buildings, etc., without the consent of the bank-creditor.

So the discrepancy between the terms of payment of the liabilities and the liquidity of the assets grew rapidly. The rate of solvency and liquidity of all private banks, and especially of the big private banks, decreased considerably, leading to bankruptcies, failure to repay deposits, and mergers between the affected banks. In the biggest banks a considerable part of the difficulties in the first years of the crisis of 1929–33 was due to the fact that under the pressure of the withdrawal of deposits and foreign credits, these banks did not succeed in realizing quickly enough their excessive share portfolios (in Bulgaria this realization was rather more difficult because of the lack of a real financial market and a real Stock Exchange in the country).

The share of the big private banks with foreign capital also decreased because of the gradual hidden withdrawal of the capital and the gradual limitation of their activity in Bulgaria (Berov, 1971). The primary reason for this withdrawal was Bulgaria's increasing economic and political orientation after 1933 towards Nazi Germany. Western capital realized that it remained in a foreign sphere of influence—the sphere of active German economic aggression. The tightening of the exchange policy of the Bulgarian National Bank in 1931 exercised an additional negative impact, and made the repatriation of the profits and of the foreign credits more difficult. The sharp decrease in the activity of the big private banks with Western capital could not be compensated for by an increase in the activity of the Bulgarian Credit Bank (with German capital), because Nazi Germany did not have sufficient free capital for export to other countries.

Co-operative banks increased substantially in number, but their relative weight could not increase in the 1920s because they generally received only the moderate resources of individual small-scale retail traders, craftsmen, some well-to-do farmers, pensioners, etc. (Dgelepov, 1940; Sprostranov, 1931–2; Kashev, 1931–32). In the 1930s, after the Depression, the situation changed negatively for the private joint-stock banks and positively for the co-operative and state-owned banks. Many private joint-stock banks failed, others merged, especially after the process of withdrawal of Western capital from Bulgaria in the second half of the decade.

The State controlled, but did not regulate, the activity of the banking system. The most important form of control was the legal obligation of the private banks to deposit a certain percentage of their deposits in the Bulgarian National Bank as a partial guarantee for the depositors. Some rules concerning the structure of the balance sheets were also introduced. The rate of interest was not regulated, but an official rate (8 per cent per year) was introduced as a lawful minimum in cases of legal decisions. In 1932 a Paying-off Office was created as a state institution to play an intermediary role between the banks and the small-scale debtors, farmers, craftsmen, etc. with the help of some money from the state budget. The majority of these small debtors were saved or assisted through spacing out their debts, lowering the rate of interest, etc., but the banks also avoided dangerous losses. Thus the banking system, with the financial help of the State, tried to play a limited stabilizing role in the 1930s.

At the same time new external factors of economic instability appeared. After the First World War Bulgaria had to look for major new export products because of the post-war changes in territory and population (the loss of southern Dobruja, the influx of a great number of refugees from Macedonia, the Aegean region, and Dobruja). These severely impeded the export of grain which had been the basis of Bulgaria's pre-war foreign trade. But the export of such new products as tobacco, eggs, poultry, and fruit also had its problems and difficulties, especially during and after the Depression of 1929–33. During the 1930s, the Great Depression and the long-term disorder of the national trade and balance of payments in many countries caused the transition to bilateral trade on the basis of clearing agreements. Bulgaria was forced to accept this kind of trade and payments with its main trade partners.

The Bulgarian economy was also hindered by financial burdens, including the payment of reparations (from 1924 until 1929), and of compensation to Belgian, French, and other businessmen for their losses during the war, as well as the repayment of the pre-war state loans in gold terms. Another new external obstacle was the growing monopolization of the greater part of Bulgarian exports and imports by Germany after 1932. Bulgaria thus lost more and more of its freedom of choice on the international market, and was forced to accept both unfavourable price conditions and a lower level of quality for many imported goods.

In this way the Bulgarian economy was adversely affected in the 1920s and 1930s by a series of new destabilizing external factors. Bulgaria was also heavily influenced by the world economic fluctuations. This was a much greater problem in the inter-war period than in the late nineteenth and early twentieth centuries, because of the greater significance of foreign trade and foreign credits relative to the national income. So we can conclude that the main destabilizing factors in the Bulgarian economy during the inter-war period were external. The banking system and the currency regime were only the channels through which these factors made their impact on the domestic economy.

It should also be noted that the relative significance of the banking system in economic activity in Bulgaria was small in comparison with most of the developed countries. In the USA in 1938, the ratio of M2 (money in circulation plus the sum of the deposits and current credit accounts in the banks) to the national income was 0.77 against only 0.39 in Bulgaria (*US Statistical Yearbook*, 1942: 294; Chakalov, 1946: 111–12; *Stat. god.*, 1942: 602–5.). This means that the Bulgarian banking system had a smaller capacity to induce additional adverse speculative weaknesses in the economy during periods of crisis. The ratio in 1938 between own capital (including reserves) and deposits plus current credit accounts in Bulgaria was also lower—only 1:4.7 against 1:8.4 in the USA, and 1:7.5 in Austria.

References

Official publications

Ekonomikata na Bulgaria do sozialisticheskata revoluzia (Ekon. Bulg.), 1969 (Sofia). *Statisticheski godishnik na Zarstvo Bulgaria (Stat. god.)*, 1925, 1942 (Sofia). *Stopanska istoria na Bulgaria (Stopanska istoria)*, 1981 (Sofia).

Books and articles

Berov, L. (1965), 'Le capital financier occidental et les pays balkaniques dans les années vingt', *Studia Balkanica*, 2–3: 139–69.
—— (1971), 'The Withdrawal of Western Capital from Bulgaria on the Eve of the Second World War', *Studia Balkanica*, 4: 222–57.
—— (1981), 'Parichnoto obraschenie v Bulgaria pri kapitalizma', *Financi i kredit*, 10: 37–49.
—— (1983), 'Inflation and Deflation Policy in Bulgaria during the period between World War I and World War II', in *Inflation through the Ages: Economic, Social, Psychological and Historical Aspects* (New York), 486–500.
—— (1985), 'The Bulgarian Economy during World War I', in *War and Society in East Central Europe, East Central Societies in World War I* xix. (New York), 170–85.

Berov, L. (1992), 'Bulgarska Narodna Banka 1879–1991', in *Bulgarska Narodna Banka, godishen otchet 1991* (Sofia), 6–14.

Chakalov, A. (1946), *Nazionalniat dohod i rashod na Bulgaria 1924–1945* (Sofia), 111–12.

Dgelepov, A. (1940), 'Stopanski problemi na kooperativnia kredit', *Spisanie na Bulgarskoto ekonomichesko drugestvo*, 39/8: 507–20.

Hadginikolov, V., and Berov, L. (1982), *Stopanska istoria* (Sofia), 541–2.

Janchulev, B. (1939), 'Novi nasoki na zemedelskia kredit', *Spisanie na Bulgarskoto ekonomichesko drugestvo*, 38/12: 316–35.

Karamikhailov, M. (1939), *Kreditnoto delo v Bulgaria i stopanskata kriza* (Sofia), 92.

Kashev, S. G. (1931–2), 'Sadachite i deinostta na Bulgarska zemedelska banka', *Stopanska misal*, 1/2: 81–97.

Kemilev, A. (1939), 'Bankovoto delo v Bulgaria prez 1938', *Spisanie na Bulgarskoto ekonomichesko drugestvo*, 38/5–6: 355–62.

Natan, G., and Berov, L. (1958), *Monopolisticheskiat kapitalism v Bulgaria* (Sofia), 131–88, 194–242.

Popov, K. (1916), *Stopanska Bulgaria prez 1911* (Sofia), 400–3.

Sprostranov, N. (1931–2), 'Populiarnite banki v Bulgaria', *Stopanska misal*, 1/3: 142–52;

Vladikin, L. (1931–2), 'Shest godini kambialen monopol', *Stopanska misal*, 1/3: 92–118.

15

Commercial Banking in Britain between the Wars

FORREST CAPIE

1. Introduction

The British economy is often grouped with other industrial economies for the inter-war years and regarded as performing poorly. In many important respects however, it was different and if output is taken as the best indicator of overall performance, the British economy appears to have done better in the 1920s and 1930s than it had done for over forty years. And after the immediate post-war period of adjustment it had a much more stable growth path than many, perhaps most, other countries. The economy grew at over 2 per cent per annum in the inter-war period. It is useful to hold this in view when considering the performance, and the contribution, of the banking sector. Economic growth depends upon a stable economy, and a stable economy is supported by a stable financial environment.

Britain also had a highly developed financial sector with many constituent parts and with most of its principal institutions having been established for around a century or more. The financial sector was made up of a variety of institutions with quite specialized functions. There was a long established central bank in the Bank of England; the accepting houses or merchant banks engaged in the finance of foreign trade and new issues in the capital market; the discount houses conducted the main business in short-term bills; the commercial banks carried out 'normal' banking business; and there were a number of other specializations such as the provision of mortgage finance where other institutions were emerging.

The British banking system contrasts sharply with those in Europe and the USA. The business of the commercial banks was quite narrow. It was often the subject of some comment. As Alfred Marshall (1927) put it: 'the charge of excessive conservatism is sometimes brought against British banks. No one disputes their unrivalled efficiency in the rather narrow range of tasks which they undertake . . . (but) . . .' As Marshall says, they did what they saw as their job, remarkably well. Banking in Britain was sound, stable, and respected but perhaps it could have been more adventurous.

This short chapter does several things: it provides a framework within which banking can be viewed; it gives some macroeconomic data that the banking sector can be set against; it describes the structure of the system; outlines the principal activities and performance of the system and its relationship with the central bank; it indicates what overseas connections there were; adverts to some of the sector's alleged shortcomings, specifically the deficiencies of the cartel; and it ends with a short guide to the monetary and financial data available for the period.

2. A Framework

There are two main ways of examining the money-supply process. The conventional approach in Britain has been the PSBR–money–debt framework, which focuses on credit. According to this the money supply is a function of government borrowing, bank lending, non-deposit liabilities, external finance, and the debt-holding behaviour of the non-bank public. The other approach is the monetary-base approach. This views money as the product of the monetary authority's control of base money, and the behaviour of banks and the non-bank public. Both approaches are useful. The latter, however, brings out more clearly the role of banks in the behaviour of the money stock. It is used in this chapter as a background to that.

The expression that is usually used is:

$$M = mB, \qquad \text{where} \qquad \left[\frac{1 + \dfrac{C}{D}}{\dfrac{C}{D} + \dfrac{R}{D}} \right]$$

B is the monetary base, and m is the money multiplier. Under a floating exchange rate the base is under the control of the authorities. Under a gold standard it is chiefly determined by the balance of payments but influenced by the monetary authorities. The money multiplier captures the behaviour of the public and the banks by the way in which they hold cash as against deposits.

The broad outline of the movements in these variables alerts us to the fact that there was considerable stability in the monetary and banking sector.

If the multiplier is stable then the behaviour of the money supply is essentially the responsibility of the authorities. A remarkable feature of the inter-war years is that the money multiplier was stable, even more stable than in the years before 1914. It is remarkable since there were several exchange-rate regimes and some turmoil in the world economy. Between the wars the money multiplier had a value of 4.4 and a standard deviation of 0.2.

This was not a result of offsetting factors. The separate elements in the multiplier were stable. In fact the public's cash/deposit ratio (C/D) can be divided into that for demand deposits (C/DD) and that for time deposits (C/TD). Both these ratios move around in response to interest rates and other influences. But the net outcome for the overall ratio was one of considerable stability, the ratio fluctuating slightly between 26 and 30 per cent.

The banks showed a similar stability (which will be returned to later), with a reserve/deposit ratio of around 11 per cent. And there was very little variation around that—a range of 10.5 per cent to 12 per cent.

3. The Macroeconomy

Table 15.1 brings out the essential features of the British economy between the two world wars. It shows that by historical standards the economy grew at respectable rates. Monetary growth was stable and for the main part prices were steady—falling gently through the 1920s and then rising slowly in the 1930s. There were of course some sharper movements in prices and also in unemployment in the two Depressions that the period is noted for, those of 1920–1 and 1929–32.

4. The Structure of Banking

The British monetary and banking system had evolved to what might be called its modern form by the third quarter of the nineteenth century. By that time the Bank of England presided over an increasingly concentrated banking system and had the buffer of the discount houses between itself and the banks.

Combination in banking was common in the nineteenth century but the pace of amalgamation, whether by merger or by acquisition, accelerated sharply in the 1890s and continued strongly through to the First World War. The fundamental motivation seems to have been a desire for increased size, regarded as more or less synonymous with strength. Also large banks, it was asserted at the time, were increasingly required to cope with an ever more complex economy.

A large number of small banks had emerged by the first quarter of the nineteenth century. By the middle of the century there was a system that had all the outward appearance of a perfectly competitive system. By the First World War there was a system that had all the outward appearance, and at least some of the behaviour, of an oligopoly. It was this structure that prevailed in British banking in the inter-war years and beyond. By 1917 the 'big five' London clearing banks dominated the system taking more than 75 per cent of all deposits. The other notable feature of the system that developed in parallel and sometimes as a direct objective or as a consequence was the branch network. Where once there had been several hundred small independent banks there were in 1920 just five big banks but with thousands of branch offices. Table 15.2 shows the pattern of development.

In fact the system had developed to such an extent that when in 1918 the Midland Bank, by that stage the biggest bank in the world, moved to take over the London Joint-Stock Bank there was widespread opposition in the country. The merger went ahead but public concern led to the establishment of the Treasury Committee on Bank Amalgamation. The Committee, made up mostly of bankers, nevertheless expressed the view that there was a danger that banks could become too large and that competition was being lost. Legislation was proposed but not enacted. Instead from this date

TABLE 15.1. *Percentage changes and annual average rates of growth in macroeconomic variables in the United Kingdom, 1922–1938*

Variables	T to T 1922–38	T to P 1922–9	P to T 1929–32	T to P 1932–7	P to T 1937–8
GNP (nominal)	27.2 (1.5)	9.8 (1.33)	− 13.2 (− 4.74)	28.2 (5.0)	4.3 (4.2)
GNP (real)	40.8 (2.1)	19.9 (2.6)	− 5.5 (− 1.9)	20.8 (3.8)	2.9 (2.8)
GNP deflator	− 15.8 (− 1.1)	− 14.2 (− 2.2)	− 7.4 (− 2.5)	3.3 (0.65)	2.6 (2.5)
M1 (nominal)	21.2 (1.2)	− 9.01 (− 1.3)	− 4.3 (− 1.5)	36.7 (6.3)	1.8 (1.8)
M3 (nominal)	20.9 (1.2)	− 4.5 (0.66)	1.2 (0.38)	24.7 (4.4)	0.39 (0.39)
Monetary base (nominal)	22.7 (1.3)	− 4.6 (− 0.67)	0.36 (0.12)	24.9 (4.4)	2.6 (2.6)
Retail price Index	− 14.5 (− 0.98)	− 10.1 (− 1.5)	− 12.4 (− 4.42)	7.8 (1.5)	0.66 (0.66)

Notes: Figures show the percentage change from beginning to end of period: T = Trough, P = Peak. Figures in brackets show the geometric average rate of growth per annum.

Sources: Capie and Webber, (1985): GNP (nominal) Table III (12)., Col. 1; GNP (deflator) Table III (12)., Col. 3; M1 (nominal) Table 1 (2); M3 (nominal) Table I (3); Monetary base (nominal) Table 1 (1); Retail price index Table III (12)., Col. 4. Feinstein (1972): Table 5, GNP (real).

onwards no mergers were permitted without the approval of the Treasury Committee.

Whether competition was being lost or not is more difficult to determine. There is no doubt that in the late nineteenth and early twentieth centuries the system became more concentrated, particularly in the years 1890–1917. By whatever measure is used there was quite clearly increasing concentration (Capie and Rodrik-Bali, 1982). However, competition and concentration are by no means perfectly correlated. It is not clear that there was as much competition as is sometimes asserted in the middle of the nineteenth century. What seems more likely is that over the period 1850–1914 regional oligopolies gave way to a national oligopoly. (One motivation for merging or acquiring was to break into an otherwise restricted geographical territory.) There was certainly much less competition than there might have been and less than is sometimes asserted.

Although the banking system that was in place by 1920 remained effectively the same structure throughout the inter-war years, there were a few changes. The Midland arranged an affiliation with the Clydesdale in 1920 and the North of Scotland Bank in 1923. There was the take-over of Drummonds by the Royal Bank of Scotland in 1924. And there was the rescue of Williams Deacons from difficulties, by absorption into the Royal in 1929. At the end of the period the Royal also acquired Glyn Mills (in 1939). Some private banks were also absorbed and there were two relatively minor mergers. In 1928 Martins merged with the Lancashire and Yorkshire Bank. And at the end of the period the District merged with the Manchester and County (1939). But the basic structure remained unchanged and the degree of concentration hardly altered. It was this structure that underpinned the stability of the system, and the stability in turn that helped to keep the structure intact. The structure allowed banks to hold well-diversified portfolios across the whole economy.

According to an old and tested organizing principle in industrial economics the structure of an industry influences the conduct of firms (usually thought of chiefly as pricing behaviour but extending to other activities such as advertising) and this conduct produces different performance. Tests of the model have invariably telescoped the exercise into an association between structure and profitability. We return below to some of these issues in a discussion of the banking system's stability. The other element that cannot be separated in the discussion of stability is the role of the central bank.

5. The Central Bank

By the inter-war years Britain had a well-established central bank. Founded in England in 1694 the Bank of England had by the middle of the nineteenth

TABLE 15.2. *Banks and bank offices in the United Kingdom, 1870–1920*

	1		2		3		4		5		6		7		8	
	a	b	a	b	a	b	a	b	a	b	a	b	a	b	a	b
1870	11	36	45	48	8	393	93	588	206	504	13	790	9	368	387	2,728
1880	16	54	49	55	10	579	98	870	160	513	10	877	9	470	357	3,423
1890	18	91	46	54	11	910	77	1,164	124	575	10	986	9	449	302	4,236
1900	15	102	26	33	14	2,223	61	1,613	56	317	11	1,088	9	511	199	5,894
1910	11	11	19	27	15	4,029	31	1,396	16	100	9	1,228	9	609	117	7,407
1920	15	15	14	16	7	6,475	13	888	8	61	8	1,291	9	921	75	9,668

Key to columns:
1 London joint-stock banks
2 London private banks
3 London provincial joint-stock banks
4 Provincial private stock banks
5 Provincial private banks
6 Scottish banks
7 Irish banks
8 United Kingdom totals
a banks
b branches

Source: Capie and Webber (1985)

century (and particularly because of the 1844 Act) adopted its modern form. It was a private bank but it had public responsibilities. It performed all the functions associated with central banking—the government's bank, issuer of the currency, and so on. But at the core of central banking is the lender-of-last-resort function.

If we take the lender-of-last-resort function to mean the provision of the necessary liquidity to the money markets in time of difficulty, then the Bank had acted as lender-of-last-resort on many occasions from the eighteenth century onwards. But there were some occasions when it did not so act. If, however, we take the function to require further (as Bagehot wanted) the pre-commitment to such action—the guarantee of the provision of liquidity in time of need—then it has to be the 1870s before the Bank can be said to have fully accepted this public responsibility. (At that time too the note issue was almost completely dominated by Bank of England note issue.)

What should also be stressed is that the function did not include the bail-out of insolvent institutions as it has since come to mean and to be extended to. It is true that the Bank organized the rescue of Barings in 1890 but at no stage did it bail out a failing firm. Banks failed almost every year between 1870 and 1914 and there were some further failures between the wars. When the market let them fail no one else moved to help them. However, as we shall see below the Bank took a more active supervisory role in the years between the wars.

By 1920 the Bank had become well practised in the art of central banking. And unlike many of its counterparts in Europe there were no restraints imposed on its functioning. In Europe as a consequence of the stabilization programmes central banks were often denied the use of open-market operations. In addition, as described, the structure had evolved to a cartel which the Bank had quietly encouraged so that it could more readily exercise its influence over a small number of bank chairmen. Moral suasion was one means of bringing about the changes in monetary policy required by the Bank. In the two decades after 1920 the Bank's tasks in relation to the banking system were limited. The Bank simply fostered the cartel and otherwise preserved the *status quo*. It was clearly the dominant institution and could exert its influence over the whole system.

An illustration of the Bank's use of its position and the pressure it could bring to bear was in the huge war loan conversion of 1932. The background to this was the size of the national debt and its relation to income and the implications of that for interest rates, monetary growth, and possible crowding-out effects. The debt had soared from £600m. in 1913 (when it was around 35 per cent of national income) to £8,000m. in 1920 (at which point it was roughly 250 per cent of national income). Much of this debt was issued at historically high interest rates and the interest payments represented a huge and long-term burden on the Exchequer. In the years of the

Depression (1929–31) the risk of growing budget deficits and the fears of their impact on confidence abroad brought pressure to act. The solution proposed—and it was one that had been in the mind of the Treasury for some time—was the reduction of interest rates. A major instrument in this operation was to be the conversion of the 1917 war loan stock from a coupon of 5 per cent to a 3.5 per cent coupon of a slightly longer-dated stock. War loan 1917 was a huge individual stock equal roughly to 27 per cent of the entire national debt which in itself was particularly large following the First World War. The commercial banks held fairly substantial amounts of the stock and their co-operation in the conversion was regarded as essential if the operation was to be a success. The bank chairmen were all invited to see Norman and were offered terms. All agreed to the terms except McKenna, chairman of the Midland and a former Chancellor of the Exchequer. In spite of the Midland's size and strength Norman was able to exert great pressure on McKenna and a price was agreed (though the price is not known). The Bank was therefore able to declare, a little misleadingly, that all the banks had converted their stock at the going rate, and great encouragement was therefore given to ordinary holders to convert.

Another illustration is found in Norman's efforts to preserve the discount market in the form it was in. Norman believed the discount houses had provided a useful function in the market and allowed the Bank direct influence over short-term interest rates. For this and historical reasons Norman organized their rescue in the 1930s when interest rates on short-term bills (the discount houses' bread-and-butter business) fell to levels that would have bankrupted them. The discount houses took loans from the clearers for short periods and provided the banks with a second line of reserves—'money at call and short notice'. Their profits depended on the margin between the rates they paid for funds and the rate at which they discounted bills. In 1929 they had signed an agreement with the cartel to pay a rate of 1 per cent below bank rate on money at call. Then short-term rates fell in the 1930s (as low as 0.35 per cent on Treasury bills), but bank rate stayed at 2 per cent throughout the decade. The discount houses were clearly bound to make huge losses. Norman persuaded the commercial banks to sign new agreements and also to give up tendering for the weekly issue of Treasury bills, leaving the discount houses with the monopoly of tender.

Throughout the whole inter-war period Montagu Norman was governor of the Bank of England. The banking system was under criticism at the time and Norman became the butt of much of the criticism. In the 1920s his preoccupation was with the return to the gold standard and the attempt to preserve the system once it had been re-established. But there were other pressures on the Bank.

There have always been those who have argued that the central bank should be more involved in the economy, that is do more than manage the currency. The part played by the Bank of England in the inter-war economy was certainly a matter of wide concern. Norman made his own views on central banking and its relationship with the rest of the economy clear in evidence given to the Macmillan Committee in the 1920s. He regarded the Bank's responsibilities as being essentially the provision of sound money and that meant the protection of the gold standard. The real economy would then achieve what it was best capable of. (There are of course serious criticisms of this position and of how the Bank operated its discount policy between the wars.) But such was the criticism that Norman and the Bank were drawn into a number of schemes designed to promote industrial recovery. One of the buzz words of the time was 'rationalization'. There were many schemes for rationalizing industry and where firms made the right moves there was assistance from the Bank in the transition.

One of the initiatives taken by Norman was an approach to the chairman of the United Dominion Trust (UDT—a finance house providing hire-purchase finance) with an offer from the Bank to increase UDT's capital base and develop further their ability to extend hire-purchase lending to a wider array of firms and to lengthen and otherwise improve their terms of lending. Bowden and Collins (1992) conclude that the outcome of this exercise was yet another demonstration that there simply was no demand for industrial finance of the kind the system was accused of failing to provide.

In summary, between the wars the Bank of England as the central bank and lender-of-last-resort performed its function well and properly according to the best principles of sound banking. As noted it went further if unenthusiastically, and not necessarily wisely, and initiated schemes for improving industrial performance. But deep down Norman did not believe in these and the evidence suggests that it was not a profitable use of resources and brought little if any benefit to industry. We return to a slightly fuller elaboration of the schemes below, in the section on banking and the real economy.

6. Overseas Connections

The early dominance of the British economy in the world economy and the scale of British foreign lending had led to the emergence and early supremacy of London as an international financial centre. London was well established as an international financial centre by the beginning of the nineteenth century, and its position strengthened throughout the century so that by 1914 it was virtually unrivalled. Britain's weakened trading and financial position after the First World War could have been expected to have damaged this position. But Paris and Berlin, two growing contenders before 1914, were in no position to take up the challenge in the 1920s. And although New York might be thought to have had many of the prerequisites for taking over the leadership, the lack of enthusiasm in the USA for participation in the world economy, and then the collapse of American banking in 1930–3 meant that London survived the inter-war years. Montagu Norman went around Europe endeavouring to promote good central-banking practice. Unfortunately, his hostility to France and his affection for centres of weakness limited his contribution.

Britain also dominated in multinational banking (a separate activity from international banking) by 1914. And this dominance continued in the inter-war years, British banks having more branches around the world than any other nationality. The very earliest British overseas banking ventures, originating in the first half of the nineteenth century, were not the outgrowth of domestic banking. In fact the firms did no domestic banking in Britain. But these were joined by the clearing banks just before the First World War and the more interesting developments in the inter-war years were those that did involve the clearing banks.

Some clearing banks had made forays into Europe just before the war. Lloyds purchased a subsidiary in Paris in 1911 and was quickly followed by London County and Westminster also purchasing a subsidiary in Paris, in 1913. (Fears were expressed at the time that these ventures would lead to contamination of the stable British system with unstable foreign practices and make London vulnerable to foreign crises.) The war provided a fillip to this European business with British troops abroad and other countries' banks closing in some territories. After the war the London clearers with their huge resources looked to extend their branch networks in Europe. Where formerly they had done their business through correspondents they now looked to acquisition.

Banks were acquired all over the world. Some of the ventures were successful and profitable. For example Stuart Jones (1988) shows that in the inter-war years two British banks (Barclays and Standard) dominated South African banking and that this brought stability to that country's banking and promoted economic development. This was probably true of other parts of the Empire. But experience in continental Europe was different. There was little success there, indeed there were large financial losses and gradually the banks pulled away from Europe.

Only four of the 'big five' had expanded into Europe. The exception was the Midland. According to Geoffrey Jones (1982) this was more by accident than design. In 1891 the Midland had moved to London. In 1898 it acquired City Bank, the leading correspondent bank overseas. Midland at that stage emerged as a leading correspondent bank. In 1918 the Midland took over the London Joint-Stock Bank, the most experienced of all banks in overseas business with more than seventy foreign agencies. The Midland was therefore well placed to carry out overseas business without the need to acquire. Holden, the chairman, did want to acquire abroad but he died in 1918 and from that time on the Midland stuck to correspondent banking—that is until its ill-fated venture into America in the 1980s.

Also, foreign banks had long done business in London. There were large numbers of them too (one of the measures of an international financial centre). But their business was essentially foreign-trade finance and not retail or commercial banking. The latter required access to the clearing-house, but in any case none of these banks showed an interest in retail banking, at least not until the last decade or so.

7. Stability

Modern British banks have taken a great deal of criticism for a long time for a variety of alleged failures. But one thing they have not been accused of for a long time is instability. This is not surprising for there has been no banking panic and no financial crisis in Britain since 1866. (1878 and 1890 are not financial crises properly defined.) And this is strikingly the case for the inter-war years.

Between the wars there were three economic recessions. One was deep, in 1921. The next was less deep but more prolonged, in 1929–32. And there was a relatively mild and brief recession in 1937–8. It is important to remember though that while these recessions reflected some of the problems in the rest of the world economy, Britain's experience was for most of the time much milder than in other countries. For example in the Great Depression of 1929–32 output in Britain fell in total by 6 per cent compared with falls elsewhere of over 30 per cent. Partly as a result of this and in contradistinction to the USA and much of Europe British banks did not get into the same kinds of difficulties as were experienced in Europe and the USA.

Some of the old staple industries were suffering throughout the period and unemployment rose to both very high historical levels and rates. But these industries were no longer dominant in output to the extent that they once had been and their impact was therefore lessened. Some of the specific actions taken by the Bank of England and the commercial banks on these difficulties are provided below.

In the years of recession banks did not fail (though mention will be made of the small Manchester bank of Williams Deacons). Indeed profitability in banking stood up quite well throughout the period. It is true that banks fudged their figures in order to promote a picture of stability. But where there are 'true' figures of bank profits (from the archives) it is possible to get a clearer picture of profits and profitability. Various attempts have been made at estimating bank profitability for the whole sector (see Capie, 1988). What these and the published series show is that for the sector as a whole there was a strong surge in bank profits from 1910 to 1920 closely paralleling those in the whole economy. There was then a sharp fall in the recession of 1921 and then recovery to a plateau that lasted through the second half of the 1920s. There was then a dip and recovery in the 1930s but this was not as deep a fall as was found in the rest of the economy. And as we have already noted that was not a serious Depression when compared with the rest of the world. The trend in profits in banking for the inter-war years can be said to have been slightly downward at least from the high point of 1920. But profitability throughout the period did not look remarkably different from what had obtained in the years before the war.

Another indicator of banking problems is the currency/deposit ratio. The course of this ratio supports the view of stability. Between 1921 and 1938 the ratio never fell outside the range 13 per cent to 15 per cent, striking stability given the upheavals and uncertainty in the international economy.

8. Some Costs of the Cartel

Between the wars the British banking sector was stable and secure. But it can also be said to have been in relative decline over the period. At one level this is quite remarkable. The British economy performed relatively well. There were fewer major shocks than there were elsewhere. When the period opened the banks had huge resources.

There was no absolute decline. Deposits per head grew from £41.6 in 1923–35 to £57.7 in 1936–8. Deposits grew at an average annual rate of 2.8 per cent in real terms between 1924 and 1937. And while the number of banks in the United Kingdom fell slightly between these years, the number of offices rose by about 20 per cent, and bank offices per 10,000 of the population rose from 2.32 to 2.6. However, growth in other parts of the financial system vastly outstripped that. For example, building-society assets grew by tenfold and the ratio of building-society deposits to bank deposits rose from 6 per cent in 1923–5 to 23 per cent in 1936–8. There were other parts of the system too showing similar growth—the Post Office Savings Bank and the trustee savings banks.

Some of the blame for the relatively weak performance of the banks can be attributed to the sclerosis that sets in with cartels. But before turning to that we consider briefly a more general phenomenon, that of the transition in an economy from one where monetization is taking place to one where financial sophistication is taking place.

Bordo and Jonung (1987) have set out the experience of several countries over a long period. They showed that in modern monetary economies the money/income ratio rises as money is increasingly adopted. But at some point there is a movement out of money—chiefly bank deposits—and into more sophisticated financial assets and the money/income ratio then falls. That is certainly a pattern that we can find in Britain, although it does not coincide in time with the other countries. British banking spread enormously in the late nineteenth century, but at about that time there was also the beginnings of the process of moving to holding more and more financial assets of a more sophisticated type. This continued between the wars and therefore some of what is observed can be explained by these trends.

However, most of the blame for the performance can be laid at the door of the banks themselves. The London clearing banks operated a price cartel and other restrictive practices. They uniformly applied a normal deposit ratio of 2 per cent below bank rate. Some variation could be found in the provinces, and some discretion was allowed on large deposits. A minimum charge of 5 per cent was placed on overdrafts. No doubt so long as business continued to grow more or less in line with the economy at large, no cause for alarm was found. But the banks were clearly losing market share in some areas of their business and some of that must be put down to the lethargy resulting from the oligopoly. Some excuse could be found in the general climate of the time because it was one in which restricted competition and protection were widely practised and encouraged.

The cartel obviously imposed some costs on the consumer and on the taxpayer via the Treasury, though it was after the Second World War before concerns over these began to be openly expressed. Various costs resulted from the collusive behaviour. One cost was that imposed on the Treasury as a result of the uncompetitive bill tender described. But the principal part of the cost fell on the consumer in the form of higher prices for banking services. We have already remarked that some parts of the financial sector were offering competition but the main part, the money transmission process, was not. This key part of the business was not a contestable market since membership of the clearing-house was required to keep costs down. The clearing-house was operated by the London clearing banks.

9. Banks and the Real Economy

There is not space in this short chapter to go into the failures that the banking system was supposed to be guilty of in relation to the real economy. Many attacks have been made (see e.g. Tolliday (1986) for the inter-war years) and many defences can also be found. We alluded above to the more active role that the Bank of England pursued in this period in relation to economic activity as opposed to price-level and exchange-rate concerns. Some more elaboration is provided here.

Concern was expressed in Britain at this time over the obvious decline of what had once been major industries (textiles and steel predominantly). With the benefit of hindsight it is possible to see more clearly what the problems of these industries were but at the time attention became focused on the need for rationalization into bigger units. It was believed that industrial productivity would be raised by adopting new techniques, removing excess capacity, and by other restructuring arrangements.

It was quite widely accepted that improved financial services could help with this process of industrial rejuvenation. The Bank became embroiled first by providing help for some of its own industrial customers but then more widely in the rationalization movement. One example of one of its own large industrial customers was that of Armstrong, Whitworth & Co. after the post-war boom collapsed in 1921. Like many other firms that had expanded productive capacity during the war, this firm faced a collapse in demand after the war. In this case the Bank took a controlling interest in the company's equity, and Bank officials actively participated in the firm's business strategy.

The Bank of England also operated on another front in this process. Although at this time it had no formal responsibilities for the conduct of the commercial banks it did concern itself in a general way with the overall stability of the system—sometimes by moral suasion. The Bank did, however, feel concerned when the Lancashire cotton industry got into difficulties. Bankruptcies were inevitable and some banks were closely involved with the industry. Williams Deacons was a small Manchester bank that had lent extensively to cotton firms. It was this that led the Bank to seek to prevent the failure of Deacons. It did this by persuading the Royal Bank of Scotland to take the firm over, indemnifying the Royal against any loss incurred. It also made sure the real reasons for the take-over were not made public.

More generally the Bank of England promoted the establishment of the Lancashire Cotton Corporation in 1931 for the purpose of rationalizing the sector. The Bank also contributed £1 million in loans to the Corporation, gave a guarantee on the issue of the Corporation's debentures, and even purchased stock outright. The Lancashire Steel Corporation was a similar vehicle.

But deep down, Norman's motives in all of this were chiefly to stave off government interference in banking; and in any case he felt that he was dealing with a relatively short-term crisis and that the Bank would be able to withdraw from its activities before long.

The commercial banks' behaviour was different. Their balance sheets show that over the 1920s and 1930s there was a trend to *greater* liquidity rather than the other way around. Whereas in the late 1920s the proportion of assets in advances to industry was 52 per cent, that fell in the 1930s to 41.2 per cent in 1936–8. (Table 15.3 provides some further detail on the changing composition of the assets side of the balance sheet.) This took place when the domestic economy was growing quite rapidly. Part of the explanation lies in the effects of the authorities' debt management. As we noted above there was a sharp increase in the public debt in the First World War and the clearing banks had been large purchasers. In the 1920s the banks managed to divert some of their resources toward the private sector. But the authorities took advantage of the low interest rates in the 1930s to shift the composition of the national debt from short term to long term. (The proportion of the debt with a maturity of more than twenty-five years rose from 32 per cent to 40 per cent between 1930–1 and 1938–9.) If long-term government securities and private advances were reasonably close substitutes, then government funding may have crowded out private finance.

It is possible of course within this that the nature of commercial-bank lending changed. The commercial banks were certainly drawn more deeply into industrial finance. For example where non-repayment of loans was threatened it was sensible for banks to extend repayment times and even lend further to ensure the survival of firms and hence the later repayment of the original loans. Added to this was pressure from the Bank of England. Holmes and Green (1986) illustrate how the Midland behaved supporting its own industrial customers. One striking case was the Royal Mail, a major rescue operation that required the deep involvement of the Midland in the 1930s. The Royal Mail group accounted for 15 per cent of the country's merchant fleet and was also in shipbuilding and steel. A Midland affiliate, the Belfast Bank was heavily extended to the group (outstanding loans of £3.5 million) and this led to deep involvement by the Midland in the group's affairs for several years.

TABLE 15.3. *Composition of London clearing-bank assets 1923–1938[a]* (ratio to total deposits, percentage)

Date (end of year)[b]	Cash	Money call and short notice	Bills discounted	Investment	Advances	(Total value)
1923–5	12.2	6.9	15.0	18.7	48.4	(£822m.)
1928–30	11.2	8.2	14.7	14.4	52.0	(£959m.)
1936–8	10.6	7.4	12.9	27.7	41.2	(£914m.)

[a] Excluding the District Bank throughout.
[b] Three-year averages centred on business-cycle peaks.

Source: London clearing-bank monthly returns, available in Capie and Collins (1983: 92–9).

The banks may not have provided venture capital, but they certainly did become closely involved with industrial customers, probably on a scale never seen before. Duncan Ross (1991) has recently provided more evidence on this and shows that the actions taken by the banks actually conflicted with the positions they adopted before the Macmillan Committee.

10. Monetary Data

The United Kingdom is now well served with collections of monetary and financial data, especially for this period. There have been many toilers in the field. The most recent attempt at providing comprehensive series of monetary data for the United Kingdom over the period 1870 to 1982 is that of Capie and Webber. These data, sources, difficulties, and where possible some solutions are presented in Capie and Webber (1985) Series are provided for the monetary base, narrow money, and broad money. For the inter-war years these are all available in monthly form. All the components of the monetary aggregates are also provided individually: notes, coin, banks' till money, money at call and short notice, time-deposits, demand deposits, and so on. This allows the construction of reserve deposit ratios, currency deposit ratios and other variables. It also allows others to construct their own series of such ratios or of monetary aggregates in cases where disagreement arises over definition. And it allows analysis of individual components where desirable.

The Bank of England is a principal source for all these data (in Bank of England *Statistical Summary* and Bank of England *Quarterly Bulletin*) though they were often supplemented from original clearing-bank data and some other sources. Bank deposits for example, the major component of the money stock, is provided by the Bank of England, but only from data reported at the time by the banks—largely from the London clearing-banks' monthly statement. In some cases better data have been found in individual bank archives. Only a limited amount of data came from the asset side of the balance sheet.

The other main source, but one that provides only annual data, does provide more asset data and a wider range of other financial data. It is Sheppard (1971).

More specifically on the inter-war years there are bank data presented in Capie and Collins (1883) These again come from the London clearing-banks' monthly statements that date from 1921. But estimates were computed for 1919 to 1921 for the Macmillan Committee and so data of these kind are available for the whole period. In particular Capie and Collins provide individual assets for the bulk of the system (the London clearing banks, which at this time comprised: Midland, Barclays, Lloyds, Westminster, National Provincial, Martins, Glyn Mills, National, Coutts, Williams Deacons. The District was added in 1936.) Coin, bank and currency notes, balances with the Bank of England, money at call and short notice, make up a small proportion of the asset side. More importantly, there are: bills discounted, investments, and advances. These latter make up the great bulk of the assets.

11. Summary

This chapter has suggested that the British banking system suffered less in the way of shocks than did banks in most other industrial countries. Also, the banks operated within an economy that suffered less violent oscillations than most other industrial economies in the same period. The stability of the banking system may have provided protection for the real economy. The recent study by Bernanke and James (1991)—an international comparison of the relationship between banking panic and output falls—provides further support for the view that countries with unit banking systems suffered badly, and those with universal banks were also vulnerable. Implicitly the British system is vindicated. That system had evolved to a stable structure where there was a small number of banks with large branch networks across the whole country and the economy. The banks were a well-defined part of the financial sector and like most of the other parts of the sector they looked after their own affairs. There was little regulation on the statute-book, and the clearing banks were left and even encouraged to regulate themselves.

This contrasts quite sharply with some recent verdicts on most other European countries' banks (James *et al.*, 1991) to say nothing of the American banks. The Canadian banking system was one that did do well and the striking feature there is the similarity between its structure and behaviour and that of the British. (Drummond, 1991, offers additional explanations.)

The banks had, however, evolved into a cartel. Some date the cartel from quite an early date such as the 1880s. While there are examples of collusive agreements in that decade, the documentation on this is weak. The cartel really developed with the amalgamations of 1895–1917 and can be properly dated from the First World War. The Bank of England is not exempt either from some blame for Montagu Norman liked, even insisted on, compartmentalization of function. Certainly the cartel made it easy for the Bank to influence the sector. But the banks in any case showed little enthusiasm for competition. They may have performed their basic functions well and contributed in big part to the stability that the financial sector enjoyed. But they failed to extend their activities into some areas that could reasonably have been expected. The relative decline in position of the commercial banks must be attributed in good part to the sluggishness induced by protection.

References

Bernanke, B., and James, H. (1991), 'The Gold Standard, Deflation and Financial Crises in the Great Depression: An International Comparison', in R. G. Hubbard (ed.), *Financial markets and Financial Crises* (NBER, University of Chicago).

Bordo, M., and Jonung, L. (1987), *The Long-Run Behaviour of the Velocity of Circulation* (Cambridge University Press).

Bowden, S., and Collins, M. (1992), 'The Bank of England and Medium-Term Finance between the Wars', *Economic History Review*, 45.

Capie, F. (1988), 'Structure and Performance in British Banking, 1870–1939', in P. Cottrell and D. E. Moggridge (eds.), *Money and Power* (London: Macmillan).

—— (1990), 'The Evolving Regulatory Framework in British Banking', in M. Chick (ed.), *Government, Industries and Markets* (Aldershot: Elgar).

—— and Collins, M. (1983), *The Interwar British Economy: A Statistical Abstract* (Manchester University Press).

—— and Rodrik Bali, G. (1982), 'Concentration in British Banking', *Business History*, 24.

—— and Webber, A. (1985), *A Monetary History of the United Kingdom, 1870–1982* (London: Allen & Unwin).

Collins, M. (1988), *Money and Banking in the United Kingdom: A History* (London: Croom Helm).

Drummond, I. M. (1991), 'Why Canadian Banks did not Collapse in the 1930s', in James *et al.* (1991).

Feinstein, C. H. (1972), *National Income, Expenditure and Output of the United Kingdom, 1856–1965* (Cambridge University Press).

Holmes, A. R. and Green, E. (1986), *Midland: 150 Years of Banking History* (London: Batsford).

James, H., Lindgren, H., and Teichova, A. (1991), *The Role of Banks in the Interwar Economy* (Cambridge University Press).

Jones, G. (1982), 'Lombard Street on the Riviera: The British Clearing Banks and Europe, 1900–1960', *Business History*, 24.

Jones, S. (1988), 'The Apogee of the Imperial Banks in South Africa: Standard and Barclays, 1919–1939', *English Historical Review*, 103.

Marshall, A. (1927), *Industry and Trade* (London: Macmillan).

Ross, D. M. (1990), 'The Clearing Banks and the Finance of Industry: New Perspectives from the Interwar years', in J. J. van Helten and Y. Cassis, *Capitalism in a Mature Economy* (Aldershot: Elgar).

Sheppard, D. K. (1971), *The Growth and Role of United Kingdom Financial Institutions, 1880 to 1962* (London: Methuen).

Tolliday, S. (1986), 'Steel and Rationalization Policies, 1918–1950', in B. Elbaum and W. Lazonick (eds.), *The Decline of the British Economy* (Oxford University Press).

16

Money and Banking in the Irish Free State, 1921–1939

CORMAC Ó GRÁDA

1. Introduction

Under the Union (1801–1921), Irish banking had developed broadly along English lines. The Bank of England had its parallel in the Bank of Ireland, and the cluster of Irish joint-stock banks founded in the 1820s and 1830s was closely integrated into the London money market. Irish interest rates were governed by London bank rate. The Bank of Ireland, chartered in 1783, prided itself on its special status, as holder of the government account in Dublin and quasi-lender-of-last-resort to the Irish banks. Because the Bank of Ireland retained far more of its commercial character than the Bank of England, the other Irish banks acknowledged its leading role with some reluctance. By and large, the Irish system had functioned smoothly, though it had not been scandal-free, nor was it a model of free competition (Ó Gráda, 1994: ch. 14).

The hallmark of Irish monetary policy after independence was caution. As Pratschke has remarked of the 1920s, 'such changes as occurred in this decade were of an institutional character, and did not immediately affect monetary policy weapons to any extent'. In the commercial banking sphere it was the same story, and the Irish banks 'continued to regard their balances in London . . . as the ultimate basis of their credit' (Pratschke, 1969: 74; Nevin, 1963: 291). The same might be said of the 1930s and 1940s. Despite the enduring popular appeal of 'crank' currency schemes, neither Cumann na nGaedheal (1921–32) nor Fianna Fáil (1932–47) administrations were keen to meddle with monetary practice.

2. The Irish Banking Sector

Commercial banking in the twenty-six-county Irish Free State (Saorstát Éireann) in the inter-war period was dominated by eight joint-stock con-

The comments of Gianni Toniolo and Antoin Murphy are gratefully acknowledged.

cerns, viz. the Bank of Ireland, the Munster & Leinster, the Provincial, the National, the Royal, the Hibernian, the Northern, and the Ulster. The Belfast Bank ceded its southern branches to the Dublin-based Royal in 1923, in order to concentrate henceforth on business in newly constituted Northern Ireland. Bank deposits in the Free State were very high relative to national income. In the south in 1932 they were worth almost £42 per head of population, compared with £48 in Britain, £40 in New Zealand, £22 in Denmark, and £72 in the USA. The bulk of deposits in Irish banks consisted of accumulated savings rather than funds for financing current spending, bearing out Andrew Jameson's quip that 'the Irishman is temperamentally a depositor, not an investor'. Other savings outlets, such as savings certificates and trustee savings banks, were less widespread in Ireland. Such outlets absorbed £5 per head of Ireland's population, compared to £22 of Britain's, £33 of Denmark's, and £40 of New Zealand's. The Irish banks converted many of their deposits into liquid resources, held for the most part on the London money market. Thus the deposits indirectly put Ireland in a very strong financial position.

The joint-stock banks differed from each other in terms of clientele, regional spread, and commercial and investment strategies. The Provincial retained its rather old-fashioned image of banker to the landed and the wealthy. The Royal was the bank of Protestant Dublin businessmen and professionals; the Munster & Leinster's orientation was towards the southern farming and business community; and so on. Still, there was ample scope for competition, which, like their confrères in England and Scotland, the Irish banks sought periodically to limit. The Ulster banks had long operated a gentlemen's agreement, and most of the banks had for several decades followed the lead of the Bank of Ireland in rate-setting. In November 1913 the Bank of Ireland had proposed to the eight joint-stock banks a system of rates and charges 'to be embodied in a formal agreement to be signed or sealed by all the banks'. However, the Munster & Leinster Bank did not attend the meeting that ensued, and the support of the Royal and the Hibernian was not forthcoming. The remaining banks considered a limited agreement, not binding in places where one of the banks not party to the agreement had a branch. But nothing seems to have come of this. At the outbreak of the Great War the banks agreed privately 'that each would retain its existing business but would not canvass for or encourage business away from any of its competitors', (Hall, 1949: 19). Rivalries about branch banking were renewed at the war's end. On a Monday evening in August 1921, for example, the chairman and manager of the traditionally staid and cautious Royal Bank travelled from Dublin to the village of Blessington, twenty miles away, in order to acquire premises for a new branch. They were prepared to act without the consent of their board, so that the Royal could begin business there on the following Thursday, one day before the Hibernian Bank (Milne, 1964: 83–4).

Yet a series of developments in 1918–19—a request from the Chancellor of the Exchequer that all the Irish banks hold interest rate on deposits to 3 per cent, the prospect of serious industrial unrest, and the uncertain future status of Irish banknotes—made for increased co-operation between the banks in other ways. This co-operation was institutionalized in 1920, when the six southern banks joined together with representatives of the three northern banks to form the Irish Banks' Standing Committee. The Committee would meet quarterly (and more often when necessary) to agree on rates for overdrafts, loans, and discounts, and to discuss other matters of common concern.

In the period under review here, banking developments were largely conditioned by the operation of the Standing Committee. This gentleman's agreement quickly acquired teeth. Not only did it set rates; members agreed in March 1920 to a scale of charges on cheques lodged in overdrawn accounts, and in May to an annual charge of one guinea on current accounts. These measures led to considerable customer dissatisfaction, but they stuck. Scales such as those shown in Table 16.1 from February 1922 give an impression of the banks' pricing policies during the inter-war period.

TABLE 16.1. *Scale of Irish banks' interest-rates*, February 1922 (%)

									(%)			
Bank of England rate	2	2.5	3	3.5	4		4.5	5	5.5	6	6.5	7
Irish banks' rate			4	4.5	5		5.5	6	6	6.5	7	7.5
Standard overdrawn accounts			5.5	5.5	6		6	6.5	7	7	7.5	8
Deposits (a) Ordinary			1.5	1.5	2		2	2.5	3	3	3.5	3.5
(b) £500–£1,999			1.5	2	2		2.5	3	3.5	3.5	4	4

The margin between standard overdraft and deposit rates—4 per cent—was wide for its day. Indeed, Irish rates were usually less attractive than those on offer in England, and there were repeated complaints in the press and from business customers about the spread between borrowing and lending rates. Delegations of businessmen and farmers[1] were met with a stock answer; the effective spread was narrower than the raw numbers suggested, and Irish customers benefited in other ways. Yet the Standing Committee's enduring concern with the loss of large deposits to English banks tells its own tale. A confidential study by Geoffrey Crowther (future editor of *The Economist*) on behalf of the Standing Committee in 1932 found claims against the banks exaggerated, yet Crowther conceded that the

---

[1] The Dublin Chamber of Commerce frequently complained about bank charges during the 1920s and 1930s. See Proceedings of the Council of the Dublin Chamber of Commerce (National Archives, 1064/3/19–20, *passim*).

typical borrower was paying 'slightly more' in Ireland than in England, but that it was in their treatment of the small depositor that the banks were 'weakest in face of criticism'. During the period under review here, individual banks grumbled at aspects of the Standing Committee's rate structure, but none seems to have systematically reneged on it.[2]

Setting standard bank charges was by no means the Standing Committee's only function. It also set out the terms for bank underwriting of government loans, and represented the banks in attempts to fend off regulation and competition. Early contacts between the Committee and the Department of Finance were none too cordial. At one story meeting in 1923, several members of the Committee wondered if the 'two young gentlemen (meaning civil servants Joseph Brennan and J. J. McElligott) who waited on them spoke with authority'. The banks were at first reluctant to underwrite government loans without a British Treasury guarantee, a politically insensitive demand that they did not continue to insist on. In the event, the government managed to raise the whole of its first national loan of £10 million without support from the banks. The terms of the second national loan of 1930 were also the outcome of tough negotiation between the banks and the Department of Finance, the banks again taking a gloomier view of the Government's creditworthiness than the outcome warranted. In November 1933 the banks wanted to know how the money sought in the next national loan was to be spent. Typically the banks sought a commission of 1.5 per cent to manage and underwrite the loans. The banks' attitude to the Financial Agreement of 1938 and the ensuing loan was one of relief. The National Bank's representative on the Standing Committee urged the banks' support for the Government, declaring the National's willingness to take up its quota of a 3.5 per cent loan at 99 or even par if the other banks went along. The other banks proved tougher, forcing 3.75 per cent at par, but were content with a one per cent commission. The Financial Agreement Loan was considerably oversubscribed.

Though it played a leading part in the Standing Committee—meetings were held at bank headquarters, usually with the bank's governor in the chair—the position of the Bank of Ireland remained rather special in the new Ireland (Fanning, 1983). Banker to the Dublin Castle administration for well over a century, the Bank of Ireland's ethos had been strongly Unionist and Protestant; in the 1920s, its court of directors was still dominated by earls, baronets, and captains. The bank had not prepared for the creation of the Irish Free State, and indeed in January 1922 a high-powered delegation crossed over to London to seek advice from the

---

[2] G. Crowther, 'Report on the Irish Banking and Currency System' (unpublished, 1932). As regards complaints about rates, e.g. IBSC. Minutes, 15 Dec. 1926, 19 Oct. 1927, 19 Jan. 1928, 23 Jan. 1928, 23 Sept. 1931, and 28 Sept. 1931.

Bank of England. Governor Montagu Norman offered little consolation, urging the creation of an independent Irish central bank on the model of the Reserve Bank of the Union of South Africa. The stark choice offered by Norman—either become a central bank or continue as a commercial bank—failed to satisfy the bank's delegation. Bank of Ireland Governor Cairnes could only reflect that Norman was 'obsessed with the pre-eminent position and conservative position of the Bank of England'.[3]

TABLE 16.2.   *Fiduciary issues of Irish banks in 1845 and 1926* (£m.)

	1845		1926	
Bank of Ireland	3.738	(58.8)[a]	1.705	(28.4)
National	0.852	(13.4)	1.365	(22.8)
Northern	0.243	(3.7)	0.243	(4.1)
Provincial	0.928	(14.6)	0.649	(10.8)
Ulster	0.311	(4.9)	0.419	(7.0)
Belfast	0.282	(4.4)	—	
Hibernian	—		0.439	(7.3)
M & L	—		0.852	(14.2)
Natl. Land Bank	—		0.055	(0.9)
Royal	—		0.273	(4.6)
TOTAL	6.354 (100.0)		6.000 (100.0)	

[a] percentages in brackets.

None the less, the Bank of Ireland adapted well to political change. It accepted the invitation from General Michael Collins, Minister of Finance of the provisional government, to become financial agent for the new administration. A few months later, in the course of a dispute with the British Treasury, 'the Court . . . animated by the feeling that in the new conditions arising out of the establishment of the Irish Free State individual interests should not be pressed to the possible advantage of the body politic, deem it a wiser and more patriotic course to merge their intests in the nation at large'. This is more than could be said at this stage of the National and Provincial, deemed by Andrew Jameson to be 'quite out of touch and sympathy with Free State affairs'. The new Government broached terms for short-term advances first with the Bank of Ireland. Early in 1923 Liam T. MacCosgair (alias W. T. Cosgrave), Collins's successor, was seeking accommodation to the tune of £500,000, and in June the Bank of Ireland joined for the first time, not without some trepidation, with the other southern Irish banks in tiding the Government over until after the general election. The bank was unhappy with its statutory allocation of the aggregate banknote issue in 1926, but its anachronistic claim for a share based on the terms of Peel's Act of 1845 rather than on business share in the mid-1920s

---

[3] IBSC file X(iii), report of meeting with Norman.

was a non-starter. (The bank's share of total Irish banknote circulation had fallen from 60 per cent in 1845 to about 45 per cent in 1880; it was still about 45 per cent in 1920–2, but its share of the note issue was lower.) Table 16.2 compares the situation in 1845 and 1926; besides reducing the share of the Bank of Ireland, the new legislation granted note-issuing rights for the first time to the Royal and the Hibernian (denied since 1845) and the Munster & Leinster (founded in 1885).

The Bank of England on occasion treated its Irish sister as a kind of satellite central bank. Changes in the London bank rate were always communicated to College Green by telegram, and the Bank of Ireland and the other Irish banks adjusted their rates without fail to maintain a margin between their minimum rate and the announced London rate. In April 1924 the Bank of England provided further evidence of the Dublin bank's special status. Governor Montagu Norman was then engaged in one of his major feats of banking diplomacy, the creation of a new German bank to finance foreign trade. The Bank of England undertook to find half the required capital, and asked the Bank of Ireland 'as a central bank to accept participation in the loan'. The Bank of Ireland duly complied, placing £250,000 at the disposal of Threadneedle Street.

Yet the vicissitudes of Anglo-Irish politics in the end ruined the special relationship between College Green and Threadneedle Street. Just a few days before the outbreak of war, a nervous Bank of Ireland court sent Deputy-Governor Sir John Keane to London to seek assurances. Keane's interview began cordially enough with his London counterpart, B. G. Catterns, with Catterns playing down Irish fears regarding the unavailability of foreign exchange and a moratorium on assets. The rest of the minute is worth quoting in full:[4]

At this point Mr Catterns retired temporarily, and on his return was accompanied by the Governor, Mr Norman, who said that notwithstanding the long and intimate relations between the two institutions he was not prepared to commit the Bank of England by promising to come to the assistance of the Bank of Ireland in an emergency of the nature under discussion. As an ordinary banking transaction there would be no question whatever about making an advance to the Bank, but in an emergency situation there was an important principal (*sic*) involved. The Bank of England looked upon Eire as a Dominion, and if they accommodated the Bank of Ireland in a crisis, there would be no reason why they should withold similar assistance from the other Dominions—the Bank was not prepared to concede this principal. Mr Norman stressed the view that the Bank 'whose centre of gravity was in Eire' should look to their own Treasury or the Currency Commission to help them over difficult periods. Sir John pointed out that the position in Eire did not admit of

---

[4] Bank of Ireland Transactions of the Court of Directors, 31 Aug. 1939. Also cited (in part) in Fanning (1983: 88). On the confidential assurances received by Dublin, see too the loaded hint in Meenan (1969: 29–30).

a solution in that way, as the Treasury came to the Bank of Ireland when it was short of funds, and the Currency Commission was not a lender of the last resort. Mr Norman then urged that as Eire was a separate political entity it should have a Central Bank of its own. He went on to say that 'two of your friends' (emphasising the word 'friends') had already approached the Bank of England for a similar assurance which the Bank of Ireland was seeking, but the Bank could not admit the principal in their case either.

After some further general remarks on the provisions of the Currency Act in regard to Consolidated Bank Notes and Legal Tender Notes, the interview terminated.

Later Mr Catterns urged the confidential nature of the information afforded as to the foreign exchange arrangements which had been discussed by His Majesty's Treasury and the Eire Government, and suggested that in any conversations which the Bank of Ireland might have with the latter, no reference be made to the fact that such information was in our possession.

Thus it took the prospect of the Second World War to switch the Bank of Ireland's full loyalty to the Irish Free State and for the commercial banks to acknowledge that an Irish central bank might have a useful role to play.

3. Official Response

The period saw two major official inquiries into banking and monetary policy options. The stance of both the Parker-Willis Commission of 1926–7 and the Commission of Inquiry into Banking, Currency and Credit (CIBCC) of 1934–8, was conservative and orthodox. So was policy, which sought simply to maintain the sterling link while gaining revenue from an Irish note issue. Yet on the question of central banking there was some ambivalence. On the one hand, though central banks were very much the flavour of the day after 1918—they had been recommended to emergent nations by the League of Nations and the Genoa Financial Conference of 1922 and enthusiastically supported by the governor of the Bank of England, Montagu Norman (cf. League of Nations, 1924)—the Irish Free State seemed not to succumb to the temptation of creating its own until 1942. On the other hand, the Currency Commission, the statutory non-political institution created in 1927 to manage the new Saorstat pound, was granted the most important responsibilities of the textbook central bank—those of defending the value of the domestic currency and generating seigniorage revenue for the Government. To that extent, the Currency Commission was a central bank by another name. The ambivalence stemmed in part from a conviction that outside the Irish Free State—and to some extent within it—central banks were being promoted as antidotes to backward or unduly risk-averse commercial banking systems. Accordingly, creating an Irish central bank might be seen as both a slight and a threat to the long-established commercial banks. The joint-stock banks were firmly opposed to any such move (e.g. *Irish Times*, 26 January 1933).

The Government quickly enacted most of the advice of the Banking Commission of 1926–7, of which the American economist Henry Parker-Willis was chairman. That Commission was dominated by bankers and their friends: its nine members included representatives of the Bank of Ireland, the National, the Munster & Leinster, and the Ulster, and neither the representatives of the Department of Finance, Parker-Willis, nor Campion (a retired Australian banker) were likely to rock the boat. Andrew Jameson of the Bank of Ireland, an old campaigner, had been the original choice for chairman. Jameson did not feel competent for the post, though it is telling that he should put the choice down to his 'reputation of being an old-fashioned conservative'.[5] Hardly surprising, then, that the Commission deemed that the soundness of Irish financial institutions vitiated the need for an Irish central bank. In this the Commission reflected the leeriness of bankers generally towards central banking (cf. Plumptre, 1940: 178–9). Furthermore, the Commission held that the virtual absence of a domestic money or capital market ruled out an independent Irish monetary policy. Such a market might develop, but could not be forced. In making this last point, the Commission was doing no more than paying its dues to the orthodoxy that 'the success of central banking depends largely upon the condition of the capital market in which it is practised' (Plumptre, 1940: 4). Now, Britain's peculiar institutional framework made it natural for the Bank of England as *de facto* central bank to control credit through open-market operations. But London's situation was quite exceptional; central bank control of the commercial banking system through reserve require-ments or moral suasion, without the intermediary of a money market, was much more important elsewhere. Bank of England orthodoxy did not prevent Norman's roving ambassador, Sir Otto Niemeyer, from recommend-ing a central bank for New Zealand in 1930. That there were 'no bill market, no short-loan market, and, generally speaking, no money market in the full sense of the term [did] not constitute insuperable objections' (Plumptre, 1940: 187; compare CIBCC, 1938: 224; Jacobsson, 1979: 131).

More important than the quality of the commercial banking system or the lack of a money market, the Irish banks' links with London and the commitment to maintain parity with sterling arguably ruled out an inde-pendent monetary policy in any case. Instead of a full-fledged central bank, the Parker-Willis inquiry therefore proposed the creation of an institution responsible for a domestic currency backed a hundred per cent by sterling notes, short-maturity British government securities, or gold as the only

[5] National Archives (SPO), S5185, minute of 29 Jan. 1926; IBSC minutes, 22 Dec. 1925.

fundamental change required.[6] In addition Irish banks were to be allowed a consolidated note issue in lieu of the fiduciary issue allowed under the Bank Act of 1845. The Commission made no provision for either bill discounting or advances. The Government's account remained with the Bank of Ireland.

The resulting Currency Commission (1927–42) guaranteed that the seigniorage from note issue belonged to the Irish authorities. How much was this worth? In a claim set out by the Irish Government during the Economic War, the seigniorage accruing to Britain while sterling remained legal tender (1922–8) was put at about £500,000 a year. This figure was reached by allowing a return of 5 per cent on the £3.9 million of British currency in circulation and another 5 per cent on the £5.5 million of British Treasury bills held by Irish banks as backing for note issue above the fiduciary allowance.[7] The estimate is probably too high; the net annual receipts of the Currency Commission in the 1930s from dividends, interest payments, and payments on consolidated banknotes, were about £200,000, or 0.1 to 0.2 per cent of national income.[8] The share of Irish legal-tender notes and coins in the total supply of outstanding money rose steadily, reaching about two-thirds by 1939 (Moynihan, 1975: 512).

The seeds of an Irish bond market were sown by the small clandestine loan raised by the First Dáil in 1919. By the mid-1930s about £25 million of government securities was being quoted on the Dublin stock market. Despite some government encouragement, this was still far from enough to create an active two-way market. Very small transactions were not a problem, but the sale of even £30,000 of national loan might take a month to complete in the mid-1930s. Such a market was little use to the Irish banks, who dealt in the London market to the tune of several hundred thousand most weeks. For example, the Bank of Ireland's short-term loans of £300,000–£500,000 to the London discount houses of Alexander, National Discount, and Union Discount stood in sharp contrast to its sales through Dublin stockbroking firms of a few thousand pounds worth of national loan or land bonds. As for markets in local industrial shares, they were typically slow. An order to sell shares at about the last quoted price might take three or four days 'as luck would have it, but it is possible you may have to wait' (Thomas, 1986: 164–71; CIBCC 1938: 395–426). Nevertheless, there was much more activity on the Dublin Stock Exchange in the late 1930s than ten years earlier. Between 1933 and 1938 the Industrial

[6] Curiously a very similar institution had been mooted in a Bank of Ireland memorandum prepared for the meeting with Montagu Norman in Jan. 1922. This scheme for a Central Reserve Bank of the Irish Free State envisaged seven directors (including three from the banks and two from the business community), and 100% backing in gold, notes and approved securities for note issue. See IBSC archive, file X(iii), Jan. 1922.

[7] Archives Dept., University College, Dublin (UCDA), P67/173.

[8] e.g. *Statement of Accounts of the Currency Commission for the Year Ended 31 March 1936*, P. 2306 (Dublin, 1936), 3.

Credit Company organized public issues worth £4.4 million, and another
£250,000 was raised without its help. Such sums, along with the £6 or so
million raised privately in these years helped to spread the investment habit
(Colbert, 1938: 14–18).

Did the Irish bank cartel result in poor service at high prices? One might
have expected a hard look at this question from the official inquiries of the
1920s and 1930s. However, both the Parker-Willis and 1934–8 Commission
were very 'soft' on the banks. In the case of the former, 'packed' with bank
representatives, and established in a hurry in order to provide a blueprint
for exchange-rate policy and seigniorage, this hardly comes as a surprise.
The banks feared much worse from the second inquiry, a creation of the
new, radical-populist Fianna Fáil administration, and tried hard at first to
quash it. Failing in that aim, they proceeded to 'capture' the inquiry though
the selection of indulgent commissioners (see below). The majority report of
the Banking Commission defended the banks against the charge of collusion
by arguing that cartels like the Standing Committee were commonplace
elsewhere, citing examples from Scotland, Britain, and the USA. Amazingly
for a commission appointed to 'examine and report on the system in
Saorstat Éireann of currency, banking, credit, public borrowing and lending', the 1934–8 inquiry failed to cross-question any representative of the
Irish joint-stock banks in public; Sir John Keane, a governor of the Bank
of Ireland and a member of the Senate, gave evidence, but only on the follies
of Fianna Fáil fiscal policy. Meanwhile, witnesses critical of the banks were
subjected to vigorous questioning by bank supporters on the Commission.
The Commission's only references to the Irish Banks' Standing Committee
(paras. 302–3) were defensive and apologetic, holding that 'it is not to the
ultimate interest of the public that competition should take the form of a
competitive reduction of charges and an increase of the rate of interest paid
upon deposits.' Perhaps so, but there were points worth at least discussing.
For example, the higher rates charged by Irish banks for loans and the slow
growth of the system might seem prima-facie evidence for a misallocation
of resources. The power of the Standing Committee to prevent individual
banks on occasion from expanding their branch networks because of
objections from other members also suggests some degree of monopoly
power. For instance, in September 1937 three banks—the Provincial, the
Northern, and the Belfast—sought permission to create several new
branches in and around Belfast. A meeting of the Standing Committee
deferred consideration indefinitely, on the basis that this would open the
door to 'unrestricted competition of a harmful nature to the offices already
established in or near these areas, and of doubtful advantage in the long-run
to newcomers'. Suspicion of bankers' monopolies was by no means confined
to cranks in the inter-war period (Plumptre, 1940: 165–70; Sayers, 1976:
236–7). But the Banking Commission, content to report overdraft rates

issued to it by the Standing Committee in its report, failed to see through the banks' strategy of not increasing overdraft rates while the Commission deliberated. Indeed, that strategy was recommended to the banks by two of their representatives on the Commission, James Sweetman and Lord Glenavy.

Two considerations possibly mitigate such criticisms. First, the banks' monopoly was countered by a powerful trade union, the Irish Bank Officials' Association. Virtually all managers and clerks were members of the IBOA, which would have been quick to capitalize on bank disunity. In the absence of the cartel, any single bank in a labour dispute would have been an easy target for the combination of a strong union and greedy business rivals. It might therefore have been slower to innovate. The problem with this argument is that the IBOA seems to have been quite adept at eating into the monopoly rents created by the cartel; in the inter-war years, Irish bank clerks were better paid than their British peers.

Second, the Irish banking sector was in the doldrums in the 1930s, and the need for some rationalization was widely conceded. Geoffrey Crowther's confidential report to the Standing Committee in 1932 highlighted the issue. Crowther found that the Irish Free State had 33 per cent more banking premises per head of population than Britain. Concerted action aimed at streamlining the branch network would result in higher profits, and enable the banks to pay a higher rate on deposits. In the following year, the Ulster Bank offered to produce at any time a list of branches that it was willing to

TABLE 16.3. *Deposits and advances of the nine Irish joint-stock banks, 1919–1938 (in percentages of the total)*

Period	B. of I.	Prov.	Natl.	Hib.	M. & L.	Royal	Belfst.	North	Ulster
(*a*) Deposits									
1919–24	16.6	8.6	21.2	7.4	14.5	2.9	9.1	7.8	12.0
1924–9	17.4	8.4	21.2	7.0	14.1	3.9	8.3	7.8	11.9
1929–34	17.7	8.2	21.1	6.6	14.3	3.7	7.8	8.1	12.4
1934–8	18.2	8.6	21.2	6.1	13.9	3.7	8.1	8.0	12.2
(*b*) Advances									
1919–24	15.8	8.5	19.9	5.7	13.3	3.6	11.7	9.8	11.7
1924–9	15.2	7.3	18.7	7.4	14.2	4.5	10.2	11.1	11.4
1929–34	16.7	7.4	19.5	6.8	13.7	4.5	8.9	10.8	11.7
1934–8	16.9	8.3	20.6	7.1	13.5	4.7	8.0	9.7	11.1

Notes: B. of I. = Bank of Ireland; Hib. = Hibernian Bank; Prov. = Provincial Bank; Natl. = National Bank; M. & L. = Munster & Leinster Bank; Royal = Royal Bank; Belfst. = Belfast Banking Company; North = Northern Bank.

The calculations exclude deposits in the National Land Bank (1919–27) and its successor, the National City Bank, a tiny fraction of the total (see Hall, 1949: 352). The Belfast Banking Company passed its southern business to the Royal in 1923, and this is reflected in the numbers. The data refer to all the banks' business, within and outside the Irish Free State.

close, and the 'redundancy of banks' was repeatedly discussed by the Standing Committee in the next few years. The results were rather disappointing, none the less. A concerted effort to effect branch closures was not made until 1938. Individual banks played bargaining games. The Bank of Ireland's articulate Lord Glenavy was the most vocal supporter of a system of branch closures, but the Belfast Bank declared satisfaction with the *status quo*, while the Munster & Leinster thought this was a matter for bank-to-bank horse-trading. Per Jacobsson's authority was invoked by Glenavy and James Sweetman (members of both the Standing Committee and Banking Commission), and eventually the Munster & Leinster conceded.[9] The result was an agreement engineered by the Standing Committee in 1939 to close twenty-five branches in twenty-three counties.

The Banking Commission defended the banks against the charge of monopoly with the argument that they engaged in various forms of non-price competition. The failure of new entrants to make an impression on the market for banking despite the healthy profits made by those already in the business, and the remarkable stability in the shares of the nine joint-stock banks in deposits and advances in the inter-war period bespeak a degree of live and let live, if not outright collusion (see below).

The 1934–8 Banking Commission had been promised by Fianna Fáil as part of its electoral programme in 1932. Finance Minister Seán MacEntee and his permanent secretary J. J. McElligott, Joseph Brennan (chairman of the Currency Commission), and representatives of the commercial banks protested both the timing and the need for such an inquiry. Brennan's objection typically contained an element of catch-22: while insisting that no institutional changes should be contemplated before exhaustive investigation, he urged that even rumours of an investigation would cause panic. Efforts to quash the inquiry were of no avail, but mention in its draft terms of reference to the 'effective control of internal and external credit' and the 'operations and methods of the joint-stock banks in regard to credit facilities' (which had alarmed MacEntee and the banks) were dropped.[10] The Banking Commission was established in late 1934 after a good deal of spadework. The Government held firm against Brennan's objections, but could hardly be accused of packing the Commission's membership with radicals. Brennan sought to spike the Commission's guns by keeping its membership small and biased towards commercial banking interests. Though he did not altogether succeed in this, his role was nevertheless paramount. Brennan was the main architect of the Commission's majority

[9] IBSC minutes, 18 Oct. 1933. See also Milne (1964). For an analogous argument see William Lazonick (1979).

[10] UCDA, P67/105(3), P67/105(2) (letters from MacEntee to de Valera, 23 Feb. 1933 and 31 Jan. 1934).

report. Other influential members included Professor George O'Brien of University College, Dublin (later a director of the Bank of Ireland), Per Jacobsson (then with the Bank for International Settlements, later president of the IMF), and Professor Theodore Gregory of the London School of Economics. The two last-mentioned were chosen as foreign experts: Charles Rist and Gustav Cassell had been invited first, but both declined. Keynes had also been briefly considered; his 1933 Finlay lecture in University College, Dublin, in support of protection and deficit spending cannot have helped his chances. George O'Brien was a trusted friend of the banks. Asked by the Standing Committee in June 1932 for advice 'as to the case which can be made by them in the event of the appointment of a Banking Commission', he felt unable to comply, but O'Brien obtained Geoffrey Crowther for them instead. Gregory and Jacobsson were both conservative in banking matters. The bishop selected, Dr McNeely, was 'unaware of any reasons why he should have been appointed, except to add an atmosphere of respectability to the conference'.[11] Brennan, who feared a commission dominated by academics, had fought very hard to get Jacobsson, then an adviser to the Bank for International Settlements.

The Banking Commission proved very indulgent to banking interests, and there was a good deal of behind-the-scenes contact between the banks and individual Commission members. Thus Lord Glenavy (repeatedly) and even Theodore Gregory urged the banks to hold their lending rates down until the Commission had reported. With Joseph Brennan at the helm, a conservative report was guaranteed.[12] The Commission's Majority Report looked back with nostalgia on the gold-standard era, and the associated 'great advance in world production, international trade and international investment' (IBCC Majority Report, para. 198). It saw little to support the policies in fashion in the 1930s, and showed little enthusiasm either for an Irish central bank. Yet in the end the majority report proposed that the Currency Commission be granted powers to engage in open-market operations, and recommended an unspecified name change to reflect this central banking feature. The Majority Report saw the main function of any such body as a restraining force on the government of the day on monetary matters. Any experimentation with the exchange rate was once more ruled out as leading to uncertainty and futile, and the Commission saw no real role for a money market in Dublin. Lord Glenavy's Minority Report interpreted the Majority Report as meaning that 'nothing whatever is wrong

[11] National Archives, S2235A (letter from Hugo V. Flinn to E. De Valera, 13 April 1935). See also Lee, *Ireland*: 199–200.

[12] As early as Apr. 1935 Hugh Flinn, parliamentary secretary to McEntee, predicted the eventual split into majority and minority camps very well in an amusing letter to de Valera. He was wrong about Sean O'Muimhneachain and Robert Barton (both government supporters), however; they signed the Majority Report (see National Archives, S2235A, 13 Apr. 1935).

with the system in Saorstat Éireann of currency, banking and credit' (Moynihan, 1975: 209, 211, 216).[13] As *The Economist*'s correspondent in Dublin put it (cited in Moynihan, 1975: 224):

The conclusions of the Commission bear all the earmarks of a compromise. The present functions are virtually limited to the issue of currency and all the holding of sterling assets against the notes issued) is to be renamed and its functions are to be enlarged. But the enlarged functions are not to include those usually attaching to a Central Bank. For example, there is to be no attempt to create a money market in Dublin, the commercial banks are not to be under the obligation of keeping reserve deposits with the new institution, and it is not even to take over the Government from the Bank of Ireland. In short, the Currency Commission is to have a new title and a research department, and that is all. It seems to be an admirable solution of the problem, which should please politicians and bankers alike.

However, *The Economist*'s correspondent was none other than Professor George O'Brien, an active member of the Banking Commission! The Commission's Majority Report was universally—and correctly—interpreted as a thinly veiled attack on the policies of Fianna Fáil. The Report sounded a warning about the balance of payments threat posed by industrialization, and was leery of the rise in public debt resulting from Fianna Fáil's social programme and the running down of foreign assets. The rhetoric of the Report anticipated that of the annual reports of that body only furtively anticipated by its authors, Ireland's Central Bank. The Government chose to ignore the Report, and it took the threat of war to produce central banking legislation. In the end, the Central Bank Act of 1942 was a compromise between, on the one hand, Brennan and the Department of Finance, and the majority of ministers on the other. Ironically, Clause 50 of that Act left open a possibility explicitly ruled out by the Banking Commission: the Central Bank's right to special deposits from the commercial banks. The aim of this clause was to induce the bank to repatriate some of their external assets for the purpose of investment at home (Hein, 1967: 13).

The Banking Commission noted that the legislation of 1927 did not envisage the Currency Commission providing advice to the Government, coyly adding that 'it does not seem to have been the habit of the Government to consult the Commission on financial questions generally'. The Banking Commission also noted the lack of co-ordinated research into

---

[13] Lord Glenavy, the Bank of Ireland's man on the Commission, was handsomely rewarded by the bank for his services (Bank of Ireland court transactions, 22 July 1937). Like other bank representatives on the Commission (though not other members), he was allowed to send a substitute to meetings. George O'Brien sat on the Commission at the behest of Lord Glenavy (Meenan, 1980: 136–8).

economic and monetary trends, and proposed the creation of a research
department in the new monetary authority.

4. Monetary Trends

Though sterling may well have been overvalued relative to foreign currencies by Churchill in 1925 (Broadberry, 1984), the effect on the Irish economy
was probably small. Higher costs in Ireland than in the United Kingdom
hardly dictated a devalued Irish pound in the late 1920s. Overall, the logic
of maintaining the link with sterling in the inter-war era was compelling,
since Irish foreign trade was almost exclusively with the United Kingdom,
and the Irish and British labour and capital markets were closely integrated.
Nevertheless, the British decision in September 1931 to suspend gold
payments was a blow to Ireland. Such a decision had been on the cards, and
the Currency Commission had even considered converting some of its
sterling balances and securities (which totalled £7.5 million at the time)
into gold or gold-backed currencies. It had failed to act out of loyalty to
the Bank of England on that occasion, though seven years later, with war
in prospect, it quietly exchanged £2.5 million of its sterling balances for
gold.

For Irish holders of sterling assets (estimated to have been worth £200
million at the time), the 25 per cent depreciation of sterling that followed
suspension constituted, in theory at least, an equivalent loss capital loss.
Their disappointment at what was seen as a breach of trust on the part of
Britain was widely shared (Bonn, 1949: 318–19):[14]

September 20, 1931, was the end of an age. It was the last day of the age of economic
liberalism in which Great Britain had been the leader of the world . . . Now the whole
edifice had crashed. The slogan 'safe as the Bank of England' no longer had any
meaning. The Bank of England had gone into default. For the first time in history a
great creditor country had devaluated (*sic*) its currency, and by so doing had inflicted
heavy losses on all those who had trusted it . . . Hitherto devaluation had been the
prerogative of improvident debtor countries. Great Britain was a powerful creditor
country, yet she had sacrificed, with apparently little regret, the fundamental
principle of an international capitalist system, the sanctity of contracts.

However, most of Ireland's external sterling assets could not have been
easily converted into some harder currency, so the implied loss of £50
million or so constituted a mere paper loss. More important, part of the loss
must have been short-term only, since the sterling value of the assets

[14] UCAD, P67/139, 'Memorandum on certain financial and economic aspects of the annual
payments by Saorstat Éireann to Great Britain' (4 Oct. 1932); Fanning (1975: 207–8); Currency
Commission, *Report for the Year Ending 31 March 1932* P. No. 729 (Dublin, 1932): 5.

probably rose to compensate for the depreciation. The dollar, which may have looked a good prospect in late 1931, was soon to depreciate even more than sterling. Still, the collapse of the gold standard provided the new Fianna Fáil administration with the opportunity to set up a public inquiry into monetary and banking policy.

Several recent studies in the Keynesian tradition have emphasized the importance of exchange-rate policy before and during the Great Depression (e.g. Broadberry, 1984; Eichengreen and Sachs, 1985; Bernanke and James, 1990). These studies show that those economies that depreciated soonest and most staged the best recoveries in the 1930s. By this reckoning British policy was a notable success, and France's loyalty to gold in the 1930s costly. Broadly speaking, the outcome of these studies is that depreciation boosted the volume of manufacturing output and exports, restored business confidence (as reflected by in the movement in Tobin's q, the ratio of an index of security to industrial output prices), dampened real wage increases, and increased the money supply. The model suggests that the sterling depreciation of 1931–3 should have given a fillip to the Irish economy. Adding Ireland as an eleventh observation to Eichengreen and Sachs's sample of ten European economies produces the result shown in Table 16.4.

TABLE 16.4. *The effects of currency depreciation: reduced-form regression results,* 1929–1935

	Adjusted R^2		Elasticity	
	Without Ireland	With Ireland	Eichengreen and Sachs	Ireland
(1) Export volume	0.558	0.405	− 0.68	+ 0.88
(2) Industrial production	0.561	0.514	− 0.50	− 0.71
(3) Real wages	0.268	0.305	0.40	0.04
(4) Tobin's q	0.467	0.291	− 1.03	− 1.78
(5) Bank deposits	0.282	0.308	− 0.54	− 0.10

Sources: (1)–(4): variables as defined in Eichengreen and Sachs (1985). Data kindly supplied by Barry Eichengreen. Irish data taken from *Statistical Abstract*. Other Irish elasticities use averages of 1929 and 1935 values. (5): data on commercial bank deposits taken from Mitchell (1975: 692–5).

The outcome shows Ireland confirming the pattern indicated by Eichengreen and Sachs as far as employment and industrial output were concerned (if one is to credit the Irish census of industrial production) and real wages. However, Irish exports fell off dramatically in real terms, despite sterling's depreciation relative to most other currencies in the sample. Moreover, viewed against the experience in the economies examined by Bernanke and

James, Irish bank deposits and advances grew very modestly relative to the depreciation against gold. Sticking with sterling cannot be blamed for this. Nor did depositors withdraw their money for fears of the banks' solvency: Irish banks were considered so safe in this period that in the wake of the US, banking crisis of 1931, several million US dollars found a temporary haven in them (*JIBI*, 1933: 74; 1934: 96; 1934: 218). The pre-1932 data are approximate, but they show that between 1926 and 1931 the aggregate deposits of Irish banks in the twenty-six counties rose by only 0.1 per cent. Between 1931 and 1939, the rise was virtually zero. These are unimpressive numbers compared to those of the London clearing banks, whose deposits rose by 5.7 per cent in 1926–31 and 28 per cent in 1931–9 (Mitchell, 1975: 683). Since the rate of inflation was about the same in both economies during the period, a *relative* decline at least in Irish macroeconomic fortunes would seem to be indicated. In support, the failure of Irish deposits to rise in the 1930s was put down to the depressed state of Irish agriculture by the Majority Report of the Banking Commission. In the eyes of the Commission, of course, the damage was largely self-inflicted, the product of an Anglo-Irish wrangle known as the Economic War (CIBCC, 1938: 190; also *JIBI*, 1935: 72; 1939: 87; Neary and Ó Gráda, 1991).

Three further reasons for the failure of deposits to rise have been suggested. The first two have less to do with the level of aggregate demand than with the structural transformation of the economy in the 1930s. First, the Banking Commission and others claimed a role for 'a higher degree of home investment' (CIBCC, 1938: 192; *JIBI*, 1938: 95; Thomas, 1986: 182–9; Colbert, 1938). Certainly, there was much more activity on the Dublin Stock Exchange in the late 1930s than ten years earlier. Between 1933 and 1938 the Industrial Credit Company organized public issues worth £4.4 million, and another £250,000 was raised without its help. A further £6 million or so was raised privately in these years. The result was a substantial increase in the paid-up capital of Irish joint-stock companies. Between 1926 and 1932 paid-up capital had risen modestly, from £35.7 million to £37.7 million; by 1938 it had reached £49.0 million. Emboldened by tax concessions and the buoyant market in Irish shares, Irish investors provided most of the capital. The process helped to spread the investment habit. But did it result in a net withdrawal of deposits from the banks? In theory, in a closed economy no such withdrawal is likely, since the expenditure of the proceeds of stock issues and other forms of company borrowing should have led to the creation of roughly equivalent flow of deposits, as the vendors of capital equipment banked their receipts. True, if the new joint-stock companies had spent the proceeds on imported capital goods, a net reduction in the deposits in the banking system would have resulted. The trade statistics show no sign of the necessary increase in the value of capital good imports: by one definition, such imports averaged £5.6 million in 1928–31, £5.0

million in 1932–5, and £6.4 million in 1936–8.[15] Overall, moreover, the sums involved are small compared to aggregate bank deposits in the Irish Free State (£114 million in 1938).

The second reason given for the sluggishness of bank deposits, that investors in Irish Government debt, culminating in the Financial Agreement Loan of 1938, financed their investments by withdrawals from the banks, is theoretically more plausible, and the sums involved more significant (*JIBI*, 1939: 87). The liabilities of the Free State Government rose from £13.9 million in 1923 to £31.8 million in 1932 to £61.4 million in 1939, and most of this debt was internally financed. Finally, the 1930s saw a big increase in deposits in the Post Office Savings Bank—£4.2 million in 1932, £10.7 million in 1939. The relatively attractive return on savings available from the post office in the 1930s was responsible for this rise, nearly double that in the United Kingdom (Mitchell, 1975: 694–5).

Reference to the picture in Northern Ireland removes some of the gloom cast by the Irish Free State bank-deposit data. In Northern Ireland deposits and cash balances fell marginally between 1926 and 1931, and dropped from £44.9 million in 1931 to £44.4 million in 1937. Admittedly, too, some other southern bank data tell a more cheerful story than the trend in deposits: the total sum of notes, bills, and cheques cleared rose from £274 million in 1932 to £324 million in 1938, while the circulation of legal-tender notes rose from £6.9 million to £10.2 million over the same period (CIBCC, 1938: 188–92; Mitchell and Deane, 1962: 448). Nevertheless, it is the sluggishness of the Irish banking sector in the 1920s and 1930s that is most striking, and this reflects, above all, the failure of the economy to grow as fast as other European economies in those decades.

References

Bernanke, Ben, and James, Harold (1991), 'The Gold Standard, Deflation, and Financial Crisis in the Great Depression: An International Comparison', in R. G. Hubbard (ed.), *Financial Markets* (Chicago: University of Chicago Press).

Bonn, Moritz (1949), *Wandering Scholar* (London: Cohen & West).

Broadberry, Steven (1984), 'The North European Depression of the 1920s', *Scandinavian Economic History Review*, 32: 159–67.

[15] Defining Class III (B–E) in the trade statistics (e.g. *Statistical Abstract 1939*: 92) as capital goods.

CIBCC (Commission of Inquiry into Banking, Currency and Credit) (1938), Report and Memoranda and Minutes of Evidence (Dublin: Government Publications).

Colbert, John P. (1938), 'The Irish Free State', *Lloyds Bank Review*, 9/95: 14–18.

Eichengreen, Barry, and Sachs, Jeffrey (1985), 'Exchange Rates and Economic Recovery in the 1930s', *Journal of Economic History* 45: 925–46.

Fanning, Ronan (1975), *The Department of Finance* (Dublin: Institute of Public Administration).

—— (1983), *Independent Ireland* (Dublin: Helicon).

Hall, F. (1949), *The Bank of Ireland* (Dublin: Figgis).

Hein, J. (1967), *Institutional Aspects of Commercial and Central Banking in Ireland* (Dublin: ERI).

Jacobsson, Erin E. (1979), *A Life for Sound Money: Per Jacobsson, a Biography* (Oxford: Oxford University Press).

JIBI (Journal of the Institute of Bankers of Ireland) (1898).

Lazonick, William (1979), 'Industrial Relations and Technical Change: The Case of the Self-Acting Mule', *Cambridge Journal of Economics*, 3.

League of Nations (1924), *Memorandum on Central Banks 1913 and 1918–1923* (Geneva: League of Nations).

Lyons, F. S. L. (1983), *The Bank of Ireland: Bicentennial Essays* (Dublin: Gill & Macmillan).

McGowan, Padraig (1990), *Money and Banking in Ireland: Origins, Development and Future* (Dublin: Institute of Public Administration).

Meenan, James F. (1969), 'The Irish Economy during the War', in Kevin Nowlan and T. D. Williams (eds.), *Ireland in the War Years and After 1939–51* (Cork: Mercier).

—— (1980), *George O'Brien: A Memoir* (Dublin: Gill & Macmillan).

Milne, Kenneth (1964), *A History of the Royal Bank of Ireland* (Dublin: Figgis).

Mitchell, Brian R. (1975), *European Historical Statistics* (London: Macmillan).

—— and Deane, Phyllis (1962), *Abstract of British Historical Statistics* (Cambridge: Cambridge University Press).

Moynihan, Maurice (1975), *Central Banking in Ireland* (Dublin: Gill & Macmillan).

Neary, J. Peter, and Ó Gráda, C. (1991), 'Protection, Economic War, and Structural Change: The 1930s in Ireland', *Irish Historical Studies*, 27: 250–66.

Nevin, Edward (1963), *Textbook of Economic Analysis*, Irish edn. (London: Macmillan).

O'Broin, Leon (1982), *No Man's Man: Joseph Brennan* (Dublin: Institute of Public Administration).

Ó Gráda, Cormac (1994), *Ireland 1780–1939: A New Economic History* (Oxford: Oxford University Press).

Plumptre, A. F. W. (1940), *Central Banking in the British Dominions* (Toronto: University of Toronto Press).

Pratschke, John (1969), 'The Establishing of the Irish Pound: A Backward Glance', *Economic and Social Review*, 1: 51–75.

Sayers, R. S. (1976), *The Bank of England 1891–1944*, i. (Cambridge: Cambridge University Press).

Share, Bernard (ed.) (1979), *Root and Branch: Allied Irish Banks Yesterday, Today and Tomorrow* (Dublin: Allied Irish Banks).

Thomas, W. A. (1986), *The Stock Exchanges of Ireland* (London: Cairns).

17

Norwegian Banking in the Inter-War Period: A Scandinavian Perspective

HELGE W. NORDVIK

1. Introductory Remarks

This chapter grows out of my research into the Norwegian banking crisis in the inter-war period with special reference to government intervention in the banking system. In view of the fact that few subjects were more hotly debated amongst contemporaries during the inter-war period, the partial collapse of the Norwegian banking system in the 1920s and the complicated and drawn-out efforts to reconstruct the banking system both in the 1920s and in the 1930s have attracted surprisingly little attention amongst Norwegian historians. In many general histories dealing with the inter-war period, the deflationary monetary policies and the return to gold is discussed, but the banking crisis and the general economic crisis of the 1920s receives a cursory treatment, and very little attention has been paid to the role of monetary and banking policies during the 1930s.

The chapter starts with a brief survey of the development of the Norwegian banking system up to the First World War and some remarks on developments during the war itself. This is followed by an examination of the monetary policies in the inter-war period in view of their special relevance to both the banking crisis and real economic variables. The extent and development of the banking crisis in the 1920s and some remarks on the early 1930s are the subject-matter for the subsequent section. The chapter concludes with a discussion of developments in the two other Scandinavian countries. The treatment of Swedish and Danish banking is necessarily brief, and the main purpose is to highlight some common and contrasting features of the three countries' respective experiences.

2. A Short Presentation of the Norwegian Banking System

The development of the Norwegian banking system exhibits several characteristic features. The Bank of Norway, established by the Norwegian parliament in 1816, two years after the dissolution of the union with Denmark, was from the start charged with two major tasks. The first was to manage the national currency and the second was to provide credit to private business. The bank was established as a private joint-stock bank, but the national parliament compelled private individuals and firms to subscribe the initial capital through a capital levy or tax. At the same time, it reserved for itself the powers to manage and control the bank through the appointment of its board of directors, who had to submit an annual report to the legislators. The Bank of Norway was given a monopoly of the note issue from its very beginning.

The first Norwegian savings bank was established in 1822 in Christiania (Oslo) and by 1850 the country had ninety savings banks. Although the savings banks secured a steadily growing share of advances in the institutional credit system, private merchant houses and individuals supplied the funds necessary for the conduct of foreign trade as well as the bulk of investments outside the agricultural sector (Knutsen, 1993). The Bank of Norway invested most of its capital in loans secured by mortgages to private individuals, while other government institutions (the so-called 'discount commissions') provided short-term credits by discounting commercial bills.

The first commercial banks were established in the major towns immediately before and during the 1850s. In the same period, the strong political agitation for an increased supply of mortgage credit resulted in the establishment of a government-controlled mortgage bank (with its directors appointed by parliament). This bank secured its funds by issuing bonds guaranteed by the State and sold both domestically and abroad. Up to the 1890s, the development of the private banking system was dominated by the strong growth of the savings banks, but commercial joint-stock banks expanded rapidly thereafter up to 1914, both in terms of numbers and asset growth.

While some Norwegian historians have maintained that the slow growth of commercial banking acted as a brake on Norwegian economic growth in general and industrial growth in particular, the institutional credit system seems on closer examination to have functioned adequately in providing finance for the growing Norwegian economy during the second half of the nineteenth century. Admittedly, the system could not on its own undertake the financing of large-scale industrial development in the two decades before the First World War, but assistance from foreign financial institutions and the rapid growth of local commercial banking after 1895 ensured that a surge in investments both in the manufacturing and shipping sectors contributed to strong economic growth before 1914 (Nordvik, 1993).

By the beginning of the First World War the Norwegian private banking system thus exhibited several peculiar characteristics. From Table 17.1 it will be apparent that the Norwegian private banking system consisted of a large

number of banks. With a population of around 2.5 million in 1914, Norway
had 525 savings banks and 119 joint-stock banks, or almost twenty-six
banks per 100,000 inhabitants. Most of these were small local banks, and
both their depositors and their borrowers were people or firms located in
the region where the bank operated. Norway had no branch banking
system. With the exception of a small minority of the large commercial
banks in the largest cities, no banks had branches outside their place of
registry (Petersen, 1986).

Another and related feature of the Norwegian private banking system was
its decentralized structure, and the close relationship between the local
economy and the local bank(s). A third characteristic of the Norwegian
banking system was the large number of savings banks. With the exception
of some fairly large savings banks in the major towns, most of these banks
were small, but taken together they accounted for 42 per cent of total assets
in the private banking system in 1914 and 27 per cent in 1919. Although
these banks by and large served small savers and small businesses, many of

TABLE 17.1. *Norwegian joint-stock and savings banks,* 1914–1939 (Kr. million)

Year	Joint-stock commercial banks			Savings bank		
	No.	Assets	Deposits	No.	Assets	Deposits
1914	116	979	630	525	724	638
1915	119	1,334	856	527	816	724
1916	138	2,483	1,441	537	1,066	952
1917	160	3,917	2,200	541	1,370	1,244
1918	193	4,720	2,721	549	1,711	1,566
1919	195	5,211	2,972	555	2,015	1,839
1920	192	5,461	3,112	562	2,253	2,053
1921	185	5,089	2,982	572	2,500	2,296
1922	170	4,532	2,697	575	2,657	2,439
1923	166	3,868	2,261	579	2,742	2,528
1924	164	3,644	2,065	580	2,776	2,555
1925	160	3,635	1,994	584	2,768	2,541
1926	162	3,259	1,993	602	2,771	2,527
1927	152	2,802	1,765	619	2,668	2,423
1928	148	2,643	1,646	624	2,597	2,352
1929	151	2,586	1,596	633	2,540	2,287
1930	151	2,401	1,498	627	2,495	2,234
1931	145	2,213	1,373	622	2,414	2,150
1932	133	2,096	1,245	617	2,399	2,114
1933	133	1,949	1,137	615	2,335	2,051
1934	120	1,859	1,048	616	2,272	1,980
1935	105	1,569	864	614	2,288	1,990
1936	105	1,571	840	605	2,181	1,863
1937	105	1,709	939	606	2,213	1,889
1938	105	1,807	1,011	606	2,307	1,971
1939	104	1,855	985	605	2,267	1,926

Source: Statistiske oversikter 1948 (Oslo: Central Bureau of Statistics, table 168).

the coastal banks in practice functioned as commercial banks inasmuch as they played a significant role as sources of risk capital to local firms and private investors (Nordvik, 1993).

A fourth characteristic feature of the Norwegian private banking system was the almost total absence of government regulation and supervision. Admittedly, the savings banks were regulated and supervised according to the Savings Bank Act of 1887. A special Savings Banks Inspectorate was set up in 1900, but a lack of resources prevented any close supervision of lending practices and policies in the savings banks. This became a serious problem during the First World War, when many coastal savings banks expanded rapidly and increased their loans to customers engaged in commerce and shipping (Nordvik, *et al.*, 1989).

The expansion of the savings banks' sector and the problems associated with high-risk loans pale into insignificance when compared to the explosive growth in the joint-stock commercial banks (Knutsen, 1991). These banks were not subject to government regulation and supervision. The Limited Liability Act of 1910 specified general rules for the establishment of joint-stock companies and these rules also applied to joint-stock banks. Apart from stipulating that banks should transfer 20 per cent of their total annual profits to a reserve fund (the general rule for other limited liability companies was 10 per cent), the Act contained no special provisions for joint-stock banks.

The rapid growth of new joint-stock banks as well as the tremendous growth in bank assets during 1916 and 1917 led to discussions between the authorities and the banking community on measures to control and supervise the joint-stock banks. A meeting held at the Ministry of Finance in December 1917 showed that there was broad agreement on the need to control the growth of new commercial banks, as well as a general commercial banking act. The latter would necessarily take some time, and in fact a general banking law did not enter the statute-book until 1924, well after the partial collapse of the banking system. A provisional Act of 9 March 1918 specified that new joint-stock banks had to obtain a concession from the Ministry of Finance, but this Act came too late to influence the banking boom during the First World War (Koefoed, 1940; Petersen, 1957; Knutsen, 1991).

Growth in the Norwegian private banking sector during the First World War was first and foremost due to a rapid expansion in joint-stock commercial banking. The number of joint-stock banks increased from 119 at the end of 1914 to 195 at the end of 1919. Total assets of the commercial banks increased from Norwegian Kr. 979 million in 1914 to Kr. 5,211 million in 1919, or by 432 per cent. The growth in bank lending was also quite spectacular. Loans outstanding from the Norwegian commercial banks increased from Kr. 751 million in 1914 to Kr. 3,754 million in 1919, or by close to 400 per cent.

The explosion in joint-stock bank lending typically took the form of so-called cash-credit loans, or overdrafts. Such loans were more often than not unsecured by mortgages in the assets of the borrowers, although it was not uncommon that borrowers deposited shares and bonds with the banks as security for their overdrafts. Cash-credit loans from joint-stock banks increased from Kr. 350 million in 1914 to Kr. 2,745 in 1919, or by almost 700 per cent (Knutsen, 1990).

Thus, the Norwegian banking system as a whole was characterized by many small commercial banks, by the existence of an extraordinary large number of both rural and urban savings banks, some of them to all intents and purposes functioning as commercial banks, and by the relatively large role played by government banks, including the Bank of Norway, in providing credit to private business, chiefly in the primary sector of the economy and in the less developed parts of the country, particularly northern Norway.

The Bank of Norway had for most of the century only hesitantly and with great reluctance assumed the role of lender-of-last-resort, and systematic support of the private banking sector only emerged in the wake of the banking crisis following the collapse of the building boom around the turn of the century. However, the banking crisis of the 1920s forced the Bank of Norway to play a much more active role *vis-à-vis* the banking sector and enhanced its importance in economic policy-making generally.

3. Monetary Policy and the Banking System

What was the relationship between the development of the banking system and the policies pursued by the monetary authorities during the inter-war period? The existing literature has tended to view the banking crisis of the 1920s first and foremost as a result of a combination of real and monetary factors with its roots in the developments during the First World War and the immediate post-war period as well as the international Depression of 1920–1. There is ample evidence to support the thesis that the banking crisis owed a lot to the war-time boom and the expansion of bank lending and domestic liquidity during the 1914–20 period (Knutsen, 1990, 1991; Nordvik, 1992). However, an examination of the monetary policies pursued in the period from 1921 up to the formal readoption of the gold standard at the old 1914 parity in May 1928, indicates that monetary policy must share some of the blame both for the severity of the banking crisis and the slow real growth of the Norwegian economy in the 1920s (Hanisch, 1979). On the other hand, the decision to leave the gold standard in September 1931, the decisive intervention of the monetary authorities in support of the two largest banks in 1931–2 and the decision to peg the value of the Norwegian krone to sterling in 1933, all contributed materially to the favourable growth record of the Norwegian economy in the 1930s (Nordvik, 1990).

The Bank of Norway suspended the convertibility of its notes for gold on 5 August 1914. The export of gold was banned, but high export earnings both from raw materials and shipping services during the war years meant both that the domestic currency rose above its pre-war gold value and that the reintroduction of convertibility on 8 March 1916 had no practical effect and that monetary expansion and inflation continued virtually unchecked during the war. An import boom during 1919 and 1920 led to the renewed suspension of convertibility on 19 March 1920 and marked the beginnings of a long period of unprecedentedly large fluctuations in the international value of the Norwegian currency (see Figure 17.1). Norway returned to the gold standard at the pre-war parity on 1 May 1928 and remained on the gold standard until 28 September 1931, when the Bank of Norway suspended gold payments following the British decision to leave gold a week earlier. Until May 1933 the krone floated, and for the rest of the 1930s it was effectively linked to sterling at a rate of 19.90, an effective devaluation of some 9.5 per cent compared to the sterling gold parity rate of 18.16 (Keilhau, 1936, 1952).

The monetary expansion during the First World War was due both to high export earnings expanding the monetary base as well as to the expansionary policy of the Bank of Norway, particularly in the years 1916–18. The rapid rate of growth in the money stock up to 1919–20 was reversed in the following years (see Table 17.2). The new governor of the Bank of Norway, Nicolai Rygg, assumed his position on 1 November 1920.

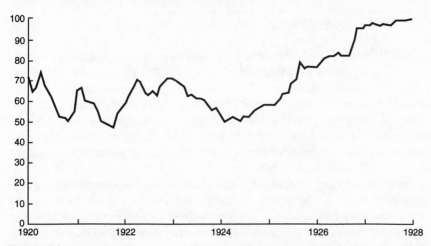

FIG. 17.1 Monthly quoted values of Norwegian kroner in per cent of gold dollars (USD), 1920–1928

Sources: Bank of Norway, *Annual Report, 1924*, and *Annual Report, 1927*:45

TABLE 17.2. *Norwegian money stock,* 1914–1918 (end-of-quarter figures) and 1919–1939 (end of month figures) (Kr. million)

Year	Currency in circulation	M1	M2
1914	126.8	170.8	1,357.7
1915	147.8	220.5	1,568.2
1916	215.1	381.6	2,262.2
1917	279.9	542.9	3,199.9
1918	369.2	700.0	4,275.3
1919	399.6	704.2	4,799.7
1920	422.8	749.6	5,241.9
1921	398.1	690.6	5,407.2
1922	364.9	607.3	5,395.3
1923	380.1	568.9	4,746.3
1924	371.3	538.7	4,450.5
1925	348.8	470.4	4,263.1
1926	314.7	436.0	4,080.3
1927	302.3	425.3	3,877.3
1928	297.6	398.5	3,558.9
1929	295.8	411.7	3,504.8
1930	295.4	422.6	3,485.3
1931	284.3	416.8	3,430.8
1932	300.4	410.7	3,251.4
1933	294.2	401.8	3,191.9
1934	311.7	413.3	3,059.9
1935	315.8	434.2	3,104.2
1936	367.9	504.3	3,111.1
1937	404.3	569.5	3,170.2
1938	431.2	608.6	3,388.8
1939	477.3	673.7	3,453.1

Source: Klovland (1984: Table 6.2).

He had already laid the necessary foundations for a reversal of the expansionary and accommodating monetary policy pursued during the war years by influencing the new rules of issuing money incorporated in the revised Bank of Norway Act of 26 November 1920. By using the traditional tools of monetary policy, i.e. keeping the discount rate high and severely tightening the loan policies of the central bank, Rygg was able to turn the rate of change in the money stock from + 11.2 per cent in 1919 to − 0.2 per cent in 1922 (Klovland, 1984).

Seen in a longer perspective the reduction in the money stock was a necessary part of the return to gold. Support to individual banks by providing lender-of-last-resort money through the discounting of commercial paper could only delay the reduction in the money stock, not fundamentally alter it. By 1925, the process was no longer mainly influenced by monetary policy (although some of the money inflow from abroad was sterilized by an agreement between the banks and the Bank of Norway), but by the developments in Norway's current account (deficit turning into substantial surplus) and by short-term capital movements (speculators buying Norwegian kroner in anticipation of a return to the gold standard).

Thus the banking crisis did not have a major impact on the course of monetary policy in the 1920s—the effect of the crisis was rather to delay the readjustments necessary to return to gold. What about the other side of the coin—to what extent did monetary policy contribute to the banking crisis? The roots of the Norwegian banking crisis must definitely be sought in the First World War boom, but the monetary policies pursued in the 1920s aiming for a return to gold at the pre-war parity were simply not reconcilable with the avoidance of a major banking collapse. With the advantage of hindsight it is clear that there was no way the policy-makers could both have their cake and eat it. The attempts in this direction led to a self-imposed recession in the middle of the 1920s and a much more severe banking crisis than would otherwise have been the case (Nordvik, 1992).

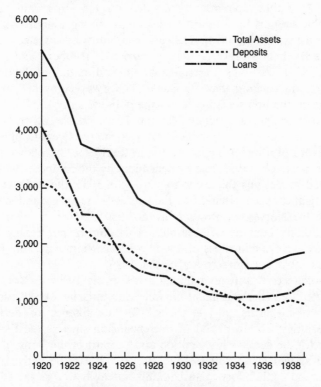

FIG. 17.2 Total assets, deposits, and loans in Norwegian joint-stock banks, 1920–1939 (Kr million)
Sources: Statistical Yearbook of Norway, 1930, Tables 110–12; *Historical Statistical, 1968,* Tables 252–3; *1978* Tables 261–2

Much of the discussion amongst historians on the return-to-gold policy in Norway during the 1920s has been concerned with the motives and viewpoints of the political parties, the central government decision-makers, and the business community in the process that led towards the resumption of the gold standard at the pre-war parity in May 1928 (Sejersted 1973, 1974; Hveding 1973, 1982; Egge, 1974; Danielsen, 1981). The debate on the reasons for and motives behind the decision to return to gold has contributed significantly towards a better understanding of the decision process behind the adoption of a deflationary monetary policy. In particular, the actions of the Bank of Norway and its strong-willed governor has to be understood not only in terms of Norwegian economic developments during and after the First World War, but must also be viewed in a wider Scandinavian and European context (Sejersted, 1973).

While there certainly was widespread opposition to a deflationary policy amongst primary producers and their political representatives (Hveding 1973, 1982), public opinion was divided on the issue, and there was considerable support for a return to gold even amongst industrialists in the export industries (Egge, 1974). The earlier attempts by some economists to depict the Bank of Norway and its governor as stubborn and misguided (Keilhau, 1952) overlooks the ineffectual and split nature of the opposition and the strong backing that the Bank of Norway enjoyed from leading politicians on the non-socialist side of the political fence.

The monetary policies pursued in the 1930s on the other hand were consistent with both real economic recovery from the Great Depression and the avoidance of a major banking crisis in the 1930s. By following sterling off gold in September 1931, and by consolidating the competitive advantage thus gained by pegging the krone to sterling in 1933, the Bank of Norway made a significant contribution to the successful recovery and subsequent growth of the Norwegian economy in the 1930s (Nordvik, 1990). This fits of course nicely into the well-established wisdom of not having an over-valued exchange rate in times of major world economic decline (Bernanke and James, 1990; Eichengreen and Sachs, 1985).

The avoidance of a major banking crisis in the 1930s in Norway must be attributed to a combination of the following three factors: (1) the severity of the banking crisis in the 1920s, (2) the absence of destabilizing factors resulting from a period of overexpansion such as the First World War, and (3) the decisive intervention and support of the Bank of Norway when the system came under strain in 1931–2. By the early 1930s, the reconstruction of the Norwegian banking system as well as the adjustment of the real economy to a significantly lower price level had resulted in a situation where the banking system was much less vulnerable to external shocks than had been the case in the 1920s. The international Depression did not really hit the Norwegian economy hard before the second half of

1930, due to lags in investment and continuing high output in many export industries.

The decision to go off gold preceded the banking crisis of November 1931, when two of the three remaining large commercial banks in Norway contacted the monetary authorities and asked for help. The two banks, Den norske Creditbank (DnC) and Bergens Privatbank (BP), were both forced to increase their borrowing from the Bank of Norway in the scramble for liquidity that followed devaluation in September 1931 and the generally fluid and insecure situation in the world economy. In Norway the situation was further complicated by a major conflict in the labour market, with strikes and lock-outs leading to further demands being placed on the banking system. These problems all contributed to difficulties for the banks on the liquidity side. However, what triggered the crisis was the realization in both banks that they would have to register major losses on lending to industrial customers by the end of the year. The banks thus found

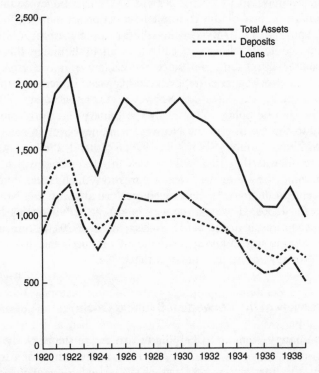

FIG. 17.3 Total assets, deposits, and loans in Norwegian joint-stock banks, 1920–1939, deflated (Kr.million)
Sources: Statistical Yearbook of Norway, 1930, Tables 110–12; *Historical Statistics, 1968*, Tables 252–3; *1978*, Tables 261–2; Index: 'Økonomisk Revues Engrosprisindeks', NOS X 178, Table 179.

themselves in both a classic liquidity situation as well as in a situation where they would lose part of their own capital (Petersen, 1982).

From the point of view of the banks, the situations they found themselves in was somewhat similar to that of the early 1920s. However, there were also differences. The most important was probably that this time the potential losses and write-off were much more easily calculated and predictable. It was thus possible to approach the capital market and ask for new share capital. The banks secured a three-month moratorium and were able to raise new capital as well as to secure a promise of unlimited liquidity support from the Bank of Norway. In this way, the banks secured their survival, and a new banking crisis was avoided (Nordvik, 1990).

The expansionary monetary policy pursued by the Bank of Norway after the suspension of the gold standard in September 1931 manifested itself through a sharp increase in the loans to the banking sector and successive reductions in the discount rate which by the end of 1932 stood at 4 per cent and was further reduced to 3.5 per cent in 1933. This policy counteracted the deflationary impact of the continued reduction in bank deposits (see Table 17.2 and Fig. 17.3). By pegging the krone to sterling in 1933, the central bank could no longer effectively control liquidity through its foreign-exchange operations, but since the exchange rate chosen in fact undervalued the Norwegian currency, liquidity was injected into the economy via continuing surpluses on Norway's current account. Thus, the foreign-exchange-rate policy followed by the Bank of Norway contributed significantly to the increase in the Norwegian money stock in spite and to an increase in bank liquidity (Nordvik, 1990; Skånland, 1967).

The net result was that the banking system as a whole withstood the stormy economic climate of the Great Depression much better than in the 1920s and contributed to the improved performance of the Norwegian economy in the 1930s. However, the weakening of the Norwegian banking sector that was a result of the banking crisis in the 1920s, also meant that the private banking system played a significantly reduced role as a source of finance for Norwegian business firms in the 1930s.

4. An Overview of the Norwegian Banking Crisis

While the banking system up to 1914 had expanded in step with the growth of the Norwegian economy and had experienced a boom during the First World War, the inter-war period was characterized by a major banking crisis in the 1920s and renewed difficulties during the early 1930s. The net result of these developments was a severe reduction in the number of commercial joint-stock banks during the inter-war years as a whole. The changes in commercial bank structure came largely through the liquidation of existing banks, as well as a limited number of more or less forced mergers. The number of commercial banks was almost halved as a result of the crisis, and the total assets and outstanding loans of the commercial banks in particular fell rapidly in the 1920s and the first half of the 1930s (see Table 17.1 and Figure 17.3). The severe fluctuations in the price level during the 1920s and the relatively stable price level in the 1930s mean that the fall in real terms was less in the 1920s, but quite pronounced in the first half of the 1930s.

The Norwegian banking crisis in the inter-war period can be divided chronologically into three subperiods (Nordvik, 1992). The years 1920–2 represents a turning-point in the sense that the expansion of the banking system was halted in terms both of the number of banks and the growth in their assets. Furthermore, a considerable number of commercial banks both in the provinces and in the capital experienced liquidity problems and many had to be assisted through the joint intervention of the Bank of Norway and the largest commercial banks (Hofstad, 1927). During 1921 and 1922 the authorities pursued a policy of forced mergers, restructing, and direct support to banks that experienced liquidity problems. However, it soon became apparent that these measures were insufficient, although they were successful in some cases.

The collapse of the commercial banks started in earnest in 1923, when a number of large regional banks as well as some major commercial banks based in the capital suspended their operations. The years 1923–8 were years of severe crisis for the Norwegian banking system. The remainder of the inter-war period can be characterized as a period of liquidation and restructuring: liquidation inasmuch as many banks were wound up and ceased to exist, restructuring inasmuch as many banks were given an infusion of fresh capital combined with a writing down of their share capital. Where the latter course proved impossible or impractical, new banks were often, but not always, established to take the place of banks that went into liquidation (Engebretsen, 1939; Nordvik, 1992).

During the winter of 1922–3 the monetary authorities gradually realized that the extent of the banking collapse necessitated some form of intervention to prevent the crisis from developing into a banking panic and collapse of the banking system as a whole. In practice, the Bank of Norway had until then acted as a lender-of-last-resort, providing the necessary liquidity to banks in trouble. The bank had also acted as an intermediary by organizing and mobilizing credit and financial assistance from other banks, the Government (through the Ministry of Finance) to supplement assistance given by the central bank itself. This strategy was no longer viable in the face of serious difficulties in some major banks and the imminent collapse of some major regional banks.

To buy time, the Bank of Norway proposed that the Norwegian parliament should pass a temporary Bank Administration Act, which essentially enabled banks to be taken into 'protective custody', i.e. to be given protection from its creditors for a limited time-period under government supervision. The Act was duly passed in March 1923, and a large number of commercial banks as well as some savings banks subsequently applied for protection under the Act.

In reality, the Administration Act implied that failed banks were allowed to continue operations, and that new deposits would have priority over old deposits if the bank later should be forced to go into liquidation. From the time the banks were given protection, the deposits were 'frozen', i.e. the banks were allowed to operate with the 'old' depositors taking all the risks, since the stockholders presumably had already lost their money and new depositors were protected through having first claim on the banks' resources. This created unforeseen problems, and may in fact have contributed to or hastened the process of bank 'closures', since depositors shifted their deposits away from banks that were perceived to be candidates for protection under the Administration Act.

A further complication was provided by the granting of a government guarantee (based on an enabling resolution passed by the Storting at the end of April 1923) to the new depositors of the two large commercial banks that ceased payments in 1923, Centralbanken for Norge and Foreningsbanken, formed in 1921 as a result of a merger between two large commercial banks in Oslo and Bergen. The guarantee was given after protracted negotiations on 5 May 1923 and was largely motivated by the fear of possible foreign repercussions if these two large banks failed to fulfil their obligations to their foreign creditors (Petersen, 1982). Foreign deposits at Centralbanken for Norge at the time when the guarantee was given totalled Kr. 89.3 million, and the large amounts owed to foreign creditors no doubt had a decisive influence on the willingness of the Bank of Norway and the Ministry of Finance to give such a guarantee (Rygg, 1950). This in effect

TABLE 17.3. *Norwegian bank failures, 1920–1928* (Number of banks and their total assets in Kr. million)

Year	Commercial banks		Savings banks	
	No.	Assets	No.	Assets
1920	3	10	—	—
1921	3	11	2	10
1922	9	166	—	—
1923	22	2,574	5	17
1924	8	398	2	2
1925	10	44	3	8
1926	13	165	3	30
1927	8	88	11	58
1928	7	32	22	110

Source: Økonomisk Revue, 8 (1932: 230–1).

gave special protection to new depositors in these banks, and probably contributed to other bank closures, since depositors in other banks could reduce their risk exposure by shifting deposits to these two banks (Brøgger, 1928; Petersen, 1957).

The purpose of the 1923 Act was to allow the Bank of Norway sufficient time to examine the banks that sought protection under this legislation. The general bankruptcy legislation did not allow the banks to seek protection from their creditors for a limited period with a view to allow financial reconstruction. After having determined their financial status and prospects, the Bank of Norway and the Ministry of Finance would make a decision on their future, i.e. whether they could be given an infusion of fresh capital

TABLE 17.4. *Norwegian banks given protection under the Administration Acts and banks placed into liquidation, 1923–1930*

Year	Protected banks		Banks in liquidation	
	Commercial	Savings	Commercial	Savings
1923	21	6	—	—
1924	5	—	—	1
1925	7	3	6	—
1926	8	3	11	3
1927	5	7	10	4
1928	1	1	11	6
1929	—	—	2	1
1930	—	—	1	—
TOTAL	47	20	41	15

Source: Rygg (1950: 144).

sufficient to enable them to survive or whether they would have to be liquidated.

The problems in the banking sector continued in 1924, and in March that year another of the large commercial banks, Den norske Handelsbank, had to suspend payments and seek protection under the Administration Act. Three of the six largest commercial banks were thus under government protection. The aim of the authorities was to restructure as many banks as possible, but it soon became clear that the extent of the losses made this unrealistic. Therefore, the original Administration Act was replaced by a new Administration Act which was passed by parliament on 17 July 1925. This prolonged the administration system for another three years. After 17 July 1928 no banks were allowed the special protection afforded by the Act, and had to be liquidated if they were unable to reach an accommodation with their creditors under the ordinary bankruptcy legislation (Nordvik, 1992; Petersen, 1982).

Altogether forty-seven commercial banks and twenty savings banks were given protection under the Administration Acts in the years 1923–8. Most of the forty-one commercial banks and fifteen savings banks were subsequently liquidated. In the period from 1 November 1922 to the end of 1930, altogether twenty-seven new commercial banks were established, with a total share capital of Kr. 35,144,000 (Engebretsen, 1939; Nordvik, 1992).

The losses suffered by the Norwegian banks during the 1920s have been estimated at around Kr. 1,500 million based on the official banking statistics. These loss figures probably represent a minimum figure, since loss figures at many small banks in the early 1920s were incompletely reported, and losses in some banks that went into liquidation and dropped out of the banking statistics were not included in the reported loss figures (Engebretsen, 1939). As will be evident from Table 17.5, losses were spread out over a long period.

This was partly a result of the protection of the Administration Acts, which allowed banks to postpone losses by carrying bad debts on their books for many years. The heaviest losses were suffered in 1923, the year when many banks had to seek protection from their creditors under the Administration Act, and in 1925. In both of these years the losses represented more than 8 per cent of total assets in the joint-stock banks. Total losses in the commercial banking sector corresponded to 30 per cent of the average annual value of the national product during the 1920s (Skånland,

TABLE 17.5. *Norwegian Bank losses (write-offs and operational losses) and profits, 1920–1930, in the commercial banking sector (Kr. million and % total assets)*

Year	Losses and write-offs		Profits	
	Kr million	% total assets	Kr million	% total assets
1920	51.1	0.96	+ 80.2	+ 1.52
1921	118.4	2.25	− 8.3	− 0.16
1922	103.9	2.16	− 31.6	− 0.66
1923	335.9	8.00	− 289.6	− 6.90
1924	117.8	3.14	− 79.6	− 2.12
1925	281.6	8.61	− 235.9	− 7.21
1926	193.2	5.67	− 151.7	− 4.45
1927	176.3	5.82	− 145.7	− 4.81
1928	66.9	2.47	− 35.8	− 1.33
1929	41.5	1.59	+ 10.7	− 0.41
1930	25.5	1.02	+ 15.0	+ 0.60
1920–30	1,512.1	—	− 872.0	

Source: *Private commercial banks 1930* (Oslo: Central Bureau of Statistics, Table k).

1990). Many of the losses written off in the years after 1923 had in reality been incurred in the 1920–3 period.

Bank losses suffered through loan defaults by borrowers were investigated by the Bank Inspectorate in 1926–7. The investigation encompassed losses on 1,030 bank customers where the losses exceeded Kr. 100,000 in the years 1920–5. Total losses in this category of debtors amounted to 74.8 per cent of all losses in the banks covered in the investigation (fifty-six joint-stock banks representing 92 per cent of total commercial bank assets, and fifty-four savings banks representing 60 per cent of total savings bank assets).

Almost a third of the losses (31.3 per cent) were due to manufacturing firms, 24.5 per cent of the losses were suffered on shipping clients, and 27.8 per cent resulted from advances made to commercial customers. Advances made to mining firms resulted in losses totalling 8.2 per cent of total losses, and the remainder (8.2 per cent) were due to losses on clients in other sectors of the economy (Nordvik, 1992).

Banks did not only lose money on their clients or debtors, but suffered losses on deposits in other banks, as well as on their portfolio investments. Generally speaking, these losses were small compared to the large losses on advances to customers, but for some of the larger banks such losses were considerable. As an example, Centralbanken for Norge A/S wrote off losses totalling Kr. 25.4 million on other commercial banks in the period 1919–25. In addition to these direct losses the bank also wrote off Kr. 9.6 million on shares in other joint-stock banks. Thus the bank lost altogether Kr. 35 million on other banks during this period, a figure that amounted to almost 23 per cent of total write-offs (Nordvik, 1992).

Bank failures were not concentrated in any particular region or area, but spread widely over the country as a whole. However, banks located in coastal towns with strong links to maritime industries or sectors such as fish exports and shipping were particularly hard hit. In many coastal towns all such banks experienced difficulties. This was the case in towns such as Haugesund, where all savings banks as well as commercial banks at one time or another suspended payments in the course of the 1920s, as well as in Stavanger, where both the town's commercial banks failed in 1923. Further north, banks in Aalesund, Kristiansund, and Molde all had to suspend payments. In general, banks in the interior as well as banks in northern Norway were less affected than banks along the coast. Very few commercial banks were unaffected by the crisis, but savings banks in general escaped serious problems. The exception were savings banks in coastal towns that had been tempted into speculative loans during the First World War, and savings banks that had overextended themselves by financing hydroelectric power stations during the war and in the early 1920s. Most banks suffered losses because they had deposits with or loans to other banks that were forced to suspend payments. The one Norwegian commercial bank that survived the crisis without serious difficulties, Christiania Bank og Kreditkasse, nevertheless had to write off Kr. 9.4 million on its loans to or shares in other banks in the years from 1919 to 1932. This amounted to 18.6

per cent of the bank's total losses of Kr. 50.5 million in the same period (Engebretsen, 1939, 1948).

It goes without saying that such a severe banking crisis led to many problems between the banks and their loan customers. In the first instance, the banking crisis was a reflection of problems in the Norwegian economy and among Norwegian business. The economic boom during and after the First World War had led to high profits, rising prices and costs. High surpluses on the balance of payments during the war were frittered away during the import-led post-war boom. The post-war Depression that struck the Norwegian economy during 1920 was made worse by rapidly rising costs due to high wage-settlements in 1920. Many firms had incurred very large debts during the last two war-years and the subsequent boom, debts that could not be serviced when prices fell in 1920–1. The combination of large investments during and after the war financed by short-term bank loans and the fall in prices was disastrous for Norwegian business firms. The wholesale price level peaked in September 1920 at 425 (1914 = 100) and fell to an index value of 269 in December 1921 and 220 in December 1922. Hardest hit by the falling price level were the export sectors of the economy, i.e. shipping and shipbuilding, fishing, and parts of manufacturing industry such as wood processing, hydroelectric energy-intensive industries particularly the electro-chemical and electrometallurgical industries, and the mining industry (Jacobsen, 1924).

As early as 1919 and 1920 many of the larger joint-stock banks had to refinance many of their industrial customers. Through these transactions many client–bank relationships were cemented in such a way that the fortunes of the bank and its client were inextricably bound together for most of the inter-war period. Through the conversion of unsecured debts into shares combined with long-term mortgage debts many Norwegian industrial firms were saved from bankruptcy, but at the cost of losing their freedom of action. The financial weakening of the banks as a result of the banking crisis in turn meant that they were reluctant to finance investments that could have increased the competitiveness and profitability of Norwegian manufacturing industry (Nordvik, 1991).

During the banking crisis there was a severe reduction in both bank deposits and bank advances. Between 1920 and 1926, the years when most of the losses occurred, total bank advances to the public declined from Kr. 5,575 million to 3,324 million. The decline was almost totally due to a reduction in the advances from commercial banks, since savings banks not only maintained their deposits from customers, but also kept up their advances. However, since savings banks were relatively unimportant as sources of finance to commerce and industry, this must have implied a severe decline in the funds available to finance the manufacturing and commercial sector of the economy.

According to one estimate, about 40 per cent of the reduction in total bank advances in this period came about through repayment of borrowings, while the remainder, or 60 per cent, was due to bank losses on loans to customers (Skånland 1967: 156). Most of the losses suffered by the banks during the worst years of the banking crisis were covered by their shareholders directly through the writing down of the value of the shares or indirectly through the use of reserves. Bank depositors suffered relatively little from the banking crisis, although they of course had the added

TABLE 17.6. *Distribution of Norwegian bank losses,* 1920–1926 (Kr. million and %)

	Kr million	% of total assets
Bank reserves and current profits	615	49.8
Write-down of shares	365	29.5
Write-down of loans from Bank of Norway	60	4.9
Write-down of government loans	59	4.8
Write-down of deposits from the public	128	10.4
Write-down of deposits from abroad	8	0.6
TOTAL	1,235	100.0

Source: Skånland (1967: 156).

problem of having their deposits frozen in the banks that had protection under the Administration Acts of 1923 and 1925.

The common destiny of banks and their industrial customers that was a result of the post-war economic crisis and the banking crisis of the 1920s is particularly apparent in the case of the banks that were given protection by the Administration Acts of 1923 and 1925. Two opposing tendencies were apparent in the relationship between such banks and their customers. On the one hand, banks given protection under the Administration Acts were under considerable pressure from their boards of administration to reduce their credit exposure by calling in loans to customers. This resulted in severe pressure on many industrial customers at precisely the time when repayment was made even more difficult by the deflationary policy associated with Norway's return to the gold standard.

On the other hand, banks that had a substantial part of their portfolio placed as advances to one or a few major industrial clients were given a breathing-space by the protection afforded by the Administration Acts. When a failed bank had a substantial part of its assets locked up in loans to major industrial customers, it was no longer only a bank–client problem, but a situation which the monetary authorities could not afford to ignore. They were well aware of the need to protect the banks as a way of preventing the collapse of important sectors of the Norwegian economy, particularly manufacturing firms that were both large employers as well as export-earners (Rygg, 1950).

The banking system suffered a further shock during the international Depression of the early 1930s. As already mentioned, two of the remaining large commercial banks were forced to apply for protection in the form of a three-month moratorium in November–December 1931. During the moratorium a concerted effort by the banks themselves and the authorities resulted in a refinancing of the banks through share issues combined with a write-down of the existing share capital and the assurance of access to unlimited liquidity provided by the Bank of Norway (Nordvik, 1990). To all intents and purposes this represented the end of the Norwegian inter-war banking crisis. Although the authorities had to intervene to rescue and in some cases liquidate several smaller banks throughout the 1930s, the banking system as a whole survived the Depression and even prospered together with the rest of the Norwegian economy during the rest of the 1930s.

The structure of the Norwegian banking system did not change in any fundamental way as a result of the inter-war banking crisis, although a considerable number of banks ended up being liquidated (see Table 17.4). The decision to liquidate Den norske Handelsbank was taken soon after it suspended payments in 1924. Centralbanken for Norge and Forenings-banken were both protected by the Administration Acts until 1928. The decision to close them down was taken by the Government and the Bank of Norway that year, but the process took several years. Many other medium-sized commercial banks, such as the Klaveness Bank, with substantial loans to manufacturing and shipping customers, were also wound up in the late 1920s and the early 1930s. In 1939 there were altogether 104 joint-stock banks, forty-six of which had been established before the First World War, twenty-five during the war, and the remaining thirty-three banks in the inter-war period, (twenty-seven under the reconstruction period in the 1920s). Altogether 143 banks disappeared as independent banking units in the period from 1914 to 1939 (Nordvik, 1992).

The number of large joint-stock banks (defined as banks controlling more than 5 per cent of total assets in the commercial banking sector) had been reduced from six banks in 1922 to three in 1935, and they controlled 58 per cent of total assets compared to 53 per cent in 1935. In general terms, it has to be said that the Norwegian commercial banking sector was substantially weakened by its inter-war experience. The savings banks did not suffer to anything like the same extent, but their ability and willingness to support the manufacturing sector was considerably reduced as a result of the crisis. Another effect of the banking crisis and the economic crisis in the 1920s was that the stock market virtually ceased to play a role as a source of funds for industry. Thus, by the 1930s, the banking sector as a whole played a much reduced role in providing funds for industrial and shipping investment. Direct financing through the bond market and internally generated funds consequently became much more important as sources of finance for the expansion of the Norwegian economy in the 1930s.

5. The Norwegian Inter-War Experience in a Scandinavian Perspective

The banking and monetary experiences of Denmark and Sweden differed somewhat from that of Norway although their wartime and immediate post-war experiences had many similarities (Cohn, 1926). Like Norway, Denmark suffered a severe banking crisis in the early 1920s. The worst crisis years was 1922, when Landmandsbanken, the largest bank in Scandinavia with total assets of Kr. 1,4 billion and equity of 140 million suspended payment. The bank was rescued by government intervention, which involved both a severe write-down of assets and the infusion of government capital, as well as a government guarantee of all claims against the bank.

Altogether thirty-five Danish banks were liquidated in the period from 1920 to 1932, while nineteen were forcibly merged with other banks, and seventeen reconstructed through the combined efforts of the Government, the central bank, and the leading commercial banks. Although the central bank supported the banking system through lender-of-last-resort policies in the first half of the 1920s, there was a shift in its policies in 1924–5, exemplified by the decision to let two large Copenhagen-based banks go into liquidation (Hansen, 1991). This shift was probably linked to the definite decision to return to gold at the pre-war parity. When this policy was made explicit towards the end of 1924, speculative buying of the Danish krone rapidly drove up its value which rose above 90 per cent of par in late 1925. The gold standard was formally reintroduced at the pre-war parity effective from January 1927. Just as in Norway, the combined effects of a deflationary monetary policy and speculative capital movements meant that Denmark also suffered a severe real economic downturn in 1925–6 and this of course also contributed to prolonging and worsening the banking crisis of the 1920s (Lester, 1937). The deflationary monetary policies of the 1920s were finally abandonned late in 1931 when the central bank intervened decisively to support the banking system after having followed Britain off gold in September 1931.

As in Norway and Denmark the basic causes of the Swedish banking crisis of the 1920s are to be found in the excesses of the First World War. However, several factors played a part in reducing the extent of the banking crisis. The Swedish banking system had undergone considerable consolidation in the years immediately before and during the war and was by the early 1920s largely a concentrated branch banking system. Compared to the Norwegian and Danish banking sectors, the Swedish was thus highly concentrated and less vulnerable to external shocks and the delayed effects of bad lending policies during the war. The wartime inflation was also less pronounced than in the other Scandinavian countries. Thirdly, the Swedish deflationary shock after the cyclical downturn in 1920, though severe, resulted in the early return to gold in 1923 and a stabilization of monetary policy. Swedish manufacturing industry, although severely hit by the post-war crisis, was stronger than its Scandinavian counterparts, and the Swedish economic recovery in the 1920s came sooner. Considerable expansion in light manufacturing industries and reorganization and rationalization in the export-based industries such as iron, steel, and the wood and pulp industries meant that the losses suffered by banks were considerably less than in Denmark and Norway (Larson, 1991). Seven Swedish commercial banks were badly affected by the economic and financial crises of the early 1920s, and four of them would have had gone under in the absence of support through the combined efforts of the Government and the large Swedish commercial banks (Larsson, 1992).

The Swedish banking system thus weathered the crisis of the 1920s relatively well, and certainly much better than the Norwegian and Danish banks. Altogether fourteen commercial banks were liquidated in the 1920s, as compared to 129 in Norway. However, the collapse of the Kreuger empire following Ivar Kreuger's suicide in 1932, subjected the Swedish banking system to new strains. Kreuger's main creditor, Skandinaviska Banken, was particularly affected by the financial troubles in the wake of the Kreuger suicide, and public confidence in the bank was badly damaged. Nevertheless, large-scale government support through a massive injection of liquidity into both the Kreuger group of companies and the banking system, saved the day and prevented any long-term serious effects to both the banking system, the Kreuger companies, and the Swedish economy in general (Larsson, 1991).

The Norwegian banking crisis of the 1920s, as was the case in the other two Scandinavian countries, had its roots in the boom years during the First World War and was triggered off by the economic downturn of the early 1920s. The long and drawn-out process of restructuring the Norwegian banking system in the 1920s was no doubt partly due to the severity of the economic crisis in the early 1920s, but also to the difficulties of untangling the bank–client relationships that locked Norwegian banks and their customers into a common destiny. The problems were further complicated by the decision to return to gold at the pre-war parity, a policy that by implication prevented a rapid reconstruction of the banking system and contributed to the weakening of many banks well into the 1930s. The flaws in the structurally weak banking system meant that the banks themselves could not provide the support and assistance needed by the manufacturing and mining sectors in need of new investment to maintain and enhance their competitiveness in the harsh economic climate of the 1920s.

By any yardstick, the Norwegian banking crisis was much more severe than in the two other Scandinavian countries. Accumulated losses of Norwegian banks were almost twice as high in absolute figures as in Denmark and Sweden. The deflationary policies in both Denmark and Norway had unfortunate consequences for real economic performance as well as for the performance of the financial sector in the 1920s. Both in Denmark, and to an even larger degree in Norway, an ambiguous and inconsistent policy with respect to lender-of-last-resort operations prolonged and deepened the banking crisis.

However, monetary and banking policies in all three Scandinavian countries were much more consistent and supportive of the financial system following the collapse of the international gold standard in September 1931. The monetary authorities of all three nations pursued a consistent lender-of-last-resort policy in the 1930s and the removal of the constraints of the gold standard in conjunction with decisive liquidity support enabled all three countries both to avoid another banking collapse and to weather the economic effects of the Great Depression. By following expansionary monetary policies, all three countries realized very satisfactory growth rates in the 1930s.

References

Bernanke, B., and James, H. (1991), 'The Gold Standard, Deflation, and Financial Crisis in the Great Depression: An International Comparison', in R. G. Hubbard (ed.), *Financial Markets and Financial Crises* (Chicago: University of Chicago Press).

Brøgger, Kr. Fr. (1926, 1928), *Kreditlivets utvikling og nutidens forretningsbanker*, i–ii (Oslo: Aschehouqs Boghandel).

Cohn, E. (1926), 'De skandinaviske papirkroner under verdenskrigen', *Nationaløkonomisk Tidsskrift*, 65.

Danielsen, R. (1981), 'F. L. Konow og paritragediens siste akt', *Historisk Tidsskrift*, 3.

Egge, Å. (1974), 'Næringslivet og paripolitikken', *Historisk Tidsskrift*, 1.

Eichengreen, B., and Sachs, J. (1985), 'Exchange Rates and Economic Recovery in the 1930s', *Journal of Economic History*, 45.

Engebretsen, E. (1939), *Norsk bankvesen* (Oslo: Johan Grundt Tanum).

—— (1948), *Christiania Bank og Kreditkasse 1848–1948* (Oslo: Christiania Bank og Kreditkasse).

Hanish, T. J. (1979), 'Virkninger av paripolitikken', *Historisk Tidsskrift*, 3.

Hansen, P. H. (1991), 'From Growth to Crisis: The Danish Banking System from 1850 to the Interwar Years', *Scandinavian Economic History Review*, 3.

Hoffstad, E. (1927), *Det norske privatbankvesens historie* (Oslo: Aschehougs Boghandel).

Hveding, Ø. (1973), 'Opposisjonen mot paripolitikken', *Historisk Tidsskrift*, 3.

—— (1982), *Landbrukets gjeldskrise i mellomkrigstiden* (Oslo: Statens Lånekasse for jordbrukere).

Jacobsen, H. S. (1924), 'Die Norwegischen Bankkrisen in Verbindung mit der wirtschaftlichen Entwicklung Norwegens seit dem Kriege', *Weltwirtschaftliches Archiv*, 20.

Keilhau, W. (1936), 'Die faktische Schillingkrone Norwegens', *Weltwirtschaftliches Archiv*, 43.

—— (1952), *Den norske pengehistorie* (Oslo: Aschehoug).

Klovland, J. T. (1984), 'Quantitative Studies in the Monetary History of Norway. Part I: The Stock of Money', mimeo (Bergen: Norwegian School of Economics and Business Administration).

Knutsen, S. (1990), 'Noen merknader til relasjonene stat-bank-bedrift under jobbetiden 1914–1920', *Research on Banking, Capital and Society, Report 13* (Oslo: Norwegian Research Council for Applied Social Science).

—— (1991) 'From Expansion to Panic and Crash: The Norwegian Banking System and its Customers, 1913–1924', *Scandinavian Economic History Review*, 3.

—— (1993), 'Bankierfunksjonen i Norge i internasjonalt perspektiv', mimeo, unpublished MS (Oslo: Norwegian School of Management).

Koefoed, H. (1940), *Den norske Bankforening 1915–1940. Trekk av norsk bankhistorie* (Oslo: Den norske Bankforening).

Larsson, M. (1991), 'State, Banks and Industry in Sweden, with Some Reference to the Scandinavian Countries', in H. James, H. Lindgren, and A. Teichova (eds.), *The Role of Banks in the Interwar Economy* (Cambridge: Cambridge University Press).

—— (1992), 'Government Subsidy or Internal Restructuring? Swedish Commercial Banking during the Crisis Years of the 1920s', in P. L. Cottrell, H. Lindgren, and A. Teichova (eds.), *European Industry and Banking Between the Wars* (Leicester: Leicester University Press).

Lester, R. (1939), 'The Gold-Parity Depression in Norway and Denmark, 1925–1928', *Journal of Political Economy*, 45.

Nordvik, H. W. (1972), 'Sparebankene og krisen i mellomkrigstiden', in *Studier i sparing og sparebankvesen 1822–1972* (Oslo: Gyldendal norsk forlag).

—— Nerheim, G., and Brandal, T. (1989), *Penger spart, penger tjent. Sparebanker og økonomisk utvikling på Sør-Vestlandet fra 1839 til 1989* (Stavanger: SR-Bank).

—— (1990), 'Penge-og valutapolitikk, bank og kredittvesen og krisen i norsk økonomi på 1930-tallet', in E. Hovland, E. Lange, and S. Rystad (eds.), *Det som svarte seg best. Studier i økonomisk historie og politikk* (Oslo: Ad Notam).

—— (1991), 'Banks and their Customers in Times of Crisis: Norwegian Experiences in the 1920s', paper presented to the International Conference on Bank–Industry relations in Inter-War Europe held at the Business History Unit, London School of Economics and Political Science, *11–14 September 1991, Papers in Business History*, (London: London School of Economics and Political Science).

—— (1992), 'Bankkrise, bankstruktur og bankpolitikk i Norge i mellomkrigstiden', *Historisk Tidsskrift*, 2.

—— (1993), 'The Banking System, Industrialization and Economic Growth in Norway, 1850–1914', *Scandinavian Economic History Review*, 1.

Petersen, E. (1957), *Den norske Creditbank 1857–1957* (Oslo: Den norske Creditbank).

Petersen, K. (1982), *Bankkriser og valutauro. Forretningsbankenes historie i mellomkrigsårene* (Oslo: A/S Hjemmet-Fagpresseforlaget).

—— (1986), *Forretningsbankenes historie. De første 70 årene* (Oslo: A/S Hjemmet-Fagpresseforlaget).

Rygg, N. (1950), *Norges Bank i mellomkrigstiden* (Oslo: Norges Bank).

Sejersted, F. (1973), *Ideal, teori og virkelighet. Nicolai Rygg og pengepolitikken i 1920-årene* (Oslo: Cappelen).

Sejersted, F. (1974), 'Paripolitikk på ny', *Historisk Tidsskrift*, 1.

Skånland H. (1967), *Det norske kredittmarked siden 1900* (Oslo: Central Bureau of Statistics).

—— (1990), 'Bankkrise og livet etterpå', *Penger og kredit*, 4.

18

Banking, Public Finance, and the Economy: Greece, 1919–1933

GEORGE B. DERTILIS and CONSTANTINE COSTIS

1. Introduction: The Economy, The Banking System

Three chronic problems afflicted Greece's economy during the inter-war period: unbalanced trade accounts, high public deficits, and heavy public debt.

The trade balance was permanently threatened by the country's dependence on the exports of a few agricultural products. Currants and tobacco alone accounted for between one-half and two-thirds of the country's total export earnings (Andreou, 1933: 136 ff.). However, invisible earnings from shipping, emigrants' remittances, and capital inflow from rich Greeks abroad, corrected the deficit at the level of the balance of payments (Kapsalis, 1927; Andreades, 1939; Stephanides, 1930).

Equally chronic and perhaps worse was the problem of a high public expenditure coupled with comparatively low revenues. From the 1870s, state expenditure came under the constant pressure of politics, patronage, and populism. On the other hand, public revenue was rather low; and while the yields from indirect taxes soon came to account for about two-thirds of the total (Andreades, 1924, 1925, 1927; Santis, 1927; Sbarounis, 1949), those from business tax remained notoriously low and those from income tax even lower (Dertilis, 1987, 1993).

This leads to the third major problem. Greece was almost always overindebted; and her poor finances greatly contributed to her more or less permanent monetary problems (Angelopoulos, 1937; Zolotas, 1928).

This was the environment in which the banking system had to operate. Ever since the nineteenth century, this system was a highly centralized oligopoly, led by the National Bank of Greece. The NBG obtained a virtually exclusive right of currency issue from the year of its institution in 1841, and kept it until 1928. Before and after the Great War, the National Bank's share of the market was huge in terms both of deposits and of lending. In 1919, for example, the NBG's share was 31.7 per cent of sight deposits, 54.6 per cent of savings, and 73.6 per cent of term deposits (Costis, 1987: 180, and 1990: tables 61–3). Active in practically every type of banking, including agricultural credit and urban mortgage, the NBG held a virtual monopoly in some of these activities. Last but not least, the NBG was the State's treasurer and its main lender.

The diversity, depth, and importance of these activities vested the NBG with immense power, both financial and political. A large bank even by Western European standards, it was on the eve of the war the uncontested leader of the Greek banking system and the privileged partner of the State.

These conditions spell out the banking system's major traits: a high degree of monopoly and a low degree of specialization. Yet these traits did not remain unchanged over time. A major change occurred in 1893, when the first real deposit bank was instituted. The new bank was the first such firm not to base its strategy upon some state privilege such as, for example, the issuing-right. Instead, the Bank of Athens aimed at the savings of the Levant and the diaspora Greeks, as well as at the thriving Greek shipping business.

TABLE 18.1. *Banks' capital as percentage of total liabilities, 1894–1928*

Year	Capital as % of liabilities
1894	41.7
1901	32.5
1910	27.1
1914	20.0
1920	7.6
1924	9.1
1928	14.5

Source: Kyrkilitsis (1934: 17, 19).

That year marks, therefore, the beginning of a gradual diversification in the strategy, the organization, and the resources of the Greek banking system.

Truly foreign capital was nearly absent in this system, with the exception of a French minority participation in one major bank's capital (Costis and Tsokopoulos, 1988: 123–152; Berov, 1965). However, Greek traders, ship-owners, and financiers from the Ottoman Empire and the diaspora contributed to the capital of almost all Greek banks. Just before the Great War, these inflows brought about a profusion of new banks and new branches in Greece but particularly in Egypt and in the Ottoman Empire. This growth continued well into the 1910s and 1920s, bolstered by Greece's substantial territorial gains in the First World War and the development of commercial agriculture in the new territories, especially of tobacco in Macedonia and Thrace.

The National Bank may have had the currency issuing privilege, but it never accepted the obligations of a typical central bank. It did not really have a discount-rate policy, it did not conduct open-market operations, and it seldom played a stabilizing role (Thomadakis, 1981). On the contrary, its often aggressive credit policies and its speculative moves in the exchange markets, had certain destabilizing effects. However, there were a few cases when the NBG was called upon to be a lender-of-last-resort and it did so, to the great benefit of the banking sector.

The strength of this system, and especially of the NBG, was probably one of the major reasons behind its stability over the inter-war period. Although it is difficult to separate causes from effects, one can safely say that this stability, in its turn, helped the Greek financial and monetary system throughout the difficult post-war years. For it alleviated the effects of the wars, of the 1929–31 recession, and of the 1931–2 financial crisis. The stability of the banking system even counterbalanced, to a certain degree, the negative effects of its members' aggressive and often speculative policies.

On the other hand, the banking system's role in assisting economic growth was not particularly positive. It tended to favour, and even to overlend to, large monopolistic firms on the basis of their mere size, often without realistic assessment of their managerial and technological potential. The reasons were not always purely economic, but also social and political. Moreover, trade got the lion's share of banking support, agriculture and industry lagging far behind. Finally, interest rates were kept high both by the power of the banks' oligopoly and by the weakness of the State's finances. There was little effort to resist or counterbalance the crowding-out effects from public borrowing, which increased enormously between 1914 and 1922, to finance initially the war, and then the economy's reconstruction after the débâcle in the 1919–22 Asia Minor campaign.

The more detailed analysis that follows, after a brief review of the years 1910–18, divides the inter-war years into four periods: 1919–24 (war, inflation and crisis); 1925–8 (partial recovery); 1929–31 (recession and crisis); 1932–9 (recovery).

2. Growth and Euphoria, 1910–1918

Between 1910 and 1918, despite the chronic trade deficit, the balance of payments seems to have behaved rather smoothly, supported by invisible inflows, mainly from shipping, emigrants' remittances, and income from capital invested abroad. Greek diaspora entrepreneurs, strong in trade since the eighteenth century and in finance since the mid-nineteenth century, had now swiftly adapted to new conditions in the world economy by a spectacularly successful diversification into shipping. The Balkan Wars and the First World War yielded wealth, territories, confidence, and high expectations. Deposits increased substantially, and the banking system made exceptional profits, increasing its reserves and capital. Finally, the drachma remained solidly at par with the gold franc, although inflation in Greece was much higher than in the UK and in France. Greece had participated in the gold exchange standard since 1910, but because of the handicaps that the war imposed upon trade, as well as the exchange pegging system, the system was not allowed to function properly, and the Greek currency was kept stable rather than being allowed to depreciate.

3. War and Débâcle, 1919–1924

Conditions changed in 1918–19 and the situation continued to worsen until 1924. Inflation had set in already in 1915; it was fuelled by war, the blockade, and speculation. Having almost full control of the exchange market, the NBG led the other banks in large-scale arbitrage operations, especially between 1919 and 1922, when inflation and monetary instability attained unprecedented heights. However, the bank's propaganda during the inter-war period and the uncritical attitude of observers and, later, of historians concealed the negative effects of the NBG's policies (Costis, 1984: 81–133). Importers and exporters also speculated by building up stocks, purchasing currency, and discounting drachmas. The country's reserves were soon exhausted and the government abandoned the gold-exchange standard *de facto* in the summer of 1919 and *de jure* one year later.

TABLE 18.2. *Price index and pound/drachma parity, 1914–1928*

Year	Price index (100=1914)	Pound/Drachma ratio
1914	100	25.16
1916	159	24.63
1918	366	24.82
1920	351	34.07
1922	636	166.54
1924	1,235	247.35
1926	1,633	386.51
1928	1,868	375.00

Source: ASG (1939: 473, 498).

Under such conditions the Asia Minor war began. As the campaign was financed mainly by fiduciary note issue, monetary growth soon became a major problem. The war ended in 1922 with the military débâcle, which left Greece's population increased by 1.3 million refugees. Meanwhile, emigrants' remittances had begun to fall. In 1922, the Government levied a peculiar form of forced loan. All banknotes in circulation were halved in value, one-half of the original value was left with the owner and the other half exchanged for Treasury bonds. The measure did not bear fruit immediately, for the deficit was too large and the Governments of the day avoided imposing heavy new taxes.

Meanwhile, problems with the outstanding war debts spoiled the State's credit in the international market. The Government turned for funds to the internal market. Even before the end of the war, the NBG had come under enormous political pressure to lend to the State far too generously. The nationalist argument was too strong for the bank to resist, before as well as after the Greco-Turkish war. The bank had to yield, only to find itself in serious liquidity trouble. Government debt of various kinds covered 75 per cent of the bank's assets in 1920, 82 per cent in 1921, 74 per cent in 1922, 65 per cent in 1924, 61 per cent in 1925; it remained then at this level until 1928 (Pyrsos, 1936: 43). It was then that the State, finally realizing its own risks, came to the bank's rescue by abandoning, after 1923, the issue of new currency, by issuing treasury notes instead and, finally, by imposing new forced loans during the year 1925.

TABLE 18.3. *Greek bank deposits total* (constant drachmas million) *and by category* (percentages), 1894–1927

Year	Total (drachmas million)[a]	Sight (%)	Saving (%)	Term (%)
1894		21.7	—	78.2
1914	397	44.7	—	55.3
1919	487	58.8	13.8	27.3
1920	671	57.9	10.8	31.3
1921	839	53.9	10.6	35.5
1922	590	58.4	9.8	31.8
1923	433	64.4	10.3	25.3
1924	552	68.5	9.9	21.6
1925	496	65.7	12.9	21.4
1926	516	64.6	18.3	17.1
1927	525	67.5	23.3	9.2

[a] At constant prices

Sources: Costis (1990: 167); Kyrkilitsis (1934: 42).

The bank's temporary weakness allowed its competitors to increase their market shares (Costis, 1987: 167–84, 220–3). Meanwhile, however, the banking system's resources as a whole had also been seriously curtailed. The refugees had swelled the country's population and the economy's demand for credit; but the volume of bank deposits had remained more or less unchanged since 1914, whilst their structure shifted in favour of the short term. Competition between the banks became thus more and more anarchic:

neither the State's authority nor the market leader's waning power could now control it.

Despite these problems the NBG's support to the State had been a crucial element immediately after the war and the huge wave of refugees; it helped keep alive not only the State itself, but the banking system as well. Thus, by 1925, Government and banks could reasonably hope that the worst days had passed and better ones would come, sooner or later.

4. Partial Recovery, 1925–1928

Better days did indeed come in 1925. Various converging factors contributed to a slow economic recovery and to the reconstruction of public finances. Pressure on the balance of payments was relieved by increased exports and by the inflow of foreign capital, especially for public works through state contracts. Monetary growth eased down and the drachma was finally stabilized *de facto* in 1927.

Pressures on the exchange market were also relieved with the prospect of new foreign loans. Although indebtedness had not increased excessively during the war, borrowing abroad had been blocked after 1919, because of the Great Powers' resentment of the restoration of the pro-German king Constantine and, later on, because of the country's outstanding war debts. The credit squeeze was eased in 1924, when the League of Nations agreed to a first loan, the proceeds of which were to finance exclusively the settlement of refugees. Further negotiations led, in 1927, to a compromise about the war debts. The exchange market had already anticipated and discounted the beneficial effects of this agreement (Zolotas, 1928, 1929).

In order to ratify the final settlement, the negotiators of the League of Nations financial committee imposed severe institutional conditions: reform of the Greek banking system through the institution of a central bank, modernization of the public finances, and stabilization of the drachma. The reform was quickly implemented; the Central Bank was created in 1928 and Greece restored the gold exchange standard.

According to the League of Nations' experts, the Bank of Greece ought not only to avoid commercial banking business, but should also become a real central bank, able to guarantee the country's finances and control the appropriate monetary and credit policies. This was mere wishful thinking, far from the realities of the local market. The State had virtually granted the new bank the right to handle the public debt, but this was a burden rather than a privilege. The bank lacked the real power that would allow it to intervene effectively in the market through open-market operations and the discount-rate policy. First, this was because the local public market for government paper was shallow; secondly, because the bulk of the business in such paper was transacted privately by the commercial banks, led by the NBG; and, thirdly, because, in this highly oligopolistic credit market supply as well as cost of money were still controlled by the NBG and its major partners. Moreover, the political leaders of the day barely suspected the role that a central bank should really play and did little to reinforce its real powers. At that time, in fact, the Bank of Greece could not even rely upon the meagre institutional powers it was to obtain belatedly, in 1930, i.e. the command of the compulsory deposits of banks' reserves and of the funds deposited by state institutions.

Armed with paper weapons, the Bank of Greece had to fight the real war that the commercial banks waged against it. When some of them met with difficulties, they refused to borrow from the Central Bank, preferring instead their old leader and familiar lender, the NBG. Even after the reforms and the institution of the Bank of Greece, therefore, and despite the fresh loans that the reforms made available, the new system was neither solid nor efficient enough to guarantee a permanent economic recovery. For institutional reform was simply not sufficient: in order to get rid of its structural defects, the system would have to go through the shock therapy of crisis.

5. Recession and Crisis, 1929–1931

Partly because of these structural weaknesses, partly under the pressures from abroad, conditions changed again in 1929. The total value of the public debt was already higher than that of most other developing countries. Public investment, an otherwise sound long-term policy, was mainly in infrastructure or public works, thus yielding only long-term benefits but no immediate returns. Public expenditure, on the other hand, traditionally too high for a small country, was further increased because of subsidies to farmers, support purchases of agricultural products, and measures of debt relief for peasants. These strongly populist tactics, not unfamiliar elsewhere in Europe during this period, now became commonplace in Greece as well; but Greek rural protectionism would prove stronger and live longer than any of its European counterparts: it was to become a structural element of the country's economy and politics until the end of the twentieth century (Dertilis, 1992, 1993).

Meanwhile, reduced international demand and falling prices for currants, tobacco, and locally produced cereals, drastically reduced peasant incomes. Recession was also felt in urban trade, although industrial output and employment continued to rise until 1931. Despite the fall of import prices, the amelioration in the terms of trade was partly offset by falling prices of agricultural produce. By 1929, the recession had already set in. Not surprisingly, it concerned the rural economy and not the industrial sector, which was not to be affected until 1931.

TABLE 18.4. *Greek national income and indices of production, prices, and employment, 1928–1934 (100 = 1928)*

Year	Index of industrial employment	Index of industrial production	Index of agricultural production	Index of export price of agricultural products	Index of consumer prices	National income (drachmas million)
1928	100	100	100	100	100	43.128
1929	108	102	75	106	105	44.529
1930	105	105	69	89	96	42.701
1931	102	109	68	83	86	39.404
1932	87	103	105	95	103	43.665
1933	94	112	130	105	116	—
1934	95	126	132	—	114	—

Sources: ASG. (1935: *passim*); national income estimates by Evelpidis (1939: 132).

Although the recession was far less dramatic for Greece's agricultural economy than for more industrialized countries, it was none the less sufficient to upset the market's confidence in the economy. The effects were soon felt on Greece's fragile currency.

A wave of speculation had already begun in 1929, led by the commercial banks and the NBG. Their network was able to control the exchange market in two ways: directly, by financing Greece's external trade; and indirectly, by financing various operations of the diaspora enterprises, whose business fed both the official exchange market and, later on, the black market (Costis, 1986: 62–73). Apart from profit, the speculators' other target was the Bank of Greece.

The Bank of Greece was unable to play any role beyond that of a clearing-house in a gold-exchange system. On the other hand, the automatic functions of the monetary system could not operate efficiently in an economy which lacked the elasticity of its more developed European competitors and partners. By 1931 these conditions meant uncontrollable currency haemorrhage (Costis, 1986: 74–97). The Central Bank, after vainly trying to borrow long-term funds abroad, and keep the drachma stable, finally saw its reserves exhausted.

In the end, recession and speculation created problems for some smaller banks; but they were not destructive for the banking system as a whole. The NBG had meanwhile recovered its strength and its control of the other banks, to which it gave some support. Although seventeen of the smaller ones did close or go bankrupt, the bigger banks managed to overcome the difficulties with the NBG's support.

Speculation may have helped the bigger private banks to survive; it may also have helped the banking system to restructure itself through survival of the fittest; but it was destructive for the drachma and the economy as a

TABLE 18.5. *Business indices, Greek banks,* 1928–1932 (1928 = 100)

Year	Big Four[a]			National Bank of Greece		
	Short-term loans	Deposits	Gross profit[b]	Short-term loans	Deposits	Gross profit
1928	100	100	100	100	100	100
1929	99	102	109	144	117	109
1930	92	107	101	173	130	117
1931	81	88	90	189	141	125
1932	65	72	81	203	145	118

[a] Bank of Athens, Commercial Bank, People's Bank, Ionian Bank.
[b] Data for the Ionian Bank not available.
Source: Kyrkilitsis (1935: 14, 16, 28–34).

whole. In 1931, the Government and the Central Bank, with the assistance and the moral support of the League of Nations, placed the banking system under strict control. Commercial banks were obliged by the Central Bank to deposit a part of their reserves at the Bank; and the Bank also took control of the management of the funds of the state institutions. In addition, the new Agricultural Bank, which was instituted in 1929 with the aim of assisting rural development, became generally the instrument of the state in checking the power of the NBG—and this not merely in the rural markets, but also within the oligopolistic hierarchy of the banking system and in the daily game of backstage politics.

All these measures, however, were taken too late; and they did not eradicate the Bank of Greece's structural weakness: it remained as unable as ever to influence the market through open-market operations and discount-rate policy. Thus, once the mechanisms of speculation and devaluation were geared together, the new powers assigned to the Central Bank proved insufficient to bring the exchange market under control (Costis, 1986: 98–113).

In fact, although pressures upon the Bank of Greece's foreign exchange reserves had started in the last months of 1930, their impact on the banking system was not very strong. Deposits were withdrawn, but there was no real run on the banks. But after the German crisis in the summer of 1931 the situation changed, and there was a turn from the drachma to foreign exchange. A gradual fall in liquidity obliged the commercial banks to meet the demand by purchasing foreign exchange from the Bank of Greece, in this way off-loading their shortage on to the Central Bank (Mazower, 1991: 149–50). However, the situation did not become critical until the sterling crisis of September 1931, which led to a stock-exchange panic in Athens and a run on the foreign-exchange reserves of the Bank of Greece. Considering monetary stability as a prerequisite for foreign credit, the Central Bank and the Government introduced corrective measures on 28 September, followed by further ones on 8 October. These measures virtually marked the end of

TABLE 18.6. *Net foreign-exchange movements at the Bank of Greece*, 1928–1932 (quarterly, in drachmas million)

	1928	1929	1930	1931	1932
1st quarter	—	− 54.7	+ 289.5	− 242.3	− 680.0
2nd quarter	—	− 248.3	− 50.3	− 290.7	+ 477.7
3rd quarter	+ 37.0	− 453.9	+ 260.5	− 13.7	+ 71.9
4th quarter	+ 284.6	− 357.5	− 476.1	− 735.0	+ 32.3
Net annual movement	+ 321.6	− 1114.4	+ 23.6	− 1281.7	− 98.1

Source: Costis, (1986: 139).

the gold exchange standard in Greece. The Bank of Greece was no longer obliged to exchange its banknotes for gold or foreign currency. The sale of foreign exchange was permitted only in the case of 'necessary' imports. Exporters were obliged to surrender their earnings to the Central Bank, and to receive their value in drachmas at the official rate. The export of capital was forbidden (Mazower, 1991: 156).

The banking system soon felt the consequences of these measures, and the commercial banks faced an acute liquidity problem. For the first time the Bank of Greece played the role of lender-of-last-resort, and played it effectively.

Although in the end the banking system did not collapse, the country's finances looked as if they soon would. The main immediate problem was the public debt. The Greek Government needed new foreign credits for the completion of its public works programme, and to this end tried to maintain monetary stability. But when it became obvious that it was impossible to raise new loans abroad, domestic resources became the only alternative, and monetary stability lost its meaning. The Government consistently requested a moratorium on foreign debt; but this was never accepted by the international finance institutions. Default was thus in the air, especially following the British crisis. After all, it was precisely the expectation of default, and of the devaluation that would necessarily follow it, that had already fuelled speculation; when both came it was, therefore, no surprise. On April 1932, the service of the foreign debt was suspended—completely for amortization instalments, partly for interest payments. On 27 April, the Government formally abandoned the gold exchange standard, and the Bank of Greece imposed new, even stricter regulations covering foreign exchange, capital movements, import restrictions, and obligatory deposits of export earnings (Mazower, 1991: 142–176)

6. The Recovery, 1932–1933

As the market had anticipated these measures, the rate of devaluation was not really dramatic: the drachma fell immediately by 15.4 per cent against the pound, and the lowest parity ever reached was at 27.4 per cent, eight months later, around the year end. This rate seems high in comparison with what happened elsewhere; it is reasonable compared to Latin American experiences. Most probably, market anticipation had already discounted in part the devaluation as well as some of its plausible side-effects. Indeed, following these fundamental changes of April 1932, there were no panics or crashes and no run on the banks. Drachma deposits remained at approximately the same level throughout the rest of the year. This was a good sign of the traditional dichotomy of the Greek economy: the behaviour of local savings-holders, basically introvert, differed deeply from the extrovert strategy and tactics of private financiers and international entrepreneurs, mostly of diaspora origin.

This dichotomy existed not only at the level of individuals; it also concerned public policy; in this sense, it was a dilemma between an open, extrovert economy and a more closed and self-sufficient one. Ever since the institution of the independent Greek State, in 1830, there was ideological controversy about whether economic development could occur solely with the country's own resources or should be based on foreign capital investment and public borrowing abroad. In the inter-war years especially, this issue became crucial and more complex. Before 1932, recovery from the wars and further development was indeed based on public debt, on foreign investment in public works, and on technology transfers. After 1932, however, the international isolation that the default imposed on Greece, even temporarily, boosted the arguments of those who preached independence and self-reliance.

These arguments came from very different people. There were, first, those who traditionally believed in and preached a lofty ideal of national independence. Close to them, but substantially different in the depth of their thinking, were those nationalists who believed, not without reason, that Greece's economy had in the past been particularly harmed by that peculiar blend of pressures from internal politics, diplomacy, foreign intervention, and public finance. The leftists' and communists' position was not too different, although for different reasons and with purposes diverging from those of the nationalists. Then there were all those radical, corporatist, populist elements, present in all parties, who adhered to the ideas and reactions of vexed chauvinism, xenophobic rejection, self-praise and self-reliance, economic isolation and autarkic pride; all reactions and ideas freshly imported from—or exchanged with—Italy, Spain, France, and the German world. Evidently, all these people had at least one simple thought in common: they did not want Greece to leave in the hands of foreign governments what Gladstone, sixty years before, had shrewdly called 'the lever of the loans' (Dertilis, 1983).

Throughout the inter-war period, therefore, there was a strong ideology in favour of financial independence and national self-sufficiency. In 1932, ideology met with the cynicism of default; thereafter it could be converted into actual policy, unfettered by any obligations toward foreign creditors.

This newly found freedom was further reinforced by a newly acquired *Drang* at the Bank of Greece. Never before had this young institution such room for manœuvre, never before had it enjoyed such force of persuasion toward small commercial banks and such prestige against its antagonist, the NBG.

The new freedom was exhibited, both symbolically and pragmatically, in the changing relationship with the International Financial Control, instituted in 1898, following the nineteenth-century default. Since then, the IFC had been assigned certain state revenues against repayment of the debt. Now, with the newly imposed exchange controls, the IFC's revenues could no longer be converted to foreign currency and the Bank of Greece blocked them in special accounts. These obligatory and very large deposits soon served not only as some sort of basis for the drachma's new credibility, or as one of the bank's best tools for an effective restrictive monetary policy, but also as a convenient reserve for expansion: by using them in full, the bank greatly increased its direct credit to the economy.

The international front was not the only one in this war against vested interest. The Bank of Greece fought it on the internal front as well, with considerable success. It imposed on the banks the requirements to convert their foreign-exchange deposits to drachmas at a discount of one-fifth the market rate (– 20 per cent). Obviously, this confiscated some genuine savings by old-time clients of the banks; but it also confiscated a good part of the profits made in the previous two years through speculation (Bank of Greece, 1978: 144–56).

These new conditions were in themselves nearly sufficient to support the ailing drachma immediately, to relieve public finances immensely, and ostensibly to boost the private sector. Within the latter, moreover, the main element lacking was confidence, and this was now restored. Other favourable factors also helped after 1932. There were soon signs of internal recovery from the recession, coupled with increased inflow from shipping and emigrants' remittances. The exchange controls helped the Bank of Greece not only to keep currency in the country but also to encourage repatriation of fugitive capital. The renegotiation of Greece's foreign debt closely followed these changes. In September 1932, a first agreement was reached, providing for temporary solutions and part payments. Thereafter, further partial agreements were negotiated year after year.

By 1933 the country's economy had not overcome its structural problems, far from it; but the crisis was certainly over.

References

(in Greek, unless otherwise stated)
ASG (1939), *Annuaire statistique de la Grèce*, 1939 (Athens).
Angelopoulos, A. (1937), *The Public Debt of Greece* (Athens).
Andreades, A. (1924), *Public Finance*, i. (Athens).
—— (1925), *Courses in Public Finance*, (Athens).
—— (1927), *Courses in Public Finance*, iv (Athens).
—— (1939), 'La Marine marchande de la Grèce pendant et après la Guerre Mondiale', in A. Andreades, Works ii (Athens, in French).
Andreou, A. (1933), *The Foreign Trade Policy of Greece* (Athens).
Bank of Greece (1978), *The First Fifty Years of the Bank of Greece, 1928–1978* (Athens).
Berov, L. (1965), 'Le Capital financier occidental et les pays balkaniques dans les années vingt', *Études Balkaniques*, 2–3: 139–64 (in French).
Costis C. (1984), 'Greece's foreign-exchange policy during the Asia Minor Campaign', in Th. Veremis and C. Costis (eds.), *The National Bank of Greece in Asia Minor* (Athens).
—— (1986), *The Banks and the Economic Crisis, 1929–1932* (Athens).
—— (1987), *Rural Economy and the Agricultural Bank* (Athens).
—— (1988), 'Banque et Industrie', in G. B. Dertilis (ed.), *Banquiers, usuriers et paysans; réseaux de crédit et stratégies du capital en Grèce (1780–1930)*, (Paris).
—— (1990), *Économie rurale et Banque Agraire. Les documents* (Athens, in Greek and French).
—— and Tsokopoulos, V. (1988), *The Banks in Greece, 1898–1928* (Athens).
Dertilis, G. B. (1983), 'International Economic Relations and Political Dependence: The Case of Greece, 1824–1878', Historica, 1.
—— (1987, 1993) 'From Tithe to Income-Tax; Greece, 1830–1940', *Colloque des Treilles* (Sept. (in English); published in Greek as *Taxation and Political Power in Modern Greece* (Athens: Alexandreia Press, 1993).
—— (1992), 'Terre, paysans et pouvoir économique (Grèce XVIIIᵉ–XXᵉ s.), Annales ESC, 2 (in French).
—— (1993), 'Terre, paysans et pouvoir politique (Grèce XVIIIᵉ–XXᵉ s.), Annales ESC, (in French).
Evelpidis, Chr. (1939), *Theory and Practice of Agricutural and Economic Policies* (Athens).
Kapsalis, T. (1927), *La Balance des comptes de la Grèce* (Lausanne, in French).
Kyrkilitsis, A. (1934), *The Banks in Greece* (Athens).
—— (1935), *The National Bank of Greece and the Other Commercial Banks* (Athens).
Mazower, M. (1991), *Greece and the Inter-War Economic Crisis* (Oxford).
Pyrsos, G. A. (1936), *A Contribution to the History of the Bank of Greece* (Athens).
Santis, D. K. (1924), *Staatschulden und Finanzpolitik Griechenlands* (Berlin, in German).

Sbarounis, Ath. (1949), *Public Finances after the Asia Minor Débâcle* (Athens).

Stephanides, D. S. (1930), *The Inflow of Foreign Capital and its Political and Economic Consequences* (Thessaloniki).

Supreme Economic Council (SEC) (1935), *The Indexes of Greece's Economic Activity during the Years 1928–1934* (Athens).

Thomadakis S, (1981), *Credit and Monetarization; Discount Credit and the National Bank of Greece, 1860–1900,* (Athens).

Tsouderos, E. (1919), *Le Relèvement économique de la Grèce* (Paris, in French).

Zolotas, X. (1928), *Foreign Exchange and Monetary Phenomena in Greece, 1910–1927,* (Athens).

—— (1929), *The monetary stabilization* (Athens).

—— (1931), *Greece's Foreign-Debt Burden* (Athens).

19

Portuguese Banking in the Inter-War Period

JAIME REIS

1. Banking in Portugal at the End of the War

At the end of the First World War, Portugal was one of the poorest countries in Europe. With a labour force which was predominantly concentrated in agriculture, a substantial rate of illiteracy and a low degree of urbanization, it is hardly surprising if, by contemporary standards, banking was also somewhat less than developed.

TABLE 19.1. *Bank sector concentration in Portugal, 1920–1935*

| | Herfindhal index of market concentration | | |
| | All bank deposits[a] | excluding Bank of Portugal and Banco Nacional Ultramarino | Percentage of total assets belonging to the 5 largest banks |
	(1)	(2)	(3)
1920	0.235	0.017	53
1925	0.181	0.045	69
1930	—	0.056	65
1935	—	0.029	68
1939	0.145	0.037	69

[a] Values cannot be calculated for 1930 and 1935 because the Banco Nacional Ultramarino published no data in 1930–8.
Source: Instituto National de Estatistica, *Situação Bancaria* (various years).

It consisted, in the first place, of some twenty joint-stock banks, the majority of which had their origins in the balmy days of the Portuguese banking boom of the 1870s. For the most part, they were small and the few which had any branches at all had only one or two—typically, in Lisbon, if their headquarters were in Oporto, and vice versa. This situation is confirmed by the low value of the Herfindhal index of market concentration for bank deposits (see Table 19.1). Geographically, too, there was much dispersion. In terms of the number of banks, the system was quite evenly

The author is grateful to Gianni Toniolo, Charles Feinstein, and Fernando Rosus for helpful comments.

distributed between Lisbon, Oporto, and the provinces. On the other hand, it should be noted that provincial banks were uniformly small, while their large counterparts were located without exception, as one might expect, in one of the two principal cities.

Although more than twenty years had passed since the crisis of the early 1890s, which had severely rocked the system, the public continued to view joint-stock banks with suspicion. Despite legislation in 1894 and 1896 to regulate the sector much more tightly than before, scarcely any banks were founded in the early twentieth century. Deposits in the old-established ones expanded slowly and contributed only slightly to the growth of the money supply. Indeed, in 1914, total bank assets were only 9 per cent larger than they had been in 1890, and the number of banks had meanwhile fallen to almost half. War and wartime inflation, in particular, had not made matters better. By 1918, in real terms, total assets, deposits, and credits had actually shrunk relative to pre-war levels. No doubt this was one of the main reasons why Portuguese banks had to have high reserve ratios (reserves/deposits plus other sight liabilities), usually of well over 30 per cent (see Table 19.3). No doubt for this reason too, this was not a country that attracted much foreign capital into this sector. In fact, one English and one French bank were the only manifestations of this kind, and they were no more than branches of much larger multinational enterprises.[1]

Portuguese banks showed relatively little functional specialization. There were neither investment nor agricultural banks and there was only one mortgage bank. In name, all of them were deemed to be 'commercial' and they were expected to deal primarily in short-term credit, of a commercial nature. The law stipulated, in fact, that all current liabilities must be backed by reserves up to 20 per cent, with the remainder being covered by commercial paper of not more than 90 days' duration. In reality, however, things were quite different. Portuguese banks had long been much more like 'mixed' banks, a substantial part of their credit being long-term in nature, even if it was not advertised in the balance sheet as such. Indeed, throughout the first fifty years of their history, it would be unusual to find one in which genuine commercial bills represented more than 50 per cent of total credits. One consequence of this was that many of the difficulties they found themselves in from time to time, and which were a major cause of bank mortality, arose from their excessive involvement in long-term operations

---

[1] On the other hand, funds accumulated in Brazil by successful Portuguese emigrants had long been an important source of capital formation in Portugal, both in banks and in other enterprises, and this continued to be the case throughout the inter-war period. It is arguable whether this should count as 'foreign' capital, however. See Pereira (1983), for the nineteenth century, and, for later years, the example of the Banco Pinto Sottomayor, which was started in 1925 mainly with 'Brazilian' money (Camara, 1989). The exception in this period was the Banco Burnay, which received an infusion of Belgian capital from the Société Générale in 1925 in order to develop the latter's interests in Portugal's African colonies.

with a view to fixed-capital formation. According to one source, they were responsible for 'the birth and development of the best part of the [country's] many and most prosperous industries'.[2]

Three other components complete this portrait of the Portuguese financial world in 1918. One of them was the savings institutions. The dominant element here was the state-owned Caixa Geral de Depositos which was able, through a well-developed national network of branches, to attract a large quantity of financial resources. With three-quarters of all savings accounts, its deposits were equal to roughly 25 per cent of the total value of demand deposits in the banking system; this made it, in a sense, the country's most powerful financial entity. This success was undoubtedly attributable to its branch network, but to a very large extent it was also the result of the safety enjoyed by these deposits thanks to the State's guarantee, something which made a favourable contrast with the joint-stock part of the system. Ever since its inception in 1876, the Caixa's main purpose had been to finance the State, either directly or by means of purchasing government bonds, and its credits were still being employed in this way at the beginning of the inter-war period.

From a functional point of view, the Bank of Portugal very much resembled the Caixa since its main activity at this time was also to finance the State. In return, it enjoyed the monopoly of the right to issue banknotes which were both legal tender and inconvertible. About four-fifths of its income-earning assets at this time represented one form or another of official loans, the remaining fifth being a commercial portfolio of short-term bills. In addition, it was the banker and treasurer to the State, something which obliged it to have a national network of branches, the only other one in the country besides that of the Caixa Geral de Depositos.

Although not yet formally a central bank, it had also played, until the war, a role as regulator of the money market and as an influence for stability in the financial system. In the first place and although itself a joint-stock bank, it was understood as its public duty that, from time to time and whenever necessary, it would act as lender-of-last-resort, and it did so on several occasions after it first intervened in this capacity during the crisis of 1876. In the second place, thanks to its dominant position in commercial banking, it had been able over the years to have a considerable effect on how much credit was made available to the market overall. In the third place, it had managed to enforce its will on the other banks in matters of interest-rate fixing, simply through the volume of its direct discounting and without recourse to more sophisticated market mechanisms, which in a country like Portugal could hardly have been expected to work anyway. To sum up in the words of a former top bank official, 'it never ceased to be the

[2] *Reforma Bancária* (1925: 5).

imposing fortress which, from the monetary point of view, has dominated and protected the entire country and has always saved it in its moments of anxiety and painful crisis'.[3]

Finally, we ought to consider the unincorporated banking houses which had always existed alongside the incorporated sector and which continued to flourish at this time. Unfortunately, prior to 1930 the data in this regard are scarce and we have only a shadowy picture of this segment of the financial system. Roughly, a dozen and a half are known to have existed at the end of the war, the larger ones in Lisbon and Oporto, with the remainder dotted all over the provinces, in smaller towns. Although for the most part not very substantial, the few individual histories available show us that some of them rivalled the largest of the joint-stock banks in assets and market influence, and they had the ability to attract a considerable mass of deposits[4]. This might be explained by the greater attraction to the public of keeping its savings, if not at the Caixa, then with institutions which had unlimited liability. Traditionally, the most important private banks specialized in investment banking and in the management of government loans, in addition to everyday commercial operations, such as discounts and remittances.

2. The Inter-war Period: An Overview

Over the course of the next two decades, important changes came about in Portuguese banking though it cannot be said that by 1939 the situation had radically altered relative to what it had been at the end of the war. Characteristic of this was the fact that the number of joint-stock banks remained stable throughout the period, at around twenty, though the turnover in the sector was heavy. Only seven of the twenty-three banks in existence at the beginning of the First World War were still in operation at the start of the Second. Meanwhile, either through fusions, bankruptcies, or reconstructions, thirty-one disappeared and thirty-two new ones came onto the scene, created either from scratch or on the basis of some pre-existing bank.

With such high rates of birth and death for banks, one might have expected a certain measure of concentration to have gradually taken place but, in fact, the opposite was the case. As can be seen from Table 19.1 (col. 2), the Herfindhal index of market concentration fluctuates but shows no trend towards higher values. Likewise, the share of total assets held by the

---

[3] Diniz (1925: 52).

[4] Information is available on Henry Burnay; Pinto e Sottomayor; Fonsecas, Santos e Vianna; and Borges e Irmão. See respectively Câmara, 1985; Câmara, 1989; Sousa, 1984; and Rocha, 1921.

five largest banks remained constant from 1925 to 1939, after rising a few percentage points during particularly agitated times in the early 1920s. The composition of this group itself is also revealing: only one of them, the Banco Lisboa e Açores, was present both at the beginning and at the end of the period. The majority of the principal joint-stock banks of the late 1930s as such did not even exist at all in the previous decade, while hardly any of the five largest of the early 1920s survived beyond 1932.

The image which these data convey changes when one enlarges the universe of financial institutions under consideration. If one adds to it the other joint-stock banks—the Banco de Portugal and the Banco Nacional Ultramarino—the degree of concentration increases (compare cols. 1 and 2 in Table 19.1). With the inclusion of the Caixa Geral de Depositos, the situation at the top of the ranking also becomes one of stability, with four of the five top financial institutions remaining the same throughout the entire period. The reason is another feature of the period, namely the persistent dominance of the system by the country's three official or semi-official institutions—the Caixa Geral de Depositos and the banks of

TABLE 19.2. *Portugal's commercial joint-stock banks, 1920–1939* (million escudos)

Year	No. of banks (1)	Capital (2)	Cash (3)	Bills (4)	Portfolio (5)	Other credit (6)	Total deposits (7)	Total assets (8)
1920	25	64	54	96	17	142	138	429
1921	26	69	93	130	28	161	221	576
1922	28	103	82	213	33	274	308	1,004
1923	28	139	104	247	60	340	372	1,092
1924	24	153	150	336	55	293	479	1,223
1925	21	127	140	387	53	299	490	1,221
1926	21	169	126	422	67	365	528	1,450
1927	21	169	154	444	78	338	610	1,603
1928	21	n/a	n/a	n/a	n/a	n/a	n/a	n/a
1929	23	n/a	n/a	n/a	n/a	n/a	n/a	n/a
1930	22	188	139	363	82	382	611	2,275
1931	23	208	203	300	70	177	640	2,239
1932	25	233	161	325	69	298	638	2,304
1933	19	209	170	370	147	391	743	2,744
1934	19	168	197	440	182	372	867	2,889
1935	18	168	188	493	174	375	900	2,915
1936	21	178	244	542	201	425	1,066	3,303
1937	22	206	282	815	228	595	1,476	4,470
1938	22	206	282	848	199	599	1,404	4,443
1939	21	201	414	881	178	651	1,635	5,107

Notes: col. (3) includes cash at other banks; col. (5) includes all shares and bonds; col. (6) includes mortgages, cash credit accounts, and a vague rubric 'General debts and credits'.
Source: Instituto Nacional de Estatistica, *Situação Bancária no Ano* (Various years). Data for 1928 and 1929 were never published.

issue for the metropolis and the colonies, respectively, the Bank of Portugal and the Banco Nacional Ultramarino. Together they consistently accounted for about two-thirds of all banking assets Given the turbulence which often beset the privately owned banks, it is only natural that the financial institutions which enjoyed special protection should have towered above the others, and that consequently the group of five largest should have witnessed hardly any change, since besides these three it included the 'perennial' Lisboa e Açores.

Growth is another aspect of this industry where an apparent dynamism, in contrast with the sluggish performance of the pre-war years, is contradicted by a closer examination of the data. In nominal terms, the total assets of the joint-stock banks expanded twelve times, which meant a fourfold expansion in real terms (see Tables 19.2 and 19.4). Savings banks did even better—their assets grew by a factor of fourteen at current prices and of five at constant prices. If we consider all financial institutions together, including the Bank of Portugal and the colonial bank of issue, which operated also in the metropolis, then nominal bank assets increased nine times between 1920 and 1939, and by 330 per cent, if price changes are taken into consideration.

The significance of these figures is twofold. In the first place, since total bank assets appear to have expanded over the period a good deal faster than economic activity—7.5 per cent compared with GDP growth at an annual rate of about 5 per cent[5]—it seems evident that there was an increasing role for financial intermediation in the Portuguese economy, unlike what had happened before the war. In the second place, bank growth was now fuelled almost entirely by growth in deposits. In contrast with that period, there was very little contribution from either share capital or retained profits, which altogether rose by a mere 1 per cent per annum. Other sources of funds, such as foreign borrowing or bonds likewise played a very minor part. The implication is that an important change of attitude towards financial institutions was taking place, with the public, both corporate and individuals, evincing a greater familiarity with them and, in particular, a new willingness to entrust them with their savings. Although we have no data on this as yet, it seems possible that besides a shift from hoarding to depositing, there may also have been an increase in the Portuguese propensity to save during these years.

Increasing deposits were not, however, the only important source of growth for the joint-stock banks during the inter-war period. Both in the 1920s and in the 1930s, the incorporation of some of the largest private banks as joint-stock banks with limited liability also contributed

[5] The GDP rate calculated from Rosas (1992) is a bit higher than this, but has been revised downwards on account of the arguments in Lains and Reis (1991).

TABLE 19.3. *Money and banking indicators in Portugal, 1920–1939*

Year	Reserve ratio (1)	Currency ratio (2)	Money multiplier (3)
1920	55	3.0	1.32
1921	60	2.4	1.41
1922	39	2.3	1.43
1923	41	2.7	1.37
1924	46	2.8	1.38
1925	39	2.8	1.36
1926	35	2.7	1.37
1927	38	2.3	1.43
1928	n/a	2.1	1.46
1929	n/a	1.7	1.60
1930	32	1.2	1.80
1931	45	1.2	1.83
1932	35	0.9	2.05
1933	32	0.9	2.09
1934	31	0.8	2.24
1935	31	0.7	2.34
1936	30	0.7	2.39
1937	27	0.7	2.44
1938	32	0.7	2.49
1939	34	0.7	2.37

Note: col. (1)—cash reserves and deposits at other banks as a percentage of sight deposits; col. (2)—cash in hands of the public divided by sight deposits at commercial banks; col. (3)—money supply (M1) divided by high-powered money.
Source: Valerio (1983).

significantly to the apparently vigorous expansion of the latter's total assets.[6] If we aggregate the statistics for these two kinds of firms, a noticeably slower performance for Portuguese commercial banks as a whole emerges. On a rough estimate, instead of the 7.5 per cent per annum given above, a more likely figure for the entire commercial sector—incorporated and unincorporated—would be 3.6 per cent.

Bank assets per capita still show a 2 per cent a year growth rate, indicating an increasing involvement and trust by the public in financial institutions. On the other hand, in this new light financial intermediation now appears

[6] The new joint-stock banks in question rapidly became some of the most important players on the financial scene. Throughout the 1930s, three out of the five largest joint-stock banks always belonged to this group of newcomers, and have indeed remained to this day the principal banks in the country. Three reasons explain their decision to incorporate at this time. One was for the families who owned them to avoid having to disclose all of their non-bank assets, as they were required to by law after 1925. A second was the growing control which the authorities tried to exercise over them, including the requirement after 1930 that they make their balance sheets known to the Ministry of Finance, thus denying the advantage of secrecy which they had previously enjoyed. Finally, it is understandable if, given the financial instability of the period, the owners of such banks should have sought to avoid the possibly disastrous consequences that the unlimited liability of one of their businesses could have on their other interests.

as retreating, given that the annual increase of bank assets was in fact one and a half percentage points below that of GDP.

For a rapidly growing economy which was also undergoing a fair amount of structural change, this is a puzzling discovery, since one would expect the contrary to have happened. But the paradox is dispelled if we consider two additional circumstances. One of them was the result of the progressive consolidation and stabilization of financial institutions, which enabled them in turn gradually to reduce their reserve ratios. These fell, on average, by almost 50 per cent between 1920 and 1939 (see Table 19.3), which made it possible for their liquidity ratios (cash reserves/total assets) to be halved too. In other words, since a falling proportion of assets was kept as reserves, the net resources made available for lending by the banks rose faster than total assets and this alone already brings the rate of growth of credit closer, by half a percentage point, to that of GDP.

The second circumstance has to do with the increasing importance of the Caixa Geral de Depositos as a supplier of credit to the market. From a negligible share at the end of the war and for reasons which will be considered later, the Caixa's contribution rose during these two decades to about one-third of total lending to the private sector. If this component is taken into account as well, then the real economy's growth performance would no longer exceed that of its financial intermediaries but would be roughly equal to it. The situation thus seems to have been one in which quite strong economic growth could take place and be compatible with a stationary level of financial intermediation, something which would be plausible in a context both of capital saving and of much self-financing by firms. This is not an unlikely situation, but it is one which has yet to be corroborated by further research.

Geographic integration of the financial system was one area where, despite continued growth, modernization was slow in coming. Banking in Portugal remained very much an affair of small and highly localized firms. The larger units continued to do their business in Lisbon and Oporto and the only ones to have truly national branch networks were those enjoying privileges in return for which they were obliged to keep offices throughout the country, i.e. the Bank of Portugal, the Banco Nacional Ultramarino, and the Caixa Geral de Depositos. Consequently, when they were not carried out by these three institutions, credit operations in the provinces were the purview of either small and weak regional joint-stock banks or of a fairly active sector of unincorporated provincial banking houses, which seem to have multiplied between the wars to fill a void created by a rising demand for credit outside the two main cities.[7]

---

[7] Compared with the eighteen which existed *c.* 1920, Valério (1983) names forty-eight such establishments as having existed at some time during the 1930s, and his list is incomplete.

The major joint-stock banks which could aspire to a 'national' status made progress in the direction of network development only very slowly, as attested by the fact that their total number of branches had risen from only thirteen in 1920 to thirty in 1939. Indeed, only the very largest had any branches at all; it is not clear how much they were a source of profit to them, or whether they meant much as a means of mobilizing financial resources, from the provinces to the principal cities and vice versa. It is worth noting in this connection, however, that as late as 1939, even the Caixa Geral de Depositos, which had offices everywhere, drew as much as two-thirds of its savings deposits from Lisbon and Oporto. It was not until the 1950s, in fact, that the commercial banks began to go in for branching on a serious scale, and succeeded in vanquishing not only their own inertia in this respect but also obstacles such as poor communications, a lack of suitable staff for branch management and an internal structure which was not designed for exercising the requisite control over its constituent parts, particularly if they were geographically dispersed.

3. The Aftermath of the War: The Early 1920s

In the years immediately after the war, the Portuguese economy faced the usual problems of adjustment that beset all other European countries. In some respects, however, it was comparatively better off. Although briefly a belligerent, it did not suffer any physical destruction. Not being an open economy prior to 1914 and in spite of having increased its sales abroad during the conflict, it did not have to face any particularly hard problems of peacetime contraction in exports. Its GDP does not appear to have fallen either, whether during or immediately after the war years, and may even have increased.

Nevertheless, the war left Portugal with two very negative legacies. One was a severe imbalance in its public finances, given that ever since 1914, while expenditure was rampant, successive governments avoided increasing tax revenues. The other was the consequence of the first. In order to finance the growing deficit, the Bank of Portugal had to lend more and more and to do this it had to be allowed, indeed compelled, to increase its note issue, which rose by 300 per cent between 1914 and 1918 and by another 600 per cent in the course of the next six years. With the supply of money rising even faster, the effect on prices was dramatic though the expected one (Table 19.4). Indeed, with the exception of Germany and Austria, Portugal could claim the sharpest post-war inflation of Western Europe.

From the point of view of the financial sector, these were turbulent and often difficult years. Bursts of euphoric activity were interspersed with the banking crises which occurred in 1920, 1923, and 1925, with the result that many banks were founded but many also disappeared—respectively, seventeen and sixteen between 1918 and 1925, for an initial total of twenty-three. In the aggregate, nominally the joint-stock sector expanded (Table 19.5), but in real terms it contracted slightly. The public increased its nominal deposits but the erosion of inflation kept their real value stagnant, and there were sharp fluctuations in this for individual banks, as a result of intense competition among them.

All three banking crises were 'classic' in the sense that there were runs by the public to liquidate financial assets, that the currency/deposit ratio rose sharply, as confidence was shaken, and that banks assumed defensive positions, cutting down on credit, reinforcing cash reserves, and allowing reserve ratios to rise (see Table 19.3). But it should be noted too that, for the most part, the origin of these troubles lay in the negative shocks experienced by the real economy, to which was added a temporary halt in the expansion of the money supply, both of which were then transmitted to the financial system, not vice versa. In 1923, for example, the causes were typically a trade recession produced by a reduction in export demand

TABLE 19.4. *Money and prices in Portugal, 1918–1939*

Year	Prices (1914=100) (1)	Money supply (M1) (million escudos) (2)	Monetary base (million escudos) (3)	Exchange rate (escudos/sterling) (4)
1918	240	358	292	7.9
1919	268	580	389	8.2
1920	420	830	626	18.3
1921	606	1,064	752	39.4
1922	707	1,531	1,071	65.0
1923	1,022	1,973	1,439	109.7
1924	1,338	2,420	1,777	134.0
1925	1,295	2,500	1,844	99.2
1926	1,250	2,583	1,890	94.8
1927	1,325	2,709	1,898	108.4
1928	1,278	2,974	2,031	108.3
1929	1,320	3,335	2,088	108.3
1930	1,266	3,674	2,036	108.3
1931	1,148	3,846	2,103	109.4
1932	1,129	4,252	2,071	110.0
1933	1,128	4,417	2,110	109.1
1934	1,138	5,121	2,282	110.4
1935	1,140	5,526	2,357	110.4
1936	1,163	5,777	2,410	110.4
1937	1,201	5,839	2,387	110.4
1938	1,170	6,081	2,441	110.4
1939	1,114	6,447	2,718	110.3

Source: as for Table 19.3.

J. Reis

TABLE 19.5. *Assets and deposits of Portuguese banks,* 1920–1939 (million escudos)

Year	Joint-stock (1)	Non-joint-stock (2)	Savings banks (3)	Bank of Portugal (4)	Banco Nacional Ultramarino (5)
Assets					
1920	429	n/a	239	745	697
1921	576	n/a	317	872	714
1922	1,004	n/a	400	1,305	1,071
1923	1,092	n/a	597	1,956	1,346
1924	1,223	n/a	653	2,572	1,521
1925	1,221	n/a	1,163	2,691	1,619
1926	1,450	n/a	1,283	2,541	1,600
1927	1,603	n/a	1,692	2,519	1,634
1928	n/a	n/a	n/a	2,774	1,754
1929	n/a	n/a	n/a	3,059	1,724
1930	2,275	1,650	2,168	2,858	n/a
1931	2,239	1,951	2,736	3,100	n/a
1932	2,304	1,638	2,757	3,072	n/a
1933	2,744	1,525	2,500	3,059	n/a
1934	2,889	1,608	2,763	3,552	n/a
1935	2,915	1,435	2,830	3,849	n/a
1936	3,303	1,575	2,923	4,294	2,144
1937	4,470	392	2,956	4,525	2,441
1938	4,443	326	3,088	4,620	2,561
1939	5,107	328	3,319	4,764	2,756
Deposits					
1920	138	n/a	204	25	145
1921	221	n/a	273	54	209
1922	308	n/a	336	59	279
1923	372	n/a	448	52	292
1924	479	n/a	452	84	320
1925	490	n/a	654	80	291
1926	528	n/a	901	86	282
1927	610	n/a	1,242	98	307
1928	n/a	n/a	n/a	77	352
1929	n/a	n/a	n/a	94	335
1930	611	418	1,561	140	n/a
1931	640	377	1,793	278	n/a
1932	638	403	2,114	543	n/a
1933	743	446	2,210	534	n/a
1934	867	493	2,421	758	n/a
1935	900	482	2,465	781	n/a
1936	1,066	532	2,550	926	664
1937	1,476	145	2,578	1,058	735
1938	1,404	125	2,694	1,071	813
1939	1,635	123	2,903	871	905

Sources: as for Table 19.3.

combined with a bad agricultural year, on the one hand; and, on the other, a monetary contraction brought on by government policies to try and stabilize the plunging exchange rate. In 1925, the trouble arose with the Government's success in raising the exchange rate, causing severe problems both to exporters and to firms facing external competitors in the home market, and consequently for their bankers. The sudden halt in the creation of base money, which was part of these stabilization efforts, by leaving the Bank of Portugal without the funds it needed in order to assist the faltering banks with extra discount facilities precipitated and then deepened the crisis.[8]

The destabilizing impact of these crises on Portuguese financial institutions was intensified by several background circumstances which magnified the latter's fragility. Inflation was probably the most important of these. One of its negative consequences was the rapid deterioration it brought about in the solvency of the banks. With no legal obligation to maintain the real value of their share capital and probably some difficulty in doing so, the ratio of assets to capital quickly increased to double what it had been in 1914, leaving many in a dangerously exposed position. The best way to avoid this situation would have been to retain most of their profits, in order to strengthen the capital account. This, however, was not open to most to do.[9] In the atmosphere of suspicion and uncertainty which surrounded the banks at this time, to have limited dividend distribution drastically would have been to invite a run by their customers. Therefore, it was only some of the unincorporated banks which were able to opt for a strategy which involved severely limiting dividend distribution.

A second harmful effect of inflation was the rapid erosion of loan values. In order to avoid a contraction of their assets, banks had to try and expand their business. At the same time, the abundance of money, which was being constantly injected into the economy, made it more difficult for banks to put their resources into short-term paper. A greater emphasis was therefore placed on the acquisition of non-financial assets, which were bound to look attractive to banks attempting to preserve their book value against a background of spiralling prices.

Tying up a fairly large part of their credit in long-term applications was nothing unusual for enterprises which traditionally were 'universal'. Before the war, this had worked quite well because a fairly close relation had generally been kept between illiquid loans and share capital. Now, however, while a growing share of assets had to be devoted to long-term loans, an

---

[8] A good account of this period is given by Telo (1980). For a banker's detailed contemporary description of some of these crises, see Diniz (1923).

[9] Lumbralles (1926: 196) also points out that by 1925 the aggregate capital of all banks had shrunk to one-third of its 1914 real value.

increasing share of the funds used by banks was money on call.[10] This created a highly vulnerable situation, a good example of which is given by a small Lisbon bank like the Banco Industrial Português. Between 1920 and 1925, it engaged in promoting medium to small industrial enterprises— bricks, salted cod, school furniture, resinous products, cement blocks, wine-bottling, and toothpicks!—and inevitably met with disaster when some of these businesses began to face trouble as a result of the strong ups and downs of the Portuguese economy in the early 1920s.

The volatility, and rapidly falling value, of the exchange rate was a third problem which threatened the banks. On the one hand, it was tempting for them to speculate in the exchange market, where the substantial profits to be made were a valuable boost to dividends which had to be high if they were to beat rising prices. On the other hand, the risks were considerable and a rapid turnover in this business was essential in order to avoid substantial losses. An example of what could happen to the less cautious comes from the Banco Economia Portuguesa which was literally wiped out in 1925 because of its delay in repaying a loan of £100,000 made to it in 1919 by the Bank of Portugal. By 1925, this debt had risen to more than the value of the bank's assets owing to a fall of 1,200 per cent in the exchange rate, and it thus became impossible for the Banco Economia to continue.[11]

Finally, public opinion placed a good deal of stress on the unhealthily speculative characteristics of the period as having some responsibility for bank instability. Fast-rising prices and the accumulation by some of wartime profits probably did breed such an atmosphere, and encouraged the multiplication of unreliable schemes to which some banks fell prey. As always on these occasions, unscrupulous operators made their appearance, even on the board of the banks themselves, a fact which was to justify a later rule empowering the government to decide whether or not a bank director was fit to occupy such a position.

Two institutional features of the period are also worthy of consideration, in that they provided an opportunity for limiting the damage which, in practice, was not utilized. One was the weak exercise of the regulatory powers conferred on the Government by the bank legislation of the 1890s, which were quite extensive. Amongst other things, it stipulated that no new bank could be created and no existing bank could issue bonds without the express consent of the Government in the form of a decree. The Government had powers to inspect any bank at any time, and could intervene by appointing a commissioner to the board of directors, should the rules governing the cover for demand liabilities or the structure and contents of the loan portfolio be breached.

[10] See Lumbralles (1926: 191–7), who points out that at the end of 1925 long-term credits were three times as large as long-term liabilities, a situation he considered fraught with risks.
[11] Based on the annual reports to the shareholders during the period in question.

Political circumstances in the aftermath of the war, however, were hardly conducive to a vigorous implementation of a law which had been devised, following the 1891 financial crisis, 'to prevent the repetition of such deplorable disorders which are so prejudicial to the country's credit'.[12] The republican parliamentary regime founded in 1910 was hardly a model of political stability—'the ministers of finance succeed each other with incredible rapidity'[13]—and the stresses of war, social unrest, and the huge financial problems of the State were hardly the best environment in which to take firm action on any front. To try and limit the strong demand for bank creation which inflation and speculation was generating was apparently impossible. To try and regulate the numerous old and new banks which pullulated in this effervescent business atmosphere was just as hard.

The second institutional factor which failed to contain bank instability was the status of the Bank of Portugal in the post-war era. Two circumstances rendered it now a much less effective arbitrator of the monetary and banking scene than it could and should have been. One was its rapidly increasing subordination to the short-run objectives of the Government of the day, chief of which was to obtain the necessary loans via the printing of money to cover the ever-widening budget deficit. Under its 1918 contract, the note issue was to be divided into two parts. One was to be used exclusively for Treasury loans, while the other was to be kept for discounts and advances. Because the authorities realized the need to limit as much as possible these overall note increases, the bank was made to keep to a minimum the part of the issue which it could use for commercial purposes so as to leave plenty for the Government's needs. Therefore, whereas in 1918 the supply of notes had been targeted for 150,000 contos for government loans and 100,000 for discounts, by 1924, a succession of further authorizations to issue had raised these figures to 1,450,000 and 195,000 contos, respectively.[14]

The upshot was that at any time the bank was fully 'loaned up' and had very little flexibility with which to intervene in the market. Indeed, it was often accused of failing to help the bank sector when in need; in fact, on more than one occasion it was forced to contract its already limited rediscount facilities owing to the pressure from the Treasury to exceed the legal limit on government loans.[15] On top of this, ever since the beginning of the war its relative position within the financial system had been constantly eroded. In 1913, its share of total bank credit had stood at 32 per

---

[12] Banco de Portugal (1946: iv. 138).

[13] Fonseca (1923: 4). (Xavier, who was a top civil servant in the Ministry of Finance at the time, later recalled that 'government instability was one of the most calamitous ills the country has suffered' (1950: 92).

[14] From 1911 the monetary unit was the escudo, with a thousand escudos making up a conto.

[15] Lumbralles (1926: 149); Morisseaux (1925: 22); Telo (1980: 225).

cent compared to 8 per cent in 1924. It had therefore lost much of its old 'clout' over the other banks, and the clearest symptom of this weakness was visible in the fact that it could no longer make its discount rate prevail. In the early 1920s, the Bank of Portugal was charging 7 to 9 per cent for discounts—in real terms, a negative rate—because this suited the government, when the market rate was 16 to 20 per cent and often more, a differential which would have been impossible ten years earlier.

A second obstacle to a reduction of the turmoil in the banking system by the Bank of Portugal was self-imposed. It arose with the continued adherence by its directors to the rule that no discount or rediscount should be conceded to paper which was not first-rate. In this, the bank followed the Bagehotian precept that lending to a client with insuperable difficulties did not help anyone, least of all the market. It was able, therefore, to pride itself on the fact that, even in the worst moments, its losses through default were minimal. In the early 1920s, however, when so much commercial and other paper was of poor quality and when so many signatures were either dubious or of a creditworthiness which was hard to ascertain, this inevitably meant that the Bank of Portugal appeared to abandon its previously more active stance, and failed to provide the temporary accommodation to bankers which would have enhanced the stability of the financial system.

4. The Recovery of the late 1920s

A turning-point in the evolution we have described thus far was clearly reached in 1925. For the economy as a whole, the significant events were the end of inflation, the stabilization of the exchange rate, and the interruption of the infernal cycle of government deficits and loans financed by the issue of fresh paper money. The policy designed to achieve these results was founded on the ruthless balancing of budgets which became the hallmark of Salazar's *Estado Novo* regime (1933–74) and the norm for decades to come, but which, in fact, was in place already in 1924 and 1925, and functioning with great success. Although its long-term benefits were manifold, the initial impact of this on the banking world was hardly positive. Rather, as mentioned above, it precipitated a severe banking crisis though one which turned out to be the last of the entire inter-war period. On the other hand, it had the virtue that it probably 'shook out' the worst elements in the banking system, and thus paved the way for the comparative stability which marked the rest of the inter-war years.

Banking was also shaken by the Bank of Portugal but for quite other reasons. In 1925, the latter suffered what was probably the greatest fraud ever perpetrated in Portuguese banking history and one which proved to be a veritable earthquake for the Portuguese political and financial world. The discredit this brought upon the Bank and upon banking in general, just as depositors were learning to return with their savings to the non-state sector, was doubtless one of the reasons for the severity of the bank crisis, since it came at a time when intervention by the reserve bank was needed more than anything else.

Nevertheless, the years that followed, down to the world crisis, were far more tranquil than those before 1925. Few new banks were created and fewer still failed. Thanks to the end of inflation, asset erosion ceased to be a problem, while the discount business picked up and grew steadily down to 1929. Notwithstanding the continuing competition by the Caixa Geral de Depositos, deposits at the joint-stock banks showed a rising trend too, which bespeaks a renewed confidence in the system. It also reflects the repatriation of Portuguese capital which had been driven to flight by the social and economic turmoil of the immediate post-war years.

As elsewhere, the late 1920s were a far more congenial environment for the banking industry. The economy was expanding but without monetary illusion, and the strong speculative element had been driven from the market-place. It was much easier now to identify and avoid dangerous loans. The problem of exchange-rate instability had also more or less disappeared. At the same time, with the shakier and more disreputable banks out of the way, thanks to the devastation wrought by the 1925 crisis, the system as a whole gained in stability, both in fact and in the eyes of the public, an externality which was important and meant lower operating costs for the survivors.

Institutional aspects again seem to have had a role, only this time for the better. On the one hand, the State armed itself with renewed and strengthened powers under a new banking law promulgated in 1925 and which, in spite of its many faults, remained in force until the late 1950s. To a large extent, this was prompted by the desire to bring the banks to heel, in the supposition that, through their selfish speculation, it was they who were the root cause of the depreciation of the escudo. A rising 'anti-plutocratic feeling' in certain political circles probably also influenced the advent of the new legislation, a further aim of which was to promote the stabilization of the financial system, with a view to re-establishing confidence and bringing back the capital which had previously fled the country in supposedly huge amounts. In spite of this, the new law met with the vehement opposition of the banks. After a violent campaign, they succeeded in having some of its original provisions watered down, though in essence it remained unchanged.[16]

[16] As a result of this campaign, the Lisbon Commercial Association was closed down by the authorities for having incited the banks to disobey the law. The banks presented no less than nineteen major objections to the first, January 1925 version of the law. However, most of these were still present in the second, March 1925 version, which was enacted. See *Reforma Bancária* (1925).

One of the interesting points of this legislation was the recognition, for the first time ever, that banking is not an ordinary business but one that influences all other business through its impact on monetary variables. Consequently, it was placed under the supervision of the Ministry of Finance and not of the Ministry of Commerce, as before. Another was the acceptance of the view that the framework for this should be laid down by the State, but that it was the bank of issue which should 'intervene' and 'orientate' in order to secure the normality of the market and 'limit its fluctuations'. A third point was the realization that the bank of issue had hitherto lacked the means to act as a bankers' bank. To get round this difficulty the bank of issue was forbidden to discount directly in Lisbon and Oporto, so that it should have the resources for rediscounting as much of the banks' paper as might be needed. In cases of emergency, it was further considered that the Caixa Geral de Depositos should be allowed, exceptionally, to rediscount paper held by banks as well. As with the earlier legislation of this kind, the new law defined the type of operations that banks were permitted to carry out and their quantitative limits, what cover was required for demand liabilities, who could be a bank director, and the periodicity and structure of the published accounts. It was completely innovative, however, in two important aspects. The first was that it was far more severe regarding the penalties for anyone infringing the rules, and spelt them out in considerable detail. The second was that it prescribed a minimum amount of capital not only for all new but also for existing banks which was significantly in excess of current levels. The amount was linked to the price of gold, and a distinction was made, in the first place, between provincial banks and those with headquarters in either Lisbon or Oporto, and, secondly, between joint-stock and unincorporated banks. The object, of course, was to bring all of them back to realistic levels of capitalization and thus put an end to the solvency problem.

The mere fact of having a better legal instrument is not in itself proof that corresponding changes take place. Unfortunately, we lack the detailed evidence on some aspects to permit an overall assessment in this case. Nothing is known, for instance, about the application of the measures on inspection and on disciplinary proceedings, or about the degree of support given by the Bank of Portugal to the market during the next few years. Nevertheless, it seems likely that in important respects the practice accompanied the theory. After 1926 and particularly after 1928, the country was under an authoritarian regime which had much less difficulty in making its will felt, and which was also a strong partisan of the view that active intervention was always justified whenever in 'the national interest'. As regards capitalization, for example, the new rule was certainly taken seriously. The assets / capital ratio for all banks, which, in 1925, had reached its highest point of 28.7, was down to 13.6 in 1930, after having started at

16.4:1 in 1920.[17] Likewise, the parsimony with which new bank licences were given out—only four in 1926–1930, a time of expansion of the economy—suggests that a more rigorous attitude towards entrants was now in place. The fact that all but one of these new banks survived the rest of the 1920s and the 1930s indicates that greater care was now taken in licensing than during the heady days of the post-war period.

Greater authority did not necessarily mean rigidity and this may have been helpful too. The capitalization rule, for example, was applied in a flexible way, with the banks in greatest difficulties being allowed several postponements. One of them—the Banco Commercial do Porto—had still not met this standard in 1931, and in 1927 only half the banks then in existence had done so even though they had been allowed to include retained profits for the purpose of capital increases. Similarly, the Bank of Portugal was permitted to go on discounting directly in Lisbon and Oporto, presumably because it was found that the other joint-stock banks were not able to fill its place and that therefore rigorous compliance with the law in this respect would have done more harm than good.

A second positive institutional influence came in the shape of the Bank of Portugal itself. Thanks to the improvement in the State's finances and to the surpluses it began to generate every year with the coming to power of Salazar, not only was there no longer any need to increase the note issue, but the part left in this for discounting and rediscounting gradually increased. In 1926, the bill portfolio of the bank had a turnover of 791,000 contos; by 1929, this had risen to 1.4 million contos. There was thus much more leeway now for the reserve bank to play the role of market regulator that the 1925 law had set out for it, but it was still not enough. Although its weight in the system was growing all through the late 1920s it remained incapable of enforcing its will in the matter of commercial discount rates. The reason, which it was the first to recognize in its annual reports, was that its share of total discounts remained too small. As a result, the other banks had no difficulty in establishing their own rates, usually two or three points above the bank's. This was a circumstance which caused the government some displeasure, as it went against its much announced fight against 'usury', and was to lead Salazar himself to write that 'the Bank should move towards a situation not only of greater financial ease but one of control over the market'.[18]

---

[17] For reasons of comparability, these ratios cover all banks except the Banco Nacional Ultramarino since there are no data for it between 1930 and 1938. 'Capital' here includes retained profits, which were becoming more and more important as a source of capital increase during the inter-war period and were accepted for this purpose by the 1925 bank law.

[18] This statement is taken from the preamble of the law which reformed the Portuguese monetary system and was probably authored by Salazar. For the text of the law, see Bank of Portugal (1946: vol. vi).

5. The World Crisis and Beyond

The most important aspect to note about the early 1930s is the comparatively mild impact of the international crisis and of the ensuing Depression on the Portuguese economy. The study of the economic history of the inter-war period is still in its infancy but the facts are clear. Prices fell only from 1930 to 1931 and then just slightly. There was a contraction of bank credit starting in 1930, but by 1933 this level had already been regained. Difficulties were experienced by firms in various sectors and the number of bankruptcies was higher than usual. However, both real GDP and agricultural and industrial output at constant prices not only had positive growth rates in every year of the decade, but performed better than in most other European economies.[19]

There are several factors to account for this. The economy was still very much based on agriculture and from this point of view,. two circumstances were of considerable import. One is the fact that the 1930s were on the whole an extraordinarily good time for agriculture, with several bumper harvests on record. The other was an extremely favourable set of policies towards this sector, whence reputedly the regime also derived much of its political support. This included price-support schemes, which were important in that they insulated farmers from the fall in international prices; incentives for technical modernization; and generous credit lines. All of this was made available via either the Bank of Portugal or the Caixa Nacional de Credito, an offshoot of a recently transformed Caixa Geral de Depositos, especially to producers of wheat, wine, cork, olive oil, and fruit. At the same time, import-substitution industrialization continued unabated, now further stimulated by a new, more protectionist tariff and by a vigorously sponsored government programme of investment in infrastructure. Special credits were made available to industrial firms in trouble and there was a determined effort to lower interest rates and to make these available to the provinces.[20]

The fact that Portugal, unlike most other countries of Western Europe, remained a not very open economy was also helpful, by sparing it from the full consequences of the contraction in international trade. The worst external shock came through the invisibles account. This was the result of the suspension of remittances from the large community of Portuguese emigrants in Brazil, and of the moratorium on the servicing of that country's foreign debt, one-fifth of which was reputedly in the hands of

---

[19] The mildness of the economic crisis was abundantly referred to at the time. See e.g. Branco (1950: 171–6) which was written in 1935. For macroeconomic data, see Rosas (1992: ch. 7).

[20] Correia (1938). This good growth performance has also been attributed in part, at least, to a Gerschenkronian type of catching up experience. See Rosas (1992: ch. 7).

Portuguese residents.[21] This, however, was compensated for by two items. One was a significant, though as yet unmeasured, inflow of repatriated capital as a consequence of the growing confidence in the country's fortunes felt by its many residents with foreign assets in their portfolios. The other was a strong expansion of receipts from tourism. The result was a balance of payments surplus in most years and a steadily rising stock of gold and foreign reserves at the Bank of Portugal.

Two further aspects stand out, this time in terms of policy. One is that while the Government, in tune with the times, followed a rigorously orthodox budgetary policy, this did not have the severe dislocative effect it had in other countries. The reason is that since this policy had already been in place for several years prior to 1931, the adjustment to it had taken place well before the crisis. The late 1920s, when it began to be consistently implemented, were a time of some prosperity, during which exports rose 50 per cent and industrial output, stimulated perhaps by investment from repatriated capital, increased 25 per cent (1926–30).[22]

The second concerns the exchange-rate policy adopted at the end of 1931, which was to peg the escudo to the pound rather than keep to the gold standard, even though Portugal had just adhered to it earlier in that year, a few months before Britain had to abandon gold. The oft and proudly proclaimed result is that the external adjustment was not severe, since exports were able to hold up reasonably well, even during the worst moments, and the domestic market was not deluged by imports from the sterling bloc, with which traditionally trade relations were close.

Banking during the 1930s fared well in Portugal, considering the bleak international economic climate and the financial difficulties experienced in so many other countries. Taken as a whole, the commercial banks kept up roughly the same asset growth—of about 3.6 per cent a year—that they had had during the preceding decade. By now, however, they were expanding much less as a result of the addition of new units and far more through internal growth. The attrition that had been characteristic of an earlier time was now greatly diminished—the number of bank creations and closures was less than half of what it had been in the 1920s. Firm size rose concomitantly, particularly at the top of the industry, where the five largest banks in 1939 were five times larger than they had been in 1920, and more than twice their size in 1930.

Greater size was accompanied by greater solidity. On the one hand, the solvency gains achieved after 1925 were retained throughout this decade, with an assets/capital ratio which barely departed from the 15 : 1 mark. At

---

[21] Most sources agree that Portuguese capital held abroad at the time of the crisis was about £50 million and that income from this was in the region of £3 million. See Telo (1980); Branco (1950); Morisseaux (1925).

[22] Nunes *et al.* (1989); Lains and Reis (1991).

the same time, although Portuguese 'commercial' banks continued to be 'universal', all through these years there was a steady erosion in the position of the long-term loan and share portfolios within assets, and thus a movement towards a healthier and more liquid composition of the balance sheet. The proportion of short- to long-term credits on average shifted from 78 per cent in 1930 to 106 per cent at the end of the period we are studying, a fact that was made much of in annual bank reports and was recorded with approval in 1938 by Araujo Correia, one of the main economic-policy formulators of the period.[23]

Improving credibility was reflected, in turn, in a greater inclination on the part of the public to convert its monetary assets into bank deposits, which expanded twice as fast in 1930–9 as they had during 1920–30. Although they could not match the Caixa's numerous branches nor its state guarantee for liabilities, in this respect it is significant that the commercial banks were no longer outpaced by the official savings bank, as they had been during the preceding decade. (see Table 19.5). With greatly increased funds at their disposal, and a government-imposed limitation on the commercial operations of the Bank of Portugal in Lisbon and Oporto, their discounts now rose more rapidly, by a healthy 250 per cent, between 1930 and 1939, even after a brief dip at the beginning of the 1930s.

Notwithstanding this fairly optimistic picture for the decade as a whole, it must be recognized that, in the short run, Portuguese banks faced all the difficulties associated with the world crisis of 1931. Clearly the negative shock suffered by the economy was transmitted to the financial sector, where in 1930–1 discounts fell by 20 per cent and 'other credits' by 60 per cent.[24] This was followed in 1932 by the closure of five banks, two of them—the Banco do Minho and the Banco Português e Brasileiro—of some import-ance and with important links with Brazil. Potentially, the greatest risk for the stability of the other financial institutions came from the Banco Nacional Ultramarino, one of the largest and also one of the worst hit. Besides being the colonial bank of issue, it enjoyed a strong presence in the metropolis through its large network of branches, in addition to its offices abroad in London, Paris, and Bombay. The origins of its troubles went back, however, over a full decade or more of bad management and political interference but were strongly compounded now by the deep recession experienced by the colonial economy. By 1931, at 300,000 contos, its losses were huge, and equal to roughly a tenth of total commercial bank assets.

[23] Correia (1938: 374) The Banco Pinto Sottomayor, for example, was declaring to its shareholders, as early as 1927, that 'we have decided to reduce systematically these (long-term) positions, whenever we have the opportunity to do so'. Long-term loans in this context refers to the values in cols. 6 and 8 of Table 19.2. We include the share portfolio because most of such assets were not very liquid, given the 'thinness' of the stock market.

[24] Data are not available for 1928 or 1929 since the *Situação Bancária*, which contains aggregate bank statistics, was not published during these years.

This led one of Salazar's closest advisers to write that 'to let it go bankrupt is something we simply cannot allow', a policy line which was successfully followed, with the result that the Banco Nacional Ultramarino was able to publish its balance sheet and operate normally again in 1938.[25] Casualties among the small, unincorporated and largely provincial banking houses by comparison were trivial in terms of the value of assets lost, though they represented a significant reduction in numbers. Between 1930 and 1931, one-third of them either closed down, were subject to government intervention, were reconstructed by creditors, or were driven to join forces and fuse with other banks.

When everything is taken into account, however, it is far from evident that these troubles amounted at any time to a full banking crisis, or to a situation as serious as that experienced in 1925. As could be expected, banks reacted with the usual defensive stance. Their aggregate reserve ratio jumped from 32 to 45 per cent, in 1930–1, but by the end of 1933 was already back to 32 per cent again. Yet despite the failures, closures, and mergers of banks and private banking houses, total commercial bank assets never fell below their 1930 level and were 8 per cent higher than this already by 1933. Above all, the currency ratio never rose in any of these years. This indicates that, though the public was nervous and there were runs on banks, there was no enduring change in its attitude regarding the basic safety of deposits.

The relative ease with which the Portuguese banking system weathered the international financial storm at the beginning of the 1930s calls for some explanation. One cause was obviously the already mentioned mildness of the domestic recession itself, the shock waves from which threatened the local banks much less than elsewhere. Besides this, a low degree of integration with other financial centres meant that the transmission of the effects of banking débâcles abroad was weak too, in contrast with the contemporary experience of more sophisticated and internationalized economies. The principal negative foreign influence of the kind was the loss of the business of remittances from Brazil, but this only hurt profits and in no way involved massive withdrawals of credits or writing down of assets abroad, since neither had been significant in the balance sheets of the Portuguese banks. Similarly, the traditionally weak integration of the banking system internally made it also less likely that the fall of any one of them would drag down the others, even when failure was visited on fairly substantial houses.

[25] Comissão do Livro Negro (1987: 145). Curiously enough, the same Quirino de Jesus who now advised Salazar had been the author of the 1925 banking law, under the previous republican regime which the *Estado Novo* execrated so. Unfortunately, little is known about the Banco Nacional Ultramarino during the 1930s, as its official history symptomatically goes no further than the 1920s, and neither annual reports nor accounts were published between 1930 and 1938.

Acute difficulties with liquidity and loss of confidence by the public are the two chief ingredients of banking crises. In this particular instance, although both were present, neither became a disruptive force. As regards the former, two circumstances were of vital importance. One was a strong inflow of expatriated capital held abroad by Portuguese investors, who, as noted earlier, were encouraged by the Government's financial orthodoxy and political stability and conservatism, which contrasted with the turmoil reigning elsewhere. The other was the Finance Ministry's policy of buying up short-term Treasury bonds—for savings, a classic alternative to deposits—which started in 1929 and by 1932 had put some 400,000 contos back into the hands of the public, i.e. the equivalent of two-thirds of all bank deposits at the time. Together, they helped to inject substantial funds into the Portuguese economy and thereby satisfied the additional demand for liquidity which is characteristic of such periods, without excessive pressure being placed on bank resources.

As regards the confidence problem, government measures also played a critical role in lessening its impact, and reveal how a highly centralized and authoritarian political system had a better chance of overcoming the crisis. The provision of credit assistance to the many financial institutions which were basically sound, but troubled by deposit withdrawals and by difficulties in collecting on loans, was one important form of intervention. This was carried out on government orders, using the considerable funds either of the Bank of Portugal or of the Caixa Geral de Depositos, to an unknown but substantial extent, at least judging by the historic high reached by the bank's rediscount portfolio in 1931. It was complemented by a flow of credit to bail out similarly sound industrial concerns which would otherwise have failed unnecessarily, and probably brought down with them the banks which financed them.[26] The second approach was to arm the Government with sweeping powers that would enable it to intervene swiftly in any financial institution in difficulty, through specially appointed commissioners. The latter could overrule any decision taken by the shareholders or directors, suspend court proceedings against the bank, including those for bankruptcy, and could decide whether to close it, put it back on its feet, or attempt a reconstruction. Extensive use was made of this legislation and altogether some twenty commissioners were appointed during this period, mainly in connection with the problems faced by the small unincorporated banking houses.

Looking beyond the early 1930s, to the rest of the decade, the persistently positive performance of Portuguese banking can be accounted for by very much the same factors as we have adduced to explain how the financial turbulence at the beginning of the decade was overcome. The overall

[26] Correia (1938: 376).

expansion of the economy and a banking system that had been purged of its weakest elements earlier, first in 1925 and again in 1931, were two obvious factors in this evolution. A continuing lack of substantial international financial links is a third. Finally, economic policy is a fourth aspect and one which deserves more detailed attention here, since it involved a significant departure from the pattern which hitherto had been followed and which, as with so many other countries, tended to be abandoned during these difficult times.

When it came to banking, the approach of the *Estado Novo* during the 1930s naturally was shaped by a combination of the regime's views regarding economic matters in general with the pressing needs of the moment. The framework was a market-oriented one, but all rules and decisions had to be subordinated to the 'superior interests of the nation', which emphasized economic growth and stability, the maximum use of national resources, and the reduction of external dependence to a minimum. While proclaiming an aversion to far-reaching intervention, except where strictly necessary, in fact, the regime's inclination was to play a strong role in shaping the course of economic events and to do so in a planned and systematic fashion.

The role of the banks in this scheme was to provide, as cheaply as possible, the support needed for the industrial, agricultural, colonial, and infrastructural development of the country, but in a prudent manner, through solid and stable firms and without upsetting the financial system. Banking institutions, although expected to remain independent and privately owned, were no longer viewed atomistically. Rather, they were conceived of as a single, integrated whole, under the strict and purposeful orientation of the State.[27] One important advantage of this was that the functional differentiation, which had never seemed possible before on any scale, now began to make sense, thus paving the way for a more efficient allocation of the banks' resources, which were also the nation's.

To achieve this, one step was to push the joint-stock commercial banks towards becoming much more 'commercial' and much less 'mixed'. As well as ensuring a useful specialization in the provision of the short-term credit that the economy needed, this had the advantage of rendering them more liquid and therefore safer, particularly at a time when they were coming to rely increasingly on sight deposits for their funds. To achieve this, one measure was to divert business to them by imposing a ceiling on the direct discount activities of the Bank of Portugal in the places where they mattered most, i.e. Lisbon and Oporto. Another was a considerable effort to improve

[27] Most of this was adumbrated already in Salazar's early financial writings of 1928–30 in Salazar (1930), and is evident again after ten years of governance in Araujo Correia (1938). Pronouncements by Quirino de Jesus and others all through the 1930s show that though the authorities reacted to events, they followed a blueprint all the same.

their balance-sheet structure by relieving them of the worst part of their long-term credits to industry, and having the Caixa Geral de Depositos take them on instead.[28] Finally, limits were imposed on the proportion in which such assets could be held.

A second step was to bring into existence a specialist 'industrial bank' under the control and ownership of the State, the lack of which had long been deemed the great shortcoming of the Portuguese financial system.[29] Instead of creating one from scratch, however, the old Caixa Geral de Depositos was reformed and made to serve this purpose. The advantages were not only that it submitted completely to the Government's will but also that it had an extensive branch network, huge deposits, and now additional funds generated by the policy of reduction of the State's debt to it, which fell from around 730,000 contos in 1929 to 140,000 in 1939. Besides serving to bail out banks with cash problems and drawing away from them their less liquid loans, it actively engaged in financing new investment in all sectors, thereby becoming a powerful instrument of government development policy.[30] By 1939, its portfolio of long-term private credits had increased fivefold and, at just over 600,000 contos, was equal to more than two-thirds of the discount portfolio of the entire commercial bank sector.

The revamped system was to be crowned by the Bank of Portugal, which under its 1931 contract with the State was committed to the task of 'regulating and distributing bank credit', in addition to that of 'implementing monetary policy at the highest level', i.e. the stabilization of the exchange rate.[31] The aim was to institutionalize it as a bankers' bank and lender-of-last-resort which would concentrate on rediscounting bank paper and avoid competition with the other banks. Although continuing to be a joint-stock company, it was to fulfil these duties under the strict supervision of the government. The number of the latter's representatives on the board of directors was enlarged and they were subordinated to a newly created committee of stabilization within the bank, where official appointees had a majority of votes. This committee was charged with overseeing 'monetary stabilization and in particular the regulation of the price and volume of credit'.[32]

[28] While applauding this measure, the 1935 report of the Corporative Chamber on banking stressed that the interpenetration of banking and industry was still such that it would be some time before this desired separation could be completed.

[29] e.g. Cabreira (1915) devotes one long chapter to this problem and how it could be solved.

[30] e.g., we know that the Caixa was directed to lend 75,000 contos to the beleaguered Banco Nacional Ultramarino in 1931. See Comissão do Livro Negro (1987: 141).

[31] The Government's philosophy regarding the central bank is laid out in the extensive preamble to the decree which authorized this contract and seems to have been written by Salazar himself. See Bank of Portugal (1946: vi. 6–37).

[32] In his memoirs, Xavier (1950), who was then a privileged spectator of state–bank relations, reveals that the objective was to increase the Government's control over what was considered a much too independent bank of issue.

Officially, the principal instrument given to the Bank of Portugal was its power to establish a ceiling for the market discount-rate, which was not allowed to exceed its own by more than 1.5 per cent. It lacked the power, on the other hand, to set minimum reserve ratios or the means to carry out open-market operations. In practice, however, its influence rested just as much on its market power, either through its rediscount facilities with the other banks or through its direct discounting, though this was being increasingly confined to the provinces. Unfortunately, we know little in detail about the manner in which the Bank of Portugal intervened in the money market but it would seem that it was an active one, something which is suggested by the answers to a questionnaire sent to it in 1938 by the Bank of International Settlements. There it stated that it used its rediscount facility to control the creation of credit by other banks, and to prevent them from acting imprudently or in a manner deemed contrary to the country's interests.[33] Finally, it should be noted that none of this would have been of much import had it not been for the Treasury's radically reduced borrowing requirements during the 1930s, which enabled the Bank of Portugal to double its bill portfolio relative to the preceding decade's level and through this to make its wishes respected by the market.

In addition to redesigning its architecture for essentially pragmatic reasons, the *Estado Novo* also sought to mould the banking system in accordance with some of its more ideological concerns. A certain 'anti-plutocratic' sentiment and a strong dislike of what was referred to pejoratively as 'speculative activity' spawned efforts to subject dealings in bank portfolio assets to a legal obligation not to 'disturb either the market or the natural order of quotations'.[34] The corporatist thinking espoused by the regime also stressed the dangers of unbridled competition and the virtues of a 'corporatist price', a latter-day version of the medieval doctrine of the 'just price'. This gave rise to limits being placed on the opening of either new banks or new branches of existing ones, and to the setting of maxima for the interest that banks could pay their depositors. While realizing that in order to have solid banks it was necessary that they be larger, and that some fusions must therefore take place, especially between the smaller or weaker ones, a strong preoccupation also existed concerning the dangers of collusion and excessive concentration of market power. Banks were discouraged from buying each other's stock, from making agreements to dominate the market, from 'disorganizing legitimate competition', or from sharing directors, auditors, or other high-ranking officials between them.[35]

---

[33] Banque des Règlements Internationaux (1938: 13).

[34] Assembleia Nacional (1935), session of 13 Feb. of the Corporative Chamber.

[35] In the absence of archival research on these issues, we may note the strongly worded opposition by Quirino de Jesus, a stalwart of the regime, to the purchase of the Banco Nacional Ultramarino by the Espírito Santo banking group in 1934. See Comissão do Livro Negro (1987: 144).

Finally, besides specific policy on banking, one has to consider the extent to which the general economic policy followed during this period influenced the performance of the financial system. The first point to be noted is the already mentioned orthodoxy in terms of budget management which permitted, after 1928, the progressive reduction of the floating debt and, when this was fully paid off, that of the funded debt. Contrary to what has been claimed, in practice this did not imply the restrictive stance one might have thought unavoidable.[36] This was because a proportion of the annual budget surplus was deposited in the current account of the Treasury at the Bank of Portugal and became a part of base money, thereby helping to expand the money supply. But budgetary policy was helpful in other ways too. Directly, it contributed towards stabilizing the banking system given that it relieved the Bank of Portugal of its traditional duties towards the Treasury and therefore allowed it to be more active in the discount market and in rediscounting for the other banks. Indirectly, it was a positive influence in that it stimulated the real economy and helped reduce unemployment by having the remainder of the surplus pumped back into the economy in the form of finance for infrastructural investments.

Two other aims of monetary policy are also relevant to our analysis. One was that of ensuring exchange-rate stability, a task which the Bank of Portugal carried out with success (see Table 19.4) and, significantly, without having to resort to monetary restriction. Indeed, what is interesting is that though the gold standard had been abandoned, policy concerning foreign reserves was very much in the spirit of the 'rules of the game'. The Bank of Portugal was not 'encouraged' to sterilize the gold and exchange reserves which the country consistently earned during the 1930s through its balance of payments surplus. Rather, it continuously issued notes in response to the increments in these reserves, thereby contributing some 40 per cent of the total increase in the money supply during these years. At the same time, thanks to a lenient attitude by the authorities regarding the creation of money by the banks, M1 grew at an annual rate of 6.7 per cent and the share of deposits in the overall supply rose from 45 to 58 per cent during the period 1931–9.

The second aim was the gradual lowering of interest rates, imposed through the agency of the Bank of Portugal and rendered possible by the expansive monetary situation. The success of this is indicated by the fact that they fell a full three percentage points in eight years.[37] This satisfied two government objectives: to economize on the servicing of the public debt, and to boost the domestic economy, in particular in the provinces, where the

[36] Bessa and Pimenta (1987: p. 304).
[37] Valério (1983: 108). The Bank of Portugal rate fell from 7 to 4%; the discount rate of the commercial banks from 7.5 to 4.25%.

cost of credit tended to be much too high. The measure was not welcomed by the banks, who felt that it squeezed their profits, but ultimately its contribution was a positive one for them. In so far as both those objectives were satisfied, it was beneficial because it helped to keep budgets in surplus and the economy growing at a good pace, both of which were favourable background features of these years for the banking community.

6. Conclusion

Between the two world wars, the Portuguese banking system changed considerably. One of the principal features of this was a high turnover in its composition which left the country with a population of banks which would hardly have been recognized in 1918. On the other hand, by 1939, nearly all the institutions on which the future development of this sector would be built, in the 1950s and beyond, were fully established. In other words, it was essentially the banks which arose during the inter-war period, and learned both to weather its financial storms and to work within the highly regulated political regime in force since 1928, which were to become Portugal's long-term survivors.

The events and the policies of these two decades produced a financial system which was becoming progressively less fragile, more concentrated, and which exhibited greater functional specialization. Its strong expansion overall, and its increasingly important role in the supply of money, provide unmistakable evidence that these changes were recognized by the public, whose trust in the banking institutions clearly increased in the course of the period. Although direct evidence for this has not been cited here, it also seems fair to infer that its contribution to the economic growth of the period was both a positive and an increasing one.

Nevertheless, Portuguese banking remained deficient in some important respects. On the eve of the Second World War, there were still too many banks, too many provincial banks, too many small banks, and still no commercial bank which could properly be called 'national'. Stability had been bought at the price of strict regulation and the credit market was dominated, perhaps more than it had ever been, by the state-controlled financial institutions. In the 1950s, the system would be criticized for being too cautious and too rigid, for not being sufficiently oriented towards the country's economic development needs, and for not using its resources as fully as it might (Wallich, 1951). To some extent at least, it is not difficult to see that these shortcomings had their roots in the problems of the inter-war period and in the solutions which were adopted to deal with them.

References

Assembleia Nacional (1935), *Diário das Sessões* (Lisbon: Imprensa Nacional).

Banco de Portugal (1946), *Legislação Própria*, 6 vols. (Lisbon: Bank of Portugal).

Banque des Règlements Internationaux (1938), *Réponses de la Banque de Portugal au questionnaire sur l'escompte et les avances* (Bâle: Banque des Règlements Internationaux).

Bessa, Daniel, and Pimenta, Carlos (1987), 'A Economia sob o Estado Novo— Estagnação ou Desenvolvimento—O Papel do Sistema Monetário—Financeiro e, em particular, do Banco Central', in António Costa Pinto *et al.* (eds.), *O Estado Novo das Origens ao Fim da Autarcia 1926–1959*, 2 vols. (Lisbon: Fragmentos).

Branco, Carlos Soares (1950), *Aspectos da Questão Monetária Portuguesa* (Lisbon: Bank of Portugal).

Cabreira, Tomás (1915), *O Problema Bancário Português* (Lisbon: Imprensa Libanio da Silva).

Camera, Joáo Sousa da (1985), *História do Banco Fonsecas e Burnay* (Lisbon: Banco Fonsecas e Burnay).

—— (1989), *História do Banco Pinto & Sotto Mayor*. (Lisbon: Banco Pinto & Sotto Mayor).

Comissão do Livro Negro sobre o Regime Fascista (1987), *Cartas e Relatórios de Quirino de Jesus a Oliveira Salazar* (Lisbon: Grafica Europam).

Correia, José Dias Araujo (1938), *Portugal Económico e Financeiro* 2 vols. (Lisbon: Imprensa Nacional).

Diniz, Augusto Alves (1923), *Crise Cambial Portuguesa (1920–1923): Aspectos e Soluções* (Lisbon: Tipografia do Diário de Noticias).

—— (1925), *O Problema do Banco Emissor* (Lisbon: Emp. Diario de Noticias).

Fonseca, Joaquim Roque da (1923), *A Migração de Capitais. Inconvenientes do Exodo dos Capitais e Necessidade de Promover a sua Imigração* (Lisbon: Tipografia do Diário de Noticias).

Lains, Pedro, and Reis, Jaime (1991), 'Portuguese Economic Growth, 1833–1985: Some Doubts', *Journal of European Economic History*, 20.

Lumbralles, João Pinto da Costa Leite (1926), *Organização Bancária Portuguesa* (Coimbra: Coimbra Editora).

Morisseaux, Jacques (1925), *Quelques aspects du problème économique au Portugal* (Gand: Imprimerie de Marneffe).

Nunes, Anabela *et al.* (1989), 'Portuguese Economic Growth, 1833–1985', *Journal of European Economic History*, 18.

Pereira, Miriam Halpern (1983), *Livre Câmbio e Desenvolvimento Económico. Portugal na Segunda Metade do Século XIX* (Lisboa: Sá da Costa Editora).

Reforma Bancária (Decreto n.10474). Parecer da Comissão Nomeada em Assembleia Geral de Bancos e Casas Bancárias de Lisboa e Porto Reunidas em 26 de Janeiro de 1925, no Banco Lisboa e Açores (1925) (Lisbon: Typographia do Banco Lisboa e Açores).

Rocha, Albino Veira da (1921), *Le Portugal au travail* (Paris: Pierre Roger).

Rosas, Fernando (ed.) (1992), *Portugal e o Estado Novo (1930–1960)* (Lisbon: Presença).

Salazar, António de Oliveira (1930), *A Reorganização Financeira. Dois Anos no Ministério das Finanças 1928–1930* (Coimbra: Coimbra Editora).

Sousa, Fernando (1984), *Banco Borges e Irmão 1884–1984* (Oporto: Banco Borges e Irmão).

Telo, Antonio José (1980), *Decadência e Queda da I República Portuguesa*, 2 vols. (Lisbon: A Regra do Jogo).

Valério, Nuno (1983), *A Moeda em Portugal, 1913–1947* (Lisbon: Sá da Costa Editora).

Wallich, Henry C. (1951), *O Sistema Financeiro Português* (Lisbon).

Xavier, Alberto (1950), *Memórias da Vida Pública* (Lisbon: Livraria Ferin).

20

Spanish Banking in the Inter-War Period

PABLO MARTÍN-ACEÑA

1. Introduction

The role and evolution of banks during the inter-war period has recently received a great deal of attention. In 1981 the Banco di Roma and the MIT jointly sponsored a seminar in which different scholars studied how the relationship between banking and industry evolved between the two wars. The papers presented on that occasion were published afterwards in a special issue of the *Journal of European Economic History* in 1984, and included the studies prepared by Bouvier (France), Tortella and Palafox (Spain), Ciocca and Toniolo (Italy), Nötel (Austria and Hungary), Hardach (Germany), and Minsky (USA).[1] Almost ten years later the International Economic History Congress held in Leuven in the summer of 1990 provided the opportunity to re-examine the same subject, also in a comparative perspective. Convened by H. James, H. Lindgren, and A. Teichova, scholars from various countries looked at the mutual ties between banking, industry, and the State and discussed the development of the financial system in the inter-war years. The proceedings of the conference have been edited by the organizers in a valuable volume (James *et al.*, 1991).

The themes that flow through all the papers are alike. They cover the impact of the First World War on the structure and later development of financial institutions; the banking expansion, or otherwise, during the 1920s; the effect on the financial system of the adherence to the gold-exchange standard; the relations between banks and industry and between banks and the State; the role of central banks and their capacity to influence monetary developments; and the impact of the Great Depression on the banking sector. The findings of the first conference have been well summarized by both Toniolo (1982) and Kindleberger (1984), while Harold James (1991) has provided a short account of the main results of the Leuven conference.

I would like to thank G. Toniolo and G. Tortella and all participants at the Venice Workshop as Banking, Currency, and Finance of the Network on the Economic History of Europe between the Wars (European Science Foundation) for their helpful comments.

[1] A book, with some of these papers, published in 1982 by the Banco di Roma and Il Mulino, predated the issue of the *Journal of European Economic History*.

Thanks to all these contributions we know a good deal more about this hitherto unexplored and neglected subject. Basically what we have learnt is that the experience of countries under observation both in the 1920s and in the 1930s was not entirely disparate. With varying degrees all experienced the impact of the First World War, the boom of the 1920s, and the bust of the 1930s. There were impressive similarities. Inflation, reconstruction, war debts, and exchange depreciation impinged on all countries one way or the other. Furthermore, the ties between industry and banks augmented and spread; with some exceptions, mixed banking became a universal phenomenon. Financial instability and vulnerability was higher after 1920 than it had been before; the 1930s were years of crisis everywhere; banks collapsed, forcing governments to intervene on a large scale and to introduce substantial reforms to restructure the financial sector. But despite these similarities, the countries under scrutiny also exhibited significant disparities. First, their financial structures stood at distinct levels of development; second, the effect of war was different for non-belligerent nations, such as the Netherlands, Spain, or Scandinavia, which in fact benefited from the conflict, and for countries directly involved in combat; third, the effect on the domestic financial structure of adherence to the gold standard varied from country to country; and finally, the impact of the Depression on the banking sector was uneven and international factors mingled with domestic affairs.

The Spanish financial experience has also received some attention. Tortella and Palafox (1984) in their contribution to the 1981 seminar examined closely the relationship between banks and industry. They noted how the financial system expanded quite rapidly during these years, and how it underwent a significant process of concentration. Secondly, they concluded that links between banks and industry were reinforced and that, unlike credit institutions in other European countries, Spanish banks were not subject to the deflationary policy imposed by adherence to the gold standard. Finally, they effectively argued that the impact of the crisis on Spain was 'muted and delayed' and this explains why banks did not collapse in the 1930s. More recently Martín-Aceña (1987, 1990), in a more quantitative vein, has looked at the same issues. In two different papers he established that the Spanish financial system experienced an important expansion during these years, and went through a conspicuous process of modernization; he also showed that the relationship between banks and industry significantly increased between 1900 and 1935, although market imperfections and the existence of discriminatory banking practices gave rise to serious inefficiencies.

The aim of this chapter is to offer a short account of the evolution and changes of the Spanish financial system during the inter-war period. Section 2 provides an overview of the structure of Spanish banking at the outbreak of the war. Section 3 deals with the impact of the First World War on the

Spanish system. Section 4 focuses on the banking events of the 1920s and the 1930s and addresses the question of why Spanish credit institutions did not collapse during the Depression. The concluding section offers some brief and general comments.

2. Growth and Structural Change in Spanish Banking, 1900–1935

At the turn of the century the number of Spanish joint-stock credit institutions approached forty, with total assets amounting to nearly 4,000 million pesetas, of which 68 per cent belonged to the Bank of Spain, 26 per cent to the non-issuing private banks, and the rest divided among saving and insurance companies and other minor financial institutions.[2] In addition, there existed a large number of unincorporated banking houses of different sizes, and private bankers operating in small markets providing commercial credit to local business. Tedde (1974) has noted that by 1900 the Spanish financial system had a strong regional orientation and was poorly integrated, and that banks operated in very limited geographical areas. The most prominent institutions were located in Madrid, Catalonia, and the Basque country. The Bank of Spain was the sole institution with extensive national coverage, thanks to its network of branches in nearly all provinces.

By 1900 the most salient banks, such as the Banco de Bilbao, the Banco de Santander, the Crédito Mobiliario, and the Compañía Mercantil de Crédito, were mixed banks of the French blend. They had participated in the construction of the railway network and also provided capital to finance relevant episodes of nineteenth-century Spanish industrialization, particularly in mining, iron and steel, shipbuilding, metalworking, and chemicals.[3] However, the overall contribution of the financial intermediaries to the process of industrialization before the First World War remains an open and cumbersome question. Furthermore, Spanish banks were characterized by their relatively small size, inadequate commercial structures, low levels of technology, serious problems of management, and underdeveloped internal organizations. The degree of financial diversification and specialization was reduced, and credit institutions were able to supply only rudimentary banking services. Finally, the links between the commercial banks and the Bank of Spain were loose; banks' managers thought of the central bank more as an unfair competitor than as a lender-of-last-resort. In short, at the end of the nineteenth century Spain's financial structure was marked by a relative lack of diversification, a predominance of the commercial banks

---

[2] The figures come from Martín-Aceña (1987: Table 6.1).
[3] Tedde (1974: chs. 3 and 4, *passim*).

over other institutions, and an excessive weight of the bank of issue—traits that are, according to Goldsmith's classification, typical of a banking system in the early stages of economic development.[4]

At the beginning of the twentieth century the transformation of the Spanish economy accelerated. From 1900 to 1930 the growth rate of GNP was about 2 per cent, above the rate registered in earlier periods, and industrial production increased at a rate close to 2.5 per cent. Simultaneously the economic structure underwent a process of modernization and Spain shortened its distance from Western Europe.[5] The financial system also displayed substantial growth and modernization. From 1900 to 1935 the number of joint-stock banks doubled, and the total assets of the financial system multiplied almost sevenfold, from 3,884 million pesetas to 25,907 million pesetas. Since the growth of financial assets was greater than that in GNP, the Goldsmith financial intermediation ratio (FIR) rose from 39 in 1900 to 75 in 1935; however, the level of intermediation of the Spanish economy in the latter year still remained below that of Western Europe.[6]

The new institutions founded after 1900 had a larger size than those established in the previous century; their average paid-up capital was higher and they carried out a greater volume of financial operations. The Banco Hispano Americano opened its doors in 1900, the Banco de Vizcaya came into existence in 1901, and the Banco Español de Crédito in 1902, as a result of the reorganization of the old Pereire's Crédito Mobiliario. A few years later the Banco de Urquijo was established in 1918, out of one of the oldest family banking houses, and finally in 1920 the Banco Central was formed, also by the transformation of an unincorporated credit establishment. These five institutions plus the other two mentioned above (the Banco de Bilbao and the Banco de Santander) formed the group of the so-called 'big seven', which have dominated the Spanish financial scene until very recently.

Many of the institutions created after 1900 were born with the character of 'mixed banks', intended to supply both short-term credit to commercial activities and long-term credit to industry, as well as to promote and participate in industrial ventures. They also intended to spread out their operations to all corners of the country by opening branches. As a matter of fact, the policy of territorial expansion allowed the new banks to capture a larger amount of resources and expand their lending activities. This policy was carried out particularly by the Madrid and Bilbao banks. Credit institutions also expanded through the absorption of small and local banks, as well as by means of amalgamations of various kinds. By 1935 the 'big seven' absorbed more than 60 per cent of the total volume of banking

---

[4] Goldsmith (1969: 33–5); for Spain, Martín-Aceña (1987: 112–21).

[5] For an account of the changes in the Spanish economy between 1900 and 1930, see the papers in Sánchez-Albornoz (1987), and more recently, Fraile (1990, 1991).

[6] Martín-Aceña (1987: 120).

operations and owned a total of 856 branches dispersed throughout the country.[7]

The relations between banks and industry in these years have been studied by Muñoz (1978) and by Tortella and Palafox (1984). They maintained that the financial institutions allotted a significant volume of resources to finance diverse entrepreneurial undertakings: banks increased their portfolio of industrial stocks and expanded the credit assigned on a long-term basis. These authors also argue that the banks participated directly in the promotion of both old and new industrial concerns, and reinforced their role in the management of firms by placing representatives on the boards of directors.

In addition, there were other significant structural changes. First, the weight of the Bank of Spain within the banking system declined substantially. The Bank's share in total assets declined from a high of 70 per cent in 1900 to only 27 per cent by 1935; conversely private non-issuing banks increased from a mere 25 per cent to 51 per cent between these dates. Savings banks also acquired a more significant weight, and reached 11 per cent by 1935. The assets of banks and savings institutions together represented nearly 65 per cent of total financial assets at the end of the period. The composition of the banks' assets also changed. External resources (deposits) grew significantly more than internal resources (paid-up capital and reserves), so that while in 1900 the ratio of internal to external funds stood at 30 per cent, by 1930 the same ratio had fallen to 17.5 per cent. The so-called cash ratio also changed: in 1900 the banking system exhibited a ratio as high as 50 per cent, while by 1930–5 it had decreased to 15.2 per cent, a clear sign of the modernization of the system. This meant that banks, rather than maintain large amounts of idle resources, started to operate on a limited cash base, trying to invest the majority of their resources in productive assets. With regard to the composition of the banks' portfolio, public securities represented approximately 30 per cent, while investment in industrial stocks stood at 20 per cent. Industry, however, received additional bank finance through direct credit and long-term loans; presumably an unknown although significant portion of the loans and credit which appears in the balance sheet of the banks under the heading of 'credit to the non-institutional private sector' (personal credit) was also a way through which banks channelled funds to industrial ventures.[8]

In short the Spanish banking system between 1900 and 1935 developed and modernized. New and bigger banks appeared, the structure became more diversified, and the institutions seem to have been able to issue new types of liabilities. More important, after 1900 the big banks extended their

[7] Some of the changes in banking during this period have been reviewed by Tedde (1988: 324–31) and García Ruiz (1990: 136–203).

[8] All the figures quoted in the text come from Martín-Aceña (1987: tables 6.1 to 6.5).

operations to all the nation's territory and the financial market became more integrated. There were also some improvements in internal organization. The big banks introduced the divisional structure, opened foreign-exchange departments, and in some cases even created small research offices in charge of collecting statistics and of preparing reports on the general situation of the economy.[9] In sum, mixed banking, diversification, specialization, and a better internal organization are some of the features and trends that characterized the Spanish financial system between the two wars.

3. Expansion and Crisis, 1914–1920

The outbreak of the war opened a short but intense period of uncertainty. The decline in the market price of domestic commodities, and the collapse in stock and bond prices, threatened to undermine the basis of the entire Spanish financial system. The lack of confidence provoked a run on bank deposits, which was directed particularly against the major commercial institutions. They were consequently induced to turn to the bank of issue with extraordinary rediscount requests. But as Spain remained neutral, confidence returned, and the economy experienced a general expansion led by a strong export boom that lasted for the entire war years. The expansion was felt by both the consumer and capital-goods industries, and the resulting demand for bank accommodation fostered a considerable expansion of banking activities.[10] The number of joint-stock banks increased from fifty-two to ninety-one between 1915 and 1920 and, as mentioned above, among the institutions founded during those years were the Banco de Urquijo in 1918, and the Banco Central in 1920, which were to become two of the more prominent credit institutions of the country. Banking operations also expanded, visible in the balance sheet of all banks, particularly that of the 'big seven'. In current pesetas, paid-up capital increased threefold and deposits multiplied by five; hence, the ratio of deposits to national income jumped from a mere 3.9 in 1914 to 9.8 by 1920.[11]

During the war the Spanish financial system made a decisive move towards mixed banking, so that by 1919 the involvement of Spanish banks in industry was much higher than ever before. Roldán and García Delgado (1973) have noted that during the war years the participation of banks in the promotion of industrial firms became a common practice. The mixed banks not only engaged in ordinary commercial operations, but also made long-term industrial investments. Financial institutions stayed ready to

[9] García Ruiz (1990: 186 ff).
[10] Still the most valuable account of the impact of the First World War on the Spanish economy is Roldán and García Delgado (1973); for a more recent review, see Sudriá (1990).
[11] Figures from Martín-Aceña (1987: table 6.2).

extend all types of loans to industrial companies and to acquire industrial securities in larger quantities than previously. Industrial credit was secured by shares, bonds, bills, and even real estate or with business mortgages. Besides, they actively participated in the formation of joint-stock companies by underwriting and purchasing securities, and bank directors sat on the boards of companies with which the banks maintained close financial relations.[12] However, the major commercial banks did not aspire to become holding companies, rather they simply pretended to benefit as much as possible from the general expansion of the economy. Finally, they also contributed to finance the public deficits by taking a substantial portion of the debt issued during the war. As the new titles could be used as collateral to obtain automatic credit from the Bank of Spain, banks became extremely liquid, which in turn allowed them to further increase their lending activities.

But the rapid process of growth predicated on mixed banking bore with it significant costs. As Ciocca and Toniolo (1984) have noted, the involvement of deposit-taking banks in industrial promotion is inherently procyclical, and lends instability to the financial system. The practices of the commercial banks made them vulnerable to fluctuations in the earning potential and in the equity value of the manufacturing firms with which they maintained relations, as if they owned the firms outright. Since banks also made commercial loans against industrial securities deposited as collateral, their loans portfolios also became extremely exposed to variations in stock prices. Further, there were many instances in which commercial loans were used to finance fixed investment; in good times, manufacturing firms would repay such credits by issuing new stocks or bonds on the securities markets; in bad times, however, the banks' commercial portfolios tended to become illiquid. Therefore, the degree of exposure of the mixed banks to a decline in industrial activity ensured that a recession in manufacturing would ripple rapidly through the banking system and the economy as a whole.

As well-informed contemporary observers anticipated, the expansion was followed by a severe crisis which affected the real and the financial sectors alike. The previous industrial boom developed without reference to post-war markets, and much of the new capacity built during and just after the war became idle. Thus the causes of the crisis which followed afterwards unfolded during the war, with high inflation, overlending, and lending on bad collaterals. The biggest risks in banks' loans emerged in credits with shares and merchandise as collateral, since it had often been given against a background of highly inflated prices and favourable valuation of the securities.[13]

---

[12] Roldán and García Delgado (1973: 242–53).
[13] André (1917: 811 ff); Ceballos Teresí (1930: iv. 393); Tallada (1926: 162 ff).

The banking crisis was especially intense in Catalonia, although other institutions in different places of the country also had difficulties. The first problems appeared in the summer of 1920, when the Banco de Barcelona, one of the oldest and most prominent Spanish credit institutions, announced important losses.[14] The depositors, fearing that the institution could not meet its demand obligations and short-term liabilities, began to withdraw their money. Eventually the bank suspended payments in November of 1920. According to different descriptions, the problems of the bank originated from extensive and continuous speculative operations in the foreign-exchange market, and from incautious lending policies; it was known that the bank lent on bad collateral and on overpriced merchandise. The crisis generated panic in Barcelona, and all banks suffered withdrawals of funds; the Catalan politicians pressed the officials in Madrid to convince them of the dangerous financial situation. The Minister of Finance summoned the governor of the Bank of Spain and told him that the central institutions should be ready to provide all the financial assistance that the Catalan bank might ask. However, the Bank of Spain was not forthcoming, and argued that all credit institutions with liquidity problems, including the Banco de Barcelona, were essentially insolvent and should not be rescued. Under pressure, the bank yielded and opened a limited line of credit, which obviously was not enough since in the end the Catalan institution had to close its doors. The effects of the failure of the Banco de Barcelona in Madrid and Bilbao, the other two Spanish financial centres, remained within certain limits. There were runs on the deposits in various institutions, but on the whole they resisted without much difficulty. Banks with good paper, or with government securities, discounted easily in the Bank of Spain and obtained all the cash they needed. In fact, by the beginning of 1921 the crisis was apparently over. However, as we shall see later, the difficulties were far from over. A few years later they would reappear and several other banks faced serious problems.

The banking reform of 1921

The authorities responded to the crisis with the enactment in December 1921 of a new Banking Law (*Ley de Ordenación Bancaria*). The Act instituted a legislative framework that was to regulate Spanish banking in the next decades.[15] The new legislation pursued two main objectives. First to re-structure and to regulate the sector, which lacked a legal framework and

[14] The crisis of the Banco de Barcelona has been studied in detail by Cabana (1978); for the role of the Bank of Spain and the impact of the crisis in the rest of the country, see Martín-Aceña (1984: 64–70).

[15] This law has been examined, among others, by Tortella (1970: 303 ff.); and also Martín-Aceña (1984: ch. 2).

had experienced an anarchic development during the war. The authorities wanted to establish certain controls on banking operations and a close supervision on the banks' activities. The notion of bank itself was defined very clearly, and financial institutions were compelled to observe certain rules and conditions before they could obtain the status of bank. The law created a new organism, the Supreme Banking Council (SBC), to supervise the working of the banking system and entrusted it with broad regulatory powers. The Act divided the country into three banking zones, and separated the credit institutions also into three categories: registered (in the SBC) banks, non-registered banks, and foreign banks. The SBC was empowered to fix the minimum amount of capital required for credit institutions and to impose certain relations between balance items, such as the ratio of the sum of equity capital and reserve funds to the volume of deposits, and the ratio of loans, investments, and real assets to demand liabilities. Further, the 1921 law compelled banks to submit monthly statements of their balance sheets to the SBC and to publish their income statements. The SBC was also given the capacity to investigate bank accounts and to supervise and impose disciplinary sanctions.

The 1921 Banking Law also sought to transform the Bank of Spain into a true central bank and to increase the control of the State over the institution. The authorities believed that the post-war crisis could have been avoided had the bank behaved as a real lender-of-last-resort. They also believed that in the past, the bank had only performed one of the functions predicated of a central institutions, that of the Government's banker, but had neglected the other two (lender-of-last-resort and monetary authority). In consequence, the law strictly regulated the relationship between the Government and the bank. It limited the amount of advances that the Treasury could obtain from the bank and fixed the quantity of banknotes in circulation (5,000 million pesetas); an issue over and above that limit required government authorization. In order to strengthen the links between the banking community and the Bank of Spain, the law forced the latter to give preferential treatment to the credit institutions; in particular, it established that financial institutions could discount paper at a preferential rate. Finally, although the Act did not forbid the Bank of Spain to operate with the non-banking private sector, it set a ceiling to the outstanding amount of private securities in the portfolio of the Bank.

In sum, the 1921 legislation aimed to introduce some order into the anarchic Spanish financial system and to regulate entry into the banking sector. It also attempted to facilitate an increase in banks' size and a reorganization of their internal structures. Simultaneously, the law gave the authorities certain powers of control and supervision. Finally, it tried to transform the Bank of Spain into a real central bank.

4. Banking in the 1920s and 1930s

As mentioned above, between 1920 and 1935 the Spanish banking system underwent continuous growth accompanied by substantial structural transformations. Both the number of banks and savings companies, and the financial magnitudes changed significantly. The volume of deposits (demand and time-deposits and savings accounts) increased from 5,171 million pesetas in 1920 to 10,917 million pesetas in 1935; as a consequence, the ratio of deposits to national income rose from 9.8 to 21.4 per cent. On the other hand, the total assets of financial institutions grew at an annual rate of 6 per cent, similar to the European average, and hence the level of financial intermediation increased. Notwithstanding, Spain's FIR level remained below Europe' average and its absolute value still indicated that Spain did not have a fully developed financial sector.[16]

The new structural features that emerged after 1900 strengthened during this decade and a half. The Bank of Spain reduced the volume of its commercial operations with the non-banking private sector, and enlarged its links with the rest of the financial community. Reluctantly and slowly the Bank of Spain was forced to accept its role as a central bank and as a lender-of-last-resort.[17] On the other hand, the Government promoted the creation of new official institutions, designed to meet the credit demand of special sectors. These institutions were born with private capital but under close public supervision and endowed with privileged statutes.[18] The first, the Banco de Crédito Industrial, came into existence in 1920 with the purpose of providing credit to new industrial projects; afterwards in 1925 appeared the Banco de Crédito Local, designed to cover the credit necessities of local authorities and to extend credit to finance public services and utilities; finally, in 1929 the Banco Exterior de España was set up to provide financing to the export sector. Although all these banks kept a low profile in these years, they certainly contributed to the diversification of the financial system. Moreover, during the 1920s there also took place a remarkable expansion of the savings institutions, whose number increased by fifty. The development of the savings banks owed much to the new favourable legal framework approved in 1926 and reformed in 1929; the legislation passed in these two years liberalized the operations of the savings companies and reduced their dependence on the Government.[19] The financial system became not only more diversified but also more integrated. The

---

[16] Martín-Aceña (1987: 119).
[17] Tortella (1970: ch. 7, *passim*).
[18] For the birth and early development of the official banks, Martín-Aceña (1991).
[19] For the savings companies during these years, see Fornies Casals (1979).

big banks established a relatively extensive network of branches which developed into real national banks. Financial concentration also intensified and contributed to blur the regional orientation that had characterized the system throughout the nineteenth century. In 1935 the so-called 'big seven' concentrated half of the paid-up capital and about 70 per cent of the total volume of deposits. Finally, two other features need to be mentioned. First, the industrial character of many Spanish credit institutions consolidated. Commercial banks undertook extensive company promotion and held a sizeable proportion of private securities in their portfolio; they augmented their operation on long-term loans and became involved in the management of industries through their representation on boards. Apparently the economic policy of the Dictatorship from 1923 to 1930 helped to foster this latter trend. As Tortella and Palafox (1984) have pointed out, the extensive programme of public works, investment in overhead capital formation (railway, roads, water projects) and other stimuli in related sectors facilitated the penetration of banks. Finally the relationship between the banks and the State grew stronger. The persistence of large budget deficits during the 1920s and 1930s covered by sales of public securities, which could be automatically pledged at the Bank of Spain to obtain credit, encouraged the banks to subscribe to the issues. The public debt not only provided banks with a highly liquid asset, but also furnished them with a quite productive asset with negligible risk. Hence it is hardly surprising that banks willingly swelled their portfolio of public securities more than of any other item in their balance sheet. Banks became perfectly liquid, ready to meet an increasing demand for credit. In addition, by loading their portfolio with government bonds they compensated for the simultaneous increase in risks associated with their rising involvement in industrial ventures.

The financial crisis of 1924–1925

The law of 1921 did not solve all the post-war difficulties of the Spanish banking system. On the contrary, the financial institutions entered the 1920s with many unsettled problems; in fact, a certain number of banks were incapable of liquidating bad loans and getting rid of devalued stocks. For a limited period banks could carry large losses by running down reserves built during earlier years. But as the recession deepened and the price of shares did not rise, industrial recovery was delayed and the financial situation deteriorated. Eventually, the difficulties re-emerged after the summer of 1924. The new crisis appeared as a continuous run on bank deposits which lasted nearly a year until September 1925. In the meantime, during these fifteen months the level of deposits decreased by 17 per cent; the run was particularly acute in the last part of 1924, and although it was over by the end of 1925, confidence in the credit institutions was not immediately restored.[20]

During 1924–6 half a dozen salient banks failed and were forced to liquidate (the Banco de Castilla and the Banco Matritense in 1924; and the Crédito de la Unión Minera, the Banco de Vigo, the Sociedad de Seguros y Crédito La Agrícola, the Banco Agrícola y Comercial, and the Banco Vasco in 1925). Particularly serious was the situation of the Banco Central, one of the biggest and most influential institutions, whose problems threatened to shatter the whole financial structure.

Contemporary observers suggested that insolvency was the basic problem of the majority of the banks that went bankrupt.[21] The persistent decline in merchandise and share prices until 1923 brought about a clear deterioration in the quality of loans and credits, as well as in the composition of the banks' investments. In particular the institutions which had intimate links with sectors severely hit by the recession suffered the most. After the war, some institutions continued to extend credit to companies to which they were linked, trying to avoid their failure; but in the end the difficulties of the firms dragged down the banks and the insolvencies in the real sector were transmitted to the banking sector. The annual reports of the banks are quite explicit with regard to these events. Bankers attributed the crisis to the industrial difficulties of the period, in particular the Bilbao-based institutions, which reported depressed conditions in the export sector, in shipping, and in heavy industry until the end of 1925.

A typical case was the failure of the Crédito de la Unión Minera. The difficulties of this company started immediately after the war, with acute liquidity problems. The company took some actions to restore its position, but unsuccessfully. The situation worsened thereafter, and both its liquidity and its solvency deteriorated during the ensuing deflationary period, since the bank continued its policy of lending to bank-affiliated companies. Confidence was reduced when the news reached the general public. The bank's shares declined, and the withdrawal of deposits that followed led to the suspension of payments. As usual, the Bank of Spain did not intervene and let the crisis run its course. The argument put forward by the board of directors to justify their passivity rested on their profound conviction that the problems of the institution were due to bad management, excessive risks, and unorthodox policy. For the Bank of Spain each institution should face its own difficulties without help, and if some banks showed signs of insolvency the best policy was to facilitate their liquidation.

Nevertheless, the Bank of Spain made an exception for the Banco Central. In this case the board was forced to intervene as a consequence of a direct

---

[20] The only modern account of the banking crisis of the mid-1920 is in Martín-Aceña (1984: 81–7).

[21] Ceballos Teresí (1930: v. 343 ff).

order from the Dictator, Primo de Rivera.[22] For a variety of reasons the Banco Central was on the verge of financial collapse, suffering from a persistent withdrawal of deposits, though the bank was essentially sound and solvent. At first the Bank of Spain prescribed its usual medicine, but on this occasion the government disagreed. The Banco Central was not only a big bank whose problems could provoke unforeseen consequences, but also there existed good relations between the directors of the bank and the Dictator, who ordered the Bank of Spain to provide assistance. The Bank of Spain could not but obey, and in a short period the Banco Central was able to overcome its problems.

The battle for the peseta

The high tide of European stabilizations occurred in 1926–7 when Poincaré put the franc back on a *de facto* gold standard and Mussolini won the battle for the *quota novanta*. In Spain, the Minister of Finance, Calvo Sotelo, persuaded Primo de Rivera of the need to establish full convertibility for the peseta and a swift adoption of the gold standard. Although the Spanish authorities failed in their attempt to stabilize the exchanges, the issue, as in other countries, has provoked a lively historical controversy.[23] But our interest here is rather in the implications for the banking system of the policy followed to introduce the gold standard, and the confrontation on the subject between the Treasury and the Bank of Spain, who forcefully opposed the operation.[24]

Initially Calvo Sotelo wanted the establishment of the gold standard at the old historical parity (25 pesetas to the pound sterling) fixed in 1868. Since the peseta had experienced a rapid and persistent upward trend during most of 1925 to 1927, he expected a full revaluation up to par. He also counted on the huge gold reserves of the Bank of Spain to defend the peseta against possible speculative movements, once convertibility had been introduced. But events in 1928 and thereafter frustrated his expectations. Contrary to what he anticipated the peseta moved in the wrong direction. In 1928 it changed its course and started to depreciate smoothly but persistently. On the other hand, the bank refused to collaborate and rejected any compromise to commit its gold reserves to defend the exchange rate. Nevertheless, Calvo Sotelo went ahead with his plans and devised a programme of stabilization whose features did not differ much from those implemented in other European countries. He was well aware of the need to impose a certain dose of deflation in the domestic economy to drive up

[22] Martín-Aceña (1984: 86).
[23] See e.g. Hernández Andreu (1986: ch. 4).
[24] For this section we follow closely the account offered by Martín-Aceña (1983, 1984: 128–69).

the exchange value of the peseta. For that he needed to raise interest rates and control the growth of the money supply. But his policy encountered first the opposition of the Bank of Spain, which was reluctant to move its discount rate, and secondly the opposition of the Dictator, who refused to introduce drastic economies in the budget, since this would have endangered the realization of his cherished public-works programme. But Calvo Sotelo was not discouraged. He set up a stabilization fund to intervene in the exchange market; the endowment of the fund came basically out of foreign credits obtained in Paris, since the Bank of Spain flatly refused to lend its gold reserves for this operation. Eventually Calvo Sotelo's plan to introduce the gold standard failed, the peseta fell in the exchange market and he was ousted from the Ministry in December 1929.

It could be argued that banks somehow benefited from the failure of Calvo Sotelo. Deflation would have meant a slower rate of growth, a lower demand for credit, and a rise in the risks of default of firms. Company failures might have produced a new crisis of confidence in the financial system. Banks did not complain about the fluctuating peseta, or the deficit spending, or stable domestic prices. If Calvo Sotelo had got his way, the economy would have suffered deflationary pressures which presumably might have led to depressed entrepreneurial expectations and a tendency for investment and consumption to stagnate. Perhaps in such case the banks might have adopted a more belligerent stance against his policy. As Ciocca and Toniolo (1984) and Forsyth (1991) have argued when considering the case of Italy, a stable currency ought not to be detrimental to banks' financial interest, but as they became loaded with industrial securities any policy affecting firms' expectations impinged on the position of the banks. In any event, Spanish financial institutions ended the decade in an extraordinarily strong situation, without apparent problems of liquidity and displaying relatively high earning ratios.

Spanish banking during the Depression

The world economic Depression of the 1930s produced a major banking crisis in many Continental European countries, particularly in those in which commercial banking was dominated by mixed or universal banking. In Italy the three largest commercial banks became insolvent in the course of 1930 and passed into state hands. In Germany and Austria too the control of important banks passed into state hands as a result of liquidity crisis. In other countries also the State had to come to the rescue of financial firms.

The Depression left minor scars on the Spanish banking system. As Tortella and Palafox (1984) wrote, Spanish institutions stood up remarkably well; no really important bank suspended payments or went into

liquidation, and there was no need to organize any large salvaging operation. As a matter of fact, there were only three liquidations which affected
again another prominent Catalan credit institution, the Banco de Cataluña,
and two of its affiliates, the Banco de Tarrasa and the Banco de Reus.
Toniolo (1982), summarizing the results of the paper by Tortella and
Palafox, indicated that the reasons why Spanish financial institutions did
not collapse, despite their potential fragility, must be found in some of the
peculiarities of the Spanish economy. First, the fact that the impact of the
economic recession on Spain was milder. The combination of economic
backwardness, a high degree of agricultural self-sufficiency, high tariff
barriers, and the early depreciation of the peseta permitted the Spanish
economy to avoid the worst of the Depression. Besides, a general rise in
wages decreed by the government in 1931, as part of an untimely income
policy distribution, stimulated consumption demand and compensated for
the fall in exports and investment. The depreciation of the peseta until 1933,
when it was pegged to the gold French franc, also contributed, as Eichengreen and Sach (1985) have demonstrated, to the escape from the crisis.
Export industries suffered less than they otherwise would have, and the
trade balance did not deteriorate excessively. Furthermore, although the
Spanish authorities attempted, following the example of other countries, to
stabilize the exchange rate by imposing a restrictive monetary policy, the
public and the banks together frustrated the efforts of the government. An
uncontrolled budget deficit also helped to prevent monetary stringency.
Banks remained highly liquid, since they had a sizeable portfolio of public
securities ready to be used, if necessary, on stand-by operations.

Spanish banks certainly did not collapse; however, during the spring and
the summer of 1931, Spanish credit institutions faced swift and significant
withdrawals of deposits that forced the Bank of Spain to intervene as a
lender-of-last-resort.[25] This situation emerged as a result of a general crisis
of confidence that affected primarily the banking system. The demise of the
monarchy, the proclamation of the republic, and the formation of a
coalition government with various socialist ministers brought anxiety and
fear to the business community and to the public in general. To make things
worse, the new Minister of Finance, the moderate socialist Indalecio Prieto,
threatened financiers and industrialists that he would block all bank
accounts. Besides, the news of the failure of the CreditAnstalt and the
difficulties of the central European institutions also contributed to darken-
ing the atmosphere. The run on banks was intense between April and June,
when approximately 900 million pesetas were withdrawn; the removal of
funds continued during the summer and by the end of September, when the

---

[25] The 1931 crisis has been studied in detail by Martín-Aceña (1984: 224–59).

crisis can be said to have been over, the total volume of deposits had declined by 1,300 million pesetas, or 20 per cent of the total outstanding in March 1931. Banks did not fail because they were able to obtain all the cash they needed to convert deposits into currency. Two reasons may help to understand what made this possible. For the first time the Bank of Spain was ready actually to behave as a lender-of-last-resort; secondly, banks had plenty of liquid assets. When the run started, the Government made a swift and surprising move to deter the crisis. Indalecio Prieto summoned the governor and the deputy governor of the central bank and all members of the Supreme Banking Council and pressed them to reach a compromise. All agreed that banks were basically solvent but could run into serious difficulties for lack of liquidity. In consequence the Bank of Spain and the Treasury agreed on a combined action to facilitate all the cash banks might need. The Government authorized an increase in the limit of banknotes in circulation up to 6,000 million pesetas, and the directors of the bank agreed to lend freely; this meant that they would discount bills on demand and would accept unhesitatingly eligible paper as collateral for credit. Since the crisis coincided with a flight from the peseta, the Government also authorized a rise in interest rates to stop the outflow of capital. As though Prieto and the governor had read Walter Bagehot, they adopted a 'lend freely but at a high interest rate' policy, as the British writer had recommended when facing a simultaneous domestic and foreign financial crisis. The other reason which contributed to prevention of a banking collapse was, doubtless, the fact that Spanish banks were loaded with gilt-edged securities; they simply pledged their unused portion of government paper to obtain cash, and in this way public securities acted as an automatic built-in stabilizer. Hence, a rapid and surprising intervention of the central bank, plus the ability of banks to monetize their holdings of government paper, explains why financial institutions did not collapse in 1931.

5. Banking in the Inter-war Years: Some Findings and Some Questions

To conclude I will enumerate very briefly some of the most salient findings that can be drawn from this chapter.

1. From 1900 to 1935 the Spanish financial system evolved from unit to branch banking; in particular the big banks extended their influence to the whole national territory, not only by opening branches but also by absorption or amalgamation with other institutions. This latter trend led to a higher degree of concentration, and by 1930 the so-called 'Big Seven' had over 50 per cent of the combined paid-up capital and more than 70 per cent of the total deposits of the system. Moreover, the structure of the financial

system became more diverse, encompassing not only commercial banks, but also an increasing number of savings institutions, insurance companies, and semi-official banks. Another relevant development was that the large banks became increasingly involved in industry: they undertook extensive company promotion, held a sizeable proportion of private securities in their portfolio, and supplied long-term loans to industrial firms. In short, mixed or universal banking became the predominant feature of the Spanish financial system. Furthermore, there was an important banking reform in 1921 which established the legal framework under which the system operated during both decades.

2. During the 1920s and 1930s the Bank of Spain was forced to accept its role as central bank and to function more as a lender-of-last-resort than as an independent credit institution. Nevertheless, the Spanish central bank usually tried to avoid its responsibility as central bank and, except on a few occasions, its performance as lender-of-last-resort was far from adequate. However, as a private deposit institution its weight within the system declined from its clearly dominant position in 1900 to a less relevant one by 1935.

3. The relationship between the banks and the State grew during the period. Mixed banks became a crucial element in the financing of the public deficit. Particularly during the 1920s they subscribed the enormous quantities of public securities issued to cover the budget disequilibria. As a matter of fact, banks' earnings and portfolio liquidity rested, to some extent, on their holdings of public debt.

4. Compared to other European financial systems, the Spanish one seems to have shown a greater stability. Certainly there were bank failures both in 1920s and in the 1930s, but they only affected a handful of institutions. Except when ordered, the Bank of Spain refrained from intervening; notwithstanding, it seems to have helped to limit the financial crisis of the spring of 1931. But the stability predicated for the system rested rather on two exogenous factors: the real shocks which hit the Spanish economy were milder than elsewhere, and banks were almost always caught in a relatively good liquidity position. As a consequence, the Spanish financial system did not require any major rescue operation or state take-over.

References

André, E. L. (1917), 'Caracteres de nuestra organización bancaria actual', *Revista de Economía y Hacienda*, Sept.
Cabana, F. (1965), *La banca a Catalunya. Apunts per una historia* (Barcelona: Ediciones 62).

—— (1978), *Historia del Banc de Barcelona, 1844–1920* (Barcelona: Ediciones 62).

Canosa, R. (1945), *Un siglo de banca privada (1845–1945)* (Madrid: Nuevas Gráficas).

Ceballos Teresí, J. C. (1930), *Historia económica, financiera y política de España en el siglo XX* (Madrid: El Financiero).

Ciocca, P., and Toniolo, G. (1984), 'Industry and Finance in Italy, 1918–1940', *Journal of European Economic History*, 13/2, special issue.

Eichengreen, B. and Sachs, J. (1985), 'Exchanges Rates and Economic Recovery in the 1930s', *Journal of Economic History*, 65/4.

Fornies Casals, J. F. (1979), 'El ahorro popular, durante la Dictadura: las Cajas de Ahorro y Montes de Piedad', *Cuadernos Económicos de ICE*, 10.

Forsyth, D. J. (1991), 'The Rise and Fall of German-Inspired Mixed Banking in Italy, 1894–1936', in H. James, H. Lindgren, and A. Teichova (eds.), *The Role of Banks in the Inter-war Economy* (Cambridge: Cambridge University Press).

Fraile, P. (1990), 'La industrialización española en el primer tercio del siglo XX: una visión alternativa', in P. Martín-Aceña and F. Comín, *Empresa pública e industrialización en España* (Madrid: Alianza Editorial).

—— (1991), *Industrialización y grupos de presión. La economía política de la protección en España, 1900–1950* (Madrid: Alianza Editorial).

García Ruiz, J. L. (1990), *Banca y crisis económica, 1930–1935*, Ph.D. thesis, Univ. Complutense de Madrid.

Goldsmith, R. W. (1969), *Financial Structure and Development* (New Haven, Conn.: Yale University Press).

Hernández Andreu, J. (1986), *España y la crisis de 1929* (Madrid: Espasa-Calpe).

James, H., Lindgren, H., Teichova, A. (eds.) (1991), *The Role of Banks in the Inter-War Economy* (Cambridge: Cambridge University Press).

Kindleberger, C. P. (1984), 'Banking and Industry between the Two Wars: An International Comparison', *Journal of European Economic History*, 13/2, special issue.

Martín-Aceña, P. (1983), 'El tipo de cambio de la peseta, 1920–1929: teoría y evidencia empírica', *Revista de Historia Económica*, 1/2.

—— (1984), *La política monetaria en España, 1919–1935* (Madrid: Instituto de Estudios Fiscales).

—— (1987), 'Development and Modernization of the Financial System, 1844–1935', in N. Sánchez-Albornoz (ed.), *The Economic Modernization of Spain, 1830–1930* (New York: New York University Press).

—— (1990), 'Economic Growth and Financial Development in Spain (1900–1930)', in E. Aerts and N. Valério (eds.), *Growth and Stagnation in the Mediterranean World* (Leuven: Leuven University Press).

—— (1991), 'Los orígenes de la banca pública', in F. Comín and P. Martín-Aceña (eds.), *Historia de la empresa pública en España* (Madrid: Espasa Calpe).

Muñoz, J. (1978), 'La expansión bancaria entre 1919 y 1926. La formación de una banca nacional', *Cuaderno Económicos de ICE*, 6.

Roldán, S., and García Delgado, J. L. (1973), *La formación de la sociedad capitalista en España, 1914–1920* (Madrid: Confederación Española de Cajas de Ahorro).

Sánchez-Albornoz, N., (ed.) (1987), *The Economic Modernization of Spain, 1830–1930* (New York: New York University Press).

Sudrià, C. (1990), 'Los beneficos de España durante la gran guerra. Una aproximación a la balanza de pagos española, 1914–1920', *Revista de Historia Económica*, 7/2.

Tallada, J. M. (1926), *Economía de la postguerra* (Barcelona).

—— (1946), *Historia de las finanzas españolas en el siglo XIX* (Madrid: Espasa Calpe).

Tedde, P. (1974), 'La banca privada española en la Restauración', in G. Tortella and P. Schwartz (eds.), *La banca española en la Restauración*, i (Madrid: Banco de España).

—— (1988), 'El sector financiero', *Enciclopedia de Historia de España, i. Economia y Sociedad* (Madrid: Alianza Editorial).

Toniolo, G. (1982), 'Per un'analisi comparata delle cause delle crisi bancarie nell'Europa dei primi anni Trenta', in *Le istituzioni finanziarie degli anni trenta nell'Europa continentale* (Bologna: Banco di Roma/Il Mulino).

Tortella, G. (1970), 'El Banco de España entre 1829–1929. La formación de un banco central', in *El Banco de España. Una historia económica* (Madrid: Banco de España).

—— and Palafox, J. (1984), 'Banking and Industry in Spain, 1918–1936', *Journal of European Economic History*, 13/2, special issue.

Vazquez, J. A. (1991), 'Notas sobre banca e industria en Asturias en su perspectiva histórica', in A. Torrero (ed.) *Relaciones banca-industria. La experiencia española* (Madrid: Espasa Calpe).

Appendix

TABLE 20.A1. *Spanish financial institutions, 1900–1935* (no. of banks and credit companies)

Year	Private banks		Savings banks and other credit companies	Official banks
	Joint-stock companies	Total		
	(1)	(2)	(3)	(4)
1900	—	—	43	2
1901	42	—	44	2
1902	—	—	47	2
1903	—	—	48	2
1904	—	—	53	2
1905	36	—	57	2
1906	—	—	59	2
1907	—	—	62	2
1908	—	—	66	2
1909	—	—	82	2
1910	51	—	85	2
1911	—	—	85	2
1912	—	—	82	2
1913	—	—	86	2
1914	47	—	89	2
1915	52	—	99	2
1916	47	—	103	2
1917	56	—	105	2
1918	72	—	120	2
1919	73	—	127	2
1920	91	—	128	3
1921	93	—	131	3
1922	93	—	134	3
1923	91	150	158	3
1924	92	147	166	3
1925	93	136	169	4
1926	93	143	171	4
1927	89	190	171	4
1928	95	199	171	4
1929	94	203	170	5
1930	90	211	171	5
1931	87	208	172	5
1932	85	216	171	5
1933	86	227	170	5
1934	86	217	169	5
1935	—	210	162	5

TABLE 20.A2. *Bank of Spain: selected asset and liabilities, 1900–1935* (million pesetas)

Year	Capital	Notes in circulation	Current accounts	Foreign assets	Treasury assets	Private domestic assets
1900	150	1,592	697	395	2,648	269
1901	150	1,639	648	369	2,633	312
1902	150	1,623	563	394	2,306	494
1903	150	1,609	602	410	2,289	541
1904	150	1,599	578	419	2,196	580
1905	150	1,550	541	437	1,966	632
1906	150	1,525	512	455	1,830	721
1907	150	1,557	490	454	1,764	775
1908	150	1,643	465	458	1,618	827
1909	150	1,671	492	491	1,672	832
1910	150	1,715	456	505	1,652	851
1911	150	1,763	446	512	1,677	871
1912	150	1,863	458	592	1,762	847
1913	150	1,931	485	650	1,706	939
1914	150	1,974	609	721	1,808	1,054
1915	150	2,100	698	972	1,870	872
1916	150	2,360	748	1,342	1,843	866
1917	150	2,799	942	2,057	1,789	1,010
1918	150	3,334	1,159	2,706	1,928	1,106
1919	150	3,867	1,060	2,985	1,701	1,597
1920	150	4,326	1,160	2,996	2,077	1,957
1921	150	4,244	1,029	2,871	807	3,123
1922	177	4,137	1,073	1,738	1,490	2,593
1923	177	4,353	1,053	2,559	1,501	2,860
1924	177	4,547	967	2,570	1,427	3,295
1925	177	4,440	1,297	2,568	1,511	3,426
1926	177	4,339	1,018	2,593	1,269	3,265
1927	177	4,202	1,079	2,642	1,713	2,904
1928	177	4,397	962	2,573	1,557	3,389
1929	177	4,458	981	2,228	1,769	3,681
1930	177	4,767	864	1,958	2,126	3,732
1931	177	4,993	1,135	1,446	2,452	4,780
1932	177	4,834	966	1,504	2,289	4,492
1933	177	4,825	934	1,549	2,181	4,493
1934	177	4,711	880	1,486	2,176	4,294
1935	177	4,837	1,323	2,099	2,430	3,852

TABLE 20.A3. *Private financial institutions: selected assets and liabilities, 1900–1935* (million pesetas)

Year	Private banks					Savings banks
	Paid-in capital (1)	Deposits (2)	Cash assets (3)	Loans and advances (4)	Investment porfolio (5)	Savings accounts (6)
1900	—	374	208	161	201	131
1901	—	413	157	204	232	138
1902	—	374	138	249	251	149
1903	—	413	106	253	283	165
1904	—	433	105	249	326	175
1905	—	447	94	277	381	191
1906	—	503	93	301	356	202
1907	—	515	79	312	370	208
1908	—	553	89	350	393	234
1909	—	593	83	388	410	244
1910	—	659	91	443	433	264
1911	—	691	87	594	445	284
1912	—	698	91	480	445	311
1913	—	707	119	464	443	349
1914	—	628	137	382	428	342
1915	258[a]	837	189	289	565	401
1916	260[a]	1,050	195	364	700	446
1917	274[a]	1,394	258	501	830	523
1918	397[a]	2,185	591	945	1,071	606
1919	467[a]	2,705	398	1,226	1,484	715
1920	730[a]	3,223	553	1,581	1,880	808
1921	784[a]	3,307	481	1,528	2,345	924
1922	789[a]	4,350	502	1,929	2,737	1,058
1923	1,025	4,448	512	1,822	3,121	1,185
1924	965	4,169	577	1,770	3,244	1,294
1925	959	3,927	616	1,654	3,250	1,437
1926	996	4135	640	1,639	3,376	1,540
1927	1,063	4,874	800	1,788	3,933	1,670
1928	1,124	5,531	1,003	1,866	4,773	1,841
1929	1,176	6,208	992	2,314	5,325	1,998
1930	1,196	6,749	1,028	2,433	5,765	2,160
1931	1,185	5,587	1,077	1,861	5,297	2,300
1932	1,161	5,942	1,076	1,875	5,488	2,489
1933	1,163	6,217	1,179	2,028	5,614	2,654
1934	1,154	6,699	1,107	2,028	6,200	2,797
1935	1,148	7,262	1,413	1,802	6,469	2,886

[a] Figures only for joint-stock banks.

TABLE 20.A4. *The stock of money in Spain*, 1900–1935 (million pesetas)

Year	Currency in circulation (1)	Deposits (2)	Money supply (3)
1900	2,204	1,167	3,371
1901	2,274	1,170	3,444
1902	2,211	1,061	3,272
1903	2,240	1,161	3,401
1904	2,211	1,166	3,377
1905	2,097	1,162	3,259
1906	2,039	1,200	3,239
1907	2,045	1,197	3,242
1908	1,954	1,234	3,188
1909	2,028	1,312	3,340
1910	2,068	1,359	3,427
1911	2,131	1,402	3,533
1912	2,244	1,448	3,692
1913	2,310	1,517	3,827
1914	2,344	1,552	3,896
1915	2,416	1,907	4,323
1916	2,678	2,214	4,892
1917	3,138	2,827	5,965
1918	3,731	3,915	7,646
1919	4,264	4,442	8,706
1920	4,769	5,152	9,921
1921	4,624	5,219	9,843
1922	4,485	6,437	10,922
1923	4,692	6,679	11,371
1924	4,858	6,378	11,236
1925	4,733	6,605	11,338
1926	4,599	6,634	11,233
1927	4,389	7,553	11,942
1928	4,491	8,249	12,740
1929	4,597	9,101	13,648
1930	4,854	9,674	14,528
1931	5,235	8,926	14,161
1932	4,987	9,299	14,286
1933	4,893	9,700	14,593
1934	4,772	10,273	15,045
1935	4,769	10,848	15,617

TABLE 20.A5. *The peseta exchange rate,* 1900–1935

Year	Pesetas per pound sterling	Pesetas per US dollars
1900	32.56	—
1901	34.78	—
1902	34.14	—
1903	33.99	—
1904	34.66	—
1905	32.91	—
1906	28.41	—
1907	28.09	—
1908	28.39	—
1909	27.15	—
1910	27.10	—
1911	27.24	—
1912	26.97	—
1913	27.09	—
1914	26.08	—
1915	24.90	5.23
1916	23.93	5.19
1917	21.17	4.43
1918	19.86	4.17
1919	22.40	5.06
1920	23.30	6.37
1921	28.51	7.38
1922	28.60	6.45
1923	31.77	9.96
1924	33.14	7.51
1925	33.66	6.97
1926	32.84	6.72
1927	28.51	5.86
1928	29.33	6.03
1929	33.17	6.82
1930	41.93	8.68
1931	47.64	10.55
1932	43.70	12.41
1933	39.98	9.71
1934	37.19	7.39
1935	37.10	7.35

TABLE 20.A6. *Spanish prices and interest rates, 1900–1935*

Year	Wholesale price index (1913 = 100)	Interest rates		
		A	B	C
1900	96.7	3.5	3.5	4.51
1901	96.9	4	4	4.48
1902	94.7	4	4	4.42
1903	97.7	4.5	4.5	4.18
1904	99.5	4.5	4.5	4.21
1905	100.0	4.5	4.5	4.10
1906	97.3	4.5	4.5	3.97
1907	101.4	4.5	4.5	3.91
1908	98.6	4.5	4.5	3.86
1909	97.3	4.5	4.5	3.74
1910	98.2	4.5	4.5	3.76
1911	94.7	4.5	4.5	3.81
1912	99.4	4.5	4.5	3.79
1913	100.0	4.5	4.5	3.98
1914	98.4	4.5	5	4.22
1915	118.3	—	—	4.47
1916	141.0	—	—	4.31
1917	165.6	—	—	4.31
1918	204.9	—	—	4.12
1919	204.2	—	—	4.16
1920	221.8	6	4.5	4.44
1921	189.4	6	4.5	4.72
1922	177.3	5.5	4.5	4.62
1923	174.8	5	4.5	4.53
1924	183.4	5	4.5	
1925	189.2	5	4.5	
1926	180.8	5	4.5	
1927	173.3	5	4.5	
1928	168.5	5.5	4.5	
1929	172.4	5.5	4.5	
1930	173.0	6	5	
1931	174.1	6.5	5	
1932	172.8	6	5	
1933	165.1	6	5	
1934	168.5	5.5	4.5	
1935	172.3	5	4	

Notes: A: Bank of Spain: official discount rate; B: Bank of Spain: rate on loans secured with public securities; C: Average yield of long-term public debt.

Sources: Banco de España, *Memorias Anuales; Consejo Superior Bancario, Boletines Trimestrales; Estadisticas Historias de España* (Madrid: Fundación Banco Exterior de España, 1985); Pablo Martin-Aceña, *La cantidad de dinero en España, 1900–1935* (Madrid, Banco de España, 1985), and 'The Spanish Money Supply, 1874–1935', *Journal of European Economic History*, 19 1 (Winter 1990).

Index